W9-COD-108

THE POPULIST PERSUASION

The Populist Persuasion

An American History

Michael Kazin

BasicBooks
A Division of HarperCollins*Publishers*

 For information, address BasicBooks, 10 East 53rd Street, New York, NY 10022-5299.

Designed by Ellen Levine

Library of Congress Cataloging-in-Publication Data
Kazin, Michael, 1948–
The populist persuasion: an American history / Michael Kazin.
p. cm.
Includes index.
ISBN 0-465-03793-3 (cloth)
ISBN 0-465-05998-8 (paper)
1. Populism—United States—History. 2. United States—Politics and government—1865–1933. 3. United States—Politics and government—20th century. I. Title.
E661.K25 1994
973—dc20 94-29404
CIP

---

96 97 98 99 ♦/HC 9 8 7 6 5 4 3 2 1

For

Alfred Kazin,

Carol Bookman Salvadori,

and

Mario Salvadori

Contents

Acknowledgments

A DECADE AGO, I began to write this book as a way of making sense of a painful experience: the decline of the American Left, including its liberal component, and the rise of the Right. Most of the people who helped me do it have agonized over the same question, although their answers often differ from mine.

I soon decided that the long course of populism was critical to the story. But to make sense of that history, I would have to learn about periods, worldviews, and movements about which I was largely ignorant. Fortunately, there were specialists in those subjects who were willing to talk about my ideas and critique my writing. For evangelical Protestantism, I relied on Tony Fels; for nineteenth-century politics, Roy Rosenzweig; for the American Federation of Labor, Julia Greene; for Father Coughlin's movement, Alan Brinkley; for the CIO, Nelson Lichtenstein; for both anti-communism and resurgent conservatism in the 1970s and 1980s, John Judis; for the New Left, Todd Gitlin; and for George Wallace and his campaigns, Tom Sugrue and Dan T. Carter. Thanks, as well, to the hundreds of scholars whose works I mined for purposes with which a number would undoubtedly disagree.

Along the way, I also got advice, clippings, and a few good lines from Eric Alterman, Robert Beisner, Leon Fink, Joshua Freeman, Sandy Horwitt, Stuart Kaufman, Timothy Meagher, Leo Ribuffo, Jules Tygiel, and Maurice Isserman, my partner in looking back on the grim and glorious 1960s. Long interviews with Heather Booth, Kevin Phillips, and Miles Rapoport cleared up the gnarled history of new populisms, right and left.

Two generous fellowships gave me time to work and the company of people who helped make that work a bit more enlightening. At the National Museum of

American History, Edith Mayo and Harry Rubenstein were indispensable. At the Commonwealth Center for the Study of American Culture down in Williamsburg, Virginia, Chandos Brown, Bob Gross, and Richard John offered excellent advice and recreation. Hard questions were also raised by the participants at graduate seminars at the University of Virginia and George Washington University, where I tried out my ideas. And course releases from American University, where I am blessed with wise and congenial departmental colleagues, gave me valuable time to think them through.

I also want to thank the wonderful staff people at the Library of Congress, where I did the bulk of my research in the elysian days when a stack pass was easy to come by. Bruce Martin was especially warm and helpful. The Library of Congress is a place where, amid esthetic splendor, one can spend days reading rare and fragile newsprint at a table shared by an Ivy League professor and a homeless man poring over the *Wall Street Journal.* Preserve the people's library!

I was incredibly lucky to have three of America's best historians spend many hours with my manuscript. Gary Gerstle read the unruly first draft and nudged me to recognize the significance of what I was trying to do. Alan Brinkley read a later draft and pointed out that a series of unconnected narratives does not make a satisfying work of history.

The third, Steve Fraser, my editor, deserves his own paragraph. Without his diligent craftsmanship, this would not be much of a book. Steve's steady encouragement, his historical and political wisdom, his acute feel for style and structure, and his sense of when and how to push an author enabled me to produce something coherent out of what was merely a grand whim. I can't believe there is a better editor of nonfiction in the United States.

At Basic Books, Justin McShea helped me track down obscure photos and drawings and kept the publication process going. Matthew Shine was a shrewd and helpful project editor, and Laura Leivick a precise and perceptive copy editor.

Finally, my family: my mother, Carol Bookman Salvadori, and my stepfather, Mario Salvadori, were immensely supportive and patient. My father, Alfred Kazin, worried with me and offered his sharp and loving advice. Neither of my children was born when I began this book. But now Danny can recognize the different species of bats and knows how many games the Orioles are out of first place. And Maia sings on key about friends, real and imaginary, and points out all the STOP signs. May they live in a far more decent world. And thanks to Jenny Lagos for playing with and caring for them in this one.

As for Beth Carrie Horowitz—physician, idea woman, copy editor, fiction fanatic, lover, and friend—I have to fall back on the immortal words of Ralph Kramden: Baby, you're the greatest.

Washington, D.C., September 1994

THE POPULIST PERSUASION

Introduction: Speaking for the People

Who shall speak for the people?
who has the answers?
where is the sure interpreter?
who knows what to say?
—Carl Sandburg, *The People, Yes,* 1936

THIS book is about the persistence of one vital way in which Americans have argued about politics. From the birth of the United States to the present day, images of conflict between the powerful and the powerless have run through our civic life, filling it with discord and meaning. The haughty financier wraps chains of debt around small farmers who grow food and fibers for the nation. The stout industrialist—top hat on his fleshy head and diamond stickpin gleaming from his silk tie—clashes with the working man dressed in overalls or secondhand suit, his jaw firm and his muscles taut. The federal bureaucrat, overeducated and amoral, scoffs at the God-fearing nuclear family in its modest home, a crucifix on the wall and a flagpole in the yard. In every campaign season, scores of politicians—both liberal and conservative—vow to fight for "middle-class taxpayers" and against a variety of "bureaucrats," "fat cats," and "Big Men."

Such images and countless others like them make up the language of populism. Whether orated, written, drawn, broadcast, or televised, this language is used by those who claim to speak for the vast majority of Americans who work hard and love their country. That is the most basic and telling definition of populism: a language whose speakers conceive of ordinary people as a noble assemblage not bounded narrowly by class, view their elite opponents as self-serving and undemocratic, and seek to mobilize the former against the latter.[1]

Through the past two centuries, most movement activists and insurgent politicians have judged certain ordinary Americans to be more virtuous or, at least, more significant than others. Populist speakers typically expressed their highest esteem for citizens who inhabited what the novelist E. L. Doctorow calls "the large middle world, neither destitute nor privileged, . . . that of the ordinary working man": yeoman farmers, urban craftsmen, native-born factory workers, home owners struggling to pay their taxes.[2]

White working men never exclusively composed this "people," but it was usually shaped in their image. Black activists had a standing quarrel with the categories at issue: for them, the elite was one to which the majority of white Americans belonged; their own people a minority whose special history and status threatened to break the mold.

Still, the language of populism in the United States expressed a kind of idealistic discontent that did not always obey demographic borders. Pitched battles between us and them often involved debates about the meaning of Americanism itself. Populist speakers in the United States voiced a profound outrage with elites who ignored, corrupted, and/or betrayed the core ideal of American democracy: rule by the common people who expected their fellow citizens to advance by diligence, practical intelligence, and a faith in God alone. There have, of course, been populisms in the history of other nations—movements and political figures that consistently expressed the belief that "virtue resides in the simple people, who are the overwhelming majority, and in their collective traditions."[3] But populism in the United States has made the unique claim that the powers that be are transgressing the nation's founding creed, which every permanent resident should honor. In this sense, American populism binds even as it divides.[4]

Resolution of this process has often been vicious and painful; violent accusations have a way of preceding or justifying repressive actions. But the fact that the political actors were fighting over a shared set of ideals helped Americans to avoid the terrors to body and mind that have characterized the hegemony of revolutionary ideologies in other nations: fascism, Nazism, Leninism, Maoism, and the type of Islam that currently rules Iran. As Alexis de Tocqueville observed during the childhood of the United States, Americans "are for ever varying, altering, and restoring secondary matters; but they carefully abstain from touching what is fundamental. They love change, but they dread revolutions."[5]

Through populism, Americans have been able to protest social and economic inequalities without calling the entire system into question. Class barriers, according to the national creed, are not supposed to exist in the United States. To maintain that most citizens—whatever their occupation or income—are moral, hardworking people denies the rigorous categories of Marxism and the condescension of the traditional Right. Believing that mass democracy can topple any haughty foe means avoiding gloomy thoughts about entrenched structures of capital and the state that often frustrate the most determined movement. Populism is thus a grand form of rhetorical optimism; once mobilized, there is nothing ordinary Americans cannot accomplish.

But what has been the consequence of these flag-waving rebellions? To appreciate the tenacity of a populist persuasion from the era of Thomas Jefferson to the era of William Jefferson Clinton is no revelation. What matters is that, within a durable frame, the language evolved; when historical actors argued about Americanism and redefined the people and their adversaries, they helped to strengthen certain political forces and to debilitate others.

The first chapter of this book explores the antebellum heritage upon which subsequent movements have drawn. Each succeeding chapter is devoted to a different, prolonged attempt to channel the vision of mass democracy and resentment against its enemies into greater power for specific social groups, usually dominated by whites, and the individuals who sought to represent them. In sequence, I profile the antimonopoly coalition that organized the People's Party; the labor and socialist movements of the Progressive era; the prohibitionists who surged to victory during the same period; Father Charles Coughlin and his largely Catholic following during the Great Depression; the industrial labor movement allied with the New Deal; conservative anti-Communists during the early Cold War; the white New Left of the 1960s; George Wallace and the white backlash phenomenon, and the new conservatism expressed by Richard Nixon, the Christian Right, and Ronald Reagan. I conclude with reflections on how Democrats like Bill Clinton and Jesse Jackson, and independents like Ross Perot, have addressed fears of a nation in eclipse.

The populist label is not normally affixed to some of these individuals and movements. And I omit certain figures, like Huey Long and Upton Sinclair, who are often called populist. My choice was not capricious. All the forces included had a nationwide impact and presence lasting at least a decade.[6] Each played a major role in one or more of the central dramas of American politics in the twentieth century: progressive reform, the Depression, the New Deal, the two world wars, the Cold War and the Vietnam conflict, the black freedom struggle, feminism, and the rise of a new conservatism.

I do not contend that my subjects *were* populists, in the way they were unionists or socialists, Protestants or Catholics, liberal Democrats or conservative Republicans. Populism, more an impulse than an ideology, is too elastic and promiscuous to be the basis for such an allegiance. Rather, my premise is that all these people employed populism as a flexible mode of persuasion. They used traditional kinds of expressions, tropes, themes, and images to convince large numbers of Americans to join their side or to endorse their views on particular issues.

The history of the populist persuasion is complex and full of ironies and contradictions; there is nothing tidy or predictable about the rhetoric of American discontents. But one can glimpse some patterns. I see two vital transitions in the way that politically active Americans have utilized the language.

The first occurred in the wake of the defeat of the People's Party—the original Populists—in the mid-1890s. Through the language of these rebels, who were based among small farmers, flowed two powerful, inherited streams of grassroots rhetoric. First was the moral revivalism of plebeian preachers and lay campaigners against slavery and strong drink; second was a spirited defense of "producers"—both rural and urban, wage earners and the self-employed—upon whose labor and loyalty the Republic depended.

In the early twentieth century, there was a parting of the ways. During the Progressive era, small farmers ceased to have the enthusiasm or the numbers to lead a national insurgency. But two other groups with dissimilar goals did: wage earners and evangelical churchgoers. A rising labor movement, including many socialists, articulated a narrowed version of the ethic that linked political virtue with manual work. It was now unions, they argued, that best represented the "average man." And a religious vocabulary had to be avoided, lest it divide labor's heterogeneous ranks. At the same time, middle-class Protestant women and ministers were mounting a righteous crusade against "the liquor trust," inevitably clashing with workers and immigrants who had no animus against the saloon.

Mutual suspicion thus estranged a movement originating in the church from one whose lifeblood was the industrial workplace. Since then, the gap between those who see ordinary Americans primarily in economic terms and those who view the people as belonging to God has never really closed. And it continues to divide populist persuaders today. Activists who blame an immoral, agnostic media for America's problems have little in common with those who indict corporations for moving jobs overseas.

The second transition helped propel a major alteration in national politics. In the late 1940s, populism began a migration from Left to Right. The rhetoric once spoken primarily by reformers and radicals (debt-ridden farmers, craft and industrial unionists, socialists attempting to make their purposes sound American, even prohibitionists eager to wipe out the saloon interests) was creatively altered by conservative groups and politicians (zealous anti-Communists, George Wallace, the Christian Right, and the campaigns and presidential administrations of Richard Nixon and Ronald Reagan).

It was a remarkable shift. The vocabulary of grassroots rebellion now served to thwart and reverse social and cultural change rather than to promote it. This turnabout can be linked to factors tangential to the movements themselves: the onset of the Cold War, the rise of a liberal state whose policies seemed to contradict its majoritarian rhetoric, the fact that most white Americans came to regard themselves as middle-class consumers and taxpayers, and the booming growth of evangelical churches whose political leanings were as conservative as their theology.

But liberals and radicals had opened the door for the Right. After World War II, the broad Left that had built the Congress of Industrial Organizations (CIO) and the Popular Front and campaigned for Franklin D. Roosevelt imploded and lost much of its insurgent spirit. Industrial unionists safeguarded their hard-won gains, Communists and their allies became preoccupied with self-defense, and liberal politicians and intellectuals took for granted the reforms of the New Deal—and the expanded, bureaucratic state that administered them—and fretted about Cold War hysteria.

Into this breach emerged, gradually and unevenly, a conservative populism that pledged to defend pious, middle-class communities against the amoral governing elite. Father Coughlin had experimented with such rhetoric in the 1930s, and the American Right began talking this way during the red scare of the late 1940s and

1950s. But conservatives didn't fully grasp its electoral potential until the domestic wars of the 1960s.

Instruction came from George Wallace and lesser-known tribunes of the white backlash. They demonstrated how to appeal to millions of former Democrats—Southern Protestants and Northern Catholics, most of them wage earners—with attacks on treasonous college kids, pro-busing judges, and politicians who, it was charged, took the people's money and wasted it on lazy minorities. The vengeful militance had a racial undercurrent that never lay far from the surface.

The New Left countered with a bold principle: the black freedom struggle should be the model for all discontented Americans. The solution to the nation's ills was the kind of direct democracy the civil rights movement was practicing in the South. Inspired by both black activists and the revolutionaries of Vietnam, most young radicals gradually replaced the "large middle world" with the Third World as the repository of political virtue. The need to build a new interracial majority was largely forgotten.

For liberal Democrats, too, the black movement took center stage in the fight for reform, a place once occupied by the struggles of farmers and wage earners (most from European roots). But liberals were yoked to a regime whose credibility and finances were running low. Unhampered by Wallace's belligerent methods, Republican conservatives leaped in to claim the taxpayers, home owners, and avid churchgoers of the great white middle.

By the 1990s, the old talk of manual "producers" versus corporate "parasites" sounded hopelessly archaic, and fragmented movements on the Left, their very definition in dispute, had found nothing compelling to take its place. Despite the results of the 1992 election, the Right's conception of a "Middle America" beset by a spendthrift, immoral political elite remained vigorous. It limited what President Bill Clinton or any other progressive leader or organization could accomplish.

My definition of populism as a persistent yet mutable style of political rhetoric with roots deep in the nineteenth century differs from two other conceptions of the term that are widely heard in late-twentieth-century America. The first, upheld by several of my fellow historians, restricts application of the term to the mass movement that arose in the 1880s among farmers in the South and Great Plains, and then crested and crashed during the crisis of the 1890s. This is the upsurge that gave Populism its name, and it deserves to be the only one graced with a capital *P*.[7] The second is a glib habit indulged in by many journalists, and even some advertisers eager to capture the volatile tastes of the public. The habit of branding as "populist" everything from Bruce Springsteen to Rush Limbaugh to loose-fitting cotton trousers also has a history, which I discuss in the final chapter.

While preferring to let my narrative do the talking, I should make clear why neither of these definitions seems satisfactory. To call populist only the People's Party and its immediate antecedents is to neglect the potent tradition to which insurgents in the late nineteenth century added their own blend of economic dread and missionary zeal. It also leads to ahistorical debates about who is or is not a true populist, debates that are just an indirect way of announcing one's political opinions.

By contrast, the cultural mode makes no useful discriminations at all. To pin the populist label on anything or anybody not associated with the glamorous and the wealthy substitutes faddishness for interpretation. For coherency, and to keep faith with the origin of the term, the political should remain central to its meaning. My own concern is with some of the men and women who articulated their collective grievances and their optimistic visions in populist ways. Populism, of course, was not the sole element in their rhetoric, but its significance is, I think, impossible to deny.[8]

It may seem strange to read a study of populism that seldom pauses to examine the language of the common people themselves, the anonymous millions whose words and pictures are rarely preserved but whose labor is present everywhere. But to do justice to that topic, over the span of two hundred years, would have been impossible—at least for me. So I chose to follow my abiding fascination with mass movements and prominent figures who sought to speak *for* the people instead of to attempt what, by necessity, would have been an anecdotal, scattershot presentation of what ordinary, nonactivist Americans were saying.

I do, however, speculate about how certain forms of expression were received and what impact they may have had on the course of political change. Where possible, these speculations are supported by evidence—from secondary works, opinion polls, election results, and the like. But I confess to making some leaps of judgment based on nothing more than an accumulated knowledge of the American past, on my sense of how political speech meshed with popular attitudes at different historical junctures. In the end, this study can, at best, capture but one aspect of a grand and elusive subject: how Americans perceived the sources of justice and injustice in their society and acted upon those views.

As readers will discover, my own sentiments about the populist persuasion are firmly equivocal. I cherish the traditional convictions of the non-Communist Left; my ideal society would be one that enhanced and protected interracial democracy, civil liberties, and the right of all its citizens to labor creatively and to live in decency.[9] Unfortunately, only a few times in American history—notably the era of the New Deal and World War II—has populist rhetoric worked to further those ends. Especially since 1945, appeals to "the people" have more commonly promoted detestable views—fear of the black and immigrant poor, a belief in conspiracies, loyalty to America and to God used as a club to beat one's rivals. In their respective heydays, Joseph McCarthy, George Wallace, and Ronald Reagan appealed as effectively to white working people as did anyone on the democratic Left. I agree with the philosopher Jurgen Habermas: "We must realize that all traditions are ambivalent and that it is therefore necessary to be critical about all of them so as to be able to decide which tradition to maintain and which not."[10]

But the contest should not be abandoned. It is only when leftists and liberals themselves talked in populist ways—hopeful, expansive, even romantic—that they were able to lend their politics a majoritarian cast and help markedly to improve the common welfare. Faith in the abilities of ordinary Americans of all races to run their society need not be blind to the logical pitfalls and mythic nature of populist appeals. It must, however, be a sincere faith—one that, I confess, does not always come easily to a Jew raised in a comfortable home who makes his living at a university. Emerson once counseled, "March without the people, and you march into the night."[11] Cursing the darkness only delays the dawn.

"The Downfall of Mother Bank": President Andrew Jackson routs Nicholas Biddle, president of the Bank of the United States, and his journalistic lackeys, c. 1833. *(Courtesy of the Collection of the New-York Historical Society)*

Chapter 1

Inheritance

Experience proves, that the very men whom you entrust with the support and defense of your most sacred liberties, are frequently corrupt, not only in England *but also in the colonies. . . . If ever therefore your rights are preserved, it must be through the virtue and integrity of the middling sort, as farmers, tradesmen, & c. who despise venality, and best know the sweets of liberty.*

—"Publius," spokesman for Philadelphia artisans, 1772

The sickly, weakly, timid man, fears the people, and is a Tory by nature. The healthy, strong and bold, cherishes them, is formed a Whig by nature.

—Thomas Jefferson, letter to Lafayette, 1823

I hold that if the Almighty had ever made a set of men that should do all the eating and none of the work, He would have made them with mouths only and no hands; and if He had ever made another class that He intended should do all the work and no eating, He would have made them with hands only and no mouths.

—Abraham Lincoln, 1859

RHETORIC FOR AMERICANS

IN 1892, Georgia Populist leader Tom Watson wrote a brief synopsis of American history intended for use in that fall's election campaign. Like any good patriot, he began with the Revolution: "Those who wished to revolt against the unjust Laws of the Mother Country were called Whigs." Then Watson detailed how long and tragic the struggle between the people and their enemies had been. He praised the framers of the Constitution as "brave men," while acknowledging they had superseded the instructions of the state legislators who sent them to Philadelphia in 1787. "Naturally, furious divisions arose" between Federalists and anti-Federalists. But the Constitution, implied Watson, was sensible and just, and it soon became "the Supreme Law under which we now live."

Only then was the battle joined. Alexander Hamilton and his followers stood up for "a strong centralized Govt." as the instrument of "a moneyed aristocracy supported by special privilege," which Watson also called "the System." According to Watson, Jefferson and his disciples (Andrew Jackson most prominent, and heroic, among them) successfully opposed this order in the name of both "individual enterprise" and "the will of the people." For a few years, the new Republican Party, at the behest of principled abolitionists, also represented "a great popular impulse." But, by the end of the Civil War, corrupt men, wielding great amounts of ill-gotten wealth, had taken control of both major parties. This "modern system of piracy" was, jeered Watson, an "improvement" over "the crude methods" of highway robbers. Now, the thieves were so dominant that "the booty is great and the risk is nought."

A former (and future) Democrat, Watson predictably scorned the Republican Party's obeisance to "Boodlers, Monopolists, Gamblers, Gigantic Corporations, Bondholders, Bankers." What, he implied, could one expect of an organization that openly admitted its support of Hamiltonian principles? But the Georgian reserved his sharpest barbs for those who were perverting the Democratic Party, created to ensure that the people would always rule. "Did [Jefferson] dream that in 100 years or less *his* party would be prostituted to the vilest purposes of monopoly; that red-eyed Jewish millionaires would be chiefs of that Party, and that the liberty and prosperity of the country would be . . . constantly and corruptly sacrificed to Plutocratic greed in the name of Jeffersonian Democracy?"[1]

Watson's vigorous polemic is cast in a familiar style of American rhetoric. Only the taint of anti-Semitism (which did not become central to his worldview until after the demise of the People's Party) distinguishes his tale from the appeals of political actors before and since who claimed to be defending the virtuous majority against its greedy, elitist foes.

But attention should be paid to familiarity. Beneath the stark dualism of Watson's history lesson ran a powerful and persistent tradition in the public language of discontented citizens. That tradition began to emerge in the Revolutionary era and became ubiquitous during the 1830s and 1840s, the Age of the Common Man—at least in popular idiom. For Watson and his comrades in the People's Party, this was a political and social Golden Age to which, in spirit, they wished to return. To understand the nature and persistence of populist language, one must return to its sources—the inheritance of most Americans who tried to speak for the people in the late nineteenth and twentieth centuries.

The embryonic populist rhetoric of antebellum America incorporated two different but not exclusive strains of vision and protest. First, there was the pietistic impulse issuing from the Protestant Reformation and continually revived by "great awakenings" that featured vivid emotional oratory, camp meetings, and the creation of new churches—all fueled by the belief in a personal God unmediated through spiritual authority. If "ALL if they choose, May enjoy the GOOD NEWS," as one evangelical writer put it in 1809, then it was every Christian's duty to attack sinful behavior, especially when it received encouragement and sanction from the rich and haughty.[2]

The second source was the secular faith of the Enlightenment, the belief that ordinary people could think and act rationally, more rationally, in fact, than their ancestral overlords. In the hands of a Thomas Jefferson or a Tom Paine, this belief was revolutionary. "Truths" about the "absolute Despotism" of King George III were "self-evident," claimed the Declaration of Independence; freed from the shackles of "ancient prejudices" and "superstition," Americans, wrote Paine that same year, saw clearly that the Crown, like all monarchies, was but an elaborate figleaf for arbitrary, self-aggrandizing rule. Paine, an erstwhile artisan, conveyed the devastating limpidity of his arguments by entitling his pamphlet *Common Sense.*[3]

Through the nineteenth century, the pietist and the rationalist coexisted in rhetoric, party politics, and coalitions of the discontented. Protestant Christianity, as a belief system, was common to both groups, although the forms of worship differed widely. Plebeian preachers and secular propagandists agreed, as one historian puts it, "that people should shake off all servile prejudice and learn to prove things for themselves."[4]

From the turn of the century to the 1830s, the democratic wave crested for both groups simultaneously. Caucasian men won universal suffrage, and working people of both sexes organized the first trade unions at the same time that evangelicals of different classes were filling thousands of new churches (Methodist, Baptist, Mormon) whose numbers dwarfed those of the older, more hierarchical denominations. The sensationalistic "penny press," read widely by plebeian audiences, mushroomed alongside Christian associations dedicated to charity, temperance, abolishing slavery, and spreading the Gospel. Charles Grandison Finney, the foremost "great awakener" in the industrializing North, was fond of comparing the conversion experience to voting for the Lord and against the Devil.[5]

Religious fervor, as Tocqueville recognized, was "perpetually warmed in the United States by the fires of patriotism." Circuit-riding preachers and union-organizing artisans (even the Painite freethinkers among them) agreed that high-handed rule by the wealthy was both sinful and unrepublican. All believed in the nation's millennial promise, its role as a beacon of liberty in a benighted world. "Vox populi, vox dei" worked in either direction.[6]

Moreover, evangelical and rationalist democrats drew from a common storehouse of imperishable linguistic goods. In parallel ways, they articulated four clusters of beliefs: about Americanism, the people, elites, and the need for mass movements. These constituted the primal grammar on which the People's Party and all subsequent American populisms would depend. Both groups constructed this grammar through what the historian Kenneth Cmiel calls "the middling rhetoric"—a marriage of bombast with informality, the bluntness of a Tom Paine with the sentimentality of a Harriet Beecher Stowe.[7]

There were differences of emphasis and meaning, of course. The pietists insisted that the Christian identity of the republic must be preserved, while for the rationalists, words like *Judas*, *sin*, and *redemption* were metaphors to bolster the emotional weight of their argument. Yet, the very intertwining of religious and democratic referents in antebellum America kept the two faces of populism from going separate ways. As the historian Gordon Wood writes: "By the early nineteenth century, America had already emerged as the most egalitarian, most materialistic, most individualistic—and most evangelical Christian—society in Western history."[8]

The first element in the shared language of politics was *Americanism* itself. This was the creed for which independence had been won and that all genuine patriots would fight to preserve. It was breathtakingly idealistic: in this unique nation, all men were created equal, deserved the same chance to improve their lot, and were citizens of a self-governing republic that enshrined the liberty of the individual. It was also proudly defensive: America was an isolated land of virtue whose people were on constant guard against the depredations of aristocrats, empire builders, and self-aggrandizing officeholders both within and outside its borders.

In recent years, scholars have disagreed about whether the Americanist creed, in the decades from the Revolution to the Civil War, can best be understood as "liberal" or "republican." Was its main ingredient free expression and the unencumbered pursuit of self-interest (liberal), or the call for a public-spirited, moral commonwealth (republican)? Like many historical dichotomies, this one is misconceived; most American patriots clearly cherished their right to speak freely and to seek prosperity (but not opulence) in the marketplace *and* still longed for a society bonded by classical and Christian notions of virtue and disinterest. Antebellum officeholders and reform activists spoke to both desires—for liberation and for community—without fear of contradicting themselves.[9]

In terms of the genesis of a populist discourse, the overriding point is that Americanism meant understanding and obeying the will of the people. Whether asserting the claims of a putatively egalitarian community or the rights of individuals against the state, it was the majority with its love of liberty that must decide. To mock the opinions and/or oppose the interests of the majority was more than foolish politics; it was un-American.

Thus, early in the history of the United States, speakers and writers transformed the country from a mere place on the map into an ideology. Ever since, dissenters from the established order have wrestled with the legacy of that achievement. On the one hand, they have not needed to offer an alternative conception of the political good; they have simply accused powerful opponents of betraying the consensual creed and marshaled the details to prove it. However, the boon is also a fetter. Because the American Revolution has already occurred, advocating a new type of polity and a new constitution seems unnecessary, dangerous, close to treason. Radical transformations undertaken in other societies under such banners as socialism, fascism, and anticolonialism are thus impossible in the United States—at once the most idealistic and the most conservative nation on earth.

Populist critics must always pinpoint which individuals and which elites have defamed the national spirit; they cannot question the terms of the civic religion itself. Richard Hofstadter elegantly described the ambivalent bargain: "It has been our fate as a nation not to have ideologies but to be one."[10]

But who were *the people* America was intended to empower? The founders of the republic seldom thought to define the term. For Washington, Adams, Madison, Jefferson, and Hancock, "we the people" was more incantation than description; like speaking of the Almighty Himself, it indicated who the ultimate sovereign was but did not specify who was actually to rule the nation. The latter should be men like themselves, planters and merchants with enough independent wealth to govern impartially for the good of the citizenry, most of whom would always be laboring for others and be immersed in petty contentions. Thus, "the people" was the homogeneous bedrock of America, the foundation upon which "a natural aristocracy" of the talented and virtuous, guided by a Constitution designed to limit democratic participation, would erect a great and just nation.[11]

Yet, soon after the Revolution, a quite different meaning of "the people" could be heard. In 1786–87, Massachusetts farmers, scissored by high taxes and low prices for their wheat and cattle, defied court attempts to seize their property for unpaid debts. One smallholder vowed, "I design to pay no more, and I know we have the biggest party, let them say what they will." In the 1790s, Jeffersonian pamphleteers praised those who toiled "with hammer and hand" as "the industrious part of the community." The New England farmer William Manning divided the population "between those that Labour for a Living and those that git a Living without Bodily Labour," making clear that the former easily outnumbered the latter.[12]

These were nascent versions of a producer ethic, the central element in populist conceptions of "the people" well into the twentieth century. By the 1830s, it had already become gospel for political candidates and mass orators. Producerism was indeed an ethic, a moral conviction: it held that only those who created wealth in tangible, material ways (on and under the land, in workshops, on the sea) could be trusted to guard the nation's piety and liberties. The Lord had told Adam, "In the sweat of thy face shalt thou eat bread," and the oft-quoted line buttressed the sentiment that manual labor was the only honest, authentic, and natural kind. It required a certain toughness then perceived as male and a practical knowledge that idle, speculative minds wholly lacked. It signified a historic shift from the old idea that hard work was necessary but dishonorable to a new belief in the superiority of those whose daily lives required exertion and strain. This was why, in 1834, Senator Thomas Hart Benton, a Jacksonian stalwart, hailed "the productive and burden-bearing classes" as one entity. Having an occupation, doing the necessary work of society, was what entitled "the people" to have power.[13]

The producer ethic was decidedly *not* an Americanized version of the class consciousness Marx and other European thinkers saw as the inevitable result of the Industrial Revolution. While many advocates of producerism arose from the growing ranks of wage earners, they cast a moral net over society instead of dissecting it with an analytical scalpel in the Marxist fashion. Besides the urban proletariat, the ranks of "producers" typically included craftsmen (some of whom owned their own shops), small merchants and manufacturers, and farmers of all regions and incomes. Until the sectional crisis took center stage in the mid-1840s, even slave-holding planters who planned and supervised the raising of crops embraced the title. To qualify as a producer, one had to be willing to rise or fall primarily on one's own efforts; intentions mattered more than results.

This blurring of class differences bothered some radical artisans. In the late 1820s, the New York City machinist Thomas Skidmore argued that entrepreneurs were not producers and that each adult man should be granted an equal proportion of the total land. But the broader definition dominated political rhetoric, providing a moral benchmark that excluded few potential voters.

It did, however, omit women—even though female garment workers, textile operatives, and shoe-binders were a major segment of the antebellum industrial workforce. Every male producer, it was assumed, strove for independence, to control his own and his family's economic fate through skilled labor and/or the steady improvement of property. A woman working for wages, the ideology held, signified the poverty and degradation of her husband, father, or brother. An independent people were thus dominated by self-reliant men.[14]

From its earliest formulations, the producer ethic was roughly synonymous with male citizens who belonged to what the Philadelphian known as Publius called "the middling sort." They paid America's taxes, fought its wars, and upheld the ideal of economic independence even if, temporarily, conditions might force some to toil for wages. The middle was a broad category, but not an all-inclusive one. Above it sat a tiny elite that lived off the labor of others. Below it was a larger group whose poverty seemed perpetual and whose behavior appeared servile, undisciplined, and childlike. Some antebellum Protestant champions of the producing classes shoved the mounting numbers of Irish-Catholic immigrants into this lowest stratum; nativist tracts are full of images of drunken Paddies, licentious Bridgets, and famine survivors who didn't mind living like pigs. But African-Americans provided a far more durable and emotionally charged subject for collective scorn.

The rising of "the people" was an avowedly white affair; the democratic vision rarely extended across the color line. Producers, especially the wage earners among them, feared slaves, not just as economic competitors, but as omnipresent symbols of what utter dependence on men of wealth and social standing could mean—the specter of feudalism on American soil. The language of the Revolution had encouraged such an opinion; in 1775, John Adams wrote, "There are but two *sorts* of men in the world, freemen and slaves." By the 1820s, workers in Northern cities routinely protested against being treated as "white slaves" and refused to call their employers by the preindustrial term "master" because it evoked the bondage of the South. Meanwhile, many of these same white workers flocked to minstrel shows where their brethren in blackface sketched the allure and vitality of a race that supposedly lived without material burdens or sensual restraints. The amalgam of loathing and fascination marked all blacks, even the minority who were free, as a perpetual other. They could never be part of the middling and productive majority. Worst of all, as their banning from Fourth of July celebrations in many cities suggested, they were not even truly Americans.[15]

This defense of cultural apartheid did not remain the sole populist sentiment on race. Later, activists in the People's Party and the labor movement would seek an alliance with blacks who shared their economic interests. But the language of white discontent never dealt comfortably with African-Americans. Even the most tolerant populist speakers tried to minimize the profound meaning of our race-divided history, to treat blacks as just one section of a glorious pluralist orchestra or to promote them into categories of "worker," "labor," and/or "producer" whose dominant images were always white.

Not surprisingly, few black activists took the bait. "Race first" was, at most times, an obligatory strategy of self-defense—even though it alienated white support. Blacks could not simply join the great majority in its struggle with a succession of elites; too often, that majority blocked their attempts to rise above the status of servile and menial labor. This uneasy stance toward "the people" often led black activists to withhold or qualify obeisance to the great patriotic abstractions. In 1829, the black abolitionist David Walker sarcastically demanded "inquiry and investigation respecting our miseries and wretchedness in this *Republican Land of Liberty! ! ! ! ! !*" And, in 1965, Malcolm X complained, "Just because you're in this country doesn't make you an American. No, you've got to go farther than that before you can become an American. You've got to enjoy the fruits of Americanism."[16]

The third major element in the populist inheritance was *the elite,* the perpetual antithesis and exploiter of "the people." For self-proclaimed outsiders, the image of the enemy took on particular importance. A persuasive rendering of political evil could transform radical dissenters into legitimate contenders for power, reversing the natural advantages possessed by those who already held it. From the 1790s on, champions of the people described the elite as being everything that devout producers, thankfully, were not: condescending, profligate, artificial, effete, manipulative, given to intellectual instead of practical thinking, and dependent on the labor of others.

Of course, these were also characteristics of monarchs and aristocrats, the very classes the Revolution had fought against. Thus, the elite could be accused of betraying the core principles of the republic, of behaving more like George III than like those who had defeated him. Because a belief in the superiority of American ideals undergirded such accusations, they could sometimes take a xenophobic turn. Future activists who called a political idea or pattern of behavior they opposed Papist, English, German, or Russian were evoking a hostile identification with Old World tyrannies that was hard to dispel. We still use words like *czar, empire,* and *robber baron* as metaphors for power—albeit with a degree of esteem as well as distrust.

While the elite, in populist discourse, retained its basic traits of character, the location of evil frequently shifted. For Jeffersonians, it lay in a pro-British cabal of merchants, landholders, and conservative clerics; for Jacksonians, a "money power" directed by well-born cosmopolitans. For activists in the new Republican Party of the 1850s, it was the "slave power" of the South that throttled the civil liberties and drove down the earnings of Northern whites.

Continuity lay in the assumption that the elite was a morbid growth on an otherwise healthy and democratic body politic; its attempt to centralize power in a few hands subverted the principles of self-rule and personal liberty. And the elite's malevolence was seldom restricted to one sphere of activity—governmental, economic, or cultural. Immoral men would pollute any segment of society they could grasp. By calling the enemy an "octopus," "leech," "pig," or "fat cat," a populist speaker suggested that "the people" were opposing a form of savagery as much as a structure inimical to their interests. Character assassination was always essential to the rhetorical game.

The fourth element of the populist inheritance followed from the very nature of the task involved. To topple a tenacious foe, spontaneous risings against injustice were not sufficient. Early in the nineteenth century, reform activists began insisting that strong *movements*—typically called "crusades," "societies," or "parties" (whether or not they competed in elections)—must gird themselves for combat and not leave the field until the elitist opponent was utterly vanquished.

Bellicose language was intrinsic to the dynamic of change. Emerging so soon after the War of Independence, it was inevitable that populist speakers frequently referred to their "battles" and "campaigns," and compared themselves to "knights" and "soldiers." One evangelical tract published in 1811 bore the title, *The Battle-Axe and Weapons of War.*[17] The American tradition of an armed force of ordinary citizens, no doubt, encouraged the ubiquity of such metaphors.

But equally significant was the need to accomplish, nonviolently, a mission analogous to that of an army in combat: to *save* the ideals of the nation and to protect the welfare of the common folk who inhabited it. To talk in populist ways meant to favor a reassertion of "traditional" national principles, to fix good institutions (such as Congress, the presidency, and local government) damaged by elites. Exhortation about a romantic vision of the "real" America was an instrument of cleansing and purification—whatever the actual policies being advanced.

Throughout the Western world during the early nineteenth century, social movements arose that were capable, for the first time, of challenging employers and entrenched state authorities on a national scale. But their healthy existence in the United States was critical evidence that "the people" remained the sons (and daughters) of freemen; that active, even unruly, discontent honored America better than did protection of the status quo.[18]

Populist rhetoric, like all attempts to sway an idealistic multitude, had some notable silences. Devotees of the public will often made only a ritualistic gesture toward their elitist opponents' right to be heard. And defenders of the majority culture saw little reason to be tolerant toward minorities who mocked their values and made no effort to shed their own. And neither, in the antebellum period nor after, did populist speakers dwell upon the acquisitive temperament and profit-mindedness so central to the engine of American capitalism. Like Tom Watson in 1892, they championed "individual enterprise" or equal opportunity in the marketplace but decried the division between haves and have-nots as a perversion of the democratic spirit. Thus, the language stayed rooted in contradiction, expressing an altruistic faith in collective uplift for a society that worshiped self-interest.

This, then, was a profound inheritance for challengers to established power, whatever their movement or the context of their particular struggle. Rationalist and pietistic rebels shared in its creation, and the language was available in equal measure to both forces. There was a difference in emphasis, of course. Descendants of the Enlightenment stressed economic grievances and reaffirmed the producer ethic, while evangelicals fixed on the ethical beliefs of the majority and called on the nation to return to Christ. Not until the twentieth century did the differences harden, separating insurgents into quarreling camps that have never reconciled.

PEOPLE'S HEROES

The antebellum United States produced not just the major concepts that future friends of the "common people" would argue about and use. It was also a Golden Age of political leadership—or so it later seemed. The battle for mass democracy waged from the 1790s to the 1860s called forth giants who fought with pen, party, and sword. Public speech was more precise, confident, and authentically idealist in those years; it had not yet been cheapened by florid excess and the mass reproduction of clichés. A man could become famous by stating the populist wisdom in fresh and bold ways. But he would not become a legend unless he had first been a victor.

A trio of populist heroes emerged in this era: Thomas Jefferson, Andrew Jackson, and Abraham Lincoln. Each sprang from a culturally specific region—the Chesapeake, the Southern frontier, the Old Northwest—and led the nation during a distinct period that bequeathed its own legacy of political contention and mythic triumph: the Revolutionary era, the Age of the Common Man, and the Civil War. Each man was remembered for inspiring ordinary Americans (assumed to be white) to participate in defending themselves, and for employing both rational and spiritual arguments to sanctify the cause of democratic rule—though Jefferson, a Deist who viewed Jesus only as a great moral teacher, rarely employed the latter. Once installed in the national canon, each man enabled postbellum reformers to claim legitimate descent from a glorious past while they railed against those who wielded power unjustly in the present.[19]

Jefferson was the one Founding Father whose very name became a signifier of democracy. Patrick Henry and Samuel Adams argued eloquently and persuasively for independence, and George Washington commanded the Revolutionary army and then the new federal state. But among the patriots any schoolchild could identify, only Thomas Jefferson had focused his intellectual energies on defining the contest between the virtuous people and a selfish elite and, over a half-century of public words and actions, had demonstrated his devotion to the side of the majority.

By quoting Jefferson, the Sage of Monticello, Populists in the South could claim a Democratic icon as their own, softening the break from the "party of the fathers" while challenging the opposition to adhere to the letter of what he had taught. The statement that "all men are created equal" caused no problem in the age of Jim Crow because its writer had always qualified it in regard to Africans and Indians. Outside the South, reformers cited Jefferson on the superior virtue of farmers, the efficacy of political rebellion, and the need for a government whose every act served the public will. In the Gilded Age, many an insurgent masthead and banner carried the great man's slogan: "Equal rights for all, special privileges for none."[20]

Central to constructing the faith were Jefferson's early statements about the fit between producerism and democracy. In the mid-1790s, Jefferson had appropriated the term *republican* for his faction in the conflict emerging within the young national government. The "anti-republicans" were, he wrote, a doomed aristocracy of pro-British merchants, unprincipled officeholders, and "nervous persons, whose languid fibres have more analogy with a passive than an active state of things." In contrast, "the Republican part" included, simply, the "entire body of landholders throughout the United States" and the "body of labourers . . . whether in husbanding or the arts." Jefferson spoke, in classical republican terms, of commercial pursuits making men incapable of disinterested rule. But later generations read him as arguing that manual pursuits were also the only moral, even the only patriotic, ones.[21]

Centralized authority, wrote Jefferson, was always a fetter on productive and resourceful citizens. In his first inaugural address, he gloried that the new nation had enough land "for our descendants to the thousandth and thousandth generation," and portrayed an ideal state that, today, we would consider libertarian: "a wise and frugal Government, which shall restrain men from injuring one another, shall leave them otherwise free to regulate their own pursuits of industry and improvement, and shall not take from the mouth of labor the bread it has earned." Originally meant to criticize Federalist pomp and ceremony, the statement and many others like it promoted the idea that the state was, by nature, an institution that common Americans should mistrust. As a body of paper-shufflers who liked to give orders, it would only episodically, accidentally represent the views and serve the interests of the hardworking masses.[22]

In the decades after his death, most champions of the people—insurgents and officeholders alike—viewed Jefferson as an indispensable, if somewhat detached, philosopher of first principles. His elegant prose was a reservoir of holy proverbs, their validity (if not their contemporary application) obvious to all. The Virginian's legacy, wrote Richard Hofstadter, was not "a [particular] system of economics or politics, but an imperishable faith expressed in imperishable rhetoric."[23] Safely ensconced in the era of perukes and knee breeches, he was remembered as a tribune who preferred the pastoral joys of Monticello to the rough-and-tumble of party conflict.

In sharp contrast, Andrew Jackson was regarded as a ruthless fighter who wielded language as a weapon to "save the republic from its enemies."[24] For him, partisanship was a necessary and permanent device to mobilize the forces of Democracy against the aristocratic "money power" of his day. Tom Watson collapsed Jackson's military and political achievements into one triumphant historical metaphor. "Oh, for an hour of that stern old warrior," rhapsodized the Georgian in 1892, "before whose Militia Rifles the veterans of Waterloo melted away, and before whose fiery wrath the combined money-kings bit the dust!" That Jackson also fiercely defended his Calvinist beliefs reassured citizens who were uncomfortable with a secular approach to politics.[25]

Populists like Watson did not label themselves Jacksonians or treat Jackson's words as holy writ (a wise decision, since close advisers wrote his most memorable statements). Jackson's concise reshaping of Jeffersonian principles merely produced an image of commonsensical toughness on which future admirers could rely for strength. A president who took every supposed slight against democracy as a personal insult encouraged his followers to do the same.

In recent years, historians have demolished the notion that, by any hardheaded social and economic definition, anything like "Jacksonian democracy" ever existed. From 1825 to 1850, income differentials in most parts of the United States actually increased; a new class of industrial capitalists subdivided and cheapened many traditional crafts while luring growing numbers of people from the countryside and abroad to slip on the harness of lifelong wage labor. Meanwhile, wealthy men dominated the leadership of both major parties (the Democrats and the Whigs) and rotated top offices, elected and appointed, among their friends and relatives. President Jackson, for all his fulminations against the "rich and powerful," owned a mansion near Nashville fully as elegant as that outside Philadelphia of his archenemy Nicholas Biddle, the president of the Second Bank of the United States. As one historian has commented, "The age may have been named after the common man but it did not belong to him."[26]

Yet, Jackson and his loyal followers (and speechwriters) did not come by their posthumous reputation dishonestly. Their rhetoric championed the cause of equal *access* to property and wealth, not the "equality of conditions" that Alexis de Tocqueville thought he had discovered in Columbia's green and informal land. Following the sainted Jefferson, Jacksonians viewed the two parts of American society in moral terms: "producers of the middling and lower classes" versus "the consumers, the rich, the proud, the privileged," as the New York editor William Leggett put it. This validated the new world of mass electoral politics by appealing to the widest possible coalition within it.[27]

In mid-nineteenth-century Europe, socialists, with the support of a sturdy press and a burgeoning workers' subculture, urged a complete break with the system they called capitalism. But in the United States, presidents, plebeian trade unionists, and "antimonopoly" editors alike only wanted the stated ideals of the "free labor system," the heritage of all citizens, to be practiced in the present and future. Left unfettered by "consumers" with inherited wealth and "special privileges," there seemed no reason why every plainspoken white male citizen could not pursue happiness in his own modest fashion.[28]

Jacksonians used the general's own biography to reinforce these convictions. Jackson was the first chief executive to rise from humble origins (he was both a small farmer and an apprentice saddler); his allies concealed details like his ownership of 150 slaves that might lead voters to doubt Jackson was truly one of them. He was also the first president referred to by a nickname, Old Hickory, which his admiring troops had given him during the War of 1812. As the novelist Joseph Conrad observed about one of his characters, "a nickname may be the best record of a success."[29]

The battle in the early 1830s over rechartering the Second Bank of the United States was the moment at which Jacksonian language crystallized into the form that grassroots activists would later claim as a tradition. Jackson's 1832 Veto Message (whose composition was directed by Attorney General Roger Taney) was a general indictment of the abuses of law and the thwarting of popular desires made possible by Nicholas Biddle's "monopoly." The president's message particularly harped on the fact that "more than a fourth part of the stock" was owned by "foreigners." The bank's congressional supporters, arguing that Jackson had given no real evidence for his most lavish attacks, that foreign capitalists had no vote in bank affairs, and that, in Daniel Webster's words, "The objection lies against all banks," missed the force of the message.[30]

The bank was perceived as evil precisely because it was a *public* creation holding public funds—but it operated as a *private* business on what seemed a tremendous scale. Did not the bank grant loans and invest capital where and when the well-educated and well-to-do directors considered it most prudent, thereby making or ruining whole industries and localities? That situation, Jacksonians argued, fostered "special privileges," unwise speculation, and an attitude of arrogance toward the lower orders. Most Americans' view of what the economy needed differed greatly from that of bankers contemplating the world from a plush address on Chestnut Street in Philadelphia. As Jackson claimed in 1834: "The Bank . . . is in itself a Government which has gradually increased in strength from the day of its establishment. The question between it and the people has become one of power."[31]

The "money power" had a particularly mysterious, nefarious character because it dealt in commodities—bonds, stocks, paper currency—that were artificial, whose value was not directly connected to human labor. Jackson knew the economy could not do without financial establishments and, in fact, his administration enabled several new state banks to compete with the Bank of the United States. But his rhetoric painted banks as an evil force whose normal functions, especially the issuance of paper money not backed by specie, corrupted the cherished principle that hard work should receive fair and reliable compensation.

This was the first concentrated salvo ever fired at a financial elite in the United States, and it echoed far beyond its immediate audience. The repetition of terms like "the Monster Bank," "the money power," and "financial monopoly" offered the emerging mass public of small entrepreneurs, ambitious shopkeepers, and strapped wage earners a way to blame their misfortunes on a haughty, unelected cabal instead of on the economic system as a whole.

To later generations of sufferers, this persistent demon, in the garb of "Wall Street" and "international bankers," demonstrated that money, whether "hard" or "soft," was not a symptom of deeper, structural ills but the problem itself. If insurgent politicians could throttle the barons of high finance, they need do little else. The federal government, Jackson lyrically proposed during the battle over the bank, should be "a plain system, void of pomp, protecting all and granting favors to none, dispensing its blessings, like the dews of Heaven, unseen and unfelt save in the freshness and bounty they contribute to produce."[32]

From the 1830s on, inexpensive urban newspapers called the penny press framed and promoted the Jacksonian viewpoint for an avid clientele of artisans, laborers, and homemakers who streamed into the cities from the countryside and the Continent. Such pioneers of the penny press as James Gordon Bennett of the *New York Herald* and Horace Greeley of the *New York Tribune* published graphic, dramatic accounts of crime, politics, and business that explicitly took the side of their working-class readers against various well-born and/or arrogant enemies in courts, countinghouses, and paternalistic moral reform associations. Bennett, an early Jackson supporter, liked to compare his periodical to what he called, in an original bit of invective, the "Wall Street press"—more expensive journals that catered to businessmen, professionals, and upper-class citizens who wanted to punish plebeian drinkers, gamblers, and brawlers. "The banks and corrupt *cliques* of men control them altogether," he charged in 1836.[33]

The penny press echoed the Jacksonian equation of toughness, maleness, and whiteness. For Old Hickory and his disciples, "manhood" was, above all, a means of self-defense. It signified protection for one's women, family, workmates, and nation against "aristocrats" who conspired with fawning blacks to undermine popular liberty. This brush tarred both abolitionists and slave-owners. In New York City, Tammany Hall, fusing partisan and racial messages, campaigned against the "Federal Whig Coon Party"; while Mike Walsh, a flamboyant radical congressman with a working-class constituency, denounced abolitionists as pawns for "wage slavery."[34] In the 1850s, most Democrats who joined the new Republican Party did so only because they believed "the Slave Power" had captured theirs. The issue that tore apart the nation's majority party frequently took the rhetorical form of a conflict over which aristocracy—that of Southern planters or of (pro-abolitionist) Northern factory owners—represented the greatest threat to the common white man.

Territorial expansion into Native American lands demonstrated another side of this phenomenon. It popularized a frontier style of producer ethic. Jackson's reputation as an uncompromising foe of the Indians, a man of action who scoffed at negotiations and legal formalities, was of immeasurable aid to his political career, especially in the South and West where "removal" of the "savages" found overwhelming support.[35] During the 1832 crisis over Cherokee lands in Georgia, Jackson's journalistic backers, many writing in the penny papers, praised him as an "untutored genius" who cut to the heart of the Indian problem and solved it swiftly. They contrasted Jackson's candid, blunt approach with the outraged opposition to Cherokee removal voiced by John Quincy Adams and Chief Justice John Marshall, whose university learning and sense of racial guilt allegedly paralyzed their manly faculties.[36]

After Jackson's time, many Americans (of both sexes) were drawn to men who emulated the virile, self-disciplined, straight-talking manner and artisanal self-confidence associated with the nineteenth-century frontier. From Natty Bumppo to Davy Crockett (who was a Whig, but no matter), and from Tom Mix to John Wayne, the scout in leatherstockings shades into the cowboy in tall hat and boots; fictional characters mix with fictionalized heroes in a seamless drama of "taming" the West. In the 1890s, the historian Frederick Jackson Turner contributed his famous argument that the frontier was essential to America's democratic attitudes and institutions. Old Hickory was the frontiersman as people's hero; three decades after his death, even a critic could write that most Americans had trusted the soldier-statesman to be "honest and patriotic . . . battling for them against corruption and extravagance, and opposed only by dishonest politicians. They loved him as their friend."[37]

Abraham Lincoln became a different kind of populist ally, one admired more for his lucid eloquence and explicit sympathy for working people than for his aggressive leadership in the war to preserve the Union and free the slaves. For Americans today, Lincoln is a figure of such monumental consensus—the masterful orator, the compassionate victor, the huge statue on the Mall—that it is hard to recapture his identity as an avatar of discontented white producers. But when movement activists in the Gilded Age and early twentieth century quoted Lincoln, it was usually to indict an entrenched foe—especially those Northern politicians who had betrayed the martyr's principles and lacked his compassion. A bogus "Prophesy" by Lincoln, warning that "the money power of the country will endeavor to prolong its reign . . . until all wealth is aggregated in a few hands, and the republic is destroyed," circulated widely at the turn of the century. A Populist poet from Nebraska reproached President Grover Cleveland:

In the sainted Lincoln's chair
Beats a heart which knows no care
For the lot of those who toil in his domain,
For the many millions poor,
Seeking work from door to door
That they may the honest needs of life obtain.[38]

For insurgents, Lincoln's legacy was, above all, that of the railsplitter as president—a man who rose to greatness but never forgot his plebeian past. "A plain man of the people," Emerson called him days after the assassination, and the image stuck.[39] For trade unionists in the Gilded Age and early twentieth century, Lincoln was an advocate of the producer as the moral cornerstone of a unified republic. Labor orators often repeated his comment on an 1860 shoemakers' strike in Lynn, Massachusetts: "I am glad to see that a system of labor prevails in New England under which laborers CAN strike." And both Christian reformers and budding Marxists welcomed his sentiment that "the strongest bond of human sympathy, outside of the family relation, should be one uniting all working people, of all nations, and tongues, and kindreds."

Activists, whether or not they represented wage earners, also found it useful to quote Lincoln's oft-stated faith in the universal potential for self-improvement and his disdain for social deference. According to the historian Gabor Boritt:

> It had all begun long ago with a poor boy's conviction . . . that a man should receive the full fruit of his labor so that he might get ahead in life. The boy became a man and a politician, and worked through the better part of his life to the end that government might always be dedicated to that proposition.[40]

After the hero's death, his career was compared with the "artificial" means by which men like the "robber barons" had climbed to a perch far above their fellows. Thus Lincoln was turned into a Jackson for Northerners, a cooler but no less determined ally of the producer in his ongoing contest with social parasites.

But what about Lincoln the Great Emancipator? Except among African-Americans who explicitly promoted that image (but not without some private misgivings about his vacillating performance), the actions Lincoln took to abolish slavery—indeed his belief that racial equality should be a core principle of Americanism—were either ignored or significantly muted in the half-century following his death. Most Northern reformers wanted to heal sectional wounds, to convince Southerners to support anti-corporate causes that, ostensibly, had nothing to do with race. At the same time, several leading segregationists pointed to Lincoln's statements about black inferiority to promote their own agenda. Thomas Dixon, Jr., a Negrophobic ex-minister from North Carolina whose 1915 book *The Clansmen* glorified the Ku Klux Klan, depicted Lincoln as a Southerner by birth and character who hated abolitionists more than slaveholders. Dixon even wrote a play about the Republican icon that had a short run on Broadway. Its title was *A Man of the People*.[41]

So, for decades, Lincoln was cherished by most political activists and propagandists for attributes other than what, besides the Union's victory itself, was the central achievement of his presidency. Besides his producer identity, he was lauded as a rough frontiersman ("a homely hero, born of star and sod" sang Illinois schoolchildren); a devout man who demonstrated his piety with what William Jennings Bryan called the "frequent use of Bible language and of illustrations drawn from

Holy Writ"; and a great public speaker who put in "simple, natural" language the basic truths of "democracy's dream."[42] Lessons drawn from Lincoln's upbringing and undeniable eloquence gained precedence over what he actually did as president—except among ideological stalwarts, both North and South, who insisted that the meaning of the Civil War could not be nudged aside with the reiteration of phrases about showing "malice toward none" and "charity for all."

As with all "invented traditions," the populist icons made of three quite dissimilar presidents represent a melding of sentiment and strategy.[43] Jefferson bequeathed a seemingly timeless set of political maxims, the creed of democracy as the chosen pursuit of moral men. Jackson presented political activists with the ideal temperament for taking on resourceful antagonists and the hope that, from the ranks of the lowly, a new type of social order could arise. Old Hickory and his compatriots also left a concrete guide to skewering opposing elites: challenge their manhood, their links to high (and corrupt) finance, and their allegiance to white producers. And Lincoln was the exemplar of the common man who stayed true to his roots, and whose behavior and prose could instruct future Americans to do the same.

Grassroots champions of small farmers and wage earners warmed themselves by such images. They gave human form to their conviction that the producing classes had both virtue and common sense on their side. Articulated, such confidence was a shield against pillars of the status quo who pelted Tom Watson and his kind with labels like "moral dynamiter" and "anarchist rabble." The people's icons had vanquished arrogant powers in the past; couldn't their ideological descendants do the same?

Populist speakers rarely paused to consider the appropriateness of hero worship. Their very reliance on icons, past and present, showed that the age of mass democracy had not destroyed the older political tradition of deference to great leaders. A people's champion, preferably one in the White House, was as significant to advancing the cause of ordinary people as absolute monarchs had once been to opposing it. Thus, an enduring irony of populism: this language that praises connections between anonymous people and mistrusts the palaver of elites has often been communicated most effectively by eloquent men who stand above the crowd.

But then, the path to success for movements that do not favor revolution has always run through reform-minded members of the existing establishment, aspiring members of a counter-elite, or both. New kinds of laws, administrative bodies, and elected officials are the harvest of all that the pamphlets, strikes, and demonstrations—the repertoire of discontent—have sown. In the United States, links between social movements and governing elites began in the 1790s with an alliance between Jefferson's Republicans and plebeian pamphleteers like William Manning. They continued, almost without pause, into the Clinton administration, two centuries later.

This symbiosis was intrinsic to the political process. Without strong movements to arouse and mobilize grievances at the grassroots, elite reformers stood naked before their stand-pat adversaries. Yet, without the aid of insiders able to speak to a national constituency and work the levers of government, movements withered away or became impotent, bitter shells. Legitimacy of this sort carries a price, of course. Movements usually have to shear off their radical edges and demonstrate that, if necessary, they can march to the rhetorical beat of an influential set of allies. The boundaries, as well as the benefits, of this relationship—in all their historical specificity—are central to what the friends of "the people" have been able to say and what they have been able to achieve.

The virtuous producer slays the twin-headed serpent of monopoly and major-party domination in a print produced by the Union Labor Party, 1888. *(Courtesy of the Library of Congress)*

Chapter 2

The Righteous Commonwealth of the Late Nineteenth Century

The day of small things was past, and I don't suppose it will ever come again in this country.
—William Dean Howells, *The Rise of Silas Lapham,* 1885

The People's Party is the protest of the plundered against the plunderers—of the victim against the robbers.
—Tom Watson, 1892

Jesus was only possible in a barefoot world, and he was crucified by the few who wore shoes.
—Ignatius Donnelly

MEETING IN ST. LOUIS

ON Washington's Birthday in 1892, hundreds of grassroots activists from all over the nation came to St. Louis to participate in a four-day Industrial Conference that concluded by launching a new political party.

This was not a unique occurrence. Third parties were common if not entirely respectable features of the frenzied political landscape of the late nineteenth century, which featured lavish partisan pageants and the highest voter participation in American history. For two decades, critics of the Democrats and Republicans had been contesting national, state, and local elections under a diversity of banners: Prohibition, Greenback, Anti-Monopoly, Labor Reform, Union Labor, United Labor, Workingmen, and hundreds of local and state Independent parties whose very name denoted repudiation of the rules of the electoral game. Established politicians had grown accustomed to deploying whatever linguistic and legal weapons were needed—ridicule, repression, co-optation—to swat down these disjointed but persistently fractious challengers.[1]

But the People's Party formed inside St. Louis's Exposition Hall appeared to be, at least potentially, a much broader vehicle than its predecessors, one capable of speaking to and for the millions of Americans who were alienated from the corporate order that had grown to maturity since the Civil War.[2] The base of the party was among debt-ridden small farmers in cotton-growing regions of the old Confederacy and wheat-growing areas of the Great Plains, many of whom were members of the Farmers' Alliance that had begun in Texas in 1877. But Populist organizers reached out, with increasing success, to some of the most visible, active reformers of their time: to the middle-class, anti-saloon crusaders of the Woman's Christian Temperance Union (WCTU) and the Prohibition Party, to the urban workers of the Knights of Labor and the American Federation of Labor (AFL), to the salon utopians of Edward Bellamy's Nationalist Clubs and the mostly working-class advocates of Henry George's single tax on land, and to Christian Socialists in seminaries and evangelical churches across the land.

To marshal such a grand coalition of outsiders required a meld of the kinds of discourse that were favored by pietists and producers, Catholics as well as Protestants. The central metaphor was salvation from an elite whose power appeared both monstrous and seamless. "There is a party that the people can trust," the journalist Henry Demarest Lloyd told a working-class audience in Chicago during the campaign of 1894, "because in the face of overwhelming odds, without distinguished leaders, money, office, or prestige, it has raised the standard of a principle to save the people."[3] Such rhetoric attempted to bridge divisions bred of class, ethnicity, religious denomination, and prior partisan loyalties. Perhaps, by adhering to principle, the David of Populism would be able to convince enough Americans to join in toppling the Goliath of concentrated wealth and corrupt state power. But failure, warned activists, would guarantee the domination of the "money power" into a dark and distant future.

The reformers who came to St. Louis late in the winter of 1892 represented this hope and this fear. In the grandiose (and, in terms of gender, inaccurate) phrase of a sympathetic reporter for Joseph Pulitzer's *Post-Dispatch,* "Every man who sat in Exposition Hall as a delegate . . . believed in his soul that he sat there as a history-maker."[4]

The meeting concluded with a unifying, inspirational moment to rival any in Gilded Age politics. A 61-year-old Minnesotan named Ignatius Donnelly—novelist, amateur scientist, professional lecturer, Roman Catholic, a man who had, for a generation, fueled the antimonopoly cause with his eloquent if somewhat eccentric energies—read the crowd of 10,000 his preamble to the conference platform. The document of twelve short paragraphs, as altered slightly for the party's first nominating convention in Omaha that July, was the pithiest—and soon became the most widely circulated—statement of the Populist credo.

"The conditions which surround us best justify our co-operation," began this "Declaration of Union and Industrial Independence." "We meet in the midst of a nation brought to the verge of moral, political, and material ruin." With the practiced modulation and cadence of a veteran (and sometime professional) orator, Donnelly made the indictment: "Corruption dominates the ballot-box . . . The people are demoralized . . . The newspapers are subsidized or muzzled . . . The urban workmen are denied the right of organization for self-protection . . . A vast conspiracy against mankind has been organized on two continents and is rapidly taking possession of the world." And what were the Democrats and Republicans doing to alleviate these "dreadful conditions"? They were ignoring them, to debate, yet again, about tariff rates, "a sham battle" that only demonstrated their venality and utter neglect of America's needs.[5]

Having reminded the delegates of the urgency of their task, Donnelly turned to the solution. As befit the tone of republican jeremiad that he had established, he pointed toward the virtues of the past. The Populists would bring the nation back to its roots of egalitarian principle and the harmony of all social classes. Donnelly vowed, "we seek to restore the Government of the Republic to the hands of the 'plain people' with whom it originated. Our doors are open to all points of the compass. We ask all honest men to join with and help us." Then he quoted, almost verbatim, the preamble to the U.S. Constitution.

Finally, Donnelly underlined the moral and political basis for the Populists' proposals, a collection of demands he and other reformers had promoted for decades: a graduated income tax, the unlimited coinage of both silver and gold, government ownership of the railroads, and more. "Wealth belongs to him who creates it," Donnelly intoned. Putting the same principle in harsher, biblical terms, he quoted St. Paul: "If any will not work neither shall he eat." And, to fuse rhetorically the two halves of the potential new majority, he asserted: "The interests of rural and urban labor are the same; their enemies are identical." Then he sat down.

It was a remarkable performance. Donnelly had summarized both the deepest fears and the most profound hopes of his audience. He had represented their cause as both radical and conservative: they would expand the power of the state only in order to restore the glories of an earlier day. They would challenge the power of the corporate, upper class and its political handmaidens only in order to expose the multiple evils of class rule itself, an incubus that was defiling the American dream.

Following Donnelly, Hugh Kavanaugh, chairman of the platform committee, read out the short list of demands. When he finished, the huge crowd exploded. According to a sympathetic journalist in attendance, "Hats, papers, handkerchiefs, etc. were thrown into the air; wraps, umbrellas and parasols waved; cheer after cheer thundered and reverberated through the vast hall, reaching the outside of the building where thousands had been waiting [*sic*] the outcome, joined in the applause till for blocks in every direction the exulation [*sic*] made the din indescribable."[6] No Populist candidate, no symbol in flesh of the reform upsurge of the 1890s ever had or ever would receive such an ovation. Cherishing principles over leaders, the men and women who had gathered in St. Louis set out to realize their mission.

CRUSADE AGAINST PLUTOCRACY

The road to St. Louis had not been an easy one. The nascent producer coalition upon which the Populists based their hopes was an unstable amalgam of social groups and political organizations with clashing priorities. Small farmers anxious about their debts wanted to inflate the money supply; while urban workers feared a hike in the prices they paid for food and rent. Prohibitionists and currency reformers both opposed the big money but differed over which of its sins was primary—the peddling of drink or the constriction of credit. And socialist voices in all their variety—Christian, Marxian, and Bellamyite—were at odds with most unionists and agrarian rebels, who affirmed their faith in private property and the malleability of the class structure. Factionalism was a perennial feature of reform politics in these years; not until 1892 did most groups cease pitching their panaceas long enough to unite behind the same third-party ticket.[7]

But, over the preceding two decades, these disparate bands agreed about two vital matters: what had gone wrong in America since Lee's surrender at Appomattox and why; and the urgent need for a messianic awakening to bring about the sweeping changes required. These commonalities made a grand coalition seem possible.

Ignatius Donnelly was speaking to every segment of the dissident throng when he evoked the misery of working Americans and blamed it on immoral men at the top. The grossly unequal character of postwar economic growth convinced activists from all social classes and regions that the days when a Jackson or Lincoln could rule were gone. The unprecedented size, market dominance, union-busting and price-gouging behavior of such corporations as Standard Oil, Carnegie Steel, and Southern Pacific Railroad led many late-nineteenth-century reformers to question the laissez-faire views which had previously seemed the best assurance that hard work would receive its just reward. Power was no longer married to principle.[8]

All the movements that rose after the Civil War used a similar vocabulary of self-defense, of urgent fortification against elitist foes. Their different constituencies and programs aside, Greenbackers and Knights of Labor, Prohibitionists and Socialists, members of the Farmers' Alliance, and disciples of Bellamy and Henry George agreed that a national crisis was at hand, comparable to the one that had led to the Civil War. Their beloved America had been wrenched from the path of righteousness and the control of the majority. Only the courageous, strenuous action of ordinary citizens could win it back.

Before the Civil War, the need for a democratic insurgency had been voiced, often eloquently, by major-party politicians. And, at first, internecine bloodletting only reinforced prior habits. Union soldiers marched into battle under the banner of "free labor," a cry that joined entrepreneurs, wage earners, and Republican politicians against a planters' society that rewarded the slothful and punished producers. For their part, Confederates and antiwar Northern Democrats viewed themselves as the authentic progeny of the Founding Fathers. Like the patriots who rose against

King George, they were compelled, they said, to oppose a regime (albeit an elected one) that was usurping their rights—of property and state sovereignty—and destroying their harmonious communities.

The sharp disillusionment that followed the war bred a bumper crop of anger. With privilege now resting securely in the saddle, the literature of reform bristled with narratives of degeneration, conspiracy, and betrayal. The only thing remarkable about Tom Watson's satiric history lesson and Ignatius Donnelly's fierce preamble was the felicity of their prose. Reform activists typically believed that they, or at least their parents, had fought a ruinous war to repel an assault on their freedom and way of life. But the war had solved nothing. Worse, in its aftermath, a new group of oppressors had captured power—armed with wealth, technology, and foreign allies far more extensive than those the antebellum lords of either lash or loom had been able to muster.[9]

In their wrath, Gilded Age insurgents made no mean contribution to the era's reputation for extravagant rhetoric. Erstwhile Republicans, whose old party had led the nation when the betrayal began, were particularly immoderate. Ignatius Donnelly came to Washington during the war as a Radical Republican congressman but left several years later, denouncing "the waste, extravagance, idleness and corruption" of the federal government and observing that "the great men of the nation dwindle into pygmies as you draw near them."[10] The suffragist Elizabeth Cady Stanton, the prohibitionist Frances Willard, the financial reformer James Weaver, and the labor journalist Andrew C. Cameron had also been dedicated Republicans. They broke with the party of Lincoln because they believed it had deserted its founding principles of free labor and moral government in the rush to court wealthy industrialists—in Donnelly's words, "the cruelest of all aristocracies, a moneyed aristocracy."[11] These reformers dedicated (or, in Stanton's case, rededicated) themselves to causes that required the same missionary zeal and certainty that a momentous choice was at hand that had earlier motivated their actions as abolitionists and/or Radical Republicans. In contrast, former Democrats like Tom Watson were restrained and ironic; they had never expected the party of Northern factory owners to serve the public interest.

For all grassroots reformers, the contemporary enemy bore many of the same names Jacksonians had employed—especially "the money power" and "monopoly." To these was added "plutocrat," a neologism all but unknown in the antebellum era. By any name, central banks and investment houses were still the main culprits. But now they were perceived as intertwined with large manufacturing concerns; men like J. P. Morgan and Andrew Carnegie had assembled a malignant force of unprecedented strength and unity of purpose. And their sway over the state dwarfed the influence of a Nicholas Biddle who, after all, had lost his earlier battle against "the people" and *their* president. The "money power" now signified a nonproductive, immeasurably wealthy octopus whose long, slimy tentacles reached from private firms on both sides of the Atlantic to grasp every household, business, and seat of government. "The money monopoly is the parent of all monopolies—

the very root and essence of slavery," asserted labor's Andrew Cameron, underlining a dread of bondage older than the republic itself.[12]

It was the unsung Greenbackers, who, starting in the late 1860s, first made elaborate arguments about the links between plutocrats and the low wages and lost chances of many Americans. Then, amid the severe depression of the mid-1870s, "the money power" trope was sprinkled generously throughout the speeches, articles, and letters of millions of people who were seeking a way to stigmatize the unseen, faraway forces that had such influence over their lives.[13] When the term *capitalist* was used, it normally referred to the men who controlled investment markets rather than, as in the Marxist sense, to the employers of wage labor.

Curiously, such attacks never explained why "the money power" had shifted from the advocacy of paper currency that had drawn Old Hickory's fire to a "hard money" position that sanctified the gold standard.[14] Clearly, what mattered, in each case, was the monster's theft of honest labor and hard-won property, not the particular brand of financial fire it spouted.

The continuity from the age of Jackson is obvious. Like that earlier generation of rhetorical democrats, Gilded Age reformers could disagree about which particular elite represented the greatest evil but were in accord on the immorality of parasitic wealth itself and the need to educate all citizens to its dangers. Neither Henry George's speculative landlords, the WCTU's liquor traffickers, nor Terence Powderly's "industrial oligarchs" had amassed their fortunes through honest toil—unless conspiracies to corner a market, to buy cheap and sell dear, or to debauch tired laborers were to be considered honest.[15]

This attack on the most successful men in American society could be crude, as in Greenback oratory about "thieves" and "frauds," or brilliant, as in *Progress and Poverty* (1879), Henry George's clear, passionate dissection of the woeful intricacies of land tenure and industrial development. In fact, long, learned arguments like George's against reigning economic orthodoxy were surprisingly popular. *Progress and Poverty* sold well over a million copies. The traveling lecturers and local editors of the Populist crusade delivered briefer but similar messages to audiences of small farmers and wage earners across the South and West. These political circuit riders assumed "the plain people" would comprehend their sermons, which were larded with metaphors drawn from European history and ancient philosophy as well as the Bible, simply because it was in their self-interest to do so.[16]

At the same time, insurgents often predicted that deliverance would have to come from a higher Power than the people themselves. "Revolution of some sort is not far off," warned Reverend George Herron, a Christian socialist, in 1895. "Either a religious movement, producing a revival such as the prophets dimly or never dreamed of, or blood such as never flowed will remit the sins of the existing order." In a plainer style, Jacob Coxey told his band of angry, unemployed followers before they set out on their small but well-publicized 1894 march on Washington, "This movement will either mark the second coming of Christ or be a total failure."[17]

Christian language was ubiquitous among those who tried to knit together an insurgent coalition. Secular arguments alone could neither evoke the scale of the problem nor incite the upheaval needed to set it right. A new surge of Christian revivalism—the third Great Awakening in American history—provided the context. In the 1870s and 1880s, hundreds of thousands of Americans flocked to tent meetings featuring the enormously popular sermons of Dwight L. Moody and the music of Ira Sankey; missionary societies sprouted from nearly every Protestant denomination. A growing number of urban ministers argued that the Lord's Prayer and the life of Jesus taught the collective nature of sin; these social gospelers—whose most prolific figures included Washington Gladden, Walter Rauschenbusch, and George Herron—aimed to create a new community of altruistic souls and rejected the conservative image of the individual miscreant left alone to face divine wrath. Mass movements had the potential to realize a solidarity that would turn America away from the worship of Mammon. Purifying society mattered more than did personal piety.[18]

Activists from a variety of social backgrounds echoed George Herron's grim, premillennialist prophecy. Many Northern evangelicals whose ancestors had once praised capitalism as a "free labor system" that allowed the entrepreneurial spirit to shine now looked with dread on "monopolies" that mocked Christian ideals of charity and brotherhood. Workers who seldom went to church and scorned conservative ministers were nevertheless fond of citing Scripture and invoking divine justice to condemn their enemies' actions and legitimize their own. For the Knights of Labor, corporate wealth was an "anti-Christ" that only a "new Pentecost" could defeat. "Brother Knights," one organizer wrote in 1882, "allow me to say that Moses, while fleeing from bondage and endeavoring to deliver his people from the hands of the Egyptian destroyer, received the imperative command from God to 'go forward.' The same injunction still comes to us, 'go forward.'"[19] Such Catholic activists as Father Edward McGlynn of New York City quieted their suspicions of Protestant perfectionism and delivered social homilies their immigrant parishioners could endorse. "Christ himself was an evicted peasant," said McGlynn. "He came to preach a gospel of liberty to the slave, of justice to the poor, or paying the full hire to the workman." *Looking Backward* (1888), Edward Bellamy's best-selling utopian novel, concludes with a febrile narrative of conversion. "I have been in Golgotha . . . I have seen Humanity hanging on a cross!" exclaims the hero after a hallucinatory walk through the streets of a mercenary, class-embittered Boston.[20]

This penchant for pious metaphor should not be understood as a desire to win more souls for Jesus. Most insurgents used a Christian vocabulary because it was the only way they knew to speak with great emotion about ultimate social concerns. Few activists called bluntly for the "application of Christian principles to politics,"[21] as did the Prohibition Party of Maine. But the contrast with prominent elite thinkers at the time is striking. In the late nineteenth century, appeals to "science" and "reason" came far more frequently from social Darwinist intellectuals like William Graham Sumner than from the ranks of trade unionists, discontented farmers, and temperance advocates.

Thus, Gilded Age insurgents wailed that Mammon and hypocrisy reigned over God, man, and principle in every major institution from the church to the factory to the once hallowed places where laws were debated and passed. Their prescription for change was, in a sense, a reactionary one. Edward Bellamy, the railroad union leader Eugene Debs, and the journalist Henry Demarest Lloyd all called for a "counterrevolution of the people" to dismantle this alarmingly radical new system that had fastened on the American republic.[22]

THE MORAL COMMUNITY

But defining "the people" created something of a problem. It was not enough to say that the majority of Americans belonged to what a Greenback propagandist called "the wealth-producing classes" and leave it at that. Such prominent conservatives as the editor of the *Nation,* E. L. Godkin, could also endorse the maxim that "labor creates all wealth" because they believed that "the industrious, prudent, self-denying, ingenious, shrewd and honest people" had *already* risen to the top of the economic order.[23] Moreover, by the late nineteenth century, the nation's social demography had become fearfully complex. Freed slaves and new immigrants from Eastern and Southern Europe and East Asia competed in the cities and on the land for work, property, and profits with those who had come earlier. How would the emerging producer coalition bridge gaps that were as much cultural as economic?

The path taken was a contradictory one, viable for a few election campaigns but ill suited to a movement seeking a long-term constituency and a secure niche in the political landscape. On the one hand, activists tended to inflate their definitions of producer and labor into a grand abstraction that ignored most differences of income and occupation. In so doing, they negated, ironically, their own impassioned charge that a yawning social gulf had made America resemble the "two nations" that had always existed in places like Britain, France, and Russia. Insurgents denounced the misery caused by unemployment, low wages, and tight money. But the humanitarian impulse led few to criticize employers or property owners as a class. To envision a political force parallel to that which Jackson or Lincoln had once commanded, it was necessary to deny that unequal economic rewards for various "producers" might hinder the search for a just, permanent solution to America's troubles.

Therefore, the most compelling definition of class standing became one's politics. Any sincere fighter against monopoly and plutocracy, regardless of occupation or social status, was, in effect, a producer. Among the "platforms of labor societies" printed in a widely circulated 1886 book about grassroots activism were statements from a variety of third parties, organizations of self-employed farmers, and groups composed mainly of wage earners. Nearly every platform—whether from the Knights of Labor, Agricultural Wheel, or Anti-Monopoly Party—hailed the "industrial masses" or "working classes" of both field and factory and cursed their "plundering" enemies.[24]

Under construction here was a moral community of self-governing citizens, not a conflict of economic classes. In fact, sympathetic local businessmen and professionals joined many local organizations of producers and sometimes served as their spokesmen. The Knights of Labor rarely allowed people other than wage earners to lead their local assemblies. But the Knights underlined the ethical core of their identity by barring only five groups from membership: bankers, land speculators, lawyers, liquor dealers, and gamblers. Such men (the gender was assumed) either preyed on human weaknesses or made a lucrative income without having to work very hard for it. Certainly, no sweat begrimed their well-fed countenances.[25]

Divisions on moral rather than class lines did inspire short-lived displays of social unity against "monopolistic" foes. The entire towns that rose up against railroad corporations during the mass strike of 1877, the explosive creation of independent parties in the 1880s, and the regional successes of the People's Party in the early 1890s all demonstrated the potential that support for a class-inclusive producer ethic had to throw a scare into local and national elites.

However, there was a danger in such an appeal that had not been evident upon its creation earlier in the nineteenth century. First, its fuzziness and hortatory style were fairly simple to imitate; Democratic and Republican competitors—who shared ideological roots and ancestral icons with the reformers—could and did co-opt it, plucking the chords of antimonopoly while rejecting enforceable measures to break up or discipline big corporations. The very suppleness of their rhetoric prevented Gilded Age reformers from blocking the political competitors who wanted to put them out of business.[26]

Second, the romance of producerism had a cultural blind spot; it left unchallenged strong prejudices toward not just African-Americans but also toward recent immigrants who had not learned or would not employ the language and rituals of this variant of the civic religion. Many insurgents who lauded the producer also stated or hinted that certain groups of people lacked the capacity to take on the monopolists in a sustained, ideologically stalwart way. This belief was clearest among unionists who asserted that "Slavs and 'Tally Annes' . . . Hungarians and Chinamen" were ignorant "black sheep" whom industrialists could easily manipulate and use to break strikes. "The republic cannot afford to have such ignorant animals within its borders," wrote one labor editor from Pittsburgh.[27]

Even those native-born activists who reached out to immigrant laborers assumed that men of Anglo-American origins had invented political democracy, prideful work habits, and well-governed communities of the middling classes. During the epic conflict with the Carnegie company in 1892, John McLuckie, a steelworker and town official from Homestead, Pennsylvania, told a mass meeting: "We are bound to Homestead by all the ties that men hold dearest and most sacred" and would have to decide "if we are going to live like white men in the future." Slovak workers in Homestead fought Pinkerton Agency guards alongside McLuckie and his "white" compatriots. But few of the latter sought to dispel the notion that they were helping backward aliens adopt a more advanced way of thinking and acting in the world.[28]

To one group of newcomers, not even the hand of paternalism was offered. Chinese (and later Japanese and Filipino) immigrants raised the specter of perpetual servility to elites that had long been associated, almost exclusively, with African-Americans. The minions of "coolie-ism" had to be banished lest plutocrats attempt to extend the system, like a slave power reborn, to Caucasian workers and farmers. Fear and loathing of the Chinese had begun among white Californians during the gold rush of the late 1840s and 1850s. A generation later, the Workingmen's Party of California made rapid political gains with vows to punish both the corrupt upper class and the Asian "coolies" who, it claimed, did their bidding. In 1877, the party vowed "to rid the country of cheap Chinese labor as soon as possible . . . because it tends still more to degrade labor and aggrandize capital."[29]

Such sentiments spread east at a rapid pace. By the 1880s, sharp, derogatory references to "Asiatics" and "Mongolians" were commonplace in the literature of the Knights of Labor and Farmers' Alliances, which aimed to attract working-class support. *Breaking the Chains,* a serialized 1887 novel by T. Fulton Gantt that championed the Knights, featured one Chinese character, the clever and unscrupulous cook for an opium-smoking land speculator and army officer. "He was among the most intelligent of the Chinamen immigrating to this country when Asia first turned loose upon us her horde of filthy, festering degradation," wrote Gantt. "He was a slave Coolie. . . . Upon getting his freedom he determined to seek employment as a body servant to the wealthiest debauchee he could find."[30]

That image of the scheming, amoral "Chinaman" starkly outlined the cultural limits of Gilded Age producerism. The regular performance of manual work was not enough to qualify one as a member of the laboring classes. As in Jackson's time, one also had to demonstrate a manly self-reliance, a refusal to defer to unjust authorities that was considered to be at the heart of Christian and American principles. Even a "most intelligent" immigrant from East Asia was still judged to be thinking and acting like a slave.

African-Americans recently freed from bondage could conceivably meet the test. But they had to eschew black nationalist sentiments, join white-dominated movements of workers and farmers, and avoid demanding a halt to the brutal regimen of Jim Crow instituted in the wake of Reconstruction. It also helped if blacks echoed the view that "Chinamen" naturally preferred submission to freedom, thus shifting the onus of dependency away from themselves. In 1879, a black coal miner wrote to a Greenback-Labor paper about "how divided the miners on the North and South railroad of Alabama are as regards a uniform price for mining coal. One would suppose that all emigrated from China or some other heathen country, to see the way they conduct themselves."[31]

For two decades before the founding of the People's Party, then, insurgents were nurturing a language of bitterness and betrayal. Sentimental about the mythic, lost world of smallholders and artisans, they demanded that elites cease their financial manipulation and political corruption and allow the people to rule once again. Millions of Americans were drawn to this critique—as the great popularity of *Progress and Poverty* and *Looking Backward* testified.

As politics, however, it fell woefully short. In no national election from 1872 to 1888 did the combined votes of all alternative parties top 4 percent of the total. The People's Party offered the best and perhaps the last chance to convert antimonopoly sentiment into a winning strategy.

THE POPULIST SYNTHESIS

Leading Populists understood that collective anger, no matter how well articulated, was not enough. To transcend despair, champions of the producing classes had to appeal to the majority of citizens whose interests they were so fond of invoking. Social differences had to be submerged, controversial moral issues played down, and regional divisions overcome in order to build a truly national organization.

A concept of Americanism unsullied by Civil War rancor could help. Opening the 1892 St. Louis conference, Benjamin Terrell of Texas counseled delegates that "the eyes of the toiling masses are upon you and they are expecting a second declaration of independence."[32] Leonidas Polk of North Carolina, a favorite for the new party's presidential nomination, received a standing ovation when he declared: "This meeting represents those men who are loyal to duty and loyal to country." And Polk, a former Confederate colonel (but never an apologist for slavery) took part in a ceremony that symbolically healed the sectional wound. Before the entire assemblage, he clasped hands with former Union Navy Commodore Van De Voort of Nebraska. A group of delegates then unfurled a huge American flag and waved it as the crowd cheered. Similar ceremonies of reconciliation were taking place elsewhere in the country as the nineteenth century neared its end—just as racial segregation was, not coincidentally, being written into law.

Also needed was a broad definition of "the people" that did not dull the term's producerist edge. Polk called on "the great Northwest, great South, and great West" to take over the government and right the economic balance upset by the financial powers of the Northeast. Orator after orator hailed "the toilers," "the industrial classes," and "farmers and laborers of the entire country" in a manner simultaneously vague and imbued with a muscular pride in manual production that men who worked for a living and were accustomed to voting for one of the two major parties could appreciate.

There were occasional hints of a more restrictive meaning. Terence Powderly of the Knights of Labor, himself an Irish Catholic, scorned new immigrants as "unfortunate" creatures whom good Americans "must educate year after year to prevent them from using bombs instead of ballots." But this narrowing of "the people" to earlier arrivals and the American-born apparently brought no protest. Few Populists were flagrant nativists. But all could applaud Powderly's implication that they were defending vital national interests "plutocrats" and their pawns in government were betraying.[33]

Rhetoric that encouraged a coalition of forces came naturally to leaders like Donnelly, Watson, and Polk. They were creatures of the age of mass politics that had begun in the 1830s with the creation of modern party structures, the public lecture circuit, and a demotic press. Their sentimental visions and cataclysmic warnings rode on the long wave of romanticism that had first swelled in the 1830s under both Jacksonian democrats and abolitionists. But their unifying grandiosity also stemmed from the wily pragmatism of the coalition builders and ticket balancers who had built the Democratic, Whig, and Republican parties into vote-gathering machines of impressive efficiency. Knowing how to whip up a massive crowd without turning off important groups not in attendance was a skill practiced by many kinds of American politicians. In a nation where no social class or ideological passion attached itself for long to any organization, even radicals had to dress up their principles to fit the occasion.

The Populists put forth a platform intended to satisfy a range of constituencies, only a few of which were already safely inside its fold. For debt-ridden agrarians, they promised an increase in the money supply, a ban on alien land ownership, and a state takeover of the railroads that so often made small farmers pay whatever they could bear. For wage earners, they endorsed the ongoing push for a shorter working day, called for the abolition of the strike-breaking Pinkerton Agency, and declared that "the interests of rural and civil labor are the same." For currency reformers and residents of Western mining states, they demanded the unlimited coinage of both silver and gold. Appended to the platform were such "supplementary resolutions" as a "pledge" to continue the healthy pensions already being granted to Union veterans and support for a boycott of a Rochester clothing manufacturer being struck by the Knights of Labor.[34]

Except for the pensions (a Republican standby), this was an agenda neither of the major parties would support. But it clearly showed a desire to move away from the monistic nostrums that had gripped the competing battalions of reform for a generation. The defeat of planks for prohibition and woman suffrage at the St. Louis conference signaled there would be no open attack on cultural attitudes that separated Northern men from Southern men, and most Catholics from most Protestants. The Populists didn't just want to be heard, they wanted to win. Through a network of over 150 local newspapers (most in the South and West) and scores of skilled itinerant lecturers attached to the movement, the Populists articulated a shrewd synthesis of beliefs grassroots reformers and radicals had been writing, orating, and praying about for the past twenty years.[35]

They first attempted to reconcile the contradictory truths inherited from antebellum and more recent champions of the common man. To keep faith with a proud (and consensual) lineage, Populist writers and orators repeatedly quoted one or more of the deceased icons of democracy. Perhaps the best practitioner of this was the popular Texas lecturer James "Cyclone" Davis. As he spoke around the nation, Davis kept the complete works of Thomas Jefferson—"the sainted sire of American liberty"—close to him on the podium. He often searched through them, as if they were scripture, for answers to audience questions about such issues as free silver and government ownership of the railroads. In a few Southern states, reformers called their new political organization Jeffersonian Democrats before adhering to the People's Party; similarly, in Kansas, the Abraham Lincoln Republicans provided one route out of the GOP. In such ways did insurgents express their hope that, with God's assistance, "the simplicity, the purity and the prosperity of the early days" might return.[36]

To this end, classical liberal cries for individual freedom and against "artificial" restraints on economic competition were combined with a classical republican emphasis on the need to enhance public virtue and oppose corporate assaults on industrious communities. The interests of the self-aggrandizing property owner could thus coexist, rhetorically, with a nostalgic evocation of a past in which champions of the people had ruled for the good of the vast majority. As one perceptive historian comments, the Populists "tried to make use of their heritage without allowing themselves to be limited by it, to recreate with new policies a society of equal rights for all and special privileges to none."[37]

While not mentioned in the Omaha Platform, the traditional Protestant concern with upright behavior was woven throughout the language of most committed Populists. A party based among evangelical, rural churchgoers could not help speaking about vanquishing all agents of corruption—saloon keepers as well as plutocrats, secular urban sophisticates as well as dishonest public officials, and occasionally "English Jew bankers" as well as more generic financiers at home and abroad—on the way to the promised commonwealth. "The party was known as the party of righteousness, and such groups as the Germans feared for their Sunday cards and beer," writes one scholar.[38]

Opponents of Populism were quick to criticize this tendency. Republican Senator John Ingalls of Kansas complained, baroquely, to a New York reporter: "The decalogue and the Golden Rule have no place in a political camp. . . . This modern cant about the corruption of politics is fatiguing in the extreme. It proceeds from the tea-custard and syllabub dilettantism of the frivolous and desultory sentimentalism of epicenes." But the fact that this interview helped the new party make Ingalls one of its first electoral victims testifies to the power of Christian moralism to motivate critics of an unethical status quo.[39]

The senator's charge of effeminancy also indicated something more than his view (common among major-party stalwarts) that politics was just another form of war. Women played a role in Populism far beyond the incidental status accorded them in Democratic or Republican circles, before or after the Civil War. They organized revivalistic camp meetings on the prairies, spoke in public and wrote articles for movement newspapers, and extended female networks already established in the WCTU and local farmers' alliances. Most Populist women spoke of their actions as extensions of the domestic ideology and evangelical fervor that had propelled them and other female activists through decades of collective struggles since the 1820s. Swore one woman: "I am going to work for prohibition, the Alliance, and for Jesus as long as I live." A male journalist from the North Carolina Farmers' Alliance viewed that stance as a political necessity: "The ladies are and always have been the great moral element in society; therefore *it is impossible to succeed without calling to our aid the greatest moral element in the country.*" To battle the manifest corruption of the old parties, the tough, manly aspect of the producer ethic was thus temporarily suspended.[40]

Morality, for Populists, meant the tacit (if not active) encouragement of state temperance legislation and even the eventual abolition of the "liquor traffic." It meant forcing nominally Christian candidates and officeholders to stop compromising with big business and urban machines and to stand up for policies that favored the meek and the exploited.[41] The notion that a democratic politics must concern itself with the enforcement of ethical standards, both public and private, was integral to the appeal of Populism. Near the end of another century, we know how explosive that conviction can be, how difficult to confine its targets to one end of the ideological spectrum.

Unlike the call for a new moral order, the issue of race posed an acute dilemma for white Populists, particularly those in the powerful detachments of the cotton-growing South. Black farmers and tenants, over 90 percent of whom lived in Dixie, shared many of the economic grievances of white yeomen and suffered to a greater degree from mounting debts to furnishing merchants and landlords. It would have been foolish for the People's Party to neglect black voters, many of whom were unhappy with a Republican Party that no longer said or did much about racial inequity. Yet, the Populists had no chance to win statewide contests or presidential electors unless they also won over a plurality of white Democrats. And not a few of the latter, the majority constituency, would certainly have agreed with the sentiments of the upcountry Alabama farmer depicted in a later novel, who grumbled: "Them black bastards is takin' the food out 'n our mouths. . . . They're down there sharin' the good things with the rich while good white folks in the hills have to starve."[42]

That almost all white Populists (Northern and Southern) shared the era's dogma about the desirability of Caucasian supremacy made the dilemma even more agonizing. How could they promise blacks enough to get their votes without unleashing fears of "nigger equality" that would send whites fleeing back to the "party of the fathers"?

The Southern Populists' solution was to appeal to blacks exclusively on matters of shared economic concern while assuring fellow whites that nothing resembling a biracial order was being contemplated. Thus, the segregated Colored Farmers' Alliance, led by the white Baptist minister Richard Manning Humphrey, grew when it attacked the crop-lien system but fell apart in 1891 after some of its members who were tenants waged an unsuccessful strike against white landowners, some of whom were Populists (which did not stop the lynching of fifteen strikers).[43] Thus, Tom Watson risked the ire of Democratic mobs when he shared speaking platforms with black Populists and derided his opponents' manipulation of race: "The argument against the independent political movement in the South may be boiled down into one word—NIGGER!" But Watson also opposed any federal intervention to protect black voters, endorsed the Jim Crow laws that Populist and Democratic legislators alike were then passing in Georgia and other states, and hotly denied allegations that he had broken bread with a black ally.[44]

Certainly, as many historians have argued, even a limited, tactical alliance with black Southerners was a dangerous, even heroic step at the time.[45] But such an alliance did not represent a break with white Americans' racial beliefs or the social hierarchy they justified. By themselves, the Populists could not have transformed the color consciousness of the Southern electorate even if that had been one of their primary aims—which it never was. Black farmers and laborers, for their part, had to be extremely courageous to join a rebellion against the Bourbon Democrats who controlled the land, businesses, and local governments on which the very survival of African-Americans depended. But the Populists continued to assume, as had their Jeffersonian and Jacksonian forebears, that "the plain people" meant those with white skin and a tradition of owning property on the land or in a craft. Not surprisingly, most blacks did not accept the Populists' circumscribed offer and instead cast their ballots, where they were still allowed to do so, either for the party of Lincoln or for that of their ancestral overlords.

Of course, Populist speakers in every region devoted most of their energy to waging a zealous and skillful assault on corporate wealth. "Old-party debaters," wrote the historian John Hicks, "did not tackle their Populist antagonists lightly, for as frequently as not the bewhiskered rustic, turned orator, could present, in support of his arguments, an array of carefully sorted information that left his better-groomed opponent in a daze." Movement publicists were pioneers of the investigative morality plays Theodore Roosevelt would later disparage as muckraking. They gathered thousands of damning details, large and small, about trusts that secretly conspired to bilk the public and bribe politicians. In the mode of alternative economists like Henry George, Populist writers educated their audiences about securities and commodities markets, business organization, and international trade while never neglecting to draw a taut battle line. "The most distressing feature of this war of the Trusts," wrote the antimonopoly reformer James B. Weaver, in a 1892 tract entitled *A Call to Action,* "is the fact that they control the articles which the plain people consume in their daily life. It cuts off their accumulations and deprives them of the staff upon which they fain would lean in their old age."[46]

As a counterbalance, the Populists argued that a stronger state could, if the electoral ground shifted their way, be the plain people's best ally—an enhancer of democracy instead of the servant of plutocracy. Weaver advocated "stringent penal statutes" against corporations that broke the law and a tax of up to 40 percent on any business controlled by a trust. The Omaha Platform called for "the powers of government" to "be expanded" and, in a revealing aside, named the postal service as a model because of its tradition of cheap, efficient, and absolutely egalitarian delivery. Party activists made clear they were not advocating socialism. In fact, they maintained that their reforms would improve not lower the status of the millions of Americans who owned small amounts of property.[47]

At the same time, the Populists remained ambivalent about a more powerful state. The American icons the Populists worshiped had left no clear guidance on the limits of federal power. Jefferson and Jackson preached the virtues of a small, non-intrusive government and insisted on a literal interpretation of the Constitution. Yet the Louisiana Purchase and the Cherokee Removal demonstrated how elastic such pronouncements could be. Even Lincoln, who vastly expanded the federal purview to defeat the Confederacy, had never advocated a nationalized rail system or laws to end land speculation.[48]

The Populists resolved their doubts in a pragmatic way. They spoke about the state as the creation and property of people like themselves. Greedy, tyrannical men had usurped that birthright; government power itself was not the problem. Everything depended on what kind of men with what ideas and ethics sat in the statehouse, the Capitol, and the White House. Otherwise, in the spirit of '76, a star-spangled fist would be raised once more against politicians who were using the people's money against the people's interests.

BOY BRYAN'S DEFEAT

In the elections of 1892 and 1894, the Populists thrust their well-crafted message into the cauldron of national politics. At first glance, the results seemed encouraging. In 1892, the presidential nominee James Weaver, a former Union officer from Iowa (Leonidas Polk, the Southern favorite, had died that June) gained over a million votes, 8.5 percent of the total. Weaver (who had also run for president in 1880—on the Greenback Labor ticket) won a majority in three states (Colorado, Idaho, and Nevada) and pluralities in two others (North Dakota and Kansas). Two Populist governors were also elected. In 1894, the party did even better. Its candidates won over 1.5 million votes; seven nominees for the House and six for the Senate were victorious, along with hundreds of state legislators. At the state level, the insurgents were not averse to tactical alliances; some of their victories were the result of a fusion with the weaker of the major parties—Republicans in the South, Democrats in the North. Nevertheless, the "producing classes" seemed, at last, to have found their national voice and to be striding forward to reshape American society.[49]

But the image of mounting strength was an illusion. The People's Party scored all its wins in two underdeveloped regions—the Deep South and the trans-Mississippi West—whose white residents had long nursed an anger against the urban, moneyed East. Aside from knots of radical unionists in such cities as Chicago and San Francisco, the Populists had failed to reach the craft and industrial workers they hoped would be responsive to their message of producer redemption. Pleasing words alone could not bridge the gap between rural evangelicals and American-born city dwellers, a great many of whom were neither American born nor Protestant. Agrarian "organizers looked at urban workers and simply did not know what to say to them—other than to repeat the language of the Omaha Platform," observes the historian Lawrence Goodwyn. Only radical workers who thought in strategic terms were willing to ignore the cultural gap, and they had little more success with the Populist standard than with earlier alternative tickets.[50]

To break out of their electoral confinement, the Populists took a fatal leap into compromise. After the 1894 campaign, a large faction in the party began to downplay the more radical planks in the Omaha Platform (like state-run railroads) and to emphasize the inflationary demand for the free coinage of silver, which appealed to underemployed and indebted citizens in several regions of the country. Meanwhile, national Democrats, severely weakened by a serious depression that began in 1893, were reborn as Jacksonian scourges of "parasites" and "privilege." In 1896, the flagging party came out for free silver and nominated for president William Jennings Bryan, a former Nebraska congressman who had built his short political career on the foundation of monetary reform and cooperation with local Populists (Republicans being the majority party in his state).

In their own national convention that year, the Populists argued long and heatedly about whether to support Bryan or to keep to the independent road. But the outcome was never really in doubt. A majority of delegates chose the hope of partnership in a governing coalition of producers over the fear that their party was being seduced and destroyed. They asked only that the Democrats accept Tom Watson as their candidate for vice president instead of Arthur Sewall, the Maine shipping magnate who'd already been nominated. The request was curtly declined.

During the presidential campaign, the major parties fought, more pointedly than ever before, to control the symbols and definitions of patriotism. The Republicans, under the tutelage of the industrialist and campaign impresario Marcus Hanna, distributed millions of American flags, many of them at "flag days" organized to honor nominee William McKinley as the nation's protector of order and, amid a depression, its "advance agent of prosperity." The fusion ticket was likened to a Confederacy controlled by Socialists. As in 1861, traitors were gathering strength, "plotting a social revolution and the subversion of the American Republic," in Theodore Roosevelt's overwrought opinion. In the Midwest, where the election would be close, Union Army veterans, calling themselves "Patriotic Heroes," perched on a flatcar filled with battlefield regalia and rode against the rebellion one last time. "So pervasive was the Republican campaign," writes Lawrence Goodwyn, "that frustrated Democrats found it difficult to show proper respect for the national emblem without participating in some kind of public endorsement of

McKinley." The most expensive campaign ever waged to that date was undertaken to save the nation from those who would destroy it in the name of reform.[51]

Against this onslaught, the only response the underfinanced effort led by William Jennings Bryan could make was to protest that the Republicans did not represent the *real* America of farms and workshops. But the message had to be conveyed almost entirely through the spoken word; almost every urban newspaper outside the South backed McKinley. And Democratic cartoons displaying the flag with a field of moneybags instead of stars only confirmed that the opposition was setting the terms of the iconographic debate.[52]

Bryan, with the help of a few Populist surrogates like the stalwart Tom Watson, did his best to redefine the electoral contest. It *was* a struggle to defend America, he said. But the assault was not coming from a half-crazed rabble but from the wealthiest men in the land—"goldbugs," "the idle rich," and the lawyers and politicians who did their bidding. Campaign buttons proclaiming free silver to be, unlike the Anglophiles' gold standard, "American Money for Americans" played a nativist variation on the same class-conscious theme.[53]

The most radical Populists never supported Bryan; they correctly, if futilely, argued that fusion for free silver would condemn the third party's broad platform to irrelevance. "The Democracy raped our convention while our own leaders held the struggling victim," Ignatius Donnelly contended in characteristically purple language.[54] Yet even he could not miss the brilliant way the 36-year-old Bryan gathered under the rhetorical umbrella of the money issue both the Populists' cherished ideals and their favorite modes of expressing them: evangelical fervor; a broad, moralistic definition of producerism; continuity with the icons of democracy; the equation of Americanism with the interests of the common people; and the need for a popular uprising to cleanse the nation.

That synthetic skill is what made the "Cross of Gold" speech, first given at the Democratic nominating convention and paraphrased by Bryan hundreds of times in his 18,000 miles of barnstorming that summer and fall, such a powerful document—inspiring to many yet threatening to more. "Bryan . . . said nothing new," one historian points out; "he had made no profound argument which men would remember and cite later. He had said, however, what hundreds of delegates, inarticulate and mute, felt and believed."[55]

Bryan's great speech framed the campaign in pietistic terms ("With a zeal approaching the zeal which inspired the Crusaders who followed Peter the Hermit" and with his final, unforgettable crucifixion image itself). He challenged the Republican claim to being the party of business—proclaiming that "the farmer who goes forth in the morning and toils all day" and "the miners who go down a thousand feet into the earth" were "businessmen" equal to "the few financial magnates who, in a back room, corner the money of the world." He declared, echoing Jefferson, that agrarian pursuits were more vital than urban ones: "Burn down your cities and leave our farms, and your cities will spring up again as if by magic; but destroy our farms and the grass will grow in the streets of every city in the country." He cited Jackson and Jefferson on the right of the people, through the government, to regulate the currency; and flayed those who allowed "foreign potentates and powers" to violate American sovereignty. Speaking to and for loyal citizens who once believed in the system, Bryan raged: "We have petitioned, and our petitions have been scorned; we have entreated, and our entreaties have been disregarded; we have begged, and they have mocked when our calamity came. We beg no longer; we entreat no more; we petition no more. We defy them!"[56]

The barrier such eloquence could never surmount was that Bryan was, despite his leadership of the nation's oldest political party, a protest candidate. Voters who did not agree that America was gripped by crisis (or who defined "crisis" as the breakdown of social and political norms) tended to view the fusionists as advocates of an unpredictable, perhaps dangerous future, in which those who had organized Coxey's Army, waged the 1894 national railway strike, and talked, like Kansas Populist Mary Lease, about "raising less corn and more hell" might actually run the government. Moreover, Bryan's pietistic rigor and his criticisms of urban life chilled many Catholic workers and other city dwellers in the East and Midwest who usually voted Democratic. Thousands heard the Republicans promise not to disturb the nation's ethnic and religious heterogeneity and marked their ballots for McKinley. Bryan drew more votes than any Populist could have, but he had cast his lot on the same side of the cultural divide.

So the man who became known as the Great Commoner went down to the first of three national defeats, and the People's Party rapidly shrank from the spearhead of a social movement into an insignificant sect (before expiring in 1908). In the decades to come, many Bryan supporters—and their scholarly defenders—would speak of the election of 1896 as a negative millennium. It was, they believed, the pivotal defeat for the grand coalition of the industrial classes and a decisive victory for corporate America, an event that had never been revenged or redeemed.[57]

In 1896, Vachel Lindsay was a teenager living in rural Illinois. In 1919, after the disillusioning struggle of World War I, he wrote "Bryan, Bryan, Bryan, Bryan," a long (and once widely read) poem that captures the blend of cultural resentment, regional pique, and producer antagonism that helped stoke the Populist revolt. Lindsay chanted, in part:

Election night at midnight:
Boy Bryan's defeat.
Defeat of western silver.
Defeat of the wheat.
Victory of letterfiles
And plutocrats in miles
With dollar signs upon their coats,
Diamond watchchains on their vests
And spats on their feet.
Victory of custodians,

Plymouth Rock,
And all that inbred landlord stock.
Victory of the neat.
Defeat of the aspen groves of Colorado valleys,
The blue bells of the Rockies,
And blue bonnets of old Texas,
By the Pittsburg alleys.
Defeat of the alfalfa and the Mariposa lily.
Defeat of the Pacific and the long Mississippi.
Defeat of the young by the old and silly.
Defeat of tornadoes by the poison vats supreme.
Defeat of my boyhood, defeat of my dream.[58]

Lindsay was not wrong to eulogize the insurgent agrarians whose spirit he had imbibed at the end of the nineteenth century. Small farmers would never again possess the numbers, the confidence, or the leadership to mount a national crusade capable of drawing in reform-minded Americans from other classes and fusing with a major party. But the significance of the People's Party transcended its own demographic and electoral fate. Through Populism coursed a rich, sometimes contradictory amalgam of dreams, demands, and prejudices whose expression, since the founding of the United States, had been indispensable to the making of democratic politics.

The People's Party stood at a point of transition for that language. On the one hand, it spoke out in pride and anger for the lost commonwealth of agrarians and artisans, the moral center of a society that had spun away from its once noble orbit. Wordsmiths like Ignatius Donnelly, Tom Watson, and Frances Willard may have been looking backward in order to vault ahead. But one cannot escape their yearning for a social harmony that could be glimpsed again only in Heaven. On the other hand, the Populists were forerunners of a more pragmatic style of expressing discontent. Blending the many hues of reform and radicalism into a single national organization, however short-lived, and maneuvering, however fatally, to take advantage of an opening at the political top demonstrated the zeal of missionaries armed with a sensible method. In the Populists' wake, activists from narrower but more durable movements would deny there was any contradiction between a faith in social progress and a defense of the hardworking people.

Vol. XXIX JUNE, 1922 No. 6

AMERICAN FEDERATIONIST

OFFICIAL MAGAZINE
OF THE
AMERICAN FEDERATION OF LABOR

PUBLISHED MONTHLY AT NINTH STREET AND MASSACHUSETTS AVENUE, WASHINGTON, D. C.

10 CENTS PER COPY $1.00 PER YEAR

The average working man takes the middle road, 1922. *(Courtesy of the Library of Congress)*

Chapter 3

Workers as Citizens: Labor and the Left in the Gompers Era

I have always had a feeling of kinship for the fellow who carries the load—the man on the under side. I understand the man who works, and I think he has always understood me.

—Senator Robert La Follette, 1913

. . . if the great industrial combinations do not deal with us they will have somebody to deal with who will not have the American idea.

—Samuel Gompers, c. 1916

. . . voic[e] your protest against autocracy in your shop. Become an exponent of American standards of Democracy in industry, of True Americanism.

—From a garment union leaflet, c. 1918

A POPULISM OF INSIDERS

THE two decades following the election of 1896 were a springtime of social movements. White collegians served the immigrant poor in settlement houses planted in urban ghettos. Black ministers, editors, and teachers (and a handful of white allies) fought segregation through the National Association for the Advancement of Colored People (NAACP) and a variety of local clubs and churches. Educated women set out to abolish the traffic in prostitutes and liquor, aid fledgling female unions, and gain the suffrage. Small farmers—more prosperous than in the Gilded Age and now assembled in diverse groups with names like The American Society for Equity and the Nonpartisan League—kept organizing to boost crop prices and ensure an adequate flow of credit. Wage earners joined unions belonging to the American Federation of Labor (AFL) in order to win a measure of workplace control, a bigger slice of the profits, and, more tentatively, a share of political power. The Socialist Party of America (SP) welcomed anyone willing to embrace the desire for a cooperative commonwealth. Increasingly, to assert a social identity—as worker, farmer, Negro, socialist, prohibitionist, or woman seeking the vote—meant joining or at least endorsing whichever organized body spoke most conspicuously for the appropriate group.

But this profusion of joiners did not attempt to knit together a new coalition of the producing classes. The internal coherence and external fragmentation of the movements prevented it; people mobilized by a bureaucratic organization to press hard for a particular agenda were not eager to back a grander scheme that might downplay their concerns and displace their leaders. And the debacle of the People's Party had all but destroyed the grand vision of a farmer-worker alliance. Future defenders of the producer ethic would be speaking from a narrower class base than that claimed by Ignatius Donnelly and his compatriots.

At the same time, there emerged a counter-elite of middle-class and upper-class progressives—in and out of government. Most worked in a profession—the law, medicine, politics, journalism, academia—but reform was their real calling. The progressives condemned, with a vigor to rival any Populist, the "privileges" of corporate wealth and the myriad ways that business corrupted politics. "Ohio . . . was not ruled by the people," recalled the civic activist Frederick Howe. "It was ruled by business . . . a small group, whose private property it protected."[1]

At all levels of government, progressives lambasted concentrated wealth as a perversion of American ideals. In Cleveland, Mayor Tom Johnson, who had once owned a string of streetcar enterprises, condemned "Big Business, corrupt bosses, subservient courts, pliant legislatures, and an Interest-controlled press," and other urban reformers echoed the indictment.[2] In the Republican Party, Robert La Follette, George Norris, and Hiram Johnson flailed away at railroads and banks while occupying governor's mansions and seats in the Senate. William Jennings Bryan, despite his failure to win the White House, led the bulk of Democratic partisans to blast "Wall Street" and other "predatory interests" and to ask, "Shall the people rule?" On the Supreme Court, Louis Brandeis—whose earlier investigations of workplace conditions had earned him the title "the people's lawyer"—made antitrust an article of faith for an entire generation of legal liberals. In leading universities, such intellectuals as Thorstein Veblen, John Dewey, Charles and Mary Beard, and John R. Commons extolled the virtues of practical workmanship and sought ways to nurture progressive schools, trade unions, and other institutions of direct democracy.[3]

A new breed of journalists popularized the anti-corporate message. In the 1890s, William Randolph Hearst and Joseph Pulitzer fueled their competition for working-class readers as much with blazing antitrust rhetoric as with Sunday color comics and exotic tales of sex and murder. Editorial cartoonists in their employ fixed all well-heeled villains in a memorable form. During the 1896 election, the Hearst cartoonist Homer Davenport caricatured plutocracy in the person of Mark Hanna—and created one of the more durable inventions of his trade. The stout, aging fellow in a tight suit checkered with dollar signs, a diamond stickpin gleaming from his cravat, and an expensive top hat in his meaty fist (but absent Hanna's recognizable features) soon became a common way for publications to signify their populist identity. The character's blend of pomposity, a slightly archaic mode of dress, and ill-gotten wealth nicely belittled a class many readers both disliked and envied.[4]

The muckrakers added a more respectable brand of outrage. Beginning at the turn of the century, reporters writing for a middle-class audience of magazine readers exposed the corrupt underside of scores of mighty institutions from the Chicago stockyards to the United States Senate. They employed a direct, consciously nonliterary style to contrast with the ornate, effete essayists of the Gilded Age. Good writing, stated the muckraking publisher Frank Munsey, was "as common as clam shells."

The new breed invented neither lampoons of the wealthy nor the detailed exposé. But they tapped a huge new market for such wares and established a new common sense about the sins of concentrated wealth. The demotic dailies soon overtook their staid competitors, and as many as five million Americans routinely read a muckraking magazine.[5]

The insiders who cursed monopoly did not succeed in sweeping away the old order—despite the conservative charge that repetitive demagogy imperiled economic growth and social peace. Notwithstanding occasional campaign statements by Theodore Roosevelt and Woodrow Wilson, no chief executive during the period consistently employed the populist idiom. It was Roosevelt, after all, who gave the muckrakers their pejorative name. In the end, the discontented insiders did more to keep alive mass suspicion of unbridled authority than to break up major corporations, end urban corruption, or give the common man and woman more control over resources and decision making.

But then, most self-styled progressives had never felt comfortable with the igneous dichotomy of producers and parasites. They spoke instead of healing the social wounds from which oozed mass strikes, third parties, and national movements of workers and farmers. The progressives' favorite synonym for "the people" was "citizens" or "the public" rather than "producers." A desire to serve the interest of the whole was the coveted virtue, not whether one made a living performing manual work. Class standing had something to do with this. Few professional reformers had held the type of jobs that give rise to grumbling about unrewarded sweat, but all were disgusted at rule by the dishonest and the greedy—whether they operated from corporate offices or legislative chambers.

Of course, the progressives meant their public to *include* wage earners and small farmers. But the former were usually equated with labor—a self-interested constituency group—while the latter got lumped together with more substantial agrarian businessmen in a "farm bloc" whose economic clout waxed even as its numbers steadily waned.[6] Progressives sought to harmonize such legitimate but partial interests for the sake of the larger "public interest." In order to assemble a new type of majority, populist-speaking insiders quietly allowed the terms "producer" and "industrial" to shed their gritty work clothes and climb the social ladder, assuming the identification with employers we take for granted today.

Linked to this change was a subtle but undeniable skepticism about the masses. The progressives no longer assumed that "the plain people" hungered to alter their powerless position. After all, crooked political machines managed to get their candidates elected time after time, and ordinary citizens had a disturbing taste for vices that made piles of money for unscrupulous men. "On the one side the People—slow to wake up, slow to recognize their own interests, slow to realize their power, slow to invoke it," wrote Tom Johnson. "On the other, Privilege—always awake and quick to act, owning many of the newspapers, . . . influencing legislatures and writing our national laws."[7] So a new "realism" about political change took hold: only when educated and guided by a skilled, perceptive counter-elite could the mass of Americans free themselves from shackles that confined their own minds as much as their institutions.

The Hearst newspaper syndicate cartoonist Fred Opper encouraged this view with a new protagonist he alternately dubbed "the Common People" or "John Public." During most of the nineteenth century, cartoonists who wanted to symbolically depict the American people (Uncle Sam stood for the *nation*) had usually chosen a robust, smiling white male who was simply dressed, had tools in hand and his enemies on the run. But John Public (the middle initial Q. was added in 1930 by another cartoonist) lacked the virility and self-confidence of his antecedents. With a hat too small for his bald head and thick glasses magnifying the bewildered frustration in his eyes (which were occasionally crossed), Opper's creation brilliantly captured the sense that "the people" were threatened from all sides but had scant comprehension of the dangers they faced—and thus little hope of resisting them without powerful allies. This middle-aged, white-collared gentleman may have held a more secure job than did his artisan forebear, though his work life was never evoked. But John Public would probably not join a mass movement unless some charismatic politician talked him into it.[8]

LABOR, EMBATTLED AND RISING

Of all the grassroots movements that did flourish during the Progressive years, only one could claim a national constituency of several million producers. This was organized labor, a force dominated by the AFL—a federation of over 100 unions ranging from the United Mine Workers, with a quarter of a million members, to the tiny Elevator Conductors and Starters. That a movement restricted to wage earners took the place of one dedicated to emancipating the "industrial classes" was fateful in the history of populist language. It forced unionists constantly to defend themselves against the accusation that they were a "special interest" incapable of speaking for most ordinary Americans.

Contemporary textbooks tend to repeat this negative opinion. They describe the

AFL as a conservative bastion composed exclusively of white male "business unionists."[9] But the organization was never so limited or unimaginative. Among the two million union members in 1910 were sizable numbers of waitresses and immigrant seamstresses, black and Slavic coal miners, and Socialists (as well as a mélange of anarchists, disciples of Henry George, and other radicals). Craftsmen in the metal and building trades did boast the most stable unions, and Samuel Gompers, president of the AFL, and his fellow leaders had themselves come up through the skilled ranks and had a special empathy with the grievances of proud artisans beset by powerful corporations.

Despite the support of some reform politicians, organized labor in the early twentieth century had to sail through almost perpetually inclement seas. From the AFL's creation in the mid-1880s until the early 1930s, its member unions could never expect either the cooperation of industrial employers or the benevolent neutrality of the state. In normal times, troops and court injunctions broke their strikes, corporate managers undermined their members' skills, and press and pulpit charged them with being class-bound, coercive, and collectivist—the very antithesis of the American way. Even when, during World War I, federal officials briefly smoothed the waters, they did so only to assemble a multi-class convoy against alien peril. When the Kaiser was defeated, the AFL got hit with the old tempests again.[10]

To confront their adversaries and advance their own hopes for workers, union leaders expressed a form of populism that spoke to three identities simultaneously: the patriotic producer, the mobilized wage earner, and the defender of rights that belonged to all American citizens. This was a discourse that echoed the grievances and visions of the original Populists but diluted their rebellious punch. There were progressives to bargain with if the nation was to change.

On the one hand, labor spokesmen were merely restating the old producer ethic when they asserted the moral superiority and practical necessity of common people and the work they performed. "We represent the part of the nation closest to the fundamentals of life," proclaimed the AFL Executive Council in 1917. Such homilies were often laced with a defiant sort of Americanism that Ignatius Donnelly would have applauded. In 1916, when New York City transit executives accused streetcar strikers of being directed by an "Alien," "outside organization," union leader William Fitzgerald responded, "My father spent four years and over as a soldier in the war of rebellion, fighting to establish the fact that one flag should wave over all the States . . . , so I leave it to the people of New York City to judge whether I am an alien or not."[11] Ready to sacrifice for democracy and country, the industrious majority remained the indispensable bedrock of the republic. Unionists still defined the enemy as the holders of corporate wealth and those government officials who did rich men's bidding. And they added attacks on intellectuals—particularly those lodged in academia and the press—who apologized or shilled for those elites. These broadsides were consistent with the rhetoric of Gilded Age insurgents.

On the other hand, a producerism that depended on strong unions was a narrower faith than that embodied in the Omaha Platform. It represented wage earners as the only producers worthy of the name, thus implicitly rejecting the old equivalence between all members of "the toiling masses"—whether or not they owned farms or other small businesses. For the AFL, only workers, acting through their unions, could build the muscle to take on the high-handed, un-American cabal. All manner of labor activists—socialists, defenders of private property, the religiously devout—proclaimed the new doctrine. Without a strong union movement, the people had nothing.

Neither did the AFL mobilize the language of Christian deliverance that had come so naturally to grassroots activists in the late nineteenth century. The heterogeneous composition of the labor movement and the personal beliefs of most leaders warned against it. Rank and filers followed a variety of creeds; Catholics may have been in the majority. Gompers himself was born a Jew but, as an adult, adhered to no ritual save Freemasonry, and his circle included few churchgoers from evangelical denominations. Most important, resorting to an idiom closely associated with Protestantism could have destroyed the often fragile bond between people who had nothing in common but their work.[12]

At the same time, the AFL needed to appeal beyond the boundaries of class to all citizens who believed the American dream of "equal rights" was endangered by corrupt officials and the power of money over principle. To be sure, the rights being emphasized were those of wage earners to protest, organize, and strike. But the stated desire for a society that rewarded merit and honest labor reached out to the millions of Americans who would never hold a union card.

AFL spokesmen could not simply roar their defiance of the wealthy and their love for the hardworking people. They were acutely conscious of operating within a political environment in which reform and social bonding headed the rhetorical agenda. With popular officeholders and periodicals damning "the Interests" and calling for the people to control their government, labor activists could not sustain a mass following by claiming that a unified, closed elite held both the economy and the state in its grasp. On certain major issues, the AFL and progressive legislators were partners—for example, in the battle to topple the autocratic Speaker of the House Joseph Cannon and the drive to regulate working hours and conditions for women and children.

Labor had much to gain from courting influential progressives: passage of a favorite bill, leniency toward an organizing campaign, or neutralization of powerful opponents. For its part, the counter-elite sought to curry favor with a large group that could deliver campaign workers, votes, and even a fresh idea or two. Such an alliance was never fully consummated. But its promise demanded that union activists live with a tension between ideological autonomy and practical accommodation. Only that minority of radicals whose eyes were fixed on the revolution to come felt free to spurn the endless dance of compromise.

The master of this rhetorical balancing act was Samuel Gompers, a former cigar maker who was the only president the AFL had (with the exception of one year) from its formation in 1886 to his death in 1924. Marxism had been Gompers's first political passion. Soon after emigrating in the 1860s from London's impoverished East End, he joined a tight community of craftsmen-intellectuals one historian calls "a who's who of socialist New York." Scorning the Knights of Labor for seeking to build a multi-class coalition of producers on little more than hope, Gompers argued that unions should be instruments of combat, whose federation would join all North American workers "in one solid phalanx powerful [enough] to resist the aggressions of the opponents of the emancipation of our class." As a good Marxist, he viewed the rise of big corporations, rather blithely, as an inevitable feature of capitalism.[13]

By the mid-1890s, however, Gompers had changed his terms of persuasion, if not his innermost convictions. He began to muffle radical expressions of class-consciousness and to glorify American ideals that all citizens held in common. The 1894 AFL convention had narrowly defeated a platform that advocated "collective ownership of all the means of production and distribution." The influence of socialists within the federation, Gompers decided, posed a serious threat to its fragile gains. With a depression on, his first priority was to ensure that the union movement survived the test of mass unemployment, as no national labor organization had done before. Arguing that wage earners should not tie their fortunes to any single electoral vehicle, he spurned calls to help organize a labor party. An end to the wage system and the "capitalist" parties had been, he decided, a youthful illusion, dangerous for the health of a movement that had to ground itself in American realities.[14]

Without entirely giving up the dream of an international working-class movement, Gompers developed a style of populist rhetoric that was a critique of and an alternative to the Marxism of his young adulthood. He rejected socialist doctrine as "un-American," "unsound," and "an impossibility." He termed campaigns to oust antilabor congressmen "a popular uprising of honest men" instead of reaching for a narrower signifier of class. AFL publications adopted a generous, openhanded vocabulary—to represent an organization of loyal Americans that could, in practice, "do more to humanize the human family than all other agencies combined."[15]

Gompers worked closely with a number of fellow officials on the AFL Executive Board and from its largest unions, all of whom were committed to labor's mission and could defend it in rational, even erudite debate. But the erstwhile cigar maker's role was singular. He was not merely the AFL's virtual president for life but often the only spokesman for organized labor whom most Americans outside the movement could identify. That was partly due to the AFL's structure. Its constitution (modeled on the British Trades Union Congress) gave individual unions almost absolute control over their daily affairs (organizing new members, going on strike, bargaining with employers). The national office was left with the responsibility of articulating positions for the federation as a whole—even though individual members could freely disagree with what it said.

Gompers performed his task with tremendous zeal. He was the editor of and most prolific writer for the AFL's national organ, the monthly *American Federa-*

tionist; gave over 100 speeches annually to audiences all over the United States and southern Canada; and frequently testified before Congress on any topic that concerned wage earners—from a literacy test for immigrants to the feasibility of socialism. As a communicator, Gompers was rather old-fashioned. Stout, owlish, and self-righteous, he spoke in public with a certain melodramatic refinement he had imbibed at the Cooper Union's free elocution classes in the 1870s. He refused to adopt the new, leaner journalistic and oratorical style of spellbinders like Robert La Follette and Theodore Roosevelt. But there was no mistaking his desire to portray unions as "embodiments of democracy" that selfish employers and benighted government officials were out to destroy.[16]

That such other AFL founding fathers as P. J. McGuire of the Carpenters and Frank Foster of the Printers underwent a similar rhetorical evolution strengthened Gompers's conviction that the balance of forces within the unions was shifting his way. So did the boom in union membership between 1897 to 1903—from 440,000 to over two million—which a return of prosperity made possible.[17]

By the turn of the century, most union leaders were following Gompers's lead. They sought to straddle the line between a workers' movement and a people's movement, hoping to avoid the repression and scorn visited on those who continued to wave a Marxist banner. They articulated the specific needs of a labor organization—recognition from employers and freedom from state interference—while also speaking optimistically of their members as simple citizens altruistically striding forward to cure the nation's ills. "Labor unions are *for* the workman, but *against* no one," wrote United Mine Workers' (UMW) leader John Mitchell in 1903. "They are for a class, . . . but the unions did not create and do not perpetuate the class or its interests and do not seek to evoke a class conflict." The search for power and legitimacy was joined.[18]

DEFENDING THE AVERAGE MAN

Critical to the AFL's strategy was its redefinition of the producer ethic, that most pregnant attribute of the "people" for any workers' movement. Superficially, union activists in the early twentieth century portrayed themselves as legatees of a proud, unaltered tradition. The axiom that "labor creates all wealth" had been the birthright of American unionism as well as a key trope of the producer ethic. From the first locals of journeyman artisans in the new republic to the inclusive assemblies of the Knights of Labor, it had enabled workers to protest the basic injustice of low wages and authoritarian bosses. In the new century, there was no reason to cede that ethical ground to soft-handed insurgents and their hortatory talk about the public interest, much less to openly hostile forces in the National Association of Manufacturers and the conservative wing of the Republican Party. John Public would not have felt welcome at a union smoker.[19]

Yet AFL leaders could not accept either of the two variants of producerism that grassroots movements in the Gilded Age had expressed. The strongest strain, that of the People's Party, they deemed too fuzzy and sentimental; it was averse to drawing distinctions between employer and wage earner and thus was of little strategic value in a trade union struggle. Marxism, the weaker strain, offered the vigorous certainty of "scientific" analysis. But its vaunting of an international proletariat rejected the consensual regard for hardworking patriots of the middling sort. As Gompers came to believe, an embattled labor movement could not afford to defy so helpful a tradition.

So he and his supporters in the AFL created a third option: the craftsperson as the most capable defender of "average" Americans and the founding principles of the republic. After about 1900, Gompers almost never publicly expressed opposition to "capitalism" as a system and seldom spoke, in the Marxist fashion, about "proletarians" or "the working class." He preferred, as he told a federal commission in 1914, "to say working people and speak of them as real human beings" with "the same desires and hopes of a better life" as anyone else.[20] AFL spokesmen normally described union members and prospective members not as a downtrodden mass but as the broad center of the population whose participation was as indispensable to civic life as it was to the process of making goods.

A revealing example of the AFL's model citizen-worker appeared in an anonymously written poem entitled "The Average Man," which, in 1910, filled an entire page in the *American Federationist*—an exceedingly rare event.

The average man is the man of the mill,
The man of the valley, or man of the hill,
The man at the throttle, the man at the plow—
The man with the sweat of his toil on his brow,
Who brings into being the dreams of the few,
Who works for himself, and for me, and for you.
There is not a purpose, a project or plan
But rests on the strength of the average man

read the first stanza. This repeated the producerist sentiments and hope for a farmer-labor alliance of the Omaha Platform.

But then, the poem took an unexpected turn:

The pride of the great and the hope of the low,
The toil of the tide as it ebbs to and fro,
The reach of the rails and the countries they span
Tell what is the trust in the average man.

Where is the old rage that the fruits of industry have been stolen, the claim that virtue belongs exclusively to the manual creators of wealth? The trust of all classes in the producer had now replaced girding the loins for battle. Moreover, in a significant departure from the image of a mass of exploited humanity battling a tiny band of parasites, the poet called his paragon "average." That label did not deprive its bearer of his indispensability. But it did remove the aura of tragic heroism. As union cartoons of the time demonstrated, Mr. Average was an archetype set squarely in the middle between an unworthy elite above and an unfortunate but equally dangerous mass of poor below. As the poet asserted: "The man who stands out between hovel and throne / The man who gives freely his brain and his brawn / Is the man that world has been builded upon."

So this was a tribute more than a protest. "In the forefront of progress, since progress began / Here's a health and a hail to the average man!" ran the concluding lines.[21]

Both the use of a quantitative term ("average") instead of a moralist one like "plain" and the embrace of "progress" showed the poet's debt to the reformist insiders enthralled by statistics who then filled statehouses and Congress. And his tribute could be extended beyond the craftsmen who were the core of the AFL to white-collar employees, those more conventional occupants of the great middle, whose "brain" labor was increasingly central to the large corporations that dominated the economy. Especially after becoming junior partners in Woodrow Wilson's coalition, union leaders, in the manner of insincere politicians, sometimes even bestowed the honorific *labor* on people who had never coveted the title. Just before the 1916 election, Gompers wrote that "Labor has a larger significance than the group that works for wages. . . . It includes all those who have spiritual and creative vision—the engineers, the great constructive and directing minds . . . who have part in supplying materials and commodities of civilization."[22]

Such images essentially ignored the female unionist. Most AFL leaders had been reared in a working-class culture that exalted physical strength, required treating other men as social equals, and disdained any wage earner who meekly obeyed his superiors. A "manly" worker, writes the historian David Montgomery, "refused to cower before the foreman's glares—in fact, often would not work at all when a boss was watching." Women workers pressed their own forms of resistance—sales clerks demanded the right to wear their own clothes instead of drab uniforms, for example—but few male unionists recognized that a wage earner could be tough without being a man.[23]

The AFL did endorse women's suffrage and encouraged female workers whose occupations did not compete with men's to organize their own unions. However, labor's guiding archetype of independence, collective power, and Americanism was a mature white male in work clothes—the stalwart figure on the hilltop of principle. In AFL iconography, idealized young women—many dressed in flowing robes and sandals—framed or stood beside these images. Women seldom appeared on their own as workers, rather than as idealized guardians of virtue and truth. Even when female wage earners went on strike, male AFL journalists described them sentimentally as noble but "helpless beings" whose travails "placed them on a pedestal of honor for the loyalty they have shown, and written across their brows a diadem that time will not erase."[24]

AFL spokesmen were more ambivalent when describing the growing number of male industrial workers, most of them unskilled, who were black or belonged to one of the newer immigrant groups from Eastern and Southern Europe. On the one hand, Gompers always vowed that unions "should open their portals to all wage workers irrespective of creed, color, nationality, sex or politics."[25] Both he and most of his closest allies were themselves immigrants or the sons of immigrants from older locations like Germany, Britain, Ireland, and Scandinavia. To exclude anyone who might, in time, become an "average man" would be self-defeating as well as a violation of labor's egalitarian principles. But he and his fellow officials worried that blacks, Slavs, southern Italians, and others new to industrial work were culturally too far outside the mainstream and might threaten the "American standard" (both economically and in terms of political rights) that white workers like themselves had sweated to achieve.

So the AFL sought to draw distinctions not on ethnic lines but on older populist ones: new workers were welcome if they manifested the same spirit of militant independence as did union pioneers and other citizen-producers. As in the Gilded Age, this criterion did not apply to industrious and efficient immigrants from East Asia (now Japanese and Filipinos as well as Chinese). Unionists still demonized them as "slavish," "diseased," and utterly incapable of raising themselves to the level of "American manhood." This attitude was a political advantage. In several Western states, AFL men took charge of the local anti-Asian movement and thereby gained acceptance as defenders of the majority race and not just a minority class.[26]

More care was given to delineating the grounds on which new immigrants from Europe should be barred from the House of Labor. In the 1906 Bill of Grievances, the AFL's first political manifesto, the organization stated it was "the constantly growing evil of *induced* and *undesirable* immigration" (emphasis added) that had to be stopped, not new arrivals per se. In the 1880s, Gompers had opposed a literacy test for newcomers because he wanted to preserve the United States as a "haven and an opportunity"; a decade later, he switched his position and argued that anyone who could not read would be unable to take advantage of those same opportunities.

A related and, for most rank-and-file workers, probably more convincing charge against immigrants from such places as Italy, Poland, and Russia was that many were or would soon become the pawns of unscrupulous elites. According to the labor editor J. W. Sullivan, the continuation of free immigration meant "more rack-rent for slum landlords, more dividends for foreign corporations subsidized by European governments, more rake-offs for contractors, . . . more voting cattle for our political stockyards, more blood for real estate sharks, more non-unionists for manufacturing combines, . . . and incalculably more misery for America's wage-earners." Still, European newcomers were more fortunate than Asians, whose passive obedience to authority was described as a congenital trait. At least any European could demonstrate, by his conduct at the workplace and in civil society, that he had transcended "his former state of servitude" on feudal overlords.[27]

Of course, union activists who were themselves "new" immigrants or were organizing them did not echo this injurious application of the producer ethic. The assumption that unskilled immigrants were helpless instruments of the powerful could, they protested, become a self-fulfilling prophecy. But leaders of only a few AFL affiliates (most notably Socialists in garment trades unions whose membership was drawn from recently arrived Jews and Italians) articulated this tolerant alternative. Others were simply overwhelmed by warnings that the only practical solution to "the racial problem" was to exclude those races with "lower standards of life and work" while slowly improving conditions for those freedom-loving common folk who *already* lived in the United States.[28]

Such formulations did not fit the one race whose ancestors had been toiling in America long before workers with names like Gompers and Sullivan arrived. Strangely, at a time when both violence against and political organization among African-Americans had reached a level not seen since Reconstruction, former slaves and their descendants seldom appeared in the statements and images, positive or negative, that the AFL presented. Apart from a few Southern unionists who forthrightly defended white supremacy, AFL officials were almost mute about the largest ethnic minority in the workforce, one whose caste status made it difficult for unions to make headway in the former Confederacy. On the rare occasions when they did make a statement about blacks, AFL spokesmen usually echoed the Southern Populists' more strenuous attempts to minimize the color line. "When black and white workers are compelled to work side by side, under the same equally unfair and adverse conditions, it would be an anomaly to refuse the rights of organization to workers because of a difference in their color," a unionist wrote in 1901.[29]

Why the perfunctory tone, so different from the smoldering phrases that union writers routinely employed when discussing other important issues? The explanation, I believe, lies in how difficult it was for AFL spokesmen to include African-Americans within their restricted categories of thought. Excluded outright by some large and important unions (the Machinists and the Railroad Brotherhoods) and feared as competitors by many of the rank and file, blacks still had to be considered native-born producers. Moreover, their emancipation was central to two historical dramas the AFL celebrated in metaphor and iconography: the abolitionist crusade and the career of Abraham Lincoln.

Outside the South, union activists could not freely indulge in racist opinions and theories; that would have betrayed their cherished principle of "equal rights." But resounding vows of color-blind solidarity would have clashed with the reigning notion of a natural racial hierarchy to which not only white Southerners subscribed. They also would have sounded too much like the pronouncements of the rival and revolutionary Industrial Workers of the World (IWW) whose brave appeal to class over racial consciousness had few notable successes. So, faced with this dilemma—a seemingly impossible choice between endorsing black equality or acquiescing in a strict separation of the races—most union leaders said as little as possible about African-Americans and spoke of working people as if they had all descended from European roots.[30]

All these positions were debated, sometimes altered, and disseminated at the state and local levels where the strength of the AFL resided. Labor was embattled in the nation at large, but, in metropolises like San Francisco and Chicago and industrial towns like Butte, Montana, and Reading, Pennsylvania, individual unions and citywide federations enjoyed a status unmatched by any earlier workers' movement. Manufacturing and transportation employers had to bargain with them, and labor activists routinely engaged in municipal politics—whether as kingmakers, appointees, or candidates.

To succeed in such locales, union stalwarts stretched beyond their own ranks to gain the majority support they craved. This could not be accomplished solely in the backrooms of political clubs where a labor leader could threaten to shut down a key industry unless he and his men got their way. It also meant using the streets and labor's own media to convince "public opinion," that protean but consistently potent beast, to look kindly on or, at least, not to obstruct greater resources and influence for America's best-organized producers.

Labor Day provided the perfect occasion. Militants had staged the first downtown parades in the early 1880s in order to promote the class-conscious ends of strong unions and a collective commonwealth; it took two decades for most employers to grant workers a day off on their holiday. But during the Progressive era, Labor Day was less an opportunity for protest than for a civic festival attended by tens of thousands of residents and lavishly covered by the local press. Union members marched in disciplined formation behind brass bands, politicians proclaimed their great admiration for the working man, and selected craftsmen practiced their trades on horsedrawn floats that were rolling representations of the producer ethic. This was the one day of the year on which unions could command the attention of millions of nonmembers. So great care was taken to fashion slogans, speeches, and visual displays that demonstrated the working-class presence without alienating anyone but sworn opponents of the AFL.[31]

Union-made films were dedicated to a similar purpose. Starting in 1907, labor activists skilled in the new technology produced a swelling number of silent movies that praised the benefits of collective action by native-born wage earners and made villains out of greedy employers and corrupt politicians. The output included brief documentaries about labor defense trials and five-reel melodramas like Frank Wolfe's *From Dusk to Dawn,* in which a romance between the iron-molder Dan Grayson and the laundress Carla Wayne blooms against a backdrop of "thugs and police beating up peaceful picketers with clubs and guns." Their makers hoped these films would compete with the numerous commercial vehicles that depicted worker activists as either wild-eyed anarchists or ugly, mannish women.[32]

Most ubiquitous in the apparatus of labor publicity was the union newspaper.

Compared to the thin, prosaic sheets that most contemporary unions publish, the typical AFL paper, circa 1910, was an intellectual feast. The *American Federationist* itself, notwithstanding the inevitable pieces by labor leaders, often resembled a general interest magazine on progressive issues. Gompers and Eva McDonald Valesh, a former Minnesota Populist who served as the managing editor from 1900 to 1909 without being graced with the title, published articles by such writers as Louis Brandeis, Jane Addams, the Social Gospeler (and prohibitionist) Charles Stelzle, the socialist William English Walling, and the feminist Charlotte Perkins Gilman.[33] In two consecutive issues, the *Union Labor Advocate* of Chicago published a learned, passionate argument for the single tax, and investigative reports on the woeful conditions at individual workplaces alongside lyrical paeans to Abraham Lincoln, drama reviews, and closely reasoned editorials on Chicago's economic future and the defense of Russian refugees. In San Francisco, the weekly organ of the Building Trades Council ran articles on a gamut of workers and industries as well as long editorials about the golden rule, Henry George's theories, and Henrik Ibsen's plays. Socialists routinely contributed to these periodicals. As a whole, the AFL press before World War I was more like the freewheeling papers attached to the People's Party than the media hitched to mere trade unionist ends.[34]

A CANCER IN THE REPUBLIC

Besides courting new friends, unionists also needed to define their enemies in a way that would gain public sympathy for both their organizations and their ultimate ends. The task was parallel to giving the aggrieved producer a fresh, optimistic image. Gompers and his associates wanted to vilify their elite opponents without placing themselves outside the consensus of middle-class reform. A common solution was to separate men of influence who dealt fairly with unions from those who threatened the republic for which the average working man so proudly stood.

Craft unionists, who seem to have recognized that most citizens did not despise the rich for simply being rich, aimed their thrusts at specific malefactors whose acts and statements were particularly egregious. This naturally included the trusts, favorite target of muckrakers and progressive politicians. Gompers liked to echo the well-publicized charges of high-level shenanigans and then remind his audience that, without the people whom he represented, the corporations could not function at all. "I have insisted, and I do now insist," he declared, "that the only power capable of coping with and (if necessary) smashing the trusts, is that much abused and often ridiculed force known . . . [as] 'The Trades Union Movement' as understood and practiced by the American Federation of Labor."[35]

But the attack on big business was selective. The growth of trade unions had led many officials, both national and local, into relationships with employers that assumed respect, though not necessarily trust or permanence. For Gompers and his allies, Mark Hanna was both a nonunion steel manufacturer and a prominent member of the National Civic Federation, a well-publicized agency that promoted mediation in industrial disputes. Few AFLers mused about an eventual harmony of interests with capital; but neither did they indulge in the emotional attacks on "robber barons" and "plutocrats" that had been so popular in the 1880s and early 1890s. A cartoonist's satirical image of generalized plutocracy was one thing; baiting men with whom you might soon have to negotiate was quite another.

Hanna and his counterparts, who no longer dismissed out of hand the idea of unionism, had to be differentiated from antilabor zealots. During the 1902 anthracite strike, the coal mine and railroad owner G. F. Baer declared, to his subsequent infamy: "The rights and interests of the laboring men will be protected and cared for—not by the labor agitators, but by the Christian men to whom God in his infinite wisdom has given control of the property interests of this country." In response, AFL spokesmen accused Baer not of being an arrogant capitalist but of sabotaging a political heritage most citizens cherished. Gompers dismissed his statement as that of a man who "clearly . . . has yet to learn the A,B,C of industrial freedom and American politico-economic organization." In San Francisco, AFL officials dubbed business foes like the National Association of Manufacturers and the Citizens' Industrial Alliance "capitalist-anarchists" and even "un-American" for trying to destroy legitimate unions.[36]

Gompers and his brethren often said the centralized state posed a greater danger to the public than did the holders of corporate wealth. Whether it used the stick of armed compulsion or the carrot of protective aid, the federal government wrested funds and control from citizens who could not afford to lose either. The People's Party had called for nationalizing the railroads and other utilities, but the AFL leadership feared this would create a permanent bureaucracy. Gompers and his associates also opposed minimum wage laws, a legislated eight-hour day, unemployment insurance, and health insurance. The AFL chief warned such measures would "rivet the masses of labor to the juggernaut of government," encouraging wage-earning men to rely on a paternalist state instead of their own power at the workplace.[37]

This proud, autonomous stance was a poor guide to labor's practice. Many local union movements quietly dissented and, as members of reform coalitions in a number of states and cities, advocated the measures Gompers opposed as well as municipal ownership of utilities and public works jobs for the unemployed. Also, to counter business support for Republicans, Gompers propelled the AFL into an alliance with the Democratic Party during the election of 1908 and continued the relationship through the presidency of Woodrow Wilson. "On Which Side Are You?" asked the AFL leader in the fall of 1916, in the contest between the "exploiters" and the "producers." But, other than Socialists, few union spokesmen at any level abandoned the nonpartisan ideal or endorsed the concept of expanding the power of the state, an institution most Americans had traditionally mistrusted.[38]

On the rare occasions when leading national unionists did advocate a greater role for the state, they usually took pains to depict the desired change as one that would promote citizen participation and a spirit of Americanism, rather than just benefit wage earners. This was the way compulsory public education was usually described. And when the Congressman and later Secretary of Labor William Wilson (a former official of the United Mine Workers, the UMW) proposed a federal pension plan for all elderly Americans in 1909, he included a provision that would have obligated recipients, whom he called the Old Age Home Guard, to submit annual reports on "patriotic sentiment" in their local communities.[39] Such devices allowed the AFL to rail at the "special privileges" that corporations received from the government, because, in principle, unionists wanted and needed none for themselves.

Toward only one part of the state—the judiciary—did the AFL regularly hurl the kind of angry rhetoric it had once reserved for profit-obsessed industrialists. The cause was plain. From 1880 until the Great Depression, state and federal judges handed down at least 4,300 separate injunctions against unions. Most enjoined strikes; others made the boycott, hitherto an effective device for mobilizing across occupational and regional lines, virtually illegal. During the Gilded Age, the courts had also struck down such reform measures as the progressive income tax (which labor supported) by ruling that legislative restrictions on wealth and property were incompatible with the maintenance of "a free, unobstructed marketplace."[40]

For the men of the AFL, these judicial acts were more than a severe hindrance; they were a symbolic cancer growing within the democratic body of the nation. The argument was reminiscent of the one Tom Watson had earlier used to legitimize the Populist rebellion: the Constitution had established a government of impartial laws, but men in high office had subverted those laws by twisting them to their own purposes. The result was a revival of hated feudal ways. "These imitators of old-world tyranny," Gompers called judges who enjoined unions. The fact that most of the judges were not elected but appointed (with lifetime tenure, if to the federal bench) seemed to clinch the case. No man who had to risk the people's disapproval could have acted in a repressive, undemocratic fashion.[41]

Equally galling to AFL spokesmen was the idea that a mere legal *opinion* could deprive laboring men of their freedom of action. In 1908, the Supreme Court of the District of Columbia granted the Buck's Stove and Range Company an injunction to stop an AFL boycott of its nonunion products. When Gompers, AFL Secretary Frank Morrison, and the UMW's John Mitchell (a vice president of the federation) publicly defied the order as a violation of the First Amendment, Judge Daniel T. Wright angrily sentenced them to prison—after delaying his ruling to aid the Republicans in the presidential election. The choice, Wright insisted in prose unusually heated for a jurist, was clear—"the supremacy of law over the rabble or its prostration under the feet of the disordered throng." "Those who would unlaw the land," Wright concluded, "are public enemies."[42]

Being thrown together with anarchists and other political undesirables was the AFL's worst fear. Rulings like Wright's, Gompers worried, "disfigured" how "newspapers . . . [and] the common people" regarded the labor movement. Unionists had long argued that *they* were the ones who stood by the democratic principles undergirding the social order. So they vigorously reversed the terms of Wright's insinuation. The *Union Labor Advocate* of Chicago portrayed the judge as a man whose ruling betrayed the "fundamental law of the land [that] was supposed to be forever assured to the citizens of the Republic." Moreover, he had broken that trust in words stiff with contempt for ordinary Americans who were merely exercising their legal rights. "The average citizen cannot understand how this judicial shell game is worked," editorialized the Chicago paper. It then added, ominously, "When he comes to thoroughly understand it there will be doings. . . ."[43]

The discrepancy between the "fundamental" law and the legal chicanery of judges and corporate attorneys also revealed a deep suspicion of anyone who made good money telling men who toiled with their hands and backs how to run their lives and organizations. Business lawyers and tyrannical judges were, for the AFL, but two elements of an intellectual class that presumed it had the best interests of working people at heart and aggressively marketed that wisdom to the general public. Labor spokesmen had long disparaged this class and its style of discourse. In 1887, Gompers urged a new labor party in New York City to "Give us a workingman's platform, not a professor's." And Frank Foster, in a 1904 pamphlet defending the closed shop against the criticisms of Charles Eliot, then president of Harvard, contrasted the plain speaking, investigatory methods of unionists and their allies with the "smug Philistinism" of "dilettante social reformers, college professors, zealous editors," and the like.[44]

Foster's outraged sneer conveys how bound up with social resentments was the attitude of labor spokesmen toward articulate opponents who were engaged in the same business of public persuasion as they were. AFL leaders were not hostile to erudition. Foster, Gompers, and a number of their compatriots drew on a range of philosophical and scientific works by Comte, Marx, Darwin, Herbert Spencer, and others. In his own writings, Foster tried to reconcile his individualist ideals with the collectivist nature of the labor movement.[45]

What rankled these men was the sermon delivered from above the battle, the finely spun theories of intellectuals (a word unionists normally encased in quotes) who had never squabbled with a foreman or scrounged for rent money. At times, this sentiment overwhelmed their usual caution toward middle-class progressives. Vexatious words battered reformers who thought the AFL too narrow in scope as well as conservatives who condemned the coercive powers of "labor bosses." Neither university-trained elite could teach anything that wage earners needed to learn. While their politics differed, their glib and condescending attitude toward workers was the same. Once preached by Jacksonians, the superiority of practical, manly knowledge over the abstract, speculative variety had found a new home in the labor movement.

THE RADICALS' DILEMMA

The bristling front against outside "-isms" posed an obvious difficulty for Socialists who worked inside the AFL. Not only did labor leftists have to convince voters to cast their lot with a party whose aims sounded utopian and whose analysis was mostly borrowed from theorists abroad; they also had to convince union members that the Socialist Party (SP) offered something that Gompers and his political allies did not.

The Industrial Workers of the World avoided such hard questions by branding AFL leaders a bunch of "labor fakirs" and declaring flatly that "the working class and the employing class have nothing in common." The IWW led several big strikes of Eastern factory workers, but their contempt for patriotism, organized religion, and elections was not much shared beyond a dedicated core of single male migrants who had little left to lose. Americans like to romanticize such heroic outlaws, but they have never followed their political leadership. So most working-class leftists opted to fight for their program from within the AFL.[46]

And they had some reason for optimism. From 1900 to 1920, the socialist movement flourished—if only temporarily—in a variety of settings that also sustained organized labor. Radical workers newly arrived from countries like Germany and Russia rallied to the American contingent of an existing international movement; some native-born craftsmen warmed to activists who really did want "producers" to run the state; thousands of former Populists from the Southwest endorsed a new agent of economic deliverance that did not ask them to give up their farms and other small businesses; and many messianic Christians of both sexes warmed to the SP's call for a new system that would establish rule by the meek and the brotherhood of man.

At its best, the SP articulated a noble vision of the "cooperative commonwealth" that could unite people who had little else in common. By 1912, millions of people read socialist newspapers in a score of different languages (the *Appeal to Reason,* a former People's Party weekly published in Kansas, had the largest circulation). That year, Debs received almost a million votes in the presidential election, and fully one-third of the delegates to the AFL convention supported the SP's program. These American Marxists believed that they, and not Gompers and his ilk, were the true inheritors of Populism. "If all the wage workers and small farmers will vote for the Socialist party, and all the capitalists, great and small, for the capitalist parties," reasoned the radical theorist Ernest Untermann, "there will be no other class in control of this country but the working class."[47]

Yet, even during their heyday, American socialists were caught in a linguistic bind. Using the Marxist vocabulary of their more powerful counterparts on the Continent bolstered their conviction of how the class struggle would end. But talk of "proletarians" toppling "bourgeois rule" also offended Americans reverential about their political heritage, capitalist though it was.

On the other hand, leftists who patched together a vernacular from more familiar materials—the producer ethic, the social gospel, and antimonopoly progressivism—risked diluting their raison d'être and seeing their followers snatched up by ever-solicitous agents of the major parties. Except for those already living within a socialist enclave—the Germans of Milwaukee, the Jews of New York's Lower East Side, the Finns of the Minnesota Iron Range, and a few others—there was no compelling reason to join or stay in the SP if its appeal differed little from that of more legitimate voices in the labor movement or among progressives.

This predicament was especially poignant for Socialists whose careers tested the outer limits of the party's fortunes. The Indiana-born Eugene Debs, its five-time presidential candidate, had backed the People's Party and did not declare himself a socialist until after Bryan's loss to McKinley in 1896. Afterward, Debs, the SP's spellbinder, continued to draw on populist themes, making frequent reference to the Bible, producerism, and the ways that "the competitive system" was crushing "American manhood" and draining "citizenship" of its democratic content. But such heartfelt appeals won him more personal esteem than votes. Debs still insisted that a "class war" would be necessary to redeem the nation.[48]

Socialists who shunned all talk of insurrection were no better able to negotiate the obstacles of legitimate discourse. The Austrian-born Victor Berger was both Milwaukee's top unionist and the leader of the city's SP, the only local in the country that regularly elected its candidate for mayor. In 1910, he won a seat in Congress (the first Socialist to do so) and exulted that, as in other "great and civilized nations . . . there will now be a representative of the working class in the national legislature."

While, in practice, Berger's focus on organizing strong unions and honest, efficient urban governments resembled the priorities of Gompers and Tom Johnson of Cleveland, he felt the need to assure his followers and probably himself that he was still a revolutionary. When the Milwaukee SP first captured city hall, Berger warned, "the management of the affairs of the city of Milwaukee are NOT the final aim of this great movement . . . I should . . . wish the victory had never been won . . . if [it] should in the least interfere with the revolutionary spirit of the Milwaukee movement."[49] Even "right-wing" socialists like Berger could not acknowledge the narrow reach of that spirit if they wanted to remain influential in the party that was their life. But such ends—particularly when expressed by a man whose first language was not English—had little impact in the rest of Wisconsin where La Follette's politics reigned.

The SP's fealty to its internal gospel caused some activists to seek a less sectarian home. Social Gospelers felt particularly uncomfortable with the drumbeat of class warfare. In Northern California, the Methodist minister J. Stitt Wilson was often at odds with the revolutionaries who controlled his state's party. Wilson, who was mayor of Berkeley from 1911 to 1913, defined socialism simply as an updated application of the golden rule—"We only want to make it impossible for the few to exploit and rob the many." "The one supreme issue," he said during his victorious campaign, "is the People versus the Plutocracy." For such talk, many comrades denounced Wilson as a "trimmer" and a sellout. By mid-decade, he had abandoned the SP altogether to campaign for both Woodrow Wilson and prohibition.[50]

Meanwhile, radicals on the Great Plains were making themselves over into militant populists. In 1915, a tiny band of socialists gave up trying to convert residents of agricultural North Dakota with a resolute, "working-class" message. They left the SP and created a new political body called the Nonpartisan League (NPL) to contest GOP primaries in that overwhelmingly Republican state. The NPL issued a program aimed squarely at the grievances of small farmers: government-run cooperatives, stringent regulation of railroads, and establishment of a state bank with branches in rural areas.

The passionate stump speaking of the erstwhile socialist (and one-time wheat farmer) Arthur C. Townley set the tone for all NPL speakers: "The struggle is between the farmers and their friends on one side and on the other side *corruption and robbery, supported by its tools, paid agents and sympathizers.* . . . The toilers or the spoilers—who shall be masters?" To accompany Townley's wrath, the young cartoonist John M. Baer drew, for the NPL's journal, a succession of grinning white-bearded farmers in overalls besting "Big Biz" and its privileged retainers (but sparing capitalism itself). Twice, the League swept to statewide victory, and Baer was once elected to Congress—probably the only American to win a House seat on the strength of his skill at political graphics. NPL contingents sprang up in fourteen other states on the Plains and in the Rockies before succumbing in the early 1920s to a consort of rivals. But the entire episode rested on the decision by Townley and his associates to "get . . . off the socialist line" and begin speaking an idiom their particular people could cheer.[51]

One of the few socialists who avoided making the choice between radical purism and populist reform was "Mother" Mary Harris Jones, the Irish-born union activist whose five decades of work in the coal fields earned her the title "the miners' angel." As a rhetorician, Jones brilliantly played against type. Stepping to the podium, the petite septuagenarian was dressed all in black save a bit of lace ringing her neck and wrists—the modest garb of an elderly Victorian. But Mother Jones was no lady. "A lady, you know was created by the parasitical class; women, God Almighty made them." Toughness and ridicule were the hallmarks of her long and frequent speeches. In a loud voice, she denounced lawyers as "grafters," claimed the press was "controlled by the Wall Street gang of commercial pirates," and, after World War I, even suggested murdering government officials who repressed strikers: "Some of the governors ought to be electrocuted. . . . Our boys are coming home in their uniforms. We sent them abroad to shoot the Kaiser. Let me tell you, we are going to get some Kaisers here at home."[52]

Mother Jones was able to avoid reproof for such statements because, in addition to her age and gender, she routinely wrapped herself in the Stars and Stripes. "One of her prized possessions was an early phonograph on which she used to play patriotic airs when no band was available," writes a biographer. She often held up the first American revolutionaries as models for contemporary workers to follow. "Be true to the teachings of your forefathers who fought and bled and raised the old flag that we might always shout for liberty," she told one UMW convention.

Jones proved the sincerity of her patriotism when the United States entered World War I in April 1917. Already an admirer of President Wilson for doing more to help "my class" than any chief executive since the sainted Lincoln, she enthusiastically supported his war policy, thus breaking with the SP majority that, at great cost, condemned the "imperialist" conflict. Her reasoning was characteristically pugnacious: "Perhaps I was as much opposed to war as anyone in the nation, but when we get into a fight I am one of those who intend to clean hell out of the other fellow, and we have to clean the kaiser up . . . the grafter, the burglar, the thief, the murderer."[53] Because she was already a legendary scourge of mine owners and other enemies of the common man, Mother Jones could support the war without losing her radical credentials. On the other hand, her Americanist brand of socialism had always contradicted the Marxist doctrine that the workers have no country.[54]

A WAR FOR AMERICANISM

All wars serve as crucibles of the rhetorics that either justify or oppose them; the original materials never emerge with their purity and potency intact. The era of World War I was a period of heated growth and divisiveness for American labor. Before the war, unionists, mindful of the military's long history of strike breaking, had overwhelmingly opposed a draft and a large standing army, though they favored a "citizen's army" over an elite force run by an officer "caste." In the populist tradition, worker activists suspected military adventures abroad of wasting public funds to help private businesses expand.[55]

But the 1917 declaration of war against Imperial Germany exploded that unity. The dominant, pro-Gompers wing of the AFL supported the war, hitching its wagon to Woodrow Wilson's star. To defend populist ideals, the world had to be made safe for democracy. But opponents, in and out of the labor movement, protested that American intervention in the European conflict betrayed those same ideals by sending working men off to die so industrialists could prosper. Phrases about the will of the majority, the tyranny of elites, and, especially, the authentic way to show one's Americanism filled the literature on both sides.

As before the war, the language of progressivism framed what unionists could say. This time, it was not insurgent politicians or muckrakers but a new, powerful agency of the federal government that presented to ordinary Americans a sophisticated rationale for belligerence.

The Committee on Public Information (CPI) was the first state propaganda bureau in United States history. Its mission was to convince Americans from all backgrounds to support what was already a monstrous, man-devouring war, whose justness even President Wilson had questioned as recently as his re-election campaign six months earlier. Hired for the task was a large staff of journalists and academics, most of whom had been quite friendly to labor and the Left during the previous two decades. The chairman was George Creel, a former muckraker and exponent of the single tax and municipal ownership who, as police commissioner of Denver, had forbidden his men to carry guns or nightsticks. The radical lawyer Clarence Darrow lent his speaking talents to the agency, and the staff included bright young men like Edward Bernays, a nephew of Freud's, who would soon create the new profession of public relations. The CPI mobilized hundreds of thousands of volunteers and distributed hundreds of millions of posters, cartoons, buttons, and pamphlets in English and eleven other languages. It was a grand exercise in what Bernays later called "the conscious and intelligent manipulation of the organized habits and opinions of the masses."[56]

From this torrent of material, one theme stood out: to endorse the war was to endorse "Americanism." This meant far more than the defense of homeland and family; for these publicists of war, Americanism signified the expansive ends progressives like Tom Johnson and Robert La Follette had fought to realize. It included (but was not limited to) the right of workers to fair representation, the freedom of immigrants (and sometimes blacks) to take advantage of available economic opportunities, and the knowledge that governments chosen by voters would work for *their* interests rather than doing the bidding of political bosses and sleazy corporations. *Americanism* meant a democracy that would make class differences obsolete. Surely, this was a vision worth dying for.

The CPI sought to appeal to everyone who lived within the borders of the United States or (through the committee's Foreign Section) shared its generous beliefs—as put forth in President Wilson's call for a "Peace Without Victory" and "self-determination" for colonized peoples. This America, as a Liberty Loan advertisement phrased it under a picture showing Hindenburg's face looming over the U.S. Capitol, "is a monument to an idea: The People ARE the Government . . . Freedom's military is the *People Embattled.* Autocracy's militarism is the *People Driven.*"[57] The United States wanted to do in only the Kaiser and his generals; as soon as average Germans embraced democratic, that is American, principles, the carnage would cease.

Union activists had long voiced the same type of Americanism, though never with the budget or skilled personnel the CPI enjoyed. When Gompers told a War Bond rally in 1917 that workers were the surest guarantors "that the spirit and methods of democracy are maintained" during "the people's war," he was extending a sentiment articulated thirty years earlier by labor party delegates in Cincinnati who wore buttons reading "Organized to Protect Our Homes, Flag, and Country."[58] At least in public, the AFL was suspicious of only those immigrants it judged incapable of standing up to "scoundrels in high places."

Like the People's Party, the labor movement had always located the most dangerous "un-American" influences at the top of society. Before the war, when coal-mine owners were cracking down on union organizers in West Virginia, the *United Mine Workers Journal* ran a jet-black map of the state with "Russia" written in place of its real name.[59] The term "industrial feudalism" was commonly applied to authoritarian employers and any government officials who backed them up.

It required no great leap to extend this habit internationally. Once Congress declared war, Gompers and his allies turned their main fire away from anti-union employers and trained it across the Atlantic, first against "the Kaiser and his immediate clique" and then also against the Bolsheviks who, by signing a separate peace treaty with Germany, left their people "powerless to maintain their own freedom or to realize their ideals."[60]

But a populist definition of Americanism was available to opponents of the war as well. As Wilson tilted toward war, a loose coalition on the left—pacifists, Socialists, and some local union officials—set up a series of ad hoc groups with names like the Committee for Democratic Control. All accused the business and political elites of wanting to throw ordinary Americans into the bloody trenches of France. They called for legislation to "take the profits out of war" by nationalizing the arms industry. But their most pressing and dramatic demand was the holding of a nationwide referendum on the question of U.S. intervention.

"Do the American People Want War?" asked a full-page advertisement in the *New Republic* that appeared early in March 1917. Its signers were three left-wing progressives—Amos Pinchot, Randolph Bourne, and Winthrop Lane—and the socialist Max Eastman. The answer was that 85 percent of voters who participated in a postcard survey had said no. Then, quoting a corporate newsletter, the trio charged that Wall Street *did* want war, and its desires were driving U.S. policy. In a passage distinguished by Bourne's characteristic irony, the timeless argument that the masses should not get embroiled in a quarrel between elites was pungently updated:

> Congress has the constitutional power to declare war, but if war comes it will not be Congress that will do the fighting. The editors will not do the fighting; nor will our bellicose lawyers, bankers, stock brokers and other prominent citizens, who mess at Delmonico's, bivouac in club windows, and are at all times willing to give their country's service the last full measure of conversation. No, the people themselves will do the fighting, and they will pay the bill. In death, in suffering, in sorrow, and in taxes to the third and fourth generations, the people who fight will pay. And therefore, we say that the people themselves should speak before Congress is permitted to declare war.[61]

Once the United States did join the conflict, such anguished pleas inspired a large antiwar movement whose main arm was the Peoples Council of America for Democracy and Terms of Peace. Socialists—especially immigrants from Eastern Europe who were enthralled by the Bolshevik takeover—and pacifists were the backbone of the resistance. They held mass rallies and distributed literature in the face of new federal laws (endorsed by AFL leaders) that forbade "uttering, printing, writing, or publishing any disloyal, profane, scurrilous, or abusive language" about the government or the military and allowed alien dissenters to be deported.

In their own way, several leading progressives also expressed distaste for the war. Robert La Follette, Jane Addams, and the leaders of the Nonpartisan League objected to the militaristic environment that was endangering social reform and enabling industrialists to become even richer. But to stay within the law, these figures also cursed the Kaiser and cheered on the doughboys. "We are against this God-damned war, but we can't afford to advertise it," the NPL's Arthur Townley confided to one of his organizers. Such equivocation did not fend off charges of aiding the enemy or hinder the sowing of populist seeds that would sprout another antiwar movement in the Midwest twenty years later.[62]

Within the ranks of organized labor, however, Gompers's fusion of loyalty with democratic ideals carried the day. It was sanctified by blood and sweetened by federal largesse. Union officials joined commissions to oversee war industries, and union rates became standard on most military projects. Employers were incensed, but organized labor finally seemed welcome as a legitimate force in American society. Even rank-and-file spokespeople for the numerous strikes that broke out in munitions plants seldom criticized the war effort itself. President Wilson's decision to address the AFL convention in November 1917 confirmed the perception of a new order; his presence alone—he was the first chief executive to enter labor's house to sing its praises—eclipsed the conventional message he delivered that day about the need for unions and the state to work together for victory.

Two months later, Wilson took the bite out of the antiwar position when he called for a generous peace treaty based on the Fourteen Points. The Socialist spokesman Morris Hillquit acknowledged that the sweeping program, proclaimed with grace by one of the great orators of his time, agreed with the "main principles" of anti-imperialism and international cooperation the Bolsheviks had put forth. The Peoples Council Treasurer Elizabeth Freeman even rhapsodized that "Trotsky, Lenin, Lloyd George and President Wilson are on our side and the People are ready to listen to us." The reformist president had forced grassroots dissidents to walk in his shadow.[63]

Most labor activists, despite grumblings about "a rich man's war," did not need to compare Wilson's words with those of Russian revolutionaries. The new members flooding into unions and a desire to trust the judgment of their two presidents—Gompers and Wilson—were probably enough to sway them, even if public opposition to the war had not been so dangerous a pursuit. So, a rhetorical precedent was set for future liberal interventionists to follow: if you would convince working-class Americans to rally to your side, stress the need to protect majority rule and to crush a tyrannical foreign elite. And give them a material stake in your mission.

THE WAR AT HOME . . . AND AFTER

Shortly after the Armistice, the AFL's short liaison with the progressive state ended. From the spring of 1919 to the middle of 1920, over four million workers participated in a wave of strikes, unprecedented in scale, that shut down nearly every major industry—steel, textiles, meatpacking, coal, and railroads. Simultaneously, growing numbers of unionists lifted their hopes to Western and Central Europe, where socialist and labor parties were thriving and often gaining a share of national power. Perhaps, American rank and filers could now realize by themselves the lofty promises the CPI and Gompers had made to win their wartime loyalty. Perhaps their swollen movement would become the engine fueling a "new majority" capable of running both the economy and the state.[64] The Bolshevik triumph also brought a new muscularity to the language of Marxists at home who had been squelched and imprisoned for opposing the war.

This lurch to the left profoundly alarmed business executives and government officials. Employers charged that anarchy was taking over the workplace and launched a national union-breaking campaign that corporate publicists called the "American Plan," evoking both wartime patriotism and the yearning for a well-ordered society. Federal and state governments, concerned with inflationary wage increases and stiffened by the GOP's takeover of Congress in the 1918 elections, responded by calling out troops and jailing organizers; the courts issued a blizzard of new injunctions.

Most leaders of labor's political upsurge were not socialists. They were mainstream AFLers who took the president and the CPI at their word when they promised a future of classless democracy. But popular rule, argued unionists, must now be extended to the workplace. A radicalized labor movement rallied around the concept of "industrial democracy." This meant independent unions for all wage earners and a degree of workers' control over production—both described as organic outgrowths of the battle for Americanism.[65]

From the industrial powerhouse of Chicago came the most impressive embodiment of that idea. In the winter of 1919, long-time officials of the Chicago Federation of Labor who were Irish and German-American joined with Slavic and Jewish newcomers, a variety of Midwestern reformers from the Nonpartisan League, and other groups to launch the Labor Party (LP). Their aim, hailed by nascent LP branches in other union strongholds, was to win control of city hall as the first step toward becoming a serious national rival to the Democrats and Republicans.

Carrying aloft this design was a rhetoric that harked back to Gilded Age producerism but also depended on the militant Americanism of wartime to motivate ends neither Sam Gompers nor Woodrow Wilson could countenance. The new party dubbed its platform "Labor's Fourteen Points." Under the label "Abolish Kaiserism in Education," it proposed that union teachers help run the public schools; an anticipated international "league" of workers (instead of nations) was portrayed as "An End to Kings and Wars." The LP welcomed merchants and white-collar workers as segments of "the whole people," whose main enemies were "the public utility corporations and other predatory financial interests, constituting the money power which fattens on special privilege."

But just before the municipal election, the LP, anxious about its prospects, abandoned its radical resolve. The party newspaper that had earlier featured huge cartoons showing crowds of determined workers (of both sexes) confronting lone plutocrats now depicted a victory for Labor candidates as the surest way to "prevent revolution." "Every businessman, big or little, who loves his country and desires to aid in saving the U.S.A. from disorders will vote the LP ticket on April 1," claimed an editorial. But only 56,000 Chicagoans—fewer than a sixth of the city's union members—voted to elect the labor leader John Fitzpatrick mayor. With an uncertain definition of who and what it was fighting for, the LP could not convince most urban workers to oppose party machines rooted in their own neighborhoods and ethnic groups.[66]

For their part, Gompers and his AFL allies mourned the loss of their wartime compact. Faced with a revolt on its Left and a new onslaught from the pro-business Right, they made a fresh attempt to capture the high middle ground. AFL publications attacked Lenin and Trotsky for disbanding independent unions and criticized militants at home who would convert craft disputes into general strikes, as occurred in Seattle in 1919. While some unionists on the industrial front lines cursed the national body for sabotaging their offensive, the aging leaders assured themselves that caution should rule until "the abnormal, troublesome times" had ended and "the hysteria shall have been stilled." After all, at least as many ordinary Americans burned to stamp out radicalism as longed for a labor government. One "A. Producer" wrote to Eugene Debs in prison, "We working people of Oregon hope that the guards throw the whip into you every day. You aren't a toiler. You never produced anything. You tried to prolong the war so that 1000000's of the US boys would be slaughtered."[67]

After the tumultuous postwar strikes were defeated, however, AFL leaders felt the need to reassert their populist credentials, lest they appear passive as the slide in union strength and the nation's economy continued. Gompers tried to match the flag-waving American Plan and the union-bashing American Legion with his own appeal to patriotic tradition. In 1920, he urged "the right thinking men and women of the Republic" to take part in the presidential campaign by intoning: "The forces of greed and plunder, the profiteers and autocrats of our political and industrial life leave no doubt as to what they desire. . . . More than in any political contest since the days of the Civil War, the issue is clearly drawn between reaction and progress." Two years later, an *American Federationist* cartoon depicted a clean-shaven, overall-clad image of "American labor" striding manfully and confidently past the twin perils of "bourbonism" (represented by the familiar top-hatted mogul in spats) and "bolshevism" (symbolized by a bearded character in rags). The artist was John M. Baer, the former congressman and cartoonist for the Nonpartisan League. The national AFL's frequent use of Baer's work in the early 1920s signified a shift to pointed, cruder images and away from the logically argued, often lengthy attacks and rebuttals that Gompers and his associates had employed before the war. Rhetorical prudence was no longer in fashion.[68]

One goad to more conflictual language came from activists, inside and outside the ranks of labor, who were, despite the defeat in Chicago, trying to organize a national third party of workers and farmers. And, for a few months in 1924, it seemed the People's Party had been reborn. Unionists (particularly on the railroads) and hard-pressed agrarians, nursing a common resentment of major-party politicians who aided their corporate enemies, were once again calling for a grand coalition to vanquish "monopoly" and grasp the levers of the economy. When Robert La Follette agreed to be their presidential candidate, nearly every prominent left-winger endorsed him, including many intellectuals and writers disgusted with the vapid, self-contented culture "normalcy" had wrought. Attempting to reverse their losses, both the AFL and the Socialist Party officially backed the ticket of La Follette and his vice-presidential choice, Burton Wheeler, a fiery senator from Montana. On paper, this was a broader alliance than the Populists had gathered in St. Louis over thirty years earlier. Only the Protestant moralists were missing.[69]

But it was a presidential campaign and not really a movement. The various groups who rallied to La Follette were not used to working together. Everything depended on the charismatic nominee. La Follette wrote the platform (it included the abolition of labor injunctions, government-owned railroads, and popular referenda before going to war), set his own minimal speaking schedule, and did almost all the fund-raising. He managed to draw an impressive 16.5 percent of the vote (and carried his own Wisconsin). But after election day, most activists quickly returned to their own agendas and constituencies. La Follette's death the following June eliminated any chance of a second battle.

Even at their most sanguine, campaigners for La Follette and Wheeler seemed to miss the days when the social conflict was starker, the lines of class division less ambiguous. A former Nonpartisan Leaguer from South Dakota declared: "This Wall Street dictatorship has got to be substituted by a dictatorship of the farmers and workers. We are the majority—we do the work—we have the right to rule." La Follette's own publicists depicted the candidate, nostalgically, as a solitary "tribune of the people" who continued the fight against "reaction" and "privilege" long after other progressives had given it up or died. John Baer drew a cartoon (captioned "The Same Spirit") that depicted a male worker casting his ballot while, in a cloud behind him, a soldier from the American Revolution looked on approvingly, musket in hand.[70]

Such appeals may have helped spur union members to the polls where their votes helped throw some of the more notorious enemies of labor out of Congress. But they did not stop a fall in the movement's membership or the gradual loss of its grassroots élan. The 1920s was, after all, the era when business mastered the art of seduction. Welfare capitalists offered their employees stock-ownership plans and group insurance, and announced that the "old dog-eat-dog theory" of labor relations was passé. Commercial advertisers invited readers to view themselves as respectable, classless consumers—whatever their occupation or income.[71]

Even within the pages of the AFL's magazine, champions of the proud producer felt the silky brush of change. In May 1920, Gompers railed at the "Congress of Negation" whose antilabor votes had, he said, violated "the true spirit of American institutions." But his words were neutralized, even mocked, by an advertisement on the facing page for Wrigley's chewing gum. Around the drawing of a shiny-faced young man about to bite into one of Wrigley's products danced the promises: "Fine after smoking," "Aids appetite," and "Thirsty? Here's refreshment to last all day—a package in your pocket means vigor, vim, encouragement."[72] The optimistic language of advertising seemed to transcend politics altogether; it made labor's combative phrases sound sour and archaic.

Admen were certainly not involved in a conscious plot to undermine working-class militancy. If they had been, the *American Federationist* would not have run their copy. But their messages presented an alluring alternative to the AFL's tarnished populism, one that even wage earners who couldn't afford many of the products being dangled no doubt found attractive. "Consumer" was no longer the pejorative label it had been at the beginning of the Industrial Revolution.

By the mid-1920s, with Gompers dead and the economy booming, the AFL turned away from the oppositional discourse that had been its stock in trade since the 1880s (taking a hiatus only during the Great War). On Labor Day, unionists in several big cities threw open their parades to anyone who cared to march, regardless of their attitude toward the movement. In Los Angeles, an officer of the American Legion was invited to give a speech, and in San Francisco, another Legionnaire judged floats. AFL publications eschewed editorial cartoons that portrayed any species of employer unfavorably and ran bland pieces on such topics as "The Use of Industrial Statistics," "The Problems of International Debt," and "Schools and Eyesight Conservation" to show that labor was a responsible partner for American industry. William Green, the new president, hacked out dry, painfully measured prose assuring employers that wages should only rise when productivity did.[73]

More skillful AFL writers, who had imbibed the opportunistic wisdom of public relations, experimented with tropes of self-improvement to convince workers to join a union. One organizing flier, entitled "Are You a Good Business Man?" asked, "Are you as wise [as an efficient employer] in managing your business of getting and keeping a job, with the right pay, with proper conservation of your precious capital—health, labor power, 'pep' and initiative?"[74] For the first time in its history, the rhetoric of the national AFL could accurately be described as "business unionist."

This shift of language had a meaning beyond the contours of a declining movement of wage earners. Never again would the activist core of organized labor and the Left employ the mode of self-reliant producerism AFL spokesmen had inherited from nineteenth-century insurgents and adapted to their own prudential purposes. Some periodicals would continue to publish images of the "ordinary" or "average"

American as an overall-clad white male craftsman or farmer who refused to be ruled by monopolists, federal bureaucrats, or professional reformers. But the movements for which they spoke tended to be conservative ones that opposed the growth of organized labor. When unionists rose again in the 1930s, their image of the people would be more ethnically tolerant, and their ambivalence toward the liberal state would all but vanish.

HAVE YOU EVER NOTICED

That this man's automobile cost $5000, While this man's only cost $500;
That this man is a power, While this man is not;
That this man is never a Prohibitionist, While this man generally is?

WHY IS IT?

From the Wholesalers and Retailers Review.

Yes, we had noticed it, but we thank the Review for calling attention to it nevertheless. The two faces are very different, and we like the old fellow in the Ford. He looks like the common people. And where did the other fellow get his four-bit cigar, and his fur-lined coat, and his jowl, and his silk hat, and his brutal eye, and his bulldog mug, and his Five Thousand Dollar automobile?

Perhaps the answer to this question would explain why it is that he is "never a prohibitionist." Somehow that big diamond smells like a bar-room. Anyhow, we climb into the Ford with the common people.

The Anti-Saloon League embraces the man in the Model T, 1915. *(Courtesy of the Library of Congress)*

Chapter 4

Onward, Christian Mothers and Soldiers: The Prohibitionist Crusade

Better that rich corporations should lose heavily on their present contracts than that the lives of men, women, and little children, who at best have a pitifully meager living, should go out in hunger and want.

—Minnie English, superintendent of work among miners, Woman's Christian Temperance Union, c. 1887

If our republic is to be saved, the liquor traffic must be destroyed.

—Purley Baker, General Superintendent, Anti-Saloon League, 1913

No concession can be made to the minority in this country without a surrender of the fundamental principle of popular government. The people have a right to have what they want, and they want prohibition.

—William Jennings Bryan, 1923

DRY OVER ALL

AS the twentieth century nears its end, most Americans regard the prohibition movement that was so powerful at its beginning as either hopelessly quaint or quaintly sinister. A college teacher who brings up the subject in class hears students use terms like "puritanical," "authoritarian," and even "fascist" to describe the evangelicals who somehow convinced the nation to undertake the idiotic, impossible task of abolishing the liquor business. The students' opinion is hardly new. In 1941, summing up an already fashionable judgment, the liberal author Edgar Kemler wrote that, when the prohibition amendment was repealed, "sin was returned to the jurisdiction of the churches where it belongs."[1] Even the Christian Right of the 1970s and 1980s seldom tried to rehabilitate the likes of Carry A. Nation.

But, in their own day, the women and men who successfully campaigned to include their moral beliefs in the Constitution viewed themselves and were widely regarded as selfless reformers, harbingers of a healthier and more democratic America. While their immediate agenda was much narrower than that of the Populists, prohibitionists insisted their goal was the same: to ensure that the "plain people"—their values and their loyal representatives—would control the society they had built instead of abandoning it to immoral "parasites" above and below. At the same time, the anti-alcohol crusaders were rhetorical progressives. Most came from the same educated, urbanizing Protestant middle class as did figures like Tom Johnson and Robert La Follette. And prohibitionists also felt more comfortable speaking of their followers as "citizens" or "the public interest" rather than "producers"—so many of whom held down sweaty, wage-earning jobs.

What set prohibitionists apart from many other zealous reformers in the early twentieth century was their explicit assumption that cleansing the nation meant bringing it back to Christ. They did not discourage ridding the cities of "boss-ism," giving women the vote, or persuading workers to join unions. But prohibition was *the* Protestant issue of the day. It had transcendent significance—both because it would cure a social evil that ruined and corrupted millions of lives and because it satisfied, better than any other issue, the urge to purify American culture that had frustrated Christian reformers since the end of the Civil War. Members of a cross section of evangelical churches dominated the drive for prohibition as they had no social movement since the heyday of abolitionism—and this time major denominations like the Methodists, Baptists, and Presbyterians were united in avid support instead of being split into bellicose camps as they were during the conflict over slavery. Ordained ministers, in alliance with thousands of laywomen and laymen, devised the movement's strategy and articulated its aims.

Opposition to strong drink was, of course, not a novel sentiment. In 1826, a band of New England awakeners founded the American Society for the Promotion of Temperance, and, since then, the cause had never lacked for enthusiasts who urged their fellow citizens to do what was good for them and their society. But by the early years of the twentieth century, the drive for prohibition had become, for evangelical activists, the supreme test of whether a moral majority could ever rule again in America. Indeed, the crusaders' influence was so great that, by 1910, a native-born white Protestant was as likely to defend the saloon as, half a century later, a liberal Democrat was to say a kind word about racial segregation.

Leaders of the dry cause in the Progressive era did not purposely exclude anyone but owners of distilleries and beer companies. This mother of all American reform movements welcomed anyone who contributed goods or moral guidance to society. In reality, however, the prohibitionists were no more representative of their fellow citizens than was the AFL, with its preference for the white skilled worker. In 1887, James McCosh, the president of Princeton College, told the Evangelical Alliance that the "middle class . . . constitute the bone and sinew of our churches, as they do of our country." The dry army never extended much beyond the educated, relatively prosperous pietists he was extolling—even though this made their claim to speak for "the people" increasingly suspect.[2]

Yet the limited orbit of the dry forces was a new phenomenon. Through most of the nineteenth century, foes of the alcohol business stressed temperance rather than legalized prohibition—though they did favor outlawing the liquor trade wherever possible. And their social concerns were as broad as those of any farmer or union activist. Temperance advocates struggled against slavery, supported the Knights of Labor, and campaigned for woman suffrage. Many routinely railed against "plutocrats" and "monopolists" for impoverishing the "producing classes." Behind this stance lay an assumption that the same corporate-political establishment that robbed ordinary Americans of the wealth they produced also lured them into debauchery. And without allies, writes the historian Norman Clark, "A [temperance] reformer could no more approach the saloon nexus than he could the Pullman Company or United States Steel."[3]

The desire for cooperation was reciprocated. Before the 1890s, most labor activists were also foes of the liquor trade. They recognized that drinking impaired the self-discipline and clear thinking necessary to educate one's fellows and mobilize them for change. What were saloons but appendages of capitalists who picked the pockets of vulnerable workers and befuddled their minds? So argued the craftsmen who joined the huge but short-lived Washingtonian Movement of the 1840s and those who organized the unions that grew rapidly after the end of the Civil War. Both the conservative railroad brotherhoods and the radical organizers of the Knights of Labor preached that workers had to break with the convivial culture of the saloon before they could liberate themselves from the wage system. Heavy drinking, wrote Andrew C. Cameron, the editor of the influential *Workingmen's Advocate,* in 1866, made a man "a slave to a depraved appetite, an appetite which robs him of manhood, erases every particle of self-respect." Two decades later, the Knights, who strictly banned liquor sellers from membership, circulated a pledge that began: "I believe that every man should be free from the curse of slavery, whether that slavery appears in the shape of monopoly, usury or intemperance. The firmest link in the chain of oppression is the one I forge when I drown manhood and reason in drink." Terence Powderly claimed that 100,000 Knights, about a seventh of the membership, had signed this document in the last half of 1886 alone.[4]

Bondage was a persistent, powerful specter for grassroots reformers in the Gilded Age. Memorably articulated by the Declaration of Independence and vigorously renewed by the abolitionists, it allowed Powderly, an Irish Catholic, to claim he was working toward the same end as were Protestant advocates of temperance and women's rights who could boast a direct link, in terms of creed and demographics, to William Lloyd Garrison and Lucy Stone. As long as temperance workers agreed that prohibition was a matter that individual towns and counties should decide for themselves, they and labor unionists could bask in the aura of a liberating cause that shone on all corners of the producer coalition. When Frances Willard, the president of the Woman's Christian Temperance Union (WCTU) stated, "the Temperance Army, the Labor Army, and Woman's Suffrage Army must unite or die," she matched the sentiments, if not the political priorities, of activists in all three groups.[5]

Yet it was also in the 1890s that the temperance forces began to stress the necessity of *prohibition* and then to go their own way—armed with a middle-class, moralistic variant of the populist persuasion. To understand how that occurred requires a look at the changing character of the once massive organization that Willard led.

THE WOMANLY VOICE

Evangelical women generated the mass upsurge that eventually outlawed the commerce in alcoholic beverages. During the winter of 1873–74, over 56,000 respectable, well-dressed housewives gathered in hometown prayer meetings and then marched with Bibles in hand to nearby saloons. Dropping to their knees, they prayed the proprietors to shut their doors and pour their noxious products down a nearby gutter. The Women's Crusade began on Christmas Eve in the southern Ohio town of Hillsboro and quickly spread to hundreds of communities throughout the Midwest, and then to Boston, Philadelphia, and the largest cities on the West Coast. In the fall of 1874, many of the crusaders met each other at the first convention of the WCTU.

Five years before, in 1869, an exclusively male group of former abolitionists had organized the Prohibition Party, vowing, in an echo of their last great campaign, to drive another "archenemy of popular government" from the land. But, despite some influence among Protestant swing voters in the Northeast, the new group had no more success prying men away from their entrenched partisan loyalties than did the Greenbackers and the other small, alternative parties of the day. No Prohibitionist nominee for president ever received more than 265,000 votes (and that was in 1892 when the Populist James Weaver was drawing over a million).[6]

The WCTU, in contrast, was able to mobilize a true mass movement whose educational and agitational efforts reached into homes, churches, schools, workplaces, and seats of government in every part of the nation. *The Union Signal,* its monthly newspaper, knit these local activities together and encouraged readers to raise their ideological sights beyond the problems caused by alcohol. By the late 1890s, the WCTU comprised more than 7,000 democratically-run chapters—some 176,000 members, all wearing white ribbons to signify their pristine motives. To that point, the WCTU was easily the largest organization of women in United States history.[7]

White-ribboners represented a cause that appealed to millions of Protestants on a number of levels. In the late nineteenth century, many women, who attended church more frequently than did men, turned their evangelistic spirit to causes intended to emancipate their sex. Members of the WCTU thus sought to reform the vulgar and violent behavior commonly associated with saloons and to save the men who frequented them. They wanted to sever the link between politicians and liquor dealers that many Americans believed was at the root of urban corruption. They hoped to replace the grasping, competitive ethic that drove many men to find relief in alcohol with a code of charity and self-discipline—"the white life"—based on the Gospels. And their dedication itself was rooted in the widespread conviction that only women of virtue could be trusted to make men more virtuous. WCTU activists, while favoring votes for women, did not feel comfortable with the sharp rhetoric of individual rights employed by suffragists like Elizabeth Cady Stanton in the 1870s and 1880s. But their all-female union was certain that the elevation of womanly values would banish the evils of a patriarchal society.[8]

The Gilded Age WCTU pressed its case through two distinct types of discourse—one applied the balm of maternal love to the conflicts searing industrial America; the other employed populist phrases to bond with the political struggle of the "industrial classes." Temperance women basked in the approval of the native-born middle class because they spoke the same language of genteel, romantic reform popularized earlier in the century by novelists like Harriet Beecher Stowe and ministers like Charles Grandison Finney. The union's disarming slogan "Home Protection" lent legitimacy to physical blockades against saloons and to such controversial proposals as government funding of child-care centers. Singing hymns and drawing metaphors from Scripture, WCTU activists pledged their lives "For Others" and offered themselves as cheerful but resolute mothers to "wronged and wrecked humanity." In the words of a contemporary propagandist, the WCTU "continually opens its windows toward Jerusalem and prays the government to make it easy for the people to do right and hard for them to do wrong."[9] That image drew one first lady, Lucy B. Hayes, and numbers of other wealthy and socially prominent Americans to the organization.

Yet, by the mid-1880s, the WCTU was becoming a voice for changes that leaped the boundaries of noblesse oblige. Emboldened by Frances Willard's view that "women as a class have been the world's chief toilers," WCTU activists endorsed the demand of women wage earners for "equal pay for equal work." They also denounced "rich corporations" for opposing safety legislation in their workplaces, established separate departments to aid miners and timber workers, and sent delegates to address a convention of the Knights of Labor. Thousands of temperance women embraced Edward Bellamy's *Looking Backward* as a beautiful and quite Christian prophecy of orderly social deliverance. Frances Willard persuaded her members to endorse the Prohibition Party (though few were eligible to vote) and then, frustrated by its poor showing, helped establish the People's Party. By 1896, the *Union Signal* was a journalistic crossroads of organized female discontent: advocates of woman suffrage, prison reform, the single tax, municipal ownership of utilities, vegetarianism, shelters for ex-prostitutes, and unions for women workers competed for space with the scourges and victims of King Alcohol. All causes fell under the expansive rubric of "God in politics."[10]

Frances Willard, who was the president of the union from 1879 until her death in 1898, skillfully crafted an appeal that brought together both images of the WCTU—the solicitous guardian and the busy evangelist of outsider grievances. "Do Everything," Willard told her followers in 1881, and the motto soon became a bridge between women whose main concern was closing down saloons that catered to uncouth immigrants and those who embraced the leader's own commitment to Christian socialism. At a time of growing tension between American Catholics and Protestants, she even praised the work of the Catholic Total Abstinence Society (which encouraged drinkers to "take the pledge" but opposed the idea of legal prohibition).

Willard's charismatic presence infused the WCTU with optimism and generosity. Members who did not share her radical views were still devoted to this slender beauty whose clear, blue eyes and ethereal composure—shining from thousands of drawings and photographs—made her seem blessed. Whether in print, in small meetings, or before audiences of several thousand people, Willard assumed the same gentle, empathetic tone. For a time in the 1870s, she had been on the staff of the great revivalist Dwight Moody, and she learned how to inspire and seduce an audience without ever stepping outside the limits of serene, ladylike address. Someday, "we might come up to the level where we can hear the cry of the world and help to hush it into peace, as a mother soothes the baby on her breast," she predicted in 1896.[11]

A century later, such pathos may seem cloying. But, accompanied by a torrent of anecdotes about battered wives and hungry children, it was the WCTU's most formidable weapon. Within the movement, Willard could promote a radical opinion—such as the idea that "poverty causes intemperance" rather than vice versa—without endangering her status as a saintly figure whose energies were entirely devoted to "whitening" the world.

Despite her renown, she failed to convince her fellow dry crusaders to fuse with a People's Party that was reluctant to endorse their cause. In January 1892, Willard had invited twenty-eight reform leaders to a Chicago hotel to prepare a party platform that might represent them all. The result was a joint address that, along with planks later included in the Omaha Platform, said harsh things about the saloon but, to Willard's chagrin, was silent about prohibition. The practical men who led the national party knew that forced temperance polarized opposing passions: it repelled as many voters (most Catholics, Eastern urbanites, industrial workers, and Democrats) as it attracted (most Southern and Midwestern farmers, Republicans, and nearly all evangelicals). Rank-and-file Populists were often more forthright. The People's Parties of three Plains states (Oklahoma, North Dakota, and Kansas) favored outlawing the liquor traffic, and, in 1896, the Georgia Populists ran a wealthy prohibitionist for governor.[12]

At the 1892 Industrial Conference at Exposition Hall in St. Louis, Willard pleaded with delegates to include her righteous imperative in their platform. With embittered officials of the Prohibition Party already damning the whole enterprise, she believed this might be the last chance to keep intact her dream of a grand coalition. But most delegates put aside their personal views and declined to take a stand that would have diverted attention from their economic demands and destroyed their embryonic producer majority.[13] Willard never renounced her support of the party she had helped birth. But her early departure from Exposition Hall amid grumbling about pressure from the "liquor element" presaged the coming rupture between two modes of populism, one based in the workplace and the other in the church.[14]

The Gilded Age alliance between comfortable evangelicals and tribunes of the horny-handed had always depended on a common foe. From the 1870s to the 1890s, the idea that monopolists were robbing Americans of both their economic independence and their Christian virtue had brought together activists who would otherwise have mistrusted each other's motives and interests. When the People's Party made its priorities clear, evangelicals reasserted their traditional judgment: only those who put the Savior first could save the nation. Producerism, never more than a minor theme for this group, now all but disappeared from the evangelical symphony. William Jennings Bryan's defeat in 1896, followed by the growing strength of a secular labor movement, only confirmed the separate direction in which most temperance advocates were already traveling.

Inside the WCTU, empathy with the exploited masses did not long survive Frances Willard's death. After 1898, the WCTU gradually but decisively severed the connections she had forged between sentimental maternalism and broadly populist definitions of reform. The soft vocabulary of motherhood and pious works still marked the statements of leaders and local activists, and Willard herself was enshrined as a demigoddess—her birthday and the anniversary of her death were fulsomely celebrated, her epigrams constantly reprinted, and the details of her life sanctified by hagiographers. But most white-ribboners now shunned any causes other than prohibition and approached workers and new immigrants with the condescending air of missionaries seeking to convert the heathen. A self-righteous, censorious tone crept into WCTU literature. Under the efficient but colorless new president, Lillian Stevens (who held office until her death in 1914), local chapters condemned as "legalized vice" the sale of cigarettes and a stimulating new soft drink named Coca-Cola.[15]

While WCTU activists still viewed the organized liquor interests as a monstrous conspiracy against "the people," they now had little faith that working people—so many of whom had succumbed to alcohol—could help defeat it. Deliverance would come only from their own kind. "The Creed of Christian Patriotism"—a popular oath to further "Christ's worldwide kingdom" through "the intelligent and faithful performance of my full duty as a citizen"—replaced expressions of solidarity with other insurgents. In a revealing phrase Willard would not have used, Stevens told the union in 1900 that "the combined liquor business . . . is morally poorer than poverty itself." Then she added, confidently:

We have with us the same class of people that has always led in all the just reforms of the past. We have on our side the testimony of science, of law and of gospel, and the Lord of Hosts is our leader. Are we not sure to win?[16]

The doctrine of enlightened self-control was replacing Willard's vision of a sober, caring society.

TO WAR WITH THE LIQUOR TRUST

By the early twentieth century, however, the maternal stewardship of the WCTU was no longer the dominant tendency in the prohibition movement—although the union did retain a large membership. The Anti-Saloon League (ASL) roared into public consciousness with a simple, uncompromising message: outlaw the liquor traffic everywhere in the nation by using all rhetorical, legal, and financial weapons available. All other remedies—third parties, moral persuasion, grand alliances—had failed.

In the North and the West, the ASL loudly invoked the precedent of the war to vanquish the Slave Power; in the South, its attacks on parasitic cities and amoral men of wealth and privilege called up the rhetorical ghosts of Jefferson and Jackson. But whatever their uses of history, the men of the Anti-Saloon League broke with the soothing, gentle ways preferred by the women of the WCTU and the dignified, often verbose habits of Victorian oratory, both political and religious. Determined to breathe a new masculinity into Protestant worship as well as into reform efforts, ASLers sounded more like the tough, plainspeaking descendants of Andrew Jackson than like the hand-wringing Jeremiahs of the crumbling producer coalition they had left.[17]

League rhetoric was charged with the tough, thrilling metaphors of war. The enemy had a "Liquor Army," many of whose commanders bore foreign-sounding names; good Christians were urged to "enlist" as "soldiers" in a "perfectly disciplined, cold-blooded fighting unit"; and neutrals were held up to scorn.[18] Whether it was the evangelist Bob Burdette summarizing his approach toward saloon-owners with the "Latin" motto "*Soc Et Tuum*" or Billy Sunday punching chairs and marching back and forth across the platform to dramatize his hatred of "booze," the ASL left no doubt it was a robust, manly campaign to protect women and children. The aggressive tone was present from the mid-1890s, but it became ubiquitous in 1913 and after, when the movement focused on campaigning for the Eighteenth Amendment. Not coincidentally, the ASL celebrated legislative victory while Americans were waging a real Great War overseas.[19]

Ironically, the WCTU, a unique veteran of the Gilded Age, had pioneered the newly muscular language. Carry A. Nation seems fixed in the historical imagination as a ridiculous figure, the grim-faced enemy of other people's pleasures whose "hatchetation" unwittingly parodied her cause. But, just as the prohibition movement itself has received less respect than it deserves, the place of Nation (who, for symbolic reasons, always insisted her middle initial be used) in that movement has been both minimized and distorted.[20] In fact, her raids on Kansas saloons in 1900 and 1901 were quite popular in her own and surrounding states. The sale of liquor had been illegal in Kansas since 1880, and so her militancy was not a form of civil disobedience but a means of enforcing the law and of embarrassing government officials who shirked their duties—even though her destruction of property earned her time in thirty-two different jails. If Carry Nation was a terrorist, she was an uncommonly compelling one who scoffed at the tender approach Frances Willard had taken. "Moral suasion!" Nation laughed. "If there's anything that's weak and worse than useless it's this moral suasion. I despise it. These hell traps of Kansas have fattened for twenty years on moral suasion."[21]

Carry Nation did not stand alone. In Topeka, she raised a Home Defenders' Army of hundreds of women to march on saloons. She had several long discussions with the governor of Kansas, was an honored speaker at local conventions of the WCTU and the Prohibition Party, and was even invited to address the state legislature, to whom she bluntly explained: "You refused me the vote and I had to use a rock."

Nation's many admirers compared her to John Brown, and, although her activist career ended on the vaudeville circuit instead of the gallows, her role in her movement did bear a stylistic resemblance to his part in the crusade against slavery. Nation, the epitome of plainspeaking commitment to her cause, was a woman unafraid to lambaste judges (one of whom she called "Your Dishonor"), politicians, equivocating ministers, and businessmen alike for betraying the votes and trust of their anti-saloon communities. But, she—unlike Brown, who detested the racism of the white majority—was translating a basic populist theme into the idiom of a rigidly moralist politics. Ordinary Kansans believed in prohibition; only a selfish elite prevented them from having it. By 1905, Nation was edging closer to the tactical mainstream. Now a resident of Oklahoma, she launched a newspaper with the motto, "Your ballot is your hatchet."[22]

The mission of the ASL was to organize that attitude into a movement whose power no class or party could deny. The organization was founded in 1893 at Ohio's Oberlin College—an early base for abolitionists and woman suffragists—and established nationwide two years later. The idea for a unified "temperance trust" capable of taking on the concentrated power of the liquor business came from John R. and Mrs. C. W. Commons, an Oberlin undergraduate and his mother, who together edited a local dry newspaper. Ironically, in his later career as a labor economist and historian, John Commons became the preeminent intellectual defender of Samuel Gompers and his fellow AFL officials, most of whom loathed prohibition.[23]

The ASL assembled a rich variety of verbal weapons: evangelical exhortation, resentment against moral laxity at both ends of the social spectrum, scientific methodology, and the call to resuscitate an America of small-town, self-reliant democrats. This blend was articulated by a band of pietistic organization men with an unparalleled talent for publicity and political pressure. If national prohibition itself had not proved unenforceable, we would today probably consider the league the single-issue group that cast the mold for others that followed.

A nonpartisan strategy enabled the ASL to break free from the doomed romance with third parties that had preoccupied many other grassroots reformers. While sharing the disgust of middle-class progressives toward blind party loyalty, league activists had a more specific reason to back any candidate who endorsed their stand: the Prohibition Party's obvious failure to win even the votes of most temperance supporters. ASL prohibitionists in the South were free to work within the Democratic Party, and Northern crusaders fought to control local Republican networks; all were skillful at mobilizing the faithful to vote in primaries, an innovation that loosened the grip of party bosses. The league's pragmatic approach to electoral politics predated Sam Gompers's injunction to "reward your friends and punish your enemies." And its steady focus on the unequivocal aim of terminating the liquor traffic offered a more straightforward basis for choosing between rival candidates than did the AFL's lengthy and mutable program of legislative demands.

From its national headquarters in Westerville, Ohio, the ASL orchestrated a swelling chorus of voices demanding prohibition. By 1913, when the final drive to pass a Constitutional amendment began, all the evangelical churches, the WCTU, a variety of social reformers, many businessmen, and even a few conservative trade unionists (particularly from the railroad brotherhoods) had joined the fold.[24] The salaried superintendents in charge of the ASL often portrayed their group as a democratic assemblage of state affiliates, religious denominations, independent temperance societies, and individual reformers who democratically made the key decisions in annual conventions. But, despite a formal structure that appeared to be as representative of the movement as Congress was of the nation, the national ASL actually operated "much like the central office of a diversified corporation." Political strategy, fund-raising, and publicity were all controlled by a handful of staff members and a few allies in key states. For them, the image of a dry army was not metaphorical; they sincerely believed themselves to be generals engaged in a war for the soul of civilization.[25]

"The Anti-Saloon League movement was begun by Almighty God," claimed its founder, Howard Russell.[26] In the Progressive era, a stormy theological debate was under way between biblical fundamentalists and their modernist foes. But the ASL and its goal were immune from this conflict; nearly every Protestant denomination, writes the historian George Marsden, viewed prohibition as "an attack on a demonic vice and a progressive reform for improving civic life." Between 1905 and 1915, the number of individual churches allied with the league doubled to almost 40,000.[27]

With such forces behind them, ASL activists confidently styled themselves the moral vanguards of progressivism. They abhorred the discourse of turn-of-century conservatism, with its fear of mass democracy and assumption that human nature was unchangeable. In most states, prohibition voters could also be counted on to back campaigns against government corruption and for corporate regulation and woman suffrage. ASL officials did not warn against involvement in such causes. They simply insisted that the liquor traffic was the root cause of social evil and thus prohibition was the only true calling for anyone wishing to perfect the world.

Every top man in the league was either an ordained minister or a reverent layman, and each played a distinct role in the organization (women were largely confined to secretarial posts). Howard Russell, a Congregationalist pastor, erected the bureaucratic structure of departments separated by function (such as publicity and finance) through which eager activists received specialized training and evaluation of their work.[28] It was also Russell's idea to offer clergymen a concrete, painless way to join the movement: the annual Anti-Saloon Sunday, when donations were collected and petitions signed for the cause.

Russell's protégé Purley A. Baker, a Methodist minister, was the ASL's general superintendent (its top official) from 1903 until his death in 1924. An inspirational speaker, Baker infused the movement's language with the tone of virtuous, patriotic uplift so common to progressive rhetoric. When critics told him other national problems were more pressing, Baker shot back: "Experience has proven that the nearer men are right on this question the nearer they are right on every great question that affects the welfare of humankind."[29]

Ernest Cherrington, a Methodist layman, directed a sophisticated, centralized publishing empire whose newspapers, billboards, and books reached both the converted and the doubtful. From 1912 on, he also controlled a fund-raising apparatus that enabled the league to spend an average of $2.5 million a year. And Wayne Wheeler, the ASL's general counsel and chief Washington lobbyist, mastered the technique of intimidating a politician with a blizzard of telegrams from constituents or a well-timed smear that he was "a tool of the liquor interests." Wheeler also co-authored the Volstead Act, the legal teeth behind the Eighteenth Amendment.

These commanders deployed a battalion of 20,000 speakers and untold numbers of writers whose rhetorical weapons had been updated and refined since their origins in the antebellum era. Fiction writers told portentous stories about upright working men whose first, innocent visit to a saloon led inexorably to their family's ruin and their own death. Physicians warned that even moderate drinking endangered the internal organs, weakened the ability to work and reason, and drastically shortened life. Social scientists furnished statistics allegedly proving that cities and states that had already adopted prohibition enjoyed lower unemployment, higher rates of production, less crime, and a healthier fiscal climate. Such details prohibitionists imparted as if they were prosecuting an airtight case. "The Brewers have the money—We Have the Facts—Come in and See," read the sign on an ASL storefront in Dayton, Ohio.[30]

This bundle of arguments was, no doubt, persuasive to most Protestant, middle-class Americans, who were increasingly demanding efficiency and probity both in their economy and civic life. But to invest prohibition with the aura of a crusade, to communicate the sense that a vital battle was being waged that absolutely *required* the public's attention and participation, more was needed than heart-wrenching narratives and statistical tables.

ASL publicists had to draw as lurid a portrait of the liquor traffic as could be imagined. At the same time, they had to identify their organization with the values and interests of common, hardworking Americans. So the league clothed itself in garments of homespun, patriotic materials designed to persuade audiences that prohibitionists wanted only to ensure that the voice of the people would be heeded.

The very name of the Anti-Saloon League promoted the idea that the evils of drink could be traced directly to an urban elite—whose public face was the street-corner tavern—that exerted its profits and power to crush the independent spirit of ordinary Americans. The ASL eagerly publicized the fact that large brewing firms owned many saloons; this gave credence to talk of a "liquor trust" that didn't even offer drinkers a choice of intoxicants. And, by the early years of the century, muckrakers were documenting collusion between the liquor business and corrupt politicians. Minions of the "trust" paid off police to ignore licensing laws, bribed railroads to carry strong drink into dry areas, and used a huge bank chest to pressure parties in big cities to nominate its friends. Lincoln Steffens, who was no fan of prohibition, recounted the tale of the anonymous St. Louis wit who "nearly emptied one house of the municipal assembly by tipping a boy to rush in and call out: 'Mister, your saloon is on fire.'"[31]

The name of the ASL also avoided the dangers of the alternatives. "Temperance" put the onus on individual tipplers. Unless they took the pledge and reformed, nothing would change. And while "prohibition" remained in use, targeting the saloon avoided the paternalistic, illiberal image of finger-wagging preachers telling people how to behave in private. It pointed the collective finger at a selfish "interest" in high places and implied that the masses were, at worst, its unwitting victims. Remarkably, it even allowed people who still used alcohol to support a movement that intended to outlaw legal drinking. "I am not a prohibitionist in the strict sense of the word," averred Senator Morris Sheppard of Texas, one of the ASL's best friends in Congress. "I am fighting the liquor traffic. I am against the saloon. I am not in any sense aiming to prevent the personal use of alcoholic beverages."[32]

Thus, for the ASL and its allies, a business that existed in nearly every American town and proliferated in its largest cities was a symbol of the broad network of manufacturers, distributors, advertisers, and urban bosses that preyed on the public. When branded a "trust" or "King Alcohol," the liquor industry became a frightening but also morally vulnerable symbol: an elite that engorged itself on the impoverishment and depravity of the entire country. "What if the saloon controls the city," asked the popular evangelical writer Josiah Strong in 1911, "when the city controls state and nation?"

To those faced with such a danger, the choice seemed as clear as the one the Populists defined when they met in St. Louis in 1892: to redeem America or watch its democratic vigor waste away. "There is but one side to the question as to the attitude of Baptists, or indeed of any Christian man and thoughful citizen concerning the liquor traffic," declared the Texas Baptist Convention in 1911, "ceaseless and truceless hostility against the entire liquor *oligarchy,* local, country, state and national, root and branch" (emphasis added). Prohibitionists said little about the split between whiskey distillers and brewers that long delayed the mounting of a common defense and then severely hampered its effectiveness. As the Populists had recognized, the specter of a unified, fiercely determined elite was much easier to comprehend and oppose.[33]

The ASL press in the years before World War I did not separate the immorality of this purportedly gargantuan foe from its economic clout. In their ubiquitous use of the phrase "the liquor traffic," prohibitionists were making a conscious connection between their movement and the contemporaneous crusade against prostitution ("the traffic in women"). Both campaigns were challenging a farflung, intersecting network of vice merchants. The ASL departed from its single-issue strategy long enough to assemble and/or join coalitions of settlement-house leaders and public-health officials that tried to close down red-light districts in New York and several other cities. Could one imagine a more diabolic partnership than that between thousands of liquor-sellers and the prostitutes who worked inside their establishments? Wrote the ASL's L. A. Banks in 1917, "If you arrest a white slaver in Alaska or San Francisco, or lay your hand on a brothel in Montana, or a gambling hall in Nevada, the whole piratical gang, with their hundreds of millions of wealth, will fight to save the scoundrels to the ends of the earth."[34]

To combat that "gang," the ASL employed two negative images that drew on both republican and anti-immigrant sentiments. The first image was that of a tycoon with fancy habits—Mark Hanna with a champagne bottle in hand and a buxom lady of the night on his arm. The Methodist bishop James Cannon, Jr., the league's most prominent official in the South, was fond of attacking what he called "the eminently respectable . . . 'high society' element" whose libertine extravagance helped him generate support among working people for prohibition.[35]

The second image was that of a paunchy, moustachioed saloon keeper with a long cigar in the corner of his mouth and a malevolent or haughty look in his recessed, beady eyes. Of obvious Central-European lineage, this urban potentate was an alien Mephistopheles who had no natural roots in the nation he was despoiling. The titles of the ASL's nationally circulated periodicals—the *American Issue* (its main organ), the *American Patriot,* and the *New Republic* (not the same magazine being published today)—emphasized that it was the ASL's mission to repel such invasive forces.[36]

One posthumous recruit was Abraham Lincoln. As an Illinois politician, the sainted Lincoln had joined the Washingtonian movement. He may even have written his own abstentionist pledge and urged young men to sign it. The Anti-Saloon League believed that tale, of course, and, in 1903, launched the Lincoln Legion—a youth contingent dedicated to embellishing the legend of the railsplitter as dry crusader. The Legion magazine published temperance speeches the martyr had given and depicted Lincoln as a humble man "earnest and active in connection with the various reform movements of his day." Later, so as not to offend white Southerners, the name was changed to the Lincoln-Lee Legion.[37]

The general superintendent of the league, Purley Baker, was fond of packing the entire indictment and patriotic vision into one sustained roar. Early in 1912, the *American Issue* published this Baker statement on its front page, set in headline type:

> We must not overlook the fact that we confront a foe that has ill-gotten wealth without limit and no conscience in the spending of it. Love for country, human character, domestic happiness, personal reputation, have no place in its code of warfare. Bribery is one of its mildest methods for accomplishing its purpose. It laughs at virtue, it mocks religion, it scoffs at common honesty, it defies every appeal of outraged womanhood and robs helpless childhood of a fair chance. It is drunk with the blood of the millions it has slain. It lowers public intelligence; it destroys public conscience; it forbids, wherever possible, right representation of public intelligence and public conscience in our law-making bodies and in the executive department of government as well. And when laws are enacted, this treasonable institution tramples upon them with impunity; it refuses to be regulated; it is incapable of reformation. . . . There is nothing left but to abolish it from every foot of territory everywhere as speedily as an advancing civilization and a developing conscience will permit.[38]

Notice how Baker, who may have learned a trope or two from Ignatius Donnelly and William Jennings Bryan, described the competing values. Traditional attributes of honor and responsibility were arrayed against "a foe" who cares for nothing but profit and power. Baker's overheated condemnation echoed the stern, many-sided attack hurled against slavery by William Lloyd Garrison and Wendell Phillips, childhood heroes to many Northern prohibitionists. Like the Slave Power, the Liquor Power subverted private and public morality, and any compromise measure (for instance, state ownership of the liquor industry) would only legitimize the beast. But, unlike the abolitionists who, before the Civil War, had smiled on self-made entrepreneurs, the ASL used language full of anticommercial implications. Thus, the resemblance between Baker and Donnelly was not merely a stylistic one.

When brewers and distillers argued that the taxes they paid and the grain they purchased were boons to the economy, dry soldiers countered with stories of mothers impoverished and children malnourished. Those innocent victims, said Billy Sunday, were the "raw material" of "the worst business this side of hell."[39] Like the Populists, foes of the saloon seemed convinced that Mammon was dominating man, and only their movement could right the balance.

No small irony attended this self-image. In fact, the dry crusaders had the support of some of the wealthiest capitalists in the land. Names like Rockefeller, Pillsbury, McCormick, and Kresge appeared on ASL donation lists alongside those of executives from several national banks and insurance companies. These men agreed with Purley Baker and his brethren that drinkers made slovenly employees, caused many accidents, and slowed the adaptation of immigrants to modern work habits. For men concerned with the future health of the economy, the saloon also represented a form of cultural backwardness, an ever-present threat to turn the fragile community of productive labor into dissolute rabble.

But most big businessmen who backed the ASL had more than future profits in mind. John D. Rockefeller was a devout Baptist; Henry Ford and the metal manufacturer Daniel Guggenheim believed their companies should try to improve their workers' individual health and moral standing as well as give them a paycheck. Ever since Robert Owen, the textile manufacturer and pioneer socialist of the early nineteenth century, there had been a number of factory owners who felt their mastery of the mechanisms of production also gave them a special insight into how society as a whole should be run. The notion that businessmen contributed to the ASL simply because they wanted an efficient and tractable workforce thins out human motivation to the unsatisfying gruel of "economic man." It also neglects the fact that contributions of less than $100 supplied more than 90 percent of the ASL's national budget.[40]

Organized prohibition was not a plot by big capital to keep workers in line; it was the latest phase of a movement to perfect individual conduct and make it rational whose wellsprings can be traced back to both the Reformation and the Enlightenment. And the ASL's very autonomy from partisan norms made some powerful businessmen quite uneasy—as did its periodic boycotts of firms that opposed prohibition. "If these church people get busy, they'll knock the devil out of politics," warned Mark Hanna. The mischievous Wayne Wheeler took the Republican kingmaker's satanic metaphor literally. "We haven't got him knocked out entirely yet, but we certainly have him on the run."[41] League officials did gather funds from some of America's richest men. But they were dependent on those men for neither money nor ideas.

Still, the fact that some big businessmen were avid supporters of the ASL points up a key difference between prohibitionists and other reformers who voiced the producer ethic. The league did not echo the kind of populist resentments expressed by organized labor and those politicians who earnestly courted the support of urban wage earners. The prohibitionists, in creating an image of the people whose interests it vowed to serve, took few jabs at patronizing elites who knew nothing of hard work. After all, ASL staff members were more likely to hire manual laborers and craftsmen than to emulate them. So the prohibitionists relied on a vocabulary of economic virtue that focused on classless American ideals instead of divisions played out on a factory floor or inside a federal courtroom.

The distinction between "productive" and "nonproductive" pursuits was a vital part of the ASL message. That message implicitly lumped together the tasks performed and the rewards received by both workers and their bosses. The liquor industry was not considered sinful only because it destroyed the health and family lives of countless Americans. It was also derided as parasitic and wasteful. In 1908, the Reverend George Hammell, an ASL publicist, wrote that "the maker or vendor of intoxicating liquors . . . can find no place in an economic society, for he cannot show that in any way he is engaged in the production of any useful commodity. He adds nothing to wealth." The businessman Oscar Todhunter was more succinct: "The saloonkeeper is a fungoid growth on the social body."[42]

To excise this growth, the ASL relied on what it took to be a broad coalition. Sometimes anti-liquor forces were referred to simply as the "decent" or "patriotic" citizenry or as "public opinion." But, whenever the specific occupations of its constituents were mentioned, they invariably included only ones we would consider solidly middle class. A 1903 editorial in a prohibitionist newspaper described league supporters as being, besides Protestant ministers, "teachers and professional men, skilled mechanics and railroad men, clerks, commercial men and successful men generally."[43] That respectable, all-male list evokes images of a complacent Babbitry or at least manifests a wish to be regarded as such. The "skilled mechanic" is merely part of the string instead of being the archetypal average man he was for the AFL.

The ASL maintained that its people were located in the hardworking, morally vigilant center of the population. It was the champion of Main Street not Wall Street (and obviously not the Bowery). When prohibition came up for a vote in several cities, the results usually followed a pattern that matched the league's self-image: middle-class, evangelical churchgoers were in favor; both rich and poor wards were opposed.[44] Several ASL spokesmen boasted of their artisanal roots, and their publications lauded small farmers and self-employed townspeople as typical citizens who had united to banish the scourge of the liquor traffic from their land. In 1903 and 1904, the *American Issue* carried a series of columns in rural dialect by Farmer Ezra Alkins (an ironic imitation of Finley Peter Dunne's enormously popular Irish bartender, Mr. Dooley). One December, Farmer Alkins told readers he had a Christmas daydream in which "All the s'loonkeepers, distillers and broorers hed quit the licker bizness an' hed gone into hon'rible trades. Some was carpenters and bricklayers an' was repairin' the houses they hed tore down with their bizness; some was doctors an' surgeons, an' was fixin' up the bodies they hed crippled."[45]

A cartoon that appeared on the cover of the California ASL newspaper in 1915 demonstrates how the group tried to locate its supporters within the humble, righteous center of the population. The drawing showed the heads and shoulders of two middle-aged men. On the left was a variant of the standard issue plutocrat: top-hatted, double-chinned, smoking an expensive cigar and scowling out of his thick, fur-lined collar. On the right was his supposed opposite: a trim, smiling man seated behind the steering wheel of an automobile. He wears a comfortable fedora and smokes a corncob pipe. The cartoon was actually a reprint from *Wholesalers and Retailers Review,* a liquor industry magazine! Originally intended as a warning about the harmful image of anti-prohibitionists as dissolute big spenders, the drawing nicely reinforced one of the ASL's favorite arguments. Below the cartoon, the league editor added the caption: "The two faces are very different, and we like the old fellow in the Ford. He looks like the common people . . . Somehow that big diamond [on the other fellow's cravat] smells like a barroom. Anyhow, we climb into the Ford with the common people."[46]

The most influential exponent of this folksy style within the prohibitionist movement was the celebrated traveling evangelist Billy Sunday. A former major league ballplayer who grew up on a marginal Iowa farm, he pioneered a preaching style that Sinclair Lewis and H. L. Mencken loved to satirize and hundreds of other ministers strained to imitate. Sunday unabashedly mixed slangy showmanship with a fundamentalist reading of the Gospel. Leaping and gyrating around the stage before delighted throngs, he made denouncing sin almost a spectator sport, a prized opportunity to hear the vernacular performed in original and felicitous ways. He once confessed: "I don't know any more about theology than a jack-rabbit knows about ping-pong," but his public sermons enthralled people whom scholarly preachers trained in divinity schools could never reach.

Billy Sunday self-consciously appealed to the hardworking male majority squeezed between the rabble and the rich. Calling himself "a rube of the rubes," he criticized both "the diamond-wearing bunch, the automobile gang, the silk-gowned" and the "low-down, whiskey-soaked, beer-guzzling, bull-necked, foul-mouthed hypocrite" who beat his wife and neglected his work. Although local businessmen financed many of Sunday's revivals, he was also quite popular with God-fearing wage earners who preferred his loose, bare-knuckled approach to that of educated, "modernist" preachers whom Sunday parodied in falsetto voice. "The calliope of Zion," Mencken dubbed him, and he blazed a clear path for theatrical pastors to follow.[47]

From the turn of the century until the end of World War I, prohibition was, besides the Lord Himself, Billy Sunday's major passion, the one cause he felt could drive a wedge between America's sacred heart and its sensual desires. Everywhere he spoke across the nation, Sunday campaigned for anti-saloon laws. According to one biographer, he took credit whenever "a town, county, or state voted for Prohibition within a year of a Sunday campaign."[48]

Of all Sunday's talks, "the booze sermon" was his best known. In it, the evangelist spiced up the ASL's stock arguments against the liquor traffic with colorful tales comparing the enemy to a rattlesnake and a voracious mongoose. He graphically described what alcohol does to the flesh, the face, and the liver. He recalled that when Jesus tried to convince pork sellers to obey Jewish law, they replied: "You are hurting our business." He challenged men in the audience to behave like a "sovereign people" by doing their moral duty, "You have a chance to show your manhood" by legally abolishing the "curse" of "your wife and the poor innocent children that climb up on your lap and put their arms around your neck." One Sunday in 1915, 30,000 men heard the booze sermon and, immediately afterward, swore a holy oath to vote for prohibition.[49]

Billy Sunday was never an official spokesman for the Anti-Saloon League, but his great appeal to ordinary, native-born Americans strummed, albeit with more panache, the same tune that Purley Baker and his associates were playing. At a time when Sam Gompers and Eugene Debs were calling on manly producers to take their country back from the rich and the haughty, evangelicals were asserting the need for Christian men to build a new order so moral that gross social inequalities could no longer survive.

EXTENDING A CLOSED FIST

Prohibitionists, however, could not fulfill that lofty mission all by themselves. The ASL's definition of "the sovereign people," like that of the mainstream labor movement, was generally limited to those groups already on its side. But some dry activists understood that recent immigrants and wage earners—among whom, after all, King Alcohol found his largest cache of victims—had, at least, to be neutralized if the great national cleansing were to succeed. One had to speak to them, sympathetically, as well as about them.

Thus, Ernest Cherrington, as director of the ASL's educational arm, distributed materials in fifteen different languages that urged newcomers to rescue themselves from the unscrupulous businessmen and politicians in their communities who profited from the saloon. Cherrington, who also planned to publish a newspaper in German and to hire speakers to reach immigrants in their own languages, eventually turned his attention elsewhere. Yet he and his assistants knew the prohibition debate sharply divided several ethnic groups—most notably Swedes, Norwegians, Finns, Hungarians, and Russians—and so they contributed funds to foreign-language papers that took a dry stand.[50]

Cherrington also harbored some hope of winning allies in the labor movement. James Duncan, the leader of the powerful Seattle Central Labor Council, was a close friend and stalwart prohibitionist. The AFL Treasurer John B. Lennon had been a temperance man since the 1880s (and a Populist in the 1890s) and wrote an occasional article for the *American Issue.* "The saloon is the enemy of the people for whom we work," he stated flatly in 1912. Enough support for prohibition existed within the AFL to convince Gompers, in 1909, to keep resolutions on the subject off convention agendas, lest they disrupt good feeling among the delegates.[51]

Inside the Socialist Party were a surprising number of ardent foes of the saloon. The orator Kate Richards O'Hare, the radical muckraker Upton Sinclair, and many of the skilled workers who moonlighted as "salesmen-soldiers" for the SP's *Appeal to Reason* endorsed prohibition for all the reasons Terence Powderly and Frances Willard had given a generation before.[52] In 1913, Jack London, a dedicated socialist in spite of his hard-earned wealth, contributed *John Barleycorn,* an affecting volume stuffed with semifictional tales of his own drinking miseries from puberty onward. London began the book by predicting that once women won the vote, they would abolish the saloon. "He [John Barleycorn] is the enemy of life. . . . He is a red-handed killer, and he slays youth," London told his wife. The immensely popular London even mused about running for president on the Prohibitionist ticket.[53] However, neither he nor any other figure from the camp of labor or socialism invested energy or political capital on reconciling the two movements.

One of the few activists who did try to mediate between urban workers and prohibitionists was the Presbyterian cleric Charles Stelzle. Unlike most white Protestant ministers from established denominations, Stelzle, the son of German immigrants, had risen from the working class. At the age of 8, he was already stripping tobacco leaves and selling newspapers on New York's Lower East Side to support himself and his widowed mother.[54]

This formative experience, Stelzle later wrote, compelled him to attract laboring men and women to the church. In 1901, seeking the key to their spiritual apathy, he mailed questionnaires to 200 leading unionists and published the composite answers in a national magazine. Predictably, the labor activists criticized ministers for preaching not "the doctrines of the meek and lowly Jesus, but the doctrines of the high and mighty ones of this earth." Churches had become a place to display individual prosperity rather than to succor the afflicted. Stelzle was struck by how favorably his informants viewed the saloon—"it is mostly here that the workingman finds occasion to become enthusiastic" about "his manifold grievances . . . his political status" and "where we go to show our appreciation of another's friendship."[55]

For most of the next two decades, the reverend tried to remake organized Christianity into a place where working men and women would feel at home. He created, inside Presbyterianism, the first Department of Church and Labor to exist in any Protestant denomination and then headed a similar commission for the Federal (later National) Council of Churches. He founded the New York Labor Temple, a center for recreation and oratory about religion and politics, whose clientele was mostly composed of Catholics and Jews. He convinced hundreds of fellow clerics to establish the morning before Labor Day as Labor Sunday, an occasion for parishioners to reflect on the condition of workers. And he wrote a regular column for union newspapers that set forth the Social Gospel as a sentimental populist creed. One Christmas, Stelzle turned to poetry:

The Christ came first to those whose aching hearts
Cried out: "How long?"—the common folk—
Who heard Him and were glad . . .
He came in largest measure to the men
Whose hearts beat to His heart most true.

If Christ should come to earth to-day,
Would He go first to temple and to mart,

To palace and to court?
Or, would He seek the cottage and the slum;
Seek those who still cry out: "How long?"[56]

But how to persuade this putative flock to endorse prohibition? Stelzle argued for the cause at several AFL conventions. He published the *Worker,* an ASL-sponsored periodical, and wrote several pamphlets and a book dedicated to the subject. In each forum, he followed a two-pronged strategy. First, he explicitly separated himself from the ugly images of saloons and saloon-goers that proliferated in dry propaganda. "I have no sympathy with the statement that all saloon-keepers and bartenders are low-browed brutes. Most of them are workingmen with all the hopes and aspirations of other workingmen." Stelzle admitted, self-critically, that "The average workingman fears being out of work more than he does going to hell." Stelzle even ridiculed his fellow prohibitionists as "long-haired men and short-haired women"—the same acid, gender-conscious terms Samuel Gompers employed. I'm still a "son of the Bowery," the preacher was saying; I know that a man who sells beer for a living hasn't sold his soul to the Devil.[57]

But Stelzle also strained to debunk rhetoric that was helping to turn workers against prohibition. In particular, he tried to expose the true meaning of "personal liberty"—a slogan the AFL shared with the U.S. Brewers' Association. Didn't union rules against working with nonunion men—and for more than eight hours a day—also violate the personal liberty of wage earners who cared about no one but themselves? Democracy, Stelzle argued, could not countenance the freedom to behave in a harmful and unjust manner. "You can't do as you please in the industrial world," he wrote. "No more dare you do as you please with regard to the liquor business. Your personal liberty is the last thing to be considered. The first consideration is the well-being of the majority." The minister supplemented these stern words with more familiar charges that the bosses of the liquor industry were "greedy capitalists" who preyed on "the weaker members of society." By helping to destroy the liquor traffic, unionists would be doing their moral duty—standing up for the needs of all producers. And their efforts would surely be rewarded. After prohibition became law, Stelzle predicted in 1918, "there will be such a revival in the labor movement as it has never seen before."[58]

All this strenuous optimism, however, essentially came to naught. The AFL welcomed Stelzle as long as he interpreted Christianity as a doctrine to aid the working man. His arguments for prohibition, however, rang hollow unless the ASL demonstrated some of the same solicitude for organized labor, and it did not. Instead, Stelzle was charged with being a union spy within the dry army, and was even tarred as an ally of Eugene Debs and the anarchist Emma Goldman. The Presbyterian church cut his budget, and few state ASLs even responded to his plea that they woo labor leaders in their own areas. Stelzle naively, if courageously, believed he could repair the broken chain of sympathy between producerist and evangelical reformers. But while the former thought him too paternalistic when he talked about the saloon, the latter abhorred his preference for the class from which he had sprung. In the 1920s, Stelzle tired of the struggle and became a public relations executive.[59]

ASL efforts to reach workers and recent immigrants were an afterthought, a messianic reflex for organizers and publicists who could never write off anyone except the liquor traffickers themselves. The single-issue strategy and hard-nosed rhetoric of the ASL made an alliance of reformers across class and ethnic lines almost impossible. With Purley Baker and his associates describing opponents of a national prohibition amendment as an invading army of sinners, all room for compromise had vanished.

The evangelical battle cries that enabled the Anti-Saloon League to inspire its own constituency incurred the distrust of most Americans who belonged to unions. The largest AFL affiliates—of building craftsmen, coal miners, garment and brewery workers—were filled with Irish Catholics, Germans, Slavs, and Jews. All these ethnic groups viewed prohibition as unwelcome coercion, not reform. Declared Mother Jones at a 1909 convention of the UMW: "We fellows have got to stick together and fight, and if we get a jag on us we have to get a ten-cent drink of rotten whiskey instead of champagne. And they are even trying to get that away from us! What we want to do is fix things so we can drink the champagne and make them drink the whiskey for a while."[60]

By World War I, the national AFL was actively opposing prohibition. Gompers joined a publicity campaign sponsored by the Brewers' Association, an employers' group, that branded the prospective Eighteenth Amendment a gross violation of American freedoms. At a time when the doughboys, many from working-class homes, were fighting to extend their ideals to benighted corners of the Old World, prohibition seemed a particular outrage.

To be sure, the Anti-Saloon League did make some effort to separate "good"—or at least harmless—immigrants from "bad." That was the purpose of donating money to the foreign-language press. But the ASL's own rhetoric was self-defeating. In 1908, the *American Issue* criticized the Chicago police for breaking up an anarchist-led parade of unemployed workers while, at the same time, protecting a march against prohibition that was sponsored by liquor dealers, in which many immigrants participated. "The worst, most dangerous anarchists of today," argued the paper, "are the hordes of foreigners who disregard their naturalization oaths of obedience to law and, under the bosses . . . , set about breaking down . . . American institutions . . . in Chicago and wherever they have the power."[61] Making a fine distinction between two types of immigrant radicals—one more dangerous than the other—was not likely to win over newcomers from Eastern and Southern Europe.

In fact, the league's praise of "Christian voters" and the drawings in its magazines that contrasted farmers who looked like Uncle Sam with bulbous-nosed, swarthy saloon keepers conveyed a sharply nativist message. Admonishments that staying dry was the surest path to "Americanization" only widened the cultural chasm. With his customary bluntness, Billy Sunday charged, in 1912: "If you don't fight the saloon, I will say that you are not an American citizen." By the time the

Eighteenth Amendment was passed, the great majority of ethnic workers—even those from evangelical churches—viewed prohibition as a coercive act imposed from outside. What, some suggested, could be more anti-American than that?[62]

In its attitude toward black citizens, the ASL lacked even the wary ambivalence it showed toward European immigrants. As a nonpartisan coalition of Southern and Northern evangelicals, the league could not afford to question Jim Crow laws or the hundreds of lynchings that enforced them. Southern ASL activists worked within the all-white Democratic Party, and separate state editions of the *American Issue* ensured that laudatory references to Lincoln and the abolitionists would not appear in publicity distributed below the Mason-Dixon line. Even in its national edition, the paper alluded to the antislavery heritage as only a metaphorical antecedent of the current crusade; sympathy for the plight of contemporary black Americans almost never found its way into ASL propaganda. Far more typical were items blaming cheap gin for inspiring black field hands to rape white women. Symbolically, the WCTU had taught the temperance army to prize whiteness—in ribbons, clothing, and as a way to designate states that voted dry. The ASL only added the lure of political opportunity.[63]

In the South, the league threw its support to a new breed of populist campaigner that combined progressive demands for railroad regulation and clean government with praise for white supremacy. In Georgia, where the first statewide prohibition law enacted anywhere for decades was passed in 1907, Governor Hoke Smith declared: "The overwhelming sentiment of the white people of Georgia is for prohibition, and the law will be enforced." For Smith and his counterparts in adjoining states, supervising the personal habits of the "undependable" and "criminally inclined" black man was part of the same agenda as "purifying" urban politics and taming the "special interests" (which, of course, included the liquor business). Moreover, the disenfranchisement of black voters allowed these progressives to attack scions of the old planter elite as "privileged" remnants who could no longer use racial appeals to divide "the people."[64]

Not all black spokesmen accepted their virtual exclusion from the dry army. Black ministers were, after all, evangelical Protestants, and they routinely denounced liquor as an instrument of the Devil. In Tennessee and a few other states, separate black temperance organizations sprang up during the Gilded Age. Their spokesmen coupled the rhetoric of Christian virtue with the suspicion that whites sold freedmen liquor "to rob them of their sense and feelings of humanity." For similar reasons, both Booker T. Washington and the aging Frederick Douglass endorsed prohibition; although, in his last major speech, in 1894, Douglass aimed a withering criticism at Frances Willard for speaking of all black men as potential rapists.[65]

Naturally, few blacks worked within the Anti-Saloon League, and those who did sometimes adopted self-deprecatory language in the urge to fit in. In 1902, Professor E. W. B. Curry asked the Ohio ASL "to tip your hat to the patriotism of the unbleached American." He added, referring to the symbolic color of the anti-liquor movement, "We are whitening within." And, in 1919, the activist Robert E. Cray thanked the national league convention for helping his people to accept "your way of thinking on this temperance question" and stated proudly that, during the recent war, teetotaling black troops stationed in the South had behaved in a thoroughly exemplary manner. "The white folks had no trouble with the negroes [sic]; they could discipline them, and make fine soldiers, and had no trouble with them."[66]

The unthinking racism of the Anti-Saloon League matched the rest of its world view. As authentic representatives of the native-born Protestant middle classes, most prohibitionists assumed that blacks, like immigrant laborers, had nasty habits that a godless elite could easily manipulate. ASL activists sincerely wanted to save all the downtrodden, eventually. But, for the present, they were too involved in mobilizing the muscle of "decent Americans" to extend their hearts to the (presumably) passive or hostile poor. Besides, a man's true task was to slay the hydra of sin and privilege before it had squeezed the moral life out of the Christian republic.

WINNING A LAW, LOSING THE PEOPLE

As it happened, victory arrived with a swiftness that astonished even the most dedicated crusaders. In December 1913, four thousand white-ribboned women and men marched down Pennsylvania Avenue to the Capitol to symbolically petition Congress to pass the freshly drafted prohibition amendment. Even though half of all Americans already lived in dry states, Howard Russell and Purley Baker predicted it would take twenty years to enact the strict language barring "the manufacture, sale, or transportation of intoxicating liquors within, the importation thereof into, or the exportation thereof from the United States." Prohibitionists prepared themselves for what they expected to be the most difficult phrase in their long struggle.

But, unexpectedly, the 1916 election swept a huge dry contingent into both the House and Senate. Insurgent lawmakers like Robert La Follette, George Norris, and Hiram Johnson who had long wavered on the issue now announced their support. Just before Christmas 1917, Congress narrowly mustered the two-thirds majority needed to submit the amendment to the states for ratification. Barely a year later, in mid-January of 1919, the Nebraska legislature, lobbied by favorite son William Jennings Bryan, became the thirty-fourth state to vote in favor, thus completing the process. "The reign of tears is over," exulted Billy Sunday. "The slums will soon be only a memory. We will turn our prisons into factories, and our jails into storehouses and corncribs. Men will walk upright now, women will smile, and the children will laugh. Hell will be forever for rent."[67]

Anti-Saloon Leaguers rushed to praise themselves for the victory. Certainly, they deserved a large slice of the credit. The nonpartisan focus on a single issue had mobilized the churches and a broad cross section of Protestant reformers. And the rhetorical contrast between a productive, pious middle class and a licentious, venal elite had attracted far more allies than critics. The ASL had convinced countless members of what was still America's dominant culture to regard themselves as a moral majority. Its most hardened opponents were recent immigrants, many of whom did not enjoy the franchise and were branded a threat if they did. When politicians for federal office realized their ambivalence toward the saloon might lose them more votes than it gained, the league's triumph was assured.

But it was in the context of global war that prohibition was transformed from a movement's proposal into a foregone conclusion. Enforced Americanism turned out to be the health of moral reform. The ASL had long suggested that "the liquor traffic" was a menace to both God and country. By 1917, it could gleefully publicize the political contributions the German-American Alliance, a group loyal to Kaiser Wilhelm, had made to the U.S. Brewers' Association, the largest employer group in the industry. Here was a brand of muckraking even Teddy Roosevelt could support. "The tyranny of this un-American system was never equaled in this or any other country," declared Wayne Wheeler in 1919. "It hastened the overthrow of the traffic."[68]

And the federal government was eager to assist. In an atmosphere of fervid readiness, Congress and President Wilson took harsh measures to curb antiwar publications, bar prostitutes from soliciting servicemen, *and* forbid the use of grain for manufacturing liquor. "Shall the many have food or the few have drink?" ran an official slogan. Just as the AFL had hitched its star to the war effort in order to enhance the status of loyal producers, so the ASL seized the opportunity to yoke the battle for "democracy" abroad to its own quest for a self-disciplined, pietistic commonwealth.

In the course of winning the Eighteenth Amendment, however, organized prohibitionists began to undermine their claim to represent the will and spirit of ordinary Americans. During the war, the *American Issue* praised any foreign leader who took a strong stand against either the liquor business in his country or those who did the imbibing. Not only did this represent a new willingness to condemn individual drinkers; the internationalist gesture also led the ASL to praise Czar Nicholas II, one of Europe's last absolute monarchs, for banning the sale of liquor in Russia, more warmly than it praised Britain's Lloyd George, whose elected government only restricted the alcohol trade. At the same time, league propagandists recognized that "the most powerful and respectable business forces in every community" were now on its side and abandoned the old images of families sacrificed to the pagan lords of profit.[69] Activists tasting the sweetness of conquest no longer needed to assert the bitter tones of populism.

In the early 1920s, as labor again waged rhetorical combat with employers and federal authorities, the ASL fused itself to what had become an increasingly conservative establishment. No longer the spearhead of a movement pressing for sweeping moral change, the league became an unofficial part of the state apparatus. It advocated strict enforcement of the Volstead Act and blocked any legislative attempts to weaken the act's single-minded pursuit of law and order—although underfinanced, undermanned, and often unmotivated police forces in many cities did little to stop citizens who broke the law.

The leading prohibitionist in this era was Wayne Wheeler, the skilled lobbyist and debater who had forged the campaign in Congress for the Eighteenth Amendment. From 1919 until his death in 1927, Wheeler's passion for personal influence led him to neglect the inspirational, nonpartisan creed that had earlier brought success. Absent the goad of an evil elite, league funds and membership steadily declined. But Wheeler kept himself ferociously busy. He vetted prospective agents hired to enforce the Volstead Act, huddled exclusively with the ruling Republicans (even though a sizable group of Democrats, particularly in the South, were steadfast drys), and crafted slogans like "Obedience to law is liberty" that repeated the authoritarian message of the contemporary red scare. In rare public speeches, Wheeler would still, in the old fashion, defend the ASL as one of the "pressure groups . . . carrying out the will of the people" for reforms like woman suffrage and the income tax that the two major parties had tried to ignore. But the common appellation of "dry boss" more accurately captured his image—an unhappy twist for an organization that had always railed against bossism in politics.[70]

Alone among well-known allies of the league, William Jennings Bryan continued unstintingly to wave the banner of popular rule. The Eighteenth Amendment, insisted Bryan, the Great Commoner, had been the fruit of a great democratic upsurge; only cynics and backsliders now doubted its value. Urban "plutocrats" might flaunt the law, but the agrarian "masses" who originally favored prohibition were still solidly behind it. "The Bryan of the 1920s was essentially the Bryan of the 1890s: older in years but no less vigorous, no less optimistic, no less certain," observes the historian Lawrence Levine. In the age of "normalcy," however, Bryan no longer commanded many followers. Neither in 1920 nor 1924 was he able to persuade his beloved Democratic Party to nominate a dry candidate for the presidency. And the mingling of religion and politics took most of his public energy, as his role in the Scopes trial demonstrated.[71]

So the ASL continued down the road to reaction. In the mid-1920s, to block a statewide referendum on prohibition that city wets might carry, the superintendent of the Michigan League even resorted to the argument that America was a republic and not a democracy. Having cut itself off from broader insurgent causes and eschewed an underdog vision, the ASL now seemed, to many Americans, to be the same kind of unfeeling, tyrannical power aligned with the state that the liquor traffic itself had once represented.[72]

The grassroots dynamism of the anti-liquor cause now passed to a new organization that flaunted its bigoted beliefs—the Ku Klux Klan (KKK). The ASL had always been nativist at heart; most of its supporters feared that immigrants, particularly Catholic ones, would tear down the bulwark of pietist values if law and public opinion didn't stop them. But league spokesmen were too shrewd to let this prejudice overshadow their message of deliverance for the American people as a whole.

In the early 1920s, the KKK candidly appealed to such fears and grew with remarkable speed. By mid-decade, it had a membership of perhaps two million white Protestants and wielded political influence in a handful of states and hundreds of municipalities from Atlanta to Portland, Oregon. Its reach was so provocative that the 1924 Democratic National Convention divided into nearly equal parts over the issue of whether or not to condemn the organization by name.[73]

Despite the Klan's grisly reputation, its stated views were probably shared by many prohibitionists frustrated by the sabotage of their handiwork. The KKK combined an appeal to "100 percent Americanism" with populist salvos against local and national elites who failed to enforce the Volstead Act, curb decadent behavior, or adequately finance public education in the face of an alleged Catholic challenge. "We are a movement of the plain people," claimed the Imperial Wizard Hiram Evans. "We demand a return of power into the hands of the everyday, . . . entirely unspoiled and not de-Americanized average citizens of the old stock." A pro-Klan Baptist magazine in Indiana threw down a challenge: "The writing of the Eighteenth Amendment into the Constitution was the crystallization of nationwide Christian sentiment. The enemy liquor gang—angry, vindictive, unpatriotic—is seeking the overthrow of the highest authority in the land. . . . They can count on the hoodlums, the crooks, the vice-joints, the whiskey-loving aliens, and the indifferent citizen to help them win. . . . Can they count on you?"[74]

Thus, in part, the Klan's revival filled a vacuum left by the deflated prohibition movement. Neither the ASL nor the WCTU had kept the brushfires of discontent burning, so a new group of militants took up the job. Thousands of evangelical Protestants, both men and women, joined the Klan in order to further the same housecleaning of public life they had once associated with the Social Gospel and movements against the traffic in liquor and prostitutes.[75]

But, unlike progressive moralists before World War I, the KKK had a decidedly conservative political agenda. Soldiers of the Invisible Empire desired only to halt the advance of a polyglot, urban America. And the Klan was just the largest and most controversial expression of a middle-class Protestant backlash against "alien" radicalism that, in varied and intersecting forms, gathered strength in the half-decade following the Armistice. Together with the American Legion and hundreds of fundamentalist churches, the Klan was waging a counterattack against pacifism, bolshevism, feminism, industrial unionism, and modernist culture—whether in Cubist art, progressive education, lewd movies, or liberal theology. The toleration of speakeasies was but the most salient of these outrages. Against the escalating danger to pietist America, the Klan's "average citizens" were a scared, defensive tribe whose elaborate oaths and exotic regalia could not hide the suspicion that their hour had passed. By the end of the 1920s, the KKK, rent by a torrent of bad publicity and the animosity of elected officials, could muster fewer than 50,000 members.[76]

The absence of a broad prohibitionist movement hastened the repeal of the Eighteenth Amendment. Certainly the end of what the unlucky Herbert Hoover once called America's "noble" experiment cannot be understood apart from the Great Depression, which diminished the electoral impact of the division between wet and dry and swept a Northern Democrat and his party into national power. But the ASL (and what remained of its penumbra) had already left itself and its cause quite vulnerable by clinging to Republican administrations that were unable to stop the commerce in alcohol or to keep criminal syndicates from making their violations of the Volstead Act pay.

In addition, league officials were slow to recognize the strength of their adversaries. After contributing propaganda and funds to Hoover's lopsided 1928 victory over the wet Al Smith (and, in their antialien fervor, occasionally sounding like Klansmen), they assumed the last serious challenge to the Eighteenth Amendment had been defeated.[77] Ernest Cherrington, who had become the ASL's chief policy maker, then launched a long-term, $15 million education project to convince Americans, yet again, that drinking was bad for them. But a dubious Congress appropriated only $50,000 for the effort, and previously supportive businesses shied away from a goal that had become anathema to their urban customers.[78]

Meanwhile, a powerful repeal campaign was under way, organized primarily by the Association Against the Prohibition Amendment (AAPA). The AAPA relied on Jeffersonian rhetoric about individual liberty and local sovereignty to lambaste the alarming increase in federal power that prohibition had allegedly caused. Directing and financing the group was a small group of extremely wealthy men—several DuPonts, the railroad executive John J. Raskob, the oil magnate Edward Harkness, and the investment banker Charles Sabin. This clique with laissez-faire convictions imitated a piece of the ASL's own, earlier strategy: the AAPA signed up members (it claimed to have 726,000 by 1926) and crafted particular messages for specific constituencies.[79] But the upper-class identity of its leaders gave mainstream prohibitionists an opportunity to rediscover their populist voice.

As it happened, the ASL and its allies waited too long and spoke too ambiguously to alter their fate. Only in 1932 did some dry crusaders seriously attempt to portray the AAPA as the tool of an economic elite. On the House floor, Congressman John W. Summers of Washington charged that the repeal drive was "not the sound, unselfish judgment of the American people" but "the culmination of a deep-laid plot of heartless millionaires to shift the tax burden from their pockets to the cravings of the helpless." Yet, dry crusaders had always stressed the moral superiority of their people; at this date, the aging Cherrington and his assistants were not about to start talking like labor organizers. In fact, the *American Issue* was still straining to link repeal forces to "subversive movements" like "Communism, gangsterism, political corruption, [and] free love," thus vitiating the attempt to capitalize on the prevailing animus against big business.[80]

The outcome was inevitable. In December of 1933, the 170 directors of the AAPA held a lavish dinner to celebrate ratification of the repeal amendment. Champagne was liberally served, and Pierre DuPont, chairman of the executive committee, presented each director with a cocktail glass inscribed to commemorate the occasion.

A quarter-century before, the ASL had mounted the most extensive publicity campaign an American social movement had ever assembled. But, on the eve of the New Deal, generals of the demobilized dry army were trying to justify a status quo that had brought the country neither public morality nor lasting prosperity. The passage and subsequent failure of the Eighteenth Amendment deprived evangelical Protestants of the one issue that could unify and direct their yearning to redeem America.

In the 1920s, many became embroiled in the debate over evolution—which was a subset of the great theological wrangle between fundamentalists and modernists over whether the Bible should be revered as absolute truth or interpreted as a historical document. In Bryan's famous 1925 defense of the law, which forbade Tennessee schools to teach Darwinian theory, his populist faith was unflagging: "When reform comes in this country, it starts with the masses. Reforms do not come from the brains of scholars."[81]

But the target was unfamiliar and insubstantial. An intellectual elite, even one whose power had been enhanced by wartime funding, was a poor replacement for "the liquor trust"—much less for the "plutocrats" and other "predatory forces" Bryan had denounced in his heyday. Experts, academic or otherwise, did not yet control government policy or get endlessly quoted in the press. They couldn't even make evolution a staple of high school biology classes.[82]

The Scopes trial did help install a thick barrier between two wings of the body politic. Liberal secularists (and some cosmopolitan believers) chuckled when H. L. Mencken quipped that Bryan loved all the "gaping primates of the upland valleys." Secure in their urban enclaves, they convinced themselves that pietistic Americans of small means were ignorant foes of social reform. For their part, evangelical Protestants (whether or not they were strict fundamentalists) grew to loathe the condescension of the learned, even when some intellectuals advocated redistributing wealth and power to ordinary people.[83] But it would be almost a half-century before large numbers of evangelicals again discovered an elite diabolic enough to make the building of their own mass movement seem both imperative and possible.

International bankers versus the people—according to Father Coughlin, 1938. *(Courtesy of the Library of Congress)*

Chapter 5

Social Justice and Social Paranoia: The Catholic Populism of Father Coughlin

Certainly, my friends, I have dedicated my life to fight against the heinous rottenness of modern capitalism because it robs the laborer of this world's goods. But blow for blow I shall strike against Communism, because it robs us of the next world's happiness.

—Father Charles E. Coughlin, 1935

The privileged princes of these new economic dynasties, thirsting for power, reached out for control over government itself. . . . And as a result the average man once more confronts the problem that faced the Minute Man.

—Franklin D. Roosevelt, 1936

THIS IS YOUR COUNTRY. DONT LET THE BIG MEN TAKE IT AWAY FROM YOU.

—Sign outside rural gas station in California, photographed by Dorothea Lange, 1938

TO CLAIM AMERICA

THE Great Depression produced a harvest of human misery, and that misery demanded explanation. Why did stocks lose almost half their value? Why did thousands of banks fail, wiping out the deposits of millions? Why did the engine of American manufacturing, once the envy of the world, suddenly begin to sputter and wheeze, knocking its operatives into unemployment for months, even years? And why were elected officials unable to fix the social machinery—until another total war in Europe got the engine up and purring again?

The available answers ranged widely from the minute to the global and from sweeping jeremiads to statistical diagrams about patterns of underconsumption. Except for conservative officeholders who assured themselves the economy was basically sound, political diagnosticians—from Louisiana's Huey Long to the Communist Party to President Franklin D. Roosevelt—agreed on a malevolent if vague culprit: concentrated wealth. In 1931, the humorist Will Rogers made the case in comfortably agrarian terms: "All the feed is going into one manger and the stock on the other side of the stall ain't getting a thing. . . . We got it, but we don't know how to split it up." A tiny elite that FDR, in his stirring 1936 acceptance speech, called, with a republican twist, "the economic royalists" had made huge profits while their countrymen and -women were struggling to survive.

But how to cure this grossly unequal condition? Somehow—whether by expanding the money supply, nationalizing key industries, building strong unions, or another remedy—the wealth amassed by the "super-rich" had to begin flowing, as Senator George Norris of Nebraska proposed, "to all the people, from whom it was originally taken."[1]

Norris's echo of the Omaha Platform was not accidental. The Depression of the 1930s was the longest and deepest economic crisis in the United States since the 1890s. It inspired both an energetic renewal of assaults on the monied and privileged, and paeans to the unalloyed goodness and wisdom of ordinary folks who were once again on the move against social injustice.[2] Few public figures questioned, as had many in the Progressive era, whether average Americans were too apathetic or confused about the sources of their collective problems to take up the burden of solving them.

Yet the political and rhetorical terrain had changed in fundamental ways since the earlier depression. This time, a reforming Democrat eager to champion the interests of "the forgotten man" was easily elected and re-elected. This time, radio was around to surpass, while subtly altering, the ability of print journalism to present emotionally stark dichotomies of bad elites and virtuous common folk. And this time, Catholic priests replaced Protestant ministers as the most prominent exponents of a Christian populism.

"The Protestant era in American life had come to its end by the mid-thirties," writes the historian Robert Handy. Many prohibitionists turned away from politics, dismayed at the public's apparent willingness to be misled by the liquor lobby and immigrant constituencies they viewed as un-American. Thereafter, Protestants who wanted to be national leaders learned to pay tribute to religious pluralism, downplaying the particulars of their own faith in the process. Public defense of the old sectarian precepts fell to such anti-Semites as Gerald Winrod and William Dudley Pelley, leader of the pro-fascist Silver Shirts. But their terrifying prophecies of the imminent appearance of a Jewish Antichrist bore scant resemblance to the democratic optimism William Jennings Bryan and Billy Sunday had once effectively preached to millions.[3]

In their wake, American Catholics—particularly the Irish among them—stepped forward to address the nation's woes in the name of all ordinary citizens with spiritual convictions. From power bases in their church, many city halls, and organized labor, the Irish (and, less often, their Slavic and German coreligionists) brandished a message that drew both on older producerist themes and specifically Catholic ones, particularly as expressed by recent papal encyclicals. They demanded respect for manual workers and curbs on speculative wealth; they warned that increasing the powers of a centralized state could lead to communism but urged politicians to aid wage earners in their conflicts with employers. They clubbed the dead horse of prohibition yet thundered against any lifting of the legal curbs on divorce, birth control, and sexy films. Like the Populists in the 1890s, Catholic activists wanted both to pull down the rich and to raise the spiritual state of the nation.

This marked a grand departure. During the nineteenth century, the Irish immigrants who ran the U.S. Roman Catholic Church—its clergy, schools, and periodicals—viewed the surrounding culture as one given to persistent spasms of nativist bigotry and Protestant rectitude. Risking the disfavor of their hierarchs, numbers of priests in mining towns and industrial cities championed the labor unions that were enrolling many of their flock. But most Catholic leaders looked inward, burnishing the distinctive identity of their faith and struggling to integrate other working-class immigrants (especially Slavs, Italians, and Germans) into one spiritual home. As putative leaders of this expanding community, Irish Catholics became a religious and political power in such places as New York, Boston, Chicago, and San Francisco but were still outsiders in the nation as a whole.

By World War I, however, the walls of the Irish-Catholic ghetto began to come down. Millions of Irishmen and -women were holding down skilled jobs, supervising other workers, or staffing offices; a few Hibernian bank executives and stockbrokers (like Joseph P. Kennedy) even made the headlines. During the war, despite their misgivings about the alliance with England, Irishmen took to combat with as much zest as any other ethnic group (and, after the Armistice, flooded the new Republic of Eire with contributions). In Chicago, by 1920, most Irish families had moved out of the slums and were voting more like their new Protestant neighbors than like their Polish and Sicilian coreligionists still mired in the lower class. The Boston Irish were still a defensive lot, but their long residence in the city helped lift them to union and political offices unattainable by new immigrants.[4]

This modest climb upward landed most Hibernian-Americans in a middling position in American society—between blacks and new immigrants on the bottom and the Protestant brahmins above. Most Irish Catholics remained wage earners, but their political and intellectual spokesmen were now "secure enough to claim America," as one scholar puts it. They began to seek a universal audience for their views about both economic injustice and moral turpitude—to express solidarity with exploited workers of all faiths while castigating Marxists and other modernists for driving the people away from God. For American Catholics, Al Smith's 1928 run for the presidency was the perfect emblem of this self-confidence—though the Protestant animus it stirred up was a blunt reminder that full acceptance was not yet won.[5]

Fortunately, the gathering Depression doused the mass fires of anti-Catholicism. The sheer reach of the economic crisis made the old charges sound petty and irrelevant. If Papists were really taking over the nation's institutions, why were so many out there on breadlines alongside other Christians? In the 1930s, no public figure of any influence still accused Catholics of being un-American.

Instead, signs of cultural acceptance abounded. Reformist Irish Catholics were elected to the governorships in several industrial states where Protestants were in the majority. A number of Hollywood films (starring Pat O'Brien and others) depicted priests as tough but warmhearted figures; rarely did a Protestant cleric receive similar treatment. The Catholic directors John Ford and Frank Capra made enormously popular movies—*Mr. Smith Goes to Washington, Meet John Doe, Young Mr. Lincoln, The Grapes of Wrath*—that featured unpretentious, God-fearing protagonists (with Anglo-Saxon names) who sentimentally embodied the egalitarian ideal.[6]

The economic debacle had given Catholic speakers and writers a historic opportunity to lift the ideological barrier separating them from other citizens. To claim America could now mean speaking a Catholic populism that seethed at the "super-rich" and rallied the millions, largely Christian, whose diligent labor and devotion to God and country had gone to smash.

The most formidable group that blended the Roman faith with a commitment to grassroots Americanism was the National Union for Social Justice (NUSJ)—initiated and led by Father Charles Coughlin. Coughlin and his followers viewed finance capital and Marxist socialism as twin faces of a secular Satan. They defended a "people" who cohered more through piety, economic frustration, and a common dread of powerful, modernizing enemies than through any class identity.

Coughlin and anyone else who desired to lead the discontented during the era of depression and world war had to cope with the rhetorical powers of Franklin Delano Roosevelt. FDR began his presidency with words that both comforted and energized fearful Americans. And, throughout his twelve years in office, he effectively communicated a fighting sympathy for their problems, foregoing the strident moralism of the Wilsonian progressives who had been his mentors. The president always seemed able to defang opponents with a nonchalant aside or an everyday metaphor—like the deadpan story of his little dog Fala's ire at GOP attacks and his equation of Lend-Lease to loaning a garden hose to a neighbor whose house was on fire. He also reassured audiences wary of enhanced federal power that the future was really in their hands. In 1936, FDR visited a throng of North Dakota farmers afraid that the government would move them off their drought-ruined lands. "I [have] a hunch that you people [have] your chins up," he told them, "that you are not looking forward to the day when the country would be depopulated. . . . I say you are not licked."[7]

FDR's generous manner, his grasp of the civil religion, and his use of memorable populist phrases—like "economic royalists" and "the forgotten man"—framed the rhetorical limits for social movements during the 1930s and World War

II. Fluent in the Christian idiom familiar to most of his constituents, he sprinkled references to the Bible and *Pilgrim's Progress* into numerous speeches. Time and again, he contrasted his defense of traditional ideals held by Jefferson, Jackson, and Lincoln with the "privileged" minority that opposed him. Not since Lincoln had a president combined so deep a compassion for ordinary people with so fierce and visionary an assault on their well-to-do enemies. "The money changers have fled from their high seats in the temple of our civilization," FDR announced at his first inaugural. "We may now restore that temple to the ancient truths . . . social values more noble than mere monetary profit."[8]

Most Americans viewed such displays of confidence as evidence of an authentic form of solidarity. And Eleanor Roosevelt's constant trips to succor the powerless closed the deal. A majority often disagreed with a given New Deal policy and were troubled by the intensification of state power it represented. But, hungry for protective leadership, they trusted the Roosevelts' concern for their plight and that kept the first couple in power until the president's sudden death in 1945.[9]

The fate of every insurgent movement was bound up with its success at developing themes suggested by FDR or accusing the president of betraying his own stated convictions. No group could blaze a more radical path—by drawing strict class lines, endorsing either communist or fascist aims, or flagrantly appealing to anti-Semitism—without suffering a sharp and permanent drop in popular support. Catholics engaged in firing up the "grassroots" (a ubiquitous term in the 1930s) had to recognize the great appeal of the president's brand of populist talk—without loosening the bonds of faith and community that had brought them this far.

MAGICIAN ON THE AIR

Father Charles Edward Coughlin had little trouble capturing the public's ear. In 1926, this Canadian-born cleric, the son of Irish immigrants, began broadcasting sermons for children and attacks on the Ku Klux Klan from his Shrine of the Little Flower in Royal Oak, Michigan, a working-class suburb twelve miles north of Detroit. Within a year, listeners in twenty neighboring states could hear him on WJR, a powerful Detroit station owned by a supportive Irish-Catholic businessman. By the fall of 1930, Coughlin was preaching more about the tumbling economy and the paralysis of the Hoover administration than about the catechism or the Klan. One network estimated that 30 million Americans tuned him in every Sunday afternoon—many, perhaps, after returning from church. Weekly, tens of thousands of admiring letters flooded into a new post office set up to handle the load. Most remarkably, Coughlin retained at least that many listeners and correspondents up to the election of 1936, when he broke decisively with the New Deal and created his own political party.[10]

What explains the tremendous popularity across denominational lines of a parish priest who never ran for elective office or sought to scale the hierarchy of his church? No doubt, Coughlin attracted millions of casual listeners who took him no more seriously than they did other radio orators. But an undeterminable number looked to him for political guidance because he stirred a potent blend of convictions: the fervent advocacy of Catholic social doctrine, hostility toward high finance and a shadowy state, and the desire for an uncompromising leader to point the way out of the Depression. Coughlin was a new kind of evangelical populist. Like the moribund prohibitionists, he spoke more to his followers' loss of psychological security and the nation's apparent fall from social harmony than to the oppression of American workers.

During the first half of the 1930s, the radio priest delivered a syncretism of messages in a lilting voice that both delighted and inflamed. He enthusiastically translated papal encyclicals about labor and poverty into the American vernacular. He unraveled the complexities of banking transactions and legislation concerning the economy. He ridiculed pompous men of wealth like J. P. Morgan and allegedly myopic government officials like General Hugh Johnson, the director of the National Recovery Administration (NRA). He invoked both Christian morality and the secular republicanism of the Founding Fathers. He advised Americans to follow wise, altruistic leaders while urging them to be suspicious of anyone who currently held national and political power. Soothingly, Coughlin showed that Catholicism and American democracy could be complementary creeds, thus helping break a long "counter-subversive" tradition (dating back to the colonial era) that argued to the contrary.[11]

Early in 1933, Coughlin compared the three years that veterans of World War I had waited for Congress to pass a bonus bill with "the three hours of agony endured by Christ on the cross." Then, he vowed:

> We are determined once and for all to attack and overpower the enemy of financial slavery; to oppose and to defeat those who still support the ancient heresy of the concentration of wealth in the hands of a few. . . . In this venture can we rely on you, on every sane American to take his place in the ranks of justice? The real fight is just beginning.

The rage of the common man at the cruel Depression was thus elevated into something akin to a spiritual principle.[12]

Coughlin articulated this fusion of piety and gall with a skill that, at least initially, captivated anyone who listened, regardless of political opinion. He possessed, remembered the novelist Wallace Stegner, "a voice of such mellow richness, such manly, heartwarming, confidential intimacy, such emotional and ingratiating charm, that anyone tuning past it almost automatically returned to hear it again." To mask a youthful speech impediment, the priest had borrowed a bit of the brogue of his Irish-born parents. He also trilled his *r*s, elongated the proper names of his adversaries for satirical effect, and swirled words like "hot," "swell," "lousy," and "damn" and epithets such as "ventriloquists of Wall Street" and "comic opera cream-puff soldier" into long disquisitions on the NRA and the Federal Reserve System.

As Stegner memorably wrote, Coughlin had "a voice made for promises." But the priest was also a superb entertainer who persuaded people by surprising and amusing them as much as by diagnosing the world's ills and prescribing a cure. What a radio fan magazine termed his "Thundering Magic of the Air" enabled Coughlin to hold his own on a broadcast menu crowded with the likes of Rudy Vallee and *The Goldbergs*. Radio also provided the stage on which the theatrical priest might turn an audience into a movement.[13]

The new broadcast medium had a ubiquitous reach. By 1936, more than 70 percent of all American families owned radios, and ownership was highest in the industrial states of the East and Midwest. A majority of listeners relied on the radio as their main source of news and kept their sets on for at least three hours a day. Working-class Americans were particularly avid. "The lower a person's economic status," observes the historian Lizabeth Cohen, "the more likely he or she preferred radio over print."[14]

The disembodied yet intensely intimate mode of communication had an ambiguous effect on political language. In contrast to the press, it made direct access to a national audience available for movement speakers. A colorful, articulate orator like Coughlin was usually a welcome addition to the broadcast schedule alongside the main fare of crooners, comics, and soap operas. Such figures as John L. Lewis, Huey Long, and the radio priest were undeniably controversial, but their voices became familiar to millions who never read their words unmediated by skeptical reporters and often hostile editorial writers. Critics of concentrated wealth routinely depicted the urban press as an oligopolistic barrier to social change and a censor of anticorporate views. But national radio networks were slow to develop, and, even when they became dominant, unorthodox spokesmen were still tolerated if they could attract listeners and advertising dollars.[15]

On the other hand, broadcasting tended to corrode the democratic roots of traditional movements. National programming implicitly encouraged listeners to take their lead from an electronically transmitted voice instead of from spokespeople in their own localities whom they could see and hear and with whom they could work and argue. The very intimacy of the medium favored a certain rhetorical style—avuncular yet authoritative, relaxed yet assertive—that usually left out women and the unpolished of either sex. Without the use of physical gestures, a political speaker had to demonstrate a mastery of subject and an empathy with those who were ignorant or confused about current affairs. Winston Churchill, John L. Lewis, and Father Coughlin all possessed these talents. And FDR—the first president to routinely broadcast his speeches, not to speak of the famous "fireside chats"—was a master of them. "The cultivated voice affected no barbarisms," writes one student of FDR's rhetoric, "The manner suggested dignity without pretentiousness." When, in 1936, Alfred Landon campaigned as the "sound, humdrum, common-sense" alternative to the charismatic Roosevelt, he was rejected by a landslide.[16]

Unlike FDR's showmanship, Charles Coughlin's was grounded in a spiritual purpose. He always regarded himself as an obedient foot soldier of the church. And, thanks to recent changes in the style of Catholic worship, his revivalistic style did not seem an aberration.

In the 1920s and 1930s, millions of parishioners flocked to huge public devotions whose emotional brilliance outshone the church's solemn Latin liturgy. The first major occasion was a 1926 Mass held at Soldier Field in Chicago that drew over 150,000 worshipers. Unlike that of the meetings held by Billy Sunday and other Protestant evangelists, the purpose of these devotions was to inspire believers to a new level of piety, to bind them closer to church symbols (the Eucharist, the Virgin, a particular saint) instead of bringing new souls to the Lord. Still the turnout was impressive. And the Depression increased both the number and passion of these events as parishioners groped for the solace of spiritual community. In Chicago, 70,000 people a week offered special prayers to Our Lady of the Sorrows; in Detroit, the Marian cult was so popular that the local Diocese had to hold devotional rallies for the Virgin at a local college football stadium. Coughlin's own parish church, whose cavernous size rivaled that of a cathedral, was named for the recently canonized St. Thérèse of Lisieux, a French girl known as the Little Flower, who died in her teens. Mass novenas to St. Thérèse held around the country became, according to one historian, "an evocative symbol of a Catholicism that was at once militant and tenderly sentimental." The same could be said of Father Coughlin himself.[17]

POPES AND MONEY CHANGERS

The radio priest was the best known of a large number of prelates and laypersons who were busy articulating their own type of social gospel. Catholic activism was based on two landmark encyclicals, *Rerum Novarum:* "The Condition of the Working Classes," issued in 1891 by Pope Leo XIII, and *Quadragesimo Anno:* "On Reconstructing the Social Order," Pius XI's 1931 updating and extension of his predecessor's work. Together, the two papal letters were a manifesto that decried the human costs of capitalism and outlined what came to be called "Catholic social action."

Rerum Novarum had roused the faithful to combat dual evils haunting the turn-of-the-century church: mass poverty and the popularity of socialism among many of Europe's working poor. "Some remedy must be found, and found quickly," wrote Pope Leo, "for the misery and wretchedness pressing so heavily and unjustly at this moment on the vast majority of the working classes." But radicals who wanted to abolish private property, weaken the family, and equalize society to "one dead level" were violating divine law as well as "striving against nature." Leo proposed a better solution: Catholic workers should form trade unions free from socialist contagion; governments should raise the living standards of the poor; and, through charity and a recognition of the mutuality of capital and labor, all members of society should work to reduce class divisions.[18]

In the United States, Catholic social reformers gave less attention to Leo's warnings and behaved as if *Rerum Novarum* had endorsed all varieties of (nonrevolutionary) unionism and the circulation of plans for uplifting the oppressed. Many priests, themselves products of a working-class background, were grateful that the Vatican had liberated them to act and speak in social arenas their Protestant counterparts had long dominated. Individual priests spoke at strike rallies and became sympathetic advisers to some AFL officials.

In the aftermath of World War I, Monsignor John A. Ryan, who as a boy in Minnesota had idolized Ignatius Donnelly, became the American church's most influential commentator on socioeconomic matters. He wrote the 1919 Bishops' Program for Social Reconstruction that endorsed unemployment and old-age insurance, the building of public housing, a steep tax on excess profits, and "participation of labor in management"—all of which went beyond anything Pope Leo had suggested or most American politicians were prepared to accept. But to conservatives who thought his ideas smacked of socialism, Ryan routinely responded that "he was about as radical as Leo XIII."[19]

In the depth of the Depression, Pope Pius bolstered the validity of that stand. *Quadragesimo Anno* purported to be only a reaffirmation of Leo's great encyclical on the fortieth anniversary of its issuance. But Pius wrote with passion and specificity about the "immense power and despotic economic domination . . . consolidated in the hands of a few." Significantly, he identified as the nub of the problem the "dictatorship" of those who "control credit . . . and rule the lending of money."

The pontiff also advocated a sweeping redesign of economic power along corporatist lines. Vocational groups—an updated form of the medieval guilds—would take control of each major industry. In outline, the plan bore some resemblance to ideas Mussolini had floated, although Pius XI was certainly no fascist. But to Catholic activists like Ryan and Coughlin, it sounded like an opening to preach economic decentralization and self-government, notions pleasing to many an American ear. Hoping to enlist such priests and their lay followers in his cause, FDR quoted the papal letter at length during the 1932 campaign.[20]

One particular expression appeared eight times in Pius's encyclical, each repetition signifying its status as the ultimate goal of worldly activism. That expression was "social justice." "The public institutions of the nations must be such as to make the whole of human society conform to the common good, i.e., to the standard of social justice," ran a typical passage.[21]

The term was not new to the reformist lexicon. Since about 1900, *social justice* had been a common, graceful label for the broad changes progressives of all faiths favored. Theodore Roosevelt employed it often in his 1912 third-party campaign for president. In 1918, the Central Conference of American [Reform] Rabbis adopted a prolabor "Social Justice Program" similar to the one John Ryan was writing for the bishops.[22]

But Pius's 1931 encyclical seemed to urge Catholics to embrace, define, and popularize the term. Many American priests were quick to oblige as were such laypeople as Peter Maurin and Dorothy Day, who founded the Catholic Worker movement. Father Coughlin proved a particularly energetic apostle. "Although I shall be called radical, my radicalism shall not exceed the doctrine of Jesus Christ, nor its development as found in the official writings of Pope Pius XI," he said in 1933, echoing (perhaps unconsciously) John Ryan's earlier words of self-defense. For Coughlin, *social justice* was a sword to wield against both the corporate right and the statist left. It pointed the sane, safely Christian middle way between an "individualism" that led to anarchy and want and a "collectivism" whose fruit was atheist dictatorship. At times, he expanded its meaning to include every measure designed to alleviate mass suffering—from breadlines to the Bank Holiday to public works. More often, he yoked it to his own star, as in a 1935 broadcast: "I need not inform this audience that since 1930 and long before then I had a plan to establish social justice."[23]

In the fall of 1934, Coughlin decided to convert his personal renown into a political movement. Inevitably, he called his new group the National Union for Social Justice. "Hitherto you have been merely an audience," he told listeners on Armistice Day. "Today, in accepting the challenge of your letters, I call upon every one of you . . . to join this Union which, if it is to succeed, must rise above the concept of an audience and become a living, vibrant, united, active organization, superior to politics and politicians in principle, and independent of them in power." The sixteen-point set of principles, the plan Coughlin claimed he had been nurturing since the 1920s, focused on economic issues. Widely disseminated, the document outlining the plan opened with a nugget of populist Catholicism, a ringing declaration that what the Lord created, no man should monopolize:

> Establishing my principles upon this preamble, namely that we are all creatures of a beneficent God, made to love and serve Him in this world and to enjoy Him forever in the next; and that all this world's wealth of field and forest, of mine and river has been bestowed upon us by a kind Father, therefore, I believe that wealth as we know it originates from the natural resources and from the labor which the sons of God expend upon these resources. It is all ours except for the harsh, cruel and grasping ways of wicked men who first concentrated wealth into the hands of a few, then dominated states and finally commenced to pit state against state in the frightful catastrophes of commercial warfare.

The priest also named the weekly paper he began publishing in early 1936 *Social Justice*. Its official editor was a Milwaukee journalist named E. Perrin Schwartz, but Coughlin always dictated most of the content. The first issue called the famous encyclicals of Pope Leo and Pope Pius "a crusader's cry, a call to arms, a practical plan of campaign, conjuring the faithful throughout Christendom to bestir themselves, to mobilize, and to apply these principles to local conditions!" It is unclear how familiar the papal letters were to lay Catholics; Al Smith once exclaimed: "Will somebody please tell me what in hell an encyclical is!" But Coughlin leaned on them for inspiration and legitimacy and, more than anyone else in the country, made the letters known to the public.[24]

For his followers, however, the priest was most persuasive as a critic of America's failed economic system. To understand the Depression, Coughlin was fond of saying, "It's a *money* question." Stripped to its oft-repeated essentials, this was his argument: Since the beginning of the republic, bankers with close ties to the great investment houses of Europe had sought to limit the amount of money in circulation. Their policy of forced deflation, when successful, allowed them to set high interest rates and to steer economic development to particular persons, industries, and regions in which they had a profitable stake. The "money-changers"—Coughlin's blanket term for any notable figure in the worlds of banking or finance—were utterly immoral and unpatriotic; they moved productive assets around the nation and the globe, never regretting the resulting joblessness, business failures, and lost sovereignty. The Morgans, Warburgs, and their ilk amassed fortunes that gave them tremendous political power. Fortunately, however, until establishment of the Federal Reserve System just before World War I, brave proponents of what Coughlin called "democratic money"—Andrew Jackson, Abraham Lincoln, and William Jennings Bryan were often cited—had periodically been able to keep the titans of greed from having their way.

But, according to Coughlin, the 1913 establishment of the Federal Reserve—a national banking network responsible only to other bankers—represented the money changers' ultimate triumph. Since then, they had been able, often at the behest of shadowy Continental figures like the Rothschilds, to manipulate the stock market, to cause or stop panics, and even to drag the United States into World War I (on the side of British financial interests). The 1929 crash was their masterstroke—"the plan was to create an artificial scarcity of money," *Social Justice* told its readers. But the Depression was proving to be the tocsin that had finally awakened Americans to their condition of financial slavery. "The sands of intrigue and of evil machinations," Coughlin stated confidently in 1933, "have filtered through the hour glass of their control."[25]

As empirical history (much less as crisis theory), this lurid tale was quite false. Yet, it is a mistake to belittle it, as did Arthur Schlesinger, Jr., with the quip, "For Coughlin, economics was a minor branch of rhetoric."[26]

The radio priest was quite happy to separate himself from the corps of trained economists, few of whom had predicted a severe depression. He often reviled intellectual specialists who took a disinterested, analytical tone when the livelihood of millions hung in the balance. His "facts" were normally presented as a string of one liners drawn from a pastiche of sources—the original Populists, various muckrakers, the famous encyclicals, and an obscure securities analyst named Gertrude

Coogan, whose 1935 book *Money Creators* posited a conspiracy by international financiers to keep Americans in perpetual debt.[27] Coughlin wanted to alert Americans that a deadly scourge was abroad in the land—rule by a financial elite that he called, expansively, "modern capitalism." And his clear, arresting prose had certainly found an audience.

Coughlin, after all, was mining a rich, historic vein of discontent. Since the heyday of Andrew Jackson, populist speakers had railed at the conspiratorial acts of a money power whose immense economic clout required no productive labor, was subject to no election, and respected no sovereign boundary. Coughlin's historical sketch echoed the vivid denunciations of "financial monopoly" in Jackson's Bank Veto message, Henry George's hatred of land speculators, the Greenbackers' attacks on overweening "plutocrats," and the Populists' indictment of bondholders and the gold standard. Like the Gilded Age insurgents, Coughlin viewed tight money as the people's curse and inflation as their redemption.

For the Michigan priest, as for his predecessors, a focus on the money question sidestepped class and ethnic differences that would have complicated the notion of a plainspeaking, hardworking majority. Nearly everyone was a victim of the money changers; so nearly all had an interest in demolishing their empire. Coughlin's obsession with bankers left the rest of the economy basically untarnished. Market relationships and private property, he assured listeners, were not the problem. Fed by a steady flow of low-interest credit, American farms and businesses could prosper and share their bounty with American workers. The problem with "modern capitalism" was that the few who held most of the capital called the tune for everyone else.

On this point, American populist language and Catholic social doctrine converged. The Church had long endorsed the accumulation of private property, but it had an abiding mistrust of the secularized world of commercial finance, expressed in its age-old ban on usury and vigorously restated by Pope Pius XI in his 1931 encyclical. This tradition dovetailed with the homegrown abhorrence of men who got wealthy manipulating "other people's money." Coughlin's proposal that Congress abolish the Federal Reserve and establish a "Government owned Central Bank" never had a chance to pass, but his insistence that Americans should control the value of their own currency was no mere gimmick. As William Jennings Bryan had recognized forty years before, it offered a symbolic way for people to comprehend and fight the distant nexus of state and corporate power, beginning with the pieces of metal and paper lying in their pockets.[28]

Coughlin's definition of the national crisis gestured toward the producerist tradition—the enemy took the form of men with clean hands who made nothing but more money for themselves. Yet, like the Anti-Saloon League, he was seldom willing to side with workers against their employers or to otherwise sharpen class consciousness. Coughlin also called for a moral regeneration of America from the grassroots to the White House. "Coughlin belongs . . . among those who see life as a struggle of Christ and anti-Christ, of good and evil, and find these forces personified in people and institutions," writes the historian David O'Brien.[29]

The priest welcomed wage earners to join a larger mass of aggrieved citizens that included small businessmen and professionals whose anonymous exertions also qualified as labor. The church's abhorrence of Marxism was one reason for his stance. Another was movement strategy. With no class-based institution or political party behind him, Coughlin had to cast his net quite wide.

A large cartoon in *Social Justice* melodramatically illustrated this inclusive posture. Entitled "The Banyan Tree of Finance," it showed five white men—labeled "farmer," "laborer," "taxpayer," "small merchant," and "independent manufacturer"—trapped by a maze of thick branches plunging into the earth. The first two characters hacked at the tree limbs with, respectively, an axe and a sharp rake while the others lay prostrate or feebly clutched a branch. The cartoonist left no doubt that the quintet (and two shadowy figures in the background) shared a common fate.[30]

In fact, Coughlin's NUSJ did seem to attract an occupational cross section of Americans, lacking only those groups he made no effort to reach—Jews and other non-Christians, the speculative rich, and racial minorities (the lack of any references to black people in Coughlin's speeches and journalism is striking; his world, like that of most Northern Catholics, was practically all white). A reporter for the *New Republic,* while unsympathetic to Coughlin's message, marveled at the "quiet, sober seriousness" of a crowd that packed Madison Square Garden in 1935 to hear the priest in person. "This was a composite, living portrait of the American people—of all ages and of every class," he wrote, ". . . roused from their lethargy and taking an active vital interest in the politics of their country."[31]

The desire for social unity did not prevent Coughlin from making a pointed appeal to industrial workers. His parish and broadcast center were located in fertile territory—the automobile capital of the world. But he had to sow it without abandoning the Catholic conception of social justice and its promised middle way between the tyranny of "modern capitalism" and a Communist hell. In the two principles of the NUSJ that directly concerned labor, the priest advocated "a just and living annual wage" for every family, "the right" of unions to organize, and the government's corresponding "duty . . . to protect these organizations against the vested interests of wealth and of intellect." Elsewhere, he urged factory owners to "share the profits with labor," an idea he magnanimously described as "God's doctrine, not mine."[32]

Coughlin's call for unions to cooperate with employers was in keeping with the moral partnership advocated by the social encyclicals. But it was at odds with a new generation of left-leaning industrial unionists as well as with the aggressive self-reliance of AFL craftsmen. The pastor of Royal Oak warned against union officials taking power for themselves. He acknowledged that workers had sound reasons to go on strike—their bosses were often brutes, their wages abysmal. But better they should follow the leadership of a wise, spiritual father who outlined the Christian path to prosperity and class peace.[33]

In the spring of 1934, Coughlin broadcast a sermon on "Capital and Labor." It spoke directly to industrial workers whose hopes for a better future had been dashed by the Depression:

> You pause to take inventory of the life you have spent. It is measured by gallons of sweat and by tons of steel. It is bounded on the east by a struggle against poverty—and on the west by a prospect of pain. . . . Let me come to you as a priest of God, caring for no living politician, but caring only for your welfare—let me counsel you, let me direct you and inspire you towards the fulfillment of your legitimate and God-given aspirations.[34]

Coughlin's prestige at the time was enormous, and at least one group of union-hungry workers took his advice. In early 1935, a knot of labor activists employed at several Chrysler plants in Detroit began meeting with Coughlin to draw up plans for a new Automotive Industrial Workers' Association (AIWA). That fall, AIWA organizers, most of whom were young and fairly new to the industry, held several mass rallies (addressed by Coughlin and several prolabor congressmen) and signed up about 10,000 members. In gratitude, the unionists dedicated their yearbook to "our adviser and supporter Father Charles E. Coughlin, the friend and educator of the masses." The following summer, with the priest's blessing, the AIWA merged into the swelling United Auto Workers (UAW). Coughlin was not the deciding force; without him, the UAW would soon have added the same workers to its rolls. Still, the priest had demonstrated that fame and impassioned appeals to frustrated self-respect could inspire the growth of an industrial union.[35]

One celebrated voice was not enough, however, to sustain a true grassroots movement. From samples of the huge correspondence Coughlin received, it seems that Irish and German Catholics formed the bulk of his loyal following. Most were skilled workers and small businesspeople—Americans of middling incomes whose sense of security had been dashed when the economy collapsed. Few mentioned engaging in any organized activity for the Coughlinite cause. While the NUSJ had perhaps a million members (and claimed many more), its local chapters seem to have been either glorified Coughlin fan clubs or abortive vehicles for individuals who linked their personal rage to a figure of national prominence. The radio priest did not help matters by forcing a rigid routine on the faithful: he decreed how often chapters should meet, ordered that the first and most important business was to read one of his statements, and even prohibited units from holding dances or raffles lest they be accused of encouraging sexual dalliance and greed.[36]

Not that a looser structure would have overcome the group's major flaw: its lack of an agenda. Coughlin rarely set out any political task for the National Union to accomplish—other than cheering and then rehashing his broadcasts. The sixteen principles of the organization were an abstract, personal credo—the proclamation of a future political heaven. Coughlin never ordered his members to wage a campaign for any plank in particular (even the narrow Number 12—"the abolition of tax-exempt bonds"). Only once did he mobilize the flock—to send letters and telegrams to Washington in late January of 1935, to oppose a treaty allowing the United States to enter the World Court. In consort with the Hearst press, Coughlin labeled the court a tool of the same "international bankers" who had pulled America into the bloody, useless world war. The torrent of mail cowed enough senators to deny the Roosevelt administration the two-thirds margin it needed. But it was Coughlin's weekly broadcast, not his vaunted National Union, that forced the Capitol post office to work overtime.[37]

The most famous priest in America thus had no conception of how to convert his adoring audience into a durable movement. With admirers arriving daily by the busload to view his elaborate, floodlit headquarters at Royal Oak, filling big arenas to hear his speeches, and buying reproductions of his portrait, Coughlin could ignore his failings as a political leader.

LOSING WITH LEMKE

When he decided to challenge the president, however, a reckoning became inevitable. During the 1932 campaign, Coughlin had vigorously backed Roosevelt as a true foe of "the money changers," thus helping wean Catholics away from the renewed candidacy of Al Smith. And, through 1934, the priest alternated between lauding the New Deal as "Christ's Deal" and ominously cautioning FDR, both in public and by letter, that his policy advisers (whom Coughlin satirically dubbed the "Drain Trust") were subverting true economic reform. The priest knew most of his radio flock also backed Roosevelt; so he often followed a blast at a particular federal program with praise for the man at the top. Sometimes, he sent word through a powerful Irish-Catholic Democrat like Joseph Kennedy that a full reconciliation was possible. But FDR was not inclined to bargain with a mercurial egotist whose following overlapped with his own.[38]

So, upon establishing the NUSJ, Coughlin moved decisively to change the "or" in his slogan "Roosevelt or Ruin" to "and." Telling his radio audience "I know the pulse of the people . . . better than do all your industrialists with [their] paid-for advice," he charged the president and his associates with serving the interests of corporate moguls and of Communist revolutionaries.[39]

This unlikely trio of enemies was not as nonsensical as it sounds. According to Coughlin, the New Deal, the Soviets, and modern capitalism had one essential quality in common: the drive to centralize power in the hands of a privileged few—whether liberal bureaucrats, international bankers, or atheistic tyrants. During their first two years in office, the New Dealers staked their economic hopes on the National Recovery Administration. The NRA encouraged big business to collude with government in signing agreements to raise prices and standardize production. A rise in investor confidence and hiring calls was the expected result. But for all the Blue Eagle emblems displayed and street demonstrations promoted from Washington, the

NRA did not dramatically cut the jobless rolls or revitalize the industrial heartland. And, for Americans still partial to a laissez-faire state, the NRA's welter of codes and regulations seemed like something out of Soviet Russia. Buoyed by this sentiment, Coughlin urged his listeners to give up the belief that a chief executive surrounded by left-wing intellectuals could really be their friend. In March of 1935, one Coughlinite wrote to FDR, "I know the truth and the truth is you have deceived the working man . . . and favored the big Business and Huge Corporations and let the Poor Working Man go starving, or go to Hell. I loved you and you have betrayed."[40]

In 1936, the radio priest gambled on the depth of such bitterness and took a leap into presidential politics. Convinced he could unite all critics of the New Deal who did not simply want to return to Republican rule, he created the Union Party (UP). The name was borrowed from the label Abraham Lincoln had used when running for re-election in 1864. America, said the priest, was now engaged in a new civil war, this time "to annihilate financial slavery" rather than "physical slavery."

Although it was supported by the evangelical stem-winder Gerald L. K. Smith and the old-age pension movement of Francis Townsend, the UP was essentially Coughlin's party. He alone nominated the ticket (rubber-stamped by a NUSJ convention): it balanced a farm-state Protestant, Representative William Lemke of North Dakota, for president with an urban Catholic, the former Boston prosecutor Thomas C. O'Brien, for vice president. The priest's campaign speeches, faithfully reprinted in *Social Justice,* overshadowed anything said by the lackluster figures who appeared on the ballot. And when the UP polled only 892,000 votes, ridiculously short of the 10 percent of the total Coughlin had vowed it would garner, his audience and influence began a gradual but irreversible decline. The hubristic misstep of the UP enabled a jeering national media to place the pastor from Royal Oak in the "lunatic fringe" of domestic Nazis and their ilk.

To explain this climacteric, scholars have focused on the break with FDR. Most of Coughlin's followers, they point out, were Democrats reluctant to vote against their president. The very creation of the UP and Coughlin's wild charges that the Roosevelt administration was "anti-God" and "bent on communistic revolution" forced millions to choose. Understandably, they rejected the side that could offer them nothing but fury.[41]

The argument is not mistaken, but it neglects what was a critical shift in Coughlin's rhetorical approach, one that sabotaged the silkily inviting public image he had carefully constructed during the preceding years and made it difficult for him to recoup support once he had lost it. Irked by the paltry coverage of the UP in the national press, the priest took to the road to promote his party, addressing rallies in over a dozen cities through the summer and fall of 1936. This left little time for the intimate radio broadcasts on which he had built his popularity. A few of his public appearances were probably unforgettable affairs for those who attended; at Cleveland's huge Memorial Stadium, he tore off his clerical collar and whipped over 40,000 mostly middle-aged NUSJ members into an adoring frenzy before collapsing on the podium.

But on the newsreel clips of these rallies, millions of moviegoers saw a harsh and feverish Coughlin. Film was not kind to the radio priest. A grinning, boastful visage replaced the pleasantly modulated rhythms of a friendly parish cleric. He strutted across the platform, clenched fists at his waist, challenging, in a tight, tense voice, the patriotism of anyone who disagreed. Hostile commentators had long described Coughlin as a demagogue. But, now, ranting on the national stump, he really did seem like an American version of Mussolini or Hitler, familiar figures to newsreel viewers.[42]

The words themselves did not help. Coughlin and lesser UP campaigners had to convince supporters of Roosevelt that the incumbent was not an authentic champion of ordinary people; that only a total break with both major parties could save America. But, since mid-1935 (when the NRA was ruled unconstitutional), FDR had been speaking like a consummate populist—lambasting "economic royalists" and "privileged enterprise," lauding "the common man," and endorsing such laws as the Wagner Act and a "soak-the-rich" tax plan that appeared to put substance behind his rhetoric. To counter this strategy, *Social Justice* descended to bald accusations that Wall Street (often in the person of Bernard Baruch) was dictating the Democrats' monetary policies and that key Roosevelt advisers were secret members of the Communist Party. In one speech, Coughlin called the president a "liar" and, in another, swore: "So help me God, I will be instrumental in taking a Communist from the chair once occupied by Washington."[43]

Candidate Lemke, a populist of the older agrarian sort, had neither stomach nor talent for such caustic fare. A generation before, the congressman had been a founder of the North Dakota Nonpartisan League, and he remained convinced that urban politicians and their coddled "interests" meant the average farmer no good. This belief turned him against FDR, especially after the president helped defeat an inflationary monetary bill Lemke had cosponsored early in 1936. Lemke made a few awkward jousts at "the money changers" and testified that he was "a real American, a farmer with large business experience, who knows the farming business, not a newspaper man."[44] But this was no way to convert Democratic voters in the cities. As a stump speaker, Lemke lacked all the zest, warmth, and originality of the man he was running against. From such an opponent, Roosevelt had nothing to fear.

Catholic supporters of the New Deal could not be so sure about the UP's true leader. Coughlin had stumbled by launching his own party and anointing Lemke its standard-bearer. But millions of lay Catholics still viewed Coughlin as their tribune of conscience—a lowly parish priest unafraid to speak truth to any source of power. Some, in fact, cheered Coughlin *because* of the internal enemies he made—hierarchs of the church who shuddered at his flamboyance and fame. In 1932, one Boston layman wrote to Archbishop William O'Connell: "Father Coughlin is a man who has tried to show the common working people the way they are being neglected by those in power." Two years later, O'Connell dared to criticize Coughlin's economic analysis and received a cascade of letters attacking him for living well "while your people starve." The results of opinion polling, an infant craft in the 1930s, suggested that Coughlin's support was greatest among manual workers and the unemployed.[45]

Monsignor John Ryan, a professor at Catholic University in Washington, D.C., decided to confront the radio priest's reputation as a man of the people. Since Ryan's first book, *A Living Wage,* had appeared in 1906, intellectuals, labor leaders, and the mainstream press had regarded him as the foremost exponent of Catholic social doctrine and a valued ally of progressive causes. In the mid-1930s, he was the elder statesman for those in the church who backed the New Deal and industrial unionism. As author of the 1919 Bishops' Program, leader of the National Catholic Welfare Council (later Conference), and participant in such secular liberal groups as the National Consumers' League and the American Civil Liberties Union, Ryan felt supremely qualified to define the true meaning of "social justice." From the standpoint of Ryan, a careful writer and flat public speaker, Coughlin's rhetorical intemperance would neither help the downtrodden nor advance the common good.

During the 1936 election campaign, Ryan took to the radio to accuse the magician from Royal Oak of deluding his followers. If ever enacted, Ryan predicted Coughlin's monetary nostrums "would prove disastrous to the great majority of the American people, particularly to the wage earners." Ryan had always viewed a stronger state committed to advancing the public welfare as the best guarantor of social justice. Coughlin's assault on the president who was implementing that aim had to be exposed and defeated.

In his broadcast response, Coughlin portrayed the aging professor as a man of the past, a once "noble priest" who now was serving a pro-Communist potentate. He reminded his audience that, three years before, Ryan had let slip the backhanded compliment, "Even though [Father Coughlin] makes mistakes, he is stirring up the animals, and that had to be done by somebody." Now, that erstwhile crusader had degenerated into what Coughlin called a "Right Reverend Democratic Politician" who lamely apologized for FDR's failure to end the Depression.

Coughlin's "animals" were not so polite. In the days following the exchange, Ryan received over 1,200 letters, most filled with curses and vitriol. He was accused of taking money from the Works Progress Administration (WPA), bankers, the Democratic campaign manager Jim Farley, or simply the "money changers"; he was branded a "Judas" who defied the teachings of popes, past and present. Throughout the correspondence ran a deep suspicion of this man who had spent most of his career teaching in universities and associating with an elite of prelates, politicians, and professional reformers. In 1936, John Ryan was on the winning side—though the UP did poll over 10 percent in South Boston and a few other working-class Irish strongholds. But the association between liberalism and intellectual condescension he seemed to personify would come to haunt the Democratic Party in decades to come.[46]

For now, however, Coughlin had to regroup. Not only had he failed to convert his disciples into a movement capable of generating its own ideas, alliances, and local leaders. He had failed to appreciate the conceptual flaw in his demonization of the banking elite. The money question was, for most Americans in the 1930s, only an ephemeral symbol of what had gone wrong in their country; bankers, while mistrusted, were not widely perceived as a modern Goliath throttling their families, jobs, and public officials. And the notion that the reassuring, jovial man in the White House was an agent of both the Kremlin and the Rothschilds defied common sense. At a time when the New Deal was trying to alleviate mass suffering through such measures as the WPA and the Social Security Act, Coughlin's lack of a concrete plan to redistribute wealth exposed his inability to be more than a phenomenally popular broadcaster. After the 1936 election, he disbanded the impotent NUSJ and found a more sensational issue on which to attempt to incite a rising of the people.

SPOILED BY WAR

From the mid-1930s to the attack on Pearl Harbor, Americans heard a lot of frightening talk about un-American tyrants bent on conquering their land. Depending on their politics, the primary danger was perceived as emanating from Rome and Berlin (seldom Tokyo) or from Moscow. Closer to home, domestic champions of fascism or communism were reputed to be hard at work, wrapped in ideological mufti. To assist an alien patron, they vigorously waved the flag and exalted the labors of ordinary people. On the Left, Sinclair Lewis's best-selling 1935 novel, *It Can't Happen Here,* portrayed a folksy politician named Berzelius (Buzz) Windrip who rides into the White House as "the Common Man twenty-times-magnified by his oratory." Once in office, President Windrip grabs dictatorial powers that his private army, the Minutemen, brutally enforce. On the Right, the new House Committee on Un-American Activities (known by the acronym HUAC) and major Republican dailies like the *Chicago Tribune* charged that the Communist Party was orchestrating sit-down strikes to undermine the American economy and make the USSR seem, by contrast, an island of class peace and plenty. Once total war broke out in Europe in the fall of 1939, the fearful scenarios multiplied and achieved a greater degree of credibility.[47]

For Father Coughlin, this jittery climate provided a good opportunity—and a greater danger. To shift his rhetorical fire away from the money-changers and train it instead on powerful individuals and groups who could drag the nation into an antifascist war might revive the morale of his followers, perhaps even add to their shrunken ranks. Into 1940, a solid majority of Americans opposed sending any troops overseas; among those without a high school education, antiwar sentiment topped 80 percent. Congress, heeding public opinion, did not vote to weaken the strict Neutrality Act until six weeks before the attack on Pearl Harbor.[48]

But a single-minded resistance to pro-war "internationalists" was also extremely risky for Coughlin. It meant abandoning a large number of people who had admired him for yoking Christian piety to economic discontent. It transformed the identity of his Social Justice movement from that of an acerbic but roughly evenhanded critic of both major parties into the (unwelcome) ally of the resolutely isolationist wing of the Republican minority. And, most perilous of all, it gave the Coughlinites' many foes a splendid opening to brand them as agents for Hitler and Mussolini.

For nearly two years after the Union Party fiasco, the charismatic priest indicated he was aware of the pitfalls he faced. Editorials and feature articles in *Social Justice* straddled the line between the older concentration on economic elites and the new emphasis on left-wing interventionists who were championing the cause of Imperial England and the atheistic Soviets. During the winter of 1937, Coughlin and his paper alternately praised and denigrated the sit-down strikes then raging in Detroit and other industrial centers. In January, *Social Justice* admonished workers for illegally "occup[ying] factories which they do not own" and suggested that the CIO head John L. Lewis was "using the front of democratic labor organization to sovietize American industry." But, in March, Coughlin urged labor to "Hold Your Lines!" "Sit-downism is illegal. What of it?" he said. "The exploitation of labor is also illegal . . . we are in the midst of a revolution . . . which was brought about, not by the laborers themselves, but by the industrialists and their petting politicians." A year later, the priest criticized FDR's call to "quarantine the [German and Italian] aggressors" by lamenting the lack of progress made in "quarantining the poverty which surrounds us at home."[49] In such statements, the populist roots of the priest's original conception of social justice were still evident.

But his loss of political strength was accompanied by the wail of lost ideals. Coughlin increasingly strummed the chords of a mournful Americanism at odds with both the mainstream version and his own sanguine past. In the late '30s, under the aegis of the New Deal, institutional patriotism was flourishing: the opening of the Jefferson Memorial and the National Archives (displaying immaculately preserved copies of the Constitution and Declaration of Independence) and the WPA's lavish sponsorship of historic guides and murals all connoted a sunny view of the American prospect. In contrast, after 1936, Coughlin's speeches and many articles in *Social Justice* bewailed the nation's declension from a glorious past when giants of principle had led the nation. For Washington's Birthday in 1937, the priest delivered an address heavy with bathetic flourishes that compared the patriotic deeds of the "Father of our Country" with the "heresy expounded by internationalists" today. The injunction to "reach back into the holy past for direction" diverged from Coughlin's earlier use of national icons to make his ideas sound like the militant updating of populist traditions.

That Fourth of July, the front page of *Social Justice* featured the photo of a man in silhouette—"The Last American"—raising a flag in a rural setting: "Who knows that by 1940 some lonely and courageous American will betake himself to a midland forest retreat and there in secret raise aloft the flag that was the Stars and

Stripes." Readers were quickly reassured that "the future of America is by no means so hopeless."[50] But the way the holiday message was presented bespoke a despair that was deeply reactionary.

On the radio, Coughlin's performances now lacked most of the wit and buoyancy that had made him so seductive. His rich timbre and musical intonations were still there, but the priest no longer satirized the foibles of bankers and "modern capitalists" or claimed his support was growing stronger by the day. "We have not lost faith in the American people," the priest wrote in an editorial in March of 1937, "although some of them have lost faith in themselves." Anguished jeremiads had replaced the upbeat metaphors of a crusade to reclaim for the majority the wealth of the earth and the powers of government.[51]

Accompanying the self-defensive pathos of this view of the nation was a new emphasis on the teachings and separate identity of Catholicism. Coughlin had always rooted his controversial statements in the doctrine of his church. But after 1936, he seldom reached beyond it to other Americans exploited by high finance and its political allies. In fact, the priest from Royal Oak and his followers began to portray themselves as the heroic builders of a new Church Militant from the ground up. Coughlin devoted entire speeches to outlining a vision of the Corporate State that would make political parties and the constitutional separation of powers superfluous. In line with the revival of medievalism then popular among Catholic intellectuals, *Social Justice* republished several arcane essays by Hilaire Belloc and other writers in praise of the blessedly harmonious order of thirteenth-century Christendom. Coughlin also tried to compete with the CIO by launching a handful of Workers Councils for Social Justice run "on the basis of Christian principles." This meant employers could join, a legislated annual wage was a substitute for engaging in "class struggle," and all cooperation with Communists or Socialists was prohibited. For the first time in his paper, the priest also allowed the church-sponsored Legion of Decency to inveigh against immoral scenes in Hollywood films and added a few outraged barbs of his own.[52]

The turn inward achieved some success. In New York, Boston, and Detroit, numbers of parish priests and editors of Catholic newspapers (most notably Patrick Scanlan of the *Brooklyn Tablet*) sided with Coughlin against the criticisms of their own archbishops. The influential Jesuit magazine *America* and several lodges of the fraternal Knights of Columbus agreed. After all, they protested, anticommunism was a pillar of the Catholic creed. Why should Coughlin be harried for applying it so zealously?

At the same time, a more compact and purposeful movement was taking the place of the defunct NUSJ. Hundreds of Irish-American policemen and other city employees joined unemployed young toughs in a shifting array of new groups with names like the Christian American League, Christian Labor Front, Christian Mobilizers, and, most commonly, the Christian Front. Some Coughlinite priests and rank and filers mounted challenges to the pro-Communist leaders of such unions as the Transport Workers. Hawked widely by a corps of aggressive street vendors, *Social*

Justice retained a weekly circulation of over 200,000 through 1940. Coughlin's own broadcasts could still command an audience in the millions, although it was no more than a third of the total at mid-decade. In January of 1939, one of the priest's radio talks opposing last-minute aid to the failing Spanish Republic elicited over 100,000 telegrams to Congress. Vehement liberal and left-wing attacks on the priest as an embezzling fraud and a cunning propagandist only testified to his enduring ability to draw a crowd.[53]

But Coughlin and his corps of loyalists misunderstood completely why ordinary Americans balked at armed intervention. Unlike the opponents of World War I whose populist arguments had targeted the bellicose rich and condemned all the warring states, the radio priest became a flagrant apologist for the European right then doing combat (armed and otherwise) with liberals and Marxists. *Social Justice* praised Franco and Salazar for governing according to Catholic principles and compared Hitler's and Mussolini's regimes favorably with those in England, Mexico, and the Soviet Union "which inaugurated the mass murder of twenty million Christians." In the summer of 1940, Coughlin's paper predicted glorious things for the new Vichy government just installed by the Nazis: "Fascist France in days to come will afford better opportunities for the mental, spiritual and social development of its people than did the France that was ruled by the spirit of the atheist Voltaire." Such comments could have gladdened no one in the United States but stalwart antimodernists and would-be Hitlers.[54]

While Coughlin had become an open admirer of fascist regimes, neither he nor his movement sought to adapt the philosophy of Franco, Mussolini, or Hitler to American society. *Social Justice* still routinely criticized a strong federal government and equated the public interest with independent, non-CIO unions and small businesses. Coughlinism never imitated the militarized, ultranationalist discourse that undergirded the "new order" in Nazi Germany and its allies. As the historian Alan Brinkley observes: "What defines a political movement is not just the intellectual currents it vaguely absorbs, but how it translates those currents into a message of immediate importance to its constituency." Those who clung to Coughlin on the eve of World War II—parish priests eager to apply their church's anti-radical dogma, bitter victims of the Depression, and newsboys spoiling for a fight with street-corner critics—knew they wanted to "kick the reds out of America" and put "real" Christians in charge. But apart from its cult of charismatic leadership, the alien creed of fascism held little attraction for such self-conscious Americanists.[55]

What Coughlin and his shrunken band did care deeply about was the alleged power of what they called "Soviet-loving Jews." Prior to 1937, anti-Semitism had lurked around the fringes of the priest's denunciations of financial barons, "modern" capitalists, and godless Communists. He once made a scornful remark about "the treachery preached by the German Hebrew Karl Marx" and, on another occasion, announced that Alexander Hamilton was a Jew "who had established the nation's banking system in the interests of the rich and well born." But Coughlin had seldom referred to the ethnicity of contemporary figures like Bernard Baruch or the Rothschilds when he attacked them as evil. And he lavished at least equal contempt on gentile financiers like J. P. Morgan and the bowler-hatted demons of the City of London—who had long held Mother Ireland in thrall. During the 1936 campaign, Coughlin told the first (and only) convention of the NUSJ that "there was never such persecution as we Christians inflicted without reason upon the Jews." At one rally in Detroit that year, he was introduced by a local rabbi. The Union Party could not afford to write off any group of voters, especially one concentrated in big industrial states.[56]

However, the shift away from skewering the financial elite to bludgeoning alleged Communists brought out a fierce ethnic antipathy that had only been hinted at before. In July of 1938, *Social Justice* began printing excerpts from the infamous *Protocols of the Learned Elders of Zion*, the specious record of a Jewish plot to conquer the world. Coughlin, aware of the furor he would cause, explained that his paper "holds no enmity for the Jew" but merely wanted "the righteous Jewish leaders to campaign openly, in season and out of season, against these communistic attempts to overturn a civilization." As his movement lost support because of the public perception that it was a haven for domestic Nazis, that remained the official line: only Jews who advanced the twin causes of atheism and communism were enemies; "religious" Jews could and should be hailed for leading their brethren away from the path of evil. With frequent citations of writings by the right-wing Irish cleric Denis Fahey, Coughlin insisted that a handful of Jews had organized the Bolshevik Revolution, thus binding themselves to what Fahey called "the Mystical Body of Satan."[57]

The pastor of Royal Oak was doubtless sincere in distinguishing between two types of Jews; it fit with his general affection for Manichean categories. But his foot soldiers in groups like the Christian Front were not particularly concerned with theological distinctions. In Brooklyn and the Bronx, bands of Coughlinite youths smashed the windows of Jewish-owned stores without inquiring into the beliefs of their proprietors. Sellers of *Social Justice* routinely used the crudest of anti-Semitic slogans to hawk their wares. On occasion, the paper published letters from readers whose fearful wrath was unchecked by considerations of spiritual doctrine. One such reader, who signed his letter J. A. B., wrote from Brooklyn in March of 1939 to oppose letting Jewish refugees enter the country. "Jews have been booted out of Europe for making a near-debacle of civilization. Shall we accept this vast, pro-Communistic Jew swarm as America's ruling and owning caste; or fight it and drive it forth; or suffer physical extinction at its hands?"[58]

A kind of populism animated the horrific challenge. Since the late nineteenth century, most American anti-Semites had, like Coughlin, identified Jews as both nonproductive manipulators of "other people's money" and the carriers of decadent, radical doctrines from abroad. J. A. B. did not hold Jews responsible for all the nation's problems. But his assumption that they could be nothing but a rapacious elite paralleled the arguments Tom Watson had made to justify the lynching of Leo Frank in 1915 and Henry Ford had circulated in his notorious 1922 publication *The International Jew.* Hitler himself defined Jews as a naturally parasitic race that gained positions of power in order to strip ordinary Germans of their hard-earned material resources and cultural cohesion.[59]

In the United States, however, Coughlin's anti-Semitism was a populism of fools. While 42 percent of Catholics (but only 19 percent of Protestants) told Gallup pollsters in late 1938 that they supported the priest, the Bolshevik Jew was failing as a mobilizing device. In New Deal America, a politics tightly yoked to a monistic conspiracy theory appealed mainly to the desperate and disorganized—the type of people who wrote bloody, chiliastic letters to *Social Justice* after it began serializing the *Protocols of the Learned Elders of Zion.* At a time when most national figures (whether in politics, labor, or business) were lauding the ideals of ethnic pluralism and grassroots democracy (at least for whites), the tribal animosities Coughlin was stirring seemed anachronistic—even though, in private, many Americans continued to grumble about "the Jews." Ironically, as another world war began, the priest whose national popularity had once signified the end of the calumny that Catholics were foreign agents was best known for accusing Jews of the same thing.[60]

So, instead of trying to build a strong antiwar and anti-Communist movement, Coughlin had to spend most of his time defending himself against verbal assaults from all directions. His supporters were active in many local chapters of the America First Committee, organized in 1940 to keep the United States out of war. But their presence embarrassed national leaders of the group and helped to stigmatize it as a haven for anti-Semites. Meanwhile, the number of stations willing to carry the priest's addresses dwindled to a handful.

Finally, in 1941, Archbishop Edward Mooney of Detroit—who had previously been wary of alienating devout Coughlinites—ordered the radio priest to stop his broadcasts for good. The next spring, after the bombing of Pearl Harbor, Mooney, at the behest of United States Attorney General Francis Biddle, also instructed *Social Justice* to cease publication. Coughlin, dutiful son of the Church, immediately complied. Until his death a quarter-century later, he remained pastor of the Shrine of the Little Flower; his superiors forbade any attempt at a national comeback.[61]

Charles Coughlin's descent into anti-Semitism and pro-fascism has tended to shape his entire political image. Living as we do in the unending aftermath of the Holocaust, it remains essential to understand how a cranky fixation on international "money changers" and their "red" allies could lead a beguiling egotist to apologize for monsters. Knowing that Coughlin, in the late 1930s, could not have predicted the Final Solution only slightly mitigates his role in portraying the Nazis as worthy men who had something to teach Americans who felt their government had abandoned them.

Yet, before he retreated to that noxious bunker, the radio priest had advanced a populism whose moment did not expire with the destruction of Berlin and the revelations of Auschwitz. At the height of his broadcast career in the mid-1930s,

Coughlin appealed to both Protestants and Catholics by speaking to their shared desire for an America whose people would control their economy and preserve their Christian values. His broad sympathy with the victims of concentrated wealth attracted both industrial workers and members of the growing white-collar class. He accused officials of an increasingly powerful and visible state of being pretentious, hypocritical, and, worst of all, ineffective. And he cited patriotic forebears and religious authorities to legitimate his unorthodox opinions.

Coughlin was too much bound by the doctrines of his church and his own prejudices to fully exploit the political potential of this meld. But, however bizarre and contradictory his proposals, Coughlin did not become a marginal figure until the eve of World War II. In his clumsy, overblown, but always entertaining way, he countered the appeal of the emerging New Deal order in the name of hard-pressed Christian Americans. Coughlin spoke with conviction to people who were concerned about the world they were losing and afraid that "big men"—liberal, secular, intellectual statists (and their wealthy friends)—would cheat them out of whatever they could gain. Soon, more astute and better-placed voices on the Right would address the same suspicions. Coughlin's mistake was to preach a bigoted and premature anticommunism when most Americans still cared more about the value of their labor.

The CIO on the march, led by the spirit of John L. Lewis, 1940. *(Courtesy of the Library of Congress)*

Chapter 6

The Many and the Few: The CIO and the Embrace of Liberalism

It's worth twelve dollars a year [in union dues] to be able to walk down the main street of Aliquippa, talk to anyone you want about anything you like, and feel that you are a citizen.

—A local leader of the Steel Workers' Organizing Committee, c. 1938

The millions of organized workers banded together in the CIO are the main driving force of the progressive movement of workers, farmers, professional and small business people and of all other liberal elements in the community. . . . They are also the backbone of the resistance to all the forces that threaten our democratic institutions and the liberty and security that Americans hold dear.

—John L. Lewis, November 1939

If I went to work in a factory, the first thing I'd do would be to join a union.

—President Franklin D. Roosevelt, as quoted on a CIO recruiting poster, c. 1936

IN THE NAME OF A NEW PEOPLE

"AM I an American?" a voice from the chorus asked the famous black singer and actor Paul Robeson during the inaugural radio broadcast "Ballad for Americans" in the fall of 1939. Replied Robeson, who was a vigorous supporter of the Congress of Industrial Organizations (CIO), "I'm just an Irish, Negro, Jewish, Italian, French and English, Spanish, Russian, Chinese, Polish, Scotch,

Hungarian, Litvak, Swedish, Finnish, Canadian, Greek and Turk and Czech and double-check American." The ballad, written by Earl Robinson, a member of the Communist Party (CP), was a symbolic roll call for a new insurgency that claimed to be representing the people in all their heartily plebeian, ethnically diverse glory.[1]

The CIO and its allies made a stark contrast with Coughlin's antimodern Christian Front. Industrial unionists were brashly attempting to represent a pluralistic majority that had its working clothes on. The Depression and the New Deal had released organized labor from the crabbed, defensive posture of the previous decade. Big business now seemed more greedy than efficient, and American culture had awakened from the long dream of Anglo-Saxon dominance. A militant brand of producerism open to everyone but bigots and millionaires had an opportunity to thrive.

The CIO was founded in 1935 by eight union chiefs disgusted with the AFL's reluctance to take on America's manufacturing combines. It quickly challenged General Motors, Goodyear Rubber, and U.S. Steel to grant their employees union recognition—and won. By mid-1937, the new organization, under the leadership of John L. Lewis of the United Mine Workers (UMW), had enrolled perhaps three million members and seemed poised to transform the industrial heartland—both on the job and in the voting booth. Then a sharp, if short, recession and unfriendly competition with the AFL stalled its growth. But World War II flooded American workplaces with new orders and new hands to fill them. By 1945, the CIO boasted six million dues payers drawn liberally from the groups Robeson extolled and any others who punched a time clock at one of America's 2,000 largest factories, its locus of power.[2]

Together with an equally prosperous AFL, the union movement had come to represent a social force unlike any in the nation's history. Wrote Eric Johnston, the president of the United States Chamber of Commerce, in 1944: "Measured in numbers, political influence, economic weight, or by any other yardstick, labor is a power in our land." A prominent scholar of unionism who was not prone to hyperbole predicted that "the United States is gradually shifting from a capitalistic community to a laboristic one . . . in which employees rather than businessmen are the strongest single influence." One could imagine broad grins creasing the faces of Terence Powderly, Ignatius Donnelly, Samuel Gompers, and Mother Jones. At last, the horny-handed producer, the average man who created all wealth, had faced down the corporate parasites and emerged triumphant.[3]

That tale of glorious continuity, narrated by many a labor spokesman at the time, has merit. During the 1930s and 1940s, millions of Americans did go on strike to achieve a measure of the respect and democratic rights at the workplace that three generations of unionists before them had demanded. The basic aims of organized labor did not change substantially from the era of Reconstruction to the era of FDR—job security, better pay, union recognition, and some power over the content and pace of work.[4]

In defining and celebrating its constituency, however, the CIO broke decisively with AFL tradition. There would be no more official suspicion that unskilled immigrants and blacks impeded the ascent of the citizen-producer. The CIO's archetypal "Joe Worker," his handsome, square-jawed white face gleaming from an educational comic book published by the organization, viewed the able-bodied poor as allies for social change, not as a threat to his status. New unionists applied the relaxed inclusiveness of the "Ballad for Americans" to the entire wage-earning population—still heavy with immigrants and their children (and increasingly black) but, due to restrictive quota laws passed in the 1920s, with far fewer newcomers than during Gompers's reign. The "cultural pluralism" that, in the Progressive era, a few intellectuals such as Horace Kallen and John Dewey had proposed as an alternative to the coercive assimilation of the "melting pot" was now the everyday faith of the CIO.[5]

Cultural diversity also implied a certain doctrinal latitude, as long as one agreed with the CIO's basic objectives. Prolabor Catholics found a secure home in the new unions. Communist organizers—their very presence a lightning rod for opponents in the AFL, business, Congress, and the churches—received a more tentative welcome if they abandoned talk of revolution. Such heterogeneity helped promote the idea that the CIO was not a narrow interest group focused on the workplace but the core of a grander "people's movement"—of small farmers, local politicians, working- and middle-class consumers, and even some small employers—that sought to level the heights of concentrated wealth and push the New Deal further leftward.

For the first time since the brief heyday of the Knights of Labor, a union movement was assembling a grand coalition of workers and the reformist middle class. *The Many and the Few* was the title of Henry Kraus's journalistic account of the 1937 sit-down strike in Flint, Michigan, that established the United Auto Workers (UAW). In 1938, a bold-faced headline in the CIO's organ read, "The interests of the people are the interests of labor, and the interests of labor are the interests of the people."[6]

Labor's many belonged no less securely to FDR. From 1936 to 1944, a class line stretched across presidential politics; urban wage earners of all ethnic origins overwhelmingly backed Roosevelt while their employers stuck with the GOP. The sentiments of the rank and file dampened occasional threats by disgruntled unionists to launch another independent party of farmers and workers. While not always smooth, the CIO's liaison with the Roosevelt administration separated it, in language and strategy, from all other populist-speaking movements since the Civil War. Forty years earlier, the People's Party had crashed in its torturous attempt to form such a relationship with the Democratic Party. While Gompers's AFL and the Anti-Saloon League had both welcomed the support of incumbent presidents, neither shaped its very identity around the success of a party that held national power. In the 1930s, the AFL, still headed by William Green, endorsed the pro-union Wagner Act but protested any "governmental intrusion" that limited its freedom of action.[7]

But the CIO had an ambitious agenda for eradicating social inequality. Its leaders endorsed measures to guarantee full employment, win civil rights for blacks and Latinos, provide universal health care, and build massive amounts of public housing. Since all these measures required congressional approval, the advocates of what came to be called "social unionism" needed the support of the burgeoning liberal state as much (if not more) than FDR and his legislative allies needed them.

There was another reason to stay close to New Dealers, even if the embrace was not always reciprocated. Despite the heroic image of labor in the 1930s, the young CIO was always a shaky proposition. Citywide strikes in San Francisco and Minneapolis and sit-downs in Akron and Flint galvanized their participants but appeared to most Americans like a sign of mass disorder and the imminent collapse of vital institutions.[8] Moreover, as in any mass organization, few members of industrial unions were committed activists or dedicated supporters of the CIO's larger program. Most refused to cross picket lines but otherwise focused on getting through life without suffering a capricious disaster. "We had seen so much discrimination," remembered a UAW activist, "people who had a lot of service and had been laid off and friends and relatives kept on. It was easy to organize people." Security in one's job and for one's family was a more critical, and concrete, need than economic rights.[9]

Thus, CIO language was an exercise in coalition speaking. Labor activists tried to fashion a populism that isolated the corporate elite but embraced the new political one—without alienating ordinary Americans who were less sanguine about an interventionist state. The CIO had to fight off conservatives who charged it was dominated by "reds" without destroying the working unity of an immature organization prey to ethnic, political, and religious squabbles. This was a feat of rhetorical acrobatics no earlier champions of American workers had performed so deftly—or with so much at stake. The prospects of the entire American Left, from liberals to Communists, essentially hung in the balance.

LABOR ON THE MARCH

The cultural and political environment of the 1930s and early 1940s required the CIO to craft a more expansive language than the one spoken by embattled artisans in the turn-of-century AFL. Didactic arguments for union principles were unlikely to win over urban workers accustomed to the intimacy of radio, the frenetic wit of the Marx Brothers, the jollity of Mickey Mouse, and the sentimental underdogs created by Charlie Chaplin and Frank Capra. Anguished pleas, in the Gompers style, to "right-thinking men and women of the Republic" would also have clashed with FDR's brimming confidence and wit.

So CIO spokesmen employed simple, repetitive phrases and images rather than closely argued speeches to reach Americans, of all classes, whose complacency the

Depression had shattered. At the crux of labor conflict was a simple desire for "industrial democracy." As John L. Lewis put it in a 1936 radio address, the question was "whether the working population of this country shall have the voice in determining their destiny or whether they shall serve as indentured servants for a financial and economic dictatorship that would shamelessly exploit our resources." Labor was "on the march" to gain a fairer, more egalitarian America for all those FDR called the "forgotten" Americans, whether or not they toiled in an industrial workplace.[10]

The sweeping, optimistic nature of this appeal owed something to the social complexion of CIO leaders themselves. Nine-tenths of them were men and, like their counterparts in the AFL at the time, most were the sons of manual workers—Catholic or Protestant—whose origins lay in Western Europe. But CIO officials tended to be younger than their erstwhile brethren in the older federation and were more likely to have participated in a radical or third party. Most had, in addition, either mastered a craft or earned the educational credentials to pursue a white-collar career. Dozens of writers and lawyers, often with Socialist or Communist affiliations, rushed to join the blue-collar insurgency they hoped would overturn the old order. Thus, the spearheads of the CIO were more sanguine about their options than were the men and women they were organizing, whose only marketable skill typically consisted of operating a machine in a repetitive manner. Working full-time for the CIO was an ideological choice—a dash into unknown terrain—that did not pay material dividends until its rebellious infancy had passed.[11]

To pursue their vision, Lewis and his associates built a publicity apparatus far more sophisticated and centralized than the labor movement had previously wielded. Two months after breaking with the AFL, the CIO began publishing the Union News Service, a weekly mailing of information and political cartoons edited for use by labor papers around the country. At the end of 1937, this was supplemented by the *CIO News,* labor's first national weekly newspaper.

Edited by the British-born Len DeCaux, a former Wobbly now close to the CP, the *CIO News* was a model for the organs published by new unions in the auto, steel, meatpacking, and electrical industries. Consistently engaging and informal, the *News* resembled—in layout, language, and graphics—the big-city tabloids most manufacturing workers already enjoyed. It offered a mix of signed columns (often written by professional journalists like Heywood Broun), upbeat news stories about advancing unions and fighting liberal Democrats, articles about professional athletes and entertainers who belonged to and/or boosted the CIO, aggressive cartoons that cheered the working man and ridiculed his "Tory" opponents, and action photos of everyone from champagne-quaffing industrialists to pretty young "union maids" in bathing suits. Such short, morale-enhancing features far outnumbered articles and speeches by union officials—items the rival *American Federationist* still highlighted. Within a year, Lewis could boast that the CIO's paper had a circulation of almost 750,000 (about 40 percent of the total membership) and appeared in over twelve editions geared to workers in different regions and industries.[12]

And the movement did not rise on print alone. In the early 1920s, AFL leaders, concerned about declining attendance at Labor Day parades, had begun giving their holiday addresses on the radio. CIO men took a more innovative approach to broadcasting. Aided by their publicity department (whose very existence signified a new self-consciousness about the media), both national and local officials made frequent broadcasts—to comment on a news event, to urge understanding and support for labor's aims and actions, and to make the larger point that the representatives of industrial wage earners could articulate the public interest as well as any politician or freelance orator. In 1940, CIO leaders spoke via a national hookup on such subjects as "technological unemployment; what the CIO means to business; labor's social outlook; jobs made in America; the CIO program on social security . . . ; the CIO and the Negro worker; labor and civil liberties; and the Wagner Act."[13]

Local activists often departed from the elocutionary format. In Chicago, the Packinghouse Workers Organizing Committee (PWOC) produced a weekly program in which rank-and-file workers talked about how the drive to organize the stockyards was progressing. The Los Angeles CIO's nightly show regularly featured a surprise guest—a worker from a local plant that was being organized. Keeping the person's name secret until the broadcast "whets the curiosity of the men in the plant," reported a labor journalist. "The men are as much interested to find out who the speaker will be as they are to hear his message. Then when he comes to work the next morning and the boss doesn't fire him, confidence grows—and so does the CIO." No audience statistics are available for such broadcasts, but they probably reached more people more quickly than did a union organ or leaflet handed out at the factory gate.[14]

The CIO also redesigned the traditional Labor Day parade to feature slogans, fantasies, and personalities drawn from the enveloping domain of mass culture. No longer were grimly purposeful male craftsmen or factory workers the main holiday attraction. Huge crowds in such union centers as San Francisco, New York, and Atlanta applauded floats topped by buxom Labor Day queens and sunny family tableaux that linked strong unions with the "American Standard of Living." In Los Angeles, both the CIO and the AFL borrowed the glamour of the movies, the city's best-known (and recently unionized) industry. On Labor Day in 1938, the Hollywood stars Robert Montgomery, Eddie Arnold, and Lionel Stander waved to spectators from open convertibles, while Count Basie's orchestra and Louis Armstrong's band "tantalized the crowd with . . . swing time antics and incomparable syncopation"—as one union reporter turned music critic phrased it. Other members of the Screen Actors' Guild appeared on floats depicting a South Sea island, a Chinese palace, and an Arabian desert complete with dashing sheikhs and a veiled harem. Organizers of these spectacles were eager to employ any device that, if only for a day, drew Americans into the expanding tent of unionism.[15]

The lead barker from the CIO's birth through 1940 was its remarkable president, John L. Lewis, the son of Welsh immigrants. He was a major reason why the organization, born during the heyday of radio and newsreels, rapidly gained national attention as a dynamic movement of the discontented and unrepresented, not merely as a practical vehicle to organize workers into unions. Lewis personified the CIO in a way Gompers, for all his ideological influence, had never done for the AFL. He was a memorable public speaker with a look and voice of great authority. And, unlike in the AFL where craft autonomy reigned, in the CIO that authority had teeth. The CIO's national leaders decided when to initiate an organizing campaign or a change in political direction and usually kept their affiliates in line.

Lewis understood the media's need for a man to symbolize a movement; an amateur actor in his youth, he knew that personal presence was as valuable an asset as cogent ideas. A bulldog-like expression and a head that journalists routinely called "leonine," a deep, resonant voice, and the sarcastic, hyperbolic phrases, many of them biblical, that flowed off his tongue at a majestic pace all gained Lewis a renown equal to Father Coughlin's at his zenith and second only to that of FDR.[16]

Yet Lewis was probably more influential as the embodiment of the CIO's early spirit than as the architect of its discourse. That language was shaped by a variety of activists, most of whom came from polyglot urban centers full of Catholics and Jews, a world apart from the Iowa coal towns in which Lewis was raised and had worked as a miner. No one, however, did more than Lewis to define the inspirational, pugnacious style of "labor on the march." One cannot imagine Gompers wielding his fists in public to make a political point. But the famous, premeditated punch that Lewis—then a man of 55—landed on the jaw of the arrogant and much taller William Hutcheson, the baron of the Carpenters' Union and a leading foe of industrial unionism, at the 1935 AFL convention was a most graphic way to announce a new departure for the labor movement.

Not that Lewis's words were insignificant. His rhetorical performance was most effective when he dressed up in regal purple what wage earners already believed. "They lie in their beard and they lie in their bowels," was his answer to red-baiting critics in 1940. But, in the same speech, Lewis scoffed at the idea that he had even a passing interest in "communist philosophy, Nazi philosophy, fascist philosophy, or any other philosophy." The CIO believed in democracy but spurned all isms. During the Little Steel strike of 1937, Lewis, like an Old Testament prophet, linked the young CIO to the oldest spiritual tradition in the West: "Labor, like Israel, has many sorrows. Its women weep for their fallen, and they lament for the future of the children of the race.[17]

As the latter incident suggests, Lewis's rhetoric sometimes overshot his target and resembled the high-flying melodrama untethered to the political moment that better suited a speaker like Father Coughlin. But most industrial workers adored Lewis, wrote the left-wing novelist Ruth McKenney, because they "liked hearing their dreams, their problems, their suffering cloaked in Biblical phrases. They felt proud that a workers' leader could use so many educated words with such obvious fluency, and they were pleased and a little flattered by hearing their own fate discussed in such rolling periods and such dramatic phrases."[18]

Indeed, Lewis never let political consistency get in the way of doing what he thought best for his people and himself. Unlike Gompers, who refined his own doctrinal code after disowning Marx's, Lewis had always been a consummate pragmatist. He enthusiastically campaigned for the Democrats when Woodrow Wilson was in power, became a staunch Republican and admirer of Herbert Hoover in the '20s, and then steered his union into FDR's camp in 1933 when UMW organizers plastered coal towns with truth-stretching signs that read, "The President Wants You to Join the Union." Such tactical shifts (and they did not end with the New Deal) seem to have reinforced a simple core of populist convictions: take advantage of centralized power, whether economic or political, but always suspect its motives; safeguard the independent strength of the labor movement; and uphold Americanism as the promise of individual mobility and the antithesis of plutocracy and greed.

In the 1930s, Lewis articulated these beliefs in a memorable style that purposely blurred the intellectual line between Right and Left. In 1933, he told a Senate Committee considering pro-union legislation, "American labor . . . stand[s] between the rapacity of the robber barons of industry of America and the lustful rage of the communists, who would lay waste to our traditions and our institutions with fire and sword. . . . Let there be no 'moaning at the bar' when we set out to sea on this great adventure." As CIO strength crested in 1936 and 1937, he blamed "the money trust" he connected to Wall Street and the House of Morgan for ordering industrial managers to resist unionization. In 1940, he told a UMW convention: "You know, after all there are two great material tasks in life that affect the individual and affect great bodies of men. The first is to achieve or acquire something of value or something that is desirable, . . . the second task is to prevent some scoundrel from taking it away from you."[19]

That few followers of Father Coughlin would have objected to these statements suggests why Lewis proved such an elusive target in the late 1930s. The CIO leader could be criticized for his bluster and intransigence, for assuming that what was good for his members was good for the country, for allowing suspected Communists to work inside his organization. National opinion polls in fact showed a preference for the stodgy William Green over this powerful labor "boss."[20] But it was difficult to portray Lewis convincingly as the captive of any force but his own ambitions.

He was too fiercely original an orator and too opportunistic an actor to squeeze into a tight ideological box. Lewis's undogmatic, unpredictable brand of populism helped to advance the perception that the CIO was a pioneering phenomenon and the militant master of its own fate—even as it boosted the fortunes of an emerging liberal elite.

THE SONG OF PATRICK HENRY, JR.

"Industrial democracy"—one of Lewis's favorite phrases—was the CIO's chief goal, posed as a fair and reasonable solution to the economic crisis.[21] But a polymorphous constituency of wage earners could not be recruited and retained so easily. Also, to avoid driving away Americans of other classes, labor spokesmen had to stress a conception of the common good that transcended the world of docks, mines, and factories.

They did so by creatively evoking three identities, often simultaneously: the industrial worker as consumer, patriotic democrat, and vanguard of liberalism. The amalgam expressed the complex responsibilities of a movement rooted in workplace conflicts but aspiring to be a bulwark against reactionaries and outright fascists everywhere. It was a secular populism for wage earners of diverse nationalities, industries, and skills who—if the threatened war broke out—might have to save the world.

Heroic images of manual workers were therefore indispensable. Before World War I, IWW artists had made countless drawings of Herculean, bare-chested workers striking hammer blows against employers, scabs, and timid AFL bureaucrats.[22] In the '30s, CIO cartoonists portrayed worker-paragons fully clothed and usually eschewed any hint that violence had a role in their struggle. The smiling, burly figures were often as tall as skyscrapers; they projected a confidence in keeping with the mood FDR, corporate copywriters, and scores of Hollywood films were setting. And they were sharply distinct from the common people described by Coughlin, those helpless victims of a monstrous conspiracy that spanned the Atlantic.

But the cheerful industrial workman had only recently realized his potency. "As the curtain rose on CIO, injustice was as commonplace as streetcars," recalled Walter Reuther of the UAW. "When men walked into their jobs, they left their dignity, their citizenship and their humanity outside."[23] CIO organizers were appealing to workers who, for the most part, had not been involved with unions before or who nursed bad memories of a disastrous postwar strike and/or failed membership drive. After several years of downward mobility caused by the Depression, many had to be convinced to take actions that might jeopardize their jobs which unemployed strike breakers could easily fill.

Thus, the producerism of the CIO was an effort to lift the self-esteem of factory workers few of whom, like the artisans and small farmers of old, had previously considered themselves sinews of the republic. While hardly any labor or left-wing publicist still called for uniting "the producing classes," a sunrise of class equality illuminated their prose. Labor's upsurge, they asserted, was bringing industrial reality in line with the civic ideal. "Finally . . . [we were] throwing off the shackles and saying to the boss, 'Go to hell! You've had me long enough. I'm going to be a man on my own now!'" as a local leader of the United Electrical Workers put it.[24] As craftsmen, past or present, Gompers and his colleagues never doubted they were indispensable to the process of production. But the CIO had to persuade people who had been treated either as malleable objects of corporate paternalism or the interchangeable servants of machines that, acting together, they could transform their working lives.

The notion of unionization as a democratic awakening had a particular appeal to the second-generation immigrants who made most of the nation's steel, garments, packaged meat, and electrical products. Even though most still lived in ethnic enclaves, these Slavs, Jews, Italians, and Greeks had grown up in a society glittering with the vision of an American standard of living that all could share. In the '20s, many had enjoyed at least some of the products advertisers identified with a comfortable existence—radios, cosmetics, even a used car. But the long Depression destroyed many community institutions—the family-run grocery store, the immigrant bank, the mutual benefits society—on which they and their parents had relied. Their faith in the American economy, if not their personal version of the American dream, was weakened. The CIO offered an opportunity to redress these grievances, to win respect from the larger society by starting at the individual workplace where the children of immigrants often formed a majority.[25]

A marvelous statement of this perspective appears in *Out of This Furnace* (1941), an autobiographical novel by a Slovak-American writer, Thomas Bell, whose immigrant grandfather and father had toiled in the steel mills of Braddock, Pennsylvania. Bell (born Belejcak) framed his narrative around three successive generations of male factory hands. The last of the trio—a young man whom everyone calls "Dobie"—helps to organize the Steel Workers' Organizing Committee (SWOC) at the huge Edgar Thomson facility of U.S. Steel. Dobie, as his nickname signifies, is a self-conscious American through and through. He speaks English without an accent, makes friends easily with coworkers from other ethnic groups, calls his father "Pop" and his wife, Julie (also a second-generation Slovak), "sweetheart," and believes organizing a union is a patriotic duty. "I want certain things bad enough to fight for them, bad enough to die for them," Dobie vows at the end of the novel. "Patrick Henry, Junior—that's me."

Earlier in his narrative, Bell sketched the SWOC activists who recruit Dobie to the cause:

> They were outspoken, fearlessly so, as though they had never learned to glance around and see who might be listening before they spoke. . . . They assumed that there was one law for the rich and one for the poor, and that it was the same law; and they talked about newspapers and radio chains and law courts and legislative bodies as though these things could be used for the benefit of ordinary people as well as against them; and there was something almost fantastic in their easy, take-it-for-granted air that Braddock burgesses and Pittsburgh police chiefs and Washington congressmen were public servants. And nobody in the steel towns had ever been heard to talk the way they talked—without stumbling over the

> words, uttering them as though they meant something real right there in Braddock—about liberty and justice and freedom of speech. . . . For lack of a handier label, [Dobie] thought of them simply as good C.I.O. men.[26]

This passage is a virtual chorus of populist melodies, sung in the key of the new unionism. "Ordinary people" can unmask the power of elites and demystify the operation of their institutions. They practice the nation's ideals every day rather than burying them in a casket of ritual. On the streets, in meetings, in Congress, they take charge of events, evincing a relaxed toughness that American men had admired in their political heroes at least since Andrew Jackson faced down Nicholas Biddle and his mighty bank. And they take it for granted that the elite institutions themselves—the press, the state, even the steel corporations—are legitimate. The point, Bell implied, is to make the loci of power serve the people, not to destroy the institutions in the name of some other system—unformed, alien, and dimly understood.[27]

In the novel, Dobie and Julie also begin to reap the material harvest of labor's new power. They own a washing machine, window shop for refrigerators, occasionally eat in restaurants, and muse about attending a Broadway show. The ordinary producer and his family were beginning to shade into a related identity—the eager, self-aware consumer.

The New Deal encouraged such thinking; policy makers counted on a higher overall wage level to soak up the excess supply that many believed was the Depression's major cause. And both the CIO and the AFL maintained that only steady work at union rates could spread the American standard of living to all corners of the land. Some retail corporations moved to take advantage of this new economic wisdom. In 1937, Sears Roebuck ran a Labor Day advertisement in union newspapers that reproduced the familiar icon of a male worker in overalls towering over the urban skyline. The copywriter linked the tribute—"Upon you the nation depends . . . upon you a nation grows"—to workers who "throughout the years" had shopped at Sears.[28]

Such an explicit consensus about the virtues of the marketplace marked a change in labor's language from the nineteenth century when *consumer* was a synonym for *parasite.* But it did not necessarily dilute the populist content—promoting the interests of the many against the privileges of a few. The kind of people who joined industrial unions were creating and participating in mass culture long before the CIO was established. What labor's tabloid-like press and jazzy celebrations signified was that movement activists finally grasped how vital that culture—movies, spectator sports, radio, chain stores, and the promise of future pleasures—had become for American workers. In fact, shared consumer tastes probably encouraged the ethnic mixing characteristic of the CIO. As Lizabeth Cohen writes: "At a time when they were all suffering from the depression and searching for collective solutions, talking about a boxing match on the radio or the latest bargain at the A&P may have done more to create an integrated working-class culture than a classless American one."[29] As with the AFL's earlier embrace of "the average man," a refinement of populist imagery brought labor closer to the ideological mainstream—this time of a nation of purchasers—without dulling its oppositional edge.

The CIO's jaunty, full-throated Americanism demonstrated the same dynamic at work. It enabled the new federation to marshal the considerable patriotic yearnings of immigrants and their children who needed to believe and then to insist that the messianic words of the Founding Fathers applied to them: "because Dobie had been born and raised in a steel town, where the word [American] meant people who were white, Protestant, middle-class Anglo-Saxons, it hadn't occurred to him that the C.I.O. men were thinking and talking like Americans." In the textile town of Woonsocket, Rhode Island, union organizers compared their employers to King George III and urged French-Canadian workers to emulate the Pilgrims and the "wise, hardy and staunch" pioneers in covered wagons who risked everything to attain prosperity for their families. In Monroe, Michigan, autoworkers carried signs with slogans like "Fordism is Fascism and Unionism is Americanism" and "Make Dearborn [Ford's headquarters] a Part of the United States." In Los Angeles, the International Ladies' Garment Workers' Union (ILGWU) told Mexican-Americans, in English and Spanish, "Remember—you are free Americans. It is your right to join the union and go on strike. . . . Don't let your employer or anybody else threaten you, frighten you, hold you or stop you." Everywhere, anti-CIO politicians and employers alike were branded as "Tories," whose actions betrayed their belief that "democracy and freedom are the bunk." The Americanization campaigns that government, corporate, and veterans' officials had waged after World War I against union militants and other radicals were bearing ironic fruit.[30]

And, as for the AFL during the Great War, labor's Americanism was also a weapon of self-defense. It helped parry (without diminishing) attacks by a formidable group of the CIO's political foes—Henry Ford, the Hearst press, the conservative Liberty League, Congressman Martin Dies of the new House Un-American Activities Committee, and leaders of the rival AFL—who charged the upstart federation was run by Communists, who preyed on innocent workers. To call Ford "King Henry V-8," to dress up as Lincoln and carry a picket sign reading "I Fought for Union Too," and to point out that the initials of the new United Steelworkers of America (SWOC's permanent name) were the same as the nation's assured CIO activists they were only doing what plebeian patriots had done before.[31] Why should such actions now raise such a fuss? Industrial unionists in the 1930s clung tightly to their democratic definition of the American creed. It was a rhetorical shield that guarded everything they were trying to achieve.

To what degree were black workers represented in the multicultural, patriotic chorus? National leaders of the CIO and most of its affiliated unions advocated giving blacks equal access to jobs and unions—and ending the larger injustices of Jim Crow. The UMW, which Lewis and his top aide Philip Murray continued to run after the CIO was established, had more black members and had long stood for a more enlightened racial order than did any other major American union (although the practice of its locals didn't always correspond to stated policy). "Behold how good and pleasant it is for brethren to dwell together in unity," a black miner from Alabama enthused in 1933 during a UMW organizing drive in the Deep South.[32] Until the wartime boom spurred a mass migration from the rural South, African-Americans were less prominent in such industries as steel, meatpacking, and auto, where together they accounted for only 4 percent of the workforce in 1940. But CIO men in the North routinely appealed to both blacks and whites to transcend racial divisions that could endanger the success of organizing drives and tarnish the public image of "solidarity." In the South, organizers of both races persevered through violence, ostracism, and red-baiting to establish small but robust interracial unions in such industries as tobacco and cotton processing.[33]

Official CIO rhetoric on the perennial dilemma of race and class was a more prosaic copy of the Alabama miner's spiritual metaphor. "Unite for common protection," "opposition to any and all forms of discrimination," and "equal economic opportunity for Negro workers" were common expressions of a desire to substitute the identity of labor for that of race.[34] Of course, the meaning of such slogans was diluted or altered as they filtered through the ranks. Some white CIO officials, especially in Southern steel mills, barely paid them lip service. Others denied any interest in "social equality" and, not wanting to be branded "nigger lovers," allowed whites to keep all the good jobs for themselves. At the other extreme were leftists in the United Electrical Workers who advocated compensatory employment policies (including, for a short time, "super-seniority" or affirmative action for blacks) and criticized fellow unionists who made racial slurs.[35]

What most white activists shared, at least outside the South, was a discourse that simultaneously deplored and transcended racial conflict. The CIO depicted itself as a rising of ordinary people who applauded ethnic "contributions" and had put the old suspicions and rancor aside. "The problems of the Negro people are the problems of all American wage earners," John L. Lewis told the 1940 convention of the National Association for the Advancement of Colored People (NAACP).[36]

This was a major advance in the history of white-dominated movements of producers. For the first time, racism was described as a malignant set of beliefs and not simply a nagging barrier to worker unity. This shift led the CIO to advocate anti-lynching laws, to call for the abolition of the poll tax, and to press integration on its own affiliates.

It also emboldened blacks and began to change, voluntarily or otherwise, the dismissive conduct of their employers and white fellow workers. In Memphis, an aged black man testified: "This CIO is a great thing. . . . After he heard about our union, our boss called some of us in his office—that never happened before. . . . He had never asked what we wanted till we had a union." One black Chicago steel-worker sang his own ballad of racial harmony. "I'll tell you what the CIO has done. Before, everyone used to make remarks about, 'That dirty Jew,' 'that stinkin' black bastard,' 'that low-life Bohunk,' but you know I never hear that kind of stuff any more. I don't like to brag, but I'm one of the best-liked men in my department. If there is any trouble, the men usually come to me."[37]

Unfortunately, solidarity was not enough. While it chipped away at prejudice on the job, the language of "black and white, unite and fight" was not equipped to uproot deeper structures of hostility and inequality that continued to keep most working people in separate camps. CIO spokesmen—despite their tolerant intentions—were, like the Populists of the 1890s, primarily making a functionalist argument based on workplace realities. Racial disunity helped only the boss, the exploiter, the forces of privilege; whether or not they liked one another, whites and blacks should find common ground.

But that logic did not extend to neighborhoods, recreation, or sexual relationships, areas where working-class whites often perceived gains for blacks as threats to their own improving status. All blue-collar workers in the same Chevrolet plant faced the same management; but General Motors didn't tell them where to live and with whom they could play and have sex. These areas were so sensitive that even unionists who protested racial epithets at work avoided talking about them.

Life off the job, however, only grew in political significance as the labor movement succeeded in making industrial jobs more bearable and, through seniority rights, more secure. After World War II, growing numbers of white workers had schools, houses, and neighborhoods whose economic value and middle-class status they wanted to preserve. It was not the task of union activists to explore the history of white supremacy in North America or the pain that history had caused. But absent such a courageous venture, they could only repeat, rather impotently, their pleas for unity as rank-and-file workers clashed at the color line.

Meanwhile, back in the '30s, the vivid images of men of all races and ethnic cultures fighting for their piece of America tended to put working-class women in the shade. The CIO did establish organizational beachheads in such industries as the retail trades, insurance, and factory farming, where large numbers of women worked and where the AFL, for the most part, had always disdained to tread. But the master tropes of industrial unionism—the solidarity of mass strikes, the muscular patriot, the beaming factory worker punching the air in triumph—were almost exclusively male. Although organized "brigades" of women played a big part in winning pivotal struggles like the 1934 Minneapolis transport strike and the 1937 Flint sit-down, union journalists reported these events as if no women had been present. Even cartoonists for the official journal of the ILGWU—whose membership was mostly female—choose as symbols of collective resolve a working man swinging a "union power" bat and another burly fellow damming "a river of runaway shops." And often, when the cartoonist for the *CIO News* wanted to ridicule William Green, the president of the AFL, he dressed him in women's clothes. Green was lampooned as a private secretary perched on the knee of an "anti-labor manufacturer," Marie Antoinette in a fur jacket carrying a cake labeled "toady policies," and a prostitute whistling down Henry Ford's car.[38]

CIO language did allow women a more visible, realistic role in the movement than had the old AFL with its ethereal, classically garbed demigoddesses, who resembled no real unionist's mate or mother. "Wives of union members can be active in many ways to promote the cause of a better life for all," suggested the CIO staff member Katherine Pollak. Among the "bread-and-butter" projects she mentioned were "demanding" quality public housing, better schools, and union-made goods in local stores. These sprang naturally from women's family responsibilities, their daily presence in neighborhoods while men were away at work, and the new consumer identity. The fact that a female journalist assumed the right of labor women to speak with an aggressiveness their men took for granted also separated the CIO from its craft-union predecessors.

The scrapping of Victorian notions of womanhood had another aspect, however. On public display went the bodies as well as the ideas of union maids. The CIO press featured, in addition to Labor Day queens, a constant stream of cheesecake photos of leggy young women linked in some way to labor organizing. "Tells All," read the caption below a seductive shot of Gypsy Rose Lee in the *CIO News.* The famous stripper had given a speech praising improved conditions in unionized burlesque houses.[39]

Neither the ancillary nor the sexy union maid was the CIO's primary constituent. Most of the workers it wooed did not labor alongside women and, like other American men, viewed hard work as a male burden to be compensated and respected as such. In 1939, a photo in the UAW's paper depicted four men in drag carrying signs reading "Help the Poor Woikin Goil—Vote CIO" and "Vote CIO—Restore Our Manhood." They were protesting the low but equal wages an employer had paid the men and women in his firm.[40]

This kind of discourse, commonplace in the 1930s, proved difficult to alter. In the quarter-century after World War II, its persistence hampered the ability and desire of the CIO to organize the increasing number of workplaces dominated by women. When, in the early 1970s, union spokesmen finally acknowledged that blue-collar America included both sexes and acted accordingly, they no longer had the ear of the nation.

During the Depression, industrial-labor activists had won an audience, in part, because they appeared to be at the center of a large new coalition that was transforming America. When John L. Lewis told delegates to the 1939 CIO convention that they were "the main driving force" of all "liberal elements in the community," he was not being hyperbolic. Embattled as the CIO was, it was the only national organization that offered Roosevelt tens of thousands of campaigners, millions of loyal voters, and support for his effort to purge the party of Dixiecrats and isolationists who had soured on most of his policies. To be sure, there was a distinction between the CIO's rhetoric and the president's. During the 1936 campaign, union spokesmen flatly equated "Tory industrialists and financiers" with the forces of "reaction and special privilege"; any antilabor businessman could consider himself included. But when FDR blasted "economic royalists," he was merely rephrasing the old Bryanite charge against monopoly that had always gladdened small employers who could least afford to pay union wages. Too obvious an embrace of the controversial CIO would have damaged Roosevelt's chances with a variety of social groups.[41]

In claiming to be the vanguard of the liberal forces, the CIO had to contend with the broader definition of *liberal* that was subscribed to by a chief executive who demonstrated his ability to muster a populist majority, albeit one that saw duty only at quadrennial elections. By the mid-1930s, Roosevelt and his speechwriters had resuscitated the liberal label, shed its individualist and libertarian connotations, and redefined it as the political courage to use the state to benefit average Americans. Liberals, explained FDR in 1938, "believed in the wisdom and efficacy of the will of the great majority of the people, as distinguished from the judgment of a small minority of either education or wealth."[42]

By the end of the decade, some CIO activists bewailed their lack of political autonomy. But, with a war in Europe and strong congressional opposition at home, most saw no alternative to depending on the president's reputation and power—and to fortifying the left wing of the Democratic Party. Although they continued to use *liberal* to mean an assemblage independent, if tactically supportive, of the New Deal, the distinction between labor's liberalism and FDR's was hard for anyone but political insiders to grasp. At the CIO's 1939 convention, Harry Bridges, leader of the West Coast longshoremen's union, hailed a great victory won by "all liberal, laboring, and progressive people." This was his way of introducing Governor Culbert Olson of California, a Democrat whom the state CIO had recently helped put into office.[43]

COMMUNISTS AND CATHOLICS

It was no secret that Harry Bridges's political judgments almost always agreed with those of the Communist Party. The tough, wisecracking Australian was one of hundreds of leaders and organizers in individual unions and the national CIO who followed the CP's line, whether or not they actually belonged to the party. Besides Bridges, the long list included Len DeCaux of the *CIO News,* the general counsel Lee Pressman, Henry Kraus and his fellow commanders of the Flint sit-down strike, the heads of the Electrical Workers (UE) and the National Maritime Union and the Transport Workers Union, and unsung activists in workplaces ranging from the forests of the Pacific Northwest to the halls of Congress. According to one scholar, "no less than 40 percent of the international unions" in the CIO were "either led by Communists and their close allies or significantly influenced by them." It was the CP's most cherished achievement, "the only thing . . . that brought them close to the reins of real power." And it probably surpassed the Socialist Party's strength in the AFL before World War I.[44]

Meanwhile, hundreds of Catholic priests and several bishops leaped into the industrial fray on the side of their working-class parishioners. In Buffalo, Father Charles A. Maxwell became spiritual adviser to steelworkers in the local SWOC; in Chicago, Auxiliary Bishop Bernard Sheil spoke to rallies of packinghouse workers and newspaper reporters and published a pro-CIO newspaper; in Pittsburgh, Father Charles Rice advised Philip Murray (the CIO vice president) and officials of the UE. Two new national groups—the Association of Catholic Trade Unionists (ACTU) and the Catholic Worker movement—and a scattering of parish "labor schools" promoted a brand of unionism in line with papal teachings.[45]

A faith in Christ and a loyalty to the Comintern were not reconcilable. But within the CIO, labor priests and labor Communists pursued a similar end: advocating a belief system that required obedience to an external, "alien" hierarchy. Both factions sought to persuade neutral unionists to lift their sights above the immediate task; both acted cautiously, knowing how fragile was the solidarity that made it possible for them to reach labor's new millions at all.[46]

The Communists were especially prudent. In the early '30s, the CP had waved the purist banner of revolution and vowed to build a "Soviet America." But, late in 1936, when the party sent its best cadre into the new CIO, it was already committed to the Popular Front—the epochal turn away from working-class insurrection and toward the broad, reformist coalitions with all "progressives" that the threat of fascism had forced on Communists throughout the world. In 1938, the CPUSA moved further in the same direction, inaugurating the Democratic Front, under whose rubric even "certain liberal sections of the bourgeoisie" were welcome. Rank-and-file Communists were now instructed to join FDR's party and/or local and state political groups (like New York's American Labor Party) allied with the Democrats. The CP lauded patriotic icons like Paine, Jefferson, Jackson, and Lincoln and swore allegiance to "the plain people" and their sturdy traditions of "farmer-labor democracy."[47]

Thus, Communists who worked inside the CIO attempted, for the most part, to mingle their language with that of the larger movement. They were typically more forthright in declaring their antiracist and antifascist principles. But that only propelled the CIO farther along the path it was already traveling, at least officially. In fact, CP members endeavored to make the new labor movement itself something of a popular front. They extended the celebration of tolerance in "Ballad for Americans" throughout the CIO; even devout Catholics were wooed (as long as they opposed Coughlinism).

In the *CIO News,* Len DeCaux kept his editorials and selection of articles scrupulously free of references to Soviet achievements or the deeds of American Communists. As director of publicity for the organization, he loyally adhered to the policies of his superior, John L. Lewis. When Phillip Murray took over as president in 1941, DeCaux, with some private misgivings, adopted the less confrontational tone toward labor's enemies that the new boss favored. "Lewis didn't interfere . . . Murray didn't interfere either," wrote DeCaux in his autobiography. His ideological self-discipline made it unnecessary.[48]

Away from CIO headquarters, individual Communists gained respect from rank and filers and won union elections by articulating a visceral resentment against specific employers, fighting for job security and higher wages, and making only the vaguest of allusions to any ultimate aims that went beyond industrial democracy and the fruits of Americanism. Louis Goldblatt, a CP member who was secretary-treasurer of the West Coast longshore union, described the approach: "I . . . discovered that those of us on the left have certain duties to perform. Among them is to learn the technique of doing 99 percent of the work and taking one percent of the credit." Across the country in Fulton County, New York, Communist leaders of a leather workers' local were so afraid to violate the political taboos of their members that they refused to allow the *Daily Worker* to be sold in their own union hall. According to a former activist there, workers knew "our union leaned a little to the left, but [their attitude was] 'I don't care what you do. You get for me. . . . But, in the same token, though, don't step on the American flag.'" John L. Lewis once told reporters he refused to turn his organizers upside down "to see what kind of literature falls from their pockets." If he had, little of it would have been emblazoned with the hammer and sickle.[49]

Despite later tactical shifts dictated by Moscow, the CP never switched back to regaling American workers with the glories of "the international proletariat" or "the class struggle." Competing groups on the Left—Socialists, Trotskyists, the IWW—accused the much larger CP of deserting its revolutionary principles. But, in so doing, they only burrowed further into the warrens of sectarianism. The triumph of populism, CIO style, as the rhetoric of the Left, was emphatic testimony that the idea of socialism had lost its appeal to all but a dwindling minority of wage earners in the United States. While the 1938 slogan "Communism Is Twentieth-Century Americanism" did not survive the decade, its spirit lived on as the quixotic fantasy of activists who craved acceptance from the same society they wanted to revolutionize. Those who lived inside the CP subculture remembered the Popular Front as the "sweetest bandwagon in history." They only wished it could have rolled on forever.[50]

Catholic clergy who worked inside the CIO also balanced self-protection with a loftier purpose. "A victory for labor in its struggles for decent conditions is a victory for Americanism and for Christianity," declared the Reverend Charles Rice in his benediction at the first CIO convention.[51] A plurality of CIO members in the late 1930s were Catholics. While they joined unions for secular reasons and knew little about the labor encyclicals, most no doubt felt more comfortable knowing the church smiled on their decision to adhere to an organization in which Marxists played an active part.

Catholic champions of industrial unionism simultaneously preached solidarity and a warning. On the one hand, they assured unionists—both leaders and rank and file—that social justice was fully compatible with social unionism. When Charles Coughlin and a mass of corporate publicists denounced individual CIO officials as "reds," labor priests counterattacked with populist vigor. "By this time we ought to be aware that certain interests in this country are trying to stop the progress of labor by smearing its leaders," remarked Bishop Robert Lucey of Amarillo in 1938. "Inspired by greed of gain and lust of power they will not tolerate the rise of strong labor unionism."[52]

On the other hand, for Lucey and his peers, a strong CIO could not mean one that deepened class hostilities. The clerics and laypersons who worked for industrial unionism agreed with Coughlin on the main point of papal teachings: Catholic social thought offered a middle way between the godless hell of communism and "modern" capitalism; it favored the security of private property *and* the need for labor to gain a greater share of the nation's wealth and power. Pius XI's vague blueprint for an industrial economy run jointly by groups of employers and workers was, the Reverend Dr. Hugh A. Donohoe, a professor of industrial ethics, told the CIO, "the only united front that the Church will recognize." But, the priest promised, "it will be a united front by human beings, seeking not the destruction of each other, but the cooperation of each other for their own and the general welfare."[53]

Donohoe's vision came no closer to being realized than did the rival one of a Soviet America. Priests who taught in the labor schools established by the Archdiocese of Detroit quickly discovered that the words of Leo XIII and Pius XI "were hard to translate into terms . . . immediately relevant to contemporary politics." Instead, they sought to assure workers that the church "was interested in their problems and helping them solve them."[54] But having their own plan for ultimate social justice enabled Catholic activists in the CIO to base their approval for working-class militancy on the traditional bedrock of charity and brotherhood.

CIO officials cautiously returned the Catholic embrace, cognizant of its power and its risks. Donohoe's words, taken from a scholarly if brisk address, received (according to the official account) "loud and sustained applause," a reception usually reserved for speeches by John L. Lewis or a favorite member of the New Deal cabinet like Henry Wallace. The CIO clearly liked to advertise its ties with the Church. The political imprimatur helped to blunt the sting of red-baiting attacks on labor, especially by foes with a pious reputation. At every national CIO convention from 1938 to 1946, the opening invocation was given by a priest or bishop from the host city. No Protestant or Jewish clergymen enjoyed anything like the prominence that such priests as Sheil, Rice, and Donohoe had as speakers at labor forums and writers for union publications.

But the benefits of pastoral support had to be weighed against the CIO's overriding commitment to a secular mode of persuasion. Only rarely did union spokesmen, of any faith, themselves cite the encyclicals or any other point of Catholic doctrine when speaking to general audiences. They were particularly wary of the corporatist vision, which, at least in outline, sounded both impractical and vaguely un-American. "I have read the encyclicals and I use them, too," John L. Lewis wrote to Bishop Lucey; "but I don't dare advocate workers' sharing in management just now. It would mean a great furor, and I would surely be put down as a Communist."[55]

When it came to religion, the CIO's approach was to refer, obliquely and blandly, to the plurality of beliefs held by ordinary Americans, thus stressing the democratic virtues they held in common. An official pamphlet on the subject concluded: "Once humanity becomes the measure of both organized religion and organized labor, we can push forward together toward the good life. . . . Both labor and religion put their faith in the people, believing in power *with* not *over* them." In local industries where Catholic workers predominated (such as New York City transit), internal union factions did, at times, fling the charge of "Christian renegade" at one another. In most venues, however, CIO rhetoric was more agnostic than spiritual. By inviting workers to mingle together under one roof where all creeds would be tolerated, movement spokesmen were, in effect, diminishing the significance of the passions that led to religious sectarianism. "We are against all forms of red-baiting, of Jew-baiting, of Catholic baiting, of alien-baiting," wrote Len DeCaux in a typical rebuke of Father Coughlin. "In this the CIO is a true Catholic organization—built upon the principles of equal treatment for all."[56]

FROM MASS MOVEMENT TO SPECIAL INTEREST

The same war that quickened Coughlin's political demise propelled the CIO into a symbiotic dependence on the liberal state. The fascist enemy represented the perfect antithesis of labor's popular front: it was avowedly racist and depised the power of liberal, independent unions. In the CIO's cartoon history of labor, a Nazi official informs a group of passive workers: "The German master race must be strong. So, no more nonsense about short hours and good pay. And you better not grumble!"[57] Only the eradication of these vermin from the planet would do.

But politicians and bureaucrats who were running the American war effort also needed industrial unions. Only strong, universally recognized organizations could discipline the millions of new workers streaming into aircraft plants, steel mills, and munitions factories and keep production at a high pitch. So, in return for a no-strike pledge, the War Labor Board required that a pro-union "maintenance-of-membership" clause be inserted in all military contracts, and the CIO doubled its numbers from 1939 to 1945—convincing some observers that the bad old industrial order was doomed. Under federal supervision (and notwithstanding persistent squabbles over many workplace issues), labor welcomed cooperation with "sophisticated" businessmen who had replaced the "Tory" exploiters of old.[58]

Important elements of the CIO's language in the 1930s had presaged this historic concord. The denial of radicalism and the ubiquity of patriotic symbolism, the pride in a movement that included all races and nationalities, and the boosting of (and participation in) the liberal coalition were easily converted into support for intervention and subsequent calls to use the heightened wartime powers of the federal state for social reform. Unlike AFL leaders, no CIO spokesman (with the partial exception of Lewis) had portrayed his movement as a supremely self-reliant force of workers whose main demand on government was that it get out of their way. Most industrial unionists wanted the state to shelter their organizations and adopt their ambitious legislative agenda. In effect, the CIO had always been a valued, if junior, member of the Democratic team. The Second World War just gave it better cards to play.

And John L. Lewis was no longer in charge. Although he had been an early and articulate opponent of fascism and anti-Semitism, the founding father of the CIO strongly opposed giving aid to the Allies after war broke out in 1939. During the following year's election campaign, he increasingly portrayed the interventionist FDR as a dangerous man whose prior good works had been but a clever means to augment an unprecedented degree of personal power. Lewis's indictment of militarism echoed that hurled by pacifists and socialists during World War I and also reflected the cynicism that gripped millions of Americans who contemplated another armed crusade for "democracy." "War has always been the device of the politically despairing and intellectually sterile statesmen," Lewis chided in a 1939 Labor Day broadcast. "It provides employment in the gun factories and begets enormous profits for those already rich. It kills off the vigorous males who, if permitted to live, might question the financial exploitation of the race." Judging from public opinion polls, Lewis's scorn for war—if not his cynical way of expressing it—was widely shared.[59]

A week before the 1940 election, the CIO leader again took to the airwaves to address the issue. By this time, the fall of France and the Battle of Britain had put isolationists on the defensive. But both the general public and the CIO rank and file remained divided and uneasy about where Roosevelt's foreign policy was leading. So Lewis could plausibly have believed his eloquence would help turn the tide.[60]

The speech some 30 million people heard Lewis broadcast on the evening of October 25 was a bitter denunciation of state tyranny, an attack on executive arrogance in the name of republican ideals. In a grim, almost weary voice, the CIO president declared: "America needs no superman . . . America wants no royal family. . . . Are we to yield to the appetite for power and the vaunting ambitions of a man who plays with the lives of human beings for a pastime?" Lewis went on to charge not just FDR but his entire party of being "in default to the American people" because, after seven years, they had not solved the problems of unemployment, hunger, increasing taxation, and a stagnant economy. The Democrats' only way out was to go to war. Roosevelt, lamented Lewis, "no longer hears the cries of the people."[61]

If he had stopped right there, Lewis would probably have retained his leadership of the CIO and even, after a hiatus, have reestablished a working relationship with the administration. But, in the last part of the speech, he endorsed Wendell Willkie and vowed to resign as CIO president if FDR won. That abruptly ended his days as a hero of prolabor liberals. Lewis's praise of the Republican nominee was campaign boilerplate, replete with abstract platform promises and devoid of any phrases that might convince the doubtful, inside or outside the labor movement, that the corporate attorney was preferable to FDR. Willkie, assured the labor leader, "is not an aristocrat. He has the common touch."

But Lewis's audience knew most bosses were Republicans, and a dab of demotic sympathy on Willkie's part could hardly compete with Roosevelt's eight years of verbal and legislative solidarity with the problems of working men and women. "We know you spoke from your heart and with conviction as you see it," cabled a UAW local to Lewis after the speech, "but . . . you are wrong in endorsing Willkie, a proven enemy in our own opinion, who would do nothing good for us. Despite Roosevelt's failures, he has done more for labor than any other past President." Even most of Lewis's miners condemned his decision. One UMW local called it "an insidious tirade"; while another promised FDR: "We shall never forget what you have done for us. We miners especially, have at last learned to live since you became a great leader of this wonderful country."[62]

The next week's election—in which Roosevelt won huge majorities in nearly every CIO precinct—revealed the limit of Lewis's rhetorical influence. Workers had cheered him as long as he was saying what they wanted to hear. But he could never hope to compete with *their* president. Lewis took his fall from national influence as an excuse to give his old bitterness against the meddling state full rein. After Pearl Harbor, he led his miners in several unpopular strikes against the War Labor Board's attempt to limit wage gains. The UMW chieftain sounded like a craft unionist of old as he blasted "the flamboyant theories of an idealistic economic philosophy" for ignoring "the facts of life in the mining homes of America." The fuzzy-minded scoundrels on high had to be taught a lesson.[63]

In contrast, Philip Murray, who succeeded Lewis as the head of the CIO, was quite content to operate inside the expanding federal umbrella. Although a longtime protégé of the UMW boss, Murray believed that labor's new status could be protected only by a permanent alliance with national Democrats and the emerging group of policy intellectuals who favored economic planning and a welfare state. This harmony between unions, the state, and liberal thinkers would result, he hoped, in "State-wide and nation-wide standards . . . to put a floor under even the best [union] contract terms." In contrast to Lewis's grandiloquent belligerence toward political and economic elites, Murray spoke simply about the need for unionists to be of "service" to America, to "stand loyally behind our President" who had helped the CIO stave off its corporate foes.

The Scottish-born Murray (of Irish parentage) had started mining coal at the age of 10, and he knew political goodwill alone could not organize industrial workers. But his soft burr, unadorned short sentences, and constant use of words like *duty, decency,* and *respect* made a disarming contrast with the fire-breathing thespian who had preceded him. Lewis indulged in a luxurious lifestyle—complete with fine antiques, expensive servants, and fancy tea parties—but Murray relaxed by returning to western Pennsylvania to chat with coal miners on their front porches. "It was

Murray's special quality," remembered Murray Kempton, "to touch the love and not the fears of men."[64]

Murray's temperament meshed with his religious convictions. The first Catholic since Terence Powderly to head a national labor federation, he hailed the celebrated encyclicals—at least in spirit. Strikes, agreed Murray, were but a necessary evil; a moral redesign of society that guaranteed workers a comfortable annual wage and a role in guiding the economy would make industrial strife all but obsolete. He endorsed the plans of John Ryan and other clerics to organize worker-employer councils with the power to run each industry. But Murray never let his spiritual principles dominate his political calculations.[65]

During the Second World War, the language of the national CIO gestured at a populist grand alliance that Murray and his associates—especially Sidney Hillman of the Amalgamated Clothing Workers—meant to augment after combat had ceased. At war-bond promotions, during election campaigns, and in their own press, CIO spokesmen fused three separate groups into one massive force that was waging a war to preserve and extend democratic rule: soldiers and partisans fighting fascism overseas, the Roosevelt administration, and progressive unionists at home together composed the common people. The world conflict, declared Murray in 1943, was a "people's war of national liberation" to achieve specific aims that each member of the trio held dear:

> We are fighting for the right of the people of every nation to be free, the right of the people to settle their own affairs and to choose their own government. We are fighting for the right of the common people to be free from want, free from fear, and their right to achieve security and to make a decent living. We are fighting for the right of the working men and women of all the countries to join labor unions of their own choosing so that through such democratic machinery they can in turn assure the continuation of democracy within their respective nations.[66]

Compared to the AFL's support for the First World War, Murray's statement was free of intimations that America's ideals were superior to those of other nations. This time, America's most visible labor official could unite with the Left (which, by 1943, chiefly meant the CP and its sizable aura) in loyally backing the commander-in-chief and praising his war aims—especially the visionary Four Freedoms. If anything, union officials wanted FDR to be more aggressive; in the last half of 1942, opening a Second Front in Western Europe was the demand of large, CIO-sponsored rallies in Chicago and New York. Wendell Willkie, Fiorello La Guardia, Charlie Chaplin, and Adam Clayton Powell, Jr., addressed the latter one in Manhattan. Thus, Gompers's counterposing of nationalist courage to internationalist passivity was reversed a quarter-century later. For the moment at least, the interests of Joe Stalin and Phil Murray were in synch.[67]

The many enemies of the CIO and its liberal allies did not let that fact go unnoticed. Overwhelming support for the war at home did nothing to silence the variety of voices complaining that "Big Government" was squashing individual freedoms and encouraging the left-wing chieftains of "Big Labor" to wield control over industry and disrupt stable patterns of ethnic and racial dominance. Critics sniped at such hated features of the new "tyranny" as automatic income tax witholding and the fact that a left-wing (and Jewish) actor like Melvyn Douglas was appointed to the Office of Civilian Defense. The New Deal–CIO alliance, writes the historian Steve Fraser, "seemed to embody everything . . . that offended the pieties and prejudices of Middle America: its gaudy cosmopolitanism, its 'Jewishness,' its flirtations with radicalism, its bureaucratic collectivism, its elevation of the new immigrant, its statism, its intellectual arrogance, and its racial egalitarianism." The strains of right-wing populism, intermittently strummed by the KKK in the 1920s and by Coughlin in the 1930s, were swelling again.[68]

And the political camp from which they emanated was getting stronger. After the midterm elections of 1938, the contours of a conservative bloc that would throttle most new social programs until the mid-1960s hardened into shape. Southern Democrats and big-city machines joined in loose coalition with Republican pols and inveterate anti-New Deal employer groups like the National Association of Manufacturers to halt and, on occasion, reverse programs the CIO and its supporters cared most deeply about. In the 1942 election, FDR's party, plagued by a light turnout, almost lost control of Congress. Its candidates for the House actually polled 1.3 million fewer votes than did the Republicans. Time and again, conservative lawmakers and employers bested the CIO in struggles over higher wages, sanctions against strikers, and the role of labor officials in regulating war production from inside the Washington beehive. Industrial unionists had become a legitimate presence in the economy and governing party of the most powerful nation on earth. But the construction of a larger people's movement that could serve both as buffer and umbrella for their aims was very much in jeopardy.

The new breed of labor patriots took a hard line against their domestic opponents. CIO spokesmen freely accused critics on Wall Street and Capitol Hill of caring more about preserving an unjust status quo than about winning the war. The thinnest of lines separated the myopic isolationist from the closet fascist. One 1942 cartoon in the *CIO News* suggested that the Nazi propaganda chief Joseph Goebbels had inspired an antilabor act by Congress. In the same vein, Harry Bridges snapped that there were "more [of] Hitler's agents per square foot in Congress than per square mile of Detroit." Union papers ran a popular series of cartoons called "The Upper Crust" that lampooned wealthy Americans for pursuing friviolous lives while workers toiled overtime to supply the armies of democracy. One drawing showed a haughty butler informing an impertinent caller that "Madam can't go on air raid warden duty unless they arrange her hours to fit in with [her poodle] Fifi's airing." While reactionaries schemed and the idle rich nattered, working Americans—civilians and soldiers together—were giving their blood and sweat to defeat the common enemy. The producer ethic had gone to war.[69]

But class-conscious bravado, however patriotic, was not enough to protect the citadel of a prolabor administration. It may, in fact, have alienated voters who identified with neither band of mudslingers. So, Murray's organization extended a gentler hand to "the common people." In the summer of 1943, the CIO set up its own electoral apparatus, the first Political Action Committee (PAC). Initiated and led by Sidney Hillman, the PAC mobilized a legion of union staffers to register voters, canvass working-class precincts, and convince potential Democratic voters that the CIO's agenda was really a "people's program" that could speed military victory and bring about sustained prosperity at high wages.

The PAC was the most ambitious political intervention the labor movement had ever attempted. Together with the middle-class National Citizens PAC created in early 1944, it aimed not just to ensure FDR's re-election but to signal that grassroots liberalism could halt the momentum of the resurgent Right and touch off a new era of social reform in which every American would find a good job in a well-planned economy.

To this end, the PAC's publicity division produced a variety of slick leaflets, pamphlets, and broadcast scripts targeted, in the pluralist mode, to discrete audiences: college students, Catholics, Negroes, Protestants, women, soldiers, even German-Americans. A "Radio Handbook" carefully demystified the secrets of radio discourse, advising a union member to talk as if "he were leaning over the back fence on a Sunday afternoon" and to "type your speech on paper that does not rattle." Overseeing the crafting of this literature was the publicity director Joseph Gaer, a Jewish immigrant from Russia who, in the mid-1930s, had interrupted his studies of history and folklore to write and edit for a series of New Deal agencies. Gaer and his assistants, many of whom were sympathetic to the CP, put forward an appeal that combined tropes of sunny, wartime consensus with energetic representations of a better world in birth.[70]

"This Is Your America" was the title of the PAC's widely distributed introductory pamphlet. Superimposed over the photo of a small farm on a gently rolling hill with cows grazing behind a picket fence, those four words were meant as a declaration and a promise. The PAC's program would enable "the Common Man of this earth" to realize his dreams. Appropriately, those dreams were framed in military terms: "the labor front," "the social security front," "the farm front," and "the conservation front." And like an efficient army, its watchwords were "planning" and "the full employment" of men and resources. One illustration compared men in suits studying the model of a new factory with generals pointing to the mock-up of an impending battle. From the Constitution, the PAC plucked a phrase that summed up its purpose. The organization "is not for workers alone but for all the common people. It is for all the people who strive to create 'a more perfect union.'"[71]

Despite its pluralist trappings, the PAC's conception of "the people" was more that of a social planner than a workplace organizer. Its publications were dotted with photos of generic wage earners with smiling, weather-beaten faces and artfully simple line drawings of cheery or expressionless men, women, and children going about the routines of daily life. Each representation gestured at an undifferentiated mass whose lot liberal policies would certainly improve. Except for a rare sketch of Hillman, Murray, or FDR, no recognizable individual appeared in any PAC publication. It was as if Gaer and company felt their core constituents looked too ethnic or radical to feature them during a pivotal election campaign in which the outcome was very much in doubt. So bland depictions of a sanitized mass public largely replaced the exuberant Jewish, Polish, Irish, and black working-class individuals who had crowded CIO materials in the late 1930s.[72]

Accompanying the visual earnestness was a sense of purpose that strained to be inoffensive instead of drawing clear ideological battle lines. "How can you tell an American?" asked the pamphlet with the bucolic cover. "He or she is an American who lives in the United States, or any of its possessions, and who believes in our way of life, which is the Democratic Way." Central to that way were such elements as "freedom of speech," "the right of every man and woman to vote," and "majority rule." The only un-American characteristic mentioned was *"to see what is wrong and not to help right it."* The PAC even addressed the maldistribution of wealth, the shared grievance of nearly every grassroots movement a decade earlier, as a matter of passively voiced principle rather than a clash of interests. "Our present economic system can be made to work," the pamphlet claimed reassuringly, "provided it is made to work *for the benefit of all.* Free Enterprise must therefore be understood as freedom of opportunity, and not freedom to waste the nation's resources and manpower to satisfy the avarice of a few."[73]

Roosevelt did win in 1944, and his victory seemed to establish CIO-PAC as a kind of national machine, able and willing to help its friends and punish its enemies on a scale previous labor activists had only imagined. Republicans had waged a vicious campaign to prevent this. They called into question both Hillman's patriotism and the PAC's self-image as the weapon of the American many. One 1944 assault on the Russian-born Hillman linked together financial policy and revolution in language reminiscent of Father Coughlin's: "He went back where he came from and returned a Communist and began injecting Communism into the labor unions of this country. . . . His idea—their idea—is to sink this country into debt so deep it will bankrupt it and then step in . . . and offer us a new form of government." Once the votes were counted, the PAC chairman could gloat, "Our opponents attempted to isolate us, to cut us off from the main body of the American people. . . . They failed because we did not pursue a narrow or selfish course. Our program was not a program for labor alone."[74]

PAC literature urged every member of the Roosevelt coalition to view the campaign as a shared wartime endeavor as well as one that would benefit each particular interest group. But what the PAC gained in breadth, it lost in forceful conviction. The literature lacked the exuberance, the specificity of detail, and the brash confidence that mark the language of a movement on the rise. The myth of a sanguine, united mass took the place of the image of a gritty insurgency of the people inspired and guided by wage earners. As the radical sociologist C. Wright Mills noted, labor's liberal rhetoric, which produced only a Pyrrhic victory, was "banalized" for the purposes of winning the election and, later, getting along with Congress and enlightened businessmen.[75] Though it helped boost the labor vote in a few key states, the PAC appealed mostly to the converted. It did nothing to allay the fears of a growing number of Americans that organized labor had become a too-powerful "special interest," part of a new liberal establishment whose concerns often diverged from theirs.

After the war ended, this suspicion seemed to grow, even though industrial unionists did their best to deny they had any privileged claims on the nation. During the UAW's long strike against General Motors in 1946 (the biggest of several major work stoppages that year), Walter Reuther demanded that the giant company open its books to prove it could not afford a wage increase without raising the price of its cars. His union was no "narrow, economic pressure group," he said; instead, it wanted "to make progress with the community and not at the expense of the community." Most voters still resented the huge strikes and, that fall, elected the first Republican Congress since the 1920s to solve what newspapers called "the labor troubles," among other postwar woes.[76] Lawmakers soon passed the Taft-Hartley Act, which invaded the internal affairs of unions and curbed their ability to organize new members.

In 1948, the CIO responded with its own version of President Harry Truman's feisty revival of economic populism and helped defeat the stiff, prosecutorial Thomas Dewey. "The simple issue," Philip Murray told a Pittsburgh crowd during the campaign, was "we don't want our government under the control of bankers and corporate interests." But, in 1950, Ohio labor, spearheaded by CIO-PAC, devoted its full attention to defeating the re-election bid of its archenemy, Senator Robert Taft—and lost, by almost a half-million votes. The Republican incumbent, blessed with a lackluster opponent, even scored well among union members who explained, "we didn't want labor to go too far" and "we didn't want labor running the country."[77]

By the late 1940s, the CIO and the liberals who defended it faced a rhetorical dilemma that helped thwart the augured shift to a more "laboristic" America. Asserting the need for organized workers to strike for their rights and economic security had provoked a backlash among citizens who longed for domestic peace after four years of international war. Yet appealing in innocuous, consensual terms to the "common people" sapped labor's ability to harness discontented Americans outside its own ranks or, for that matter, within them. In the desire to cooperate with big employers and to identify their aims with those of Democratic politicians, labor spokesmen abandoned the witty, bold images of flag-waving factory hands who could "talk to anyone you want about anything you like" that John L. Lewis and his admirers had evoked so effectively when the CIO was young and very definitely a movement.

The priority now was to be responsible—to speak the language of partnership, negotiation, and the law. The struggling vessel of "industrial democracy" sailed into an agreeable port labeled "collective bargaining." The boss became "management" and "grievance" the universal term for any form of worker discontent. The multiyear contracts that CIO unions signed with GM, U.S. Steel, and other major corporations were lengthy, complex documents designed to minimize strikes and ensure that employers would control the work process—while guaranteeing members a more generous level of pay and benefits than they had ever enjoyed. With dim prospects for the revival of a broader people's movement, officials became absorbed with a sphere they could control and let their attorneys work out the details. In the late '40s, a bill that would have provided national health insurance failed to pass Congress, in part because unions did not mobilize workers to campaign for it. When CIO publicists claimed that Taft-Hartley was a "slave labor law," even most rank and filers didn't take them seriously.[78]

Soon after the war, thanks to strong unions and the politicians they supported, millions of blue-collar Americans (especially those with white skin) began to experience a new prosperity that enabled them to buy new homes and cars—and to gripe at paying the federal income taxes now, for the first time, required of all but the poorest citizens. Slovak-Americans working in Pennsylvania steel mills, Finns on the docks of San Francisco Bay, and Poles in the slaughterhouses of Chicago were no longer at the mercy of any barking foreman or dictatorial manager. Grateful for union protection, they could now leave the marching and sloganeering to others. So labor's success was also its failure. Perhaps inevitably, it dissipated the insurgent spirit, the will to take risks and to make short-term sacrifices, upon which the growth of any social movement depends.[79]

Big changes in American society were also undermining labor's base. Just as industrial unionism came of age and ended the bad old days of shop-floor autocracy, the manufacturing workforce itself began a slow but relentless decline. And employers in the growing Sunbelt and white-collar firms everywhere were determined to block unions. But a reckoning was delayed until the 1970s, when the postwar boom ended.

World War II was the last time that the men and women of organized labor could realistically imagine themselves to be combative and optimistic representatives of the ordinary people as a whole. The rhetoric of class had always been bound up with indignities suffered at work—with "aristocratic" employers and their "slave-driving" ways. For antebellum artisans, Knights of Labor, the "average men" of the AFL, and the patriotic plebeians of the early CIO, life on the job was a microcosm of American society. The fight for democracy, equality, and decent compensation there mirrored and fostered the larger quest for an order free of high-handed monopolies and the privileged characters who ran them.

That conviction also lay at the core of a producer ethic whose appeal was never limited to wage earners. From Greenbackers to Coughlinites, activists who championed the interests of small farmers, shopkeepers, and homemakers agreed with the precept that power should be wielded at least as much by those who create wealth as by those who possess it. If the majority of Americans shared little else, they shared the experience of work—difficult, long, anonymous labor for, at best, a moderate reward. And that ordeal made them eternally suspicious of "big men" in corporate offices who held the whip of money and influence over people whose hands, wits, and small pieces of property produced everything the country really needed.

The CIO was the last mass insurgency on the Left to stress the centrality of work to any notion of a democratic polity. When, for compelling reasons, the industrial-labor movement embraced the new liberal order and got enmeshed in the coils of bureaucratic responsibility, there was no other force to carry on the tradition. The American Left, stretching from CP loyalists to progressive Democrats like Adlai Stevenson, never recovered from that lost grounding in the lives and language of ordinary Americans. Gradually, after the war, most liberals and radicals abandoned faith in the desire and capacity of "the people"—still mostly white and now securely, if not happily, employed—to endorse their political agenda. "The burden-bearing classes" Jacksonians had saluted a century before would soon attract some unfamiliar champions.

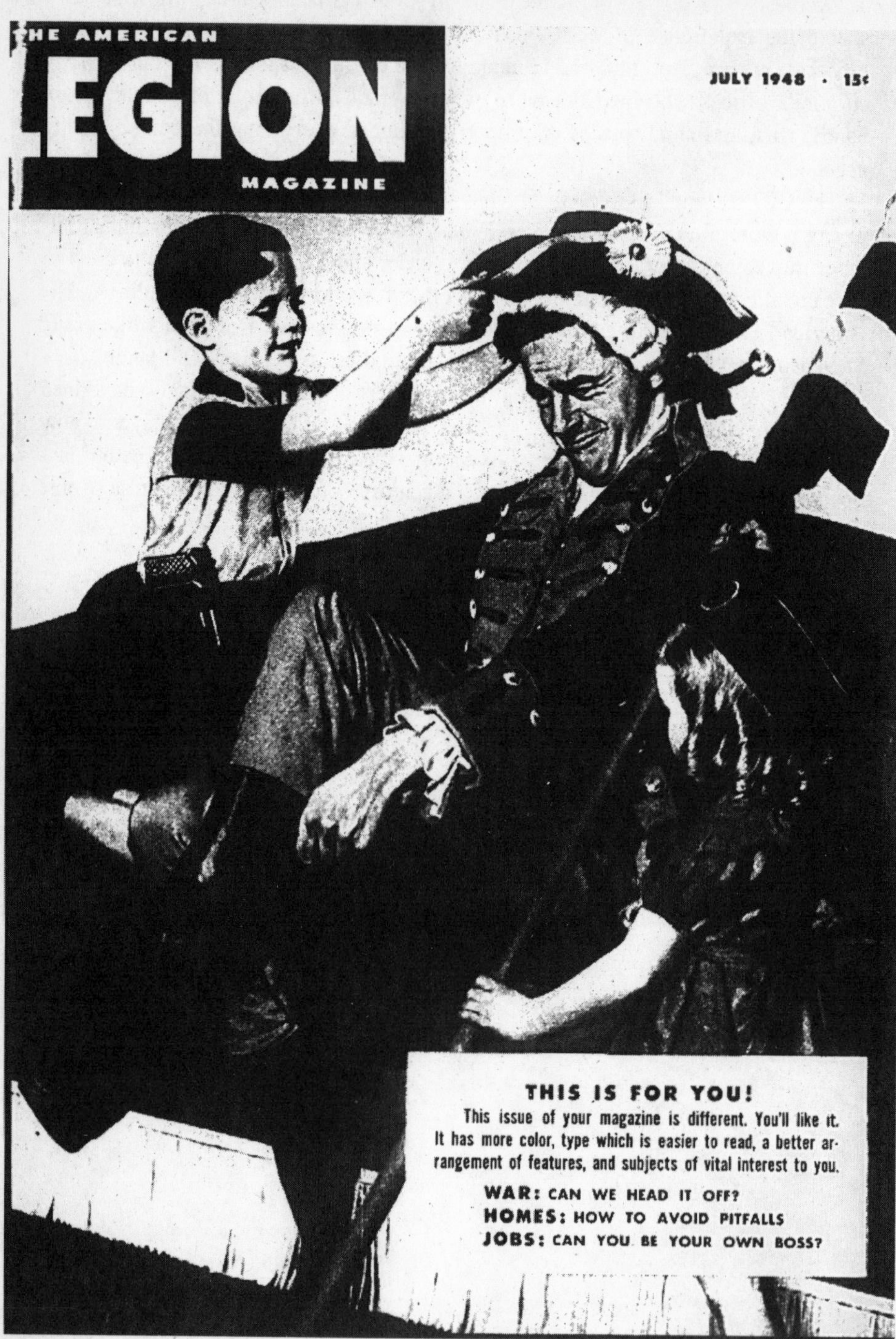

Patriot Dad, 1948. *(Courtesy of* American Legion Magazine *and the Library of Congress)*

Chapter 7

A Free People Fight Back: The Rise and Fall of the Cold War Right

The common man . . . can grasp the idea of treason without reading about it in a book, and he values his citizenship in a free country enough to fight for it.

—James Rorty, 1950

A farm boy learns early in life that the smelliest jobs are the ones that sometimes the nice *little boys don't do.*

—Senator Joseph McCarthy, 1953

Nobody loves McCarthy but the People.

—Anti-Communist song, c. 1954–55

Was not populism the forerunner of "grass roots" democracy? Did it not seek to subject the government to the people's will, to tumble the mighty from their high seats, to turn legislators into registrants of the people's will. . . . Did not populism allege to protect the people and their government from . . . cells of conspirators who, contrary to the people's will and through the complacency or collusion of their rulers, were enabled to gain control of society?

—Edward Shils, 1956

THE POWER OF UN-AMERICANS

UNTIL the 1940s, conservative populism was an oxymoron. From the Gilded Age through the Great Depression, the hallmark of mainstream conservatism had been its support for unregulated capitalism and of private riches honestly obtained. For Americans who cherished property rights and the maintenance of public order, rebellions from below were to be feared, discouraged, and, if necessary, put down by force.[1] Sensational foes of modernist culture such as the Ku Klux Klan of the 1920s and Father Coughlin in the late 1930s did attempt to stir up the pious masses against an elite they accused of having un-Christian designs on the nation. But neither sought to preserve the economic status quo. And their bigoted language reaped a whirlwind of notoriety that landed them in the province of the "lunatic fringe"—from which no movement has ever escaped to regain national influence.

But the Cold War and the diffusion of irreligious mass culture gave conservatives a historic opportunity to marry two impulses that had seldom been joined: the critique, memorably voiced by Andrew Jackson, of high government officials who secretly abet their foreign friends and the evangelicals' persistent horror of moral anarchy fostered by a cosmopolitan elite. A new Right battened on these dual suspicions—of the spread of secular decadence and of great federal power in the hands of liberals.

This mode of populism had little to say to Americans whose discontent stemmed from other causes—the economy and race relations in particular. Despite strenuous efforts, conservatives were unable to shake the specter of Herbert Hoover or to defeat their adversaries in both major parties. But they did scare them, profoundly, and they charted the main course the American Right would follow for the next two decades.

Fed by constant tensions with the Soviet bloc, the anti-Communist movement was certainly broader and more varied in the decade following World War II than in the late 1930s. Conservative red-hunters now sprang from both Protestant and Catholic churches, veterans' groups, middle-class neighborhood and professional organizations, and the Republican Party. Activists belonged to bodies as well established as the American Legion and Knights of Columbus and as obscure as the Friends of Frank Fay Committee, which filled Madison Square Garden in 1946 to support an actor whose trade union had censured him for making charges of subversion against some fellow thespians.[2]

Fear provided the crucial adhesive. In Eastern Europe, China, Southeast Asia, and in the nuclear laboratories of the Soviet Union, the "reds" were making alarming gains. This could not happen, many conservatives charged, unless some of America's most powerful and privileged had lent a hand.

During the Depression, opponents of the New Deal had argued that the interventionist state—directed by liberal planners and allied with industrial unions—was a giant step toward socialist dictatorship. In 1941, Father Coughlin wrote: "Too many of us do not realize that the Marxists' greatest victory, to date, has been won not in Europe nor in Asia but at the city of Washington, D.C."[3] Although FDR's wartime leadership enabled his followers to discount them, such accusations surfaced again in the 1944 election.

Linked to the Soviet menace, however, the sins of the new establishment—from the advocacy of national health insurance (called *socialized medicine*) to the patronage of abstract art (created, according to the Republican Congressman George Dondero, by a "horde of foreign art manglers")—seemed to imperil the very survival of an independent, God-fearing America. Conservatives viewed with scorn the many liberal Democrats who now agreed that the USSR must be "contained." Why had these equivocators taken so long to draw the line? Why did they still refuse to take responsibility for the nation's slow descent into a statist hell?[4]

The new conservatives took more adept positions than had their prewar counterparts who often sounded like fascists or social Darwinists. Conservatives were now largely free of some bad habits that had crippled haters of FDR—whether populist figures like Coughlin or the corporate executives of the Liberty League, whom the epithet "economic royalist" fit like a handmade suit. Most had ceased blaming Jews (or, for that matter, international bankers) for the rise of communism and tried to forge a united front of religious Americans from all Western faiths.[5] They stopped talking about the Constitution as if it sanctified laissez-faire, and they even acknowledged that some limited federal measures were necessary to alleviate poverty. And they hinted at the middling nature of their putative constituency: small home owners and tax payers with steady jobs.

Conservatives of this new breed had clearly learned something from their political adversaries. Tutored by repentant ex-Leftists, they adapted majoritarian images once associated with industrial labor and the New Deal. Right-wing portraits of plainspeaking, clean-living patriots from a variety of ethnic backgrounds resembled similar ones CIO-PAC had designed during World War II—with the critical omission of wage earners in the foreground while African-Americans were barely visible.

Conservatives were now fixed on a domestic foe that resembled, at least superficially, hoarders of concentrated wealth during the Great Depression: well heeled and well educated, arrogant and secretive, this enemy engaged in deeds that would undermine the system of democratic rule. From the late 1930s through the war, liberals had charged that isolationists and labor-bashers were lackeys, willing or not, of fascism. Now, the Right returned the barbs of this "Brown Scare" with its own talk of an "underground elite" filled with secret reds and their dupes—some of whom were even wealthy employers who "always pick up the fat checks in the 'right' places."[6]

Conservatives thus found in the storehouse of populist language a potent weapon for their anti-statist crusade. A conspiratorial elite organized both inside government and in the wider culture was forcing Americans into a regimented system that would destroy their livelihoods and tear down their values. The power of big business, implied the Right, looked puny compared to that of the new leviathan. Liberal intellectuals from the booming universities allegedly hatched the dangerous ideas, and wealthy celebrities from radio and screen shrewdly translated those into alluring images. A free people had to fight back or lose its freedom altogether.[7]

This was quite a departure. For the first time in United States history, large numbers of activists and politicians were employing a populist vocabulary to *oppose* social reform instead of support it. They even cheered the FBI for serving the cause and aided its investigations whenever possible. The Anti-Saloon League and the Coughlinites had sounded conservative themes of a moral nature. But universal prohibition and the nationalization of banking were hardly defenses of the status quo. In contrast, few red hunters advocated any political reforms other than the extirpation of a grandiose, alien growth. The only serious problem they wanted the state to solve was its own subversion by "un-Americans."[8]

Such a limited agenda seemed appropriate for the late 1940s and early 1950s. With labor spokesmen nurturing their hard-won legitimacy, the traditional contest between "producers" and "parasites" was diluted of its old force. No new domestic conflict had yet taken its place. Social scientists probing for class consciousness among American wage earners found a good deal of dissatisfaction with the content of blue-collar jobs but little belief that class position was either the cause of the problems or the basis for a solution. Most workers, thankful for secure employment at better wages, now described themselves as part of the great American middle class.[9] Such terms as *regular guy, average Joe,* and *average American,* evoking an agreeable personality rather than a political opinion, eclipsed ones like *working man* and *Joe Worker* that suggested a more biting distinction.

Wealthy individuals still aroused their share of suspicion, of course. But major corporations now had a dual identity: they were efficient dispensers of technological wonders for work and pleasure as well as profit-hungry behemoths. Wherever one looked in the national media—especially on television—the white middle-class consumer (of both sexes) was depicted as the generic American. Working people—their polyglot reality intact—did not blindly submit to this marketing strategy. But its tone of smothering optimism inspired rebellions of cultural taste (by both conservatives and rock and rollers) instead of class-conscious indignation.[10]

The Right also benefited from an upsurge in religious feeling and church membership. Polls taken in the late '40s found that about nine-tenths of all Americans believed in God, viewed the Bible as His "revealed word," and prayed regularly. Church membership in the 1950s—roughly two-thirds of the population—was the highest ever recorded in the twentieth century. To affirm their faith, devout Catholics and Protestants both routinely mounted street rallies and created a variety of radio and television programs; the young Billy Graham rapidly became—with an initial push from the Hearst press and a love affair with the camera—the most popular evangelist since the heyday of Billy Sunday. Doctrinal sniping across the Catholic-Protestant boundary also decreased. And broad acceptance of a newly named "Judeo-Christian" tradition helped inoculate Americans against a fresh outbreak of anti-Semitism. As in the nineteenth century, religiosity and patriotism seemed indivisible. In Washington, D.C., a well-known Protestant minister called an American atheist "a contradiction in terms."[11]

The claim that one people under God was waging a momentous struggle against the reds, both at home and abroad, flowed naturally from this environment. Since the Bolshevik Revolution, American conservatives of all faiths had linked communism with secular thought and modernist culture. Now, they could counterpose their own ringing loyalty to God and country with the perfunctory, often defensive statements made by members of a liberal "establishment" whose beliefs, it was charged, weakened the nation's resolve. In their aims and constituency, the red hunters were quite different from the militant prohibitionists whose cause was lost for good. But their call for an uprising to drive a God-denying elite of un-Americans from power belonged to that same revivalistic tradition.

A COMMUNITY AT WAR

The Right's image of the good people it wanted to save was abstract in all but moralist fervor. The American majority was portrayed as a devout, modest, productive bloc under siege. Conservative anti-Communists did not exclude blacks and other Americans not of European background; they simply assumed everyone on their side lived and thought as did pious whites of the middling classes.

Central to describing this "people" was the newly popular concept of "community." By mid-century, the term evoked universal contentment—murmuring as it did about relationships more voluntary, informal, and emotionally compelling than ones experienced through the state or in the larger society. Although that meaning dated from the nineteenth century and was common among academic writers (especially sociologists), no insurgent movement until the 1940s had prized the word. Activists who spoke for "Christians," "producers," "working people," and "ordinary Americans" had taken a certain residential and psychic rootedness for granted.[12]

But the social upheavals of wartime and, in their wake, the blooming of automobile suburbs with their luxuriant forests of television antennae provoked intellectuals to analyze the connections being lost. In the early 1950s, the conservative philosopher Robert Nisbet thought it "ominous" that so many Americans longed for the type of "community" that rampant "individualism and secularism" had methodically destroyed. Perhaps, he feared, they would reach for the "sense of moral coherence and communal membership" a Marxist party could offer. Nisbet did not ask people fleeing small towns and ethnic ghettos for new subdivisions if they felt a similar craving. Perhaps, community was a cherished value only when transfigured by memory.[13]

Activists on the Right, however, talked as if the orderly, virtuous communities of old had largely survived; with a fresh prosperity, they remained the spiritual bedrock of the nation and the popular base of its redemption. Carpenters and pharmacists, priests and ministers, veterans and housewives alike were cheered for engaging in "community action" to purge "reds" from top positions in labor, government, the media, entertainment, and education where they were imperiling the national interest.

Yet conservative anti-Communists did worry that ordinary Americans were too complacent; flush with new homes, cars, and televisions, most lacked the spontaneous indignation toward a powerful foe on which any grassroots movement depends. While supporting the exposure and banishment of traitors, the public did not appreciate the extent of the problem and the ways that well-placed figures caused and exacerbated it. As one ex-Communist turned FBI informer wrote: "Mr. and Mrs. Average American simply live so far from mental imprisonment like that of the Reds that they cannot conceive of its existence here." Members of the enemy elite, it was argued, hid their true purposes behind seductive ideas like "free speech" and "disarmament." So the red hunters made language itself a key battleground between "the plain people" and their adversaries.[14]

"Mr. and Mrs. Average American" were addressed as members of a community still at war—now against *red* fascists. Many anti-Communist writers, like speakers for the Anti-Saloon League forty years before, employed a tough, colloquial vocabulary fit for soldiers who needed to wake up the apathetic civilians in their midst. The enemy were "pinkos," "reds," "Commies," and "crypto-Commies" who used any weapon from slander to murder to get their way. In 1948, a group of "real Americans" published in a Hollywood trade paper a "Memo to a Bunch of Suckers" who had signed petitions in support of civil liberties. Calling this behavior "fronting and stooging" for Communists, the advertisement jeered, "Give them the shelter of the Constitution, so they can roll it up and stuff it down your throats when the moment pleases them."[15]

Slang was an obvious boon to headline- and scriptwriters. Tabloids like the *New York Daily News* and vituperative columnists like Westbrook Pegler also fed working-class readers a steady diet of muscular lingo crafted to resemble remarks that might have been overheard at a waterfront tavern or lifted from one of Mickey Spillane's best-selling novels about a he-man private eye who enjoys killing "Commies . . . in cold blood."[16]

But the punchy style signified a larger political purpose: the refusal to dignify a ruthless opponent by actually engaging his arguments about capitalism, socialism, and racial inequality. Trench warfare of the mind seemed to require a sharp, pain-inducing prose to cut through the soothing phrases about "peace" and "human rights" found in both Stalinist propaganda and the homilies of liberalism. In 1952, Richard M. Nixon, then a candidate for vice president, scorned mere "nicey-nice little powder-puff duel[s]" with the enemy. Those who were "soft" on communism were leaving the nation defenseless before a "clever, relentlessly thrusting force."[17]

A dread of effeminancy shivers through such phrases. *Real* men were not fooled by sweetly romantic visions of a better world. Neither did they shrink from ripping the lid off government to expose the subversives inside. Intent upon defending true manhood, conservative journalists and politicians often spied a connection between communism and homosexuality. Just before the 1950 election, a columnist for the *Daily News* named John O'Donnell wrote that "the primary issue" was "that the foreign policy of the U.S. . . . was dominated by an all-powerful, super-secret, inner circle of highly educated, socially highly placed sexual misfits in the State Department, all easy to blackmail, all susceptible to blandishments by homosexuals in foreign nations." Billy Graham hailed congressmen who revealed "the pinks, the lavenders, and the reds who have sought refuge beneath the wings of the American eagle."[18] Sexual perversion was a form of weakness the patriotic community could not tolerate.

INTELLECTUALS

Despite the Right's mistrust of professional thinkers as inveterate "softies" and liberals, it was a new group of intellectuals that catalyzed the making of a new conservatism. Three streams of thought flowed into a common pool of opinion. Ex-Marxists like James Burnham, Whittaker Chambers, Max Eastman, Will Herberg, Wilmoore Kendall, Eugene Lyons, and James Rorty agreed with such young conservatives as Brent Bozell, William F. Buckley, Jr., and Russell Kirk, and such veteran foes of statism as Frank Chodorov, John T. Flynn, and Suzanne La Follette that communism and socialism—both as doctrine and practice—were the antitheses of self-governing communities and traditional liberties. A new establishment, claimed these intellectuals, had gradually taken hold of America's institutions and was running them in a manner as haughty and inimical to the interests of most citizens as had the robber barons of old.

Conservatives launched new journals of opinion to disseminate their beliefs. *Plain Talk, The Freeman, Human Events,* and the *National Review* were aggressive, often witty periodicals written and edited by men and women who courted the public at large. Together, they alerted a few thousand readers that the battle of ideas would no longer be ceded to liberals and the Left. And viewpoints first aired in the small-circulation journals spawned numbers of articles in popular periodicals like the *Reader's Digest* and *American Legion Magazine.* Critical of the leftward leanings of most academics, intellectuals on the Right wrote an arresting prose that any high school graduate could understand.

Not all these thinkers and journalists were of the same mind on key issues. Libertarians like Chodorov, who opposed a militarized state, clashed with ex-radicals like James Burnham, who argued that a third world war had already begun, a war in which the United States must either liberate "captive nations" (through propaganda and armed intervention) or risk its own destruction. The Yale professor Wilmoore Kendall, who worshiped majority rule, quarreled with the unabashed elitist Russell Kirk, who inveighed against "uniformity" and "economic leveling." But all shared a mission: to loosen the grip of liberal, secular opinions over American politics and culture and to invigorate a new conservatism free from the ghosts of the Great Depression.[19]

It was Kendall, a little-known political scientist, who taught key thinkers on the Right to identify their cause as that of the always-virtuous American majority. An erstwhile Trotskyist from Oklahoma who was the son of a blind, itinerant preacher, Kendall argued that a true democrat must be willing, even eager, to enforce the beliefs of the "community." In the 1930s, this meant suppressing the rights of

Nazis; a decade later, it meant banning all Communist activity and even deporting leftists if they continued to promote their noxious cause.

Kendall's praise of "public orthodoxy" and his brilliant, idiosyncratic style strongly influenced many thinkers on the Right, particularly two men who had been his students at Yale, William F. Buckley, Jr., and Brent Bozell. The conviction that liberals were, as Kendall later put it, "a small minority in the American community" gave the young duo the confidence to defend Senator Joseph McCarthy as a hero whose enemies in the press and government did not represent the sentiments of the public. And much of the editorial fire in Buckley's *National Review* stemmed from a zeal to challenge not just the hegemony of liberal thought but that of a liberal "establishment" that had lost touch with the American mainstream.[20]

Among the most vigorous and widely read exponents of the new right-wing appeal was John T. Flynn, a writer today forgotten by all but a handful of scholars. In the late 1940s, Flynn wrote two best-selling books and many articles in the *Reader's Digest* that set forth the anti-Washington message in blunt prose stuffed with details about wasted funds and bungled programs. The Tennessee Valley Authority (TVA), he wrote, while its aims were laudable, was "soaking the taxpayers" as much as private utilities were "soaking the customers"; its "blather" aside, the "Government" (he always capitalized the word) had no intention of lowering the cost of homes to a price that "the self-respecting citizen . . . who doesn't want to become a public charge" could afford. At the top, men Flynn labeled "National Socialist Planners" (to exploit memories of the recent war), hidden from public view, were busily substituting worship of the state for "the American system." In the tradition of Tom Watson and the Anti-Saloon League's Purley Baker, the writer meant to alarm, educate, and mobilize his readers all at the same time.[21]

Flynn's popularity as a polemicist was due, in part, to his skill at recycling concepts he had once employed as a *left*-wing populist during the Depression. In the 1930s, he had been a prolific scourge of financial speculators. A regular columnist for both the Scripps-Howard Syndicate ("Plain Economics") and *The New Republic* ("Other People's Money") and the author of several books with titles like *Graft in Business,* he demanded that the government assure workers and small businessmen a fair chance to hold their own against the major corporations.

But Flynn soon turned against the New Deal. He condemned the National Recovery Administration as a "scheme" the Chamber of Commerce had long desired, and, in 1936, supported the Socialist Norman Thomas for president. By the end of the decade, Flynn's hatred of big government led him into the America First Committee, for whom he gave speeches reminiscent of those given by radical opponents of World War I. If Americans marched off to war again, Flynn predicted in 1940, "the Big Shots of the nation and towns, the politicians, and the generals will be in the reviewing stands, exhibiting themselves, wallowing in the acclaim of the troops and the cheers of the people. But . . . the dying will be done by the boys who parade. And they will die in the fog and smoke of battle, in the stench, the filth, the terrors and the obscenities of the fight upon distant fields in Europe or Asia."[22]

After the war, this visceral suspicion of the governing elite allowed Flynn to update his enemies list without departing too much from his original script. The victories of Communists and social-democrats after World War II simply allowed him to draw a more frightening image of a state run amuck. The most influential statement of his views was *The Road Ahead: America's Creeping Revolution,* a short volume that sold over two million copies in 1949, four million more in a condensed version published in the *Reader's Digest,* and was widely distributed by the Republican Party during the midterm campaign of 1950. Enthusiastic reviews in the right-wing press highlighted Flynn's muckraking method. As the *New York Daily News* put it: "This book names names, rips off disguises, exposes many a fake lover of the people, and cites chapter and verse. Better read this book. They're after you and they're playing for keeps."[23]

The premise of *The Road Ahead* was that liberal Democrats owed their faith to England's Fabian Society, the band of genteel socialists founded at the turn of the century whose proposals for a welfare state the current Labour government was busy implementing. Their rule, warned Flynn in the type of language he had once trained on Wall Street, was a more insidious form of tyranny than the Kremlin engineered and a far greater threat to American liberties than pro-Soviet regimes in the Third World (in fact, he would later criticize the United States' intervention in Korea and Indochina). Flynn used metaphors like "sneak attack," "hooded Socialism," "slow poison," and "assassination" to link the liberal establishment to such loathsome (and moribund) forces as the Japanese military and the KKK. Disgusted by "compromising leaders," Flynn concluded that only a new mass movement could defeat the collectivist "revolution" at home. "We cannot depend on any political party to save us," he wrote. "We must build a power outside the parties so strong that the parties will be compelled to yield to its demands. . . . We must begin to dismantle the tyrant State in America and to build up once again the energies of a free people."[24]

By sandwiching Flynn's exhortations between homespun features like "My Most Unforgettable Character" and "Seed Catalogue Contagion," *Digest* editors presented an ideal of decent, unassuming folk at odds with the sophisticated urban liberals—in and out of government—who would take their money and control their minds. Liberal "eggheads" like Adlai Stevenson viewed the masses as easily sated and hoodwinked; conservatives like Kendall and Flynn viewed them as America's salvation.[25]

CATHOLICS

It was no coincidence that a good many of the new right-wing intellectuals were pious Roman Catholics. Whether born to the faith like Flynn and Buckley or converts like Kendall and Bozell, they found in the church a majestic, stable, fully realized ideological alternative to both the nonchalant secularism of liberals and the atheism of the far Left. Moreover, being Catholic allowed conservative writers to bond, at least in spirit, with millions of working-class and lower-middle-class Americans whose hostility to communism and affection for "traditional" morality nearly equaled theirs—even if they didn't share Flynn's hatred for the "tyrant State" at home.

Protestants were not so unified. While Billy Graham and many of his fellow evangelicals were certainly militant foes of "reds and pinkos," some liberal Protestant clergymen had lauded the Soviet "experiment" and lent their names to CP fronts. Methodists were bitterly split over the left-wing activities of the church-affiliated Federation for Social Action. Such a rift never appeared within the oldest denomination in Christendom.[26]

Catholic organizations constituted the largest and best financed—as well as most uncompromising—battalion in the anti-Communist movement. Its generals were such powerful hierarchs as Cardinal Spellman of New York and Archbishop (later Cardinal) Cushing of Boston. Its troops were priests and laypersons who distributed pamphlets for the Catholic Information Society, started Mindszenty Circles (named after the imprisoned cardinal of Hungary) and discussion groups affiliated with the Knights of Columbus Crusade for the Preservation and Promotion of American Ideals, organized chapters of the Catholic War Veterans, contributed articles to *Our Sunday Visitor* and the *Brooklyn Tablet,* marched in Loyalty Day parades, and denounced union officials who strayed too close to the CP line.

Such flag-waving militance overshadowed the liberal, pro-union tendency in the church. A reviewer for *Catholic World* remarked, defensively, that William F. Buckley "rightly fears the totalitarian state but what does he know of the totalitarianism of the mining patches of West Virginia?" Priests in some industrial areas kept up their Labor Schools and pointed out the gap between televised affluence and their many parishioners who could not pay the tab.[27] A majority of American Catholics continued to vote Democratic; they appreciated programs like the GI Bill and subsidized federal housing, and the GOP had not yet effaced the memory of its snobbish, nativist past. But, in the decade after the Axis surrender, messianic ardor among parishioners and prelates alike was found mainly on the Right.

The language of Catholic anticommunism during the early Cold War was rooted in the church's established antipathy to all varieties of godless collectivism. The brutal imposition of Stalinist regimes on Poland, Hungary, and Czechoslovakia gave renewed life to papal warnings about the rise of a "barbarism outside Western civilization" that, according to Catholic opinion, had earlier rampaged through revolutions in Russia, Spain, and Mexico. As part of the same tradition, a few church spokesmen and Catholic intellectuals still insisted on admonishing all who held materialist beliefs. New York's Bishop Fulton Sheen, a magnetic speaker whose weekly *Life Is Worth Living* was one of the most popular shows on television in the mid-1950s, patiently reminded his vast audience that "Communism is related to our materialistic Western civilization as putrefaction is to disease . . . what the Western world has subscribed to in isolated and uncorrelated tidbits, communism has integrated into a complete philosophy of life. There is no identity between the two, but there is affinity." This was a far cry from Coughlin's ad hominem harangues against "modern capitalists." But the underlying sentiment was the same.[28]

Most Catholic anti-Communists, however, gave up the habit of pointing out resemblances between the American system and that of its mortal enemy. Such equivalences sounded faintly unpatriotic; moreover, they had the unpleasant echo of the ghettoized past, when immigrants felt the need to protect themselves against the alien influences of a new land. By 1950, Catholics were dispersed through nearly every American institution and knew their votes and dollars could make or break politicians with national ambitions. With barely a trace of self-consciousness, their leaders could speak of themselves and their flock as Americans whose loyalty was greater than that of the Alger Hisses and Dean Achesons, State Department officials who had allegedly betrayed the nation despite the regard denoted by an Ivy League education and a high government post.

For Catholic activists in the postwar period, Americanism meant discarding public words and symbols that separated them from citizens of different faiths. There would be no more "Christian Fronts" or "Christian" unions, no more tolerance of anti-Semitic harangues or wistful evocations of the medieval order. While occasionally glancing over their shoulders at critics who continued to doubt the church's support for the First Amendment, Catholic anti-Communists were now leading Protestants and even Jews in a defensive purification of an American community that included them all.[29]

One can sample the ecumenical, populist flavor of this domestic crusade in the weekly *Brooklyn Tablet,* whose chief editor was the ardent layman Patrick Scanlan. Despite its local name, the independent *Tablet* was available in parishes throughout the East and boasted a circulation of over 120,000—higher than that of any other Catholic newspaper in the United States at the time. And Scanlan's medley of editorials, news, columns, book and movie reviews, political cartoons, and sports probably ensured that the paper was actually read.[30]

His political message, a call to vanquish elite immorality and treachery, implicitly invited non-Catholics to join the struggle. From time to time, the *Tablet* reported on progress the church was making toward racial integration. Jews were seldom referred to as such and never in a pejorative manner; the paper published articles by Rabbi Benjamin Schultz, head of the small Jewish League Against Communism, and ran a letter from a reader named Nathan D. Schapiro that concluded, "Let us all help to clean our Government from strange and foreign philosophies."[31]

Cultural pluralism was an innovation for Scanlan and his paper. As late as 1941, the editor had been one of Father Coughlin's most faithful supporters—a dedicated isolationist and a leading defender of the Christian Front in New York City. But the defeat of fascism and the new legitimacy of anticommunism gave him a chance to escape the ranks of the politically uncouth. He thrust the *Tablet* into the mainstream of a mobilization close to his heart, and thereby gained a measure of revenge on old liberal enemies.

"There is no double standard—one for the rich, the famous, the celebrities, another for the rest of us," wrote George Sokolsky, a Jewish journalist whose column appeared regularly both in the Hearst papers and the *Tablet.* In this instance, Sokolsky was associating Alger Hiss with Hollywood's tolerance of a well-publicized, adulterous affair between the actress Ingrid Bergman and the director Roberto Rossellini. "There can only be one standard for society. Our standard is based on moral law," wrote Sokolsky. "From it we dare not depart in principle, even if we sometimes slip in action. And the unrepentant, the flagrant, the boastful defies moral law—and it is so to be spoken." Since the nineteenth century, Catholic authorities had accused all manner of secular radicals of wanting to destroy marriage and the family. By the 1950s, as Sokolsky indicated, this was not just a Catholic issue but an American one.[32]

Patrick Scanlan drove the unity between politics and spiritual ethics through nearly every opinion piece he published. Saving America required the application of a stern moral code to public life. There was thus no significant difference between allowing a homosexual to retain his security clearance and an alleged Communist to keep his job in the State Department. "Moral perverts" and "base betrayers" were an equal, interlocking peril to the nation.

In addition to laying down firm ideological guidelines, the *Tablet* cheered on specific acts of moral witness. In 1949, Scanlan hailed the national rechristening of May 1 as Loyalty Day and published front-page photos of thousands of marchers striding up Flatbush Avenue "in one of the most impressive demonstrations of loyalty to God and country ever seen in Brooklyn." Street demonstrations inspired by what were said to be recent messages from the Virgin Mary predicting the conversion of Russia also drew lavish coverage.[33]

Although the editor gladly printed speeches by Democrats willing to denounce "so-called liberal intellectuals," his true sympathies lay farther to the right. At the beginning of the Korean War, Scanlan gloated that "only now" the "diplomatic 'genuises'" were "learning what the man on the street has known for years" about the evils of world communism. Two weeks later, he called for the resignation of Secretary of State Dean Acheson—ridiculing him as "a product of the tea-cozy camarillas (composed of Washington press and politicos) with whom the Secretary's synthetic English accent and oh-so-cute ventures in humorous understatement went over great guns." Scanlan's talent for ridicule helps explain why William Randolph Hearst made him a "standing offer" to write a regular column for his chain of right-wing dailies.[34]

What was missing from the *Tablet*'s vigorous polemics was a clear description of "the people" who would or should rise up to banish perfidy and sin. Absent from the paper—as from the propaganda of the entire anti-Communist movement—was the type of interest-based constituency earlier grassroots activists on both the Left and Right had urged to follow their lead: producers, workers, small businessmen, even the Anti-Saloon League's common man in the Model T who wanted to drive liquor-dealers out of his community. On occasion, the *Tablet*'s editorial cartoonist depicted a group of exemplary Americans—one Loyalty Day drawing included a standard-bearing soldier, a man in overalls, a mother and child, and an older man in a suit—all of them white. But neither here nor in Scanlan's prose was there an explicit statement of what connection such people had to each other, besides their identity as anti-Communist and God-fearing citizens.[35]

Yet, the *Tablet*'s editor and his counterparts on similar Catholic publications had no doubt they were speaking on behalf of what later right-wing activists would call "the moral majority." When Scanlan wrote, "The American people know that their country is in peril," the "people" he envisioned were extrapolated from those Catholic city dwellers whose names and faces filled the columns of his newspaper—parish priests; members of Catholic Youth Organization (CYO) basketball teams and Holy Name Societies; young married couples with Irish, Italian, and Polish names; the roofers and grocers and undertakers whose small advertisements dotted the back pages. There was a natural fit between this undefined but undeniably extant community and the rhetorical thunder against "high officials" that frequently occupied the front and editorial pages.

Scanlan assumed that all observant, employed Catholics with close-knit families shared a cultural understanding with other Americans who led similarly uncelebrated but decent lives. His assumption underlined how far Catholic activists had traveled since the days of mass immigration. Scanlan felt no need to delineate who these Americans were or to contrast them explicitly with the "perverts" and "betrayers" about whom he and his contributors had so much to say. As a result, the enemy's identity, like that of Satan himself, was sharply etched while the forces of good were bathed in a warm, fuzzy glow.[36]

To drive their populist demonology home, right-wing Catholics relied on the assistance of a number of former Communists from working-class backgrounds. The best-known of these was Louis Francis Budenz, a former managing editor of the *Daily Worker,* who became a well-paid "expert" witness at a lengthy series of trials and congressional hearings during the height of the red scare. Before bolting the CP in 1945, Budenz had put in over three decades as a labor and left-wing activist who always sought, or so he later claimed, to combine his religious beliefs with an equally strong desire for an authentically American form of radicalism. Budenz was, consecutively, a devotee of *Rerum Novarum* who promoted "our Christian Social program" within the Wilson-era AFL, the editor of an independent socialist paper during the 1920s, and a fiery organizer of strikers and the unemployed during the worst years of the Great Depression.

As a leader of the tiny American Workers Party in the early 1930s, Budenz urged the Left to stop using a revolutionary vocabulary borrowed from abroad and to adopt patriotic symbols like the Fourth of July and the "Don't Tread on Me" flag. A "realistic radical movement," Budenz wrote in 1935, "will refuse to consider itself an exotic, conspiratorial outfit, but will audaciously declare that it *is* the America of the future, and that in its hands lies the carrying out of the 'free and equal' promise of this country." He joined the CP that same year because its shift to the Popular Front resembled his own "American Approach."[37]

What made Budenz a credible spokesman for anticommunism a decade later was his charge, made plausible by his insider's knowledge, that the CP betrayed the nationalism and populism it rhapsodically professed. Moscow's control, he told HUAC in 1946, "stamps [the CP] immediately as something set off from the rest of America, as a quisling organization as much under the heel of the Kremlin . . . as the Nazi bund was the agent of Hitler's Germany."

Budenz's subsequent testimony and abundant writings amplified the point. The Communists actually had "contempt for things American"; they were run by a small band who met in secret atop a building in lower Manhattan; their notion of revolution as "devotion to the totalitarian state" clashed with his definition of it "as something which welled up from the people, as had our own American Revolution and the fight against chattel slavery." He also averred that the church in the United States, far from being a supporter of the status quo, had furthered democratic rights by struggling for religious tolerance and independent labor unions. In effect, Budenz was saying that he had left the CP when, under the guidance of Bishop Sheen, he realized the Party had turned its back on pious Americans. With such arguments did Catholic red hunters build around themselves the aura of a grassroots movement against the clear and present danger of domination by the godless.[38]

Veterans

One group of ordinary Americans got special billing from the postwar Right. In a domestic Cold War, there could be no more desirable allies than the men who had just fought and won a hot one abroad. Catholic anti-Communists had to be discreet about claiming that their minority religion gave them any superior purchase on political truth. But organized military veterans could engage in the most viciously ad hominem campaigns against "subversives" with the confidence that their right, even their duty, to speak for the nation as a whole could not be effectively challenged. The triumphant conclusion of the recent war only enriched a long tradition of viewing military service as the highest form of patriotism. The citizen-soldiers who fought under George Washington, the Grand Army of the Republic that still waved the bloody flag decades after Lee's surrender at Appomattox, and the six war heroes elected to the presidency before 1900 had all prepared the stage on which veterans' groups strode out to save the nation from the reds.[39]

During the first decade of the Cold War—when roughly half the seats in Congress were occupied by veterans—four different national groups concerned themselves with political issues transcending their quite effective lobbying for benefits reserved for ex-service personnel.[40]

Alone on the liberal Left was the American Veterans Committee (AVC). Founded in 1944, the AVC, under the slogan "Citizens first, veterans second," tapped the one-world idealism of those returning soldiers who were beginning to show up on college campuses. But, despite the leadership of such liberal paragons as Franklin D. Roosevelt, Jr., and the publisher and editor of the *New Republic,* the organization soon got embroiled in a savage internecine battle between pro- and anti-Communists—a feud the right-wing press did everything to encourage. By 1949, the AVC survived only in the minds of its beleaguered staff members.[41]

A longer-lived but only slightly less marginal group was the Catholic War Veterans (CWV), which, at its postwar zenith, claimed 200,000 members. Organized in 1935 by an Irish-born priest from Queens, N.Y., the CWV voiced an apocalyptic anticommunism with occasional swipes at "the moneyed interests" that vainly attempted to keep the flame of Coughlinism burning. Its working-class membership saw no contradiction between praising Joe McCarthy and endorsing more funding for social security and public housing. Individual champions of the New and Fair Deals might be traitors; but was that any reason to oppose measures to help the working man?

But the CWV was avowedly sectarian. Its recruiting literature advised that "The Catholic war veteran should remember that he is first and foremost a Catholic" and should be "ready to do and die for [his] faith." Outside a few strong enclaves of the church, the organization seems to have had little presence.[42]

The much larger American Legion and the Veterans of Foreign Wars (VFW) framed their anti-Communist message within the popular, if self-serving, image of combat-hardened men as the exemplars of civic virtue. In the two years immediately following the war, membership in the two organizations swelled to a total of almost seven million. This unprecedented growth made possible a sophisticated lobbying campaign and extensive "community service" programs like junior baseball leagues, automotive-safety classes, and local holiday commemorations—all swathed in patriotic bunting by a large corps of skilled publicists. The apparatus of the Legion and VFW together equaled what the largest national unions, combined, could muster and dwarfed the resources of any other nonreligious private association in the land.[43]

A good portion of this capital was spent establishing veterans as men who could be trusted, above all others, to identify who "the Commies" were and then to rout them. Here is Omar B. Ketchum, legislative director for the VFW, writing in 1949:

> Down through the years, in every community of the United States, urban and rural, those citizens who have served the nation in the armed forces during time of war have been the ones who keep their feet solidly on the ground with faith and belief in the American way of life. They have been alert to ferret out and combat phony panaceas advanced as a rosy substitute for sound and proven values. . . . The social planners, and the new order advocates, want to change all this.[44]

That Ketchum's words were part of a warning to veterans (and other readers) about an impending assault in Congress against the GI Bill only underlines their salience. Just as Gompers, Lewis, and Murray had invoked the indispensability and stalwart patriotism of manual workers in order to demand a higher wage or an end to political harassment, so Ketchum expected that the universal regard for men who had risked their lives to defend their "community" and "the American standard of living" would make his specific end appear to be modest compensation for invaluable services rendered.

Of course, the difference between the producer ethic and the veterans' code indicates the political distance traveled since the days of victorious sit-down strikes and of jeering at "economic royalists." The major national issue was now the contest with a rival, tyrannical world power and its domestic apologists, a contest that might require (or so the authorities insisted) a permanent warfare state. In this climate, the veteran represented the common man at his most heroic—he had established his mettle in a bloody contest between freedom and slavery.

Ketchum's organization was actually less vigorous than the American Legion in waging the rhetorical battle. Founded in 1913 by veterans of the Spanish-American War, the VFW tended to have a more working-class, locally focused membership than did its counterpart. During the early Cold War, VFW publications generally followed the Legion's lead in denouncing "world government" and a variety of liberals and fellow-travelers in high places. But only one or two articles in each issue of its monthly magazine were devoted to political matters, and even those were often reprints of HUAC pamphlets. Judging from the paucity of original material about subjects other than GI benefits, and the multiplicity of ads for self-employment schemes like metalizing baby shoes and courses in radio repair, the editors seemed to assume VFW members cared more about their personal security than the menace of a treasonous elite.[45]

In contrast, American Legion publications were determined and precise about what the nation's priorities should be. "With 17,000 Posts, the Legion should have at least 17,000 fairly well trained and qualified specialists on subversive activities," wrote National Commander James O'Neil, a small-city police chief, in 1948. And with an active Women's Auxiliary, a glossy, high-circulation monthly magazine, a biweekly newspaper, and ancillary publications like the *Firing Line* expressly intended for such "specialists," the Legion's impact was akin to that of a battleship sailing into combat with all its guns blazing.[46]

The ferociousness of the attack matched the scale of the danger. In tandem with such ex-Communists as Louis Budenz who regularly contributed to its press, Legion officials argued that the enemy was not just advancing overseas; it had taken hold of the main levers of American culture. Featured articles in the Legion magazine asked "Does Your Movie Money Go to Commies?" and "Do Colleges Have to Hire Red Professors?" Others revealed how "The Commies Go After the Kids" by peddling "progressive" comic books and folk songs and attacked "Our New Privileged Class" of "scientists clearly implicated in the Soviet atomic thefts," "crimson professors," and "habitual red-fronters" who "still write and perform for radio and television." Without persistent exposure, Legionnaires insisted the menace would only continue to intimidate honest citizens and expand its influence, reducing Americanism to the status of a minority ideology. Aided clandestinely from Moscow, Hollywood, and parts of the federal government, left-wing subversion was, wrote one contributor, "like a cancer. . . . Allowed to grow, it affects the vitals of the organism in such a way that its removal is a critical and sometimes fatal operation."[47] The vocabulary of malignance was employed to reverse the course of a potentially deadly social disease.

Legion publicists also sought a constituency larger than their own healthy membership. To pursue this goal, some adjustments in language were necessary. Since the organization was founded, in the wake of World War I, Americanism had been its creed. Before 1945, it was a faith defined more by what it shunned than by what it favored. Legionnaires, who often had close ties with anti-union employers, took an active, often violent part in repressing labor organizers, radical gatherings, and individual speakers whose ideas were out of step with what one historian calls "a community defined both morally and historically." It hardly needs to be said that the Legion community excluded all but the most subservient blacks (posts were segregated) and women who didn't object to joining an auxiliary in which they would be addressed by the husband's name ("Mrs. John Smith"). Homer Chaillaux, the director of the Legion's Americanism Division from 1934 through World War II, struck a characteristically belligerent posture when asked if he would debate the CP leader Earl Browder. "I'll meet him in an alley any time, but I'll never dignify Communists by meeting them on a platform."[48]

But its postwar leap in membership and participation in a crusade whose purpose all but a few Americans supported brought a rhetorical shift from law-and-order conservatism to the new right-wing populism. Without repudiating their old positions, Legion writers, bolstered by the new posts blooming in thousands of real communities, increasingly suggested that the powerless many thought more clearly and acted more sensibly than did the privileged few. "There can be no compromise between the truths embodied in our Declaration of Independence and the error behind the Communist Manifesto," declared *The Firing Line* in 1953. "Those who deny this are deceivers or deluded fools, be they statesmen or street-cleaners. The ditchdigger who understands this is better able to guide our foreign policy than the diplomat who does not understand it."[49]

With both visual images and graphic prose, Legion publicists staked their claim to a broader, more generous community. Most covers of the monthly magazine featured a color illustration showing ordinary (always white) Americans at play or work: a teenage boy waxing his jalopy and grinning at two girls walking by; two fire fighters rushing to finish a game of checkers before dashing to their waiting truck; a young woman glancing at a photo of her uniformed husband as she sews an American flag. Here were the wholesome, amusing touches made famous by Norman Rockwell's illustrations for the *Saturday Evening Post,* a style also widely copied by canny advertisers out to celebrate middle-class family life.[50]

Numerous articles in the Legion magazine implicitly contrasted such folksy vignettes with the elitist foibles of reds and fellow travelers. In 1951, a two-page spread was devoted to photos of large houses owned by "Commies and party-liners . . . in some of the better suburbs of New York and Los Angeles." The magazine commented sarcastically that "most of them don't let their love for the poverty-stricken cramp their own luxurious way of life." Two years later, a writer on the Rosenberg case gleefully noted that, at a fund-raising dinner for the condemned couple, "The invitations were elegant and the price was a mere twenty-five dollars per person." Evidence that radicals' chic lifestyle clashed with their plain-folks rhetoric underscored the moral superiority of the humble, anti-Communist majority.[51]

Calling for "a united front against the commies," Legionnaires occasionally welcomed a notable African-American or CIO leader into their patriotic tent. In 1950 and 1951, the black novelist and folklorist Zora Neale Hurston, whose resentment of patronizing liberals led her to become an apologist for segregation, contributed two feature articles to the Legion magazine. One accused radical "bosses" of buying black votes in a close Florida senatorial primary; the other lampooned Communist attempts to convince American blacks, as "colored peoples of the world," not to fight against "Mao's hordes" in Korea. In 1950, Commander George N. Craig praised the CIO for "bouncing the Commies" and invited James Carey, then secretary of the labor body, to speak at the Legion's All-American Conference. Carey's vow, "there's less danger of the CIO being captured by the Communists than there is of the National Association of Manufacturers being captured by the Communists," needled his hosts for their purer-than-thou stance.[52]

Carey had reason to be sarcastic. Union spokesmen were quite aware of the Legion's union-busting past. And more recently, the organization had disbanded a group of Union Labor Legionnaires in order to ward off any danger of radical "infiltration." While many posts outside the South were desegregated, the Legion seldom defended its black members against discriminatory treatment by employers, hospitals, or local governments. When the premier veterans' organization opened its doors to blacks or industrial workers, the overture remained strictly on its own terms.[53]

To keep the issue of domestic subversion burning, Legionnaires engaged in scores of local "communitywide" actions. The benign face of these appeared in the frequent marches and rallies promoted by the *Brooklyn Tablet* and other religious periodicals and educational events such as the "Day Under Communism" staged in the small town of Mosinee, Wisconsin, on May 1, 1950. The punitive side was driven by a felt need to identify and then expel the internal enemy. Equipped with a tactical repertoire that included letter-writing campaigns, picketing, house meetings, and mass attendance at public hearings, the Legion helped force the dismissal and blacklisting of numerous teachers, entertainers, and union officials with left-wing sympathies and/or backgrounds. In the summer of 1949, Legionnaires in Peekskill, New York, even used stones and fire to break up a concert starring Paul Robeson, then notorious for his pro-Communist views. The Legion did not try to control what its oft-mentioned 17,000 posts did to combat the "reds"; it was content to motivate them.[54]

Critics branded such exploits "witch-hunts," and the continuing popularity of Arthur Miller's play *The Crucible* (first performed in 1953) has helped give the metaphor almost universal currency. Yet perpetrators and champions of the nonviolent affairs described them as courageous acts that confirmed the ability of ordinary citizens to unite against a common foe.

In 1951, the American Legion press hailed one Josephine Baker, "a young American housewife" from Buffalo who "sparked a movement" that drove organizers of a pro-Soviet peace pledge campaign out of her neighborhood. A sympathetic (male) reporter suggestively described Baker, whose husband was an army engineer and a Legionnaire, as "a slight but oh-my girl whose small build and smiling eyes give little hint of a reserve of energy and mental power." Baker, whose tactics included a counterpetition and a local protest march that drew 2,500 people, explained her success:

> I guess I just got my Irish up. I made up my mind that if they had the nerve and gall to come into our Project, we could show them how we felt about it. We were a small group, but everybody worked hard. We didn't have any money, and none of us ever held public office. We wanted to keep it on a high plane—pro instead of anti—and we wanted it to be a grassroots, non-political, spiritually-based effort. We enlisted the support of priests, ministers and rabbis. Democrats and Republicans worked together.[55]

One would expect to read such phrases in a description of neighbors getting together to stop a highway project or, more recently, to expel drug dealers from their streets and schoolyards. Putting them to a grander purpose suggests that red hunters perceived themselves as continuing the cooperative spirit, the scrap-metal drives and victory gardens, prevalent in many towns during World War II.

It evidently never occurred to Baker or the Legion correspondent that "they," the agents of "the communist machine," had a constitutional right to circulate their petitions. The discourse of populist anticommunism precluded such considerations. Communities of otherwise apolitical, anonymous Americans were rising up to stop one detachment of a self-evidently evil force that was killing GIs in Korea. From Yalta to the United Nations to China, the Communist "conspiracy" had been responsible for squandering the gains of total victory in World War II, a failure that emboldened new aggressors like the North Koreans and the Chinese. Citizens, soldiers, and housewives who had cheerfully done their duty for God and country before were merely doing it again. To question the purpose of such spirited diligence was deemed unneighborly, cowardly, and elitist. It was, in a word, un-American.

MR. McCARTHY GOES TO WASHINGTON

It should be evident by now that the political nightmare we associate with Senator Joseph McCarthy of Wisconsin had already been dreamed up by people like John

T. Flynn, Patrick Scanlan, and Josephine Baker. Out of the materials of communitarian self-defense and the terror of another world war, they fashioned an image of the enemy that cried out for determined action on a national scale. Exposing how the red cancer could spread to your school or neighborhood only increased the urgency of striking at its domestic source—no matter how high it went. The Wisconsin senator did not emerge as a national figure until February of 1950, when, in a notorious speech to a Republican women's group in Wheeling, West Virginia, he accused the State Department of keeping 205 (or was it 57?) Communists on its payroll. By that time, citizen-activists had already spent years identifying their targets, developing their style, and building an infrastructure to communicate their message.

McCarthyism, as many scholars have noted, was not itself a mass movement; "it never had members, organized chapters, offered candidates, or formulated a platform." But with a ready-made, institutionalized constituency in churches, veterans' posts, ethnic societies, editorial rooms, and businesses throughout the land, the senator and his Washington allies didn't need to create their own.[56]

Yet, one cannot deny McCarthy's importance to the anti-Communist cause. A decade earlier, HUAC, under the chairmanship of Representative Martin Dies (a Texas Democrat), had exposed the "Trojan horse" of CP front groups, naming hundreds of names of individuals associated with them, and declaring that "a half-dozen dupes high in the federal government are more useful to Stalin and Browder than are ten thousand ordinary dues-paying members of the Communist Party." Beginning in 1947, Richard Nixon and his HUAC comrades grabbed the front pages with dramatic hearings that resulted in jail terms for Alger Hiss and the left-wing scriptwriters known as the Hollywood Ten. Little HUACs in states such as California and Florida followed suit.[57]

But McCarthy thrust himself and his investigations into the center of national politics in a way no red hunter had been able to do before him or since. He dominated the news and gave birth to an eponym that still carries a powerful charge. In the context of his time, his skill as a rhetorical populist must be appreciated, odious though it may be to contemporary sensibilities.

By upbringing, temperament, and invention, McCarthy was an ideal specimen of the political outsider come to rattle the halls of power. Grandson of Irish immigrants, he was born in 1909 on a small farm in northern Wisconsin and energetically took up growing chickens and managing a grocery store before earning a law degree at Marquette University. Later, McCarthy often traded on his rural background for earthy, aggressive metaphors like the one that serves as an epigraph for this chapter. Traitors in government, he told a national television audience, were like "potatoes under a hill"; they never grew alone. He also was capable of mining the more elegiac vein of agrarianism, describing a 1952 vacation in the Arizona hills as an opportunity to make "contact with real Americans without any synthetic sheen . . . those real people who are the heart and soul and soil of America."[58]

At the same time, McCarthy unabashedly played the tough Irishman battling to upset a game rigged by the WASP establishment. "McCarthyism is Americanism with its sleeves rolled," he once said. He concocted tales about combat he had never seen, reveled in long poker games and hard drinking, was known to be adamantly loyal to friends and assistants, and, when attacked, vowed to fight on until "crucified" by powerful foes. To sympathizers steeped, as were so many Americans, in cinematic images, the senator may have appeared a hybrid of James Cagney as a charismatic gangster and Jimmy Stewart as the title character in Frank Capra's *Mr. Smith Goes to Washington.* The wisecracking, overgrown street kid fused with the idealistic country boy out to clean up a national scandal.[59]

The way Mr. McCarthy made himself a Washington phenomenon enraged most insiders in government and the press but endeared him to untold numbers outside the capital. He showed no deference to the hallowed norms of senatorial etiquette, the rules of seniority, or even the legal protocol governing the release of classified information. Aided by anonymous admirers throughout the federal bureaucracy (including J. Edgar Hoover), he posed as an indefatigable sleuth, wielding sheaves of paper containing names of "subversives" and hinting that an innocuous-looking list or letter would cause a whole network of traitors to unravel.

McCarthy knew a good punchline was often the best offense. He grew fond of renaming newspapers that were critical of him; the *Milwaukee Daily Journal* became the "Milwaukee Daily Worker" and the *New York Times* the "New York Daily Worker." The populist intent was clear. Pointing to one correspondent for a liberal daily, he snapped, "I'm not saying Dick's a Communist, it's just the two percent at the top of his paper that are Communists." In the Wheeling speech that launched him, he accused "the bright young men who are born with silver spoons in their mouth" of "selling this nation out." Later, he would revel in denouncing "parlor pinks and parlor punks" and ridiculed famous adversaries with epithets like "Alger—I mean Adlai" (Stevenson) and "the elegant and alien [Dean] Acheson—Russian as to heart, British as to manner."[60]

Such antics made him a political lightning rod and an instant celebrity. Opinion polls conducted in the early 1950s showed that McCarthy was more popular than his own pet issue of Communists in government. A fixture in newspapers, in magazines, on the radio, and on popular interview shows on television, he managed to draw support from people whose social resentments had little to do with the absence or presence of Soviet agents in the federal bureaucracy.[61]

McCarthy's disruptive skills did not please all those who shared his politics. Some voices in the anti-Communist Right were understandably wary of connecting their cause to the conduct of a junior senator from a rather unimportant state. Most conservative intellectuals defended McCarthy's motives and damned those of his liberal critics in the media; John Flynn was a particularly zealous champion. But, being intellectuals, many recoiled, as did Max Eastman and Will Herberg, from methods deemed not "mature and thoughtful" or, worse, a species of "government by rabble-rousing."[62]

Some leading Catholics, most notably Cardinal Spellman and Patrick Scanlan, maintained that McCarthy, a dependable churchgoer, was doing both their work and God's. The senator courted such allies with statements like: "Today we are engaged in a final, all-out battle between Communistic atheism and Christianity . . . the chips are down—they are truly down." The diocesan press overwhelmingly defended him, as did the Knights of Columbus. But the influential Fulton Sheen took no stand on the controversial figure, and the many priests and laymen who had supported both Roosevelt and Truman were either embarrassed or infuriated by McCarthy's talk of the "twenty years of treason" that began with FDR's 1933 recognition of the USSR. Bishop Sheil of Chicago, a staunch labor liberal, told a UAW audience in the spring of 1954 that the senator was a "carnival man" running "a kind of shell game" that "distract[s] us from our real problems, including the problem of Communism." But no other member of the church hierarchy was equally outspoken.[63]

Of the veterans' organizations, only the marginal CWV publicly rallied to McCarthy's side. During his four years in the limelight, neither the VFW nor the American Legion ran a single article in their national magazines about the senator—even though their alarm at Communist "penetration" of American life paralleled his and he frequently spoke at local veterans' events.[64]

But right-wing Republicans saw no reason to demur. McCarthy was their best chance to close the gap between ideological conservatives and white working people (especially Catholics) that the Depression had opened wide. As late as the summer of 1951, Gallup pollsters found that a majority of respondents, when asked "what the Republican party stands for today," chose "For privileged few, moneyed interests, big companies" over any other proposed reply. And the children of the white ethnics who had rallied to the Democrats in the '30s were now registered to vote. Notwithstanding their new middle-class identity, most were not inclined to desert the "party of the people" that had forged the New Deal and military victory. As the first national figure from the GOP capable of expressing plebeian resentments, McCarthy could begin to reverse the partisan imagery—if he could avoid the kind of scandalous slipup to which maverick politicians are so vulnerable.[65]

McCarthy, with his slashing style and ridicule of patrician policy makers, was already making inroads into a number of Irish, German, and Eastern European neighborhoods that traditionally voted Democratic. Most of the 6,000 New York City police officers who came out to cheer a McCarthy speech in April 1954 were still registrants in the party of FDR and Tammany Hall. That same year, John Fitzgerald Kennedy refused to publicly criticize his fellow senator, explaining, "Hell, half my voters in Massachusetts look on McCarthy as a hero."[66]

Absolving the mass of Democrats from the sins of the "lace-handkerchief crowd" helped spur McCarthy's popularity among his coreligionists in cities like Boston, New York, and Chicago. A Democrat himself in the 1930s, he charged, in a 1950 debate, that "a group of twisted-thinking intellectuals" had "taken over the Democrat Party" and made President Truman their "prisoner." And, while partially financed by Texas oilmen, he didn't engage in the kind of union-bashing that made some of his political allies, like Robert Taft and Barry Goldwater, anathema to organized labor.

McCarthy cultivated the image of a relentless red hunter who didn't mind making enemies in high places because his only true support came from "the people," whatever their class or political affiliations. Their "good common sense and inherent decency" shone, said McCarthy, through each of the thousands of letters he received. In the words of his biographer: "He often stood alone, challenging the largest and most powerful organizations—the State Department, the army, and, at times, a few of the nation's great journalistic and industrial concerns. In a certain sense, McCarthy was the hero of the little man as he attacked the well-dressed, well-educated, self-assured managers of modern society."[67]

Reading McCarthy's words today, it is difficult to recapture that heroic quality. Apart from a few colorful insults and taut expressions of alarm (like "a conspiracy so immense"), his speeches and statements—most of which were written by a corps of right-wing journalists and senate aides—contain almost nothing that could not be found in contemporary utterances by less formidable politicians like Senators Pat McCarran and William Jenner, and columnists like George Sokolsky and Westbrook Pegler.

McCarthy was an effective if not memorable speaker at banquets and other party functions. But when he tried to strike a grander pose, he usually failed. In July of 1951, he read to a nearly empty Senate the first third of a 60,000-word attack on General George Marshall that was full of scholarly references to military strategy and European history. The entire speech, entered into the *Congressional Record,* angered moderate Republicans and was noticed mainly by his critics.[68]

The audience McCarthy wanted to reach, however, was not in the habit of reading long speeches or worrying about the originality of a senator's prose. The man everyone called "Joe" was one of the first politicians to exploit the ability of television to boost an individual who is witty, alert, and at ease before a camera. As the media scholar Daniel Hallin observes, television news has always been strongly receptive to populist figures, whether average citizens with a good story to tell or the idealistic "'little guy' who stands up to the 'powers that be.'" McCarthy understood instinctively how to play an Everyman, and one whom the viewing public would not switch off.[69]

During his brief years of glory, the popularity of TV soared. By the end of 1954, Americans owned 35 million sets—representing a tenfold increase since the beginning of the decade. To see McCarthy's frequent performances on such interview programs as *Meet the Press* was to discover a clever showman who knew his severe charges would go down easier when mixed with a seemingly guileless humor and informality.[70]

The interview show was a perfect setting for an anti-establishment politician. Seated across from several primly dressed, tightly-wound journalists, McCarthy acted the part of the average citizen incensed by the shenanigans of the powerful but full of confidence about what needed to be done. He smiled his slow, broad-jawed grin and waved a meaty hand or outstretched finger to the camera, addressed the reporters by their first names ("Now, listen here, Frank"), alternated between satirical quips and stern promises to "clean out" the reds, and clearly enjoyed jousting with his mostly liberal interrogators on a network owned by wealthy liberals. After all, as the newsworthy guest, he always had the last word. And with the simple gesture of placing his briefcase beside him on the table, McCarthy put the broadcast itself in perspective. Even while answering reporters' skeptical questions, he was fully engaged in the people's business.[71]

Besides his breezy demeanor, the senator made effective use of the kind of crisp, memorable phrases that would come to be known as "sound bites." Some were clever—defining McCarthyism as "calling a man a Communist who later is proved to be one" and answering a question about his preference for a new Secretary of State with, "I would say that almost any one of the 150 million normal Americans would do a better job than Acheson." Some were sober, like his comment that the ouster of the China expert John Paton Davies "is many years and many lives too late." Others were determined: "I'll make you one promise, that Leavenworth [penitentiary] won't hold them," referring to what he'd do as chair of a senate investigations committee.[72]

Buried in the middle of a long speech or columns of newsprint, such lines were relatively insignificant. But on television, they were a kind of blunt revelation. Here, it seemed, was a straight-talking politician not afraid to speak his mind before these arrogant, badgering journalists. When, in July 1950, the *Meet the Press* moderator Martha Rountree (a rare woman panelist) asked the senator whether he'd consider using different "tactics," McCarthy manfully refused to retreat. "I'm not equipped to use lace-handkerchief kind of tactics. We may have to use lumberjack tactics, bare-knuckle tactics, because these are the only kind of tactics the Communists understand." With the Korean War under way and military recruiting ads festooning the broadcasts, that comment put smug, gritless journalists on the defensive (and, by extension, anyone who shared their opinions). Sure, my methods may be a bit rough, implied the man named Joe, but what are *you* doing to fight communism?[73]

However, the pugnacious populist whom TV nurtured it could also destroy. From April to June of 1954, the Senate's Subcommittee on Investigations looked into allegations McCarthy and United States Army officers had made about each other. The nationally broadcast hearings threw a harsh, sustained light that no public figure had encountered before. McCarthy flopped and shriveled under the glare. During almost six weeks on camera, the formerly calm and sanguine enforcer sounded shrill and looked irritated and mean. His crisp, witty charges against vulnerable liberals now became rambling, anxious flailings of such unlikely targets of Communist "infiltration" as hydrogen-bomb factories, the CIA, and the officer corps of the army.

In the most dramatic exchange of the hearings, McCarthy accused the army's counsel Joseph Welch of concealing the brief radical past of one of the young lawyers in his conservative Boston firm. Welch responded as a righteously indignant patriarch: "Until this moment I think I never really gauged your cruelty or your recklessness," he said, and went on to explain the whole innocent story. When McCarthy tried to renew the attack, Welch interrupted, asking the now famous rhetorical question: "Have you no sense of decency, sir, at long last? Have you left no sense of decency?" With this refreshing, spontaneous break from parliamentary procedure, Welch turned the tables on his adversary, the iconoclastic, would-be guardian of political morality, who smiled at inappropriate times and perspired heavily under the hot lights.[74]

Historians have offered several good reasons for McCarthy's poor performance before an audience that, at some time during the hearings, included about 80 million people. He was drinking heavily; he was forced to defend special favors he had demanded for an aide; an eloquent (though belated) attack by Edward R. Murrow on prime-time television had just reproached him for "confus[ing] dissent with disloyalty"; President Dwight David Eisenhower had finally turned against him, and the army was too powerful and revered an opponent.

All these factors, however, might not have been enough if the embattled politician had been able, as before, to capture the high ground of principle. But unlike broadcast interviews and the many earlier hearings he himself had chaired, the floodlit forum in the spring of 1954 was one McCarthy could not control. Other senators and skillful attorneys—not left-wing intellectuals, liberal journalists, or executive appointees—were challenging him now. Forced to defend himself against *their* facts and *their* principles, the most feared man in American politics was transformed into a whining, boorish fraud. Six months later, the Senate, by a four-to-one margin, voted to censure him. As much as a third of the public disagreed with their decision, but McCarthy's power was lost forever. He died in 1957, a victim of chronic alcoholism.[75]

With McCarthy's fall, the anti-Communist movement lost its élan and momentum. The cause had attracted a complex assortment of activists spread throughout thousands of localities and hundreds of organizations. But its very heterogeneity was a cause of weakness. Most anti-Communists had never clearly articulated any aim more ambitious or idealistic than hunting down reds and expelling them. So when the most ambitious, flamboyant red hunter of them all belly flopped before his critics, they could do little but protest that he'd been framed by "the establishment." In a eulogy, William Schlamm (a former Communist) wrote in the *National Review* that the uncompromising lawmaker had been "tarred and feathered by genteel Ivy Leaguers, by gracious leaders of Women Voters Clubs and by noble princes of the press" who abhorred his style and discounted his message.[76]

Through the remainder of the decade, the Catholic Right and the American Legion continued to repeat the old charges to a public that had found good reasons for complacency—the death of Stalin, the end of the Korean War, the obvious impotence of the Communist Party, and the re-election of a Republican president.

In 1954, the unflappable, fatherly Murrow had counseled viewers to "remember always that *accusation* is not proof and that conviction depends upon evidence and due process of law. . . . We will not be driven into an age of *unreason.*" The responsible anticommunism of men like Murrow, Welch, and Eisenhower triumphed over the irresponsible brand that McCarthy had come to symbolize.[77]

In the end, the activists of the postwar Right had focused in too tightly on an enemy with less influence than they imagined. Executive appointees like Alger Hiss and policy intellectuals like Owen Lattimore and J. Robert Oppenheimer were little more than servants of the men who held political power; their expertise was useful to the liberal order only so long as they skirted controversy. Once in trouble, they proved to be quite dispensable. And the left-wing notions, past or present, of some screenwriters and professors caused barely a ripple on the slick surface of mainstream culture in the 1950s. Pragmatists in the White House, Congress, the major networks, and the press were not about to allow right-wing crusaders to imperil America's unrivaled prosperity and imperial dominion.

Public confidence in government, raised during World War II, wavered little as a result of the stormy debate about the presence of traitors within. Near the end of the decade, pollsters found that only one-fourth of their respondents did not "trust the government to do right most of the time."[78] For the time being, the tones of contented moderation had driven out the discourse of anguished zeal.

THE GREAT LIBERAL FEAR

But red hunters on the Right gave liberal intellectuals a terrible shock. How could millions of Americans—perhaps a majority—share such irrational, inchoate resentments against thinkers and high officials who were on the same side as they in the Cold War? Perhaps grassroots insurgencies that spoke a populist idiom were themselves the problem. Perhaps "the people," who were all but deified in the age of FDR, could no longer be trusted in the age of Joe McCarthy.

In 1955, an anthology of essays appeared whose main ideas rapidly became established wisdom among academics and journalists seeking to understand mass support for the red scare. *The New American Right,* edited by Daniel Bell, featured articles by such well-known writers as Richard Hofstadter, Seymour Martin Lipset, David Riesman, and Bell himself. The seven contributors—five of whom were Jews—approached the problem from a variety of sociological and historical perspectives. But, as Bell wrote, "they showed a remarkable convergence in point of view." Most salient was a suspicion of mass democracy unrestrained by institutional rules and rulers and unmediated by rational intellects like themselves. "[I]n a populistic culture like ours, which seems to lack a responsible elite with political and moral autonomy," wrote the Columbia historian Hofstadter, ". . . it is possible to exploit the widest currents of public sentiment for private purposes." Given the right circumstances, Hofstadter warned, "it is at least conceivable that a highly organized, vocal, active and well-financed minority could create a political climate in which the rational pursuit of our well-being and safety would become impossible."[79]

This was the great fear of the liberal intellectuals: social movements of the ill-educated could destroy what made America such a good place in which to live, write, and teach. In the 1930s, most of the future contributors to *The New American Right* were youthful activists in one faction or another of the Marxist Left. But, twenty years later, American socialism was moribund, and industrial unionists, newly reunited with their old AFL antagonists and seemingly content to protect gains already made, seldom proposed transforming America from the shop floor upward. Liberal intellectuals responded by discarding nearly all sentimental vestiges of the producer ethic. Most also made peace with what appeared to be the unquestionable success of corporate capitalism, although they did not entirely abandon hope for a new opening on the Left.

At any rate, these writers maintained, their erstwhile embrace of socialism and the CIO had been a *rational* passion, rooted in class grievances and informed by a body of theory—rigorous, erudite, Talmudic. While riddled with naive and romantic flaws, the proletarian cause, it was argued, had nothing in common with the verbal crudities of anti-Communist crusaders like McCarthy or the thousands of vigilantes around the nation who were banning books from libraries, sacking teachers and entertainers with left-wing pasts, and generally treating heterodox expression as un-American. The red scare, Hofstadter implied in his essay, smacked more of fascism than of true conservatism, which had always honored the legitimacy of learning and deferred to responsible elites. And a mere decade after the Holocaust, there could be no greater fear for Jewish intellectuals than the spread of mass intolerance associated with demagogues on the Right.[80]

The threat was particularly poignant because postwar America had elevated intellectuals to a position unique in their and the nation's experience. The federal government required an expanding corps of hard scientists to create and refine new technologies and social scientists to explain and, perhaps, aid in modernizing a complex, often hostile world. The universities—their luxuriant growth fertilized by the GI Bill, government largesse for construction and research, and a middle class flush enough to afford tuition—tendered well-paid positions and a supportive environment in which to pursue a (non-Communist) life of the mind. For the first time in American history, secular thinkers gave up their stance as alienated aesthetes and, despite a bundle of misgivings, became an essential adjunct of what C. Wright Mills was calling "the power elite." The sociologist Edward Shils, a Jew from working-class origins who rode atop the academic wave, later wrote: "From the condition of being peripheral in a society which they believed was culturally provincial, American intellectuals came to see themselves as effective members of the center of an intellectual metropolis."[81]

Contributors to *The New American Right* argued that much of the public support for red-hunting paranoia stemmed from "status anxiety." The postwar boom had raised the majority of Americans above lives of mere subsistence, but their good fortune was too new to allow much generosity. "Having precariously won respectability in paycheck and consumption style," wrote David Riesman and Nathan Glazer, many Americans opposed the social leveling and foreign aid promoted by liberals in government, academia, and the arts. The literary critic Leslie Fiedler observed that the words "liberal" and "intellectual" were "for better or worse, historically synonymous in America."[82]

But such individuals were no less the captives of "status strain" than were the people who ridiculed them as "eggheads." Having traveled in less than one generation from Union Square soapboxes to seminar rooms off Harvard Square and Morningside Heights, liberal thinkers could never be truly secure. Sufficiently whipped up into a conformist frenzy, the "populistic culture"—within which nativist and anti-Semitic attitudes still simmered—might seriously erode or even wash away the islands of elite civility to which Jews of immigrant parentage had so recently been welcomed.

The fragility of their new status renders more understandable the intellectuals' assault on the original Populists, whose very name no political group had seen fit to adopt since the demise of the People's Party a half-century before. For Bell and his colleagues, the Populists were a useful template for designing a theory of social movements. Viewing them as cranky provincials instead of a coalition of producers, liberal thinkers argued that the delusions of the Populists reverberated through progressivism, the ideology of Coughlin and Huey Long, and the fulminations of McCarthy and his admirers.

Since the late '50s, historians and other scholars have persuasively demolished both the portrait of the initial Populists as irrational bigots and the idea that those who supported Populism were linked demographically to McCarthy's followers. On the basis of a handful of bombastic documents, Bell and his fellow authors essentially conflated small farmers and wage earners who railed against private monopolies with right-wingers, often of comfortable means, who despised the New Deal state. It was tempting to fuse haters of "the money power" with scourges of "twisted-thinking intellectuals," to cast a disapproving glance over the whole enterprise of mobilization for anti-establishment ends, to brand as populist any prejudices held by large numbers of Americans. But to do so violated not just the need to draw careful distinctions between past and present; it also contradicted the very democratic ideals Bell, Hofstadter, and their colleagues believed they were upholding.[83]

Yet a nugget of meaning lay buried within the dross of simplistic history. There *was* a close resemblance between the *rhetoric* of Populist campaigners and that of conservative anti-Communists. Both appealed to the will and interests of a self-reliant, productive majority whose spiritual beliefs, patriotic ideals, and communities were judged to be under attack at the hands of a modernizing elite, a "civilized minority," in the historian Christopher Lasch's ironic term. To neglect the presence of common threads of expression that stretched beyond the People's Party itself is as mistaken as to force that tradition into a container brimming with repugnant beliefs. John T. Flynn and Patrick Scanlan were pursuing quite different ends than were Ignatius Donnelly and Tom Watson in the 1890s. But, as a language, populism could leap ideological boundaries and attract Americans hostile to modern liberalism as well as those who continued to think fondly of labor unions and FDR's Four Freedoms.[84]

The more resourceful activists of the postwar Right may have had the last word in this debate. Besides helping to saturate American culture in the fear of "Commies," they succeeded in frightening many liberals into mistrusting the very kinds of white Americans—Catholic workers, military veterans, discontented families in the middle of the social structure—who had once been foot soldiers of causes such as industrial unionism, Social Security, and the GI Bill. A little more than a decade later, liberalism would indeed be in crisis, and more skillful politicians than McCarthy would rush to fill the vacuum the Left had created. While losing, the red hunters of the 1940s and 1950s had planted the seeds of future victory.

Antiwar march on the Pentagon, 1967. *(Courtesy of the Library of Congress)*

Chapter 8

Power to Which People? The Tragedy of the White New Left

The powers of ordinary men are circumscribed by the everyday worlds in which they live, yet even in these rounds of job, family, and neighborhood, they often seem driven by forces they can neither understand nor govern . . . [they] accordingly feel that they are without purpose in an epoch in which they are without power.

—C. Wright Mills, radical sociologist, 1956

Thus far the war in Vietnam has only dramatized the demand of ordinary people to have some opportunity to make their own lives, and of their unwillingness, even under incredible odds, to give up their struggle against external domination.

—Paul Potter, President of Students for a Democratic Society (SDS), 1965

For lots of us our whole life is a defiance of Amerika. Everything we do and have—our street actions, our friendships, our ideas—all show our contempt for the pig death culture of this country.

—Weatherman faction of SDS, 1969

The boy from the state of Wisconsin gave precise instructions, "Hey, newspaperman, don't call us students, we're the People."

—Nicholas Von Hoffman, reporting on an antiwar demonstration, 1971

OUT FROM LIBERALISM

THE liberals who anxiously turned back the assault of the postwar Right were confronted in the 1960s by a very different adversary: a radical movement led, in the main, by their own children. The white New Left was not the exclusive property of young people from professional, secular, intellectually aware families who revered the memory of FDR and wanted the United Nations to be strong. But liberal sons and daughters, joined by a healthy contingent of "red-diaper babies," as children of Communists were known, set the dominant tone in nearly every New Left group—especially Students for a Democratic Society (SDS) and the shifting array of local committees and national coalitions that mobilized against the Vietnam War. Confident of their own ideas and eager to publicize them both in the mass media and through underground newspapers and radio stations, the progeny of privilege gave new meaning to the defense of ordinary people and the bashing of their establishment foes.

The populism of what its adherents called, simply, the Movement was unique. Never before in the United States had a radical upsurge that sought to win power for the common folk sprung from within the dominant order itself.[1] And the ideals of this order were ones a budding populist could support. "Becoming a radical," observed the psychologist Kenneth Keniston in 1968 after conducting a study of the breed, ". . . involves *no fundamental change in core values*."[2]

The young leftists who began emerging from universities in the early 1960s shared the major principles that had evolved from the New Deal through the Fair Deal to the New Frontier: the desirability of a welfare state, democratic labor unions, a rapid end to poverty and racial discrimination, even opposition to the bureaucratic autocracy of the Soviet Union. Until it became an antiwar storm center in 1965, SDS got most of its funds from industrial unions, particularly the UAW.[3]

But in this historical niche was born a sense of responsibility. Young radicals nurtured on altruism and compassion were appalled when liberal rulers betrayed their own stated beliefs—and then lied about it. These liberals allowed racist legislators to control Congress, managed the poor with paternalistic regulations and ghettoized housing projects, neglected to outlaw segregationist practices inside many unions, and attempted to crush anticolonial revolutions they branded Communist inspired—thereby making Soviet claims about "U.S. imperialism" sound credible. Content to govern a society of middle-class conformists, liberals had lost their soul. "What kind of system is it," asked Paul Potter, the president of SDS, in 1965, that "creates faceless and terrible bureaucracies and makes those the place where people spend their lives and do their work. . . , that consistently puts material values before human values—and still persists in calling itself free?"[4]

New Leftists had grown up in a political culture that stressed the division of the world into absolute good and absolute evil, freedom versus totalitarianism. The images of Nazi Germany and the Stalinist USSR were of advanced bureaucratic states that lost their moral bearings and committed unspeakable crimes. The

Nuremburg trials, memories of which were revived during the Israeli trial of former SS leader Adolf Eichmann in 1960–61, served as a potent analogy—particularly for the many Jews in the New Left. Not to act against an unjust system was to acquiesce in its behavior.[5] William Lloyd Garrison and Frances Willard would have understood.

For the young moralists of the 1960s—missionaries of a secular persuasion—only a self-conscious rebellion from below could topple the corrupted liberal order. To accomplish that task, the New Left sought to break the particularistic fetters that had bound previous conceptions of the virtuous majority. Workers and consumers, blacks and whites, Asians and Latinos, women and men, the oppressed of other nations, and later gays and straights were all deemed to be victims of what was vaguely but ominously called "the System." With the romantic urgency of youth, radicals insisted that no group be demonized, patronized, devalued, or excluded.

At the head of the System stood a slick, self-perpetuating club that radicals called "the power structure" or "the power elite" (the latter phrase was the title of the sociologist C. Wright Mills's most influential book). Jointly, the members of this club held in their hands the authority of big business, the federal government, the military, the press, and the major universities. Their worldview was described by radical historians as "corporate liberalism"—a smooth blend of demotic sophistry, symbolic legislation, and fantasies of endless consumption. "It performs for the corporate state a function quite like what the Church once performed for the feudal state," explained SDS president Carl Oglesby in 1965. "It seems to justify its burdens and protect it from change." The wealth and political clout of industrialists that earlier left-leaning populists had so reviled was now just one feature—and not the most alarming one—of what Mills called the "higher immorality." A pervasive powerlessness that washed over distinctions of occupation, income, and property would be the primary motive for social change.[6]

This analysis led young radicals to reach beyond the aims of earlier mass movements on the left. The Populists, the AFL, the CIO, and Marxists (in their reformist mode) had not challenged the legitimacy of a government of parties and bureaucrats tethered to the holy Constitution. And they assumed the division between leaders and followers—in the state and within their own organizations—to be a natural one.

But New Leftists found the very forms of modern politics frustrating, alienating, and inauthentic. No matter how good their intentions, lawmakers and bureaucrats eager to satisfy a bundle of powerful constituencies (big business, big labor, and the military) always ended up telling unorganized Americans what they should want—and then consistently failed to deliver. In 1965, one SDS leader suggested that elections were "irrelevant" to the process of change because a closed elite determined who the nominees would be.[7]

Citizens should reject this phony democracy and build their own system of "participatory democracy." The governed should govern themselves directly—in a patient, caring manner. The result would be a "beloved community"—a society in which, as two renowned young radicals had written on the eve of the revolutions of 1848, "the free development of each is the condition for the free development of all."[8] In the words of SDS's Port Huron Statement, drafted in 1962 by Tom Hayden and revised by fifty-eight of his compatriots:

> We would replace power rooted in possession, privilege, or circumstance by power and uniqueness rooted in love, reflectiveness, reason, and creativity. As a *social system* we seek the establishment of a democracy of individual participation, governed by two central aims: that the individual share in those social decisions determining the quality and direction of his life; that society be organized to encourage independence in men and provide the media for their common participation.[9]

The decision to begin the main body of the manifesto with a long section called "Values" made SDS's priorities clear: people must treat one another democratically if they would become capable of genuine self-rule. Although his fellow activists admired Hayden for his ability to convey ideas in vivid, uplifting phrases that sounded "American," no one in SDS was a leader in the traditional sense. All wanted to be known as organizers without rank, not foot soldiers in anyone's army.[10]

A phrase from a recent papal encyclical that described human beings as "infinitely precious" had a prominent place in the Port Huron Statement. The gentle if urgent tone of the entire document contrasted explicitly with both the language of the "tough-minded" elite (exemplified by President John Fitzgerald Kennedy) and those Communists and anti-Communists who had once huddled around rival "old slogans" like "United Front Against Fascism" and "No Cooperation with Commies and Fellow Travelers."[11]

As many critics pointed out, participatory democracy (P.D.) was a utopian notion to which no framework of theory was ever added. But as rhetoric that married "a patriotic aura with a revolutionary ring," it was quite powerful.[12] "P.D." represented, on the one hand, the ultimate extension of rule by "the plain people" and of "industrial democracy" that earlier left-leaning populists had cherished in words but had compromised in practice. The entire society would be run like a New England town meeting or an agrarian cooperative. On the other hand, the New Left's distrust of representative institutions separated this kind of populism from its predecessors—as well as from the liberal elite whose global rivalry with the USSR threatened all of humanity.

Young radicals were pressing the existential conviction that people had to take control of *how* decisions were made, coupled with the unspoken faith that, once empowered, they would pursue tolerant, egalitarian ends. To the interest-group politics of Cold War America, whose higher circles mouthed liberal jargon to rationalize injustice, the New Left impelled an heroic alternative: let the people decide everything and get out of their way.[13]

MODEL IN BLACK

But who *were* the people? Clearly, white radicals argued, the old answer wouldn't do. The organized working class offered no true alternative. In fact, both union leaders and many of the rank and file colluded with corporate liberalism because they were, according to the Port Huron Statement, "lulled to comfort by the accessibility of luxury and the opportunity of long-term contracts." Even worse were the salaried and securely housed masses of the great white middle class; their soul-destroying materialism and trust in immoral leaders made the system hum. "Cheerful robots," C. Wright Mills called them. Mills, intellectual hero to the New Left, ridiculed the Marxists' "labor metaphysic" and, by extension, any other predigested theory about which social group should be the major agent of change. Think for yourselves about who is on the move, he advised; then act accordingly.[14]

In the early 1960s, that could only mean the black crusade for freedom. The creators of the white New Left proudly modeled themselves on the young African-Americans who—with a small number of white compatriots—were braving bombs, bullets, firehoses, and jail to bring authentic democracy to the South. Whites in SDS and its sister group, the Southern Student Organizing Committee (SSOC), wore the work shirts and overalls, sang the freedom songs, and, most important, imbibed the political vision of the black organizers in the Student Non-Violent Coordinating Committee (SNCC). In their individual variety—the elegant selflessness of Bob Moses (who had broken off his philosophy studies at Harvard), the taut brilliance of Stokely Carmichael (graduate of the select Bronx High School of Science), and the eloquent fury of Fannie Lou Hamer (who had labored all her life on a cotton plantations)—SNCC workers seemed to demonstrate that an entire people was in glorious revolt against centuries of brutal prejudice and exploitation.

Any "beloved community" of true democrats would be indebted to the black activists who had coined the phrase. SNCC workers, wrote Howard Zinn of Boston University in his book-length tribute to the group, "are as compassionate and as brave as human beings with human failings can be . . . they nurture a vision of a revolution beyond race, against other forms of injustice, challenging the entire value-system of the nation and of smug middle-class society everywhere."[15]

This was a more momentous break with the populist past than was participatory democracy itself. For the first time, significant numbers of white activists proclaimed a desire to take their cues from a primarily black movement. As Carl Oglesby wrote, "I see SNCC as the Nile Valley of the New Left. And I honor SDS to call it part of the delta that SNCC created."[16] Until the late 1930s, every mass insurgency had either ignored blacks or insisted they talk and behave like members of the white majority. The CIO and the Popular Front tried to be sensitive to the special plight of what they called "the Negro people" but never considered the possibility that the victims might become the leading force on the Left.

By the 1960s, however, white radicals could no longer accept the image of a resolute assembly of ordinary white faces with a few darker ones mixed in for the sake of solidarity. Having been raised "in at least modest comfort" and with a commitment to the egalitarian ideal, they responded to the black struggle with shivers of guilt as well as gobs of admiration. One Southern SDS member agonized about "the Original Sin of our ancestry," and "white skin privilege" became a favorite response to the question of why most American workers had always been racist.[17] For the New Left, the meaning of *freedom* began with the struggle of African-Americans at the grassroots—the struggle to win equal rights and power by and for people who suffered under the legacy of slavery, Jim Crow, and liberal attempts to patronize and assimilate them.

At the time, this seemed the only honest and principled way to solve the American dilemma. Black liberation, aided by unselfish whites, would destroy the highest and oldest barrier to achieving a democracy worthy of the name. To vault the boundary of race, the young Left had to focus on racial injustice.

Not until later in the decade—when civil rights gave way to black power—did the political costs of this stance become clear. For white activists, a racially specific definition of the people tended to drown out the thin strains of majoritarian, color-blind language that had resonated from the Popular Front. If Vietnam was "a white man's war" against a poor, yellow nation—as SNCC and other black groups charged—then white radicals inevitably took the side of the Vietcong. The American military had to be defeated for true freedom and democracy to triumph.

Its defiance of liberal shibboleths was one of the elements that spurred the New Left's growth among young people in a flamboyantly antinomian era. But the character of that growth was self-limiting. Young white radicals based in and around university campuses generally rejected the kind of public language most insurgents on the Left had employed, with a good deal of success, since the era of Andrew Jackson. Undeniably, the populist tradition had little room for blacks, women, or Third World people as articulate makers of their own history. Yet if ordinary Americans did not share a common identity as hardworking patriots set upon by an arrogant, grasping elite, how could they ever cohere? How would the movement achieve the "democracy of individual participation" that was its founding purpose?

TO THE COMMUNITY, AMBIVALENTLY

Through the first half of the 1960s, young radicals were reluctant to shed all inherited patterns of language and strategy. Organizing still meant assistance to reform efforts by working-class and lower-middle-class Americans of all races—ordinary people who, a generation earlier, had been courted by the New Deal. College leftists walked on picket lines with typographers and autoworkers, brought food to striking coal miners in Kentucky, aided the creation of reform factions within the Democratic parties of New York City and Los Angeles, and moved into poor urban neighborhoods. Although New Leftists showed a preference for grassroots insurgencies unsullied by ties with the system, few wanted to impose a doctrinal line or shut off any sincere attempt to mobilize ordinary Americans, however defined, to help themselves.[18]

The intent of such undertakings was the same as that of populist-speaking activists in the past: to convince the hard-pressed millions to reclaim their society from an exploitative, self-seeking minority. And despite their self-conscious break with the Old Left, a nostalgic fondness for protest songs and raised fists joined the young radicals to their forebears in the 1930s. Bob Dylan, a dropout from the University of Minnesota, traveled to New York City to meet his dying idol, the leftist folksinger Woody Guthrie, and was soon recording, in a distinctly Guthrie-like drawl, songs called "Masters of War" and "The Times They Are A-Changin'." Before he got fed up with sending "messages" and became an icon of the international counterculture, Dylan sang freedom songs to field hands on a Mississippi cotton plantation, visited union organizers in Appalachian mining towns, and even showed up at an SDS national meeting.[19]

While critical of organized labor and the Democratic Party for resting on their New Deal laurels, New Leftists also hesitated to break completely with such powerful figures as Walter Reuther and Lyndon Baines Johnson. After all, wasn't the Republican Right, now led by Barry Goldwater, a greater evil? Several SDS chapters began life as study circles with "liberal" still in their name. For the 1964 election, the organization adopted the equivocal slogan, "Part of the Way with LBJ." Until escalation of both the Vietnam War and the movement to stop it, most activists retained some hope that liberals would grasp the need to move to the left.[20]

Yet for all its diligent organizing, the New Left could not shake its ambivalence about the political will and opinions of the white majority. Radicals worried about the inertia of consumers, workers, and students and about the tenacious appeal of anticommunism. They agonized that racism prevented most whites from seeing that freedom for blacks might liberate them, too.

In 1961, Tom Hayden wrote a public letter to SDS from a segregated drunk tank in Albany, Georgia, where he'd been jailed for participating in a freedom ride. He reported, "I listened in pity and outrage to the stories of our still-sobering cellmates. 'No nigger has life so bad as me' . . . 'the poor whites can't get no jobs even when them niggers can. We should be fighting for OUR equal rights . . . you nigger-lovers can go home after this, but me—I have to walk to Atlanta.'"[21]

Young radicals wanted to empathize with such people; only a biracial coalition of outcasts could bring about the kind of fundamental change they desired. Moreover, they had learned from the black freedom movement that the most humbled Americans could take on the establishment that ruled their lives. From the labor movement's militant past, they retained an understanding of the distinction between the rank and file and union "bureaucrats" as well as a sense that working people were never as content as the pro-business press supposed them to be. And the natural optimism of youth led them to hope that almost anyone, however lulled or apathetic, who did not belong to the power elite might be persuaded to understand the truth about the awful state of the nation. So they fanned out from their campuses to test their convictions in poor black and white communities.

In this venture, they had a seasoned precursor named Saul Alinsky. During the 1940s, Alinsky, the son of a prosperous Jewish tailor, had moved away from the orbit of the Communist Party and become the chief philosopher and entrepreneur of community organizing. The method of Alinsky's Industrial Areas Foundation (IAF) amounted to a mass psychology of urban populism. With tough talk and imaginative tactics, he and the corps of organizers he trained sought to convince residents of declining urban neighborhoods to take on the outside elites that belittled and exploited them.[22]

Only when tenants had dumped garbage on a slumlord's front porch to protest a neglect of repairs or parishioners had staged a children's Mass to pray for a municipal lunch program would they understand how to cure their overlapping, collective ills. Community organizing in the Alinsky mode was an emancipatory device to end internecine squabbles, to foster a neighborhood's identity and purpose, and, in the very long run, to establish the "broad, popular democracy" advocated by his idols Paine, Jefferson, and Whitman.[23] Nicholas Von Hoffman, once Alinsky's star pupil, advised: "The organizer's first job is to organize, not right wrongs, not avenge injustice, not to win the battle for freedom." Once citizens—Alinsky's term of preference—learned how to convert their discontent into protest, they could decide for themselves what they wanted and how to get it.[24]

In the 1960s, young radicals applauded that emphasis on democratic process over product. But they questioned how much IAF organizers had really achieved in the scattering of urban enclaves where they'd set up shop. One New Left critic scored the IAF as "basically an effort to provide therapeutic experiences to 'deprived' people." The Alinsky dictum to speak only about issues pertaining to the "self-interest" of a particular community seemed self-defeating; it could never knit together a radical movement whose members would have to make sacrifices for the common good. At worst, the narrow focus excused aid to working-class whites who wanted to resist blacks moving into their neighborhoods (though the IAF initiated projects in black and Mexican-American communities, too). Such rank opportunism New Leftists could not abide.[25]

Yet it was impossible to sink deep roots in working-class communities without diluting the intellectual purity of one's principles. Alinsky was a middle-class Jew in love with great books and social theory. But he had served his apprenticeship in the proletarian milieu of the 1930s Left and still frequented the company of streetwise priests and union officials. Without such seasoning, New Leftists were attempting to bridge the gulf between student union and street corner, between a "beloved community" of activists and everyday communities of white and black working people who craved security and mistrusted condescension.

The most ambitious attempt to reach beyond the campus and the educated middle class occurred from 1963 to 1965, when most of SDS's leading activists moved into poor urban neighborhoods, both white and black, under the aegis of the Economic Research and Action Project (ERAP). The poor, whom Michael Harrington had called "the Other America" (in his influential 1962 book of the same title), were not the sturdy producers earlier populist speakers had championed. Often unemployed and plagued by alcohol and family violence, the urban poor had never seemed a reliable base for political organization of any kind, let alone one that might spark a society-wide upheaval. Marxists had often written them off, in the Continental idiom, as "the lumpenproletariat." Saul Alinsky and his disciples had always concentrated on those community residents who already belonged to churches, unions, or other stable bodies.

But 1960s radicals viewed the negative imagery as part of the problem. Except for their heroes and heroines in SNCC, no one who professed to be helping the poor really wanted them to take power over their own lives, to transform the very limited welfare state that was supposed to serve them. The social workers who regulated them, the social scientists who studied them, and the politicians who manipulated them were all judged to be agents of a system that caused the very degradation they sanctimoniously deplored. At a time when the Johnson administration was trumpeting a "war on poverty," SDS maintained that only the poor could defeat poverty and, in so doing, bring real democracy to America. Young radicals who understood "the needs of ordinary men for a decent life" were eager to help them get started.[26]

Several hundred organizers (including Tom Hayden, his former wife Casey Hayden, and Paul Potter) moved in small clusters to ten run-down black and white neighborhoods, most in the North, to forge what they hoped would be "an interracial movement of the poor." They knocked on thousands of doors, held community meetings (which few local people regularly attended), and survived for long stretches in their collectives on little more than peanut-butter-and-jelly sandwiches. Like the muckrakers of old, ERAP activists researched and exposed the way "power structures" of local government officials and corporate executives kept themselves wealthy and in control.[27] Urging the unemployed and underemployed to turn their frustration against elites rather than one another, ERAP organizers hoped to build "a new and commanding force in American politics" to rival or even surpass that which organized labor had mustered during the New Deal.[28]

Yet, unlike CIO activists in the 1930s, these young radicals were clearly outsiders in such neighborhoods as Chicago's Uptown, Newark's Clinton Hill, and the black ghetto of Chester, Pennsylvania. They had taken on the task of translating conceptions of participatory democracy that were rooted in an academic Left into the language of mostly apolitical people. These people, whether white or black, certainly liked the idea of having the power to make decisions that vitally affected their own lives. But any talk that smacked of radicalism or communism bred mistrust, and the all-day meetings the ERAP organizers held in communal settings were a most unusual style of political behavior.[29]

During its short life, ERAP did establish a handful of viable community groups—especially Chicago's JOIN (Jobs or Income Now) and the Newark Community Union Project (NCUP)—which, ironically later latched onto the swelling apparatus of the federal antipoverty program. And, through ERAP, activists learned practical lessons in "face-to-face communication" they would put to use in later phases of the movement—particularly the feminist awakening. The thousands of counterinstitutions radicals created through the rest of the decade and beyond—underground papers, health clinics, and cooperative food stores—observes the historian James Miller, "all would try their hand at direct democracy and rule-by-consensus." So P.D. turned out to have a concrete meaning after all.[30]

But few ERAP activists were able to merge an internal discourse that spoke of their projects as chances "to test our ideas," to cure the poor of "ideological hang-ups," and to build "counter-societies" with the language of the people they were organizing. As a result, the impression persisted that these middle-class kids were in but not of the community; that they were only the most sincere of political missionaries. "Students and poor people make each other feel real," gushed Tom Hayden. Evidently Saul Alinsky was not the only activist who indulged in therapeutic experiences.[31]

In 1965, Dorothy Perez, an Uptown resident and member of JOIN, unintentionally acknowledged a deep cultural gap between the organizers and the organized even as she praised the commitment of the radical outsiders. "I find it uplifting to know that we are not really a forgotten people," she said at an ERAP-sponsored conference of the poor; "that students and young adults in JOIN care enough to give so much of themselves to help us to help ourselves, by leading, guiding and instrusting [sic] us to form a union for and of ourselves."[32]

Even though ERAP failed to galvanize a new interracial insurgency, the idea that organizers must share the lives of downtrodden Americans in order to make fundamental change—a notion the New Left shared with earlier generations of ascetic radicals—retained its ethical attraction. But during the rest of the decade and beyond, most leftists would ground their collectives in college neighborhoods and towns that offered a more inviting cultural terrain and a surer base for challenging America's rulers.

LIBERATED AREAS

Returning to campus, the New Left transformed itself from a network of activists into a mass movement. Midway through 1964, the SDS National Office was delighted to report a membership of close to 1,000 spread across twenty-nine chapters. Four years later, as a new school year opened, the organization had at least 100,000 members in perhaps 400 chapters (by then, the accuracy of SDS's record keeping had gone the way of crewcuts and saddle shoes).[33]

And that was just the indicator of radical strength easiest to chart. Colleges and high schools across the nation featured a potpourri of unheralded local groups that supported black rebellion, opposed the Vietnam War, and were engrossed in a culture of drug-assisted good times and harmonious visions. Hundreds of underground newspapers, most selling thousands of copies per week, sported such whimsical names as *The Great Speckled Bird, All You Can Eat, Daily Planet,* and *Dock of the Bay,* phrases borrowed from popular songs, television shows, and other effusions of mass culture. In 1968, one national poll reported that three-quarters of a million college students (over 10 percent of the whole) identified themselves as adherents of the New Left; most were probably affiliated with no organization at all.[34]

Disgust with America's long war in Vietnam fueled this conflagration. But the intellectual-activists who started SDS could still glimpse their handiwork in the language being spoken—although few remained at the head of the blazing, centrifugal movement. There was, in the late 1960s, the same "alienation" from middle-class repression and complacency, the same anger at the hypocrisy of liberal authorities, the same insistence on collective decision making as the only genuine form of democracy. As in the early 1960s, mimeographed pamphlets—their prose bulging toward the margins with analysis, reproach, and resistance—were the most common form of propaganda on campus.[35]

And young radicals continued to match their language to that of black activists on the militant cutting edge. In the days of freedom rides and voter-registration campaigns, that had meant emulating SNCC's talk of building a "beloved community" while groping for a principled way to convince poor whites and blacks that they should work together. By 1967, it often meant using hip slang and pugnacious epithets like "pig" while periodically donning the sunglasses and leather jackets favored by members of the Black Panther Party. The Panther maxim "Power to the People" quickly became the unofficial slogan of white radicals as well.

To organize their fellow young whites, some New Leftists tried to talk black. "Students are niggers," began a popular pamphlet by a (white) California state college professor named Jerry Farber. "When you get that straight, our schools begin to make sense." The SDS National Office, in 1967, offered a "special 4-poster package of revolutionary heroes." One idol was the Latin-American guerrilla leader Che Guevara; the other three were Malcolm X, Stokely Carmichael, and Muhammad Ali. "White kids are moving against this racist decadent system too," proclaimed the supermilitant Weatherman faction of SDS in 1969. "If we accept the honkey lives that Amerika forces on us—and don't move on the side of the people of the world, we are keeping their struggle down."[36]

The new white student Left, at its zenith, did not sprout evenly throughout the land. By the end of the '60s, half of all Americans between the ages of 18 and 21 had taken at least some college classes; the result was a considerable diversity of rhetoric and experience.[37] The nucleus of each major—and well-reported—New Left center was a large, internationally renowned university: the University of California (Berkeley), the University of Michigan (Ann Arbor), the University of Wisconsin (Madison), Harvard University (Cambridge), and Columbia University (the Upper West Side of Manhattan).

In those locales, one could glimpse a kind of populism blooming in rather small and rarefied spaces. Activists—most of whom sprang from reform-minded, professional families and majored in the liberal arts—were genuine leaders of a "people." They found the bulk of students at least mildly supportive, the faculty willing to listen, the administration defensive, and surrounding neighborhoods that offered cheap lodging (sometimes on the edge of a black ghetto) and a tolerant attitude toward young people fond of recreational drugs and rock and roll.

This was more than student power, although it depended upon congregations of college kids willing to stand up to administrators and boards of trustees on a more or less regular basis. It signaled that large numbers of young, white middle-class Americans felt themselves "to be unfree," as the SDS spokesman Greg Calvert declared in 1967, and not merely fighters in other peoples' battles.[38] When they took on a university "target" linked to the war or another evil wrought by the system, it seemed like masses of citizens—albeit young ones—with righteous grievances were opposed only by an elite scared of losing its lofty titles and federal funding.

At the time, some critics belittled New Leftists for remaining on campus instead of trying to "radicalize" the larger society. But every movement of the discontented initially seeks to rally the segment of society from which it comes to challenge those in immediate authority. Small farmers fought the banks and railroads; union workers clashed with bosses and federal judges. In the 1960s, students attacked university officials, think tanks doing military research, and ROTC buildings. The difficulty comes when a movement seeks to broaden its scope beyond the community for which it can credibly speak. The New Left attempted to make that leap with ERAP; it never consistently did so again.

The premier model of a youth community existed in and around Berkeley, the flagship campus of the University of California. Since the 1930s, Berkeley, together with San Francisco across the bay, had been host to a large popular front of leftists, bohemians, and folksingers. The landmark student uprising took place at Berkeley in the fall of 1964. Ignited by the refusal of President Clark Kerr (a labor specialist and liberal Democrat) to allow the Friends of SNCC to collect money on campus, the Free Speech Movement (FSM) charged that managers of the "multiversity" were handling college students in a fashion that paralleled the way the Southern elite mistreated blacks. "In Mississippi an autocratic and powerful minority rules, through organized violence, to suppress the vast, virtually powerless majority," charged the FSM spokesman Mario Savio. "In California, the privileged minority manipulates the university bureaucracy to suppress the students' political expression."[39]

Paternalistic bureaucrats, however, were hardly the same as brutal Delta sheriffs, and the students who responded to Savio had dreams most other citizens didn't share—and a hip vocabulary to match. The FSM, like the campus insurgencies that followed it, employed a language that effectively appealed to young people hungry for a politics of courage and imagination but that puzzled or enraged Americans who viewed a college education as a privilege whose essential value should not be questioned.

A few weeks before Savio's speech, the FSM activist Brad Cleveland published an open letter to undergraduates. He challenged students to stop acting "as a herd of grade-worshiping sheep" and to become "the seeds of an educational revolution unlike anything which has ever occurred." At the end of his letter, Cleveland asked readers to "Remember one thing: The task of genius, and man is nothing if not genius, is to keep the miracle alive, to live always in the miracle, to make the miracle more and more miraculous, to swear allegiance to nothing, but live only miraculously, think miraculously, to die miraculously." The passage was written earlier by Henry Miller, whose sexually explicit, autobiographical novels had recently been cleared by the Supreme Court for American distribution.[40]

Few Berkeley radicals saw a contradiction between aligning themselves with both poor blacks and with a symbol of the erotic beat culture. They were fighting the power elite because it stifled a creative life of the mind and spirit *and* because it ignored the persistence of want and inequality. Brandishing Miller's words and advocating revolution were both ways to shock a society addicted to managing its problems with the latest in psychobabble and advanced technology. "Do not fold, spindle or mutilate" read the IBM registration cards that hundreds of FSM members pinned to their chests in one demonstration.[41]

Then there was the popular protest song, "Little Boxes" by the Bay Area folksinger Malvina Reynolds. "Little Boxes" satirized tract housing just south of San Francisco (most of it occupied by working-class people on their way up) as

Little boxes on the hillside,
Little boxes made of ticky tacky,
Little boxes on the hillside . . .
And they all look just the same.

Reynolds, a Berkeley Ph.D. and erstwhile follower of the Communist Party, intended, like Brad Cleveland, to wake up the suburban masses and their children—who, she mistakenly believed, "all go to the university." To revise Woody Guthrie, this land *was* their land; and she didn't like what they'd done with it.[42]

Such foes of conformity helped make Berkeley a liberated area, the base for New Left organizing up and down the West Coast. By the late 1960s, a radical coalition was electing candidates to the city council, and the alternative weekly *Barb* outsold the conservative *Berkeley Daily Gazette*. A 1968 *Time* poll of Berkeley students about the Vietnam War found fewer than 10 percent who supported American policy. Whenever California Governor Ronald Reagan vowed, as he did regularly, to "clean up the mess at Berkeley," a shifting but durable community of what Tom Hayden called "the dropouts, the freaks, and the radicals" was able to defy him.[43]

But the student movement boasted only a handful of Berkeleys. On hundreds of unprestigious campuses that the national media generally ignored, New Leftists were an embattled minority who could count on neither tolerant authorities nor supportive classmates. The majority of students came from white working-class families and often resented radicals for disrupting classes and condemning a war their friends and relatives were fighting. In the spring of 1969, an SDS rally of 200 at Kent State University in Ohio was attacked by 700 college protesters, some armed with motorcycle chains and baseball bats. The New Left in such places was split between activists who clung to older ideals of peace and racial integration and those who emulated the bolder, confrontational rhetoric common in more "liberated" locales.[44]

It was not easy to be a radical at Kent State. The only publicly funded university in the industrial triangle between Cleveland, Akron, and Youngstown, Kent attracted a student body seeking credentials and professional training more than a voyage of self-discovery through the liberal arts. Many were sons and daughters of men who made cars, rubber, and steel; freedom, to them, meant never having to work in a factory, unionized or not. The student population at Kent State increased more than 400 percent from the mid-1950s to mid-1960s with majors like business administration and engineering leading the way. Robert White, the university's president through most of the 1960s, viewed any left-leaning student as either a nihilist or a "bleeding heart," and most of the faculty backed him up when he refused to discipline the students who attacked SDS. The city of Kent itself was a Republican stronghold on guard against "pot-smoking Communists." Sanctuary for leftists came only from a small number of sympathetic clergymen.[45]

In this environment, radicals at Kent State usually talked more like Berkeley liberals. The campus movement began in 1963 with protests against the town's segregated swimming pools, and spokesmen for the local antiwar committee spent a good deal of their time simply defending their right to be heard and making guarded arguments like, "The Asian Communists have such a vast job to do to feed their millions that they are in no position to take us on, even if they wanted to. . . . " An SDS chapter wasn't formed on campus until the fall of 1968. It quickly got embroiled in caustic debates between revolutionaries spoiling for a fight and moderates who wanted to continue holding peace forums. The National Guard troops who opened fire on May 4, 1970, had been called to campus because Kent's mayor overreacted to a night of rioting by drunken students and because Ohio's Republican governor wanted to illustrate his toughness during a difficult primary campaign. Four students were killed; not one was a radical.[46]

The mass student movement thus exhibited a rarefied mode of populism. The academic communities where radicalism became the authentic voice of a people were atypical, dominated by budding intellectual-activists from comfortable backgrounds who lived in stimulating separation from the evil society outside. On campuses where career-minded students from working-class backgrounds were the norm, the New Left struggled to stay afloat in a hostile sea. Only after the shootings at Kent State did activists breach this cultural barrier; that May, some sort of protest occurred at 44 percent of American colleges.[47] But no radical organization knew how to use the brief explosion to turn the student movement in a majoritarian direction.

CLEAN IT OFF OR RIP IT DOWN

To understand that failure means exploring the rhetoric used by radicals in the larger antiwar movement they influenced but did not control. Major protests began in the spring of 1965 after President Lyndon Baines Johnson ordered United States troops into combat in South Vietnam and bombers to raid the North; they continued to build, in size and intensity, for six years until President Richard Nixon ended the draft and began to withdraw most GIs from that devastated country. At its height, the antiwar movement drew supporters from nearly every political camp, excluding only stalwart red hunters, whose number was decreasing. As befit such a diverse lot, demonstrators had a variety of reasons for their opposition—from practical warnings against fighting a land war in Asia to pacifist cries that military force was nothing but mass murder.[48]

New Leftists, armed with their sense of moral urgency and tactics of direct action, played a major role in building this antiwar movement into the largest and most successful one in the nation's history. But their rhetoric pulled in different directions. The most conspicuous option was to indict America root and branch for fostering the misery of Indochina; only an anti-imperialist revolution led by Third World people inside and outside American borders could exorcise the nation's sins. The quieter course was to appeal to the nation's democratic principles, which usually included the traditional populist argument that ordinary people were fighting and paying for a war that benefited only a privileged elite.

How activists handled the American flag said a lot about the path they preferred. Third Worldists defamed the banner—tearing holes in it, replacing the stars with skulls, or waving instead the tricolor of the National Liberation Front of South Vietnam (the NLF or Vietcong). Few United States flags were actually burned. Radical populists carried the Stars and Stripes upside down—the naval signal for distress—or superimposed a peace sign. Some, insisting *they* were the true patriots, defiantly waved the nation's banner before police and counterdemonstrators. Citizens of that rare nation whose anthem speaks adoringly of its flag, antiwar protesters were quite earnest about the play of symbols in cloth.[49]

Many activists, of course, did not fall neatly or immediately into either camp. Anti-warriors often felt attracted to both Third Worldist and populist sentiments; they appreciated the power of the civil religion (in its left-wing variant) and hesitated before the enormity of desecration.

One could condemn the war, say kind words about the enemy, and still seek to represent plainspeaking Americans and their ideals. The Vietcong, explained Paul

Potter at a peace march sponsored by SDS in April 1965, was composed of "ordinary people" fighting "to have some opportunity to make their own lives." The growing war was not so complicated or foreign; like the civil rights movement, it was a struggle for democracy. Potter did not welcome a Communist victory; he retained a distrust of Leninist parties. But if most Vietnamese wished to be led by one, Americans must respect their choice.[50]

Seven months later, Carl Oglesby, the new president of SDS, struck up a more direct quarrel with rhetorical tradition. At a peace demonstration sponsored by the liberal group National Committee for a Sane Nuclear Policy (SANE), he questioned whether it were possible to cling to the faith of New Dealers and still understand why the United States was in Vietnam. The 30-year-old Oglesby, whose bearded angularity reminded some of D. H. Lawrence, was not himself a rebel against the urbane, progressive middle class. Son of an Akron tire builder, he had attended Kent State in the late 1950s on a debate scholarship and ended up with an engineering degree. He had left a good job with a military contractor to join SDS. So Oglesby was already something of a stranger to the assumptions he was challenging.[51]

His speech posed a conflict between "humanist" liberals, like the ones in the crowd, and the corporate variety:

> The original commitment in Vietnam was made by President Truman, a mainstream liberal. It was seconded by President Eisenhower, a moderate liberal. It was intensified by the late President Kennedy, a flaming liberal. Think of the men who now engineer that war—those who study the maps, give the commands, push the buttons, and tally the dead: Bundy, McNamara, Rusk, Lodge, Goldberg, the President himself.
>
> They are not moral monsters.
> They are all honorable men.
> They are all liberals.[52]

In similarly rhythmic prose, Oglesby went on to detail the then little-known pattern of American support for right-wing coups and dictatorships—in South Africa, Iran, Guatemala, the Dominican Republic, and elsewhere.

Oglesby urged liberals to assist in dismantling the structure of horrors—"help us shake the future in the name of plain human hope." But his speech presaged the scorn at such an alliance and the embrace of militant Third Worldism that would typify the New Left for the rest of the decade. Unlike Potter, Oglesby defined what was going on in Vietnam as a "revolution" and explained that the violence of the other side was unavoidable: "Revolutions do not take place in velvet boxes. They never have. . . . Nuns will be raped and bureaucrats will be disemboweled. Indeed, revolution is a fury. For it is the letting loose of outrages pent up sometimes over centuries." Absent was any hint that corporate liberalism might be harming his fellow citizens as well as the Vietnamese. Oglesby acknowledged, "I sound mighty anti-American," adding "Don't blame *me* for *that!* Blame those who mouthed my liberal values and broke my American heart."[53]

Anguish soon hardened into iconoclasm. By 1967, the escalating war shone a national floodlight on young radicals who viewed any statement of patriotism as a compromise with imperialism. Echoing the angry young men and women of the Black Panther Party, these New Leftists opposed their own wicked "mother country" to the noble Third World. Some took to spelling the country's name "Amerika," hinting at a resemblance with Nazi Germany. "American radicals are perhaps the first radicals anywhere who have sought to make a revolution in a country which they hate," observed the black writer Julius Lester in 1970.[54]

Leftists who cultivated an outrageous, if humorous, style of talk and dress captured the mass media's rapt disapproval. Instead of the troubled rationality of Potter and Oglesby came Abbie Hoffman, the Yippie jester, telling his many fans to make "revolution for the hell of it," and steal food, clothing, and education instead of working for them. On television and in the underground press, budding celebrities like Hoffman and Jerry Rubin crowded out local radicals who sounded only slightly different from their fellow students.[55]

Certainly, Abbie Hoffman believed he was a patriot, even a populist. As he later explained: "To me the country is the land and the people, not necessarily the guy who happens to be president." But the networks depicted him as the kind of radical who waved the Vietcong's flag and burned the American one, and he made no effort to deny it.[56]

In fact, Hoffman and other revolutionaries (the term *organizer,* with its connections to labor was now less common) exulted in their heretical image. Streams of young people from a variety of regions and social backgrounds were flowing into the movement precisely because its speakers and press lampooned the civil religion and glorified in symbols of total rebellion—which their elders abhorred.

When SDS vaulted into antiwar prominence in 1965, thousands of new members from the Southwest and rural Midwest joined up, bringing with them a deep alienation from the pious, pro-military, work-obsessed culture in which they'd been raised. A large minority in the organization, this new breed, collectively dubbed "prairie power," cared little about the conflict with liberalism and the Old Left that had molded the writers of the Port Huron Statement. The establishment they knew was a conservative one, and they were eager to kick it in the shins.[57]

Elated with their escape from the clutches of the system, such rebels seldom wondered who would make the revolution. Television newscasts, despite their verbal censure, showed abundant footage of angry young blacks, young whites with long, glistening hair, and a variety of antiwar protesters who were at once determined and ecstatic. The underground press displayed the same alluring images—enveloped by articles implying that, in combination, campus revolts, ghetto rebellions, rock music, psychedelic drugs, and the Vietcong were sapping the power of the establishment, of "straight" America. "Something is happening here,/But you don't know what it is,/Do you, Mister Jones?" sneered Bob Dylan in a song Black

Panther leaders quoted admiringly. Day by day, to paraphrase "The Internationale," the alienated were becoming the human race.[58]

In 1969, after he and other self-described "weirdos" watched the telecast of the first moon landing, Abbie Hoffman fantasized that "some day we too will fly off in some communal capsule, Blacks, Puerto Ricans, Hippies, liberated women, young workers on the line, and G.I.'s sitting in stockades because they don't want to go to Vietnam. There will be a whole mess of us laughing and getting stoned on our way to OUTERSPACE, and the first thing, the very first thing we're gonna do out there is to rip down that fuckin' flag on the moon."[59]

Away from the cameras, other young radicals were propounding a different vision, one that displayed their faith in what America had once meant and should mean again. They sought, in effect, not to rip down the flag but to cleanse it of crimes done in its name. In 1967, an SDS member from Michigan State wrote in his local paper: "A nation is not defined by the particular policy, of a particular administration, in power at a particular point in time. Rather, the genius of a nation is expressed in those lofty ideals and broad spiritual currents which have threaded their way through the fabric of its history . . . our commitment to the real core values and ideals that have made this nation great demands that we oppose the war." The writer was David Stockman. Two years later, Stockman, raised a pious Methodist, deserted a New Left bent on revolution and began the political migration that landed him in Ronald Reagan's first cabinet.[60]

Echoing such sentiments in the late 1960s were a number of radicals who wanted to fill the political gulf that existed between their movement and the many white working people who liked neither the war nor demonstrators who rooted for the enemy. In spirit, these activists resembled Max Eastman and Randolph Bourne—the left-wing intellectuals who, half a century before, had demanded a national referendum on the question of entering World War I. They, too, hoped a version of class-conscious Americanism would speed an end to the killing.

Artifice plagued some of these efforts. *The Little Red White and Blue Book* was a palm-size compilation of radical quotations by "Great Americans" from Thomas Jefferson to Eldridge Cleaver. This militant updating of Popular Front platitudes was the creation of Johnny "Appleseed" Rossen, an ex-Communist and the landlord of SDS's national office. Rossen believed that only a genuine patriotism could make the New Left more than a vehicle for protest. But his title (a comment on Mao Zedong's *Little Red Book* of aphorisms) and the mélange of statements made centuries apart probably amused more readers than it inspired. An alternative Americanism could not be crafted simply by stringing together shards of evidence that the nation had an energetic left-wing past.[61]

More auspicious efforts came from antiwar activists who focused on the draft. The Selective Service System purposely discriminated against young men who either could not or would not pursue a higher education. One of the New Left's most-quoted pamphlets was the 1967 reprint of a government memo that described this bias as "the American or indirect way of achieving what is done by direction in foreign countries where choice is not permitted." In response, the SDS slogan "Not With My Life You Don't" tapped a deep vein of resistance to federal prerogatives that, since the 1930s, had been more common on the Right than on the Left. The draft-counseling centers that proliferated in college towns and big cities offered a multitude of ways to act on that conviction.[62]

In some places, the draft brought fresh purpose to the dormant practice of community organizing. Late in 1967, *The Movement* newspaper in San Francisco (formerly the voice of Friends of SNCC) urged radicals to form draft-resistance unions in white neighborhoods as opening moves in a long-term strategy "to reach our own people." "Let's be straight," the monthly declared in terms reminiscent of both ERAP and Saul Alinsky: "What's got to be done is to get the people in this country who neither support nor confront the government's misuse of power MOVING . . . we've got to find issues on the local level, in the community, around which people can demand control of what the political machine, or a minority of landlords and businessmen now control."[63]

A scattering of ambitious projects did get started. While in college, I occasionally participated in one called the Boston Draft Resistance Group (BDRG). The BDRG rented a tiny office in a white working-class neighborhood of Cambridge where, to most residents, military service seemed the most secure and most honorable option available to an unmarried young man without a steady job. For several months, our major task was to call on every local man classified 1-A (fit for induction) and urge him to consider legal and quasilegal ways to avoid going in. While we fixed on individual circumstances, phrases like "a rich man's war" and "it's not our fight" inevitably punctuated the encounters. Unlike David Stockman, I saw no contradiction between marching down the street chanting "Ho, Ho, Ho Chi Minh, the NLF is Gonna Win" and professing, in private conversation, the patriotic ideal that citizens should defy the government when it commands them to abet injustice.

The one place antiwar radicals made a sustained attempt to reach working-class Americans was inside the military itself. Starting in 1967, hundreds of civilian activists joined with servicemen (and a few servicewomen) on active duty to run off-base coffeehouses, stage protests, and defend GIs being court-martialed for refusing to fight in Vietnam and for other political offenses. They also helped publish newspapers that, because they seldom could circulate freely, were the only ones to deserve the title of an "underground" press. The GI movement did not make its national presence known until April 23, 1971. On that day, Vietnam Veterans Against the War (VVAW) mobilized some 700 of its members to march to the Capitol, where every protester "solemnly announced his name and unit and then threw his medals over a makeshift fence toward the nation's seat of authority."[64]

The GI movement gratified two impulses dear to radical activists. First, it challenged American intervention at its most sensitive point: toiling at the point of war production, soldiers and sailors could stop the military machine by themselves if only they found the will to do it. The idea that fighting men were the most reliable arbiters of national policy, proclaimed by the VFW and the American Legion during the red scare, was thus stood neatly on its head. Second, college-educated leftists were able to interact politically with people from working-class and poor backgrounds who wanted and needed the help of supportive civilians. Only one-fifth of the men who served in Vietnam had more than a high-school education; thus, most "had to learn about the war the hard way, by fighting it."[65] For men who had escaped the draft and women tired of the fist-clenching campus Left, the GI struggle was a unique opportunity to weaken the vulnerable heart of imperialism and perhaps build a true people's movement.

As Abbie Hoffman knew, a shared fondness for rock music and smoking dope and a mutual aversion to inherited authorities helped smooth the connection. Early in the 1970s, New Left cartoonist Ted Richards created a GI character named Dopin' Dan, who spent his time getting stoned, dreaming about sex, and trying to outsmart discipline-happy "lifers." Dan, like most disgruntled soldiers at the time, did not complain about the war being immoral; his beef was simply that the government had given him no convincing reason to risk his young life in its service.[66]

Of course, radical civilians had to confront a good deal of mistrust about their own motives. While most GIs in Vietnam and elsewhere had decided, by the end of the sixties, that the war was a worthless enterprise, few warmed to an antiwar movement that seemed full of pampered kids having a quite safe and wonderful time. A television documentary filmed in 1969 depicted a group of American infantrymen in Vietnam who resisted combat orders and wore love beads around their necks and peace signs on their helmets. Notwithstanding the raiment of rebellion, all nodded their heads when one of them snapped: "The first thing I'm going to do when I get back to the world is beat up a hippie."[67]

To change such attitudes, activists from outside the military modulated the brashness common to SDS and other radical anti-warriors. "Probably you resent the fact that peace demonstrations include kids who can wait out the war in college. You have every right to be mad about that," acknowledged a leaflet addressed to GIs in the fall of 1968. "But do you know that the antiwar movement is trying to do away with the draft laws that give special privileges to some?" The populist strategy of turning class resentments against those who ran the system seemed the only way to cut through inequalities that divided the young and disaffected. "In fact," the leaflet continued, "the antiwar movement is trying to do away with all the laws that force people to fight and die in Vietnam while a few politicians haggle over how to keep the war going forever."[68]

COMING APART

As it happened, the war outlasted the mass movement against it, which mounted its last big demonstrations in the spring of 1971 and then rapidly declined. By the end of the 1960s, neither radical voice—the populist or the Third Worldist—spoke for more than a minority of the swelling numbers of citizens who wanted the killing to stop and the GIs to come home. Organizing on hundreds of campuses and marching down countless streets, New Leftists had made a good deal of noise and trouble. But they had not been able to convert antiwar sentiment into a demand for the kind of radical democracy proclaimed at Port Huron.

Meanwhile, buoyed by the growing demand for peace, a group of liberal senators had emerged as the conscience of the Establishment. The best known were Robert Kennedy, Eugene McCarthy, and George McGovern—all of whom ran for the Democratic presidential nomination in 1968 (McGovern only briefly) and coaxed thousands of protesters to believe that the system could once again serve the people. The revival stalled after the police assault on demonstrators at the party's convention in Chicago that summer; SDS mounted fall protests under the slogan "Vote With Your Feet, Vote in the Streets." But once Richard Nixon moved into the White House, liberal Democrats began denouncing the war with a new vehemence. In 1972, McGovern, now the Democratic nominee, pledged to pull all remaining United States troops out of Vietnam. His campaign gathered in most of the radicals then active on campuses and elsewhere—a fact Nixon's re-election campaign did not fail to exploit.[69]

Antiwar liberals failed to win the presidency, but they did steal the New Left's fire with language reminiscent of the movement in earlier days—before Vietnam became the cause that crowded out all others. The poignant strains of an idealism betrayed, of American values reasserted to oppose rulers who had lost touch with the needs and desires of "ordinary people" pulsed through the speeches of prominent lawmakers who hoped to preserve the interracial, cross-class electoral base that had elected every Democratic president since FDR.

In the months before his assassination in June of 1968, Robert Kennedy showed how to oppose the slaughter in Indochina without sounding either unpatriotic or elitist. He challenged conservative male undergraduates at the University of Oklahoma to give up their student deferments if they truly supported the war. At the University of Kansas, he called the Vietcong "a brutal enemy" and labeled immediate withdrawal "unacceptable to us as a country and as a people." But, in the same speech, he castigated American policy makers for putting their awesome power to a bloody, immoral, and profoundly undemocratic end:

> Can we ordain to ourselves the awful majesty of God—to decide what cities and villages are to be destroyed, who will live and who will die, and who will join refugees wandering in a desert of our own creation? If it is true that we have a commitment to the South Vietnamese people, we must ask, are they being consulted?[70]

The death of Kennedy—admired alike by black, Latino, and white working-class Catholic voters—doomed his mission to bridge the divide of race and culture. But antiwar liberals did gain the allegiance of those middle-class Americans, of all ages, who hated the war but could not endorse a revolution to bring down "the mother country." Tom Hayden didn't become a Democrat until the mid-1970s. But, in 1968, he privately supported RFK for president and wept as he sat near the slain candidate's coffin in New York's St. Patrick's Cathedral. "He identified with the alienated," Hayden later recalled. The erstwhile Catholic liberal was beginning a voyage back to his first political home.[71]

Both paths blazed by New Leftists in the antiwar movement thus came to dead ends. Liberals like Kennedy and McGovern co-opted the quieter, populist option; certainly a new president could cleanse the flag more quickly if not more completely than could any radical movement. And the young rebels who cheered on the Weathermen and admired Abbie Hoffman prized gesture over organizing and controversy over strategy. Power would not flow to the people through a forest of television cameras. Looking back in 1973, the writer and activist Elinor Langer remarked: "Because revolution was effectively impossible one did not have to dirty one's hands in compromise, nor mingle much with the hoi polloi (meaning: the middle class, the un-Chosen) along the way . . . [we] mistook revolution, a rare historical event, for a moral choice."[72]

The loose alliance that, in 1969, Abbie Hoffman had imagined sending off to the moon was even then a quixotic construction. Most politically engaged blacks and Puerto Ricans were busy crafting their own proud identities and, like the European immigrants who had swarmed into the cities before them, demanding their share of the pluralistic pie. Young (male) workers and antiwar GIs shared the anti-authoritarian message of the New Left but mistrusted the privileged messenger.

And new feminists were increasingly losing patience with the antics of radical men. Basic to the feminist awakening was a rejection of the violence-tinged jargon that male New Leftists had learned from black revolutionaries and made their own badge of honor. Loose talk about "picking up the gun" and "offing pigs" repressed the doubts and fears of its speakers and ignored women's concerns about how "the revolution" was affecting personal life. It was also self-defeating. "I know one woman who grew up in the Old Left," wrote Marge Piercy in 1969, "and who will not use language she associates with that type of life and politics. In the small group of organizers she operates in, her refusal is viewed by the male ideological clique as a pitiful weakness. . . . If she cannot talk their language, they cannot hear her, although she speaks the language of the kind of workers they are attempting to organize."[73]

Of course, some radical feminists asserted their own kind of linguistic arrogance. Talk about "smashing the nuclear family" and about "male supremacy" being the one "contradiction" that dwarfed all others demonstrated the same desire to impose a simple, moralistic framework that had stymied the growth of the "male-dominated" Left.[74]

But a greater number of feminists forged a more sensitive style of political work that voiced and affirmed the common sense and common experiences of housewives and secretaries, mothers and blue-collar workers in a world controlled by men. Such "consciousness raising" harked back to the gentle optimism of the Port Huron Statement and the ERAP projects. The spawning of the New Left had been a rebellion against the hypocritical bluster of powerful men; the "beloved community" was an inchoate version of the sentiment feminists would later enshrine in the phrase "the personal is political."

But the women's liberation movement gave birth to a separate community numbering in the millions. Widespread and decentralized, it included women's health clinics and restaurants, newspapers and bookstores, publishing houses and recording companies. Feminist writers and organizers, working both in their own media and mainstream outlets, propelled such issues as day care, rape, abortion, and birth control into the center of national debate.

Yet, for all its eloquent passion, the rhetoric of women's liberation was as alien to the left populist tradition as were defiant curses at "Amerika." Radical champions of the people had long depended on exhortations of class, however flexible their conceptions; the division of humanity into halves, one of which had always oppressed the other, made male wage earners as guilty as their affluent adversaries. The avalanche of discontent feminists had started allowed basic truths to be expressed about the inequality of women and safe havens to be set up for everyday life and political action. But the unprecedented insurgency made it difficult to imagine a new alliance capable of advancing the Left's traditional agenda of income distribution and power to the workers.

Radicals in the 1960s rattled the sacred vessels containing American ideals and the images of virtuous producers in struggle with the rich and the venal. Unlike previous grassroots movements, the New Left tried hard to look America straight in the face and confront its wrenching passions of race, sexuality, violence, and egotism—all displayed on an international stage.

But in rejecting the myth of a hardworking, patriotic people, the young white rebels from university enclaves did not think seriously about how to build an alternative majority. They directed their moral fire at specific political authorities—most of whom, until the end of the decade, were Democrats. In contrast, New Left attacks on big business, an elite whose power was both permanent and increasing, tended to be either abstract, glancing blows at corporate liberals or focused on the murderous hardware of war—napalm made by Dow, bombers by Boeing—and ignored the workers who made it. The major villains were bureaucratic "masters of war" who showed up every evening on the television news. When Maoists argued that the destruction of Vietnam only "serve[d] the interests of business" and urged antiwar students to get jobs in factories, they sounded like dogmatic relics of another age.[75]

While it was natural to curse a government that wasted so much life and treasure, the fixation on an evil, liberal state had an unintended consequence. Conservatives had long articulated their own version of "Not With My Life You Don't" and should have been grateful for the damage the New Left was doing to their liberal opponents. Never having articulated a producer ethic, young radicals had no effective way to counter the rise of a right-wing populism that inveighed against "welfare bums" and "pointy-headed intellectuals." Millions of Americans, white and black, still suffered from injuries of class that had not vanished with the oft-trumpeted arrival of a middle-class majority. And contemporary workers, like generations before them, bristled at educated critics who sought to correct their prejudices and refine their style. When 1960s radicals tore off the ideological blinders worn by past friends of the people, they donned some thick ones of their own.

Moral outrage at a violent, paternalistic state had enabled the New Left to help build the largest antiwar movement in the nation's history. But the inability of radicals to transcend their own backgrounds, to speak both authentically and empathetically to Americans outside the educated middle class, prevented them from waging a serious struggle for domestic political change—one that, as in the past, would need cooperation from a liberal elite. Activists had hoped to replace a corrupt system with a mass movement committed to face-to-face, interracial democracy. But, notwithstanding the remarkable gains of feminism, they only discredited the old order without laying the political foundation for a new one.[76] That was the New Left's tragedy—and America's.

George Wallace in Pittsburgh, 1968. *(Courtesy of the Bettmann Archive)*

Chapter 9

Stand Up for the Working Man: George Wallace and the Making of a New Right

We notice some of our elected representatives, and some other people who get their names in the papers, scream for Civil Rights for the Negro . . . Yet they happen to be just the people least affected. They have expensive homes on 2 to 5 acre estates, far from the common man, and that is the way they like it and want it to remain . . . IT IS EASY TO TELL SOMEONE ELSE WHAT TO DO, WHEN YOU DON'T HAVE TO DO IT YOURSELF.

—Two white residents of Chicago, 1966

I think that if the politicians get in the way. . . , a lot of them are going to get run over by this average man on the street, this man in the textile mill, this man in the steel mill, this barber, the beautician, the policeman on the beat, they're the ones—and the little businessman—I think those are the mass of people that are going to support a change on the domestic scene in this country.

—George C. Wallace, 1967

Now people say we're only out for ourselves and we're against the Negroes and all that. Well, I don't know. I've never been asked. If they did come around and talk with us at work and ask us their questions, I'll bet we'd confuse them. One minute we'd sound like George Wallace, and the next we'd probably be called radicals or something.

—A union welder, c. 1970

UPSET AND FORGOTTEN

AT the end of the 1960s, I met two white working-class men whose political opinions didn't fit into neat categories of right or left.

One was a 19-year-old named Nick who came from a small town in North Carolina. I met Nick in what now seems an unlikely place—Cuba. Both of us were cutting sugarcane as part of the Venceremos Brigade—a group of several hundred Americans who'd traveled, without passports, to that revolutionary island to symbolically break our government's economic blockade. Some time before, an SDS chapter had recruited Nick. White working-class kids were a prize catch for the New Left at the time; so, as I remember, the chapter paid for Nick to go to Cuba to soak up some radical seasoning.

But Nick was no political naif. In 1968, he had worked for George Wallace's presidential campaign in North Carolina. He was attracted to SDSers because they exuded a cocky rebelliousness similar to Wallace's and because they opposed the war and the draft, neither of which he saw much reason for.

Nick had a wonderful time in Cuba and didn't take the countless political lectures we heard too seriously. By the time we embarked for home, I suspected he was drifting away from the Left. Earlier, he had automatically dismissed Wallace as a racist, but now he was talking fondly of the man's "guts," his feistiness. I never saw Nick again. Some years later, I heard he had returned to North Carolina, found work as an auto mechanic, and, in 1972, had again campaigned for George Wallace.

The second man, named Bill, was a machinist in his middle thirties. He lived across the street from me in a section of Portland, Oregon, where inexpensive, well-kept houses abutted the railroad tracks. We talked now and then about politics; Bill was an active shop steward in his union and hated Richard Nixon, and those affinities drew us together. But one afternoon in May of 1972, he surprised me. "A great, great man died today," Bill volunteered. George Wallace had just been shot while addressing a rally in Maryland, and television reporters at first assumed the wounds were fatal. "A great man?" I asked. "He sure was," said Bill, mournfully. "He was the only politician who stood up for the working man."

Bill and Nick shared certain political impulses. Toward the men who held national power, especially those Bill called "wheeler-dealer liberals," they were, at best, suspicious and, at worst, hostile. They were defensively proud of people like themselves—whites with steady jobs or small, local businesses. While not overtly racist, they were also not particularly sensitive to or concerned about the specific problems of black people. Their attitudes toward the world of politics ranged from a cynical disgust at elected officials who "wasted" tax money on welfare programs and the war in Indochina to a flickering hope that, left to themselves, ordinary people could fix whatever the establishment had screwed up. And they expressed these views in a plain, blunt language that equated their own values and principles with those of America.

At the end of the 1960s, the mass media and the major parties suddenly discovered people like Nick and Bill. Giving them labels like "the silent majority" and "hard hats," television commentators, newsmagazines, and presidential candidates rushed to define the discontent of citizens who usually considered themselves to be middle class and had, since the 1930s, normally voted Democratic. Now these people no longer felt their income and cultural status were secure in a society that seemed to be unraveling. "There are times when I wonder who really runs this country," a steamfitter's wife complained. "It's not people like us, that I know. . . . There are some big people, in Washington I guess, and they make all the decisions; and then it's left for us to go and send our boys to fight, and try to pay the high prices that the politicians have caused us to have."[1]

Two decades of relative prosperity had not wiped away the economic and cultural insecurities that had fueled mass movements during the Depression. Millions of whites had benefited from union strength in and federal largesse to the defense, education, transportation, and construction industries. But now many felt their good jobs, their modest homes, and their personal safety were under siege both from liberal authorities above and angry minorities below. No one in power, it seemed, realized that *they* were the real, the indispensable America. Dick Sinnott, a Boston columnist beloved by anti-busing forces in that city, explained: "We're the poor sunavabees who pay our taxes and sweat tuitions, sweat mortgages and car payments and the cost of groceries and fuel, get no handouts, give our blood, take our turn in line, volunteer for charities, and work two jobs, sometimes three."[2]

This was the voice of the unrepresented producer, updated for an age of anxious, newly "middle-class" consumers dependent upon but wary of the liberal state. Sinnott, like bygone agrarian rebels and Knights of Labor, spoke for creators of wealth and makers of moral communities done wrong by the system. In the 1960s and early 1970s, government officials who spent public money on the unworthy poor took the place of the "plunderers" and "monopolists" at the turn of the century who were accused of fattening off the cheap labor of immigrants from backward regions of Europe and Asia.

It was liberals, those "big people" in Washington, who got the blame for leading the nation into a shooting war it couldn't win and a war on poverty whose promise grossly overshot its achievements. A bloated state appeared to be meddling, ineptly, in areas where it didn't belong—and damaging the lives and pocketbooks of the hardworking white middle in the process. At least big corporations provided employment and, under union pressure, a decent level of wages and benefits.

But the political allegiance of Bill, Nick, and the steamfitter's wife seemed up for grabs. Were these restive Americans tending more to the Right—part of the backlash against black power and antiwar protests—or were they possessed of a new, anti-authoritarian, leftish spirit demonstrated in a wave of wildcat strikes, consumer boycotts, and the pervasive mockery of higher-ups in business as well as the state? A movement or party that could channel the growing resentment of such people—as had the grassroots reformers and insurgent politicians of an earlier day—might break the grip of the New Deal order.

Some radicals in the 1960s believed they could win such fellow rebels to their movement. That was a prime purpose of GI organizing and the reason Nick got a free trip to Cuba. "Not With My Life You Don't" might have a class-conscious meaning. After all, white working people had been exemplars of left-wing populism since the heyday of the Knights of Labor in the 1880s. They were the embodiment of the horny-handed producer, the AFL's average man, and the CIO's citizen-proletarian. In the mid-1950s, C. Wright Mills had written movingly about "ordinary men . . . driven by forces they can neither understand nor govern." And, by the late 1960s, their alienation from all manner of authorities—mainstream politicians, big businessmen, liberal journalists, military commanders, and national labor leaders—approached that of the typical SDS member.[3]

But radicals had little to offer. Based in university enclaves, New Leftists included few who comprehended the tangled emotions of envy and indignation that shaped the response of less privileged whites to ghetto rebellions and antiwar demonstrations. Radicals ached to realize their own international, antiracist vision. Not many could speak empathetically to people who felt their needs were being ignored in the well-publicized conflicts between governing liberals and college radicals over the escalation of black demands and the war in Indochina.

As the only institutions run by working people, labor unions should have been able to speak to a large segment of the disgruntled white millions. Many union officials certainly shared their feelings about the culture of protest. The president of the International Association of Machinists drew cheers at his 1968 convention when he declared that "union members who have worked so hard to build this country are pretty sick of rioters, looters, peaceniks, beatniks and all the rest of the nuts who are trying to destroy it." But he and his fellow officials still led a force whose considerable political clout depended upon electing liberal Democrats. Moreover, they remained locked into the New Deal assumption that a better standard of living for all would quiet racial strife. So rebels from the AFL-CIO's own uneasy ranks—whether they supported Wallace, black nationalism, or wildcat strikes that disrupted production—had to be squelched lest they destroy a status quo that "big labor" had helped create.[4]

Conservatives thus had a grand opportunity. Never had so many working-class whites who remained at the core of the New Deal coalition been so hostile to liberalism and so open to changing their political loyalties. The Right, however, would have to link its antistate convictions to everyday concerns that nagged at the insecure white middle.

George Wallace's campaigns for president in 1964 and 1968 pointed the way. Schooled in the vernacular of ordinary Southern whites, Wallace posed as the champion of any citizen harassed by arrogant but inept bureaucrats, slovenly and unpatriotic protesters, and criminal minorities—none of whom did anything useful for society. His "people" had unglamorous jobs and a culture that prized close families and an unswerving faith in God and country. And, assured Wallace, they were "gettin' fed up and are gonna turn this country around."

Though he never got close to winning the White House, Wallace ensured that the 1960s would be a decisive era for the Right. While the New Left soared and then crashed to earth, conservatives were appealing to resentment of neglect and betrayal by the elite that had deep roots among white Americans. Both Right and Left drew inspiration from the mass outrage against powerful liberals and the system they governed. But only the Right learned how to express that anger in populist ways that gained a respectful hearing among a majority of voters.

RACE FIRST

The lesson, however, did not come easily. Emerging from the debacle of McCarthyism, American conservatives still clung to rhetorical habits that bound them in a tight community of the aggrieved but enabled critics to successfully brand them as irresponsible and radical—a threat to public civility and the First Amendment.

After World War II, the Right had tried, with a fair degree of success, to transform its old image as a front for greedy corporations and officeholders unmoved by human suffering. It was hard to accuse red-hunting zealots like Patrick Scanlan and John T. Flynn of being motivated by profit or social position. Their brand of Catholic passion was certainly at odds with the upper-class manner of the Liberty League.

But in their very zeal, postwar conservatives came to represent an equally distasteful alternative: the abrasive messiah, the stiff-necked fanatic who keeps warning of vast conspiracies to which the average citizen is blind. And a sprinkling of new organizations created in the late 1950s and early 1960s to carry on McCarthy's mission were almost instantly labeled "extremist"—an unwelcome tag nearly everyone but their own members employed. Robert Welch, the Catholic founder of the John Birch Society (largest of the new groups, it had perhaps 30,000 well-heeled members in 1962), never recovered from his claim that President Eisenhower was "a dedicated, conscious agent of the Communist conspiracy." And the Birch Society's rejection of unions, the minimum wage, and Social Security and its insistence that "the United States is a *republic,* not a democracy" harked back to the kind of conservatism that predated the Bolshevik Revolution. The only thing radical about this right was its terror of the enemy.[5]

Neither did Barry Goldwater, despite his capture of the 1964 Republican nomination for president, chart a clear path out of the wilderness. The Arizona senator, the last major presidential candidate without a college degree, was imbued with the entrepreneurial optimism of his mushrooming region and understood the nature of power too well to engage in conspiracy mongering. But he hesitated to criticize the Birch Society, a bulwark of his grassroots support. And the language of his 1964 campaign often resembled the second coming of James Madison and Edmund Burke—the principles of Robert Welch without his paranoid flailings. Goldwater, for example, began his acceptance speech with abstract paeans to "freedom" and "order": "*Freedom—balanced* so that order, lacking liberty, will not become the slavery of the prison cell; *balanced* so that liberty, lacking order, will not become the license of the mob and the jungle."[6]

Similarly, Young Americans for Freedom—the Right's equivalent of SDS, the organization was founded at William F. Buckley's family estate in Sharon, Connecticut—articulated a gentlemanly conservatism that spoke of "eternal truths," "God-given free will," and "the genius of the Constitution"—as well as the need for "victory over, rather than coexistence with . . . the forces of international Communism." Evidently no one at the Sharon gathering reflected that the "eternal truths" of working-class citizens might not coincide with those of well-educated conservatives gathered at a sprawling New England manse. Buckley's own self-consciously elegant prose, studded with terms like "apodictically" and "*ceteris paribus,*" displayed the same myopia. The most powerful wordsmiths on the Republican Right were using an elitist idiom to combat the liberal elite. Not surprisingly, in 1964, the party that clung to the memory of FDR crushed the party that still attracted the legatees of economic royalism.[7]

But down South, conservatives could glimpse a brighter future. During the early '60s, GOP candidates for statewide office in Alabama and Mississippi had stridently defended segregation, while Goldwater wrote off the black vote and advised "hunting where the ducks are." In 1964, the Republican nominee carried five states of the old Confederacy and ran competitively throughout the region. Millions of registered Democrats deserted their own party's candidate, Lyndon Johnson, even though he was a son of Texas. The major reason for the sea change was Goldwater's vocal opposition to the 1964 Civil Rights Act, a decision he based on antistatist principle rather than any belief in white supremacy (in fact, as a Phoenix businessman, he had hired blacks and contributed to the local NAACP).[8]

Of course, Goldwater's public rationale mattered less than did his stand on the most pressing and divisive issue in American politics. Amid the ashes of a crushing national defeat, the GOP's Southern Strategy was launched. "The Republican Party has become the white man's party," exulted Gerald L. K. Smith, erstwhile ally of Father Coughlin. Opposition to what black activists demanded and their white liberal and New Left allies endorsed might bear fruit where scare talk about red conspiracies and principled appeals to individual freedom had failed.[9]

The accumulated tinder of racial backlash was abundant, and not only in the South. Since World War II, European ethnics, liberated from poverty and abusive employers, had been declaring their identity as mainstream *white* Americans. Interracial workplaces and union rhetoric about solidarity did little to calm the dread, sexual as much as economic, of having blacks as neighbors.[10]

As early as the mid-1940s, African-Americans who came to industrial cities like Detroit and Chicago in search of jobs were often attacked by mobs when they tried to move into white working-class districts. White residents, many of whom had recently purchased their first homes with federal financing, claimed a right, as

Americans, to live in peaceful, ethnically stable communities. In 1945 and 1949, conservatives running for mayor in the union bastion of Detroit twice defeated prolabor Democrats who favored building public housing in areas dominated by Catholic home owners. The rhetoric of white civic groups was full of accusations that "government bureaucrats, many influenced by Communism or socialism . . . misused tax dollars to fund experiments in social engineering for the benefit of pressure groups." In the 1960s, politicians like Louis Day Hicks in Boston and Mario Procaccino in New York echoed this sentiment when they taunted "limousine liberals" for busing children to integrated schools while doing nothing to curb urban crime.[11]

Such talk represented one of the more persistent strains in the populist tradition. The attack on domestic subversion in city hall was new, but the charge that a haughty elite and a rabble of black or yellow hue were ganging up on the industrious Caucasian middle was nearly as old as the republic. Before the Civil War, urban wage earners protested that their employers were treating them like "white slaves"; later, most participants in the bloody 1863 draft riot in New York City were Irish-Catholic workers fearful that Republican, Protestant businessmen and newly emancipated slaves would destroy stable trades and homogeneous neighborhoods.[12] The archetypal Alabama farmer of the 1890s who thought black sharecroppers were "down there sharin' the good things with the rich while good white folks in the hills have to starve" had a complaint capable of endless mutations.[13]

Such fears explained why ordinary whites were losing things of great value—good jobs, hospitable communities, values of self-discipline, and advancement through merit—all secured by diligent work. Overt race baiting gradually disappeared from public discourse in the North during the two decades following World War II. The consecutive battles against fascism and communism had given the belief in "equal rights" for individuals, black and white, a legitimacy that could not be shaken. But the meaning of *rights* was not fixed to the advantage of liberals like Martin Luther King, Jr., and Lyndon Johnson—much less to such radicals as Stokely Carmichael and Tom Hayden. Conservatives could capture votes by protesting that average whites deserved equal treatment, too.

In the South, a long line of canny politicians had voiced a similar brand of populism that seldom defied the dogma of white supremacy. Hostility toward big business meshed with cultural resentments of sophisticated city dwellers; it was Bryanism with a drawl. In the 1920s and 1930s, Huey Long of Louisiana labeled Standard Oil his state's true "invisible empire" and thundered, "I don't want the bosses. I want the people on my side." During the height of the New Deal, Theodore Bilbo wooed white Mississippians with passionate denunciations of "rich corporations" and "paid lawyers" who trod on the interests of "the farmer, the soldier, and the laboring man." In 1946 and 1954, James E. (Big Jim) Folsom was elected governor of Alabama by attacking county rings of corrupt politicians and the "Big Mules" who ran industrial Birmingham and heaping praise on organized labor, old-age pensioners, and the TVA. Folsom was also a hard-drinking "country boy" who loved telling rural voters that his mother's turnip greens were far superior to any he could buy in a big-city restaurant.[14]

Not all Southern tribunes delivered an anticorporate, pro-welfare-state message. But the down-home *style* proved irresistible. Across the region, candidates hired string bands, collected donations in washtubs, and made fun of elites whose urban addresses and urbane habits cut them off from the redneck masses.

None of these politicians, whatever their views on concentrated wealth, took the radical step of advocating that blacks enjoy the rights already granted them by the federal Constitution. Like the original Southern Populists, the insurgents who began their careers from World War I to the 1930s targeted social distinctions between whites; at best, they sought to minimize the significance of race.

But deliberate neglect of the reality of Southern life could be sustained only so long as local authorities and their vigilante irregulars kept black citizens from participating in politics. When African-Americans, with some help from Washington, mounted their historic challenge to homegrown apartheid, most Southern populist orators switched quite easily from ridiculing the well-off to voicing the racial fears of their constituents—a dread that always lurked just below the surface. In the 1940s, Bilbo stopped roasting "the money power" and turned exclusively to flagrant Negrophobia. As the civil rights movement gathered strength, "outside" forces that promoted integration—the CIO, federal judges, powerful national politicians— were thrust into the adversarial role earlier played by local economic elites. "The boys at the Barber Shop understand what the [1957] civil rights bill has done to them and they don't like it," the Young Democrats in one Texas town wrote to Lyndon Johnson, then majority leader of the Senate; "they will not long stand for a federal dictatorship."[15]

Among major figures in the Deep South, Jim Folsom was unique in his reluctance to join the chorus of bigotry. In the face of massive resistance, he suggested that racial hatred was, at bottom, a matter of class: "The funny part about it is that most of these fellows doing all the hollering live with the Negroes, work with the Negroes and get their living made by the Negroes," he observed in 1956. "And most of them inherited those big plantations where they used to have slaves, and a lot of them wish they had slaves on them now." Yet, only a week later, Folsom assured the White Citizens' Council, "I was and am for segregation." And he opposed all federal civil rights bills, claiming they meant to substitute the "rule of a few" for the sovereignty of individual states.[16] Folsom did not intend to commit political suicide. Even for him, the grassroots idiom, like nearly everything else in the South, bore the label "Whites Only."

It was from this particular fountain of populism, fed as it was by the tortured history of the South and the insecurities of newly middle-class white Northerners, that American conservatives learned the rudiments of a majoritarian vernacular. Their prior motifs—the cranky vision of a monolithic evil and hosannas to a stateless free market—had failed to crack the liberal consensus. While capable of mobilizing bands of activists, the combination did not persuade discontented white Americans that the Right was truly on their side. A clever Democrat from rural Alabama would blaze a better way.

A REDNECK GOES NATIONAL

From the beginning of his career, George Corley Wallace portrayed himself as a principled fighter from humble origins who was eager and able to challenge entrenched power. He "has stood, glued steadfast to his position, without giving a second thought to the political consequences," wrote an admiring biographer. Such phrases evoked the well-known image of the governor who, in 1963, "stood in the schoolhouse door" for four hours in a courageous, albeit fruitless, attempt to stop the United States Attorney General and thousands of National Guard and federal troops from opening up the University of Alabama at Tuscaloosa to two black students. Not surprisingly, the biographical details are neither so simple nor so heroic.[17]

Wallace was born in 1919 in the little town of Clio, on a sparsely populated edge of the Black Belt. His grandfather was a prosperous physician, so esteemed that he was elected to a probate judgeship without having to campaign for the post. As through most of the South, local politics in that corner of southeast Alabama meant county politics. Barbour County, where Clio is located, was, according to the Wallace biographer Marshall Frady, "probably the most virulently political" jurisdiction in Alabama. "Growing politicians has been its chief industry and its major pastime." Wallace's father, George Sr., was a perpetually sick and bitter man, an unlucky (but hardly poor) farmer who died young. He was also an avid campaigner who once managed to get himself elected chairman of the powerful county Board of Revenue.[18]

Perhaps to compensate for his father's frailty, George Jr. enjoyed picking fistfights and, as a teenager, was a good enough boxer to win the state Golden Gloves title in the bantamweight division twice. As a freshman at the University of Alabama, he ran for class president, defeating the candidate put up by the fraternities—the haughty campus establishment. "He wouldn't wear a tie, and his manner, his affiliates, everything about him indicated the part of a poor country boy working his way through college," recalled a former student. Even then, Wallace was already planning to run for governor. When he enlisted in the army during World War II, he pointedly avoided the officer track favored by most collegians because he knew that voters who had been privates and corporals would always outnumber the erstwhile captains and majors.[19]

This populist instinct drew the young man on the make to Big Jim Folsom. Wallace began his first term as a state legislator in 1947, the same year that Folsom, whose home county was adjacent to Barbour, moved into the governor's mansion. The young assemblyman proved himself a diligent apprentice. He sponsored several bills favored by the administration and helped the governor formulate legislative strategy. More important, he drank from Folsom's fount of homey metaphor and anti-elitist bombast, emulating his "country boy's relish in disconcerting, even disheveling ceremony and citified starchiness," as Frady puts it. Wallace began to give talks around the state, honing his furious, crowd-pleasing style at Kiwanis clubs and union halls. The student had learned his lessons well. When Folsom won a second term in 1954, Wallace wrote several of his speeches.[20]

At first, Wallace, like Folsom, refused to take a rigid stand against black rights. He asked the governor to appoint him to the board of trustees at Tuskegee Institute, repository of the small amount of political leverage wielded by Alabama blacks. In 1948, although he opposed the historic civil rights plank adopted by the Democratic National Convention, Wallace refused to walk out with the rest of his state's delegation or to endorse the Dixiecrat ticket that swept his state's presidential vote that fall.[21]

But, with the rise of the civil rights movement, space for ambivalence on the race question rapidly narrowed, and the ambitious Wallace went with the flow. Elected a state circuit court judge in 1952, he found ways to pose as an aggressive, flamboyant defender of what were euphemistically called the "traditions" of the South. The "fighting judge" issued injunctions to stop the removal from railroad stations of signs marking segregated facilities, threatened to order the arrest of any FBI agent who insisted on peeking into the racial makeup of Southern grand juries, and declined to wear judicial robes that would symbolically separate him from constituents. Early in 1956, he broke with Folsom, telling anyone who'd listen that Big Jim had always been, "soft on the nigger question." Plucking a trope from the arsenal of anticommunism indicated Wallace's desire to be viewed as a reliable, tough crusader against white Alabama's external enemies. His populist phrases would now serve the embattled cause of segregation.[22]

Wallace hoped to ride his growing reputation into the governor's mansion in 1958. Yet, wary of Folsom's reputation for needlessly offending the powerful, he often pulled his punches. In the Democratic primary (the only election that mattered), Wallace portrayed himself, somewhat blandly, as a "farm boy-soldier-lawyer-legislator-judge" whose background guaranteed "fair play" for all Alabamians but no tolerance for "the crowd above the Potomac River" who try "to tell us how to go about it."

Although he repudiated Folsom (who, by law, could not succeed himself), the candidate from Barbour County continued to display his stylistic debt to the outgoing governor. Wallace hired a hillbilly band and the comedian Minnie Pearl (star of the *Grand Ole Opry*) to warm up crowds, cursed his opponents for employing "smut and smear" tactics, and stressed his support for organized labor and expansion of the TVA. But he was defeated, in a runoff election, by the state Attorney General John Patterson, who was endorsed by the KKK—a fact Wallace hoped would discredit him among moderate voters who abhorred violence.[23]

It would be many years before George Wallace again ran as the candidate of peace and reason. In 1962, he was elected governor after a campaign whose militant tenor presaged his later races for the presidency. With the slogan "Stand Up for Alabama," he wielded a rhetorical sword that slashed repeatedly at a single, powerful enemy—the federal judiciary (and, by extension, any politicians who supported it).

Wallace did not bother to argue the legal merits of rulings by such men as District Judge Frank M. Johnson, who sought to enforce school desegregation, protect civil rights workers, and restrain the Klan. The candidate's charge was a populist one: judges "not even elected by the people" were controlling the lives of the majority of Alabamians. His denunciation of Frank Johnson (a classmate and friend when both were in law school) as a "carpetbagging, scalawagging, integrating, race-mixing, bald-faced liar" seldom failed to draw a standing ovation. To critics of this approach, the candidate associated himself with sainted company. "Why shouldn't I attack the federal courts?" he asked. "Thomas Jefferson attacked them, Andrew Jackson attacked them, and Franklin Roosevelt attacked them more than any President." He also stressed, in contrast to the alcoholic Folsom who was seeking a third term, that he and his wife, Lurleen, were teetotaling, churchgoing people who would refuse to serve liquor in the governor's mansion.[24]

Although few commented on it at the time, this was a rhetorical strategy that held great promise for the American Right. Wallace, in 1962, was combining hostility to an overweening, undemocratic state with a defense of biblical values and citing icons of the majority party for justification. Moreover, he avoided making racist comments about blacks (at least in public), repeating instead the homily that segregation "serves the best interests of all our people" (which was enough to get support from the KKK and the White Citizens' Council). And Wallace, ever alert to the vitality of class feeling, stayed away from wealthy areas like the Birmingham suburb of Mountain Brook. "I wouldn't make a speech in Mountain Brook if they paid me," he told an aide, "'cause they too busy riding around in limousines and going to the country clubs to care about the working people of Alabama."[25]

Upon taking office, Wallace promptly became the best-known segregationist in America. His inaugural speech in January 1963 was a declaration of war; "government has become our God," he asserted, "it is a system that is the very opposite of Christ." His melodramatic peroration—"In the name of the greatest people that have ever trod this earth, I draw the line in the dust and toss the gauntlet before the feet of tyranny. And, I say, segregation now! Segregation tomorrow! Segregation forever!"—was replayed on countless broadcasts. It immediately transformed the new governor into a champion of the entire white South, constantly in demand as the evangelist for a particularly contentious version of freedom. Banished forever was the courtly defense of Southern customs; now a plebeian Saint George had come to slay the federal dragon.[26]

Six months later, Wallace's carefully arranged barring of "the schoolhouse door" made him seem a man of action and not just words. Standing defiantly, cleft chin out and back straight, before Attorney General Nicholas Katzenbach, a much taller man, Wallace told the cameras: "There can be no submission to the theory that the central government is anything but a servant of the people." It was, as the journalist Taylor Branch has noted, an event that defined the "conservative standard" for the next two decades. Remarkably, Wallace had converted his failure to stop two black students from attending a public university into a forceful symbol of protest against the centralized government about which most Americans always felt uneasy.[27]

The staged confrontation ensured him a national audience. In the following months, Wallace gave speeches all over the country, many at college campuses where he enjoyed alternately baiting and joking with packed audiences of liberal students. "In the midst of enemies," wrote Marshall Frady, "his instinct is to become almost cuddlesomely kittenish, to innocently spank and paw at their rage. At Harvard he told his audience, 'You left-wing, pinko liberals should appreciate me puttin' money into your treasury.'" At the same time, Wallace was sharpening his appeal to the mass of white Americans, half of whom were telling pollsters that the Kennedy administration was "moving too fast on civil rights." He told a friendly crowd in Cincinnati: "When you and I start marching and demonstrating and carrying signs, we will close every highway in this country!" Getting booed at elite colleges enhanced that message. And it was after a speech at the University of Wisconsin that a local admirer gave Wallace the idea of running in a few 1964 presidential primaries.[28]

The governor's growing fame, or notoriety, stemmed, in part, from his skill at manipulating the electronic media. Like Joe McCarthy before him, Wallace knew that vigorous jousting with interviewers made for entertaining broadcasts. By refusing to accept the civic-minded, rather solemn parameters of a television or radio news program, the Alabamian could grab control of the occasion, posing as a plain-spoken man willing to stand up for his beliefs, whatever the political consequences. With most Americans now getting their news from television, his was a stance capable of winning friends in the North and the West as well as the South.

In June 1963, just before the confrontation in Tuscaloosa, Wallace appeared, for the first time, on *Meet the Press.* All the panelists were from leading Eastern networks or publications; all seemed determined to expose their guest's statements as mere rationalizations for racism. Given the supremacy of the U.S. Constitution of the United States over that of Alabama, asked Anthony Lewis of the *New York Times,* "What is your *true* purpose" in staging the upcoming charade? Wallace threw a series of deft counterpunches. He denied that blacks in Alabama were prevented from using public facilities (he mentioned Tuskegee Institute); he asked why federal troops were never sent to quell violence in *Northern* states; he quoted FDR on the need to save the Supreme Court "from itself."

Perhaps his best moment came in answer to a prosecutorial question from Lewis about why his state prevented blacks from voting. "We don't have any utopia in Alabama," Wallace acknowledged. "But neither do you have one here in New York City where you can't walk in Central Park at night without fear of being raped, or mugged, or shot." At no point did the former bantamweight boxer give in to the clever, legalistically inclined journalists. Even the most critical viewers had to be impressed (or scared) by his ability to look and sound the pugnacious underdog whose faults were no greater than those of other, less controversial public officials. Thousands of favorable letters soon arrived in Montgomery from all over the nation.[29]

Wallace's new image helped him do surprisingly well in the three state primaries he entered in the spring of 1964. Against stand-ins for President Lyndon Johnson, he gained 45 percent in Maryland, 34 percent in Wisconsin, and 30 percent in Indiana. Small farmers and blue-collar workers, both those of Eastern European ancestry and Southerners who had started migrating North during World War II, were his strongest supporters. But, as Wallace certainly understood, few pulled his lever because they had a principled objection to federal tyranny. A rising "racial backlash" (the term was coined that year) against the civil rights movement—which many whites linked with a rise in black crime—was the primary cause of his good showing. At one Wallace rally in Milwaukee attended mostly by Polish-Americans, the local sponsor, a tavern keeper and ex-Marine named Bronko Gruber, ordered two black people who refused to stand for the "Star-Spangled Banner" to leave. Then he asked, "Who is it that beats up our newsboys, rapes our women, attacks old women? You know who it is—it's your colored brothers. How long can we tolerate this? Did I go to Guadalcanal and come back to something like this?"[30]

In 1964 and during the next three presidential elections in which he ran, George Wallace was labeled the "backlash" candidate. Of course, he always denied that either he or his supporters were motivated by racism. Ever the adroit counterpuncher, he even charged that "the biggest bigots in the world are . . . the ones who call others bigots," because they—liberal journalists and radical protesters—dismissed, as a smokescreen for prejudice, the concerns of ordinary whites about job security and safe streets. But, fueled partly by the national media that wished him no good, the impression persisted that Wallace's political strength was the direct product of antiblack feelings that he skillfully whipped up with the use of code phrases like "law and order" and "neighborhood schools."[31]

No one knows exactly why a particular group of voters cast its ballots for Wallace—although he did best in areas like Gary, Indiana, and parts of Milwaukee whose white residents confronted a mass of black newcomers and the beginning of layoffs in nearby factories.[32] But we can understand the Alabamian's rhetoric in historical context.

Wallace was using the racial crisis of the 1960s to draw a class line between two different groups of *white* people. In this sense, he remained true to the Southern populist tradition from which he had sprung. After 1964, Wallace routinely answered reporters' needling questions about segregation with his own attacks on establishment hypocrisy. He would needle liberal congressmen for sending their own children to private schools and insist that all he wanted was for parents to have a *choice* about where their children would be educated. "We're not talking about race," he protested, "we're talking about local democratic institutions."[33] From 1964 on, his main targets were powerful judges, "bureaucrats," and "theoreticians" (their whiteness assumed) who wanted to foist "absurd" blueprints for change on average men and women. That many of those blueprints were attempts to aid black people was an essential element in the resistance mounted against them. But so was a widening cultural gulf between European-Americans that had as much to do with differences of class and with moral judgments as it did with their opinions about the rights of African-Americans.

Wallace was seeking to represent the same virtuous, masculine middle of America that earlier populist speakers had often embraced. For Jacksonians, it had been the "sinews of the republic" who stood between African slaves and Indians below them and "aristocrats" above. For the AFL before World War I, it was the "average man" threatened by both greedy industrialists and new immigrants willing to work for almost nothing. For Billy Sunday's prohibitionists, it was the "rubes" against "the diamond-wearing bunch" and their "whiskey-soaked" accomplices. For the red hunters after World War II, it was pietistic patriots who would turn back the challenge of a treasonous elite and its liberal dupes. Notwithstanding obvious differences of credo and demography, each of these forces mistrusted the same interlocking elite of government officials and cosmopolitan intellectuals; each fervently contended that the common sense, moral values, and toughness of white working people were superior to the supposed wisdom of urban sophisticates who seldom got their hands dirty.

But, as a populist spokesman on the Right, Wallace accomplished something unique. He managed to look and sound more like an ordinary, working American than did anyone of prominence on the contemporary white Left, dominated as it was by activists bred in at least modest comfort. In his personal style as well as the words he spoke, Wallace exuded a feisty self-confidence, a combative defensiveness, a pride in his background that appealed to my acquaintances Bill and Nick and several million other Americans (more of them male than female) who worked with their hands or felt close to those who did.

His rhetorical success stemmed from two interrelated sources: his own emblematic qualities and the ways he sarcastically skewered the foes of his kind of people.

Wallace was the first serious presidential candidate in the twentieth century who identified himself as a working man. "Can a former truck driver married to a dime-store clerk and son of a dirt farmer be elected President?" asked his 1968 campaign literature. The first part of his self-description was a bit misleading; Wallace's entire experience as a member of the white-line proletariat consisted of a few months he spent behind the wheel of a dump truck, just after college (when he met his future wife, Lurleen, then a teenager selling cosmetics at a Kresge's department store).

But the slogan demonstrated his canny regard for the particulars of wage-earning, small-property-holding white society. No fatuous abstractions about "labor" or "workers" or "the middle class" for him; Wallace, unlike most mainstream politicians, fondly *named* the specific kinds of (white) Americans for whom he claimed to speak, thereby dignifying their occupations and honoring their anonymous lives: "the bus driver, the truck driver, the beautician, the fireman, the policeman, and the steelworker, the plumber, and the communications worker, and the oil worker and the little businessman. . . ." It was a tactic Sam Gompers, who never doubted the link between one's craft and one's politics, might have appreciated.[34]

Wallace's tastes and bearing amplified his words. He had a common, rough quality that fascinated and/or repelled observers who expected aspirants for the presidency to carry themselves with relaxed dignity and to dress like big-city bankers. The governor slicked back his hair, wore inexpensive suits, and unapologetically admitted that he "put ketchup on everything." Moreover, his performance before crowds was designed not to inspire but to incite; he told hecklers to cut off their beards, dared "anarchists" to lie down in front of his car, and mused about how "mean" a steelworker in the White House would be. One conservative writer compared him to "Edward G. Robinson in the days of Little Caesar" and quipped, "he can strut sitting down."[35]

Blue-collar belligerence was a major element in Wallace's appeal. But his authenticity did have a softer side. A true son of the plebeian South, he declared his adherence to evangelical Protestantism and his love for country music. The former allowed him to scorn "the liberal circles" for thinking "their minds are the greatest things in the universe" and denying that "there is a God Who made all of us." The latter, aided by endorsements from such popular recording artists as Marty Robbins and Hank Snow, gave him a connection to a musical style whose popularity was exploding: in 1970, there were over 650 AM radio stations exclusively broadcasting country songs; a decade earlier, fewer than 100 had existed. "People that listen to the kind of music you are playing tonight," Wallace said on a television show in Oklahoma City, "are the people that are going to save this country." In sharp contrast to rock (which enjoyed a simultaneous boom), country lyrics lamented the heartaches of white working-class love, drinking, and jobs—typically sung with a pronounced drawl or Southwestern twang.[36]

The same traits that endeared Wallace to certain Americans tended to strike his critics as the embodiment of evil. In the *New York Review of Books,* Elizabeth Hardwick dissected the Alabamian's appearance with a contempt that bordered on the pornographic:

> Wallace in his plastic-like, ill-cut suits, his greying drip-dry shirts, with his sour, dark, unprepossessing look, carrying the scent of hurry and hair oil: if he were not a figure, a star, he would be indistinguishable from lowest of his crowd. . . . [His] natural home would seem to be a seedy hotel with a lot of people in the lobby, and his relaxation a cheap diner.

According to Hardwick, the men in Wallace's crowds, "our ordinary people," were even worse; they were perpetually exhausted, self-destructive, "joyless," "sore and miserable." Thus, one of the leading contributors to a major intellectual journal that was then close to the New Left deemed Wallace's politics a natural extension of his and his supporters' cultural perversity. At the time, activists on the

Right were deriding the "freaks" of the antiwar movement in analogous ways. But only the Left did their adversary the favor of equating his outlook with that of ordinary, patriotic citizens: the *New York Review* sarcastically entitled Hardwick's essay "Mr. America."[37]

George Wallace courted such elegant loathing. The elite, in his view, was composed of precisely those people who thought their privileged upbringing and higher education had taught them how to identify and solve everybody else's problems. His favorite terms of reproach were "bureaucrat," "theoretician," and "pseudo-intellectual." Some of his best applause lines came at the expense of the anonymous professor who "knows how to run the Vietnam war but can't park his bicycle straight" and the *New York Times* for calling Fidel Castro "'the Robin Hood of the Caribbean' when every taxi driver in Montgomery knew he was a Communist."[38] In Wallace, white people who resented being regarded as intolerant, ignorant, and crude had found a champion to manifest their frustrated pride.

While such emotions were reminiscent of those the red hunters had tried to exploit in the 1940s and 1950s, Wallace was far from an updated version of Joe McCarthy or Patrick Scanlan—though he did appeal to some of the same conservative Catholics and veterans' groups as they had. Wallace was respectful of spiritual values (and jumped into the controversy over school prayer from the outset) and militant about national security, but those issues were never central to his message. He urged his audiences to laugh at the ineptness and impracticality of liberal intellectuals, not to fear them as agents of a red Antichrist. Moreover, as a post-FDR Democrat and the governor of a poor state, he explicitly favored a government that aided the common folk—as long as it stayed out of their schools, their unions, and their family lives. His grievances against federal power began and usually ended with its measures to force integration. A decade before, the anti-Communist zealots had all but ignored the issue of race; Wallace, despite his denials, rose to prominence because of it. And unlike the conservative moralists who had backed McCarthy, he spent no time rhapsodizing about the ideal American community. For this man who lived for politics, harvesting discontent was all.

In one sense, however, Wallace was proposing a type of regime quite different from the one being administered by liberals. His focus on lawlessness and street crime, his hostility toward lenient judges, and his unstinting praise of the police amounted to a demand for a state that would be markedly more severe.

But it would be populist as well as authoritarian. A Wallace administration, promised the candidate, would guarantee both the individual freedom and the security that average, law-abiding Americans desired. It would somehow get rid of the appointed judges who took over local schools but let violent criminals go free. Most critical to meeting these needs were rank-and-file policemen. Only they could restore the safety of neighborhoods and obedience to "law and order." "Let the police run this country for a year or two and there wouldn't be any riots," Wallace told several audiences. The harassment of cops by liberal courts and politicians, ghetto rioters and long-haired protesters who shouted "pig" was an assault—from above and below—on the people's first line of defense. "Law and order" was a public good that had grown scarce with the "pseudo-intellectuals" in charge. Better that governor's chairs be filled by furious factory workers "with about a tenth-grade education" than by "genteel" politicians who let the cities burn. A state, Wallace-style, would restore both local control and self-control, in abundance.[39]

Provocative calls for the common folk to straighten out the nation did not gladden erstwhile leaders of the Goldwater campaign. Despite their earlier flirtation with McCarthy, conservatives like William F. Buckley, Jr., cherished the calm defense of laissez-faire economics and moral order. The Alabamian's constant jibes at "pseudo-intellectuals," his support for welfare entitlements in his own state (though paid for by a regressive sales tax), and his appeal to prejudice smacked of a demagogue willing to shout anything to win votes. As the 1968 election campaign approached, several *National Review* writers tried to convince their readers that, as Frank Meyer put it, Wallace's populism was "the radical opposite of conservatism" and would "poison the moral source of its strength." Buckley privately referred to the Alabamian as "Mr. Evil" and, in a televised debate, branded him a racist and a would-be dictator.[40]

However, the "radical" Right saw not menace but opportunity. For the Birch Society and its ilk, Wallace was a veritable angel of deliverance from the political margins to which a hostile media and their own paranoid theories had relegated them. The alliance had a reciprocal rationale: the far Right needed some way to reach beyond its own dwindling membership; Wallace required a grassroots network if he was to mount a serious independent campaign for the presidency. So, in the years between the 1964 and 1968 elections, a national Wallace movement was gradually created.

While its precise composition is still unknown, the operation outside the Deep South had many local Birchers at its heart. The governor and his Alabama cronies made all the key decisions, but local conservative zealots staffed campaign offices, distributed literature, and did much to collect the 2.7 million signatures that put Wallace's American Independent Party (AIP) on the ballot in all fifty states—an unprecedented third-party achievement. Smaller numbers of activists came from the White Citizens' Councils, the Ku Klux Klan, and the Liberty Lobby (a well-funded group whose melding of nativism, anti-Semitism, and fear of financial elites was reminiscent of Father Coughlin's doctrine in the late 1930s).[41]

Ever the shrewd political entrepreneur, Wallace freely exploited the labor of these people but never let them set the direction or rhetoric of his campaign. The candidate occasionally employed a far Right slogan—such as the Birchers' "Support Your Local Police." But he eschewed talk of conspiracies, international or otherwise, and said little about the danger of communism at home or abroad. Despite his affiliation with a third party in 1968, Wallace remained, at heart, a pro-union Democrat whose expectations for what the government should do had been formed by the New Deal. His only concession to the Birch Society and its smaller brethren was to refrain from denouncing them in public.

The far Right's relationship to the Wallace campaign was analogous to that which the Communist Party maintained with CIO leaders from the late '30s through World War II. In both cases, "extremists" worked diligently and, for the most part, anonymously for an end they alone could never realize. To reach their goal, they had to adopt the language of the more legitimate partner. Like the CP journalists who had continued to praise both Stalin and John L. Lewis, the Birch Society press was able to endorse Wallace without ceasing, elsewhere, to warn about the perils of mass democracy. But when they talked about the man from Alabama, Birchers sang his tune. In the Society's organ *American Opinion,* Susan L. M. Huck asked, who supports Wallace? It is, she answered, "the hardworking, taxpaying, ultimately burden-bearing majority—which is still NOT on welfare, learning Leftist slogans in college, or engaged in writing, shuffling, or enforcing 'guidelines.'"[42]

THE GREAT INCITER, 1968

It was one thing to define this worthy majority but quite another to win its votes. The 1968 presidential campaign was George Wallace's season to preen in the spotlight, the one time in his life that a share of national power appeared to be within his grasp. Mainstream commentators were concerned, with reason, that the feisty Alabamian would throw the election into the House of Representatives by adding enough border states and perhaps even a Northern state or two to his strong base in the Deep South. If that had occurred, the former truck driver would have played a major role in deciding who became chief executive.

Yet, Wallace's effort in 1968 also exposed the weaknesses of his political method and the shortcomings of his blunt variety of populism. Unable to win the nomination of a Democratic Party dominated by liberals, he decided to create his own AIP—but was unwilling to make it anything more than an ad hoc instrument for the current campaign. Already expert at thrilling vengeful whites, he made little attempt to sketch a positive agenda that might have helped him break through the distrust that dogged him outside the heart of Dixie. Wallace sincerely believed he was more than a protest candidate; that he had a chance, albeit a slight one, to win a plurality of the vote in the fall campaign against Richard Nixon and Hubert Humphrey.[43]

The support he was drawing in 1968 looked to many liberals like a fascist movement on the rise. It was a year engorged with the symptoms of national crisis: the Tet Offensive that began the American withdrawal from Vietnam, violent campus and ghetto uprisings, Lyndon Johnson's decision not to run for re-election, the assassinations of Martin Luther King, Jr., and Robert Kennedy, and election rallies routinely punctuated by battles between cops and demonstrators. Wallace's people and their New Left antagonists often seemed like two national gangs (perhaps the

Nazis and Communists in 1932 Berlin) eager to bash one another as the cameras rolled.

Believing the Deep South was already theirs, the AIP campaign directors concentrated on white working-class areas in the urban Midwest and border states. Aside from the predictable buttons and leaflets, Wallace was virtually the whole campaign; lacking the institutional apparatus and constituency group backing the major parties had, he had to show up, give a rousing speech, and rely on the media's unflagging curiosity. Personal appearances on local television interview shows were a substitute for expensive network ads.

The campaign was not without resources: $25-a-plate dinners and the brisk sale of hats, buttons, and other paraphernalia supplemented the contributions of some rich men with right-wing sympathies. John Wayne, normally a Republican, sent three $10,000 checks, and Colonel Sanders kicked in some of his poultry profits. But the attractive young Southern women who roamed the crowds at every event with plastic buckets in hand indicated that the drive was somewhat of a throwback to campaigns before the ubiquity of radio and television. Like William Jennings Bryan in 1896, George Wallace largely rose and fell in 1968 through the powers of his own voice.[44]

There were other parallels between the man from Alabama and the Great Commoner from Nebraska. Both Wallace and Bryan sought to represent a coalition of middling white producers—the wage earner, the small businessman, the family farmer—who believed Eastern elites were harming their interests and devaluing their culture. Both men were polarizers whose message seemed hostile to subaltern groups (Catholic immigrants in the 1890s and African-Americans in the 1960s), a fact that contradicted their claim that only the rich and powerful had anything to fear.

The differences, however, were equally telling. Unlike Bryan, Wallace had no major national party behind him. And his campaign was driven by pure resentment, an ability to whip up the hostilities of certain average whites and channel them in his direction. Bryan, on the other hand, was a genuine idealist who spun his vision of America as a small-town democracy motivated by evangelical beliefs and preserved by a reformist state. Compared to the Great Commoner's defiant, if sentimental, faith in grassroots altruism, George Wallace was only a Great Inciter.

To follow the AIP candidate through the maelstrom he helped create was, depending on one's viewpoint, either invigorating and colorful or a descent into the sordid psyche of the white backlash. Instead of Bryan's stemwinding exuberance, Wallace threw pugnacious one liners, curt testimony to the state of political rhetoric in the emerging age of sound bites. The typical Wallace rally began innocently enough with a country music band and a prayer. Then, after a warmup speaker or two had urged the crowd to donate "to the fastest-growing political movement in the history of our nation," the man himself strutted on stage, waving to his thousands of fans, his media entourage, and the handful of (multiracial) hecklers who had been allowed, even encouraged, to attend. He deftly evoked a sense of danger.

Reported Garry Wills: "The crowd is ripe. He radiates a gritty nimbus of piety, violence, sex. Picked-on and self-righteous, yet aggressive and darkly venturous, he has the dingy attractive air of a B-movie idol, the kind who plays a handsome garage attendant. . . . He comes rubbing his hands on invisible garage rag (most of the pit grease out of his nails), smiling and winking, Anything-I-can-do-for-you-pretty-girl?"[45]

Wallace knew his advocates felt that liberals and their sometime critics in the counterculture were monopolizing the public debate; his people hungered for a way to fight back. So he first let the hecklers have their (often obscene) say. Then he reduced them to slovenly parasites: "You young people seem to know a lot of four-letter words. But I have two four-letter words you don't know: S-O-A-P and W-O-R-K"; or "You just come up to the platform afterward, and I'll autograph your sandals."[46]

The aura of producer outrage at all soft-handed elitists pervaded Wallace's rhetoric as never before. He trumpeted every local union endorsement he received and made a point of introducing the labor officials (most from lily-white building trades locals) who showed up at his rallies. While castigating the press for calling his people racist, he immediately turned the crowd's anger away from the "hard-working reporters" in attendance and toward the "*editors,* back in *offices,* that write all that stuff." He attacked the two parties for running "a Tweedledee and Tweedledum system" and quipped "there isn't a dime's worth of difference" between them. He went through his honor roll of unsung occupations before accusing the federal courts of "look[ing] down their noses at Alabamians and Tennesseans and the workingman in California."[47]

For a man running a campaign whose slogan was "Stand Up for America," the candidate was conspicuously reticent about endorsing the raging war in Indochina. Wallace knew the liberal hawks in power had failed to make a convincing case for intervention; most citizens, including his own stalwarts, no longer believed the United States was truly defending the freedom of the South Vietnamese. So he took the safe position of supporting the troops, adding that antiwar dissenters who backed the Communist enemy should be tried for treason. The latter advice was, characteristically, used to flail "the intellectual incompetents" lodged at fancy universities. "If you can't distinguish at Harvard between honest dissent and overt acts of treason," he told a (perhaps apocryphal) "Boston Harvard professor," "then you ought to come down to Alabama, we'll teach you some law down there."[48]

One month before the election, Wallace's brash he's-one-of-us posture had gained him 21 percent in the Gallup Poll—only seven points behind the Democratic candidate, Hubert Humphrey.[49] But then the AIP candidate began to slide. One reason was that the same style responsible for his rise also alienated many people who otherwise agreed with his anti-elitist, anticrime message. Just as the later New Left's tough rhetoric bound its loyalists tighter to the cause but scared away many potential converts, Wallace's quick, snarling jibes and the heckling corps he attracted made him seem part of the same disorder he was condemning. He was the very opposite of the calm steward of the nation's affairs that most Americans wanted a president to be, especially at a time of social upheaval.

Outside the South, women of all classes and cultural backgrounds particularly shied away from the candidate's trigger-happy demeanor. Wallace's belated decision, in early October, to make retired General Curtis LeMay, the former Air Force chief of staff, his vice-presidential nominee only exacerbated his problem with female voters. At his first (and only) campaign press conference, LeMay told astonished reporters: "I don't believe the world would end if we exploded a nuclear weapon." Then he praised the impact of the twenty hydrogen bomb tests held in the South Pacific by observing that the rats on Bikini atoll "are bigger, fatter, and healthier than they ever were before." In November, two-thirds of Wallace's vote came from men, a far larger gender gap than for either Nixon or Humphrey. In one historian's succinct, if overstated, conclusion, "women simply did not like George Wallace."[50]

At the same time, a furious late challenge to his image as a prolabor populist undercut the AIP candidate's support among white working-class men in the North. The United Auto Workers and the AFL-CIO flooded their blue-collar members with sophisticated pamphlets documenting Alabama's high rates of illiteracy and low expenditures for schools and workmen's compensation, its poor record of adhering to child labor laws, and its regressive tax structure. The literature asked workers if they were ready to vote for a man whose campaign was dominated by "racists, bigots, Birchers, and assorted other Far Rightists." Labor publicists could not convince white unionists to despise Wallace, whose campaigners in states like Michigan included quite a few of their members. But they did make him appear a bad risk, a potential tyrant whose actual policies had done the working man no good. On election day, Wallace carried only five Southern states, four of which Goldwater had also won, and 13.6 percent of the vote. Nationwide, the Alabamian received almost twice as much support from nonunion manual workers as from their union counterparts.[51]

The pattern of Wallace's vote in 1968 sketched the depth—and the limits—of the country's alienation from national political leaders and their civil rights positions. In the South (where he drew over one-third of the ballots cast) he was indeed the candidate of the "average man" and his poorer white brothers and sisters: farmers and workers, skilled and unskilled, gave him most of their votes. In the North and West, however, Wallace only sheared off protest votes from the major parties. His 8 percent of the ballots was drawn disproportionately from angry young men with low-paying jobs and no education beyond high school. Outside the South, he did better among Catholics than Protestants. But the efforts to reach ethnic voters from the struggling middle class in places like Milwaukee, Detroit, and Boston were essentially wasted. Interracial coalitions of voters were coming apart in such locales, but no major segment was breaking toward George Wallace.[52]

Wallace's style made him seem part of the social crisis that had beset America rather than essential to solving it. In his clever, snarling way, he was *too* authentically populist, too candid and impolitic an outlet for the rage of his mostly male, mostly working-class followers to attract other voters who simply wanted the nation's troubles to end.

At the same time, Wallace neglected, more obviously than had Father Coughlin thirty years earlier, to build a movement independent of his own political ambitions. Other than continuing to back a candidate who had no chance of being elected president, men like Bill and Nick lacked any national forum for voicing their urgent grievances and acting to redress them. It was left to a Republican Party, spearheaded by an erstwhile scourge of domestic communism, to try to harvest the discontent Wallace had sown.

The burden of Middle America, 1979. *(Courtesy of Tribune Media Services)*

Chapter 10

The Conservative Capture: From Nixon to Reagan

This country is going so far to the right you are not even going to recognize it.

—Attorney General John Mitchell, speaking to reporters, 1971

If there is a role for the Republican Party, it is to be the party of the working class, not the welfare class. It is to champion the cause of producers and taxpayers, of the private sector threatened by the government sector, of the millions who carry most of the cost of government and share least in its beneficence.

—Patrick Buchanan, 1975

The problems of the nation—abortion, the schools—can all be traced to humanism. . . . Our basic values, even the Ten Commandments, have been thrown out. The values of the community aren't controlling things anymore; the courts and the government are.

—Bob Whorton, Christian activist, 1987

They called it the Reagan Revolution. Well, I'll accept that, but for me it always seemed more like the Great Rediscovery—a rediscovery of our values and our common sense.

—Ronald Reagan, presidential farewell address, January 1989

WHIP THE LIBERALS AND PRAISE THE LORD

THERE is no political boon greater than the ineptitude of one's foes. At the end of the 1980s, the three easy electoral wins of Ronald Reagan and George Bush seemed to represent a wholesale rejection of liberalism—both as policy and ideology. The New Deal order, intoned commentators across the political spectrum, had expired in a hail of outmoded nostrums, estranged constituencies, and bumbling standard-bearers. Its death appeared as epochal and inevitable as that of the dinosaurs. In white ethnic neighborhoods that, until recently, had been bastions of the Democratic Party, liberalism had become associated, observes the sociologist Jonathan Rieder, with "profligacy, spinelessness, malevolence, masochism, elitism, fantasy, anarchy, idealism, softness, irresponsibility, and sanctimoniousness."[1] In most areas of the country, politicians on the way up mouthed the very term with the utter distaste once reserved for socialism.

But liberalism did not topple simply from the weight of its own failures. Beginning in the late 1960s, conservative activists and politicians—most of whom were Republicans—re-created themselves as the authentic representatives of average white Americans. They learned to harness the same mass resentments (against federal power, left-wing movements, the counterculture, and the black poor) for which George Wallace had spoken but was unable to ride to victory. The Grand Old Party turned itself into a counter-elite and a welcome home for white refugees from the liberal crack up.

This required broadening and softening the Alabamian's contentious definition of "the people." Rather than suggesting a takeover by angry steelworkers and street cops, emblems of the blue-collar backlash, conservatives announced their solidarity with the concerns of an imprecisely defined "silent majority" of producers and consumers—taxpayers, white ethnics, housewives, "Middle Americans" who felt scorned by the New Left and besieged by powerful liberals.

The Republican Party had always been rooted among white middle-class voters. As liberalism crumbled, astute minds in the party recognized that the defense of middle-class *values*—diligent toil, moral piety, self-governing communities—could now bridge gaps of income and occupation that the GOP had been unable to cross since the Great Depression. This became possible only because, away from the workplace, millions of white wage earners now proudly identified themselves as consumers and home owners.[2]

The labor-liberal alliance forged in the 1930s was the victim of its own success. The social programs and long-term union contracts that, in the context of the postwar boom, had enabled millions of white working people to enjoy a measure of job security and to afford homes of their own also made possible a new coalition that demolished the New Deal order. By the end of the 1960s, whether one earned a wage or owned a small business, carried a union card or chafed at the restrictions imposed by labor was often less important than a shared dislike of a governing and cultural elite and its perceived friends in the ghettos and on campus.

The United States was a very different country than it had been at the end of World War II. The cultural and political fault lines split open in the 1960s had yielded a jagged, racially defined landscape not reducible to haves and have-nots. And organized labor—once a reliable bastion of left-wing populist imagery—was often unwilling and increasingly unable to challenge the legitimacy of the big corporations that employed thousands of union members.

Unlike Wallace, most conservatives did not have to choose between building their own third party or returning to a political fold controlled by their sworn enemies. Since the Goldwater campaign, they had become the dominant grassroots force inside a major party that was on the rebound. In contrast to Wallace, they enjoyed a legitimate platform from which to speak in grand, optimistic terms appropriate to a force that would govern the nation and not merely trade blows with its despoilers.

And the Republican Right enjoyed another advantage the one-time AIP candidate lacked: a normative vision. From the mid-1970s on, the rhetorical defense of hardworking Americans against the liberal elite was yoked to a discourse of values that were considered "traditional" as well as middle class. Organizers based in fast-growing evangelical Protestant churches led the fight to make both policy and social custom reflect their biblical code of sexual self-discipline, patriarchal families, and a Calvinist type of producer ethic. As one minister explained his opposition to welfare payments: "It's immoral to take money from people who work and give it to those who won't work. . . . This is God's morality, not ours. Our laws were founded on God's word and not on Man's will."[3]

Liberals accused the Christian Right of wanting to coerce citizens into a mythic, small-town regimen of bigoted uniformity. And loose talk that "God Almighty does not hear the prayers of Jews," though untypical, seemed to confirm the charge.[4] But, like prohibitionists early in the century, the evangelical Right wanted to save ordinary people, not repress them. In its view, the liberal elite wasn't merely arrogant, bumbling, and spendthrift; liberals' tolerance of abortion, homosexuality, and atheism demonstrated a higher immorality. Conservative Protestants—in alliance with a large number of sympathetic Catholics and even some orthodox Jews—understood the need to transform collective perceptions of right and wrong if they would change not just the rulers of society but the nature of their rule.

To carry out the desired reformation, the Republican Right could marshal a formidable array of resources and constituencies. Conservatives talked like grassroots activists but were able to behave like a counter-elite. Within their coalition were Sunbelt corporations opposed to federal regulation and high taxes; churches mobilized to reverse the spread of "secular humanism"; local groups that protested school busing, sex education, and other forms of bureaucratic meddling in "family issues," and foundations that endowed a new generation of intellectuals and journalists. All these groups were skilled in the art of impressing politicians with their organizing capacity, if not their convictions. The multi-issue, multiconstituency offensive was more potent and sustainable than the crusade against the domestic red menace had ever been.[5]

From its beginnings, the newest Right bloomed in symbiotic liaison with a fresh crop of standard-bearers. Conservative politicians gave up talk of repealing the

New Deal (or hunting down its Communist foot soldiers) to focus, in populist ways, on cultural ruptures. First came George Wallace, eager to invoke a mass movement of the unpolished and neglected. Then, in 1966, Ronald Reagan won the governorship of California by campaigning as a straight-talking "citizen-politician" who vowed to clamp down on ghetto rioters, welfare cheats, permissive academics, and unpatriotic college students (but not unions or Social Security). He did quite well with white working-class voters.[6] And, at the end of the 1960s, a refashioned Richard Nixon tried his hand at wooing the plain but alienated people.

Left behind in these efforts was the Madisonian rigidity of Barry Goldwater—as well as the antiradical paranoia of Joe McCarthy and Robert Welch. Anticommunism remained basic to the worldview of the Right; it made it possible to draw a line in the sand between "captive" nations and free ones and to attack the peace movement and its liberal allies for being unpatriotic. But, as Nixon's 1972 visit to China demonstrated, the leader of a conservative party could bend the old orthodoxy when it no longer served his purposes.

Without abandoning their core beliefs, activists and politicians on the Right became skilled at courting white Democrats, both North and South, with praise of their labor, their families, their ethnic identities, and their moral beliefs. Such language did not guide the domestic programs of either the Nixon or the Reagan administration—both of which aided the interests of large corporations and did nothing to stem the decline in real wages and good industrial jobs. But it did help frame their policies as correctives to the damage that had supposedly been done by haughty liberals who ignored the desires of the virtuous majority. By capturing the language of populism, conservatives were able, at last, to dominate national politics and to force their long-time adversaries onto the defensive.

THE NIXON DEPARTURE

Richard Nixon was not the dream candidate of the Republican Right. After becoming vice president in 1953, he had worked hard to transform himself into a statesmanlike moderate in order to dispel memories of the red-hunting zealotry that had first made him a national figure. Those who fondly remembered Nixon calling Adlai Stevenson an "appeaser . . . who got a Ph.D. from Dean Acheson's College of Cowardly Communist Containment" mistrusted his attacks on Joe McCarthy and the compromise he made with the GOP liberal Nelson Rockefeller to secure the 1960 nomination.[7] Nixon had, however, regained the esteem of figures like William F. Buckley, Jr., by campaigning for Goldwater in 1964 and then working, tirelessly, to pick up the pieces after that year's landslide drubbing.

And Nixon's loathing of what conservatives called "the Eastern establishment" was as visceral as theirs. He still resented the attempt by Eisenhower's corporate backers to dump him from the GOP ticket in 1952. And the privileges of sanctimonious liberals chafed against his prepolitical past: a childhood spent on a small, unprofitable orchard in Southern California; his family's subsequent struggle to keep their garage and grocery store afloat; the self-discipline and constant work regimen demanded by his devout, ever-serious Quaker parents; his failure as an entrepreneur of frozen orange juice during the Depression. This was, at heart, the same man who, as a first-term congressman, had labeled Alger Hiss "the darling of the elitists" and helped send him to jail.

Despite the nearly two decades Nixon spent at or near the pinnacle of a rich man's party, his old wounds had not healed. In his White House diary, Nixon spilled out his contempt for members of the "American leader class" who came to "whine and whimper" and his preference for "labor leaders and people from middle America who still have character and guts and a bit of patriotism." Unlike Wallace, Nixon had not sounded anti-establishment themes throughout his career. But he had no trouble deciding what side he was on in the raging cultural conflict.[8]

During the 1968 race for president, however, he played it safe. The Nixon campaign followed the perennial strategy of any challenger running against an unpopular administration—hammer away at the incumbents and say as little as possible about what you might do. In his acceptance speech, the Republican nominee drew a dismaying portrait of "cities enveloped in smoke and flame . . . sirens in the night . . . Americans dying on distant battlefields . . . hating each other; killing each other at home." His television commercials, more ingenious than any previous examples of the genre, employed the unsettling devices of rapid montage and electronic music to remind viewers that "America is in trouble today," trouble that only a shift in leadership could remedy.

Nixon made no serious attempt to articulate a conservative vision to replace the liberal one. His 1968 campaign, orchestrated by advertising executives and television producers, cleverly remade the image of a candidate widely perceived as a vindictive loser. Nixon welded together shiny scraps of rhetoric without acknowledging the sometimes antagonistic political vehicles from which they had fallen. He sought to straddle the racial gulf—sternly promising a crackdown on "criminal forces" and blaming urban violence on "government programs" while vowing to promote "black capitalism." He made a feint toward the idealistic young by endorsing "participatory democracy which puts personal liberty ahead of the dictates of the state." The point was not to win over activist blacks or left liberals. It was, as Garry Wills observed, to "throw up a protective screen around his actions." Nixon spoke as a congenial centrist who needed to transcend the bitter internal struggle that had plagued the Republicans in 1964. This stance befit the man whom Patrick Buchanan, his admiring aide, called "the least ideological statesman I ever encountered." Nixon's guiding slogan "Bring Us Together"—lifted from a poster carried by a young supporter—could have been directed to his own party as much as to the country at large.[9]

But the victor's campaign was not all bathos and shadows. Working out of their headquarters on Park Avenue, Nixon and his handlers were beginning to develop a populist message that borrowed from Wallace's themes while avoiding their caustic sting and Southern provenance. We need to listen, advised the Republican nominee, to "the voice of the great majority of Americans, the forgotten Americans, the non-shouters, the nondemonstrators." This spoke to and for people who disliked the New Left and its sympathizers. But it avoided Wallace's suggestion, born of his region's damaged pride, that forgotten whites should smash their way to recognition. And while the AIP threw in its lot with "workingmen and -women," the Nixon campaign defined the majority in more comfortable economic and moral phrases, unmoored to specific ways of earning a living: "They're good people. They're decent people; they work and they save and they pay taxes and they care."[10]

Muting Wallace's thinly veiled attacks on blacks, such verbal markers placed the onus on the self-centered, the lazy, and the disorderly—on people who yelled about change but wouldn't (or couldn't) pay their taxes. The majority of Americans, Nixon implied, were content to obey the law—including civil rights laws—and to go about their business; they didn't want to run over bearded protesters or let the cops take over the cities. In this sanguine vein, the Republican National Committee put out a license plate emblazoned with the popular motto, "I Fight Poverty—I Work."[11]

Nixon carefully distinguished his racial politics from those of the segregationist Right. He endorsed the egalitarian, color-blind principles embodied in *Brown v. Board of Education* and the 1964 Civil Rights Act. However, like Wallace, he directed his fire at judges and federal officials who tried to implement such principles through remedies like affirmative action and school busing. In measured phrases, Nixon invoked the primacy of community: "to force a local community to carry out what a federal administrator or bureaucrat may think is best for that local community—I think that is a doctrine that is a very dangerous one." As the sociologist Jonathan Rieder observes, "If Wallace offered rollback, Nixon suggested containment."[12]

Helping to devise Republican strategy in 1968 was Kevin Phillips, an Irish Presbyterian from the Bronx who worked directly under the campaign director John Mitchell. Still in his twenties, Phillips was also engaged in writing an audacious interpretation of American political history that placed populism in the center. With the imaginative use of a voluminous array of statistics, Phillips argued that ethnic, racial, and regional antagonisms had been the keys to party supremacy in every electoral cycle from the era of Jefferson to the 1960s. When a party convincingly placed itself on the side of the hardworking, culturally mainstream masses and against the moneyed, Northeastern establishment, it usually gained national dominance for a generation or more. Phillips traced his own populist awakening to his initial days as a student at Harvard Law School in the early 1960s. The Young Democrats there, he remembered, had gone to prep schools, dressed expensively, and looked down on Young Republicans like him—public school graduates in bargain-store clothes. "Knowing who hates who" and acting accordingly was, he claimed, the key to electoral success.[13]

In the late 1960s, Phillips exulted, the only reliable Democratic voting blocs were committed liberals and the poor blacks and Latinos the government was attempting to uplift. This was a coalition of minorities, held together by a combination of guilt, rage, and domestic programs the taxes paid by middle-class whites made possible.

Contemporary Democrats, argued Phillips, had made a fatal political error. They foolishly leaped "beyond programs taxing the few for the benefit of the many (the New Deal)" to pass "programs taxing the many on behalf of the few (the Great Society)." In response, whites across the Sunbelt (a term he invented) and Catholics in the North and Midwest were moving toward the GOP. The establishment—which Phillips defined as "Wall Street, the Episcopal Church, the great metropolitan newspapers, the U.S. Supreme Court, and Manhattan's East Side"—had opposed FDR. But now it was composed of genteel liberals who disdained the conservative wave that "has invariably taken hold in the ordinary (now middle-class) hinterlands of the nation." George Wallace was only riding the froth of this breaker; the new breed of upwardly mobile, college-educated Republicans, Phillips predicted, were far better equipped to gain the allegiance of "the productive segment of society" that "resents the exploitation of society's producers."[14]

This was the first time a leading conservative had linked his cause to an explicitly "populist" identity, albeit one with a middle-class rather than blue-collar flavor. Upon taking power, the president and his men built on Phillips's predictions and carried most conservatives (even those who had despised Wallace-style populism) along with them. During Nixon's first term, which climaxed in his landslide reelection, the wooing of the forgotten majority proceeded along two main tracks: a critique of the mass media as a new type of elite and the use of the phrase "Middle America" as a seductive definition of the people. At the time, the advice Phillips gave to Nixon reminded one journalist of Machiavelli's relationship with the Florentine ruler Cesare Borgia, "describing in naked words what his hero had all along been doing by instinct."[15]

The new administration certainly did not abandon the levers of domestic reform. In fact, Nixon officials designed an affirmative-action plan to speed up integration in the construction industry, and they proposed tougher environmental laws and a guaranteed annual income to replace the welfare system. Brilliant opportunist that he was, the president talked like a grassroots conservative while often governing like a liberal.[16]

But he would never allow the barons of the old, declining order to think he had become one of them. To neutralize opposition, the new administration waged a rhetorical offensive against the television networks and erudite liberal dailies, particularly the *Washington Post* and the *New York Times*. In 1969, Vice President Spiro Agnew gave several speeches in which he indicted the networks in terms once used by leftists to describe corporate power in toto: "a tiny and closed fraternity of privileged men, elected by no one, and enjoying a monopoly sanctioned and licensed by government . . . the airwaves do not belong to the networks; they belong to the people." Administration figures began popularizing the term "media" itself—believing it had a colder, more sinister sound than the traditional "press."[17]

The alleged sins of the electronic moguls were not economic in nature. Unlike the leftists of old who had lambasted "lords of the press," the dapper Agnew (who was fond of making impromptu references to his golf game) said nothing about the wealth or labor policies of the men who decided what Americans should know about the world. His aim was patently partisan: to reveal that prominent reporters and anchormen posing as objective in reality had a "radical-liberal" agenda. How could these people portray the antiwar movement and counterculture kindly yet refuse to accord the president and his supporters the benefit of the doubt? Clearly, the media was trying to substitute its views for those of the citizens it was supposed to be serving. "There is no element in American life more out of touch with the concerns and beliefs of the common man than the liberal press," wrote Patrick Buchanan, then a presidential speechwriter. In late 1969, at a time of huge antiwar demonstrations, the president asked "the great silent majority" to support his Vietnam policy. "It was almost as if the media, not Hanoi, were the enemy," reflects a biographer.[18]

Targeting the media satisfied some old personal grudges. Since his days as a red-hunting congressman, Richard Nixon had waged frequent skirmishes with the press; it was to a corps of political correspondents that he had spat, erroneously, in 1962, "You won't have Nixon to kick around anymore. Just think how much you're going to be missing."[19] Buchanan was the principal writer of both the "silent majority" speech and Agnew's major critique of the networks. A former Goldwater activist who viewed himself as the conservative conscience of the administration, he still bore a grudge against Edward R. Murrow and his colleagues for helping to bring down Joe McCarthy.[20]

But at the end of the 1960s, with most Americans disgusted with both the war and those protesting it, blaming the biased messenger also seemed like good politics. If the nation was indeed becoming a society whose major commodity was information, then exposing the motives of one's adversaries who controlled its production and distribution was vital to sapping their power. And television news *was* controlled by executives and reporters who tended to favor cultured, liberal Democrats like Adlai Stevenson and John Kennedy and to disdain politicians like Richard Nixon who rose from the provincial, lower-middle class and often appeared stiff and defensive on camera. "They own the word factory," complained Agnew's press secretary; "they make the words."[21]

Such arguments, planted in vengeful soil, helped to germinate the conservative critique of a new class, organized in academia as well as the media, that continued to undermine American values and national security—even after the New Left had withered. They also led the Nixon administration to create its own image-making apparatus to counter the hostility of what the then–White House aide David Gergen called "the great outside they." The perpetual selling of the president had begun.[22]

Its original consumer base was Middle America—the antithesis of slick cosmopolitans who mocked the patriotic, the un-hip, and the blue-collar. The political idiom was coined in 1967 by Joseph Kraft, a national columnist worried that he and his liberal colleagues "in what is called the communications field are not rooted in the great mass of ordinary Americans—in Middle America." Under the guidance of Attorney General John Mitchell, it became the GOP's identity of choice, one that could unite loyal, "Elm Street" Republicans with white working-class Democrats who had soured on their party's liberal ideas and leadership—an alliance between Rotary Club, American Legion post, and union hall that embodied Mitchell's talk of a government and economy "close to the people."[23]

As a metaphor, Middle America evoked, simultaneously, three compelling meanings: the unstylish, traditionalist expanse that lay between the two coasts; an egalitarian social status most citizens either claimed or desired; and a widespread feeling of being squeezed between penthouse and ghetto—between a condescending elite above and scruffy demonstrators and welfare recipients below. The wholesome connotations of Middle America functioned somewhat like a Frank Capra film or a Norman Rockwell painting to repel critics. Other than revolutionaries or cynics, how many people would want to be permanently located on the edges of the body politic? The very ubiquity of Middle America indicated that conservatives had successfully steered populist sentiments in their direction.[24]

At the beginning of 1970, *Time* magazine bestowed its imprimatur on the term by crowning Middle Americans its "Man and Woman of the Year." The lengthy cover story summarized the attitudes toward race, dissent, Vietnam, and morals of this group estimated, for no apparent reason, to number about half the population; it also listed their presumed tastes in entertainment—baton twirling, the Rockettes, football, and *The Green Berets* (a pro-war movie starring John Wayne). Hedging a bit, the article concluded: "The present shift to the right is in one perspective illusory": average folks no longer considered adulterous movie stars or moderate black spokesmen outside the pale. But by anointing Nixon "the embodiment of Middle America," *Time* suggested how difficult it would be for opponents on his Left to apply the designation for their own purposes.[25]

Alongside the optimistic thrust of Middle America, the president and his men expressed a tougher, militant brand of populism that echoed George Wallace's defense of blue-collar prejudices. In the spring of 1970, groups of construction workers in New York City and St. Louis—union members all—beat up demonstrators (many of whom were college students) protesting Nixon's decision to send American troops into Cambodia. A few weeks later, the president invited leaders of the New York Building and Construction Trades Council to the White House and donned a hard hat for photographers to dramatize his gratitude that someone had put people he had recently dubbed "these bums . . . blowing up the campuses" in their place. Almost immediately, buttons emblazoned with a hard hat showed up at demonstrations organized to support Nixon's war policy, and the headgear became synonymous with white backlash politics.[26] In that fall's midterm elections, the president and his allies focused so tightly on Middle America's hostility to radicals, rioters, and permissiveness that their stridency may have cost the Republicans votes from people who preferred "a sense of calm mastery and consensual order" the Nixon of 1968 had projected.[27]

For Wallace, however, this strategy posed a grave problem: an administration of rhetorical conservatives was co-opting his message. Nixon, Agnew, and their subalterns attacked many of the same enemies and courted the same productive middle as he did. And they did not adopt the heated, class-conscious barbs and fondness for country music and stock-car racing that, taken together, seemed to limit Wallace to a Southern, largely blue-collar constituency. The governor complained that the administration was stealing his issues without acknowledgment. But in national polls from 1969 to 1971, he drew no more support than he had won in the last election.[28] Clearly, he had to make some changes.

Thus, as the 1972 campaign began, Wallace turned down the emotional volume and began to sound more like a conventional politician—albeit one who could never escape his contentious image and who probably would have demoralized his loyal followers without it. Hankering for legitimacy, he decided to run in Democratic primaries, consigning the jilted AIP to a marginal existence. An avowed Bircher, former Representative John Schmitz, became its presidential nominee.[29]

Wallace's own literature—slicker and better financed than before—now portrayed the seemingly perpetual candidate as a safer, saner tribune of the (white) common man. With few radical protesters still in evidence, he no longer talked about running over any anarchist who lay down in front of his car. Accepting the enfranchisement of African-Americans, the governor of Alabama had himself photographed with a black homecoming queen and told a conference of black mayors: "We're all God's children. All God's children are equal." Wallace focused on the issues of high, regressive taxes and the "senseless, asinine busing of little children" to make concrete his indictment of a spendthrift government run by incompetents and liars.

Wallace also took tentative aim at a more traditional populist target: concentrated wealth. His glossy campaign organ, *The Wallace Stand,* proclaimed a populist siege on "super-rich, tax-free" foundations. "If the Supreme Court is so interested in busing, why don't they bus some of this money from Wall Street back to the Treasury?" Wallace asked in 1971 at a stop in Toledo. Yet he soon dropped this gambit, which failed to gain the type of response accorded attacks on minions of the state.[30]

These adjustments helped, somewhat, to lift the onus of being the backlash candidate, but they got him no closer to the prize. During the presidential primaries of 1972, the Democrats were split in three irreconcilable directions; the old Capitol hands Hubert Humphrey, Edward Muskie, and Henry Jackson competed for the middle while Wallace and the antiwar liberal George McGovern occupied the wings. Before he was shot and paralyzed on May 15, the Alabama governor's white working-class base had gained him a plurality of delegates in the crowded field. But the Wallace campaign seemed a disgruntled cry of protest rather than a fresh groundswell of formerly silent citizens demanding redress from an unyielding system. "Send Them a Message," Wallace's 1972 slogan, unintentionally revealed his finite prospects. The antiwar and feminist activists who were increasingly powerful at the party's grassroots would never have abided as their nominee this former segregationist, who was still the darling of the far Right.

In self-evident frustration, Wallace and his loyalists claimed that an old pattern of domination was simply being repeated. "They"—the elite Eastern media, the Nixon administration (suspected of aiding the assassination attempt), and the whole permanent system undergirded by courts, inherited wealth, and the milieu of top universities—seemed determined that the Alabama governor and his kind of people would never gain national power. It was the same lament the followers of Tom Watson and William Jennings Bryan had made at the end of the previous century. "If they're against it, why don't they change it?" Wallace chided his electoral competitors. "They been in power a hundred years, all together."[31]

In 1972, the Nixon-Agnew re-election campaign demonstrated how a rising political elite could take advantage of an anti-elitist message. The Republicans portrayed George McGovern and his supporters as the embodiment of everything Middle America abhorred: "giveaway" antipoverty programs, the "reverse discrimination" of recent civil rights rulings, the sexual anarchy allegedly promoted by radical feminists and gay liberationists, and a willingness to surrender Vietnam to the enemy. In the words of a secret Nixon campaign memo, McGovern was portrayed "as the Establishment's fair-haired boy and RN postured as the Candidate of the Common Man, the working man." Of course, the Democrats were quite capable of goring themselves. They angered the chieftains of the AFL-CIO, denied a delegate seat to Mayor Richard Daley (whom the media had made a symbol of white ethnic power), and botched the selection of a vice-presidential nominee.

Still, Nixon's landslide that fall was the culmination of a project the Right had been developing since the end of World War II. A champion of the hardworking, plain-living majority had finally vanquished the candidate of the cosmopolitan liberal establishment (albeit one who hailed from South Dakota). Despite or because of his opportunistic nature, Richard Nixon had showed conservatives how to profit from the crackup of their adversaries.[32]

THE NEW PROHIBITIONISTS

But opportunism was not enough. Nixon had never offered more than the gauziest of alternatives to the ideology of the liberals he was deposing; and his domestic agenda, however described, was clearly intended to be a refinement of the welfare state, not an attempt to dismantle it. The Watergate scandal that began to build only months after the 1972 landslide seemed to prove that "Tricky Dick" had never really changed his spots. Other than Pat Buchanan, few conservative activists were willing to mount a campaign to defend a president who spoke profanely, acted deviously, and had done little to weaken the leviathan state. Nixon's accusations of a conspiracy by the Eastern press and assorted other liberal "enemies"—a chord he had strummed since the Hiss case—could not slow the wreck of his presidency.

That debacle opened up space for grassroots activists who knew quite clearly what kind of America they wanted and what stood in the way of realizing it. The religious Right emerged as a national force in the half-decade just after Watergate and a severe jolt of "stagflation" (recession plus high prices, particularly for energy) highlighted the impression that American society was flailing about in a septic tank of corruption, ineptitude, and decline. In 1976, the movie *Network* attracted large audiences who readily grasped why the protagonist, a renegade television anchorman, might achieve nationwide popularity simply by exhorting people to shout in public, "I'm mad as hell, and I'm not going to take it anymore."[33]

Mainstream politicians—whether they called themselves liberals or conservatives—were seen as either having caused or made a major contribution to the mess. By thinking primarily of personal and partisan advantage, they had forgotten what had made the United States so prosperous, stable, and free in the past. With such arguments, reminiscent of jeremiads hurled by the original Populists, the call for a moral and spiritual revival caught on among many Americans who had never sympathized with the Right before. Perhaps the lack of leaders and of a citizenry imbued with "traditional values" was what ailed the nation.

For the first time since the victory of the prohibition movement a half-century earlier, conservative religion meshed with conservative politics to produce a bumper crop of discontent. Defenders of the old-time religion in the 1970s expressed their grievances and hopes in spiritual terms that had not been prominent in the public realm since the 1920s. A consuming desire to cleanse sinful institutions led them to chastise judges who forbade school prayer but authorized abortions, television executives whose productions smashed sexual taboos, and school authorities who promoted an agnostic stance toward moral questions. Activists on the religious Right were spearheading a traditionalist backlash against cultural changes they identified with the stylish professionals of "the new class" who allegedly controlled the mass media, the educational system, and the federal government. In contrast to Wallace and Nixon, who focused almost exclusively on tearing down the liberal battlements, the Christian Right had a coherent, albeit nostalgic, vision of what needed defending: the family headed by the father, a moral code based on the Bible, and an economic order that favored the self-reliant entrepreneur and worker.

The local terrain was already well seeded. Evangelical Protestant congregations had been growing rapidly since the 1940s, particularly in the booming Sunbelt. And a florescence of new seminaries, radio and cable-television stations, and riveting young preachers supplied a fervor and moral purpose lacking in theologically staid (and politically liberal) denominations. By the late '60s, the Southern Baptist Convention had become the largest denomination in the United States and the source of many votes for George Wallace. But not until the mid-1970s did this missionary zeal focus on the same liberal establishment that the Right had long been assaulting with secular terms. Billy Graham's well-known friendship with President Nixon had a meager impact compared to the sophisticated national institutions—part business, part movement—run by Jerry Falwell, Pat Robertson, and other paragons of conservative evangelism.[34] Not since the heyday of the Anti-Saloon League had masses of Christian activists had the determination and the resources to place themselves and their grievances in the vanguard of a grassroots campaign to change American culture.

Unlike earlier attempts to bring the political world back to God, this crusade leapt across the divide of the Reformation. Catholics repelled by legal abortion, homosexuality, and the advance of secular mores joined the same organizations—the Moral Majority, the Conservative Caucus, Committee for Survival of a Free Congress, and others—as did conservative Protestants.[35] The public image of the movement reflected its ecumenical nature; leaders from Catholic backgrounds such as Phyllis Schlafly, Paul Weyrich, Richard Viguerie, and Pat Buchanan echoed the same "back-to-basics" message voiced by Protestants like Falwell and Robertson. The first denunciations of "secular humanism," in fact, had come from conservative Catholics in the 1950s.[36] The flame of the old social encyclicals still flickered wanly in phrases about government having a responsibility, as Weyrich put it, "to protect the helpless, be they unborn or senile, against the self-interest of others."[37] But Catholics on the Right no longer advocated a guaranteed annual wage or a corporatist order. The welfare they wanted the state to promote was almost completely spiritual.

To combat the shared danger of liberal secularism, Christian conservatives revived the notion of an aroused "community" of ordinary men and women. Red hunters had employed such rhetoric a quarter-century earlier to justify expelling "subversives" from schools and workplaces. But the 1970s Right applied it more broadly. The communities they spoke for were filled with pious, self-reliant individuals who gathered together to safeguard "traditional values" acquired either through upbringing or conversion. And political activism was mandatory because the state—its courts, its schools, its bureaucrats, and its untrustworthy politicians—was trying to dictate how "the ordinary man" taught his children and conducted his business. Such an appeal echoed that of the original Populists, though the context was vastly changed. "Certainly the rebels from the towns and countryside would have preferred to fight where they felt at home, in the very communities they were striving to protect," writes the historian Robert Wiebe about the movement of the 1890s. "But this much they had already learned: to free the community they would have to free the nation."[38]

For the communitarian Right of the 1970s, no issue was more salient than education. The dawning information society appeared to put liberal academics, and school officials who followed their lead, in a position of unusual influence: by deciding what knowledge students should absorb, they could shape the views of whoever held power. And, over the previous two decades, contention had wracked the whole arena of education—from the fight over desegregating public schools to the revolt on college campuses. George Wallace, Ronald Reagan (as governor of California), and Richard Nixon had already attracted support from many white Democrats by standing up for "neighborhood schools" and against student "riots."

What the Christian Right added was the element of spiritual self-defense. The power of this stance could be glimpsed in a variety of local settings filled with white working-class people. In the mountain towns of Kanawha County, West Virginia, the spark was textbooks that allegedly encouraged students to take a relativist attitude toward diverse religions and sexual practices. In 1974, thousands of coal miners and their families—led by fundamentalist ministers and Alice Moore, a member of the local board of education—walked off their jobs and boycotted school. Their statements and songs breathed an outrage that bunched together all elite outsiders—big coal companies, the National Education Association, the American Civil Liberties Union, the Supreme Court—as irreligious "experts" who wouldn't listen "to us little old hillbillies." In the words of "Ballad of Kanawha County" by Mary Rose (an alias):

Our bridges fell in, the dams gave way, and they strip-mined our beautiful hills.
We turned our cheek when the bridges blew up, but they even blew up our stills.
Yes, we turned our cheeks seventy times seven, we did not resist
Till they came for the souls of our precious ones, and now we're gonna resist.
Now they come for our kids with their dirty books and their one-world plan,
But they got a surprise from us mountain folk, because now the Lord said stand.[39]

In Boston, that same year, the issue was a busing plan handed down by Judge W. Arthur Garrity, Jr., a liberal. The angry white protesters, most of whom were devout Catholics, utilized both church rituals and anti-authoritarian symbols and slogans borrowed, unapologetically, from the civil rights movement and the New Left. Affixing handfuls of militant buttons to dresses and windbreakers, they chanted "Hell, no! We won't go" and sang "We Shall Overcome." Hundreds of mothers marched through their neighborhoods loudly reciting the rosary. While most journalists depicted the revolt as a racial one, the anti-busing movement took pains to depict its adherence to a Catholic ethic of selfless service to one's community, family, and faith. The struggle was to "preserve neighborhood schools" against "judicial tyranny," not to oppose integration per se. George Wallace never said it better.[40]

The fact that women played a central role in such local movements indicated an important shift for the Right. With rare exceptions, the main activists backing Father Coughlin, crusading against domestic communism, and campaigning for George Wallace had been men. And their discourse assumed it was a man's job to rescue the citizenry being robbed and tyrannized. To turn back the enemy, Americans would have to be as aggressive and resourceful as combat soldiers or policemen under fire.

But women such as Alice Moore, Mary Rose, and the thousands who turned out to oppose busing in Boston articulated a more benevolent rhetoric of resistance. Not since the turn-of-the-century heyday of the WCTU had the urgent tones of collective moralism been so closely associated with the concerns of wives and mothers. Inspired by a love of God, this new conservative sisterhood was acting to protect children—"our precious ones"—and to prevent an amoral state from trespassing on such intimate family matters as sex education and religious training. In the early '70s, Phyllis Schlafly put aside her speeches against nuclear arms control to lead the campaign against the Equal Rights Amendment (ERA). "The most tragic effect of ERA," she warned, "would . . . fall on the woman who has been a good wife and homemaker for decades, and who can now be turned out to pasture with impunity because a new, militant breed of liberationist has come along." The Middle American woman—like her feminist foe—would be silent no longer.[41]

The same "pro-family" stance motivated the growing right-to-life movement—although favoring a ban on abortion would seem to contradict one's antipathy to a meddling state. Both Protestant and Catholic women in the religious Right placed the "sacred" lives of "unborn children" in opposition to the "self-centeredness" of career women, who allegedly cared only about their own pleasure and personal freedom. The overwhelming majority of grassroots workers against the ERA and abortion, like those on the opposing side, were women. And, despite their antifeminism, they presumed that a womanly conception of politics was the soul of common sense.[42]

None of this repudiated the conservative animus against big government. Schlafly told her audiences: "If you like ERA, you'd better like congressmen and Washington bureaucrats and federal judges relieving you of what little power you have left over your own life." Banning abortion posed no contradiction for Schlafly and her antistatist sisters. It was intended to restore an older and superior moral code, not to create a new layer of official guardians and regulators (which had also been the perspective of the Anti-Saloon League—until the prohibition amendment became law).[43]

Like Richard Nixon, the grassroots Right was convinced that the mass media was a hostile force that might be manipulated but could not be persuaded. To get its message out, the new conservative movement turned to other outlets, some of them fresh creations, that "moral Americans" could both own and control: direct mail, radio talk shows, cable television stations, right-wing magazines, and newspapers. Direct mail received the most attention—because of its emotional, polarizing style as much as for the funds it generated. Political copywriters had to alarm readers into reaching for their checkbooks instead of their wastebaskets. A letter from Jerry Falwell's Moral Majority, for example, named the television producer and liberal activist Norman Lear "the number one enemy of the American family." A solicitation for Senator Jesse Helms warned: "Your tax dollars are being used to pay for grade school education that teaches our children [that] CANNABALISM, WIFE-SWAPPING, and the MURDER of infants and the elderly are acceptable behavior."[44]

Producers of this alternative medium often described their work in populist terms. Richard Viguerie, a pioneer in selling conservative views by mail (who had worked for George Wallace in the 1970s), explained in 1982:

> The liberals have had control not only of all three branches of government, but of the major universities, the three major networks, the biggest newspapers, the news weeklies, and Hollywood. . . . So our communication has had to begin at the grassroots level—by reaching individuals outside the channels of organized public opinion. Fortunately, or rather providentially, a whole new technique has become available just in time—direct mail, backed by computer science, has allowed us to bypass all the media controlled by our adversaries.[45]

The newest wrinkle in political advertising—delivered, ironically, by a legion of government employees—thus became the ordinary people's best friend.

The right-wing movement being born struck many journalists as a frightening and quite novel phenomenon. But, as Kevin Phillips (who coined the phrase "new right" in 1975) commented, it actually represented a blend of "three powerful trend patterns that recur in American history and politics": white lower-middle-class resentment of urban elites, a moral crusade akin to prohibition, and a "Great Awakening" of religious zeal.[46] Jimmy Carter, with his background in the rural South and his born-again Baptist convictions, benefited from these impulses in his 1976 presidential campaign when he promised Americans "a government as good as its people." But, once in office, as leader of what was still a liberal party, he ignored or opposed the issues dearest to the Christian Right.[47]

This cleared the way for the Republicans to reclaim the Lord's people. Unlike earlier populist-speaking movements that had denounced the power of governing elites, the traditionalist Right after World War II had never really been politically autonomous. Its roots lay in the revengeful GOP of the 1940s that had mounted the first national charge against a left-wing, modernist capture of the state. Not all leading figures in the Christian Right were lifelong Republicans. Falwell and Robertson had been raised as Southern Democrats; others had flirted with the Wallace campaign or mused about starting a party of their own after Gerald Ford appointed Nelson Rockefeller vice president in 1974.[48] But most conservatives who considered that option—like William Rusher, Pat Buchanan, and Viguerie himself—had begun as GOP stalwarts. The presidential candidacy of a buoyant senior citizen from California brought them back to the fold.

THE REAGAN RESOLUTION

In rhetorical terms, Ronald Reagan was the most effective chief executive since Franklin Roosevelt. The conservative Republican encouraged the resemblance.

FDR had been his youthful political hero and, through the 1940s, the lodestar of his beliefs. Even after Reagan turned sharply against the legacy of the New Deal, Roosevelt's rhetoric remained his model of how a president should talk: affably, anecdotally, with concern and confidence for the problems of individual Americans as well as the welfare of the people, writ large.

Reagan was fond of quoting the Democratic icon to signify that he, too, was engaged in transforming a hapless government that no longer served average citizens. In so doing, the GOP leader touched cultural chords in many white Democrats who had soured on their party's liberal standard-bearers but were uncomfortable with the traditional Right. Observes the biographer Lou Cannon: "When Reagan spoke, ordinary Americans did not have to make the mental translation usually required for conservative Republican speakers. He undermined the New Deal in its own vernacular." One could thus become a Reagan Democrat without ceasing to venerate FDR and John F. Kennedy.[49]

During his presidency, most analysts of Reagan's prowess as a communicator focused on matters of style: his sonorous voice, first trained for radio and then mastered during his decade as a spokesman for General Electric; his low-key, conversational tone (whether delivering the State of the Union address or giving a personal interview); and his ability to use body language and wit to persuade television viewers he truly believed whatever he was saying. Reagan turned all the jibes about selecting a second-rate actor for president on their head. In an age saturated with the mannerisms and drama of the visual media—when "TV in a way *was* the presidency," as the White House speechwriter Peggy Noonan put it—an agreeable performer in the role of Everyman could be a devastating presence.[50]

But thespian skills, while essential to building Reagan's popularity, did not by themselves convince millions of Democrats and independents that he was their kind of president. The populist content of his speeches dovetailed smoothly with his direct, relaxed, quip-ready approach. What Reagan said seemed to flow naturally from the way he said it.

The erstwhile New Dealer could switch deftly from a spiritual to a secular mode as he conveyed his mistrust of haughty liberals and his faith in the American people. He charmed the moralistic Right while never separating himself from middle-class citizens whose collective anxieties were more bound up with income lost through taxes and inflation, and homes and families imperiled by crime than with the issues that fired up Jerry Falwell and Phyllis Schlafly. With party loyalties crumbling and a clear desire for change in the air, Reagan depicted himself not primarily as a Republican but as an insurgent outsider who fit none of the preconceived categories of American politics. Richard Darman, a close economic adviser, insisted Reagan was more a "populist" than a conservative or Republican. Allies and critics alike compared him to Andrew Jackson. Like Old Hickory, Reagan seemed "the authentic echo of a groundswell voice" of "freedom from government"—one who felt as comfortable in a tuxedo and limousine as clearing brush on his California ranch.[51]

Despite glib allusions to the "revolution" he was making, Reagan was actually reconciling the different strands of conservative populism. He shared evangelical Protestant concerns about school prayer, evolution, and the imminence of Armageddon while also appealing to pious Catholics who worried about abortion and the "evil empire" of communism (and it didn't hurt to call attention to his Irish surname, though he was raised in the fundamentalist Disciples of Christ). He gave Americanism a fresh prominence and optimistic meaning; it was the natural creed of plainspeaking, industrious citizens who were capable of improving their lot without government assistance. And his speeches and television ads, especially during the 1984 campaign, revitalized the myth of the national community as a homogeneous small town, stocked with friendly people of middling incomes who had "a quiet, unselfish devotion to our families, our neighbors, and our nation."[52]

The Anti-Saloon League, the red hunters, George Wallace, Richard Nixon, and the Christian Right had minted their own versions of these durable coins of discourse. But Reagan cleansed them of all but a modicum of resentment and bitterness, making an ideology that had once sounded extreme appear to be the bedrock of common sense and consensual values. As the journalist Sidney Blumenthal wrote, "without Reagan, conservatism would never have become a mass cultural experience; he gave life to abstractions."[53]

At the same time, the Republican president maintained the Right's traditional silences: his frequent references to Jesus Christ made Jews seem a spiritual other, the "federal establishment" he derided never included anyone in a military uniform or the weapons business (who did exceedingly well during his administration), and his vaunting of ordinary people rarely mentioned the existence (much less the merits) of African-Americans or the impoverished newcomers flooding in from Latin America. Yet Reagan's omissions seemed myopic rather than mean-spirited, and the Democrats were unable to exploit them. Except during the severe recession of 1982–83, the president enjoyed solid support from the white majority.[54]

Reagan's most striking rhetorical tactic was his updating of the traditional opposition between "special interests" and "the people." In place of the old pejoratives about trusts and economic royalists, the president and the right-wing activists who followed his example spoke of "the interests" the way neoconservatives did about "the new class"—as a group of liberal insiders who wielded their great power to thwart the public will.

The exact identity of these "interests" remained quite vague. Reagan's 1984 statement that "national Democrats used to fight for the working families of America, and now all they seem to fight for are the special interests" suggested that a bundle of privileged minorities were the problem: organized feminists, homosexuals, advocates of affirmative action, public schools, and government unions—all elements of the Democrats' weakened coalition.[55] But he seldom attacked any of the groups by name. Imprecision was vital to describing this putative elite; many voters, after all, were connected to one or more of its specific parts.

Reagan's reworking of the venerable dichotomy was vital to Republican hopes of becoming the majority party. It allowed conservatives to blunt attacks on his administration and the GOP as apologists for the corporate rich—the second coming of Coolidge and Hoover. Updating the decade-old focus on "the silent majority" and Middle Americans, Reagan and his handlers (several of whom had also served in the Nixon White House) described a conflict between bureaucrats greedy to enhance their power and a hard-pressed majority tired of paying for welfare programs it neither wanted nor needed. As earlier, this invocation of the moral middle depended on a belief that elite interests and the black poor were colluding in parasitic embrace.

What made this message compelling to independent voters was the issue of taxation. At the end of the 1970s, middle-class home owners in several states—California, most prominently—mounted and won initiative campaigns to sharply cut local property taxes that had risen along with the inflationary surge of the decade. Most of the leaders of this tax revolt were conservative Republicans like Howard Jarvis, a retired businessman from Southern California, who had traveled on Herbert Hoover's campaign train in 1932 and had long insisted that the best way to combat big government was "not to give them the money in the first place." But now this kind of argument drew approval from millions of home owners "mad as hell" (the slogan Jarvis borrowed from *Network*) about bearing the financial burden of liberal programs. The image of their movement as a populist insurgency rapidly passed into conventional wisdom—along with the language its organizers had used to describe themselves. In 1984, a team of reporters for the *Los Angeles Times* described the "tax rebels" as "led by political outsiders . . . from groups on the fringe of the dominant institutions in American society" who "found themselves arrayed against a coalition of establishment forces comprising most elected officials, public employees, the trade unions, and the large corporations."[56]

Ronald Reagan, who aimed to slash all levies, quickly aligned himself with the insurgent spirit blowing from his own state. The rage of small home owners was extended to taxpayers in general, regardless of position or income. Productive Americans, declared the president, should not have to transfer any more of their just rewards to the Goliath state. "The people have made it plain already," asserted Reagan during his commencement address at Notre Dame in May 1981. "They want an end to excessive government intervention in their lives and in the economy, an end to . . . a punitive tax policy that does take 'from the mouth of labor the bread it has earned.'"[57]

Like past conservatives who engaged in populist talk, the president never attempted to define "the people" too closely. The rage for tax cuts had given Republicans an advantage they had long desired: an economic issue that placed a majority of voters on their side in apparent conflict with an unresponsive elite. But the GOP was, as much as ever, the party favored by employers and wealthy individuals, and their tax rates generally plummeted under Reagan's policies. It wouldn't do to call attention to class divisions that could upset the new coalition.

So, in his unique fashion, Reagan simply transcended the problem. He offered glittering tributes to the indispensable masses and stern warnings to their foes and let an improving economy and the disarray of the Democrats do the rest. In his first inaugural address, Reagan called a rhapsodic roster of producers that, with one exception, could easily have appeared in literature the CIO published during FDR's last campaign: "men and women who raise our food, patrol our streets, man our mines and factories, teach our children, keep our homes, and heal us when we're sick—professionals, industrialists, shopkeepers, clerks, cabbies, and truck drivers . . . this breed called Americans." And in his 1985 Labor Day speech (given in Independence, Missouri—the hometown of the now legendary "plainspeaking" Harry Truman), Reagan promoted a new income tax "simplification" plan (originally designed by the Democrats Bill Bradley and Richard Gephardt) as the salvation of the struggling middle class:

> I'm here to declare to the special interests something they already know, and something they hope you won't find out: Our fair share tax program is a good deal for the American people and a big step toward economic power for people who've been denied power for generations.[58]

The Republican president had captured the language of the New Deal and of earlier populists on the Left. And the "fair share" proposal he was advocating cut rates dramatically for the wealthiest 5 percent of Americans while raising, slightly, the taxes most families had to pay. It was quite a performance.[59]

In the wake of his sweeping re-election in 1984, Reagan was so well liked that reporters were loath to point out such a clear contradiction between his words and his program. An aura of mysterious strength enveloped him; it was hard to belittle a man in his seventies who kept smiling after being shot by a would-be assassin and who gave uplifting, entertaining speeches on a regular basis. Even jokes about his lack of attention to the details of policy may only have burnished his image as a leader with the common touch who understood as much as the job required. The novelist John Updike remarked, through his fictional alter ego Rabbit Angstrom, "the powerful thing about [Reagan] . . . was that you never knew how much he knew, nothing or everything, he was like God that way, you had to do a lot of it yourself."[60]

For vivid testimony of the spell Reagan cast over the faithful, one can turn to the memoir of Peggy Noonan, who spent 1984 to 1986 as a lyrical and much-appreciated presidential speechwriter. An Irish Catholic from a working-class family who adored the Kennedys, she credits her move rightward to a Wallace-like resentment of rich liberals who made "the nonrich" pay for their expensive, unworkable domestic programs. Her favorite White House official was coreligionist Pat Buchanan, then the communications director, whom she describes as "effortlessly egalitarian," the kind of conservative "happy to sit for an hour with a janitor and talk about life and the world in a way that one suspects [prominent liberals] never could. . . ."[61]

Like most Washington memoirs, Noonan's book is full of witty put-downs of former associates and hard lessons learned about the exigencies of political power. But when she writes about Ronald Reagan, the sun shines brightly and harps are playing. "He was probably the sweetest, most innocent man ever to serve in the Oval Office," she gushes. "'I'm not odd,' he would say, 'I'm only odd for a president.'"[62] The man at the top was a man of the people.

Down in the ranks, however, rejoicing gradually gave way to carping and competition. While all sections of the Right cheered Reagan's unexpected victory in 1980, many Christian conservatives came to doubt whether his talk of defending traditional values was being matched by action. The administration's energies went into cutting taxes and building up the military; Reagan avoided waging congressional battles on such divisive issues as a Human Life Amendment and public funding for religious schools. Neoconservative intellectuals praised America's new pugnacity abroad, and free-market ideologues cheered measures to curb regulation and unleash entrepreneurs. But the sunny populist in the White House was putting a large section of the conservative movement in the shade.

The reaction was pained, though sporadic. Richard Viguerie charged that Reagan had "turned his back on the populist cause" by dining with the likes of Nelson Rockefeller and Henry Kissinger "to stroke them and assure . . . other members of the establishment that things would not be very different under Reagan, that they had nothing to worry about." Paul Weyrich, an influential proponent of "family issues," made similar, if more muted, complaints.[63] In several states, corporate donors to the GOP tried to drive the Christian Right out of the party. Evangelicals saw it as a matter of class shoving conviction. Claimed one member of Christian Voice in northern Virginia: "The majority of the big money men are three Martini Episcopalians who belong to the Country Club and drive a Rolls or a Jag or something and they despise these unwashed low-income Christians coming in singing their hymns and trying to take the Party away."[64]

But not many Christian activists blamed their president. They understood that Reagan was succeeding by making conservatism sound like common sense, not a spiritual call to arms. Insurgents on the Right were discovering a truth that labor leftists had learned during the height of the New Deal: grassroots criticism loses its sting when the president captures the people.

And success encouraged demobilization. Following the 1984 Reagan landslide (and the beginning of Mikhail Gorbachev's dismantling of the "evil empire" from within), contributions to right-wing organizations dropped precipitously. Only the most paranoid conservatives could still argue that veterans or emulators of the Great Society and New Left were dominating the governing elite. Bathed in the nostalgia of "oldies" music, the conflicts of the 1960s that had given the grassroots Right a new birth now seemed more quaint than persistent.

Populism of the confrontational variety was an icing on the old cake of bitterness that fewer people now needed to consume. In the late '80s, Viguerie's direct-mail firm almost went bankrupt; it survived only by securing contracts from the fanatical Reverend Sun Myung Moon. The Moral Majority dissolved, and evangelical activists were thrown on the defensive as the mainstream media charged them with censorship and authoritarianism.[65]

For two decades, from the end of the 1960s to the end of the 1980s, conservative Republicans had posed authentically in populist dress by keeping cultural resentments uppermost in the public mind. Adhering to a disciplined script, GOP politicians ran against a "liberal establishment" composed of federal bureaucrats, the mass media, arrogant academics, and other amoral "special interests." This nexus of power supplanted big business and its political cronies as *the* main threat to the beliefs (and pocketbooks) of the hardworking white majority. In a 1980 poll, even two-thirds of union members agreed that business was over-regulated.[66] The Right's definition of what was at stake in American politics gained wide acceptance, even though the GOP itself never attained majority status—with the great exception of presidential elections.

But populist policies did not follow from populist rhetoric. At the end of the 1980s, the taxes of middle-class Americans were higher than ever. And, despite the entreaties of the Christian Right, neither the Reagan nor the Bush administration did much to ban abortion, curb homosexuality, or weed "secular humanist" texts and teachers out of America's schools. The GOP was, after all, still the party of business, and the only priority of business in an era distant from the days when John D. Rockefeller and Henry Ford denounced the saloon was to sell products, not to worry about the spiritual health of its customers. Praise of workers and taxpayers with "traditional values" was one thing; to take on the institutions—television, malls, advertising—that peddled all kinds of sensual gratification would have been quite another.

The Christian Right might also have learned a hard lesson from its (unacknowledged) forefathers and foremothers in the prohibitionist movement. At the stage of protest, a language of moral revival is enormously useful; it gives voice to people who feel the nation is slipping away from its righteous moorings. But the same language sounds mean and divisive when spoken by people in or close to power. It seems a peril to majority rights instead of a cry of outrage by the unrepresented. When Pat Buchanan bluntly announced at the 1992 Republican National Convention that "there is a religious war going on for the soul of America," he triggered a backlash that helped the Democrats win that fall. Ordinary citizens were no less angry at big government, but the declining value of their jobs and education now seemed to alarm them more than did the values of any secular cabal.

Ross Perot in Little Rock, Arkansas, 1992. *(Courtesy of the Bettmann Archive)*

Chapter 11

Conclusion: Populisms of Decline

Based on the populist notion that the paying customers are entitled to air their feelings when things go wrong, booing has become Everyman's revenge, the only recourse when a millionaire hangs a curve or muffs an easy field goal or blows two free throws.

—Sportswriter Ray Ratto, 1986

The Bush administration and the vice president represent an economic elite of the country. . . . The people who made more in the 1980s by doing less and paid less taxes and are now giving lectures to the people who worked harder for less money and paid more taxes.

—Bill Clinton, 1992

I love the American people and I am sure that you do, too. I owe them a debt I can never repay and so do you. Today, their government is a mess, and they want it fixed. By joining together as the owners of this great country, they can solve these problems.

—Ross Perot (addressing other presidential candidates), 1992

Our rhetoric speaks in the terms of another day, another age. It does not seem to express our present reality. And yet our politicians and those to whom they speak are surprised and troubled by the lack of fit, concerned less to find a new rhetoric than to find an easy formula to make the old rhetoric apt again.

—Robert N. Bellah, 1980

BY NO OTHER NAME

IF Tom Watson and Ignatius Donnelly had lived into the 1990s, they would have heard several familiar themes animating the language of electoral politics. Candidates were once again bemoaning the distress of small property holders and wage earners, shaken by an economic sea change that was increasing the gap between rich Americans and everyone else. Insurgent voices were once again charging representatives of both major parties with using public funds to sabotage the public interest. As it had been a century before, Congress was accused of being more responsive to corporate lobbyists, foreign as well as domestic, than to ordinary citizens' demands for good jobs and efficient, egalitarian services. And, again, there was a palpable longing to return to earlier days when, at least in rose-tinted memory, the nation was wealthier and its prosperity widely shared.

But, of course, the Gilded Age was not really making a comeback. Radicals in the 1890s had condemned "monopolists" and "plutocrats" for degrading the labor and corrupting the morals of the producing majority; they did not worry that American power was in its sunset days—that foreign competition was dooming the nation's future. A century later, however, the loudest expressions of populist sentiment were being driven by precisely that fear; voices of antimonopoly were mute in comparison. As framed by a media obsessed with signs of crisis, the contemporary alarm had multiple, intersecting sources: the evaporation of unionized manufacturing jobs, a long-term drop in real wages for both white-collar and blue-collar workers, the growth of violent crime, the deterioration of public institutions (schools, hospitals, police departments), the hostility between fragmented cultural identities (such as gays versus evangelical Christians, and Afrocentrists versus Eurocentrists)—and the inability of the state, whichever party was in power, to cope successfully with any of it.

The rhetoric of crisis and the further erosion of faith in politicians made one thing clear: American conservatives had not succeeded in establishing a new political order. Ronald Reagan left office with a plurality of Americans still adhering, however nominally, to the Democratic Party. Opinion surveys still registered a mistrust of big business that almost equaled the contempt for big government. Aside from the Southern Baptist Convention, the Right controlled no major institutions on which to base a remaking of American government and culture.

And the very meaning of conservatism was in question. The end of the Cold War exposed how much rightists had been bound together by what they hated instead of what they wanted to change. Deprived of both the Soviet foe and Reagan's harmonious balm, activists engaged in furious quarrels over issues like foreign trade, immigration, and the outlawing of abortion. "There is no longer any set of fixed beliefs that characterizes conservatives," observed an astute journalist midway through the Bush administration.[1]

With the nation's political future up for grabs, populist contenders emerged from every part of the ideological spectrum. Jesse Jackson quipped that Republicans "engage in reverse Robin Hood—took from the poor, gave to the rich, paid for by the middle class." Bill Clinton and Al Gore vowed to establish an administration that would take America back from "the privileged few" and "put people first." Pat Robertson waged a presidential campaign "aimed at Main Street as opposed to Wall Street."[2] And erstwhile neo-Nazi David Duke, who ran as the presidential candidate of a tiny Populist Party in 1988, was almost elected governor of Louisiana (as a Republican) by blaming racial quotas and welfare payments for squeezing the livelihoods of white workers and taxpayers.

Accompanying the ubiquitous rhetoric about a people in peril was a locutionary sideshow that would probably have shocked bygone defenders of the toiling masses. Beginning in the mid-1980s, populism became something of a fashion statement. Journalists and copywriters affixed the term not just to campaigners and officeholders (a habit begun in the early 1970s) but also to talk-show hosts, cable networks, rock musicians, film directors, low-priced bookstores, even sports fans who booed when rich athletes play poorly. Hewlett-Packard, one of the largest corporations in America, advertised a new product as neither "liberal" nor "conservative" but "Populist . . . the perfect printer for the masses"; while Banana Republic, a clothing outlet geared to young professionals, unveiled its "Men's 100% Cotton Twill POPULIST pants . . . steeped in grass-roots sensibility and the simple good sense of solid workmanship . . . No-nonsense pants for the individual in everyman."[3]

Defining what the common people want and then selling it to them has long been the forte of both merchandisers and politicians. Snapped a comedian in 1992, "To be a populist, all you have to be is popular."[4] Yet the promiscuous applications of the term conveyed something more compelling—the discrediting of alternatives.

Other words that once evoked a vision of universal improvement as well as a set of collective grievances now seemed exhausted, their relevance blunted by careless use and the obvious failures of those who carried their standards. *Democratic* lost much of its value after years of duty for nearly every political force on earth—from North Korea (the Democratic Peoples' Republic) to the Nicaraguan Contras (the Democratic Force). Outside a small circle of theorists, *liberalism* connoted a worldview defined in the 1930s and reborn in the early 1960s that no longer inspired many activists or voters. *Radicalism* had come to indicate emotional vehemence and a willingness to defy conformity rather than any specific point of view. *Socialism* pointed to a creed that had never shed its alien provenance (and, with the end of the Cold War, also lost its power to provoke). Even *conservatism*—so recently transformed into a synonym for one version of change from below—was, thanks to the failure of Reaganomics, gradually returning to its familiar perch among the staid and well born.

But no American president or victorious social movement had ever called themselves "populist." The term was thus free from the scorn visited on its rivals. It became a convenient label for left, right, center, and anyone simply out to make a profit, a handy way to signify that one was on the side of the *real* people—those with more common sense than disposable income—and opposed to their elite enemies, whoever they might be.

One accepted truth about politics since the 1960s was that most Americans, whatever their specific opinions, were fed up with inauthentic, manipulated prose that covered up the squalid deeds of those on high. Ronald Reagan did little to stem the tide of cynicism about the powerful; he may even have increased it with repeated digs at the "special interests" who, he maintained, were still entrenched in government. What better proof could a public figure or private firm give of its concern for the troubled millions than to don a new name implying that the people, in their abiding disgruntlement, had been right all along?

Thus, populism—the supposed discourse of ordinary, apolitical Americans—became, in the 1980s and after, a deliberate rhetorical project. Political consultants, now considered a necessity for any serious candidate, advised their clients to smother in praise "working men and women" and "the middle class" (the terms were usually synonymous) and to damn their opponents for favoring the rich (through selective tax cuts, for example) and/or trying to live like them.[5]

The ensuing blare did not drown out dissenting voices. The furious competition between media outlets benefited anyone with a large bank account who could turn a phrase and seemed to have a simple, grand solution to the enveloping crisis. But grassroots activists who stuck to the hard work of local organizing could seldom gain a hearing in the electronic marketplace. Without such attention, they found it difficult to build alliances capable of challenging individuals—whether presidents or billionaires—who routinely appeared on television.

NEW SUITORS OF THE MIDDLE CLASS

The dethroning of conservatives did not mean their brand of populism had lost its influence. Even after the economic boom of the Reagan years ended, there was a rhetorical lag. The assumption persisted that the key conflict in American politics was between the government—spendthrift, inept, and immoral—and nearly everyone else. Leading voices of discontent continued to reproach public officials for being too liberal with other people's money. Political talk filled up with concerns about jobs and income, but no national movement or major presidential candidate inveighed against the modern-day plutocracy—big corporations that now tap labor as well as markets all over the globe.[6]

The largest mass movement since the heyday of the Christian Right revolved around Ross Perot, a wealthy man who demanded huge cuts in the federal budget and wanted the government run more like a business because, he said, "in business, people are held accountable."[7] At the turn of the last century, both Populists and progressives had argued that business corrupted politics; Perot reversed the premise.

Linked to the virtual absence of an anticorporate perspective was the lack of a national movement that, like many before World War II, could credibly represent itself as "composed primarily of the classes who work."[8] Organized labor, the only secular institution in America that brought together poor and middle-class wage earners, made intermittent stabs at reaching those whose interests were hurt by predatory capital. The AFL-CIO and individual unions circulated petitions calling for higher taxes on big business, denounced leveraged buyouts by "corporate raiders," and waged a fervent if losing battle against the North American Free Trade Agreement.

But these efforts were patently defensive, cries for help from organizations that were losing members, strikes, and political sympathy—even from many Democrats who, like Bill Clinton, had routinely received union support, financial and otherwise. That liberal journalists, few of whom sprang from working-class backgrounds, often echoed the Right's characterization of labor as a pampered special interest revealed and helped to widen the gulf between the proud self-image held by union activists and their frayed reputation in the nation at large. Politicians from both parties showered praise on the "blue-collar work ethic" of the "lunchbox kind of guys" whose wives or mothers spoke "kitchen table" wisdom. But very few invoked the ethical link between labor (of all kinds) and the creation of wealth that had been at the core of populist language from the nineteenth century through the 1940s. The rhetorical border between workers and the great, spongy middle class remained as permeable as ever.

Meanwhile, the Left, its most vocal and visible adherents still located on college campuses, was absorbed with issues of gender and racial identity. The collapse of the Soviet bloc seemed to confirm the utter bankruptcy of the Marxist "labor metaphysic" C. Wright Mills had faulted a generation before. To once again "privilege" class, argued contemporary radicals, would only mean throttling the energetic styles of expression and fellowship that feminists, gay activists, and black nationalists had forged. The chrysalis of community formed around each identity, enrobing it with fragile pride.

But Democrats hungry to regain the White House did not need a working-class insurgency to teach them how to exploit the economic crisis. In the late '80s, they began reinventing themselves as champions of the middle class and set out to woo their own version of the discontented majority. "For more than a decade our government has been rigged in favor of the rich and special interests," contended a 1992 pamphlet issued by the Clinton-Gore campaign. "While the wealthiest Americans get richer, middle-class Americans work harder and earn less while paying higher taxes to a government that fails to produce what we need."[9]

In highlighting the economic gap between the privileged few and the industrious many, the party of FDR was returning to a definition of political conflict that had proved so fruitful during both the 1830s and the 1930s. And, like Roosevelt in 1932, Clinton had the great advantage of running against a failed presidency. This time, the role of Herbert Hoover was played by George Bush. Unable to banish the specter of a permanent recession, Bush turned the once-potent talk of family values from a normative vision into a clumsy attempt to change the subject.

But Clinton, the "new" Democrat, was also borrowing from a script written by a more recent political breed—populist-minded Republicans like Richard Nixon,

Kevin Phillips, and Ronald Reagan. The critical people Clinton's campaign put first were the same hardworking, rule-following, God-fearing white middle-class Americans whom Nixon's speechwriters had dubbed the "silent majority." As a candidate and as president, Clinton, who was raised a Southern Baptist, urged "those of us who have faith" to embrace social policies that were anathema to the Christian Right.[10] Unlike the dirt farmers and industrial workers who had been loyal to FDR, the pious middle class was a group that had experienced something of the good life and now felt it slipping away.

Kevin Phillips himself proved more faithful to his populist principles than to his party. His 1990 book, *The Politics of Rich and Poor,* handed the Democrats a virtual campaign blueprint. With a cascade of "plutographics," Phillips attacked the GOP under Reagan and Bush for enriching "upper America" and degrading the jobs and income of nearly everyone else. Middle Americans were anxious about their present and future livelihood; but their identity as populist archetypes hadn't changed.[11]

Of course, the Clinton campaign was also careful to give trusty Democratic constituencies some reasons for hope: promises to appoint pro-choice judges, to support black and gay rights, to pursue an ambitious environmental agenda, to consider laws making it easier for unions to organize. But it was the struggling middle, the former Democrats wooed by George Wallace and won by Ronald Reagan, to which the Clinton campaign devoted the most thought and effort in hopes of luring them back to the fold. "I got into this race because I did not want my child to grow up to be part of the first generation of Americans to do worse than her parents," the Democratic nominee told audiences, and his barnstorming bus tours through predominately white areas in the Midwest drove the point home in a relaxed and quite telegenic way.[12]

Clinton was also consciously rejecting the bland, managerial behavior of his immediate predecessors, Walter Mondale in 1984 and Michael Dukakis in 1988. Both losing candidates, recalled a speechwriter for all three campaigns, always seemed to be "indoors, wearing suits, pointing at charts . . . looking like officials of the government." In contrast, Clinton routinely cracked jokes, loosened his tie or donned a sports shirt, and was most comfortable in talk-show settings where he could soothe and persuade anyone with a problem. The party branded, for over two decades, as the property of arrogant liberals and ungrateful minorities was turning back, with an informal empathy, to average Americans in trouble.[13]

Clinton's campaign persona signified the climax of a voyage toward political realism that many left-wing and liberal activists began at the end of the 1960s. In his twenties, the future chief executive helped to organize peace demonstrations, ran the Texas operation of George McGovern's 1972 campaign for president, and told an ROTC official of his "great sympathy with those who are not willing to fight, kill, and maybe die for their country."[14] Clinton never changed his mind about the Vietnam War, but he and many other Democrats of his generation consciously began wooing the very kinds of people who had once recoiled at their youthful rebellion.

This shift had its origins among New Leftists who had asserted the virtue of American ideals, even as their movement was self-destructing. In the early '70s, clusters of white radicals who felt uneasy with the rhetoric of the fist and wanted to reach the white majority began to craft what they called a "new populism." This meant articulating optimistic conceptions of "democracy" and "citizenship," talking about how a movement should and could help change the lives of people of all races and most classes by drawing on resources they already possessed and by using a political language they already spoke. "If you lose faith in people, then you shouldn't be in this line of work," reflected the organizer Heather Booth, a pioneer of the new movement.[15]

Booth and several thousand others set out to rebuild the Left in a variety of working-class areas, most of whose residents were white. Economic grievances, precise if limited demands on local businesses and state legislatures, and a careful avoidance of racially charged subjects like busing and affirmative action would, they hoped, revive the dream of radical democracy. The very names of the new grassroots bodies advertised their amiable, if militant, mission: Active Clevelanders Together, Richmond United Neighborhoods, Illinois Public Action Council, and the most popular, Fair Share.[16]

In Chicago, Heather Booth and Steve Max, a fellow survivor of SDS, created a training institute called the Midwest Academy that offered new populist organizers a shared perspective to guide their work. Instructors urged students to shelve talk of "the working class," "socialism," and "revolution." Such concepts, remembers Booth, led to discussions that were "intellectual and abstract and vacuous and insulting." Instead, in traditional populist style, the trainers described "our forces" with such murky but meaningful phrases as "the 90 percent" or "the overwhelming majority." The other side were simply "people whose interests are against you." One graduate of the academy remembers Booth stressing the need for organizers to dress and wear their hair in "normal" ways in order to communicate with average Americans. "It was a specific part of the training," he says.[17]

Yet the new populism, for all its sensitivity to mainstream discourse and its commitment to gender equality, could not brake the rightward course of national politics. Booth and her fellow activists, unlike the Christian Right, made no attempt to exploit new media technologies, relying instead on such methods as house-to-house canvassing that consciously eschewed the tainted world of political self-advertising. And the new populists had no solution to the lack of good jobs and good wages but to blame those at the top. They wrote lengthy briefs for "economic democracy" but ignored the need for policies that, as in the heyday of liberalism, would increase the nation's wealth and not merely redistribute it.[18]

The idea of a new populism also appealed to a less radical breed of political operatives. Beginning in the early 1970s, a scattering of disgruntled liberals inside the party—Jack Newfield and Fred Harris, most prominently—urged a return to "bread-and-butter issues" that could separate "the little guy" (of both races) from the corporate elites that were the backbone of the GOP. No nominee for president adopted such a strategy, often derided as "class warfare." After Reagan's second landslide, however, the call for a "populist" idiom reminiscent of that which Roosevelt and Truman had spoken rapidly gained adherents. A growing number of Democratic consultants and politicians in the mid-1980s advocated an explicit focus on economic discontent—but one that neither encouraged grassroots protest nor abstained from the techniques of commercialized politics. In 1987, the liberal journalist Robert Kuttner summarized the new-old wisdom: "Democrats can regain their status as majority party only by rebuilding a majority coalition of ordinary, wage- and salary-earning people, whose political and economic interests are not identical to those of the wealthy."[19]

The populist turn received a strong impetus from Democratic opinion researchers schooled in the methods of Madison Avenue. After the 1984 disaster, Stanley Greenberg, a former political science professor at Yale University, helped to conduct focus groups (normally used to identify product preferences) in Iowa, New Hampshire, and blue-collar suburbs of Detroit. His purpose was to discover why so many white Democrats who had ascended to the middle class had soured on their party and defected to Ronald Reagan.

Greenberg's team found that, among such voters, the dual animus of producers toward the social top and bottom was alive and unmoored to either party. On the one hand, white wage earners from Macomb County, Michigan (adjacent to Detroit, with its black majority), voiced backlash sentiments that had hardly changed since George Wallace stopped running for president. "Blacks constitute the explanation for their [white defectors'] vulnerability and for almost everything that has gone wrong in their lives," Greenberg concluded; "not being black is what constitutes being middle class; not living with blacks is what makes a neighborhood a decent place to live."

Yet there was hope for Democrats who could learn how to speak like populists. White defectors in Iowa and New Hampshire, states with very small numbers of African-Americans, resented the power of big corporations fully as much as they did the federal government for "giving away" money to the undeserving poor. These people, wrote Greenberg, identified themselves as middle class but "live paycheck to paycheck, with frozen meals and hot dogs, without genuine savings; they cannot rest assured, for all this work, that their children will escape this marginality." While they were fond of Reagan, they still perceived the GOP as the bastion of "wealth and business." So they remained Democrats, hoping at each election cycle that the party would nominate men and women who, as they put it, really understood their economic problems and spoke their language.[20]

In the 1986 midterm elections, a few dozen candidates based their campaigns on the assumption that, as Greenberg put it, "The American public . . . is profoundly populist." In his race for a Senate seat from South Dakota, Tom Daschle attacked "the corporate giants" and their allies in the Reagan administration for driving long suffering farmers off their land. Jim Jontz, campaigning for a House seat from northwest Indiana, told factory workers anxious about their jobs: "It's not how well

Wall Street is doing that's made us a great country." And in his run for a Senate seat from Georgia, Wyche Fowler sponsored television advertisements that slammed the Republican incumbent for accepting contributions from "forty-two no-tax corporations" and then cut to a posh restaurant "where the liquor was flowing freely." All three candidates won close races in areas that had voted strongly Republican in 1984; though only Fowler, a liberal by Deep South standards, had to put together a coalition of both blacks and whites.[21]

Such victories—which helped the Democrats win back control of the Senate—fueled the conviction that a full-fledged revival of economic populist talk could move the nation leftward. Greenberg, Robert Kuttner, Kevin Phillips, and others argued that Democrats had become the majority party in the 1930s by offering to protect ordinary people from hardship and leaving their moral views and behavior alone. They now advised candidates to downplay social issues like abortion and affirmative action that divided the hardworking middle and to take the offensive, as had Fowler's television spot, against the lifestyle of the rich and faddish who had benefited handsomely from the reign of Reagan. We populists identify, said Jim Hightower, Texas commissioner of agriculture, with the people who "are down at the Seven-Eleven picking up a Budweiser and a Slim Jim" and not with the "yuppies enjoying a midday repast of cold melon mélange and asparagus and goat cheese and a delightfully fruity and frisky California white wine."[22]

This kind of language marked a tactical advance for the Democrats. For the first time in a quarter-century, politicians with an essentially liberal agenda were putting the concerns of ordinary whites first, while promising not to forsake the particular needs of African-Americans.

Yet, in a fundamental sense, the entire strategy floated on air. Unlike the 1930s, there was now no dynamic social movement or mood of left insurgency forcing the Democrats' hand. No wave of activists had emerged from the white middle class to articulate a fresh vocabulary of discontent and hope—one reason why, in 1988, Michael Dukakis resisted advice to bash the rich until the last days of his campaign. And, like new populists on their left, these Democrats skirted or minimized matters of race instead of confronting their obvious severity and speaking honestly about their causes.

The Democrats' turn to populism, therefore, remained a strategy hatched by candidates and their consultants who sought an honorable and efficacious way to abandon the liberal label. It did respond to mass emotions but was not connected in any organic way to the "workingmen and -women" whose sentiments candidates ritually invoked. This was a populism that saw no need for organized movements from below to support and extend its achievements. Like the copywriters for Hewlett-Packard and Banana Republic, Democratic campaigners were trying to pitch populism to a certain segment of the national market. But, in politics as in any sales effort, the consumers could always select a competing product or simply decline to buy any goods at all.

Ironically, the only figure within the Democratic fold who departed from this pattern and sought to galvanize a movement was Jesse Jackson—a fierce opponent of language aimed at enticing white defectors back to the party. Jackson's presidential campaign in 1984 revealed how hungry black people were to see their social perceptions and their demands legitimated by the media and the political elite. Jackson, the ambitious preacher who had, over the years, taught tens of thousands of his people to chant, "I Am Somebody," brought the crusade against "institutionalized racism" at home and abroad into venues where it had never before gained a serious hearing—editorial boards, television news shows, and presidential primaries. By the time Jackson told the Democratic National Convention in San Francisco, "No lie can live forever. Our time has come," his passionate cadences were as familiar to the public as were Reagan's homilies and jests. And both men had risen primarily through the power of their oratory.[23]

But Jackson was not content to be the black candidate for president. Tentatively during his 1984 campaign and consistently in the 1988 one, he articulated a sweeping vision of an America where political power and material resources would gradually shift from the top to the bottom. Jackson eschewed liberal clichés about fairness and equality that had grown stale since the mid-1960s. He spoke instead of the "economic violence" committed by runaway factories, "merger maniacs" on Wall Street, and politicians who funded nuclear weaponry instead of adequate education and housing. While Jackson's actual program featured such longstanding (but unrealized) liberal proposals as national health insurance and full employment, his method was that of a revivalist, indicting the system's sins and demanding repentance.[24]

Journalists often called Jackson a populist, though the insurgent candidate himself never adopted the term. Indeed, he was the first African-American leader of national stature to prominently champion the self-interests of workers, farmers, and others of *all* races who were in economic distress.

Yet, from the first, black was the only strong hue in Jackson's Rainbow Coalition. Apart from scattered groups of strikers and radical professionals, whites either shied away from or were antagonistic to the eloquent preacher who was so clearly an instrument of black empowerment (Latinos were somewhat more receptive). Jackson, by holding up the civil rights movement and its individual heroes and heroines as the exemplars of social change, installed a usable past, but it was one few of the whites he wanted to reach would adopt as their own.[25]

The obstacle Jackson was unable to bridge was one of country as well as color. The people he evoked were a transnational assemblage: black South Africans, white Iowa farmers, and Palestinian villagers all belonged with no pecking order of geography or suffering. And his most effective images were always of the poorest Americans, men and women whom most politicians neglected because they were unorganized and often didn't vote. Jackson reminded his listeners that most poor people were working people. As he told the 1988 Democratic convention:

> They catch the early bus. They work every day. They raise other people's children. They work every day. They drive vans and cabs. They work every day.

> They change the beds you slept in at these hotels last night and can't get a union contract. They work every day.... No job is beneath them.... They're not lazy. Someone must defend them because it's right, and they cannot speak for themselves.[26]

Unfortunately, this moving passage did not spring from the traditional core of American populism, even the left-wing variety. Its sentiments, along with Jackson's concern for the oppressed in other nations, were more those of "The Internationale" ("Arise, ye wretched of the earth") than of generations of sturdy producers who *did* feel some jobs were beneath them and were ready to fight to prevent falling to the lowest class. In the 1980s, such Americans—who now called themselves "middle class"—were still firmly convinced they were the bedrock of the republic, albeit one undergoing a severe economic jolt. Jackson appealed to working people regardless of race. But when he urged more money for the poor and the enforcement of affirmative-action decrees, white swing voters perceived him more as a threat than a savior.[27]

STILL MAD AS HELL

Bill Clinton gained the White House in 1992 partly because he clearly separated himself from such politics, which smacked too much of the New Left whose environs he had inhabited two decades before. With Stanley Greenberg running his polling operation and the self-styled populists James Carville and Paul Begala directing his strategy, Clinton denounced the economic policies responsible for the "middle-class squeeze" and championed the people who suffered from it. His campaign trinity of jobs, health care, and education was certainly designed to appeal to voters of all races. But the candidate's handlers made sure the media focused on his speeches and question-and-answer sessions in Macomb County and similar venues full of Reagan Democrats. Later, his inaugural address strummed chords of a Middle American populism that Reagan just as easily could have played:

> This beautiful capital ... is often a place of intrigue and calculation. Powerful people maneuver for position and worry endlessly about who is in and who is out, who is up and who is down, forgetting those people whose toil and sweat sends us here and pays our way.... Americans deserve better ... let us resolve to reform our politics, so that power and privilege no longer shout down the voice of the people.... Let us give this capital back to the people to whom it belongs.[28]

The rising of "the people" against the politicians was the favorite motif of nearly all presidential campaigners in 1992. Contenders with little chance to win opened the throttle to nostalgic intensity. On the Left, Jerry Brown donned union windbreakers and scorned "the greedy elite on Wall Street," while, on the Right, Pat Buchanan charged, "It is the sons of middle America who pay the price of reverse discrimination advanced by the Walker's Point [George Bush's vacation home] GOP to salve their consciences at other people's expense."[29] And reporters who covered Clinton's inaugural address assumed the passage about "people whose toil and sweat sends us here" was a device to convince followers of Ross Perot that the new president was a man they could trust, that he had truly come to fix the mess he had inherited.

Perot's drawing power illustrated that an updated form of conservative populism could still move millions. His talk of Americans as "owners" of their country was reminiscent of the tax revolt's image of hard-pressed suburbanites burdened with funding the guilt-ridden schemes of the welfare state. His homespun, Texas-accented ridicule of overdressed lobbyists and the "country clubbers" and "preppies" in Bush's White House was a softer variant of the class-conscious barbs thrown by George Wallace at "limousine liberals" and the "pointy-headed intellectuals" in their service. And his reverence for combat veterans and successful entrepreneurs as "smart, tough, and self-reliant" dovetailed with the ethos of leadership Nixon and Reagan had both promoted. Perot was a devastating critic of "the decade of greed, the era of trickle-down economics," but his main remedy was a balanced budget. Such rhetorical convergences were no accident; Perot was a lapsed Republican who had worked closely with Nixon presidential aides, and his base lay among the same whites of middling income who had been the GOP's prime supporters in the 1970s and 1980s.[30]

The Texas billionaire had learned from the mistakes of conservatives who, after more than a decade in power, had squandered their insurgent élan and lost their sensitivity to cultural trends. He communicated directly with voters through televised talk shows and electronic presentations of his own lucid, if facile, explanations of the economic troubles; he was like a secular Father Coughlin armed with four-color charts and graphs. He shunned talk of a Christian America and refused to take sides in any culture war. While pro-choice on abortion, he paid little attention to the issue. Meanwhile, he made sure that some blacks and women spoke for his organization, United We Stand America. Perot was even able to parry, if not defuse, charges that a man with so much wealth could not credibly represent the downwardly mobile. "He's buying [the White House] for the people," quipped one critic, "because it's out of our price range."[31]

What inspired and united Perot's supporters was the same "mad as hell" conviction that had animated campaigners for George Wallace, the last serious presidential candidate to run outside and against the two-party system. "When Perot supporters talked about 'us' against 'them,'" two analysts reported, "they meant the people—all the people—against the politicians."[32] This was the same rage that Bill Clinton and other Democrats were trying to channel. But Perot's brand of populism represented a more profound disillusionment because it was grounded among people who had once believed in Reagan's pledges to "get government off our backs" and "bring America back." Once betrayed, they would be difficult to attract to a new governing coalition.[33]

Like the appeal of Wallace and other twentieth-century insurgent campaigners for president, Perot's was self-limiting. The nature of the constraint was both personal and ideological. Perot was unwilling to build a movement that was more than a network of his admirers, and his unproven charges of conspiracies against him and his family left him open to ridicule by cynical reporters. United We Stand was all but invisible unless its creator appeared regularly on television, saying tough and controversial things.[34] The same dependence on one man plagued Father Coughlin's flock during the nation's last sustained economic crisis and had already reduced the Rainbow Coalition to a debating society awaiting Jesse Jackson's next campaign.

Moreover, Perot, the big businessman as maverick, could not convincingly recast himself as the hero of a desperate congeries of wage-earning people. He chose employers, not workers, as models of civic virtue and insisted on blaming a shifting cast of politicians for the poor economy instead of pointing to a more permanent establishment of international corporations. Change a few deluded policy makers and their "stupid" ideas about how the world works, and America would be as prosperous as ever. It was an easy, rather painless solution to the alarming, many-faceted decline.

The flaws in Perot's approach became evident during the debate on the North American Free Trade Agreement (NAFTA) in the fall of 1993. Here was an issue that seemed to symbolize perfectly the conflict between a suffering middle class scared of losing jobs and income and a globe-trotting elite concerned only with enhancing its profit and influence. "Citizens beware," announced Ralph Nader. "An unprecedented corporate power grab is underway in global negotiations over international trade." A remarkable ad hoc alliance of Left and Right—Nader and United We Stand, the AFL-CIO and most environmental groups, Jesse Jackson and Patrick Buchanan (who labeled NAFTA a device to speed "world government")—mobilized demonstrations, television ads, and hard lobbying to stop Congress from ratifying the trade pact with Mexico.[35]

Opinion polls showed a classic split: Americans with incomes higher than the average supported the agreement; those with lower incomes opposed it. Robert Reich, the secretary of labor admitted, "The dirty little secret buried inside the NAFTA debate is class consciousness. Low-skill, low-wage workers don't think NAFTA will help them. . . . The suspicion is that NAFTA will help the elite." Perot's popular quip about "a giant sucking sound" emanating from Mexico illustrated the visceral nature of the fear.[36]

Perot was the trade pact's most prominent antagonist, the only national figure capable of speaking not for a "special interest" or a discredited partisan faith but for America's economic future. Thus, his failure to make the case that NAFTA was indeed a cause worth fighting against did much to sink the opposition. During a climactic televised debate with Vice President Al Gore, Perot was forced to defend his own involvement with American firms in Mexico; he also engaged in fruitless squabbles over how much money he'd spent to defeat NAFTA and whether the television networks would run his ads. Instead of attacking companies who absconded with American jobs, he made an ill-tempered feint at an old conservative bogeyman: presidents who predicted their programs would cost less than they actually did. When the press reported that Gore had won the debate, a United We Stand activist complained, "All our calls, from average Americans, say Mr. Perot did a wonderful job. . . . If you bash our spokesperson, you're bashing us."[37]

It would have been extraordinary if the Texas mogul *had* struck out at the very types of corporate institutions he himself had created. A big businessman could not be expected to seriously question whether big business was good for ordinary Americans. But the polymorphous opposition had no other spokesman to crystallize the discontents it held in common. The anti-NAFTA movement, such as it was, disintegrated after losing the vote in Congress. "Working men and women" still had no effective means of speaking out for themselves.

THE LANGUAGE WE NEED?

Is the language of populism, continually renewed to chill a fresh elite and warm a fresh array of ordinary folk, still the language we need? As this glorious and terrible century nears its end, there is a disjunction between the language of electioneering and the self-evident realities of American culture. The traditional rhetoric of the people versus the establishment sounds, to many ears, naive if not offensive in its assumption that "the people" share anything beyond a geographic space.

The domestic body politic is shot through with gendered, multiracial identities that do not translate into old categories of producer and parasite, the authentic community and the artificial powers-that-be. The feminist scholar Elizabeth Kamarck Minnich criticizes populism for trying "to add women onto its agenda rather than re-forming its most basic thoughts and goals and ways of acting from the perspective of women," while Cornel West points out how necessary to black freedom were the quite unpopulist levers of presidential decrees and Supreme Court decisions. Both the Emancipation Proclamation and the *Brown v. Board of Education* case, he writes, "would have lost in a national referendum."[38] Most liberals and radicals no longer believe that America is the chosen nation, that "we, the people" could march forward together to prosperity and equality if only we could throw "the establishment" off our backs.

The popularity of skeptical views is due, in part, to the historical era through which we are passing. All the universal identities created during the Reformation and Enlightenment and renewed by liberals and socialists in the nineteenth century are in retreat. It is a rare intellectual who can still speak of Christians, or the proletariat, or even the common people in the old messianic fashion, as a vision embracing all humanity. Assertions of cultural and political difference have also disabled ideals like the producer ethic and the rights of man that flowed from the inclusive visions. Because left populists in the United States always criticized their rulers in the name of those ideals, the old rhetoric inevitably suffers from the postmodern disenchantment with fixed concepts and universal dreams.

Bill Clinton's reclamation effort notwithstanding, the populist idiom still resonates more routinely on the Right. Not since the 1940s has talk of "the people" gripped a coalition of the middle and bottom of society and included (not without some friction) people of all races and both genders. Scaling that progressive pinnacle of New Deal and Popular Front depended on a unique conjuncture of factors—the shared privation of the Depression, the shared faith in insurgent labor and FDR, and the common purpose of crushing fascism. And the great contest between the many, represented by a working-class movement, and the few "economic royalists" cannot be re-created in a postindustrial world. In the near future, liberals and leftists will probably spend a good deal of their time challenging attempts by populist speakers on the Right—including the resurgent Christian Coalition—to recapture white middle-class affections. The Left's own affinity with the will of ordinary people of all races remains an abstraction in search of movements that can realize it.[39]

But perhaps the continuing weakness of left populism is not so grim a prospect. After all, the most serious problems we face are global in nature, driven by dynamics not reducible to nationally or racially bounded categories of "people" and "elite." Figuring out "who hates who," in Kevin Phillips's phrase, can still win an American election and pleases our impulse to revolt in traditional ways. But it is of little use in regulating corporations that operate in scores of different nations, in helping impoverished people to develop their own economies without jeopardizing the health of the planet, in convincing Americans that their self-interest requires having compassion for the poor and transplanted both at home and abroad. In the whirlpool of decline, populism too easily becomes a language of the dispirited, the vengeful, and the cynical—of young men spoiling for a fight and of candidates with more cleverness than conviction. Its assertion of resentments based on class and status may be a barrier to constructing a new type of universalism—what the eco-anarchist Murray Bookchin calls "the ability to voice broadly human concerns." The alternative to campaigns that quickly descend into skirmishes between image makers is, writes the neoliberal Mickey Kaus, to behave as if "Politics is about what we think our lives together should be like."[40]

Yet the desire to transcend populism is also shortsighted. It ignores the very persistence of the language, rooted in the gap between American ideals and those institutions and authorities whose performance betrays them. That continuity occurs for a good reason. At the core of the populist tradition is an insight of great democratic and moral significance. No major problem can be seriously addressed, much less nudged on a path toward solution, unless what an antebellum politician called the "productive and burden-bearing classes"—Americans of all races who work for a living, knit neighborhoods together, and cherish what the nation is supposed to stand for—participate in the task.

Such citizens, many of whom are now frustrated and confused, have always brought their prejudices and self-interested myths along with them. But then so have people who write and read books like this one, usually guarding a not-so-secret wish that other Americans were as rational and tolerant as we imagine ourselves to be. When an attack of hauteur masked as civility strikes, one would do well to recall Sam Gompers's reply to Mark Hanna's complaint about the "undiplomatic" behavior of the Buffalo steelworkers in his employ who had gone on strike to protest abuse by their foremen. "We don't raise diplomats," said Gompers, "at thirteen, fourteen, or fifteen cents an hour."[41]

To move any closer toward redistributing wealth and revitalizing mass democracy, intellectuals have to take part in social movements that knit such people together. Without silencing the spirited voices of gender and racial community that emerged from the 1960s, we have to help chisel away the hardened self-righteousness that has grown up around such identities.[42] Otherwise, we risk spending the future as spectators to the endless competition between spin doctors and copywriters, captives to anyone who seems to make the old rhetoric sing again, if only for one acceptance speech or thirty-second spot. Such passivity is a cultural disease, and some form of populism is needed to cure it.

When a new breed of inclusive grassroots movements does arise, intellectuals should contribute their time, their money, and their passion for justice. They should work to stress the harmonious, hopeful, and pragmatic aspects of populist language and to disparage the meaner ones—without forgetting that evangelical zeal cannot be expunged from our culture. Like the American dream itself, populism lives too deeply in the fears and expectations of American citizens to be trivialized or replaced. We should not speak solely within its terms, but, without it, we are lost.

A Note on Method

ANY contemporary historian who chooses to write about language strolls, intentionally or not, into a methodological minefield. In recent years, the spirited argument that a focus on language and imagery should be central to the study of societies past and present has whipped up a complex and contentious debate among historians (as well as other academics in the humanities and social sciences). To oversimplify, the insurgents hold that power is inherently discursive and thus indeterminate. The ability to define and invent, to delimit and legitimate is basic to making war and winning elections, to waging a strike and deciding who will change the diapers. As the historian Lynn Hunt writes about the French Revolution: "Political symbols and rituals were not metaphors of power; they were the means and ends of power itself."[1]

On the other side, Marxists and neoconservatives alike protest against the substitution of language for life. They argue that power is fundamentally material and interpersonal, and that historians, with some precision, can determine its nature and function. How symbols are wielded is less important than the wealth and repressive might of those who wield them. "The language of politics articulates social relations . . . but it is never severed from its social moorings," write Elizabeth Fox-Genovese and Eugene Genovese.[2]

My own perspective falls between these two poles. Critics of what is called the "linguistic turn" are correct to emphasize the tangible components of power—such as property, armed force, access to goods and services—that frame debate and constrain behavior. In revolutionary France, heads did roll, people did starve, châteaux and churches were demolished and expropriated by those passionate about expunging the brutalities of the Ancien Régime. Discourse preceded, informed, and interpreted all these events but it did not invent their horror or the misery they caused. We are, after all, biological vessels who cringe before the fate of our bodies.

Yet one cannot grasp the struggle to control perception without paying close attention to language. Political texts tell us what power means, even if they don't rule the process of crafting those meanings. "The spectacle that widely publicized political language constructs," writes the sociologist Murray Edelman, "bemuses people's minds and places them in a social world marked by constant threats and constant reassurances." Any political text worthy of our attention brims with a multitude of voices—old, new, contradictory, playful, earnest, and otherwise. But it is nonetheless strategic, an instrument of purposes not always consciously recognized by the user.[3]

To capture the evolving language of American populism, I have tried to retain that tension between the social world of language users and the types of expression they employed. Political discourse does not speak itself; it is the creation of people engaged in institutions with varied resources and agendas. With that in mind, I discuss the role played by parties, unions, voluntary associations, universities, and the state—as well as media institutions, from the Jacksonian penny press to cable television. My aim has been to write what the labor historian Donald Reid calls "linguistically informed history," a pragmatic exercise that "never ceases to ask who speaks, who listens, who acts, when, where, why, how often, and to what effect."[4]

Other than that, I surrender the terrain of theory to more qualified thinkers. My own method is quite traditional. I assume that the people who worked in major social movements and electoral campaigns were not fools, though they sometimes behaved in foolish ways, and I view their rhetoric and symbols as rational acts that were intended to gain followers and political power. My exploration of populism as an ideal type of language is embedded in a familiar sort of narrative—with characters, events, rises, falls, changing sensibilities, and a dash of drama.[5] The choice of method was a natural one; storytelling with a political purpose has always been the kind of history I most enjoy reading and writing. Fortunately, that taste has not gone out of fashion, the academic rage for explicit theorizing notwithstanding.

Notes

INTRODUCTION: SPEAKING FOR THE PEOPLE

1. For my modest approach to studying the history of political language, see "A Note on Method," pp. 285–86.
2. E. L. Doctorow, "Theodore Dreiser: Book One and Book Two," *Jack London, Hemingway, and the Constitution: Selected Essays, 1977–1992* (New York: Random House, 1993), 37. The list of identities is mine.
3. Peter Wiles, "A Syndrome, Not a Doctrine: Some Elementary Theses on Populism," in *Populism: Its Meanings and National Characteristics,* ed. Ghita Ionescu and Ernest Gellner (London: Weidenfeld and Nicolson, 1969), 166. Wiles supplies a short list of populist movements that includes the Chartists in Britain, the Narodniki and Socialist-Revolutionaries of Russia, Social Credit of Western Canada, and the forces led by Mohandas Gandhi in India and Julius Nyerere in what became Tanzania (p. 178). Most interpreters would add the Peronistas of Argentina and the APRA party of Peru.
4. I am fond of Richard Hofstadter's formulation: "Conflict and consensus [in America] require each other and are bound up in a kind of dialectic of their own." Hofstadter, *The Progressive Historians: Turner, Beard, Parrington* (New York: Knopf, 1968), 463. For a similar statement, see John Higham, "Hanging Together: Divergent Unities in American History," *Journal of American History* 61 (June 1974): 7.
5. Alexis de Tocqueville, *Democracy in America,* vol. 2 (New York: Shocken Books, 1961), 306.
6. In contrast, Huey Long's Share the Wealth Clubs existed for less than two years in the mid-1930s. And the novelist Upton Sinclair's roughly simultaneous career as a Democratic candidate was limited to California.
7. See especially Lawrence Goodwyn, *Democratic Promise: The Populist Moment in America* (New York: Oxford University Press, 1976).
8. Two valuable syntheses of populism as a political style in the United States and

other nations are Ionescu and Gellner, *Populism,* and Margaret Canovan, *Populism* (New York: Harcourt Brace Jovanovich, 1981). Also see the excellent anthology of documents, *American Populism,* ed. George McKenna (New York: G.P. Putnam's Sons, 1974).

9. For a recent declaration, see [Todd Gitlin, Paul Berman, and Irving Howe], "Democratic Vistas 1991: A Statement for the Democratic Left," *Dissent* (Fall 1991): 473–81.
10. "'More Humility, Fewer Illusions'—A Talk Between Adam Michnik and Jurgen Habermas," *New York Review of Books,* March 24, 1994, 25.
11. Quoted by Merle Curti, "Intellectuals and Other People," *American Historical Review* 60 (January 1955): 282. For an incisive argument on the need for intellectuals to have an empathetic relationship with their national culture, see Michael Walzer, *The Company of Critics* (New York: Basic Books, 1988), 225–40.

CHAPTER 1. INHERITANCE

1. Tom Watson, *The People's Party Campaign Book, 1892* (New York: Arno, 1975), 1–23.
2. Elias Smith, "On Predestination," quoted by Nathan O. Hatch, *The Democratization of American Christianity* (New Haven: Yale University Press, 1989), 228.
3. The best study of Thomas Paine's thought in historical context is Eric Foner, *Tom Paine and Revolutionary America* (New York: Oxford University Press, 1977).
4. Hatch, *Democratization,* 136.
5. On the plebeian involvement with evangelical religion and moral reform in one critical region, see Teresa Anne Murphy, *Ten Hours' Labor: Religion, Reform, and Gender in Early New England* (Ithaca, N.Y.: Cornell University Press, 1992).
6. Alexis de Tocqueville, *Democracy in America,* vol. 1 (New York: Knopf, 1945), 317; Edward Pessen, *Jacksonian America: Society, Personality, and Politics,* rev. ed. (Homewood, Ill.: Dorsey Press, 1978), 67–73; Ernest Lee Tuveson, *Redeemer Nation: The Idea of America's Millennial Role* (Chicago: University of Chicago Press, 1968).
7. Kenneth Cmiel, *Democratic Eloquence: The Fight over Popular Speech in Nineteenth-Century America* (New York: Morrow, 1990), 55–93.
8. Gordon Wood, *The Radicalism of the American Revolution* (New York: Knopf, 1992), 230.
9. On this point, see James T. Kloppenberg, "The Virtues of Liberalism: Christianity, Republicanism, and Ethics in Early American Political Discourse," *Journal of American History* 74 (June 1987): 9–33. A guide to literature on the controversy is the special issue of *American Quarterly* 37 (Fall 1985), which includes synthesizing articles by Joyce Appleby, Linda Kerber, Jean Baker, James Oakes, and John Diggins. Also see Daniel Rodgers's debunking essay, "Republicanism: The Career of a Concept," *Journal of American History* 79 (June 1992): 11–38.
10. Quoted in Hans Kohn, *American Nationalism: An Interpetative Essay* (New York: Macmillan, 1957), 13.
11. On this concept and its genesis in the English revolution of the 1640s, see Edmund S. Morgan, *Inventing the People: The Rise of Popular Sovereignty in England and*

America (New York: Norton, 1988). Also see Daniel T. Rodgers, *Contested Truths: Keywords in American Politics Since Independence* (New York: Basic Books, 1987), 80–111.

12. Quotes from George McKenna, ed., *American Populism* (New York: G.P. Putnam's Sons, 1974), 69–70; Wood, *Radicalism,* 278–79. On Manning and other plebeian democrats of his day, see *The Key of Liberty: The Life and Democratic Writings of William Manning, "A Laborer," 1747–1814,* ed. with an introduction by Michael Merrill and Sean Wilentz (Cambridge: Harvard University Press, 1993).
13. Thomas Hart Benton, quoted in Alexander Saxton, *Indispensable Enemy: Labor and the Anti-Chinese Movement in California* (Berkeley: University of California Press, 1971), 21–22.
14. On Skidmore, see Sean Wilentz, *Chants Democratic: New York City and the Rise of the American Working Class, 1788–1850* (New York: Oxford University Press, 1984), 194–95. On the failure of working women to break through male constructions of producerism, see Christine Stansell, *City of Women: Sex and Class in New York, 1789–1860* (New York: Knopf, 1986), 130–54, and passim.
15. The awful irony, as Judith Shklar points out, is that black spokesmen like Frederick Douglass were then demanding to be allowed to join and profit from the free labor system and denied they wanted any special treatment from the government. Judith N. Shklar, *American Citizenship: The Quest for Inclusion* (Cambridge: Harvard University Press, 1991), 83–84.

    On the complex appeal of minstrelsy, see Alexander Saxton, *The Rise and Fall of the White Republic* (New York: Verso, 1990), 165–82. On the connections between producerism and race in antebellum America, see David Roediger, *The Wages of Whiteness: Race and the Making of the American Working Class* (New York: Verso, 1991). Adams quoted in Wood, *Radicalism,* 179.
16. *David Walker's Appeal* (New York: Hill and Wang, 1965 [orig., 1829]), 2; *Malcolm X Speaks,* ed. George Breitman (New York: Pathfinder, 1965), 172.
17. Cited in Hatch, *Democratization,* 231.
18. John D. Eaton in 1824, quoted in Robert V. Remini, *Andrew Jackson and the Course of American Freedom, 1822–1832,* vol. 2 (New York: Harper and Row, 1981), 77. On the international dimension, see Charles Tilly, "Social Movements and National Politics," in *Statemaking and Social Movements: Essays in History and Theory,* ed. Charles Bright and Susan Harding (Ann Arbor: University of Michigan Press, 1984), 297–317.
19. It was seldom mentioned that Jefferson thought Jackson unfit to be president and that, at the beginning of his career, Lincoln was a Whig and thus a bitter opponent of Jackson's. Alexander Hamilton, foil of many a populist attack, had been particularly critical of jeremiads. In the Sixth Federalist Paper, he asked, "Have we not already seen enough of . . . those idle theories which have amused us with promises of an exemption from the imperfections, the weaknesses, and the evils incident to society in every shape? Is it not time to awake from the deceitful dream of a golden age?" Quoted in Sacvan Bercovitch, *The American Jeremiad* (Madison: University of Wisconsin Press, 1978), 139.
20. On the Populists and Jefferson, see Merrill D. Peterson, *The Jefferson Image in the American Mind* (New York: Oxford University Press, 1960), 257–65; Lawrence Goodwyn, *Democratic Promise: The Populist Moment in America* (New York: Oxford University Press, 1976), 373–75; Norman Pollack, *The Just Polity:*

Populism, Law, and Human Welfare (Urbana: University of Illinois Press, 1987), 113–14. In 1906, after imbuing his populism with racist and anti-Semitic overtones, Tom Watson changed the name of the periodical he edited to *Watson's Jeffersonian Magazine*. See C. Vann Woodward, *Tom Watson: Agrarian Rebel* (New York: Oxford University Press, 1938), 381.

21. Jefferson, from a 1795 letter, quoted by Winthrop Jordan, *White over Black: American Attitudes Toward the Negro, 1550–1812* (New York: Penguin, 1969), 476. Also see Wood, *Radicalism,* 106.
22. Thomas Jefferson, *Writings* (New York: Library of America, 1984), 494.
23. Richard Hofstadter, *The American Political Tradition and the Men Who Made It* (New York: Knopf, 1948), 43. Hofstadter claimed that Jefferson usually stated the "generous and emancipating thoughts for which his name is so justly praised" in his letters rather than in public statements. But readers of his inaugural addresses will find this an exaggeration; at any rate, by the late nineteenth century, Jefferson's letters were widely available.
24. Marvin Meyers, *The Jacksonian Persuasion: Politics and Belief* (Stanford: Stanford University Press, 1957), 2. Despite its abstract tone, Meyers's book is still a splendid guide to the Jacksonian image.
25. Watson, *Campaign Book,* 26. Like many polemicists, Watson was not too meticulous about historical details. He alludes to Jackson's command during the Battle of New Orleans, which took place six months *before* the Battle of Waterloo. On Jackson's religiosity, see Remini, *Jackson and the Course of American Freedom,* pp. 9–11.
26. Edward Pessen, *Jacksonian America: Society, Personality, and Politics,* rev. ed. (Homewood, Ill.: Dorsey Press, 1978), 100. On Jacksonian society, see pp. 77–100, and passim; Wilentz, *Chants Democratic;* and Charles Sellers, *The Market Revolution: Jacksonian America, 1815–1846* (New York: Oxford University Press, 1991).
27. Leggett quoted in Russell Hanson, *The Democratic Imagination in America: Conversations with Our Past* (Princeton, N.J.: Princeton University Press, 1985), 128. Joseph Dorfman once pointed out that, even for "radical" leaders of antebellum trade unions and short-lived workingmen's parties, the language of class was loosely generic, intended more to attract a broad majority than to draw clear distinctions. "Only your political opponents and the terrible aristocrats and the lazy idlers were clearly not honest 'working men.'" Joseph Dorfman, "The Jackson Wage-Earner Thesis," *American Historical Review* 54 (January 1949): 305.
28. Eric Foner states this contrast well: "The ideologies of nineteenth-century labor and farmers' movements, and even early twentieth-century socialism itself, owed more to traditional republican notions of the equal citizen and the independent small producer, than to the coherent analysis of class-divided society. . . . Not the *absence* of non-liberal ideas, but the *persistence* of a radical vision resting on small property inhibited the rise of socialist ideologies." Eric Foner, "Why Is There No Socialism in the United States?" *History Workshop* 17 (Spring 1984): 63.

The negative meaning of "consumer" derived from the Latin verb *consumere*—"to take up completely, devour, waste, spend." Raymond Williams, *Keywords: A Vocabulary of Culture and Society,* rev. ed. (New York: Oxford University Press, 1985), 78–79.

Many European socialists and anarchists viewed the United States as an exceptionally free nation whose accomplishments should be emulated. For example,

Mikhail Bakunin, after traveling in America, wrote, "Class antagonism hardly yet exists" because "all workers are citizens" to whom the colonists had bequeathed a "traditional spirit of liberty." Quoted in Paul Avrich, *Anarchist Portraits* (Princeton, N.J.: Princeton University Press, 1988), 23.

29. The nickname, referring to a wood of particular hardness, was given to Jackson after he led his troops on a march of several hundred miles through swamps and dense forests. John William Ward, *Andrew Jackson: Symbol for an Age* (New York: Oxford University Press, 1955), 54–56; Joseph Conrad, *Nostromo* (New York: Modern Library, 1951), 351.
30. For the quotes from Jackson and Webster, see Richard Hofstadter, ed., *Great Issues in American History: From the Revolution to the Civil War, 1765–1865* (New York: Vintage Books, 1958), 292, 298. On the drafting of the veto, see Remini, *Jackson and the Course of American Freedom,* 353–73.

    Astonishingly, Nicholas Biddle and his supporters believed the Message was a "manifesto of anarchy" that had fatally discredited Jackson's cause. They even spent the bank's money to reprint and distribute thousands of copies of the speech. Harry L. Watson, *Liberty and Power: The Politics of Jacksonian America* (New York: Hill and Wang, 1990), 150–51.
31. Quoted in Arthur Schlesinger, Jr., *The Age of Jackson* (Boston: Little, Brown, 1945), 123–24.
32. "Protest to the Senate," April 15, 1834, quoted by Arthur Schlesinger, Jr., "The Ages of Jackson," *New York Review of Books,* Dec. 7, 1989, 49.
33. Quoted in Michael Schudson, *Discovering the News: A Social History of American Newspapers* (New York: Basic Books, 1978), 52. On Bennett's career, see James L. Crouthamel, *Bennett's New York Herald and the Rise of the Popular Press* (Syracuse, N.Y.: Syracuse University Press, 1989). Small artisan papers had been the first to marry democratic outrage to a fascination with the misdeeds of elite institutions. But this pioneering labor press did not survive the depression of the late 1830s and early 1840s. See Dan Schiller, *Objectivity and the News: The Public and the Rise of Commercial Journalism* (Philadelphia: University of Pennsylvania Press, 1981).
34. Wilentz, *Chants Democratic,* 327, 333.
35. As Richard Hofstadter noted, "The task of fighting the Indians gave all classes a common bond and produced popular heroes among the upper ranks." Hofstadter, *American Political Tradition,* 48.
36. On the contrast, see Ward, *Symbol for an Age,* 46–78; Daniel Walker Howe, *The Political Culture of the American Whigs* (Chicago: University of Chicago Press, 1979), 40–42; Michael Rogin, *Ronald Reagan, the Movie and Other Episodes in Political Demonology* (Berkeley: University of California Press, 1987), 168.
37. Nathan Sargent in 1875, quoted in Robert Remini, *The Legacy of Andrew Jackson: Essays on Democracy, Indian Removal, and Slavery* (Baton Rouge: Louisiana State University Press), 22. For a historically diffuse, largely apolitical, but still fascinating view of such imagery, see Rupert Wilkinson, *American Tough: The Tough-Guy Tradition and American Character* (New York: Perennial Library, 1986).
38. The sham document is quoted and discussed in Merrill D. Peterson's encyclopedic *Lincoln in American Memory* (New York: Oxford University Press, 1994), 160; poem by Mrs. J. T. Kellie, quoted in Pollack, *Just Polity,* 188.
39. Emerson, speech in Concord, Mass., April 19, 1865, reprinted in *Building the*

Myth: Selected Speeches Memorializing Abraham Lincoln, ed. Waldo W. Braden (Urbana: University of Illinois Press, 1990), 31.

40. Gabor S. Boritt, *Lincoln and the Economics of the American Dream* (Memphis: Memphis State University Press, 1978), 284. Boritt points out that Lincoln also admired self-made men (whom he contrasted with those like John Jacob Astor who employed unscrupulous means to amass tremendous wealth), and "did not see the working class as a well-defined stratum with its own special interests because he did not see any permanent classes in America." In fact, Lincoln was proud that most Northerners were "neither hirer nor hired" and claimed that, numerically, wage earners were a rather insignificant group (less than one-eighth of all "labor" in the United States). Borritt, 182, 178, 179.
41. Michael Davis, *The Image of Lincoln in the South* (Knoxville: University of Tennessee Press, 1971), 146–53. On blacks and the Lincoln image, see Scott A. Sandage, "A Marble House Divided: The Lincoln Memorial, the Civil Rights Movement, and the Politics of Memory, 1939–1965," *Journal of American History* 80 (June 1993). On Lincoln's attempt to enshrine equality as the civil religion, see Garry Wills, *Lincoln at Gettysburg: The Words That Remade America* (New York: Simon and Schuster, 1992). I am less sanguine than Wills that the attempt was a success—until a century later.
42. Quotes from David Donald, *Lincoln Reconsidered* (New York: Knopf, 1956), 144; Bryan speech in 1909, in *Building the Myth,* ed. Braden, 144; Ida Tarbell speech in 1932, ibid., 213.
43. Eric Hobsbawm, "Introduction: Inventing Traditions," in *The Invention of Tradition,* ed. Eric Hobsbawm and Terence Ranger (Cambridge, Eng.: Cambridge University Press, 1983), 1–14.

CHAPTER 2. THE RIGHTEOUS COMMONWEALTH OF THE LATE NINETEENTH CENTURY

1. While none of these parties drew more than a small fraction of the popular vote in any presidential election, alternative tickets did take control in perhaps a hundred towns and cities from Vermont to California. For the labor parties, see Leon Fink, *Workingmen's Democracy: The Knights of Labor and American Politics* (Urbana: University of Illinois Press, 1983), 28–29, and passim. On the tenor of Gilded Age politics, see Michael E. McGerr, *The Decline of Popular Politics: The American North, 1865–1926* (New York: Oxford University Press, 1986), 3–183; Morton Keller, *Affairs of State: Public Life in Late Nineteenth Century America* (Cambridge: Harvard University Press, 1977).
2. This meeting culminated a rather protracted process of party building. In the summer of 1890, a coalition of Kansas reformers had formed a People's Party and run a slate of nominees for state and local office. Then, in May 1891, a mass gathering in Cincinnati had voted to set up a provisional committee for a national party with the same name. The meeting in St. Louis nine months later formally established the party organization and drafted its platform. In July 1892, the Populists held their first nominating convention in Omaha and officially ratified the platform.

3. Lloyd speech of October 6, 1894, quoted in Chester McArthur Destler, *American Radicalism, 1865–1901* (Chicago: Quadrangle, 1966), 219.
4. *St. Louis Post-Dispatch,* 22 February 1892.
5. Quotes from the version printed in Watson, *People's Party Campaign Book,* 123–26. On Donnelly's career, see Martin Ridge, *Ignatius Donnelly: The Portrait of a Politician* (Chicago: University of Chicago Press, 1962).
6. Quoted by John D. Hicks, *The Populist Revolt: A History of the Farmers' Alliance and the People's Party* (1931; reprint, Lincoln: University of Nebraska Press, 1961), 228. The preamble received a similar response when it was read at the first nominating convention of the People's Party on July 4 of that year. The entire document is now known as the Omaha Platform, but it was essentially completed and first read at the St. Louis Conference.
7. There is no adequate survey of the politics of this shaky coalition. But see Nell Irvin Painter, *Standing at Armageddon: The United States, 1877–1919* (New York: Norton, 1987), 72–109, and Destler, *American Radicalism.*

   A perceptive discussion of the pro-capitalist contours of the ideology of most insurgents is Paul Krause, "The Life and Times of 'Beeswax' Taylor: Origins and Paradoxes of the Gilded-Age Labor Movement," *Labor History* 33 (Winter 1992): 32–54.

   The discussion in this section concerns only those activists—variously called reformers, insurgents, or radicals—who spoke from and for social movements of wage earners, farmers, and the prohibitionists. That omits the so-called "mugwumps"—elite literary figures like James Russell Lowell, Henry Adams, and a number of lawyers and other professionals—who protested major-party corruption and proposed the establishment of the federal civil service. Even though the mugwumps shared some of the same grievances as did those within the Populist orbit, their distaste for mass democracy was quite alien to populism in any form. "When I am in a small minority I believe I am right. When I am in a minority of one, I know I am right," boasted the mugwump William Everett. Keller, *Affairs of State,* 551.
8. For examples of this cross-class opposition to the corporate power, see Herbert Gutman, "The Workers' Search for Power: Labor in the Gilded Age," Gutman, *Power and Culture,* ed. Ira Berlin (New York: Pantheon, 1987), 70–92; Fink, *Workingmen's Democracy,* passim.
9. A good sample of such texts produced by adherents of the Farmers' Alliance and/or the People's Party is *The Populist Mind,* ed. Norman Pollack (Indianapolis: Bobbs-Merrill, 1967), esp. 3–327.

   According to the literary theorist J. Hillis Miller, "the basic elements of any narrative" include "an initial situation, a sequence leading to a change or reversal of that situation, and a revelation made possible by the reversal of situation." Miller, "Narrative," *Critical Terms for Literary Study,* ed. Frank Lentricchia and Thomas McLaughlin (Chicago: University of Chicago Press, 1990), 75. The myth of antebellum virtue, the post–Civil War capture of power by "monopolists" and "plutocrats," and the various grand escapes outlined by Greenbackers, Frances Willard, Henry George, Edward Bellamy, and other Gilded Age reformers fit this model perfectly.
10. Quoted in Ridge, *Ignatius Donnelly,* 91.
11. Donnelly quote from 1886 platform of the Minnesota Farmers' Alliance, published in Knights of Labor, *Labor: Its Rights and Wrongs* (1886; reprint, Westport, Conn.: Greenwood Press, 1973), 155. A Greenback pamphlet of 1878 denounced Republi-

can "robbery" but included several protest songs set to such Union melodies as "John Brown's Body" and "Rally Round the Flag Boys." J. H. Randall, *National Greenback and Labor Shot and Shell* (Clyde, Ohio: self-published, 1878).

12. Quoted in Robert P. Sharkey, *Money, Class, and Party* (Baltimore: Johns Hopkins University Press, 1959), 194.
13. For examples, see Herbert G. Gutman, "Black Coal Miners and the Greenback-Labor Party in Redeemer, Alabama, 1878–1879," *Labor History* 10 (Summer 1969): 509, 532.
14. Robert P. Sharkey traces this change to the suspension of specie payments during the Civil War and the ubiquity of greenbacks, which became known as "the money of the people." Sharkey, *Money, Class, and Party,* 195–97.
15. Leon Fink shrewdly points out that the depiction of working people as more competent than their oppressors implied that government regulation of corporations might not be required. With "the minimal resources necessary to sustain their productive activities (e.g., credit, land, the ballot, and cooperatives)" and "control [over] those parasitic or monopolistic elements that would destroy or hoard society's resources, then civil society could carry on with a minimal state." Leon Fink, "Looking Backward: Reflections on Workers' Culture and Certain Conceptual Dilemmas Within Labor History," in *Perspectives on American Labor History: The Problems of Synthesis,* ed. J. Carroll Moody and Alice Kessler-Harris (DeKalb, Ind.: Northern Illinois University Press, 1989), 9.
16. At the end of another century, it is hard to imagine any single cultural production—let alone a book—having the political impact that Bellamy's *Looking Backward* and George's *Progress and Poverty* did. For examples of Greenback propaganda, see the songs in Randall and Lurton, *National Greenback and Labor Shot and Shell,* 39–61. On the Populists, see Pollack, *Just Polity,* passim.
17. Herron quoted in *The Rhetoric of Christian Socialism,* ed. Paul H. Boase (New York: Random House, 1969), 95; Coxey in Carlos Schwantes, *Coxey's Army: An American Odyssey* (Lincoln: University of Nebraska Press, 1985), 41. The official name of Coxey's group was the Commonwealth of Christ.
18. On the general nature of this revival, see William G. McLoughlin, *Revivals, Awakenings, and Reform* (Chicago: University of Chicago Press, 1978), 141–78; Mark A. Noll, *A History of Christianity in the United States and Canada* (Grand Rapids: William B. Eerdmans, 1992), 286–307.
19. Bruce Laurie, *Artisans into Workers: Labor in Nineteenth-Century America* (New York: Hill and Wang, 1989), 152; Herbert Gutman, "Protestantism and the American Labor Movement," in his *Work, Culture, and Society in Industrializing America* (New York: Vintage, 1977), 94–95. Also see Ken Fones-Wolf, *Trade Union Gospel: Christianity and Labor in Industrial Philadelphia, 1865–1915* (Philadelphia: Temple University Press, 1990).
20. McGlynn quoted in Eric Foner, *Politics and Ideology* (New York: Oxford University Press, 1980), 188; Edward Bellamy, *Looking Backward* (New York: New American Library, 1960), 215.
21. Quote from Keller, *Affairs of State,* 548.
22. Quoted in Fink, "Looking Backward," 9; Destler, *American Radicalism,* 217. Similar "counterrevolutionary" sentiments were voiced at the time by Eugene V. Debs and Edward Bellamy. See Nick Salvatore, *Eugene V. Debs: Citizen and Socialist* (Urbana: University of Illinois Press, 1982), 134; John L. Thomas, *Alternative America,* 274–75.

On the other hand, "revolution" had a positive connotation in the writings of some Populists. In 1892, Tom Watson's *Campaign Book* was subtitled, "Not a Revolt, It Is a Revolution"; the phrase came from a comment supposedly made to King Louis XVI on the night the Bastille fell. That same year, a woman Populist propagandist wrote, "Put 1,000 woman lecturers in the field and the revolution is here." Mari Jo Buhle, *Women and American Socialism, 1870–1920* (Urbana: University of Illinois Press, 1981), 89.

But Populists normally referred to their side as the "reform" forces and never, to my knowledge, as the "revolutionary" ones. The former was a legitimate abstraction from the days of the Founding Fathers. But the latter would have implied a commitment to methods likely to alienate discontented but conservative Americans whom the Populists were courting.

23. Quoted in Daniel Rodgers's perceptive study, *The Work Ethic in Industrial America, 1850–1920* (Chicago: University of Chicago Press, 1978), 221. Rodgers notes that Gilded Age advocates of social transformation did not adhere to an economic definition of the labor theory of value: "For most radical spokesmen the central issue was not the source of prices but the source of wealth, and the force of the slogan derived far less from economics than from its stubborn moral affirmation of the indispensability of those who toiled and produced" (p. 213–14).
24. Knights of Labor, *Labor: Its Rights and Wrongs,* 29–33, 153–69. An exception was the Central Labor Union of New York and Vicinity, which declared, "The combined wages-working class represents the great majority of the people" (p. 165).
25. Fink, *Workingmen's Democracy,* 9. Sometimes, the coalition was even broader. In Kansas City, Kansas, the leadership of the insurgent Citizens' Alliance included two high officers of local banks (p. 137).
26. On this subject, as applied to the labor component of the producer alliance, see Leon Fink, "The Uses of Political Power: Toward a Theory of the Labor Movement in the Era of the Knights of Labor," in *Working-Class America,* ed. Michael Frisch and Daniel Walkowitz (Urbana: University of Illinois Press, 1983), 104–22.
27. Michael McGovern, "The Puddlers' Jubilee, August 1896," in *Labor Lyrics and Other Poems* (Youngstown, Ohio: [self-published], 1899), thanks to David Montgomery for this reference; Paul Krause, *The Battle for Homestead 1880–1892: Politics, Culture, and Steel* (Pittsburgh: University of Pittsburgh Press, 1992), 217.
28. Paul Krause, "Labor Republicanism and 'Za Chlebom': Anglo-Americans and Slavic Solidarity in Homestead," in *"Struggle a Hard Battle": Essays on Working-Class Immigrants,* ed. Dirk Hoerder (DeKalb: Northern Illinois University Press, 1986), 143–69 (quote, 145).
29. See Alexander Saxton, *The Indispensable Enemy: Labor and the Anti-Chinese Movement in California* (Berkeley: University of California Press, 1971).
30. T. Fulton Gantt, *Breaking the Chains: A Story of the Present Industrial Struggle* in *The Knights in Fiction: Two Labor Novels of the 1880s,* ed. Mary C. Grimes (1887; reprint, Urbana: University of Illinois Press, 1986), 47. On the anti-Chinese opinions of Kansas workers, see Scott G. McNall, *The Road to Rebellion: Class Formation and Kansas Populism, 1865–1900* (Chicago: University of Chicago Press, 1988), 153.
31. Quoted in Herbert G. Gutman, "Black Coal Miners and the Greenback-Labor Party in Redeemer, Alabama, 1878–1879," *Labor History* 10 (Summer 1969): 531. For a nuanced discussion of white workers' attitudes toward free black labor after the

Civil War, see David Roediger, *The Wages of Whiteness: Race and the Making of the American Working Class* (New York: Verso, 1991), 167–84.

32. Terrell quoted in *St. Louis Globe Democrat,* 23 February 1892, p. 12. On the popularity of the Declaration of Independence among nineteenth-century reformers and radicals, see Philip S. Foner, ed., *We, the Other People* (Urbana: University of Illinois Press, 1976).
33. Powderly quoted in *New York Times,* 23 February 1892, 8. The immigration stance was one of ten "supplementary resolutions" that were not formally included in the platform but were listed as "expressive of the sentiment of this Convention." For the entire document (actually the final one ratified that summer in Omaha), see Hofstadter and Hofstadter, *Great Issues,* vol. II, 139–45 (quote on 144).
34. See Hofstadter and Hofstadter, *Great Issues,* vol. II, 139–45.
35. For a vivid portrait of the educational network, see Goodwyn, *Democratic Promise,* 351–86. William Sewell points out that all social movements use several kinds of historical discourse simultaneously. A movement's success depends, in part, on the effectiveness of the meld. William H. Sewell, Jr., "How Classes Are Made: Critical Reflections on E. P. Thompson's Theory of Working-Class Formation," in *E. P. Thompson: Critical Perspectives,* ed. Harvey J. Kaye and Keith McClelland (Philadelphia: Temple University Press, 1990), 68–75.
36. On Davis, see Goodwyn, *Democratic Promise,* 373–77. On the transitional parties, Peter H. Argersinger, "Editor's Introduction," William A. Peffer, *Populism, Its Rise and Fall* (Lawrence: University Press of Kansas, 1992), 5–6. Quote from Ignatius Donnelly in 1895, cited by Frederic C. Jaher, *Doubters and Dissenters: Cataclysmic Thought in America, 1885–1918* (New York: The Free Press of Glencoe, 1964), 136.
37. Bruce Palmer, *"Man over Money": The Southern Populist Critique of American Capitalism* (Chapel Hill: University of North Carolina Press, 1980), 209.
38. Quote from a letter to a Populist newspaper in Nebraska, Stanley B. Parsons, Jr., *The Populist Context: Rural Versus Urban Power on a Great Plains Frontier* (Westport, Conn.: Greenwood Press, 1973), 101; Michael Rogin, *The Intellectuals and McCarthy: The Radical Specter* (Cambridge: MIT Press, 1967), 179.

    The degree and nature of Populist anti-Semitism was once a hotly disputed topic. I tend to agree with the view, best expressed by John Higham, that it was a minor element of the movement's language that stemmed more from a nationalist hatred of international bankers than from a specific antagonism toward Jews. Higham also argues that anti-Semitic rhetoric (and actions) were more prevalent among urban Protestant elites than they were among agrarian reformers at the time. Higham, "Ideological Anti-Semitism in the Gilded Age," in *Send These to Me: Immigrants in Urban America,* rev. ed. (Baltimore: Johns Hopkins University Press, 1984), 111 and passim. Also see Jaher, *Doubters and Dissenters,* 130–37.
39. Quoted by Vivian Hart, *Distrust and Democracy: Political Distrust in Britain and America* (Cambridge, Eng.: Cambridge University Press, 1978), 97.
40. Quotes from Edward L. Ayers, *The Promise of the New South: Life After Reconstruction* (New York: Oxford University Press, 1992), 233; Julie Roy Jeffrey, "Women in the Southern Farmers' Alliance: A Reconsideration of the Role and Status of Women in the Late Nineteenth-Century South," *Feminist Studies* 3 (Fall 1975): 79.

    The slim body of literature on women and Populism includes Mari Jo Buhle,

Women and American Socialism, 82–94; Pauline Adams and Emma S. Thornton, *A Populist Assault: Sarah E. Van De Vort Emery on American Democracy, 1862–1895* (Bowling Green: Bowling Green State University Popular Press, 1982); and MaryJo Wagner, "Women in the Farmers' Alliance," paper given at the 1990 Meeting of the Organization of American Historians. Wagner concludes that women leaders of the agrarian crusade "were middle-class women espousing traditional family-centered values that they combined without contradiction with public roles and radical economic and political views." A good study of "moral suasion" as a political strategy is Lori D. Ginzberg, *Women and the Work of Benevolence: Morality, Politics, and Class in the Nineteenth-Century United States* (New Haven: Yale University Press, 1990).

41. Even though the national People's Party endorsed neither prohibition nor woman suffrage, many populist women were or had been quite active in both campaigns. See Wagner, "Women in the Farmers' Alliance," 7. On the state level, several People's Parties did endorse prohibition. On the Nebraska case, see Parsons, *Populist Context,* 106. On the relationship between Populism and prohibition, see chap. 4.

42. Carl Carmen, *Stars Fell on Alabama,* quoted in Gerald Gaither, *Blacks and the Populist Revolt: Ballots and Bigotry in the New South* (University, Ala.: University of Alabama Press, 1977), 68. In fact, small farmers in the Black Belt who had belonged to the Farmers' Alliance were less likely than upcountry agrarians to vote for the People's Party. Morgan Kousser, *The Shaping of Southern Politics: Suffrage Restriction and the Establishment of the One-Party South, 1880–1910* (New Haven: Yale University Press, 1974), 35. The best study of Southern Populist views on race is Palmer, *"Man over Money,"* 50–66.

43. William F. Holmes, "The Demise of the Colored Farmers' Alliance," *Journal of Southern History* 41 (May 1975): 187–200; Goodwyn, *Democratic Promise,* 292–93. For a heroic exception to the pattern, see Lawrence Goodwyn, "Populist Dreams and Negro Rights: East Texas as a Case Study," *American Historical Review* 78 (1971): 1435–56.

44. Watson (from his *People's Party Paper*) quoted in Barton Shaw, *The Wool-Hat Boys: Georgia's Populist Party* (Baton Rouge: Louisiana State University Press, 1984), 80; on laws, see Gaither, *Blacks and the Populist Revolt,* 70–71, and Charles Crowe, "Tom Watson, Populists, and Blacks Reconsidered," *Journal of Negro History* 55 (April 1970): 99–116. Crowe's article is couched as a criticism of C. Vann Woodward's well-known biography of Watson.

Of course, the Populists' stance toward blacks was quite different than that of Southern Democrats. The latter were spewing out race hatred and passing disenfranchisement laws (some of which, like the poll tax, also limited the participation of poor whites) that both Populist and Republican legislators vehemently opposed. See Kousser, *The Shaping of Southern Politics.*

45. See, for example, Goodwyn, *Democratic Promise,* 276–306. For a judicious summary of this issue, see Ayers, *Promise of New South,* 269–74.

46. Weaver quoted in *From Populism to Progressivism: Representative Selections,* ed. Louis Filler (Huntington, N.Y.: Krieger, 1978), 25.

47. In Nebraska, the Hamilton County Independent Party, a direct antecedent of the Populists, allayed the fears of local merchants by stating, in 1891, "The Independence Party is formed for the purpose of making money plentiful and relieving the general public . . . among which are towns and its businessmen . . . from the grasp

of monopoly." Quoted in Parsons, *Populist Context,* 73. For a good discussion of the relation of antimonopoly to private property, see Norman Pollack, *The Just Polity,* 114–17.

48. While calling for a graduated income tax, the Omaha Platform added the proviso that "all State and national revenues shall be limited to the necessary expenses of the government, economically and honestly administered." Hofstadter and Hofstadter, *Great Issues,* vol. II, 143.

For a good discussion of Populist views on the state, see Norman Pollack, *The Humane Economy: Populism, Capitalism, and Democracy* (New Brunswick, N.J.: Rutgers University Press, 1990), 121–26.

49. See the discussion of national, regional, and state results in McMath, *American Populism,* 170–99.

50. Goodwyn, *Democratic Promise,* 310. On the failure of the Chicago People's Party, see Destler, *American Radicalism,* 162–211.

51. Roosevelt quoted in C. Vann Woodward, *Tom Watson: Agrarian Rebel* (New York: Oxford University Press, 1938), 305–6; Goodwyn, *Democratic Promise,* 528–29; Stanley L. Jones, *The Presidential Election of 1896* (Madison: University of Wisconsin Press, 1964), 291–93. Other McKinley supporters adopted the more genial tactic of describing their opponents as deluded by crackpot monetary theories and frustrated by economic failure. See William Allen White's much reprinted editorial, "What's the Matter with Kansas?" Hofstadter and Hofstadter, eds., *Great Issues,* vol. III, 165–69.

52. James E. Wright, *The Politics of Populism: Dissent in Colorado* (New Haven: Yale University Press, 1974), 238. After tremendous debate and division, the Populists ran a joint ticket with the Democrats in twenty-eight states. Robert Durden, *The Climax of Populism: The Election of 1896* (Lexington: University of Kentucky Press, 1965), 125.

53. Roger A. Fischer, *Tippecanoe and Trinkets Too: The Material Culture of American Presidential Campaigns, 1828–1984* (Urbana: University of Illinois Press, 1988), 157. Other Democratic campaign items betrayed the party's defensiveness on the matter of patriotism. For example, under a drawing of the Stars and Stripes, a ribbon included the words, "Mark Hanna, what we say: The Flag of our Country waves for ALL our people." Ibid., 156.

For a creative discussion of the literary meanings of the monetary issue, see Walter Benn Michaels, *The Gold Standard and the Logic of Naturalism: American Literature at the Turn of the Century* (Berkeley: University of California Press, 1987), 137–80.

54. Quoted in Martin Ridge, *Ignatius Donnelly* (Chicago: University of Chicago Press, 1962), 357.

55. Jones, *Election of 1896,* 229.

56. Bryan quoted in Hofstadter and Hofstadter, *Great Issues,* vol. III, 158–65. For the most influential scholarly dismissal of Bryan and the fusion campaign as having any similarities with the authentic Populist movement, see Goodwyn, *Democratic Promise,* 426–514.

57. The best example is Goodwyn, *Democratic Promise,* 515–64. Bryan himself did not agree. His book about the 1896 campaign was entitled *The First Battle.*

58. Vachel Lindsay, "Bryan, Bryan, Bryan, Bryan," *Collected Poems,* (New York: Macmillan, 1919), 103–4. On the close links between Lindsay's politics and

poetics, see Ann Massa, *Vachel Lindsay: Fieldworker for the American Dream* (Bloomington: Indiana University Press, 1970).

CHAPTER 3. WORKERS AS CITIZENS: LABOR AND THE LEFT IN THE GOMPERS ERA

1. Frederick C. Howe, *The Confessions of a Reformer* (New York: Scribner's, 1925), 173.
2. Tom Johnson, *My Story* (1911; reprint, Seattle: University of Washington Press, 1970), 33.
3. A good brief survey is Arthur S. Link and Richard L. McCormick, *Progressivism* (Arlington Heights, Ill.: Harlan Davidson, 1983). Also see Daniel T. Rodgers, "In Search of Progressivism," *Reviews in American History* 10 (December 1982): 113–32. On the antitrust tradition and its decline, see Alan Brinkley, "The Anti-monopoly Ideal and the Liberal State: The Case of Thurman Arnold," *Journal of American History* 80 (September 1993): 557–79.
4. Stephen Hess and Milton Kaplan, *The Ungentlemanly Art: A History of American Political Cartoons,* rev. ed. (New York: Macmillan, 1975), 127. Vachel Lindsay reflexively called up the image in his 1919 lament over "Boy Bryan's defeat."
5. Munsey quoted in Christopher P. Wilson, "The Rhetoric of Consumption: Mass-Market Magazines and the Demise of the Gentle Reader, 1880–1920," in *The Culture of Consumption*, ed. Richard W. Fox and T. J. Jackson Lears (New York: Pantheon, 1983), 49. The figure of five million is cited in Samuel Huntington, *American Politics: The Promise of Disharmony* (Cambridge: Harvard University Press, 1981), 101.
6. Farmers' organizations did not abandon populist rhetoric, of course. For example, an organ of the Texas Farmers' Union opined in 1908, "It must be the destiny, the proud privilege of the South and West to give our nation industrial and financial freedom, for the Republic of the Fathers must not perish from the faith of the earth." Quoted in Theodore Saloutos and John D. Hicks, *Agricultural Discontent in the Middle West* (Madison: University of Wisconsin Press, 1951), 222.
7. Johnson, *My Story,* ix.
8. On John Public and his ancestors, see Hess and Kaplan, *Ungentlemanly Art,* 38–39; Charles Press, *The Political Cartoon* (Rutherford, N.J.: Fairleigh Dickinson Press, 1981), 208–31; Richard Samuel West, *Satire on Stone: The Political Cartoons of Joseph Keppler* (Urbana: University of Illinois Press, 1988), Figure P, 316–18; Albert Bigelow Paine, *Thomas Nast: His Period and His Pictures* (New York: Macmillan, 1904), 295.
9. See Dorothy Sue Cobble and Alice Kessler-Harris, "The New Labor History in American History Textbooks," *Journal of American History* 79 (March 1993).
10. For the best history of this conflict, see David Montgomery, *The Fall of the House of Labor: The Workplace, the State, and American Labor Activism, 1865–1925* (New York: Cambridge University Press, 1987). Also see my case study, *Barons of Labor: The San Francisco Building Trades and Union Power in the Progressive Era* (Urbana: University of Illinois Press, 1987).
11. Quotes from *American Federationist* (hereafter, *AF*) (April 1917): 277; Philip S.

Foner, *History of the Labor Movement in the United States*. Volume 6. *On the Eve of America's Entrance into World War I, 1915–1916* (New York: International Publishers, 1982), 78–79.

12. For a limited period (1912–16), the AFL did sponsor a campaign, known as Labor Forward, that couched unionism in spiritual terms. "Employers who exploited innocent women and children or who refused to pay a fair wage for a fair day's work were breaking their sacred trust with God, who commanded that all righteous people share in society's wealth," write the campaign's historians. But, aside from this limited effort, the national federation rarely tried to invest unionism with a divine rationale. Elizabeth Fones-Wolf and Kenneth Fones-Wolf, "Trade-Union Evangelism: Religion and the AFL in the Labor Forward Movement, 1912–16," in *Working-Class America,* ed. Michael Frisch and Daniel Walkowitz (Urbana: University of Illinois Press, 1983), 165. Also see the more extensive study of workers and religion, Ken Fones-Wolf, *Trade Union Gospel: Christianity and Labor in Industrial Philadelphia, 1865–1915* (Philadelphia: Temple University Press, 1989).

13. Quotes from Bruce Laurie, *Artisans into Workers: Labor in Nineteenth-Century America* (New York: Noonday Press, 1989), 177; editorial in the *Union Advocate, The Samuel Gompers Papers,* vol. 2, ed. Stuart B. Kaufman (Urbana, Ill.: University of Illinois Press, 1987), 58; and Stuart B. Kaufman, *Samuel Gompers and the Origins of the American Federation of Labor, 1848–1896* (Westport, Conn.: Greenwood Press, 1973), 168. Such opinions were not meant only for working-class audiences. In 1883, Gompers testified before the United States Senate Committee on the Relations Between Labor and Capital in much the same way: "There are two classes in society, one incessantly striving to obtain the labor of the other class for as little as possible . . . and the members of the other class being, as individuals, utterly helpless in a contest with their employers . . . " (pp. 114–15). The most incisive biographical treatment of the man is Nick Salvatore's introduction to the abridged version of Gompers, *Seventy Years of Life and Labor: An Autobiography* (Ithaca, N.Y.: ILR Press, 1984), xi–xli.

14. Gompers also opposed an official endorsement of the People's Party even though several AFL unions sent delegates to the 1892 Industrial Conference in St. Louis. The AFL president did leave a door partly open for future political cooperation between workers and farmers. He praised the new party for representing "a healthier public opinion, a sturdier manhood and independence, and a promise to maintain the liberties that the people now enjoy" and announced that he was casting his own ballot for James Weaver. He also voted for Bryan in 1896. Gompers, "Organized Labor in the Campaign," *North American Review* (July 1892): 91–96.

15. Quotes from Gompers's address to 1903 AFL convention, Gompers, *Labor and the Common Welfare,* ed. Hayes Robbins (1919; reprint, Freeport, N.Y.: Books for Libraries, 1969), 179; *AF* (August 1906): 531; report to the 1909 AFL convention, cited in Christopher Tomlins, *The State and the Unions: Labor Relations, Law, and the Organized Labor Movement in America, 1880–1960* (New York: Cambridge University Press, 1985), 59.

    In 1914, the socialist Morris Hillquit remarked that Gompers was "the most class conscious man I [ever] met." Quoted (anonymously) in Salvatore, *Seventy Years,* xvii. And Gompers once commented that, were he a citizen of Germany, he would have been a member of that nation's huge Social-Democratic Party.

16. My comments on Gompers's style are based on a reading of many of his speeches

and on hearing what may be the only extant recording of his voice—a speech at a War Bonds rally in 1918. Recording at the George Meany Memorial Archives, played for me by Professor Stuart Kaufman. On the new spellbinding style, see Kenneth Cmiel, *Democratic Eloquence: The Fight over Popular Speech in Nineteenth-Century America* (New York: Morrow, 1990), 248–50. On Gompers's reluctance to give up his "stilted manner," see "The Reminiscences of Eva McDonald Valesh," Columbia University Oral History Research Office, 1952, microfiche ed., 87.

17. Over the next decade, however, AFL membership stayed relatively constant in the face of resistance from organized employers and the courts. It rose dramatically again during World War I. See figures in Leo Wolman, *The Growth of American Trade Unions, 1880–1923* (New York: National Bureau of Economic Research, 1924).
18. John Mitchell, *Organized Labor* (Philadelphia: American Book and Bible House, 1903), ix. Interpretations of AFL ideology have undergone a major revision in recent years. For the classic version that praises its job- as opposed to class-consciousness, see Selig Perlman, *A Theory of the Labor Movement* (New York: Macmillan, 1928) and *A History of Trade Unionism in the United States* (New York: Macmillan, 1929). For a sophisticated rethinking from which I have learned much, see Leon Fink, "Labor, Liberty, and the Law: Trade Unionism and the Problem of the American Constitutional Order," *Journal of American History* 74 (December 1987), 904–25. Also see William E. Forbath, *Law and the Shaping of the American Labor Movement* (Cambridge: Harvard University Press, 1991), and Julia Maria Greene, "The Strike at the Ballot Box: Politics and Partisanship in the American Federation of Labor, 1881–1916," Ph.D. diss., Yale University, 1990. On the federation's political heterogeneity, see Montgomery, *Fall of the House of Labor,* 1–8, 257–329.
19. On the tradition from which the AFL sprang and continued to draw, see Laurie, *Artisans into Workers.*
20. Quote from Gompers 1914 debate with the socialist Maurice Hillquit before the United States Commission on Industrial Relations, *Gompers: Great Lives Observed,* ed. Gerald E. Stearn (Englewood Cliffs, N.J.: Prentice-Hall, 1971), 53. As late as 1898, Gompers "referred to himself as a Socialist" in conversation with Milwaukee socialist leader Victor Berger. Nick Salvatore, *Eugene V. Debs* (Urbana, Ill.: University of Illinois Press, 1982), 173. And, as long as Gompers was its president, the preamble to the AFL constitution began with a ringing reference to "the struggle . . . between the oppressors and the oppressed of all countries, a struggle between the capitalist and the laborer which grows in intensity from year to year." Quoted in Kazin, *Barons,* 287.
21. "The Average Man," *AF* (August 1910): 667. A few years earlier, the Boston editor and labor official Frank Foster had written a didactic, autobiographical novel that also sought to ennoble the typical union member. His hero, the scion of "an average middle-class American family," is briefly attracted to the Socialist Labor Party but in the end resolves simply to combine trade union activities with personal altruism: "If I make myself a good citizen, help my neighbor and cultivate my own faculties, such as they are, I rather fancy it is a fair amount of business for one man to attend to." Frank K. Foster, *The Evolution of a Trade Unionist* (Boston: Allied Printing Trades Council, 1901), 173.
22. *AF* (November 1916): 1067.

23. David Montgomery, *Workers' Control in America* (New York: Cambridge University Press, 1979), 13; Salvatore, *Debs,* 63–64. For excellent discussions of two groups of women workers, see Dorothy Sue Cobble, *Dishing It Out: Waitresses and Their Unions in the Twentieth Century* (Urbana: University of Illinois Press, 1991), and Susan Porter Benson, *Counter Cultures: Saleswomen, Managers, and Customers in American Department Stores, 1890–1940* (Urbana: University of Illinois Press, 1986).
24. Quotes from Stephen H. Norwood, *Labor's Flaming Youth: Telephone Operators and Labor Militancy, 1878–1923* (Urbana: University of Illinois Press, 1990), 80; a 1916 issue of the *Cigar Makers' Official Journal,* quoted in Ann Schofield, "Rebel Girls and Union Maids: The Woman Question in the Journals of the AFL and IWW," *Feminist Studies* 9 (Summer 1983): 347. In the early 1920s, union telephone operators did construct an image of the purposeful and courageous "trade union woman." Norwood, ibid., pp. 254–94.

    In Europe at this time, female images put out by labor and the Left were only slightly more active and proletarian in dress and manner. See Eric Hobsbawm, "Man and Woman: Images on the Left," *Workers: Worlds of Labor* (New York: Pantheon, 1984), 83–102.
25. Quoted by David Brody in his survey article, "Labor," in *Harvard Encyclopedia of American Ethnic Groups,* ed. Stephan Thernstrom (Cambridge: Harvard University Press, 1980), 613.
26. See Alexander Saxton, *The Indispensable Enemy: Labor and the Anti-Chinese Movement in California* (Berkeley: University of California Press, 1971); Catherine Collomp, "Unions, Civics, and National Identity: Organized Labor's Reaction to Immigration, 1881–1897," *Labor History* 29 (Fall 1988): 450–74; Gwendolyn Mink, *Old Labor and New Immigrants in American Political Development: Union, Party, and State, 1875–1920* (Ithaca, N.Y.: Cornell University Press, 1986).
27. Quotes from A. T. Lane, *Solidarity or Survival? American Labor and European Immigrants, 1830–1924* (Westport, Conn.: Greenwood Press, 1987), 88, 148; Edward F. McSweeney (the assistant United States commissioner for the Port of New York), *AF* (January 1902): 1.

    Mexican-American workers were usually subjected to the same standard. Many Anglo unionists regarded them as "peons" accustomed to a bestial standard of living but did try to organize them. In 1903, Gompers told Mexican farm laborers working near Los Angeles that he would grant them a union charter, but only if they broke an alliance with fellow workers who were Japanese. The Mexicans refused. Tomas Almaguer, "Racial Domination and Class Conflict in Capitalist Agriculture: The Oxnard Sugar Beet Workers' Strike of 1903," *Labor History* 25 (1984): 325–50.
28. Gompers, *Seventy Years,* vol. 2, 153. The custom of referring to different nationalities as "races" encouraged the drawing of invidious distinctions between groups we now consider part of the same broad categories. For an insightful survey of labor's ideology and behavior toward "new" immigrants, see James R. Barrett, "Americanization from the Bottom Up: Immigration and the Remaking of the Working Class in the United States, 1880–1930," *Journal of American History* 79 (December 1992): 996–1020.
29. *AF* (April 1901): 118; for the grudging concurrence of one Southern state federation, see Philip S. Foner, "An Additional Short Note on the Alabama State Federation of Labor," *Labor History* 18 (Winter 1977): 120–21.

30. At times, even IWW spokespeople expressed the belief, common among disgruntled white workers, that a life of wage labor was more onerous than the conditions blacks had endured in the Old South. In 1905, "Big Bill" Haywood told the founding meeting of his organization, held in Chicago: "Why, folks, rather than be one of the [immigrant] residents of the ghetto down here, a place that I was through last night, I would rather be a big buck nigger on a plantation in the South before the days when chattel slavery was wiped out." *The Founding Convention of the IWW: Proceedings* (1905; reprint, New York: Merit, 1969), 579.
31. For details see Michael Kazin and Steven J. Ross, "America's Labor Day: The Dilemma of a Workers' Celebration," *Journal of American History* 78 (March 1992): 1294–1323.
32. *From Dusk to Dawn* had a cast of over 10,000 and was quite popular, at least in New York City. Steven J. Ross, "Struggles for the Screen: Workers, Radicals, and the Political Uses of Silent Film," *American Historical Review* 96 (April 1991): 342–44.
33. AFL officials wanted such figures to embrace labor's strategy. Wrote Gompers in 1915: "If all the welfare workers, the social uplifters, the social legislative enthusiasts would apply the efforts and money they are now diverting to other causes to the work of promoting organization, they would greatly shorten the time necessary to put all workers in a position where they could solve their own problems, fight their own battles, and promote their own welfare as free, equal men and women." Reprinted in Gompers, *Labor and the Common Welfare,* 33.
34. *Chicago Union Labor Advocate,* January and February 1909; Kazin, *Barons of Labor,* 101 and passim.
35. Quoted in Laurie, *Artisans into Workers,* 210.
36. *AF* (March 1902): 119; (July 1904): 583; Kazin, *Barons of Labor,* 118.
37. The AFL did favor wage and hours laws for women and federal workers who were judged to be unable to help themselves. Gompers quote from Theda Skocpol, *Protecting Soldiers and Mothers: The Political Origins of Social Policy in the United States* (Cambridge: Harvard University Press, 1992), 207. See pp. 205–47 for an insightful discussion of the AFL's attitude toward a more interventionist state.
38. Quote from Greene, "Strike at the Ballot Box," 600; for a good summary of the AFL's political position, see chapter one.
39. Ann Shola Orloff, "The Political Origins of America's Belated Welfare State," in *The Politics of Social Policy in the United States,* ed. Margaret Weir, Ann Shola Orloff, and Theda Skocpol (Princeton, N.J.: Princeton University Press, 1988), 57; Skocpol, *Protecting Soldiers and Mothers*, 215–16.
40. William E. Forbath, *Law and the Shaping of the American Labor Movement* (Cambridge: Harvard University Press, 1991). For the quantitative estimate of injunctions, see pp. 61, 193–98. Also see the discussions of judicial power in Fink, "Trade Unionism and the Constitutional Order," and Victoria C. Hattam, *Labor Visions and State Power: The Origins of Business Unionism in the United States* (Princeton, N.J.: Princeton University Press, 1993).
41. Gompers quote from Tomlins, *State and the Unions,* 64–65.
42. Quotes from Tomlins, *State and Unions,* 67.
43. Quotes from Forbath, *Law and the Shaping,* 125; "The Sentence of Gompers," *Union Labor Advocate* (January 1909): 38. For a good summary of the case, see Barry F. Helfand, "Labor and the Courts: The Common-Law Doctrine of Criminal

Conspiracy and Its Application in the Buck's Stove and Range Case," *Labor History* 18 (Winter 1977): 91–114.

44. Gompers in the New York *Leader* (July 1887), from *Samuel Gompers Papers,* vol. 2, 48; Foster, "Has the Non-Unionist a Right to Work How, When, and Where He Pleases?" pamphlet issued by the AFL, 1904, p. 7. In AFL and CIO Pamphlets Collection, George Meany Memorial Archives. Also see Skocpol, *Protecting Soldiers and Mothers,* 209–10.
45. On this neglected subject, see George Cotkin, "The Spencerian and Comtian Nexus in Gompers' Labor Philosophy: The Impact of Non-Marxian Evolutionary Thought," *Labor History* 20 (Fall 1979): 510–23.
46. William Z. Foster, then a leading radical unionist and later a Communist, advocated "boring" inside the AFL because it expressed "the same language of the broad masses of workers." Quoted in Edward P. Johanningsmeier, *Forging American Communism: The Life of William Z. Foster* (Princeton, N.J.: Princeton University Press, 1994), 109.
47. Reprinted from *Appeal to Reason,* 27 June 1903, in *"Yours for the Revolution": The Appeal to Reason, 1895–1922,* ed. John Graham (Lincoln: University of Nebraska Press, 1990), 78. The best one-volume work on the SP is James Weinstein, *The Decline of Socialism in America, 1912–1925* (New York: Knopf, 1967). But also see Nick Salvatore, *Eugene V. Debs: Citizen and Socialist* (Urbana: University of Illinois Press, 1982).
48. For numerous examples see Salvatore, *Debs.*
49. Sally Miller, *Victor Berger and the Promise of Constructive Socialism* (Westport, Conn.: Greenwood Press, 1973), 76, 72. Also see Daniel Bell, *Marxian Socialism in the United States* (Princeton, N.J.: Princeton University Press, 1967), 84–85.
50. Douglas Firth Anderson, "The Reverend J. Stitt Wilson and Christian Socialism in California," in *Religion and Society in the American West: Historical Essays,* ed. Carl Guarneri and David Alvarez (Lanham, Md.: University Press of America, 1987), 375–400.
51. Quotes from Paul J. Dovre, "A Study of Nonpartisan League Persuasion, 1915–1920," Ph.D. diss., Northwestern University, 1963, 583, 73. On the Nonpartisan League generally, see Robert L. Morlan, *Political Prairie Fire: The Nonpartisan League, 1915–1922* (Minneapolis: University of Minnesota Press, 1955), and Scott Allen Ellsworth, "Origins of the Nonpartisan League," Ph.D. diss., Duke University, 1982. The Minnesota Farmer-Labor Party, which was a power in the state during the 1920s and 1930s, was directly descended from the Minnesota Nonpartisan League.
52. Quotes from *The Speeches and Writings of Mother Jones,* ed. Edward M. Steel (Pittsburgh: University of Pittsburgh Press, 1988), 59, 30, 43, 197–98.
53. Steel, ed., *Mother Jones,* xv, 21, 187. Ironically, most of those who broke with the SP to support the war were middle-class and upper-class intellectuals like William English Walling and Algie Simons, and Christian Socialists like George Herron and J. Stitt Wilson.
54. Mother Jones was no feminist. She dismissed woman suffrage as a cause limited to "parlor parasites" (even though most female unionists of the time supported it). And her very identity as a brazen old lady bucking up the mettle of male miners—whom she addressed as "we fellows"—emphasized the strongly masculine face of the labor movement.

55. For examples, see *AF* (December 1898): 203–4; Montgomery, *Fall of House of Labor,* 363; David Montgomery, *Citizen Worker: The Experience of Workers in the United States with Democracy and the Free Market During the Nineteenth Century* (New York: Cambridge University Press, 1993), 103. Gompers himself had been a vocal foe of American imperialism at the turn of the century.
56. Edward L. Bernays, *Propaganda* (New York: Horace Liveright, 1928), 9. On the CPI, see Stephen Vaughan, *Holding Fast the Inner Lines* (Chapel Hill, N.C.: University of North Carolina Press, 1980); George Creel, *How We Advertised America* (1920; reprint, New York: Arno, 1972).
57. Reprinted in Vaughan, *Holding Fast,* 63.
58. Gompers, 1918 speech for War Bonds; Stephen J. Ross, *Workers on the Edge: Work, Leisure, and Politics in Industrializing Cincinnati, 1788–1890* (New York: Columbia University Press, 1985), 386.
59. Map reprinted in David Corbin, *Life, Work, and Rebellion in the Coal Fields: The Southern West Virginia Miners, 1880–1922* (Urbana: University of Illinois Press, 1981), after page 154.
60. Gompers, "Labor's Attitude," a speech published by the CPI, contained in AFL Pamphlets, Meany Memorial Archives, 4, 5.
61. *New Republic,* March 3, 1917, 145. On Bourne's antiwar position, see Bruce Clayton, *Forgotten Prophet: The Life of Randolph Bourne* (Baton Rouge: Louisiana State University Press, 1984), 203–30.
62. Townley quoted in Morlan, *Political Prairie Fire,* 257. Townley and other orators who supported the war but opposed "profiteering" and restrictions on free speech often identified their domestic enemies with the nation's external foes. Condemning men who made "billions of dollars of war profits" while average Americans scraped to make a living, Arthur Townley told an audience in St. Paul: "Get a German helmet, place it upon THEIR head, and YOU SEE THE KAISER himself." "Address of A.C. Townley of the Farmers and Workers Conference," 18 September 1917, Papers of the National Nonpartisan League, Microfilm Edition, Manuscript Division, Library of Congress.
63. Frank L. Grubbs, Jr., *The Struggle for Labor Loyalty: Gompers, the A.F. of L., and the Pacifists* (Durham, N.C.: Duke University Press, 1968), 90–91, 113–14.
64. On the national and international context, see the essays in James Cronin and Carmen Sirianni, ed., *Work, Community, and Power: The Emergence of Labor in Europe and America, 1900–1925* (Philadelphia: Temple University Press, 1983).
65. See Joseph A. McCartin, "'An American Feeling': Workers, Managers, and the Struggle over Industrial Democracy in the World War I Era," in *Industrial Democracy in America: The Ambiguous Promise,* ed. Nelson Lichtenstein and Howell John Harris (New York: Cambridge University Press, 1993), 67–86.
66. Quotes from *New Majority,* 4 January 1919, 1, 15; 29 March, 1919, 4. Many of the cartoons were by such former artists for *The Masses* as Art Young, Fred Ellis, and Boardman Robinson. On the failure of the LP, see Lizabeth Cohen, *Making a New Deal: Industrial Workers in Chicago, 1919–1939* (New York: Cambridge University Press, 1990), 49–51; Weinstein, *Decline of Socialism,* 222–29.
67. Letter from Gompers to James Duncan, 4 May 1920, quoted in Montgomery, *Fall of House of Labor,* 332; letter to Debs, 30 April 1921, in *Letters of Eugene V. Debs,* vol. 3, 1919–1926, ed. J. Robert Considine (Urbana: University of Illinois Press, 1990), 216. Thanks to Maurice Isserman for sending me this document.

68. *AF* (August 1920): 745. Baer continued to draw cartoons for labor and liberal publications until his death in 1970. See Bill G. Reid, "John Miller Baer: Nonpartisan League Cartoonist and Congressman," *North Dakota History* 44 (Winter 1977): 4–13; *Biographical Directory of the American Congress, 1774-1971* (Washington, D.C.: Government Printing Office, 1971), 538.
69. Among the famous names were Frederick Howe, Amos Pinchot, Charlotte Perkins Gilman, Florence Kelley, Upton Sinclair, H. L. Mencken, and Sinclair Lewis. For a recent account of the 1924 campaign, see Stanley Coben, *Rebellion Against Victorianism: The Impetus for Cultural Change in 1920s America* (New York: Oxford University Press, 1991), 112–35.
70. Quotes from Weinstein, *Decline of Socialism,* 293; *The Facts: La Follette-Wheeler Campaign Text-Book* (Chicago: La Follette-Wheeler Campaign Headquarters, 1924); *AF* (July 1924): 539. Despite its official support, the AFL gave La Follette only $25,000 for his campaign.
71. On labor's political gains in 1922 and 1924, see Montgomery, *Fall of the House of Labor,* 434–37; on business image making, David Brody, "The Rise and Decline of Welfare Capitalism," in Brody, *Workers in Industrial America* (New York: Oxford University Press, 1980), 48–81. On advertising, see Roland Marchand, *Advertising the American Dream: Making Way for Modernity, 1920–1940* (Berkeley: University of California Press, 1985).
72. *AF* (May 1920): 416–17. For a similar juxtaposition of angry rhetoric and pleasant commercial copy (for soap), see ibid., November 1922, p. 808.
73. Kazin and Ross, "America's Labor Day," 1311. On Green's ideology in the 1920s, see Craig Phelan, *William Green: Biography of a Labor Leader* (Albany: State University of New York Press, 1989), 29–47.
74. "Are You a Good Business Man?" AFL Pamphlets, no date but clearly between 1924 and 1930. The cover of this pamphlet depicts two men in business suits seated at a desk with, below, inexplicably, black field hands picking cotton. For a blunt comparison of unionists to salesmen, see *AF* (December 1928): 1482.

CHAPTER 4. ONWARD, CHRISTIAN MOTHERS AND SOLDIERS: THE PROHIBITIONIST CRUSADE

1. Edgar Kemler, *The Deflation of American Ideals* (1941), quoted in Norman H. Clark, *Deliver Us from Evil: An Interpretation of American Prohibition* (New York: Norton, 1976), 211.
2. For a large sample of (mostly male) leaders of the Prohibition Party and Anti-Saloon League from 1890 to 1913, see Jack S. Blocker, Jr., *Retreat from Reform: The Prohibition Movement in the United States, 1890–1913* (Westport, Conn.: Greenwood Press, 1976), 8–38.
3. Clark, *Deliver Us from Evil,* 67. In 1892, the Prohibition Party of Tennessee confidently declared, "economic law requires each citizen to be a producer, to receive as such his equitable share of the profits of his production and to bear his proportionate share of the burden of the state." Quoted in Paul E. Isaac, *Prohibition and Politics: Turbulent Decades in Tennessee, 1885–1920* (Knoxville: University of Tennessee Press, 1965), 68.

4. Quoted in Ronald M. Benson, "American Workers and Temperance Reform, 1866–1933," Ph.D. diss., University of Notre Dame, 1975; 44, 163–64. Also see David Brundage, "The Producing Classes and the Saloon: Denver in the 1880s," *Labor History* 26 (Winter 1985): 29–52.
5. Willard quoted in Benson, "American Workers," 189–90.
6. The preeminent historian of the Gilded Age prohibition movement is Jack S. Blocker, Jr. See his *"Give to the Winds Thy Fears": The Women's Temperance Crusade, 1873–1874* (Westport, Conn.: Greenwood Press, 1985) and *Retreat from Reform.*
7. Besides Blocker's books, valuable sources on the WCTU and the female milieu of evangelical activism include Mother (Eliza Daniel) Stewart, *Memoir of the Crusade* (Columbus, Ohio: William G. Hubbard, 1889); Ruth Bordin, *Women and Temperance: The Quest for Power and Liberty, 1873–1900* (Philadelphia: Temple University Press, 1981); Barbara Epstein, *Politics of Domesticity: Women, Evangelism, and Temperance in Nineteenth-Century America* (Middletown, Conn.: Wesleyan University Press); Lori D. Ginzberg, *Women and the Work of Benevolence: Morality, Politics, and Class in the Nineteenth-Century United States* (New Haven: Yale University Press, 1991).
8. On the differences between the early WCTU and the suffrage movement, see Jack S. Blocker, Jr., "Separate Paths: Suffragists and the Women's Temperance Crusade," *Signs* 10 (Spring 1985): 460–76. Men could join the WCTU on an ex officio basis, but they had to pay annual dues higher than the 50 cents required of women. Kerr, *Organized for Prohibition,* 45.
9. Mrs. Susanna M. D. Fry, "The Flower of Temperance Chivalry—Frances E. Willard," WCTU pamphlet, c. 1900, in Collection of Political History Division, National Museum of American History, p. 7.
10. Willard quoted in Louise Newman, "Laying Claim to Difference: Ideologies of Race and Gender in the U.S. Woman's Movement, 1870–1920," Ph.D. diss., Brown University, 1992, 238; *Union Signal,* 3 December 1896. On the WCTU's appeal to Populist and Christian socialist women, see Mari Jo Buhle, *Women and American Society 1870–1920* (Urbana: University of Illinois Press, 1981), esp. 60–69. The Prohibition Party supported many of the same aims, but its organizers spent most of their time vainly attempting to lure temperance supporters away from their more traditional electoral loyalties.
11. *Union Signal,* 3 December 1896. For a good sample of Willard's prose, see her autobiography, *Glimpses of Fifty Years: The Autobiography of an American Woman* (Chicago: H. J. Smith, 1889). The author's selfless image is immediately presented on the title page, which states that the book was "written by order of the National Woman's Christian Temperance Union," and in the "Dedicatory" note: "To Mother as a Birthday Gift on January 3, 1889, the eighty-fifth anniversary of her undaunted life, I dedicate her eldest daughter's self-told story."
12. Worth Robert Miller, *Oklahoma Populism: A History of Populism in the Oklahoma Territory* (Norman: University of Oklahoma Press, 1987), 123; Barton C. Shaw, *The Wool-Hat Boys: Georgia's Populist Party* (Baton Rouge: Louisiana State University Press, 1984), 150–52.
13. The Omaha Platform stated equivocally: "While our sympathies as a party of reform are naturally on the side of every proposition which will tend to make men intelligent, virtuous, and temperate, we nevertheless regard these questions, impor-

tant as they are, as secondary to the great issues now pressing for solution, and upon which not only our individual prosperity but the very existence of free institutions depend." Quoted in Richard Hofstadter and Beatrice K. Hofstadter, *Great Issues in American History,* vol. III, *From Reconstruction to the Present Day, 1865–1981* (New York: Vintage, 1982), 142.

14. On this dispute, see Blocker, *Retreat from Reform,* 39–67; Ruth Bordin, *Frances Willard: A Biography* (Chapel Hill: University of North Carolina Press, 1986), 175–85. When asked about the People's Party in 1896, Willard insisted she was still "with it heart and soul." Quoted in Kerr, *Organized for Prohibition,* 65. A year before, Donnelly, still hopeful about forging a grand alliance of reformers, declared, "I am sure ninety-nine out of a hundred Populists are Temperance men." Quoted in Paul Kleppner, *The Cross of Culture: A Social Analysis of Midwestern Politics, 1850–1900* (New York: Free Press, 1970), 354.
15. For example, see *Union Signal,* 24 November 1904. The organization also supported a Georgia state law that required blacking out any liquor advertisements that appeared in periodicals sold in the state. Ibid., 13 January 1916, 15.
16. *Union Signal,* 18 February 1904, 1. Anna A. Gordon, *What Lillian M. N. Stevens Said* (Evanston: National Woman's Christian Temperance Union, 1914), 2–3.
17. On one aspect of this change, see Margaret Lamberts Bendroth, *Fundamentalism and Gender: 1875 to the Present* (New Haven: Yale University Press, 1993), 13–30.
18. For example, see Carrington A. Phelps, "Liquor's Fight Against Prohibition," in D. D. Hammell, ed., *Passing of the Saloon* (Cincinnati: Tower Press, 1908), 224–34. For an earlier interpretation of this aspect, see Richard Hofstadter, *Anti-Intellectualism in American Life* (New York: Knopf, 1963), 118–22.
19. On the traditional connection between citizenship, war, and masculinity, see Genevieve Lloyd, "Selfhood, War, and Masculinity," in *Feminist Challenges: Social and Political Theory,* ed. Carol Pateman and Elizabeth Gross (Boston: Northeastern University Press, 1986), 63–76.
20. The only book-length biography of Carry A. Nation is breezy and mocking: Robert Lewis Taylor, *Vessel of Wrath: The Life and Times of Carry Nation* (New York: New American Library, 1966). On the significance she placed in her full (married) name, see p. 62. The most recent survey of the prohibition movement, in Jack S. Blocker, Jr., *American Temperance Movements: Cycles of Reform* (Boston: Twayne, 1989), omits her entirely as does K. Austin Kerr, *Organized for Prohibition: A New History of the Anti-Saloon League* (New Haven: Yale University Press, 1985). For a short survey of her life, see Clark, *Deliver Us from Evil,* 81–84.
21. Will Carlton, "Carry A. Nation—Heroine of the Hatchet," in Hammell, *Passing of the Saloon,* 318–19; Robert Bader, *Prohibition in Kansas: A History* (Lawrence: University Press of Kansas), 140. On her ability as a writer and speaker, see Taylor, *Vessel of Wrath,* 21–23.
22. A supporter named Annie Diggs, the Kansas state librarian and a former Populist, said of Nation, "an old Hebraic personage has stepped into our lax and nerveless time." Quoted in Bader, *Prohibition in Kansas,* 155. Other quotes, pp. 147, 154; Carlton, "Carry A. Nation," in Hammell, *Passing of the Saloon,* 318.
23. Kerr, *Organized for Prohibition,* 78–79. Kerr's study is the best modern treatment of the ASL, though he does little with language per se. Also see the pioneering work, Peter H. Odegard, *Pressure Politics: The Story of the Anti-Saloon League* (New York: Columbia University Press, 1928).

24. The Catholic Archbishop John Ireland had been a founding member of the national ASL. But he was one of the few priests to support the league's work. On the rather ineffectual temperance work done by the Paulist fathers in the Progressive era, see Sister Joan Bland, *Hibernian Crusade: The Story of the Catholic Total Abstinence Union of America* (Washington, D.C.: The Catholic University of America Press, 1951).
25. On the ASL's organization, see the meticulous account in Kerr, *Organized for Prohibition,* 115–22 and passim.
26. Quoted in Odegard, *Pressure Politics,* 6.
27. On the near-universal support for the ASL and prohibition among Protestants, see George Marsden, *Fundamentalism and American Culture: The Shaping of Twentieth-Century Evangelism, 1870–1925* (New York: Oxford University Press, 1980), 88; Robert T. Handy, *A Christian America: Protestant Hopes and Historical Realities* (New York: Oxford University Press, 1971), 88–92, 149–50; Sydney E. Ahlstrom, *A Religious History of the American People* (New Haven: Yale University Press, 1972), 870–72. The only dissenters were the Episcopalians, who frowned on evangelicalism generally, and German Lutherans, who saw the crusade as an attack on their beer-loving ethnic group.
28. The ASL was quite self-conscious about its training methods. By the turn of the century, it was holding internal conferences at which instruction was given in such topics as "How to Elect a Friendly Legislature," "The Use of the Press, Secular and Religious," "The Use of the Stereopticon," and "How to Prepare for and Conduct Local Option Contests." *American Issue,* 21 October 1904, 6.
29. Kerr, *Organized for Prohibition,* 143.
30. Kerr, *Organized for Prohibition,* photo facing p. 114. For the figure of 20,000 speakers, see Clark, *Deliver Us,* 107.
31. Lincoln Steffens, *The Shame of the Cities* (New York: McClure Phillips and Co., 1904), 34.
32. Quoted in Clark, *Deliver Us from Evil,* 95.
33. Strong quoted in Paul Boyer, *Urban Masses and Moral Order* (Cambridge: Harvard University Press, 1978), 208–9; Lewis L. Gould, *Progressives and Prohibitionists: Texas Democrats in the Wilson Era* (Austin: University of Texas Press, 1973), 47.
34. L. A. Banks, "The Romance of the Anti-Saloon League Movement," in Banks, ed., *Ammunition for Final Drive on Booze: An Up-to-Date Arsenal for Prohibition Speakers* (New York: Funk and Wagnalls, 1917), 63–64. For an earlier example of the attack on the liquor industry, see Carrington A. Phelps, "Liquor's Fight Against Prohibition," in Hammell, ed., *The Passing of the Saloon,* 224–34. On the ASL's aid to the antiprostitution effort, see Boyer, *Urban Masses and Moral Order,* 205–17; Timothy J. Gilfoyle, *City of Eros: New York City, Prostitution, and the Commercialization of Sex, 1790–1920* (New York: Norton, 1992), 303–6.
35. Virginius Dabney, *Dry Messiah: The Life of Bishop Cannon* (New York: Knopf, 1949), 51.
36. For cartoon examples of the archetypal saloon keeper, see *American Issue* (Ohio edition), 20 January 1912, cover; Odegard, *Pressure Politics,* after 42.
37. Louis Banks, *The Lincoln Legion: The Story of Its Founder and Forerunners* (New York: The Mershon Co., 1903); Merrill D. Peterson, *Lincoln in American Memory* (New York: Oxford University Press, 1994), 247–51.

38. *American Issue* (Ohio edition), 6 January 1912.
39. Billy Sunday, "The Famous 'Booze' Sermon," in William T. Ellis, *"Billy" Sunday: The Man and His Message* (Philadelphia: John C. Winston, 1914), 112–13. For an ASL cartoon showing the corpse of a young girl stretched on a monument labeled "PROFIT," see Sean D. Cashman, *Prohibition: The Lie of the Land* (New York: Free Press, 1981).
40. For a book-length statement of the contrary position, see John J. Rumbarger, *Profits, Power, and Prohibition: Alcohol Reform and the Industrializing of America, 1800–1930* (Albany: State University of New York Press, 1989). On ASL funds, see Clark, *Deliver Us from Evil,* 113; Kerr, *Organized for Prohibition,* 149–50.
41. Quoted in Justin Steuart, *Wayne Wheeler: Dry Boss* (1928; reprint, Westport, Conn.: Greenwood Press, 1970), 46. On boycotts, see Boyer, *Urban Masses,* 215.
42. Hammell, ed., *Passing of the Saloon,* 43, xiv.
43. Blocker, *Retreat from Reform,* 16.
44. Boyer, *Urban Masses,* 213.
45. Despite such agrarian references and frequent praise for the virtues of rural life, most ASL activists lived in towns and cities. Their demonization of saloon keepers thus served more to mobilize prohibitionists against their local foes than to add fuel to a weakening conflict between country and metropolis. *The American Issue,* (Ohio edition), 25 December 1903, 2. For an antebellum example of such temperance rhetoric, see the speech by Lyman Beecher quoted in Clark, *Deliver Us,* 35.
46. *The Searchlight,* September 1915, 1.
47. The best study of Sunday remains the biography by William G. McLoughlin, Jr., *Billy Sunday Was His Real Name* (Chicago: University of Chicago Press, 1955). For insights on his language, also see William T. Ellis, *"Billy" Sunday: The Man and His Message* (Philadelphia: John C. Winston, 1914); Homer Rodeheaver (Sunday's song leader), *Twenty Years with Billy Sunday* (Nashville: Cokesbury Press, 1936); Marsden, *Fundamentalism and American Culture,* 130–35; Lyle W. Dorsett, *Billy Sunday and the Redemption of Urban America* (Grand Rapids: Eerdmans, 1991), passim; Kathleen M. Blee, *Women of the Klan: Racism and Gender in the 1920s* (Berkeley: University of California Press, 1991), 45. On his popularity among workers, see Fones-Wolf, *Trade Union Gospel,* 184–88, 191–92, and Clark, *Deliver Us from Evil,* 99–101.
48. McLoughlin, *Billy Sunday,* 233. Sunday never became part of the ASL's organization because he did not want to be bound by its electoral endorsements.
49. "The 'Famous Booze Sermon," in Ellis, *"Billy" Sunday,* 86–120; Timberlake, *Prohibition and the Progressive Movement,* 18.
50. See "Americanizing the Foreigner," *Union Signal,* 20 January 1916, 8.
51. In 1908, the ASL and AFL did cooperate in an unsuccessful attempt to defeat conservative Speaker of the House Joseph Cannon for re-election. Cannon opposed the agendas of both organizations and, under the rules of the House at the time, could prevent the bills each desired from ever coming up for a vote. Julia Greene, "The Strike at the Ballot Box," Ph.D. diss., Yale University, 1990, 456–58.
52. James R. Green, "The 'Salesman-Soldiers' of the '*Appeal* Army': A Profile of Rank-and-File Socialist Agitators," in Bruce Stave, ed., *Socialism and the Cities* (Port Washington, N.Y.: Kennikat Press, 1975), 29.
53. Norman H. Clark, *The Dry Years: Prohibition and Social Change in Washington*

(Seattle: University of Washington Press, 1965), 71–72; *American Issue,* 17 February 1912, 1; Jack London, *John Barleycorn* in *Novels and Social Writings* (New York: Library of America, 1982), 935–36; Carolyn Johnston, *Jack London—An American Radical?* (Westport, Conn.: Greenwood Press, 1984), 151–53.

Even those unionists who opposed prohibition still spoke of heavy drinkers as men incapable of helping themselves or the movement. "Lots of booze is full of 'kick,'" wrote a left-wing labor journalist in 1919, "but, after all, only the man not full of booze can make his kick count for something." *The New Majority* (Chicago), 5 April 1919, 5.

54. The scholarship on Stelzle is meager. But see George H. Nash III, "Charles Stelzle: Apostle to Labor," *Labor History* 11 (Spring 1970): 151–74; Fones-Wolf, *Trade Union Gospel,* passim; Susan Curtis, *A Consuming Faith: The Social Gospel and Modern American Culture* (Baltimore: Johns Hopkins University Press, 1991), 254–65, and Stelzle's own autobiography, *A Son of the Bowery: The Life Story of an East Side American* (1926; reprint, Freeport, N.Y.: Books for Libraries Press, 1971).

55. Reverend Charles Stelzle, "The Workingman and the Church: A Composite Letter," *The Outlook,* 27 July 1901, 719.

56. Stelzle, "If Christ Should Come Today," Chicago *Union Labor Advocate,* December 1908, 7. Stelzle avoided theological comments that would offend workers who were not evangelical Protestants, and his column appeared in a variety of union papers, several of which had a predominately Catholic audience.

57. Charles Stelzle, *Why Prohibition?* (New York: George H. Doran, 1918), 16, 57, 15. Gompers used the phrase a year earlier at a meeting of the Council of National Defense; see Bernard Mandel, *Samuel Gompers: A Biography* (Yellow Springs, Ohio: Antioch Press), 491.

58. Stelzle, *Why Prohibition?* 79–80, 76, 157, 156; Kerr, *Organized for Prohibition,* 153. The dry press also tried to satirize the cry of "personal liberty." See the editorial cartoon reprinted in James H. Timberlake, *Prohibition and the Progressive Movement* (Cambridge: Harvard University Press, 1963), 91.

59. Ferenc Szasz, *The Divided Mind of Protestant America, 1880–1930* (University: University of Alabama Press, 1982), 55.

60. Mother Jones, quoted in Edward Steel, ed., *Mother Jones: Speeches and Writings* (Pittsburgh: University of Pittsburgh Press, 1988), 29.

61. *American Issue* (Ohio edition), 28 March 1908.

62. Sunday quoted in *American Issue* (Ohio edition), 13 April 1912, 6. In 1922, Czechs in Chicago held a rally against the Volstead Act that featured "women costumed as Liberty serv[ing] refreshments . . . the Liberty Bell, the Spirit of 1776, and other such symbols of independence from tyrannical government." Lizabeth Cohen, *Making a New Deal: Industrial Workers in Chicago, 1919–1939* (New York: Cambridge University Press, 1990), 210–11.

63. In *The Birth of a Nation,* the director, D. W. Griffith, portrayed inebriated blacks abusing the virtuous white women of the South. Griffith, a prohibitionist, died from the complications of alcoholism.

64. *American Issue,* 6 June 1908; Hoke quoted in Hammell, *Passing of the Saloon,* 270; Dewey Grantham, *Southern Progressivism: The Reconciliation of Progress and Tradition* (Knoxville: University of Tennessee Press, 1983), 161. For the classic statement of Southern progressivism as "for whites only," see C. Vann Wood-

ward, *Origins of the New South, 1877–1913* (Baton Rouge: Louisiana State University Press, 1951).

65. Statement by the National Colored Labor Union, quoted in Benson, "American Workers," 54; Hanes Walton, Jr., and James E. Taylor, "Blacks and the Southern Prohibition Movement," *Phylon* 32 (Fall 1971): 247, 256; William S. McFeely,. *Frederick Douglass* (New York: Norton, 1991), 368–69. The anti-lynching campaigner Ida B. Wells also lambasted Willard for her statement. Bordin, *Frances Willard,* 216–17. On the racial attitudes of Willard and other women reformers of the era, see Newman, "Laying Claim to Difference."
66. Blocker, *Retreat from Reform,* 167; Anti-Saloon League of America, *Proceedings,* Nineteenth National Convention (Westerville, Ohio: American Issue Publishing Co., 1919), 118–19. Cray's speech does contain hints that he had more subversive intentions. Throughout the talk, he referred to his people as "Africans in America," a term identified with the fledgling Pan-Africanist movement. And immediately after making the statement about black troops, he added, "You know this country was infested with German spies. We can't trust a white face now." Ibid.
67. Quoted in Lawrence W. Levine, *Defender of the Faith, William Jennings Bryan: The Last Decade, 1915–1925* (New York: Oxford University Press, 1965), 128. The legislative history of the amendment is fairly complicated, involving many strategic gambits and compromises. Good summaries include Clark, *Deliver Us,* 118–39; Kerr, *Organized for Prohibition,* 185–210. The congressional vote on the amendment was 65 to 20 in the Senate and 282 to 128 in the House.
68. Wayne Wheeler, "America's Marvelous Escape from the Secret Domination of the Breweries," speech given 26 January 1919, quoted in *Briefs for Prohibition,* 167. On the brewers' unholy alliance, see Steuart, *Wayne Wheeler,* 123.
69. Banks, *Ammunition for Final Drive on Booze,* 42–43.
70. On Wheeler and the ASL in the '20s, see Steuart, *Wayne Wheeler,* 210–11 (quote); Kerr, *Organized for Prohibition,* 211–41; Clark, *Deliver Us,* 140–80; Blocker, *American Temperance Movements,* 119–25.
71. Bryan, "Prohibition," in Ray Ginger, ed., *William Jennings Bryan: Selections* (Indianapolis: Bobbs-Merrill, 1967), 214–15; Levine, *Defender of the Faith,* vii. Although he had always endorsed temperance, Bryan, a career politician, was a relative latecomer to the cause of total prohibition. See Paolo E. Coletta, *William Jennings Bryan,* vol. III, *Political Puritan* (Lincoln: University of Nebraska Press, 1969), 60–79.
72. Blocker, *American Temperance Movements,* 124.
73. No reliable membership statistics exist for the Klan in the 1920s. But for one sensible estimate, see David H. Bennett, *The Party of Fear: From Nativist Movements to the New Right in America History* (Chapel Hill: University of North Carolina Press, 1988), 222–23.
74. Evans quoted in Bennett, *Party of Fear,* 221; magazine quoted in Leonard J. Moore, *Citizen Klansmen: The Ku Klux Klan in Indiana, 1921–1928* (Chapel Hill: University of North Carolina Press, 1991), 35. For cogent summaries of recent scholarship on this Klan (discontinuous with the first organization of that name, which expired in the 1870s), see Leonard J. Moore, "Historical Interpretations of the 1920s Klan: The Traditional View and the Populist Revision," in *The Invisible Empire in the West: Toward a New Historical Appraisal of the Ku Klux Klan of the 1920s,* ed. Shawn Lay (Urbana: University of Illinois Press, 1991), 17–38; Stanley

Coben, *Rebellion Against Victorianism: The Impetus for Cultural Change in 1920s America* (New York: Oxford University Press, 1991), 136–56.

75. For a richly documented argument, see Blee, *Women of the Klan.*
76. Figure taken from Blee, *Women of the Klan,* 175. For a longer discussion of the rise and fall of the Klan, see my review-essay, "The Grass-Roots Right: New Histories of U.S. Conservatism in the Twentieth Century," *American Historical Review* 97 (February 1992), 140–45. For a convincing argument about the conservative nature of Klan populism in one of its strongholds, see Robert D. Johnston, "From Direct Democracy to the Ku Klux Klan: Lower Middle Class Populism in Portland, Oregon, 1900–1925," Paper given at the 1992 Convention of the Organization of American Historians.

    Tom Watson aided the Klan's rebirth—in his later persona as a religious and racial bigot employing a populist vocabulary. See Nancy McLean, "The Leo Frank Case Reconsidered: Gender and Sexual Politics in the Making of Reactionary Populism," *Journal of American History* 78 (December 1991), 917–48.
77. The Methodist Bishop James Cannon told a rally in Cambridge, Maryland, that "Governor Smith wants the Italians, the Sicilians, the Poles and the Russian Jews. That kind has given us a stomach ache. . . . He wants the kind of dirty people that you find today on the sidewalks of New York." Quoted in Dabney, *Dry Messiah,* 188.
78. See Kerr, *Organized for Prohibition,* 260–65.
79. The best study of the AAPA is David E. Kyvig, *Repealing National Prohibition* (Chicago: University of Chicago Press, 1979). The membership total appears on page 46. Also see the muckraking, anti-repeal interpretation by Fletcher Dobyns, *The Amazing Story of Repeal: An Exposé of the Power of Propaganda* (Chicago: Willett, Clark, 1940).
80. Quotes from Clark, *The Dry Years,* 222; Nixon Carver, "Lack of Perspective Common Trait of Leaders of Subversive Movements," *American Issue,* 12 March 1932, 5. Also see Clark, *Deliver Us,* 199.
81. Bryan quoted in Garry Wills, *Under God: Religion and American Politics* (New York: Simon and Schuster, 1990), 102.
82. Garry Wills notes that Scopes lost his challenge to the Tennessee law and that, under pressure from state legislatures, most textbooks failed to treat evolution as more than a debatable theory until the 1960s. *Under God,* 113. Also see Marsden, *Fundamentalism,* 184–95.
83. Here I follow the insights of Garry Wills in *Under God,* 97–114. Mencken quoted in Marsden, *Fundamentalism,* 187.

CHAPTER 5. SOCIAL JUSTICE AND SOCIAL PARANOIA: THE CATHOLIC POPULISM OF FATHER COUGHLIN

1. Quotes from Lawrence W. Levine, "American Culture and the Great Depression," *The Yale Review* 74 (Winter 1985): 210; Mark H. Leff, *The Limits of Symbolic Reform: The New Deal and Taxation, 1933–1939* (New York: Cambridge University Press, 1984), 99.
2. In the 1890s, a Populist editor penned an indictment of big businessmen, every phrase of which would have been widely cheered forty years later: "They have the

power to impoverish the farmers, make millions of good men tramps; to reduce their employees to silent slaves; to ruin great cities; to plunge a happy and prosperous nation into sorrow and bankruptcy." Quoted in Norman Pollack, *The Populist Response to Industrial America* (Cambridge: Harvard University Press, 1962), 21.

3. Robert T. Handy, *A Christian America: Protestant Hopes and Historical Realities* (New York: Oxford University Press, 1971), 213. On Winrod and Pelley, see Leo P. Ribuffo's excellent *The Old Christian Right: The Protestant Far Right from the Great Depression to the Cold War* (Philadelphia: Temple University Press, 1983).
4. Ellen Skerrett, "The Development of Catholic Identity Among Irish-Americans in Chicago, 1880–1920," in *From Paddy to Studs: Irish-American Communities in the Turn of the Century Era,* ed. Timothy J. Meagher (Westport, Conn.: Greenwood Press, 1986), 117–38; John F. Stack, Jr., *International Conflict in an American City: Boston's Irish, Italians, and Jews, 1935–1944* (Westport, Conn.: Greenwood Press, 1979), 29, 40.
5. Quote from William M. Halsey, *The Survival of American Innocence: Catholicism in an Era of Disillusionment, 1920–1940* (Notre Dame, Ind.: University of Notre Dame Press, 1980), 3. Halsey notes there was "a remarkable unanimity of general outlook" between Catholic intellectuals and workers and professionals of the same faith (p. 6). Also see the comments of Jay P. Dolan, *The American Catholic Experience: A History from Colonial Times to the Present* (Garden City, N.Y.: Doubleday, 1985), 351.
6. On the Irish-Catholic ascendancy, see William V. Shannon, *The American Irish* (New York: Macmillan, 1963), 131–348.
7. As Bruce Miroff observes of FDR: "Every facet of his complex political identity was called into play to win over the public." Miroff, *Icons of Democracy* (New York: Basic Books, 1993), 233. FDR quoted in Catherine McNicol Stack, *Main Street in Crisis: The Great Depression and the Old Middle Class on the Northern Plains* (Chapel Hill: University of North Carolina Press, 1992), 119–20.
8. Quoted in *Great Issues in American History: From Reconstruction to the Present Day, 1864–1981,* ed. Richard Hofstadter and Beatrice K. Hofstadter (New York: Vintage, 1982), 345. An excellent discussion of FDR's rhetoric is Ann Ruth Willner, *The Spellbinders: Charismatic Political Leadership* (New Haven: Yale University Press, 1984), 153–71. Warren Susman's succinct judgment was on the mark: "Whatever else might be said about the New Deal, its successes and its failures, it is obviously true that it was a sociological and psychological triumph." Susman, *Culture as History: The Transformation of American Society in the Twentieth Century* (New York: Pantheon, 1984), 159.
9. As Lawrence Levine observes, several popular films during the 1930s featured wise leaders who went outside constitutional bounds to help the common people. Levine, "Hollywood's Washington: Film Images of National Politics During the Great Depression," in Levine, *The Unpredictable Past* (New York: Oxford University Press, 1993), 243–45.

   For a thoughtful discussion of how FDR used traditional kinds of rhetoric to justify significant shifts in policy, see Stephen Skowronek, *The Politics Presidents Make: Leadership from John Adams to George Bush* (Cambridge: Harvard University Press, 1993), 288–324.
10. For a record of the dates and titles of most of Coughlin's radio addresses, see George A. Condon, "The Politics of the Social Justice Movement," Ph.D. diss.,

University of Tennessee, 1962, appendix A. The figure of 30 million was provided by CBS. Ibid., pp. 23–24.

11. David Brion Davis, "Some Themes of Counter-Subversion: An Analysis of Anti-Masonic, Anti-Catholic, and Anti-Mormon Literature," *Mississippi Valley Historical Review* 47 (September 1960): 205–24.
12. "To the Ex-Service Man," given in March 1933, in *Father Coughlin on Money and Gold: Three Pamphlets* (1933; reprint, New York: Arno, 1973), 87.
13. Wallace Stegner, "The Radio Priest and His Flock," in *The Aspirin Age, 1919–1941,* ed. Isabel Leighton (New York: Simon and Schuster, 1949), 234; Richard Akin Davis, "Radio Priest: The Public Career of Father Charles Edward Coughlin," Ph.D. diss., University of North Carolina, Chapel Hill, 1974, 22; David H. Bennett, *Demagogues in the Depression: American Radicals and the Union Party* (New Brunswick, N.J.: Rutgers University Press, 1969), 35; *Radio Guide,* 6 January 1934, 5.
14. *Radio Today,* January 1936, 9; Daniel Czitrom, *Media and the American Mind: From Morse to McLuhan* (Chapel Hill: University of North Carolina Press, 1982), 86; Paul Lazarsfeld, *The People Look at Radio: Report on a Survey Conducted by the National Opinion Research Center* (Chapel Hill: University of North Carolina Press, 1946), vii, 42–43; Cohen, *Making a New Deal,* quote on 327.
15. For contrasting perspectives on the ideological openness of radio networks, see Ruth Brindze, *Not to Be Broadcast: The Truth About the Radio* (New York: Da Capo Press, 1974), quote on 7; George Seldes, *Lords of the Press* (New York: Julian Messner, 1938), 3, 211, 394. Brindze's own subtitle suggests her critical view was not a common one.
16. Landon later derided the influence of radio on the campaign. "The important thing I had to say was the idea I would convey and what I stood for. The Presidency is primarily an elective office, not a broadcasting station." Barnet Baskerville, *The People's Voice: The Orator in American Society* (Lexington: University of Kentucky Press, 1979), 178–79, 189. Also see Arthur M. Schlesinger, Jr., *The Politics of Upheaval* (Boston: Houghton Mifflin, 1960), 601–2.
17. On changes in spiritual practice after 1920, see Dolan, *American Catholic Experience,* 384–87; Leslie Woodcock Tentler, *Seasons of Grace: A History of the Catholic Archdiocese of Detroit* (Detroit: Wayne State University Press, 1990), 408–13 (quote on 412). For the roots, see Jay P. Dolan, *Catholic Revivalism: The American Experience, 1830–1900* (Notre Dame, Ind.: University of Notre Dame Press, 1978), esp. 185–203.
18. For *Rerum Novarum,* I have used the abridged translation in *The Papal Encyclicals in Their Historical Context,* ed. Anne Fremantle (New York: New American Library, 1956), 166–95.
19. Marc Karson, *American Labor Unions and Politics, 1900–1918* (Carbondale, Ill.: Southern Illinois University Press, 1958), 212–84; Mary Harrita Fox, *Peter E. Dietz: Labor Priest* (Notre Dame, Ind.: University of Notre Dame Press, 1953); Msgr. John A. Ryan, *Social Doctrine in Action: A Personal Story* (New York: Harper and Bros., 1941), 146–47; Francis L. Broderick, *Right Reverend New Dealer, John A. Ryan* (New York: Macmillan, 1963), 69.

    In his autobiography, Ryan wrote: "Inasmuch as I had for almost a decade been listening sympathetically to the proposals made by the Farmers' Alliance and the Populists for state regulation of industry, I found Pope Leo's pronouncements on this subject not only pleasing but reassuring. The doctrine of state intervention which I had come to accept and which was sometimes denounced as 'socialistic' in those benighted days, I now read in a Papal encyclical." Ryan, *Social Doctrine,* 44–45.

20. On the 1931 encyclical, see Fremantle, ed., *The Papal Encyclicals,* 228–35; Ryan, *Social Doctrine,* 234, 243–45. On FDR's citation, see George Q. Flynn, *American Catholics and the Roosevelt Presidency, 1932–1936* (Lexington: University of Kentucky Press, 1968), 17–18.
21. See Leo W. Shields, "The History and Meaning of the Term 'Social Justice,'" Ph.D. diss., University of Notre Dame, 1941, 48–49.
22. Shields, "History and Meaning," 26, 51, 59–60; Roland B. Gittelsohn, "The Conference Stance on Social Justice and Civil Rights," *Retrospect and Prospect: Essays in Commemoration of the Seventy-Fifth Anniversary of the Founding of The Central Conference of American Rabbis, 1889–1964,* ed. Bertram Wallace Korn (New York: The Central Conference of American Rabbis, 1965), 86–89. Thanks to Pam Nadell for this reference.
23. Charles Coughlin, "The New Deal in Money," broadcast December 1933, in *Father Coughlin on Money and Gold: Three Pamphlets* (1934; reprint, New York: Arno, 1973), 7; Coughlin, "A Reply to General Hugh Johnson," 11 March 1935, in Charles Coughlin, *A Series of Lectures on Social Justice* (1935; reprint, New York: Da Capo, 1971), 225.
24. "National Union for Social Justice," broadcast of 11 November 1934, reprinted in Coughlin, *A Series of Lectures,* 18; NUSJ preamble quoted in Brinkley, *Voices of Protest,* 287; *Social Justice* (hereafter, *SJ*), 13 March 1936, 4. On Coughlin's influence, see Aaron Abell, *American Catholicism and Social Action: A Search for Social Justice, 1865–1950* (Garden City, N.Y.: Hanover House, 1960), 240; James Terence Fisher, *The Catholic Counterculture in America, 1933–1962* (Chapel Hill: University of North Carolina Press, 1989), 73, 75; John Cahalan, Jr., "The Hour of Power," *Commonweal,* 28 January 1931, 343–45. Al Smith quoted in James Hennesey, S.J., "Roman Catholics and American Politics, 1900–1960," in Mark A. Noll, ed., *Religion and American Politics: From the Colonial Period to the 1980's* (New York: Oxford University Press, 1988), 313.
25. Coughlin, "The New Deal in Money," December 1933, in *Coughlin on Money and Gold,* 43. "1929 Crash Plotted by Bankers as Final Bid for Supremacy, *SJ,* 14 September 1936, 15. For a fine summary of Coughlin's economic views, see Brinkley, *Voices of Protest,* 148–53.
26. Schlesinger, *Age of Upheaval,* 20.
27. Gertrude M. Coogan, *Money Creators: Who Creates Money? Who Should Create It?* (Chicago: Sound Money Press, 1935). Coogan's book, dedicated "To the American People, from Whom the Truth Has Been Too Long Withheld," presents many of the same anecdotes and accusations Coughlin used but lacks his felicity of style. Coogan later charged Coughlin had stolen her ideas. Stegner, "The Radio Priest," 242.
28. Eight of the NUSJ's sixteen principles directly involved either monetary or fiscal policy, including the call for nationalizing banking. "Other people's money" was a trope widely used by populists from the early 1900s to World War II. Prominent examples include Louis Brandeis's 1913 book about the insurance industry and John Flynn's weekly column in the *New Republic* during the mid-1930s.

29. David O'Brien, *American Catholics and Social Reform: The New Deal Years* (New York: Oxford University Press, 1968), 170.
30. The cartoon by an artist named Wyrick (the paper supplied no other identification) appeared in *SJ,* 21 January 1938.
31. Hamilton Basso, "Radio Priest—in Person," *New Republic,* 5 June 1935, 36, 96. For a necessarily inexact demographic analysis of Coughlin's following at this time, see S. M. Lipset and Earl Raab, *The Politics of Unreason: Right-Wing Extremism in America, 1790–1977,* 2nd ed. (Chicago: University of Chicago Press, 1978), 175–76; Brinkley, *Voices of Protest,* 194–207.
32. Brinkley, *Voices of Protest,* 287–88; "Social Justice and a Living Wage" and "Share the Profits with Labor," broadcasts of 18 November and 2 December 1934, both in Coughlin, *A Series of Lectures,* 31, 46–47. A third NUSJ principle presaged the rhetoric of right-wing tax revolts: "I believe in the simplification of government, and the further lifting of crushing taxation from the slender revenues of the laboring class." Coughlin also endorsed the Wagner Act. *SJ,* 10 April 1936, 5.
33. Douglas P. Seaton, *Catholics and Radicals: The Association of Catholic Trade Unionists and the American Labor Movement from Depression to Cold War* (Lewisburg, Pa.: Bucknell University Press, 1981), 36.
34. Speech of 25 March 1934, in Coughlin, *Eight Lectures on Labor, Capital, and Justice* (Royal Oak, Mich.: The Radio League of the Little Flower, 1934), 115–16.
35. On the short history of the AIWA, see Steve Jefferys, *Management and Managed: Fifty Years of Crisis at Chrysler* (New York: Cambridge University Press, 1986), 63–67; Warner Pflug, *The UAW in Pictures* (Detroit: Wayne State University Press, 1971), 30; Henry Kraus, *The Many and the Few: A Chronicle of the Dynamic Auto Workers* (1947; reprint, Urbana: University of Illinois Press, 1985), 13–14. Coughlin was invited to the 1936 UAW convention in order to attract Polish and Irish-Catholic members. Irving Howe and B. J. Widick, *The UAW and Walter Reuther* (New York: Random House, 1949), 12–13.

    In an oral history interview, R. J. Thomas, the president of the UAW during World War II and earlier a vice president of the AIWA, said of Coughlin: "He was doing in those days a constructive job in my opinion of trying to give the workers some guidance." But Thomas turned against the priest when the latter began to criticize FDR and seemed to be "putting himself in a position of trying to be a dictator to the labor movement." "The Reminiscences of R. J. Thomas," transcript, Oral History Research Office, Columbia University, 1956, 24, 35, 37.
36. Coughlin justified his authoritarian hold by saying he was only a temporary "virtual dictator. . . . It was either that or let some crooked politician gain control of the organization and use it for his own ends." Condon, "Politics of Social Justice," 165. On how the chapters were run, pp. 162–69; Brinkley, *Voices of Protest,* 186–92, 194–215.
37. The fight against joining the World Court was led by such progressive Republicans as Hiram Johnson and George Norris, who supported most of the New Deal's domestic initiatives. See Ronald L. Feinman, *Twilight of Progressivism: The Western Republican Senators and the New Deal* (Baltimore: Johns Hopkins University Press, 1981), 61–64; Brinkley, *Voices of Protest,* 134–37.
38. Here I follow the discussion by Brinkley, *Voices of Protest,* 124–27. Also see the valuable studies by Charles J. Tull, *Father Coughlin and the New Deal* (Syracuse,

N.Y.: Syracuse University Press, 1965); James P. Shenton, "The Coughlin Movement and the New Deal," *Political Science Quarterly* 73 (September 1958): 352–73.

39. Coughlin, "The National Union for Social Justice," in Coughlin, *Series of Lectures,* 7–19.
40. Tull, *Father Coughlin,* 61, 80, 90.
41. Quotes from Stegner, "The Radio Priest" and "Enlightenment vs. Revolution," editorial in *SJ,* 5 June 1936, 4. For the dominant interpretation, see Brinkley, *Voices of Protest,* 252–61; Bennett, *Party of Fear,* 260–61.
42. This description is based on several edited sequences contained in Irv Drasnin's documentary film "The Radio Priest," 1988, part of "The American Experience" series. During the campaign, one of Coughlin's supporters wrote to him from Los Angeles: "Not a sentence of your newsreel speeches can be heard for the hissing and booing here." Quoted in Geoffrey S. Smith, *American Counter-Subversives, The New Deal, and the Coming of World War II* (New York: Basic Books, 1973), 46. For a disarming contrast to his 1936 speeches, see the interviews Coughlin did with Universal Movietone News from 1933 to 1935, copies of which are available in the National Archives.
43. Quoted in Bennett, *Party of Fear,* 262.
44. The swipe at journalists was probably aimed at Secretary of Agriculture Henry Wallace, who had gained prominence by publishing a popular magazine for Midwestern farmers.

    Lemke promised his audiences that after four years in the White House, he would not run again because the "money changers will have been driven out of the temple forever, and anyone with ordinary ability will then be able to make a good president." Lemke, "When I Am President," *SJ,* 19 October 1936, 5. Also see Edward C. Blackorby, *Prairie Rebel: The Public Life of William Lemke* (Lincoln: University of Nebraska Press, 1963).
45. Stack, *International Conflict,* 74, 54–55; Lipset and Raab, *Politics of Unreason,* 173. For evidence from Chicago of lay resentment against the church's wealth and alleged avarice, see Cohen, *Making a New Deal,* 225–26.
46. Broderick, *Right Reverend New Dealer,* 223–28; Shenton, "Coughlin Movement," 367–69; Fisher, *Catholic Counterculture,* 77–79; *SJ,* 19 October 1936; Stack, *International Conflict,* 55; Gerald H. Gamm, *The Making of New Deal Democrats: Voting Behavior and Realignment in Boston, 1920–1940* (Chicago: University of Chicago Press, 1989), 154–55.
47. Sinclair Lewis, *It Can't Happen Here* (New York: P.F. Collier and Son, 1935), 88; Ribuffo, *Old Christian Right,* 22–24, 178–215. For a detailed local study of the frenzied debates, see James C. Schneider, *Should America Go to War? The Debate over Foreign Policy in Chicago, 1939–1941* (Chapel Hill: University of North Carolina Press, 1989).
48. On public sentiment toward the impending war, see Michael Leigh, *Mobilizing Consent: Public Opinion and American Foreign Policy, 1937–1947* (Westport, Conn.: Greenwood Press, 1976), 29–51.
49. *SJ,* 11 January 1937, 12; 18 January 1937, 1, 15; 15 March 1937, 1; Coughlin speech, 13 February 1938 in *Sixteen Radio Lectures, 1938* (Royal Oak, Michigan: [self-published], 1938), 51. Archbishop Michael J. Gallagher of Detroit, Coughlin's supportive superior, had strongly condemned the Flint sit-down strike. Kraus, *Many and the Few,* 121.

50. *SJ,* 1 March 1937 (speech of 21 February 1937), 6–7; 5 July 1937, 1.
51. *SJ,* 8 March 1937, 4, 9.
52. Davis, "Radio Priest," 272–73; *SJ,* 21 June 1937, 1, 3.
53. No detailed study of the nature and extent of Coughlin's active support has been published. But for evidence that Coughlinism had a sizable following through the 1930s, see O'Brien, *American Catholics,* 147–48. Citing public opinion polls, the author states that 9 percent of the American public listened to Coughlin regularly in the spring of 1938 as opposed to 30 percent before 1936. However, 84 percent of the 1938 audience approved of his ideas.

    Also see Sheldon Marcus, *Father Coughlin* (Boston: Little, Brown, 1973), 182; Joshua Freeman, *In Transit: The Transport Workers Union in New York City, 1933–1966* (New York: Oxford University Press, 1989), 143–48; Ronald Bayor, *Neighbors in Conflict: The Irish, Germans, Jews, and Italians of New York City, 1929–1941* (Baltimore: Johns Hopkins University Press, 1978), 87–108; Davis, "Radio Priest," 459; John L. Spivak, *Shrine of the Silver Dollar* (New York: Modern Age, 1940); Alfred McClung Lee and Elizabeth Briant Lee, *The Fine Art of Propaganda: A Study of Father Coughlin's Speeches* (New York: Harcourt Brace and Co., 1939); Theodore Irwin, "Inside the Christian Front," *Forum and Century* (March 1940), 102–8. The latter estimates that the Christian Front had 12,000 members in New York City alone.
54. *SJ,* 4 April 1938 (regarding Salazar); 21 March 1938, 1, 8; Davis, "Radio Priest," 458 (regarding Franco); Coughlin speech, "Not Anti-Semitism but Anti-Communism," December 4, 1938, Recorded Sound Division, Library of Congress; *SJ,* 22 July 1940, 3 (regarding Vichy).
55. Brinkley, *Voices of Protest,* 280; James T. Farrell, "Tommy Gallagher's Crusade," *The Roosevelt Era,* ed. Milton Crane (New York: Boni and Gaer, 1947), 195–224.
56. Davis, "Radio Priest," 270, 268–69; Lipset and Raab, *Politics of Unreason,* 182; Brinkley, *Voices of Protest,* 175 (introduced by rabbi).
57. *SJ,* 18 July 1938; *An Answer to Father Coughlin's Critics by Father Coughlin's Friends* (Royal Oak, Mich.: The Radio League of the Little Flower, 1940). On Fahey's influence, see Mary Christine Athans, "A New Perspective on Father Charles E. Coughlin," *Church History* 56 (June 1987), 224–35.
58. *SJ,* 27 March 1939, 16–17. The most vitriolic letters were, like those sent to John Ryan during the 1936 campaign, rebuttals of a prominent Catholic's sharp criticism of Coughlin. "Well, Judas, how much richer are you tonight for having sold your despicable mouth to the Jews?" began a letter from one Joan Christian, replying to a radio speech by Frank Hogan, then president of the American Bar Association, *SJ,* 2 January 1939, 10.
59. The literature on anti-Semitism is, of course, voluminous. For an excellent historical summary of the American version and its connection to the New Deal, see Ribuffo, *Old Christian Right,* 3–24.
60. On the changing nature of Coughlin's audience, see O'Brien, *American Catholics,* 175; Lipset and Raab, *Politics of Unreason,* 171–78. Citing public opinion polls taken during World War II, John Morton Blum wrote that "Americans distrusted Jews more than any other European people except Italians." Blum, *V Was for Victory: Politics and American Culture During World War II* (New York: Harcourt Brace Jovanovich, 1976), 172.
61. On Coughlinites and America First, see Wayne S. Cole, *America First: The Battle*

Against Intervention, 1940–1941 (Madison: University of Wisconsin Press, 1953), 134–38. On Mooney's actions, see Tentler, *Seasons of Grace,* 332–42.

CHAPTER 6. THE MANY AND THE FEW: THE CIO AND THE EMBRACE OF LIBERALISM

1. Quoted in Maurice Isserman, *Which Side Were You On? The American Communist Party During the Second World War* (Middletown, Conn.: Wesleyan University Press, 1982), 22. Even though Robinson was a member of the Communist Party, his "Ballad" was so popular that it was performed in 1940 at the conventions of both the CP and the Republican Party. Joel Lewis, "Earl Robinson's Red, White, and Blue," *In These Times* (25 September–1 October 1991), 18.

   Two years later, in a characteristic statement, Paul Robeson told the press: "The future of America depends largely upon the progressive program of the CIO . . . the Negro people, for the most part, understand that the CIO program is working for all laboring groups, including their own minority." Quoted in Martin Bauml Duberman, *Paul Robeson: A Biography* (New York: Knopf, 1989), 249. Also see Philip S. Foner and Ronald L. Lewis, eds., *The Black Worker from the Founding of the CIO to the AFL-CIO Merger* (Philadelphia: Temple University Press, 1983), 36.
2. The CIO routinely inflated its membership totals, especially in the late '30s, when thousands of workers considered themselves to be members but did not pay regular dues. For estimates, see Nelson Lichtenstein, *Labor's War at Home: The CIO in World War II* (New York: Cambridge University Press, 1982), 80; Steve Rosswurm, "An Overview and Preliminary Assessment of the CIO's Expelled Unions," in Rosswurm, ed., *The CIO's Left-Led Unions* (New Brunswick, N.J.: Rutgers University Press, 1992), 14.
3. The scholar was Sumner Slichter. Quoted in David Brody, *Workers in Industrial America: Essays on the 20th-Century Struggle,* 2nd ed. (New York: Oxford University Press, 1993), 158. There now exists a large and sophisticated literature on the rise and maturation of the CIO. But the best single narrative remains Irving Bernstein, *Turbulent Years: A History of the American Worker, 1933–1941* (Boston: Houghton Mifflin, 1969).
4. However, most industrial workers in the 1930s were schooled in the discipline of mass production and thus downplayed workers' control, a vital matter to the craftsmen of Samuel Gompers's day.
5. Nat Schreiner and Jack Alderman, "Joe Worker and the Story of Labor," CIO Publication 180, c. 1945, in library of the Department of Labor, Washington, D.C. On the history and politics of cultural pluralism, see Philip Gleason, *Speaking of Diversity: Language and Ethnicity in Twentieth-Century America* (Baltimore: Johns Hopkins University Press, 1992), and Gary Gerstle, "American Liberals and the Quest for Cultural Pluralism, 1915–1970," unpublished manuscript in collection of author.
6. *CIO News,* 2 April 1938, 4.
7. On the AFL in the 1930s, see Craig Phelan, *William Green: Biography of a Labor Leader* (Albany: State University of New York Press, 1989); Christopher Tomlins, *The State and the Unions: Labor Relations, Law, and the Organized Labor Movement in America, 1880–1960* (New York: Cambridge University Press, 1985),

148–96; Philip Taft, *The AFL from the Death of Gompers to the Merger* (New York: Harper, 1959).

8. On public disapproval of the sit-down strikes, see Michael Barone, *Our America* (New York: Free Press, 1990), 111–12.
9. Quote from David Brody, "Workplace Contracturalism in Comparative Perspective," in *Industrial Democracy in America: The Ambigous Promise,* ed. Nelson Lichtenstein and Howell John Harris (New York: Cambridge University Press, 1993), 179. On this topic see Melvyn Dubofsky, "Not So 'Turbulent Years': A New Look at the 1930s," in *Life and Labor: Dimension of American Working Class History,* ed. Charles Stephenson and Robert Asher (Albany: State University of New York Press, 1986), 205–33; John Bodnar, "Immigration, Kinship, and the Rise of Working-Class Realism in Industrial America," *Journal of Social History* 13 (1980), 44–64.
10. John L. Lewis quoted in "Industrial Democracy in Steel," 6 July 1936, recording in Recorded Sound Division, Library of Congress. I have borrowed the title of this section from Edward Levinson, *Labor on the March* (1938; reprint, New York: University Books, 1956 [1938]).
11. On the demographic characteristics of the two cohorts of leaders, see Walter Licht and Hal Seth Barron, "Labor's Men: A Collective Biography of Union Officialdom During the New Deal Years," *Labor History* 19 (Fall 1978), 532–43. A number of recent works—by Ronald Schatz, Gary Gerstle, and others—have revealed that the men and women who formed CIO unions typically held skilled jobs and had prior political commitments, unlike most of the rank and file. See the bibliographical appendix, "Good Reading," for titles.
12. Lewis report, CIO, *Proceedings of the First Constitutional Convention,* Pittsburgh, 1938 (Washington, D.C.: CIO, 1939), 43; Lichtenstein, *Labor's War at Home,* 80. Of course, individual unions and some local and state CIO federations also published their own journals. Many of these reprinted the brisk dispatches and irreverent graphics issued by the left-wing Federated Press as well as those the national CIO provided.
13. CIO, *Proceedings of the Third Constitutional Convention, 1940* (Washington, D.C.: CIO, 1941), 52.
14. Cohen, *Making a New Deal,* 343; CIO News, 8 December 1941, 7. Access to the airwaves was not always available. KYA in San Francisco, one of the city's most powerful stations, refused to renew the local CIO's contract for a daily program because the fare was deemed too "controversial"; CIO, *Convention Proceedings, 1940*, 52.
15. Material in this paragraph comes from Michael Kazin and Steven J. Ross, "America's Labor Day: The Dilemma of a Workers' Celebration," *Journal of American History* 78 (March 1992), 1313–15.
16. The essential source on Lewis's life is Melvyn Dubofsky and Warren Van Tine, *John L. Lewis: A Biography* (New York: Quadrangle, 1977), abr. ed. (Urbana: University of Illinois Press, 1986). Unfortunately, the authors say little about Lewis as a speaker. For impressions by insightful contemporaries, see Louis Adamic, *My America, 1928–1938* (New York: Harper and Bros., 1938), 385–403, and Saul Alinsky, *John L. Lewis: An Unauthorized Biography* (New York: G.P. Putnam's Sons, 1949).
17. Quotes from CIO, *Convention Proceedings, 1940;* Dubofsky and Van Tine, *John L. Lewis,* abr. ed., 241.

18. Ruth McKenney, *Industrial Valley* (New York: Harcourt, Brace, 1939), 250.
19. Dubofsky and Van Tine, *Lewis,* 183, 292; Lewis, "Industrial Democracy in Steel," speech broadcast 6 July 1936, recording, Recorded Sound Division, Library of Congress. John Brophy, who knew Lewis as a bitter foe in the UMW and then as his ally in the CIO, said that the labor titan never saw himself as a "member of the proletariat. . . . I think while he recognized that there were a mass of people who did the work of the country; I think in his Middle-western background he got the sense that as far as American society was concerned, it was a fluid situation." "The Reminiscences of John Brophy," Oral History Research Office, Columbia University, New York, 1957, 607–8.
20. Green's margin was smallest among lower-income respondents. *The Gallup Poll,* vol. 1: *1935–1948* (New York: Random House, 1972), 62–63; 120–21.
21. Adamic, *My America,* 397. This was not a new concept for either the labor movement or labor intellectuals who had used it since the late nineteenth century. But the CIO raised it to new prominence as a guiding slogan for its activities. On the historical evolution, see the excellent volume *Industrial Democracy in America: The Ambiguous Promise,* ed. Nelson Lichtenstein and Howell John Harris (New York: Cambridge University Press, 1993).
22. For examples of the IWW producer image, see Joyce L. Kornbluh, ed., *Rebel Voices: An IWW Anthology* (Ann Arbor: University of Michigan Press, 1964). A brilliant discussion of the Herculean image at an earlier date appears in Lynn Hunt, *Politics, Culture, and Class in the French Revolution* (Berkeley: University of California Press, 1984), 94–112.
23. Reuther, intro. to the 1956 reprint of Levinson, *Labor on the March,* xiv.
24. Ronald Schatz, *The Electrical Workers: A History of Labor at General Electric and Westinghouse, 1923–60* (Urbana: University of Illinois Press, 1983), 117. For a rare use of the old populist terminology, see "The C.I.O. and the Farmers," *Union News Service,* 30 August 1937.
25. On the destruction of immigrant institutions and views toward and participation in mass culture, see Cohen, *Making a New Deal.* On the pivotal role of second-generation immigrants in the CIO, see Thomas Gobel, "Becoming American: Ethnic Workers and the Rise of the CIO," *Labor History* 29 (Spring 1988), 173–98.
26. Thomas Bell, *Out of This Furnace: A Novel of Immigrant Labor in America* (1941; reprint, Pittsburgh: University of Pittsburgh Press, 1976), 412, 385.
27. At the end of the novel, Dobie does briefly muse, "they might try finding a satisfactory substitute for bosses and bossism," Bell, *Furnace,* 408–9. But earlier, the author portrays Dobie's father's vote for Eugene Debs in 1912 as an impotent gesture. And the weight of Dobie's section of the narrative is all on the side of cheering SWOC, the Democratic Party, and the common sense of average workers—all of which precluded political leaps of faith.
28. *Journal of Labor* (Atlanta), 3 September 1937.
29. Cohen, *Making a New Deal,* 357; also see Lary May, "Movie Star Politics: The Screen Actors' Guild, Cultural Conversion, and the Hollywood Red Scare," in *Recasting America: Culture and Politics in the Age of Cold War,* ed. Lary May (Chicago: University of Chicago Press, 1989), 125–53.
30. Quotes from Bell, *Furnace,* 410; Gary Gerstle, *Working-Class Americanism,* 153–95; Warner Pflug, *The UAW in Pictures* (Detroit: Wayne State University Press, 1971), 62; ILGWU leaflet entitled "General Strike Call," c. 1935, Political

History Collection, National Museum of American History; Len DeCaux, *CIO News,* 5 June 1939; Bruce Nelson, *Workers on the Waterfront* (Urbana: University of Illinois Press, 1988), 183.

In western Pennsylvania, one SWOC activist kicked off an organizing drive by reading a "Steel Workers' Declaration of Independence," which imitated the original in its recitation of "a history of repeated injuries and usurpations" committed by U.S. Steel. William Serrin, *Homestead: The Glory and Tragedy of an American Steel Town* (New York: Times Books, 1992), 191.

For a good overview of this subject, see Gary Gerstle, "The Politics of Patriotism: Americanization and the Formation of the CIO," *Dissent* 33 (Winter 1986), 84–92.

31. Pflug, *UAW in Pictures,* 85; *CIO News,* 24 February 1941, 1; 25 August 1941, 1; 25 May 1942, 1.

At times, the symbolic campaign descended to self-parody. One week, the front page of *CIO News* included a photograph of a young woman holding a rock brought up from a Pennsylvania mine. On it appeared the initials "CIO." The caption read, "The letters C.I.O. are a natural crystal formation, produced by nature thousands of years back in geological time. Each letter is perfect, and was produced without help by man. Evidence enough—say C.I.O.-ers—that the C.I.O. has its roots deep in American history and American soil!" *CIO News,* 19 February 1938.

32. Quoted in Robert J. Norrell, "Caste in Steel: Jim Crow Careers in Birmingham, Alabama," *Journal of American History* 73 (December 1986), 672–73.

33. On this issue see Norrell, "Caste in Steel," and Michael Goldfield, "Race and the CIO: The Possibilities for Racial Egalitarianism During the 1930s and 1940s" with responses by Gary Gerstle et al., *International Labor and Working-Class History* 44 (Fall 1993), 1–63. On the struggle in an important Southern city, see Michael K. Honey, *Southern Labor and Black Civil Rights: Organizing Memphis Workers* (Urbana: University of Illinois Press, 1993).

34. Quotes from "The CIO and the Negro Worker," 1942 CIO pamphlet, in Foner and Lewis, *The Black Worker,* vol. VII, 37–41; Meier and Rudwick, *Black Detroit and the Rise of the UAW* (New York: Oxford University Press, 1979), 26.

35. Norrell, "Caste in Steel"; Schatz, *Electrical Workers.* On the CIO's attempt to sidestep the issue of race in a key Southern state, see Robin D. G. Kelley, *Hammer and Hoe: Alabama Communists During the Great Depression* (Chapel Hill: University of North Carolina Press, 1990), 138–51.

36. Quoted in Meier and Rudwick, *Black Detroit,* 26.

37. Quotes from Honey, *Southern Labor,* 137; Horace R. Cayton and George S. Mitchell, *Black Workers and the New Unions* (Chapel Hill: University of North Carolina Press, 1939), 218.

38. Susan Hartman Strom, "Challenging 'Women's Place': Feminism, the Left, and Industrial Unionism in the 1930s," *Feminist Studies* 9 (Summer 1983): 359–86; Elizabeth Faue, "'The Dynamo of Change': Gender and Solidarity in the American Labour Movement of the 1930s," *Gender and History* 1 (Summer 1989): 138–58 (quote, 152). *CIO News,* 12 February 1940; 5 February 1940; 10 February 1941. According to his biographers, John L. Lewis had, since the early '30s, "cast aspersions on Green's manhood, no small insult to an ex-coal miner who shared the exaggerated sense of manliness associated with that occupation." Dubofsky and Van Tine, *Lewis,* 247.

Female union membership did increase by 300 percent during the 1930s, a figure comparable to that for men. But women had started from a much smaller numerical base. Sara Evans, *Born for Liberty: A History of Women in America* (New York: Free Press, 1989), 215.

39. Katherine Pollak, "Building Union Strength," *Union News Service,* 22 August 1936, 1. *CIO News,* 20 February 1939, 4. In South Chicago, wives of steelworkers went door to door "to convince other wives that they should encourage their men to join SWOC." Cohen, *Making a New Deal,* 347.
40. Nancy F. Gabin, *Feminism in the Labor Movement: Women and the United Auto Workers, 1935–1975* (Ithaca, N.Y.: Cornell University Press, 1990), 30.
41. I borrow this point from Michael Miles, *The Odyssey of the American Right* (New York: Oxford University Press, 1980), 12. For examples of the rhetoric of the 1936 campaign, see Fraser, *Labor Will Rule,* 368–70.
42. On Roosevelt's capture of the term "liberal," see David Green, *Shaping Political Consciousness: The Language of Politics in America from McKinley to Reagan* (Ithaca, N.Y.: Cornell University Press, 1987), 119–34 (quote on 121–22). Green points out that FDR ceased calling himself a "progressive" because so many older political figures who identified with that term (like Al Smith, Herbert Hoover, Amos Pinchot) were bitterly opposed to the New Deal. Father Coughlin once described Senator Burton Wheeler, a Roosevelt opponent, as a "true liberal." *SJ,* 18 March 1940, 20. But three years earlier, the priest had snapped, "It takes no brains to be liberal with other peoples' money," quoted in Charles J. Tull, *Father Coughlin and the New Deal* (Syracuse, N.Y.: Syracuse University Press, 1965), 176.
43. CIO, *Proceedings of 1939 Convention,* 68–69. On the CIO's debt to the New Deal, see Steve Fraser, "The Labor Question," in Fraser and Gerstle, ed,. *The Rise and Fall of the New Deal Order, 1930–1980* (Princeton, N.J.: Princeton University Press, 1989), 70.
44. A generation later, the former CP leader Earl Browder recalled, "The rise of the C.I.O. trade unions carried the whole labor movement with it. It was the basis of the Communist advances in all other fields." Browder, "The American Communist Party in the Thirties," in *As We Saw the Thirties: Essays on Social and Political Movements of a Decade,* ed. Rita James Simon (Urbana, Ill.: University of Illinois Press, 1967), 231–32. On the CIO and the CP, see Harvey Klehr, *The Heyday of American Communism: The Depression Decade* (New York: Basic Books, 1984), 223–51 and passim (quote, 238); Bert Cochran, *Labor and Communism: The Conflict That Shaped American Unions* (Princeton, N.J.: Princeton University Press, 1977); Harvey A. Levenstein, *Communism, Anticommunism, and the CIO* (Westport, Conn.: Greenwood Press, 1981).
45. Ronald Schatz, "American Labor and the Catholic Church, 1919–1950," *International Labor and Working-Class History* 20 (Fall 1981): 46–53; Schatz, *Electrical Workers,* 182–83; Douglas P. Seaton, *Catholics and Radicals: The Association of Catholic Trade Unionists and the American Labor Movement, from Depression to Cold War* (Lewisburg, Pa.: Bucknell University Press, 1981); Steve Rosswurm, "The Catholic Church and the Left-Led Unions: Labor Priests, Labor Schools, and the ACTU," in Rosswurm, *Left-Led Unions,* 119–37.
46. On the comparison, see Leo Ribuffo, *Right Center Left: Essays in American History* (New Brunswick, N.J.: Rutgers University Press, 1992), 149–50.

47. A. B. Magil and Henry Stevens, *The Peril of Fascism: The Crisis of American Democracy* (New York: International Publishers, 1938), 171.
48. DeCaux, *Labor Radical,* 268. On the opening to Catholics, see Klehr, *Heyday,* 221–22.
49. Louis Goldblatt, "Working-Class Leader in the ILGWU, 1935–1977," Regional Oral History Office, Bancroft Library, University of California at Berkeley, 1980, 425; Gerald Zahavi, "'Communism Is No Bug-a-Boo': Communism and Left-Wing Unionism in Fulton County, New York, 1933–1950," *Labor History* 33 (Spring 1992), 175. The union to which the Fulton County local was affiliated, the Fur and Leather Workers, was the only one in the CIO whose top national officials openly admitted their membership in the CP.

    At the same time, several of the CP-led Unemployed Councils were opening their meetings with a prayer or a Hail Mary, depending on the religious composition of the area. Robert Fisher, *Let the People Decide,* 38.
50. Joseph Freeman quoted in Ribuffo, *Left Center Right,* 134. After the CP swung to the Left after World War II, its major spokesman, William Z. Foster, still spoke in populist terms of basing a third party on "a broad antiwar, antimonopoly coalition among workers, poorer farmers, African Americans, and 'progressive' sectors of the middle classes." Edward P. Johanningsmeier, *Forging American Communism: The Life of William Z. Foster* (Princeton, N.J.: Princeton University Press, 1994), 316.

    In contrast to the American situation, the British Left in the 1930s "continued to equate patriotism with jingoism. . . . The same instincts which made people vulnerable to jingoism, it was assumed, left them open to fascism as well." Miles Taylor, "Patriotism, History and the Left in Twentieth-Century Britain," *The Historical Journal* (1990), 980.
51. CIO, *Proceedings of the First Constitutional Convention,* Pittsburgh, November 14 to 18, 1938 (Washington, D.C.: CIO, 1939), 10.
52. *CIO News,* 24 September 1938, 6.
53. Donohoe speech, CIO, *Proceedings of 1939 Convention,* 65–66. Some supporters of Coughlin were also active in the ACTU, most notably Father Edward Lodge Curran, a prominent Brooklyn churchman, and a few local chapters of the decentralized organization sometimes sided with Coughlinites against union officials with ties to radical groups. Seaton, *Catholics and Radicals,* 99, 183; Joshua Freeman, *In Transit,* 148–51.
54. Leslie Woodcock Tentler, *Seasons of Grace: A History of the Catholic Archdiocese of Detroit* (Detroit: Wayne State University Press, 1990), 343.
55. Lewis quoted in Aaron Abell, *American Catholicism and Social Action: A Search for Social Justice, 1865–1950* (Garden City, N.Y.: Hanover House, 1960), 253. For one CIO leader's speech that did include such references, see John Brophy, "The Church and the CIO," *CIO News,* 7 May 1938, 6. Brophy, however, was speaking to a most receptive audience, the National Catholic Social Action Conference.
56. "Labor and Religion," CIO publication 111 (October 1944), 11 (in library of Department of Labor); DeCaux, *CIO News,* 9 February 1939, 5. On the local workers mentioned, see the excellent studies by Joshua Freeman, *In Transit,* and Gary Gerstle, *Working-Class Americanism.*
57. Schreiner and Alderman, "Joe Worker."
58. On wartime unionism, see Lichtenstein, *Labor's War at Home*; Fraser, *Labor Will*

Rule; Joshua Freeman, "Delivering the Goods: Industrial Unionism During World War II," *Labor History* 19 (Fall 1978), 570–93. For a critical postwar assessment, see C. Wright Mills, *New Men of Power: America's Labor Leaders* (New York: Harcourt Brace, 1948).

59. Lewis, radio address of 4 September 1939, recording in Recorded Sound Division, Library of Congress.
60. On public opinion toward the war, see Michael Leigh, *Mobilizing Consent: Public Opinion and American Foreign Policy, 1937–1947* (Westport, Conn.: Greenwood Press, 1976), 29–51.
61. Quotes from the speech, *New York Times,* 26 October 1940.
62. Quotes taken from the excellent unpublished study by Bruce Nelson, "'A Class Line Across the Face of American Politics'? Workers, Organized Labor, and the Presidential Election of 1940," 27, 29.
63. Quoted in Dubofsky and Van Tine, *Lewis,* 305.
64. Kempton quoted in Irving Bernstein, *Turbulent Years,* 443; Murray quoted on p. 446.

There is no full biography of Murray. The best account of his life is Ronald Schatz, "Philip Murray and the Subordination of the Industrial Unions to the United States Government," in Melvyn Dubofsky and Warren Van Tine, ed., *Labor Leaders in America* (Urbana: University of Illinois Press, 1987), 234–57. Also see Juanita Diffay Tate, "Philip Murray as a Labor Leader," Ph.D. diss., New York University, 1962. My characterization of his oratorical style is taken from these sources, several of the speeches he gave from 1937 to 1945 that are stored in the Recorded Sound Division of the Library of Congress, and several newsreels stored at the National Archives.

65. Upon Murray's assumption of the CIO presidency, *Social Justice* praised him as "an American who believes in the spiritual concept of life without neglecting to care for those material things without which it is well nigh impossible for a man to save his immortal soul." *SJ,* 6 January 1941, 4.
66. Murray report, CIO, *Proceedings of Sixth Constitutional Convention, November, 1943* (Washington, D.C.: CIO, 1944), 36–37.
67. Ralph B. Levering, *American Opinion and the Russian Alliance, 1939–1945* (Chapel Hill: University of North Carolina Press, 1976), 84–86.
68. Blum, *V Was for Victory,* 224–25; Fraser, *Labor Will Rule,* 526.
69. *CIO News,* 30 March 1942, 1, 4; Delbert D. Arnold, "The CIO's Role in American Politics, 1936–1948," Ph.D. diss., University of Maryland, 1952, 128 (Bridges); *CIO News,* 6 July 1942, 8.

Such rhetoric was a continuation of the Brown Scare—the equation of all reactionaries with Nazis—that had bedeviled Father Coughlin before Pearl Harbor. See Leo Ribuffo, *The Old Christian Right: The Protestant Far Right from the Great Depression to the Cold War* (Philadelphia: Temple University Press, 1983), 178–224.

70. "Radio Handbook," in Joseph Gaer, *The First Round: The Story of the CIO Political Action Committee* (New York: Duell, Sloan and Pearce, 1944), 325, 327. Fortunately, most of the key PAC publications are compiled in this volume. For the bare details of Gaer's life, see *Contemporary Authors,* vols. 9–12, first rev. ed. (Detroit: Gale Research, 1974), 310–11.
71. Gaer, *First Round,* xv, 188, 190, 93, 43. Also see Murray's statement, "Labor's Political Aims," CIO publication 102 (1944) in Department of Labor library.

72. For examples, see Gaer, *First Round,* 194–203 and passim.
73. Gaer, *First Round,* 37–38, 57.
74. Quoted in Fraser, *Labor Will Rule,* 529, 536.
75. See the ironic chapter on "The Liberal Rhetoric" in Mills, *New Men of Power,* 111–21.
76. Reuther quoted in *New Republic,* cited by Nelson Lichtenstein in his forthcoming biography of the UAW leader.

    Some striking union members also grumbled about the privileges of their leaders. A Baltimore steelworker complained to Philip Murray: "I know plenty with very little [money] ahead of them, whereas you fellows in high places travel via Pullman, or Air-plane, broadcast speeches over high price Broadcasting systems, and take up residence in high-class hotels, while they stand in the cold, 'picketing' plants that have no intention of trying to operate." I am indebted to Kenneth Durr, a graduate student at American University, for bringing this document from the Murray Papers to my attention.
77. Murray, speech given 23 October 1948, CIO Press Releases, bound copy in George Meany Memorial Archives; Samuel Lubell, *The Future of American Politics,* 3rd ed. rev. (New York: Harper and Row, 1965), 184.

    See also Fay Calkins, *The CIO and the Democratic Party* (Chicago: University of Chicago Press, 1952), 12–36. For public opinion hostile to postwar strikes, see *The Gallup Poll,* vol. 1, *1935–1948* (New York: Random House, 1972), 521, 568, 583.
78. This paragraph benefited greatly from correspondence with Nelson Lichtenstein. Also see his *Labor's War at Home,* 238–44. On the campaign for national health care (in which the AFL was an equal participant), see Alan Derickson, "Health Security for All? Social Unionism and Universal Health Insurance, 1935–1958," *Journal of American History* 80 (March 1994): 1333–56.
79. On the historic shift during the 1940s from "an elite to a mass tax," see John F. Witte, *The Politics and Development of the Federal Income Tax* (Madison: University of Wisconsin Press, 1985), 110–37.

    I don't mean to minimize the considerable benefits to union workers of collective bargaining and increased political clout. Two insightful assessments are Howell Harris, "The Snares of Liberalism? Politicians, Bureaucrats, and the Shaping of Federal Labor Relations Policy in the United States, ca. 1915–47," *Shop Floor Bargaining and the State: Historical and Comparative Perspectives,* ed. Steven Tolliday and Jonathan Zeitlin (New York: Cambridge University Press, 1985), 148–91, and David Brody, "Workplace Contracturalism in Comparative Perspective," in *Industrial Democracy,* ed. Lichtenstein and Harris, 176–205.

CHAPTER 7. A FREE PEOPLE FIGHT BACK: THE RISE AND FALL OF THE COLD WAR RIGHT

1. See Robert G. McCloskey, *American Conservatism in the Age of Enterprise* (Cambridge: Harvard University Press, 1951); George Wolfskill, *Revolt of the Conservatives: A History of the American Liberty League, 1934–1940* (Boston: Houghton Mifflin, 1962); Clinton Rossiter, *Conservatism in America: The Thankless Persuasion,* 2nd ed. (New York: Vintage, 1962).

2. On the Fay Committee, see *Brooklyn Tablet,* 19 January 1946, 1, 4, 5.
3. Charles Coughlin quoted in Charles J. Tull, *Father Coughlin and the New Deal* (Syracuse, N.Y.: Syracuse University Press, 1965), 231–32.
4. George Dondero, who lived in Royal Oak, Michigan, represented Coughlin's district. Quoted in Jane De Hart Mathews, "Art and Politics in Cold War America," *American Historical Review* 81 (October 1976), 773.
5. Anti-Semitism did not completely vanish from the Right. But vocal anti-Semites like Merwin K. Hart and John Owen Beaty did not lead mass organizations and received little publicity.
6. Harry Serwer, "Lefties in Business," *Human Events,* 27 September 1950; Ralph de Toledano and Victor Lasky, *Seeds of Treason: The True Story of the Hiss-Chambers Tragedy* (New York: Funk and Wagnalls, 1950), 52.
7. Business associations—the National Association of Manufacturers and the United States Chamber of Commerce—and individual employers contributed funds and publicity to the postwar Right. They usually represented their views as those of discontented ordinary Americans and eschewed suggestions of self-interest. See Peter Irons, "American Business and the Origins of McCarthyism," in *The Specter: Original Essays on the Cold War and the Origins of McCarthyism,* ed. Robert Griffith and Athan Theoharis (New York: Franklin Watts, 1974), 72–89.

   A good example of postwar business propaganda was a 1952 advertisement for Republic Steel in which a bus rider in casual clothes tells his friend across the aisle: "You know me, Ed . . . I'm strictly a sports page guy. But when I was home in bed last week with that blasted head cold, I didn't have much to do but read the paper. . . . And Ed, what I read in those editorials made me mad enough to forget how I felt. . . . One was about 'Creeping Socialism'. It told what's going on right under our noses . . . a lot of undercover work to turn us into a bunch of spineless dummies, instead of free citizens." *Freeman,* 11 August 1952, 783.
8. On the activities of the FBI, see Kenneth O'Reilly, *Hoover and the Un-Americans: The FBI, HUAC, and the Red Menace* (Philadelphia: Temple University Press, 1983).
9. Good examples, from different political positions, are Richard T. Morris and Raymond J. Murphy, "A Paradigm for the Study of Class Consciousness," *Sociology and Social Research* 50 (April 1966): 297–313; Michael Mann, *Consciousness and Action Among the Western Working Class* (London: MacMillan, 1973); Kay L. Scholzman and Sidney Verba, *Injury to Insult: Unemployment, Class, and Political Response* (Cambridge: Harvard University Press, 1979).

   Poll data on attitudes toward corporations are sketchy before the late '50s. But it is clear that, up to the mid-1960s, antimonopoly sentiments were in the minority during the postwar era. For a useful synthesis of the data, see Seymour Martin Lipset and William Schneider, *The Confidence Gap: Business, Labor, and Government in the Public Mind,* rev. ed. (Baltimore: Johns Hopkins University Press, 1987), 29–39.
10. See Jackson Lears, "A Matter of Taste: Corporate Cultural Hegemony in a Mass-Consumption Society," in *Recasting America: Culture and Politics in the Age of Cold War,* ed. Lary May (Chicago: University of Chicago Press, 1989), 38–57.
11. Robert Wuthnow, *The Restructuring of American Religion: Society and Faith Since World War II* (Princeton, N.J.: Princeton University Press, 1988), 17; Stephen J. Whitfield, *The Culture of the Cold War* (Baltimore: Johns Hopkins University Press, 1991), 83. Quote, p. 87.

12. As Raymond Williams succinctly put it, "**Community** can be the warmly persuasive word to describe an existing set of relationships, or the warmly persuasive word to describe an alternative set of relationships. What is most important, perhaps, is that unlike all other terms of social organization . . . it seems never to be used unfavourably, and never to be given any positive opposing or distinguishing term." *Keywords: A Vocabulary of Culture and Society,* rev. ed. (New York: Oxford University Press, 1985), 76.

    In the mid-1950s, a careful study of how social scientists employed the term found ninety-four definitions and sixteen concepts. George A. Hillery, Jr., "Definitions of Community: Areas of Agreement," *Rural Sociology* 20 (June 1955): 111–23. For a useful critique of the academic discourse, see Gerald D. Suttles, *The Social Construction of Communities* (Chicago: University of Chicago Press, 1972), 3–18.

13. Robert A. Nisbet, *The Quest for Community: A Study in the Ethics of Order and Freedom* (New York: Oxford University Press, 1953), 34, 37, 47.

14. Louis F. Budenz, *This Is My Story* (New York: McGraw-Hill, 1947), 233. In the fall of 1953, the Americanism Commission of the American Legion sent out a membership ad featuring a "gaunt Korean veteran POW" that was expressly "directed at apathetic arm-chair Americans." "The threat of expanding world Communist [sic] doesn't lessen over the weekend," the Commission warned. "Malenkov and his Red morticians operate on a round the clock, seven day a week schedule. We've got to fight the fire of Communism with the fire of enthusiastic Americanism." *The Firing Line,* 1 November 1953, 1.

15. Quotes from R. Wilson Brown, "Hollywood Has the Jitters," *American Legion Magazine* (hereafter *ALM*), March 1948, 30.

16. On Spillane's contribution to the red scare, see Whitfield, *Culture of the Cold War,* 34–37.

17. On Pegler, see Oliver Pilat, *Westbrook Pegler* (Boston: Beacon, 1963).

18. Quoted in Whitfield, *Culture of the Cold War,* 44–45.

19. For a balanced, comprehensive history of right-wing thought after World War II, see George H. Nash, *The Conservative Intellectual Movement in America Since 1945* (New York: Basic Books, 1976). Kirk's phrases quoted on p. 73. An excellent biographical account is John B. Judis, *William F. Buckley, Jr.: Patron Saint of the Conservatives* (New York: Simon and Schuster, 1988).

20. Although he may have helped write Brent Bozell and William F. Buckley's apologia, *McCarthy and His Enemies* (Chicago: Henry Regnery, 1954), Kendall became increasingly estranged from Buckley and *National Review,* often calling the latter "the Right-wing organ of the Establishment." On his thought, see the lucid discussion in Nash, *Conservative Intellectual Movement,* 120–22, 227–48 (quote, 408; note 130); Judis, *Buckley,* 60–61. The longer quote is from a debate in 1964 between Kendall and James MacGregor Burns, *Dialogues in Americanism* (Chicago: Henry Regnery, 1964), 120.

21. Quotes from John T. Flynn, "The Hidden Red Ink in TVA's Books," *Reader's Digest,* December 1947, 133; Flynn, "Low-Cost Housing CAN Be Provided," *Reader's Digest,* January 1948, 95; Flynn, *The Road Ahead: America's Creeping Revolution* (New York: Devin-Adair, 1949), 70–75. An explicit statement of the need to "educate our electorate on the true nature of the grave crisis which menaces our civilization" appears on pp. 154–55.

Unfortunately, there is no full biography of Flynn or complete study of his works. The most useful secondary sources are Richard Clark Frey, "John T. Flynn and the United States in Crisis, 1928–1950," Ph.D. diss., University of Oregon, 1969; Ronald Radosh, *Prophets on the Right: Profiles of Conservative Critics of American Globalism* (New York: Simon and Schuster, 1975), 197–273.

22. Quote from Frey, "John T. Flynn," 200. Flynn made a point of criticizing anti-Semitic statements by Charles Lindbergh and other America First Committee spokesmen and fought against followers of Father Coughlin who were active in the New York City chapter.
23. Quoted in *Reader's Digest,* February 1950, 1.
24. Flynn, *The Road Ahead,* 67, 79, 126, 154, 158, 160.
25. *Reader's Digest,* February 1950. The term "egghead" was coined by the journalist Stewart Alsop and his brother John during the 1952 presidential election. It was meant, in part, as a caricature of Adlai Stevenson's thin, balding skull. The Democratic nominee was popular among educated liberals because of his elegant evocations of civic virtue. John Alsop's definition was "a visual figure of speech tending to depict a large, oval head, smooth, faceless, unemotional, but a little haughty and condescending," quoted in Horace Coon, *Triumph of the Eggheads* (New York: Random House, 1955), 294.
26. In 1953, J. B. Matthews, the lead investigator for Joseph McCarthy's Senate committee, accused Protestant ministers of being "the largest single group supporting the Communist apparatus today," Mark Silk, *Spiritual Politics: Religion and America Since World War II* (New York: Simon and Schuster, 1988), 89. For one local conflict within Methodism, see Don E. Carleton, *Red Scare! Right-wing Hysteria, Fifties Fanaticism and Their Legacy in Texas* (Austin: Texas Monthly Press, 1985), 103–11. On Catholic condemnation of the wartime Soviet alliance, see George Sirgiovanni, *An Undercurrent of Suspicion: Anti-Communism in America During World War II* (New Brunswick, N.J.: Transaction, 1990), 147–63.
27. Christopher Fullman quoted in Patrick Allitt, *Catholic Intellectuals and Conservative Politics in America, 1950–1985* (Ithaca, N.Y.: Cornell University Press, 1993), 78. On the activities of one labor school, see Ronald W. Schatz, "Connecticut's Working Class in the 1950s: A Catholic Perspective," *Labor History* 25 (Winter 1984), 83–101.
28. Sheen also advocated a watered-down form of corporatism in which workers would, in some vague way, share the control and profits of industry. But, unlike his counterparts on both the CIO Left and the Coughlinite Right in the 1930s, he showed little interest in the issue. Fulton J. Sheen, *Communism and the Conscience of the West* (Dublin, Ireland: Browne and Nolan, 1948), 9, 51, 146–67. At the same time, the Knights of Columbus crusade listed nine "abuses of unrestricted capitalism" that were indebted to the social encyclicals. Christopher J. Kauffman, *Faith and Fraternalism: The History of the Knights of Columbus, 1882–1982* (New York: Harper and Row, 1982), 361–62. On these issues, see Allitt, *Catholic Intellectuals,* 70–81.
29. The most prominent critic was Paul Blanshard whose *American Freedom and Catholic Power* (Boston: Beacon, 1949) was sharply condemned by both the church and most non-Catholic reviewers. For the historical context, see Barbara Welter, "From Maria Monk to Paul Blanshard: A Century of Protestant Anti-Catholicism," *Uncivil Religion: Interreligious Hostility in America,* ed. Robert N. Bellah and Frederick E. Greenspahn (New York: Crossroad, 1987), 43–71.

The chief counsel of Joseph McCarthy's Senate Investigations Subcommittee was, of course, Roy Cohn. And a number of other Jews were active in the anti-Communist cause—the columnist George Sokolsky, the writer Eugene Lyons, and Alfred Kohlberg, a prime organizer of the pro-Chiang "China Lobby." Moreover there was an American Jewish League Against Communism that supported McCarthy throughout his career. See Roy Cohn, *McCarthy* (New York: New American Library, 1968), 249–50.

30. Scanlan's actual title was managing editor. But he clearly guided the paper's editorial policy. For the paper's influence, see Donald F. Crosby, S.J., *God, Church and Flag: Senator Joseph R. McCarthy and the Catholic Church, 1950–1957* (Chapel Hill: University of North Carolina Press, 1978).
31. Quotes from *Tablet,* 15 April 1950, 6; 22 April 1950, 8. For evidence of antidiscrimination, see ibid., 22 April 1950, 9. For a denial of Coughlinite connections, ibid., 29 April 1950, 11. Despite Scanlan's new attitudes, Jews in New York still suspected the *Tablet* of anti-Semitism. See Richard Gid Powers, "The Roy Cohn Dinner," paper presented at 1991 convention of the Organization of American Historians, 17.
32. *Tablet,* 4 March 1950, 14. On the family issue, see Jeffrey M. Burns, *American Catholics and the Family Crisis, 1930–1962: An Ideological and Organizational Response* (New York: Garland, 1988).
33. Quotes from *Tablet,* 7 May 1949, 1, 9. Marian tributes, usually connected to apparition cults at Fatima and elsewhere, were quite popular during the early Cold War. See Thomas A. Kselman and Steven Avella, "Marian Piety and the Cold War in the United States," *Catholic Historical Review* 72 (July 1986), 403–24.
34. Quotes from *Tablet,* 1 July 1950, 1; 15 July 1950, 11; John Cooney, *American Pope: The Life and Times of Francis Cardinal Spellman* (New York: Times Books, 1984), 220.
35. Cartoon in *Tablet,* 29 April 1950.
36. Quote from *Tablet,* 15 July 1950, 11.
37. Quoted in Budenz, "For an American Revolutionary Approach," *Modern Monthly,* (March 1935), 16. I am grateful to Roy Rosenzweig for lending me copies of Budenz's writings from the 1930s.

    On Budenz, see Marc Karson, *American Labor Unions and Politics, 1900–1918* (Carbondale: Southern Illinois University Press, 1958), 265, 268–69; David Caute, *The Great Fear* (New York: Simon and Schuster, 1988), 123–25; A. J. Muste, "Sketches for an Autobiography," in *The Essays of A.J. Muste,* ed. Nat Hentoff (Indianapolis: Bobbs-Merrill, 1967), 170–74; and Budenz's own confessional books, *This Is My Story* (New York: McGraw-Hill, 1947) and *Men Without Faces: The Communist Conspiracy in the U.S.A.* (New York: Harper and Bros., 1950). Also interesting is his wife's memoir, Margaret Budenz, *Streets* (Huntington, Ind.: Our Sunday Visitor, 1979).
38. Budenz testimony, "Investigation of Un-American Propaganda Activities in the United States, Revised Hearings Before the Committee on Un-American Activities," 79th Congress, 22 November 1946 (Washington, D.C.: Government Printing Office, 1947), 3; quotes from Budenz, *My Story,* 100, 128, 124, 7–12. On Budenz's sometimes controversial mixture of anticommunism and Catholicism, see Crosby, *God, Church, and Flag,* 58–62.

    Similar avowals of liberal views appear in other memoirs of former Communists who became prominent red hunters. For examples, see Benjamin Gitlow, *The Whole of Their Lives* (New York: Scribner's, 1948), and Herbert Philbrick, *I Led Three Lives: Citizen, "Communist," Counterspy* (New York: McGraw-Hill, 1952), 307–8.

39. The six heroes were Washington, Jackson, William Henry Harrison, Grant, Garfield, and McKinley. Other well-known military figures—Winfield Scott and George McClellan—were nominated for the presidency by major parties. And wartime experience was also an asset for successful candidates like James Monroe, Franklin Pierce, and Rutherford B. Hayes. On the early debate over the place of the military in American life, see Marcus Cunliffe, *Soldiers and Civilians: The Martial Spirit in America, 1775–1865* (Boston: Little, Brown, 1968). On workers' ambivalence toward that tradition, see David Montgomery, *Citizen Worker* (New York: Cambridge University Press, 1993), 89–104.

40. In 1953, the *VFW Magazine*—hardly a disinterested source—reported that, all together, over 300 representatives and senators were veterans. "Annual Conference Salutes 310 Veterans Serving in Congress," April 1953, 11. Stephen J. Whitfield reports that 195 congressmen and forty-four senators belonged to the American Legion alone in the late 1940s. Whitfield, *Culture of the Cold War,* 188. Of course, Presidents Truman and Eisenhower were war veterans, and the latter owed his office directly to his military success.

41. Scholarship on the AVC is quite meager. But see Robert L. Tyler, "The American Veterans Committee: Out of a Hot War and into the Cold," *American Quarterly* 18 (Fall 1966), 419–36, and Richard Severo and Lewis Milford, *The Wages of War: When America's Soldiers Came Home: From Valley Forge to Vietnam* (New York: Simon and Schuster, 1989), 309–14.

42. On the CWV, see Caute, *Great Fear,* 110 and passim; Crosby, *God, Church, and Flag,* 16–17 and passim; *Catholic Vet* (Milwaukee), February 1948 ("moneyed interests" and defense of Father Coughlin). The *Catholic Vet* changed its name to *Wisconsin Catholic Vet* in January, 1952. Ibid., July 1952, 1; Reverend Edward J. Connor, "Why CWV," ibid., February 1952, 1–5. I was unable to locate files of any other CWV publication, and current staff members at the national office were uncooperative.

43. Like other grassroots components of the anti-Communist movement, the VFW and the American Legion have not attracted much scholarly interest. The best book, William Pencak, *For God and Country: The American Legion, 1919–1941* (Boston: Northeastern University Press, 1989), does not cover the Cold War era, and there is no separate study of the VFW. But see Rodney G. Minott, "The Organized Veterans and the Spirit of Americanism, 1898–1959," Ph.D. diss., Stanford University, 1960, and Raymond Moley, Jr., *The American Legion Story* (New York: Duell, Sloan and Pearce, 1966), a semiofficial account. According to David Caute, the Legion owned property worth $100 million. *The Great Fear,* 350.

44. Ketchum, "It's Up to World War II Vets," *Foreign Service* (name changed in January 1951 to *VFW Magazine*), June 1949, 18, 34.

    In 1947, the VFW had 3.2 million members (and 1 million in its women's auxiliaries), Caute, *The Great Fear,* 350. A year earlier, the Legion reported a total of 3.5 million (compared to only 1 million in 1941). No auxiliary total was given. Pencak, *For God and Country,* 319.

45. *VFW Magazine,* December 1948; January and March, 1949 (HUAC pamphlet);

October 1950 (ads). In the same period, the *American League Magazine (ALM)* ran many advertisements from national tobacco, liquor, and automobile companies. And its career-oriented ads included guides to becoming a hotel executive and a real estate agent alongside ads for courses in meat-cutting and machinery repair. William Pencak refers to the VFW before World War II as providing "a more down-to-earth alternative [to the Legion] with a similar attitude toward patriotism and veterans' benefits." Pencak, *For God and Country,* 50.

An exception was a fascinating article by Edward A. Rossit, "Why I Am a Revolutionist," *VFW Magazine*, January 1954, which advocated, much as Louis Budenz did, recapturing terms like *revolutionary, democracy, comrade,* and *people's government* from "the Red regime in the Kremlin."

46. James F. O'Neil, "How You Can Fight Communism," *ALM*, August 1948, 16–17.
47. Quotes from *ALM:* May 1949, 42; November 1951, 11; December 1949, 14–15; September 1951, 11; Karl Baarslag, "Slick Tricks of the Commies," February 1947, 19 (cancer).
48. Quotes from Pencak, *For God and Country,* 5, 10. For the only coherent definition of *Americanism,* taken from the preamble to the Legion constitution, see Moley, *American Legion Story,* 369. On the Legion's support for segregation and opposition to unions, see Pencak, ibid., 68–69; 208–34.
49. *The Firing Line: Facts for Fighting Communism,* 1 May 1953, 1.
50. *ALM,* April 1951, March 1951, July 1951. Such covers had been the norm in the late 1940s. By 1951, the magazine occasionally featured a pointedly political message: General Douglas MacArthur striking a heroic pose or angry, screeching leftists marching against the Korean War, ibid., February 1952; September 1951.
51. *ALM,* April 1951, 20–21; S. Andhil Fineberg, "They Screamed for Justice," ibid., July 1953, 22. Covers for the *VFW Magazine* had a similarly comfortable, small-town flavor, although most featured young veterans with their families.
52. Zora Neale Hurston, "I Saw Negro Votes Peddled," *ALM,* November 1950, 12–13, 54; "Why the Negro Won't Buy Communism," ibid., June 1951, 14. On her political stance at this time, see Robert E. Hemenway, *Zora Neale Hurston: A Literary Biography* (Urbana: University of Illinois Press, 1977), 328–36.

Craig also revised the Legion's former suspicion that unionists were lax about subversion: "Many younger Legionnaires are probably of the erroneous impression that this CIO housecleaning marks the first positive steps by American organized labor to do something practical and tangible about the menace of Moscow's Fifth Column in this country. Nothing could be further from the truth. Organized labor in this country has waged an unrelenting and bitter war against the bolshies almost as long as the Legion's own fight against subversion." George N. Craig, "Labor Sets an Example," *ALM,* April 1950, 14–15. For Carey's talk, see American Legion, *Proceedings of All-American Conference, New York City, January 28–29, 1950* (Indianapolis: American Legion, 1950), 21. In addition, the magazine began to run photos of black Legionnaires in this period.

53. Gray and Bernstein, *Inside Story,* 179–84, 191–206.
54. For case studies of Legion-supported vendettas, see James Truett Selcraig, *The Red Scare in the Midwest, 1945–1955: A State and Local Study* (Ann Arbor: UMI Research Press, 1982), 87–100; Charles H. McCormick, *This Nest of Vipers:*

McCarthyism and Higher Education in the Mundel Affair, 1951–52 (Urbana: University of Illinois Press, 1989); Carleton, *Red Scare!*

During the early 1950s, 110,000 Legionnaires also served as unpaid contacts for the FBI, which urged them to report on alleged threats to national security. See Athan Theoharis, "The FBI and the American Legion Contact Program, 1940–1966," *Political Science Quarterly* 100 (Summer 1985): 271–86.

55. Fred Turner, "How a Housewife Routed the Reds," *ALM,* November 1951, 25, 63.
56. Quote from Seymour M. Lipset and Earl Raab, *The Politics of Unreason,* 2nd ed. (Chicago: University of Chicago Press, 1978), 220. For a good guide to recent literature on McCarthy and McCarthyism, see Robert Griffith, *The Politics of Fear: Joseph R. McCarthy and the Senate,* 2nd ed. (Amherst: University of Massachusetts Press, 1987), ix–xxv. Griffith's own thesis is sound: "I saw in Joe McCarthy the creature of America's postwar politics, not its creator." Ibid., xi.
57. Martin Dies, *The Trojan Horse in America* (1940; reprint, New York: Arno Press, 1977), 302–3. Robert Griffith comments, "Martin Dies named more names in a single year than Joe McCarthy did in a lifetime. The membership of the Dies Committee perfected all the gambits that McCarthy would later use," *Politics of Fear,* 32. On the California legislature's committee, see *Red Fascism: Boring from Within . . . By the Subversive Forces of Communism,* compiled by Senator Jack B. Tenney (1947; reprint, New York: Arno Press, 1977 [1947]).

    For a sample of transcripts from HUAC hearings, see *Thirty Years of Treason: Excerpts from Hearings Before the House Committee on Un-American Activities, 1938–1968,* ed. Eric Bentley (New York: Viking, 1971).
58. Quotes from "Meet the Press," 2 July 1950, in Motion Picture Division, Library of Congress; Richard Rovere, *Senator Joe McCarthy* (New York: Harcourt Brace, 1959), 8.
59. On McCarthy's resemblance to the characters Cagney played, see James T. Fisher, *The Catholic Counterculture in America, 1933–1962* (Chapel Hill: University of North Carolina Press, 1989), 161. Though released in 1939, the Capra film was still the best-known example of a movie about an insurgent politician. The best biography of McCarthy is David M. Oshinsky, *A Conspiracy So Immense: The World of Joe McCarthy* (New York: Free Press, 1983).

    Fred Siegel compares McCarthy's "bold and brazen" persona to that of "the 1940s movie tough guys Humphrey Bogart and John Garfield." Though he has a point, I think Cagney and the Stewart character correspond better to McCarthy's identity as an Irishman and outsider politician. Frederick F. Siegel, *Troubled Journey: From Pearl Harbor to Ronald Reagan* (New York: Hill and Wang, 1984), 77.
60. Quotes from Griffith, *Politics of Fear,* 123; Edwin R. Bayley, *Joseph McCarthy and the Press* (Madison: University of Wisconsin Press, 1981), 126–67; *A History of Our Time: Readings on Postwar America,* 2nd ed., ed. William H. Chafe and Harvard Sitkoff (New York: Oxford University Press, 1987), 65–66; Allen J. Matusow, ed. *Joseph R. McCarthy* (Englewood Cliffs, N.J.: Prentice-Hall, 1970), 62, 56.
61. McCarthy scored his highest "favorable" to "unfavorable" rating—50 percent to 29 percent with the rest having "no opinion"—in a poll taken in late December 1953. But, at the same time, a plurality of 47 percent disapproved of his methods, and, when asked "what is the most important problem you would like to see Congress take up in the new session starting up in January?" more chose "taxes" and "the farm problem" than "Communists in the Government." *The Gallup Poll,* vol. 2,

1949–1958 (New York: Random House, 1972), 1201, 1203, 1199. For a compilation of poll data, see Michael Rogin, *The Radical Specter: The Intellectuals and McCarthy* (Cambridge: MIT Press, 1967), 232.

In a study conducted during the summer of 1954, less than 1 percent of a sample of 600 people volunteered that communism was an internal threat to the nation. Samuel A. Stouffer, *Communism, Conformity, and Civil Liberties: A Cross-section of the Nation Speaks Its Mind* (Garden City, N.Y.: Doubleday, 1955), 68.

62. Quotes by Eastman and Herberg, in Nash, *Conservative Intellectual Movement,* 111, 112.
63. McCarthy from the Wheeling speech, quoted in Chafe and Sitkoff, ed. *A History of Our Time,* 65. Sheil quoted in Saul D. Alinsky, "The Bishop and the Senator," *The Progressive,* July 1954, 4–9. On the official Catholic position see Crosby, *God, Church, and Flag,* and Vincent P. De Santis, "American Catholics and McCarthyism," *The Catholic Historical Review* 51 (April 1965): 1–30. De Santis states convincingly: "Though Catholics were split over the McCarthy issue, the greater majority of those who publicly expressed an opinion, supported the Wisconsin senator (p. 2)."
64. The Legion's silence about McCarthy continues in its two authorized histories, Moley, *The American Legion Story,* and Thomas A. Rumer, *The American Legion: An Official History, 1919–1989* (New York: M. Evans, 1990). His name is absent from the indexes of both books.
65. On the underlying strength of the Democrats, see Michael Barone, *Our Country: The Shaping of America from Roosevelt to Reagan* (New York: Free Press, 1990), 256–67. For a summary of McCarthy's support among conservative Republicans, see William B. Hixson, Jr., *Search for the American Right Wing: An Analysis of the Social Science Record, 1955–1987* (Princeton, N.J.: Princeton University Press, 92), 27–37.
66. McCarthy was also a family friend who dated one of JFK's sisters. Quoted in Whitfield, *Culture of Cold War,* 209. Professor Joshua Freeman of Columbia University assured me about the political affiliations of New York policemen.
67. Quotes from Matusow, ed., *McCarthy,* 51; *Major Speeches and Debates of Joe McCarthy, 1950–51* (New York: Gordon Press, 1975), 6, 17, 36, 66; the biographer is David M. Oshinsky, *Senator Joseph R. McCarthy and the American Labor Movement* (Columbia: University of Missouri Press, 1976), 170. On McCarthy's political clout in the 1950 election, see Griffith, *Politics of Fear,* 124–31. On his social base more generally, see Lipset and Raab, *Politics of Unreason,* 224–35; Hixson, *Search for the American Right Wing,* 3–48.
68. For insights on McCarthy's speaking style, see Vaughn Davis Bornet, "An Eyewitness Account of Senator Joseph R. McCarthy on the Hustings, San Mateo County [California], February 10, 1954," *The Pacific Historian* 29 (1985): 69–74. On the Marshall speech, see Griffith, *Politics of Fear,* 144–46. The speech was reprinted as a book, Joseph R. McCarthy, *America's Retreat from Victory* (New York: Devin-Adair, 1951).
69. Daniel C. Hallin, "Network News: We Keep America on Top of the World," in *Watching Television,* ed. Todd Gitlin (New York: Pantheon, 1986), 14–15.
70. The television statistic is taken from Bayley, *McCarthy and the Press,* 176. In 1954, the majority of American households owned a television, as compared with only 9 percent in 1950. Barone, *Our Country,* 269. For a critical analysis of the way televi-

sion "lowers politicians to the level of their audience," see Joshua Meyrowitz, *No Sense of Place: The Impact of Electronic Media on Social Behavior* (New York: Oxford University Press, 1985), 268–304.

71. These comments and those that follow are based on a viewing of four editions of the thirty-minute *Meet the Press* (2 July 1950; 3 June 1951; 25 January 1953; and 3 October 1954); two editions of the fifteen-minute *Longines Chronoscope* (November 1951 and 25 June 1952), and a variety of brief clips from Paramount newsreels from the period. *Meet the Press* can be viewed in the Motion Picture Division, Library of Congress; the other shows are in the National Archives.

72. Quotes from *Chronoscope,* November 1951; *Meet the Press,* 3 June 1951 and 25 January 1953; *Chronoscope,* 25 June 1952.

73. Both the United States Navy and Air Force were sponsors of this particular program, *Meet the Press,* 2 July 1950. Occasionally, McCarthy was also capable of slipping in a hint that he was an educated man. Once he quoted from *Macbeth. Chronoscope,* November 1951.

74. On the Army-McCarthy hearings, see Griffith, *Party of Fear,* 254–63; and the documentary film by Emile DeAntonio, *Point of Order* (1964).

75. For a summary of historical opinion on the hearings, see Oshinsky, *A Conspiracy So Immense.* For the text of Murrow's famous peroration to the *See It Now* program of March 9, 1954, see *In Search of Light: The Broadcasts of Edward R. Murrow, 1938–1961,* ed. Edward Bliss, Jr. (New York: Knopf, 1967), 247.

In the middle of November 1954, as the Senate debated the censure resolution, the Gallup Poll reported that 36 percent of respondents who had been following the proceedings were against an affirmative vote. *The Gallup Poll,* vol. II, 1289. A few weeks later, just after the Senate vote, McCarthy was fourth on the list of "most admired men"—trailing only Eisenhower, Churchill, and Adlai Stevenson and ahead of such luminaries as Douglas MacArthur and Pope Pius XII (p. 1296).

In his last appearance on *Meet the Press* on October 3, 1954, McCarthy already looked like a defeated man. He asked for sympathy for the sacrifices he had made, shook his head sadly when talking about the Communist threat, and often mumbled and repeated himself. He also seemed noticeably older and heavier than during the televised hearings of the past spring.

76. Schlamm's obituary from May 18, 1957, reprinted in Matusow, ed., *McCarthy,* 126–30.

77. On Murrow's rhetorical victory, see Robert L. Ivie, "Diffusing Cold War Demagoguery: Murrow Versus McCarthy on 'See It Now,'" in Martin J. Medhurst et al., *Cold War Rhetoric: Strategy, Metaphor, and Ideology* (Westport, Conn.: Greenwood Press, 1990), 81–101 (quote, 94). For accusations that the liberal elite did McCarthy in, see Schlamm, ibid.; Cohn, *McCarthy,* 214, 224, 248–52; Medford Evans, *The Assassination of Joe McCarthy* (Boston: Western Islands, 1970).

78. Lipset and Schneider, *Confidence Gap,* 17.

79. Daniel Bell, "Interpretations of American Politics—1955," 48–49; Richard Hofstadter, "The Pseudo-Conservative Revolt—1955," 78–79, both in Bell, ed., *The Radical Right* (rev. ed. of *The New American Right*) (Freeport, N.Y.: Books for Libraries Press, 1971 [1963]). The other contributors were Nathan Glazer and the two gentiles, Talcott Parsons and Peter Viereck, the latter the only conservative in the group (but one hostile to McCarthy).

80. On the Jewish connection, see Peter Novick, *That Noble Dream: The 'Objectivity*

Question' and the American Historical Profession (New York: Cambridge University Press, 1988), 339–41.

81. Government and corporations had begun to call on the advice of university-trained experts during the Progressive era, and the New Deal administration made extensive use of their talents. But not until the postwar era did academic intellectuals come to be regarded, and to regard themselves, as a critical part of networks of established power.

    Shils, "Intellectuals and the Center of Society in the U.S.," in Shils, *The Constitution of Society* (Chicago: University of Chicago Press, 1982), 245. The essay was first published in 1970. For a critical view of the same phenomenon, see Christopher Lasch, *The New Radicalism in America, 1889–1963: The Intellectual as a Social Type* (1965; reprint, New York: Norton, 1986), 316–18.

82. Riesman and Glazer, "The Intellectuals and the Discontented Classes—1955," in Bell, *Radical Right,* 87–113; Fiedler, "McCarthy and the Intellectuals," in *An End to Innocence: Essays on Culture and Politics* (Boston: Beacon Press, 1955), 68.

83. Influential critiques and revisions include C. Vann Woodward, "The Populist Heritage and the Intellectual," *The American Scholar* 29 (Winter 1959–1960): 55–72; Walter T. K. Nugent, *The Tolerant Populists: Kansas Populism and Nativism* (Chicago: University of Chicago Press, 1963); Norman Pollack, *The Populist Response to Industrial America* (Cambridge: Harvard University Press, 1962); Rogin, *McCarthy and the Intellectuals;* Lawrence Goodwyn, *Democratic Promise: The Populist Moment in America* (New York: Oxford University Press, 1976). For a good summary of the argument in *The New American Right,* see Hixson, *Search,* 17–26.

84. The term "civilized minority" appears in a scathing chapter of Christopher Lasch's *The True and Only Heaven: Progress and Its Critics* (New York: Norton, 1991), 412–75.

CHAPTER 8. POWER TO WHICH PEOPLE? THE TRAGEDY OF THE WHITE NEW LEFT

1. The prohibitionist crusade had been rooted in established, evangelical churches. But its agenda was much narrower than that of the New Left; the dry army wanted to reform the nation, not transform it utterly.

2. Kenneth Keniston, *Young Radicals: Notes on Committed Youth* (New York: Harcourt, Brace and World, 1968), 113.

3. Most of the funds were channeled through SDS's parent group, the League for Industrial Democracy, an offshoot of the Socialist Party. Peter Levy, "The New Left and Labor: The Early Years (1960–1963)," *Labor History* 31 (Summer 1990): 298–300; Keniston, *Young Radicals,* 113.

4. Paul Potter, "The Incredible War," speech given on April 17, 1965, at an antiwar march in Washington, D.C., sponsored by SDS, *The New Left: A Documentary History,* ed. Massimo Teodori (Indianapolis: Bobbs-Merrill, 1969), 246–48.

5. I have borrowed a few phrases in this paragraph from Maurice Isserman and Michael Kazin, "The Failure and Success of the New Radicalism," *The Rise and Fall of the New Deal Order, 1930–1980,* ed. Steve Fraser and Gary Gerstle (Princeton, N.J.: Princeton University Press, 1989), 219.

6. Mills, *The Power Elite* (New York: Oxford University Press, 1956), 343; Carl Oglesby, "Trapped in a System," in Teodori, *New Left,* 183. Radical historians at the University of Wisconsin originated the concept of "corporate liberalism." For examples of their work, see *For a New America: Essays in History and Politics from "Studies on the Left," 1959–1967,* ed. James Weinstein and David W. Eakins (New York: Vintage, 1970).
7. Todd Gitlin, "Power and the Myth of Progress," *New Republic,* 25 December 1965, 19–21.
8. Karl Marx and Friedrich Engels, "Manifesto of the Communist Party," in *Marx and Engels: Basic Writings on Politics and Philosophy,* ed. Lewis S. Feuer (Garden City, N.Y.: Anchor, 1959), 29.
9. Quoted in James Miller, *"Democracy Is in the Streets": From Port Huron to the Siege of Chicago* (New York: Simon and Schuster, 1987), 333. This book contains the full text of the statement as well as a fine discussion of the New Left as an intellectual phenomenon.
10. Ironically, Hayden had grown up in Royal Oak, Michigan, and worshiped at Father Coughlin's church—several years after the priest beat his forced retreat from politics.
11. The phrase was suggested by Mary Varela, one of the few Catholics at Port Huron—besides Hayden. Quotes from Miller, *"Democracy,"* 331, 332.
12. Miller, *"Democracy,"* 152.
13. Mills, *Power Elite,* 3.
14. C. Wright Mills, *White Collar: The American Middle Classes* (New York: Oxford University Press, 1951), 353–54; "Letter to the New Left," in Priscilla Long, ed., *The New Left: A Collection of Essays* (Boston: Porter Sargent, 1969), 22.
15. Howard Zinn, *SNCC: The New Abolitionists* (Boston: Beacon Press, 1965), 216.
16. Oglesby, "Democracy Is Nothing if Not Dangerous," 1966. SDS Papers, Microfilm edition, reel 38, no. 265. On the New Left and SNCC, see Clayborne Carson, *In Struggle: SNCC and the Black Awakening of the 1960s* (Cambridge: Harvard University Press, 1981), 175–90.
17. Quotes from Port Huron Statement in Miller, *"Democracy,"* 329; Robb Burlage, "On Being Young and Southern," c. 1962, in SDS Papers, reel 36, no. 44.
18. Tom Hayden, *Reunion: A Memoir* (New York: Random House, 1988), 53–72; Jeff Shero, "Chapter Reports: U. of Texas," in SDS Papers, reel 35, no. 19; Levy, "The New Left and Labor," 306; Peter Barbin Levy, "The New Left and Labor: A Misunderstood Relationship," Ph.D. diss., Columbia University, 1986, passim.
19. The best of an unsatisfactory lot of biographies of Bob Dylan is Robert Shelton, *No Direction Home: The Life and Music of Bob Dylan* (New York: Morrow, 1986). On his SDS appearance (in 1963), see Kirkpatrick Sale, *SDS* (New York: Random House, 1973), 106; Todd Gitlin, *The Sixties: Years of Hope, Days of Rage* (New York: Bantam, 1987), 198.
20. In 1964, Paul Potter, then president of SDS, wrote "A Letter to Young Democrats" that charged the Johnson administration with "tokenism" and proclaimed his organization's "common commitment to participatory democracy." But he also cited the arch-liberal Democrats Walter Reuther and New York City Congressman William Fitts Ryan as two of the "prominent Americans" who "supported" SDS. SDS Papers, reel 38, no. 276.

21. Hayden letter, 11 December 1961, SDS Papers, reel 1. On his involvement with the Albany movement, see Hayden, *Reunion,* 66–72.
22. The best single source on Alinsky is Sanford Horwitt's *Let Them Call Me Rebel: Saul Alinsky—His Life and Legacy* (New York: Knopf, 1989). Also see P. David Finks, *The Radical Vision of Saul Alinsky* (Ramsey, N.J.: Paulist Press, 1984), and Joan E. Lancourt, *Confront or Concede: The Alinsky Citizen-Action Organizations* (Lexington, Mass: Lexington Books, 1979).
23. Saul Alinsky, *Reveille for Radicals* (Chicago: University of Chicago Press, 1946), 25. See also 207–20.
24. Quoted in John Hall Fish, *Black Power/White Control: The Struggle of the Woodlawn Organization in Chicago* (Princeton, N.J: Princeton University Press, 1973), 27.
25. Danny Schechter, "Reveille for Reformers: Report from Syracuse," *Studies on the Left* 5 (Fall 1965): 86–87. For a later statement of this position, see Alan S. Miller, "Saul Alinsky: America's Radical Reactionary," *Radical America* 21 (January–February 1987): 11–18.
26. Quote from 1963 SDS position paper, *America and the New Era,* quoted in Sale, *SDS,* 98. For a well-argued SDS critique of federal policies, see Robb Burlage, "The 'War on Poverty': This Is War?" (1964), SDS Papers, reel 36, no. 47.
27. For a list of the projects and a rough estimate of the number of organizers, see Sale, *SDS,* 113–14, 146. A popular guide to doing radical muckraking is Jack Minnis, "The Care and Feeding of Power Structures," published in 1963 or 1964, SDS Papers, reel 38, no. 247.
28. Richard Rothstein, "JOIN Organizes City Poor," SDS Papers, reel 38, no. 298. On ERAP generally, see Sale, *SDS,* 95–115, 131–50; Wini Breines, *Community and Organization in the New Left, 1962–1968: The Great Refusal* (New York: Praeger, 1982), 123–49; Sara Evans, *Personal Politics: The Roots of Women's Liberation in the Civil Rights Movement and the New Left* (New York: Knopf, 1979), 126–55. A fascinating set of oral histories from the Chicago project is Todd Gitlin and Nanci Hollander, *Uptown: Poor Whites in Chicago* (New York: Harper and Row, 1970).
29. See the perceptive analysis in Miller, *"Democracy,"* 208–17.
30. Miller, *"Democracy,"* 216.
31. Quotes from Rothstein, "JOIN Organizes"; Miller, *"Democracy,"* 213; Evans, *Personal Politics,* 127.
32. Dorothy Perez, "The Need for JOIN," SDS Papers, reel 38, no. 271. For a discussion of how "the scholar-activist" could help remedy "the basic economic inadequacies of the American system" as well as some anxiety about erstwhile college students "invading" poor communities, see Carl Wittman, "Students and Economic Action," a pamphlet published by SDS in April 1964, Teodori, *The New Left,* 128–33.
33. Sale, *SDS,* 122–23, 479.
34. The poll, taken in October 1968 by Yankelovich, also found that more students "identified with" Che Guevara (who had been dead a year) than with any of the three major presidential candidates. Gitlin, *Sixties,* 344–45. On the underground press and the culture it both represented and fostered, see Laurence Leamer, *The Paper Revolutionaries: The Rise of the Underground Press* (New York: Simon and Schuster, 1972), and Abe Peck, *Uncovering the Sixties: The Life and Times of the Underground Press* (New York: Pantheon, 1985). For an example of campus radi-

cals who sought to merge with the counterculture, see Glenn W. Jones, "Gentle Thursday: An SDS Circus in Austin, Texas, 1966–1969," in *Sights on the Sixties,* ed. Barbara L. Tischler (New Brunswick, N.J.: Rutgers University Press, 1992), 75–85.

35. The use of mimeograph machines instead of offset printers, a matter of speed as much as penury, gave the literature a homemade, informal quality. For numerous examples, see the SDS Papers.

36. Jerry Farber, "Student as a Nigger" (1968), SDS Papers, reel 36, no. 85; *New Left Notes,* 7 August 1967, 7; "Bring the War Home" (1969), an SDS Weatherman pamphlet, reprinted in *Vandals in the Bomb Factory: The History and Literature of Students for a Democratic Society,* ed. G. Louis Heath (Metuchen, N.J.: The Scarecrow Press, 1976), 374.

37. On the sociological differences between students, see Godfrey Hodgson, *America in Our Time* (New York: Random House, 1976), 387–91.

38. Greg Calvert quoted in Sale, *SDS,* 318.

39. Mario Savio, "An End to History," in Teodori, *New Left,* 159. The most detailed guide to this remarkable local history is W. J. Rorabaugh, *Berkeley at War: The 1960s* (New York: Oxford University Press, 1989).

40. Bradley Cleveland, "A Letter to Undergraduates," in Teodori, *New Left,* 150–51.

41. The protest is remembered by Barbara Garson, *The Electronic Sweatshop: How Computers Are Transforming the Office of the Future into the Factory of the Past* (New York: Penguin, 1988), 73.

42. Malvina Reynolds's song was first recorded in 1962 (by Schroder Music Company) but remained popular in the mid-'60s. During the FSM strike, she labeled U.C. Berkeley a "robot factory." Rorabaugh, *Berkeley at War,* 29, 89, 127.

43. Rorabaugh, *Berkeley at War,* 110, 113, 121; Lou Cannon, *Reagan* (New York: Putnam, 1982), 148; Tom Hayden, *Trial* (New York: Holt, Rinehart and Winston, 1970), 160.

44. See especially Kenneth J. Heineman, *Campus Wars: The Peace Movement at American State Universities in the Vietnam Era* (New York: New York University Press, 1993). For the impact of pacifism on the New Left of the late 1960s, see Maurice Isserman, "You Don't Need a Weatherman but a Postman Can Be Helpful," in *Give Peace a Chance: Exploring the Vietnam Antiwar Movement,* ed. Melvin Small and William D. Hoover (Syracuse, N.Y.: Syracuse University Press, 1992), 22–34.

45. Quotes from Heineman, *Campus Wars,* 37, 120.

46. Heineman, *Campus Wars,* 177, 226–28.

47. Charles DeBenedetti with Charles Chatfield, *An American Ordeal: The Antiwar Movement of the Vietnam Era* (Syracuse, N.Y.: Syracuse University Press, 1990), 280.

48. For details on the movement, the best sources are Nancy Zaroulis and Gerald Sullivan, *Who Spoke Up? American Protest Against the War in Vietnam, 1963–1975* (Garden City, N.Y.: Doubleday, 1984); DeBenedetti with Chatfield, *American Ordeal;* Tom Wells, *The War Within: America's Battle over Vietnam* (Berkeley: University of California Press, 1994).

49. For abundant details, see Rosalind Urbach Moss, "'Tangled in the Stars and Covered with the Stripes': Symbolic Struggles over Flag Use and National Direction in the 1960s," unpublished manuscript. Thanks to Cecilia O'Leary for lending me a copy.

50. SNCC had a slogan with the same message: "One Man, One Vote—Mississippi, Vietnam." And one of the favorite radical arguments against the war was that the United States had refused, in 1956, to allow the Vietnamese to hold a free election because, according to none other than Dwight David Eisenhower, Ho Chi Minh would have won.
51. On Oglesby's background, see Sale, *SDS,* 195–96; Gitlin, *The Sixties,* 258–59; Jack Newfield, *A Prophetic Minority* (New York: New American Library, 1966), 89–90; Heineman, *Campus Wars,* 114–16; Joan Morrison and Robert K. Morrison, *From Camelot to Kent State* (New York: Times Books, 1987), 297–99.
52. Carl Oglesby, "Trapped in a System," in Teodori, *New Left,* 182.
53. Ibid., 183, 184, 187.
54. Julius Lester, "Aquarian Notebook," *Liberation,* July 1970, 34.
55. The indispensable study of this process is Todd Gitlin, *The Whole World Is Watching: Mass Media in the Making and Unmaking of the New Left* (Berkeley: University of California Press, 1980).
56. Abbie Hoffman, "A Brief History of Student Activism (1987)," *The Best of Abbie Hoffman* (New York: Four Walls, Eight Windows, 1989), 398.
57. See Carl Davidson, "Has SDS Gone to Pot?" *New Left Notes,* 3 February 1967, 4; Sale, *SDS,* 279–97; Gitlin, *The Sixties,* 186.
58. "Ballad of a Thin Man," in Bob Dylan, *Lyrics, 1962–1985* (New York: Knopf, 1985), 198. On the Panther connection, see *The Movement Toward a New America,* ed. Mitchell Goodman (Philadelphia: Pilgrim Press, 1970), 129.
59. Abbie Hoffman, *Woodstock Nation* (New York: Random House, 1969), 124–25. On television imagery in the late '60s, see Gitlin, *Whole World Is Watching.*

Describing one large antiwar demonstration, the radical journalist Dotson Rader rhapsodized, "It is a kind of theatre, with banners and songs and ritualistic language, a moment unto itself creating the illusion of power, absolutist, making the unreal, the wished-for, seem within reach. It is a place where one can say things and mean them which one could never speak anywhere else." Quoted in Breines, *Great Refusal,* 32.

60. Quoted in Heineman, *Campus Wars,* 89.
61. Johnny Appleseed, *The Little Red White and Blue Book* (Chicago: n.p., 1969). My impression of the booklet's reception comes from discussions I had with fellow activists at the time.
62. Sale, *SDS,* 319–20.
63. "The Movement: We've Got to Reach Our Own People," November 1967, in Teodori, *The New Left,* 303–9. For a similar proposal written by two ERAP veterans, see Rennie Davis and Tom Hayden, "Movement Campaign 1968," SDS Papers, reel 36, no. 67; Miller, *"Democracy,"* 284–85.
64. DeBenedetti and Chatfield, *American Ordeal,* 309–10. For photographs of the event and accompanying oral testimony, see John Kerry and Vietnam Veterans Against the War, *The New Soldier,* ed. David Thorne and George Butler (New York: Collier, 1971). There is little written about the GI movement. The only full-length study is by an activist—David Cortright, *Soldiers in Revolt: The American Military Today* (Garden City, N.Y.: Anchor Press, 1975).
65. Christian Appy, *Working-Class War: American Combat Soldiers and Vietnam* (Chapel Hill: University of North Carolina Press, 1993), 25, 51.
66. *Dopin' Dan,* April 1972 (Berkeley: Last Gasp Eco-Funnies). On the culture of dis-

senting GIs, see Steve Rees, "A Questioning Spirit: GI's Against the War," in *They Should Have Served That Cup of Coffee,* ed. Dick Cluster (Boston: South End Press, 1979), 148–79. On the scale of resistance in the military, see Cortright, *Soldiers in Revolt, and* Lawrence M. Baskir and William A. Strauss, *Chance and Circumstance: The Draft, the War, and the Vietnam Generation* (New York: Knopf, 1978), 109–66.

67. Appy, *Working-Class War,* 217, 223.
68. National Mobilization Committee, "A Message to GIs and to the Movement," in Teodori, *New Left,* 315. For a perceptive discussion of GI attitudes toward the New Left and the war, see John McDermott, "Thoughts on the Movement" (September 1967), SDS Papers, reel 38, no. 223.
69. For a detailed discussion of the "normalization of dissent" in the late '60s and early '70s, see DeBenedetti with Chatfield, *American Ordeal,* 238–347.
70. Quotes from *RFK: Collected Speeches,* ed. Edwin O. Guthman and C. Richard Allen (New York: Viking, 1993), 299, 325, 326.
71. Miller, *"Democracy,"* 287–88, 293–94.
72. Elinor Langer, "Notes for Next Time: A Memoir of the 1960s," *Working Papers for a New Society* 1 (Fall 1973): 62.
73. Marge Piercy, "The Grand Coolie Damn," *Sisterhood Is Powerful: An Anthology of Writings from the Women's Liberation Movement,* ed. Robin Morgan (New York: Random House, 1970), 481.
74. For numerous examples, see Alice Echols, *Daring to Be Bad: Radical Feminism in America, 1967–1975* (Minneapolis: University of Minnesota Press, 1989).
75. The Progressive Labor Party (PLP) was the most significant exponent of this view. For an example of PLP rhetoric, see "Cambridge Vote on Vietnam," April 1967, SDS Papers, reel 36, no. 50.
76. For a parallel argument that focuses on the libertarian aspect of the New Left, see E. J. Dionne, *Why Americans Hate Politics: The Death of the Democratic Process* (New York: Simon and Schuster, 1991), 31–54.

CHAPTER 9. STAND UP FOR THE WORKING MAN: GEORGE WALLACE AND THE MAKING OF A NEW RIGHT

1. Quoted in Robert Coles and Jon Erikson, *The Middle Americans: Proud and Uncertain* (Boston: Little, Brown, 1971), 7. For a fine discussion of what she calls "The Discovery of the Working Class," see Barbara Ehrenreich, *Fear of Falling: The Inner Life of the Middle Class* (New York: Pantheon, 1989), 97–143.
2. Dick Sinnott quoted in Ronald P. Formisano, *Boston Against Busing: Race, Class, and Ethnicity in the 1960s and 1970s* (Chapel Hill: University of North Carolina Press, 1991), 189. Formisano describes Sinnott, whose column appeared in several local newspapers, as "the most popular print spokesman of the antibusing legions," 187.
3. A fine study of this estrangement is Richard Sennett and Jonathan Cobb, *The Hidden Injuries of Class* (New York: Vintage, 1972).
4. The machinist union head P. L. Siemiller, quoted in Seymour Martin Lipset and Earl Raab, *The Politics of Unreason,* 2nd ed. (Chicago: University of Chicago

Press, 1978), 363. For the AFL-CIO's position on ethnic and racial divisions, see George Meany, "New Dimensions for Labor's Urban Ethnic Priorities," in *Pieces of a Dream: The Ethnic Worker's Crisis with America,* ed. Michael Wenk et al. (New York: Center for Migration Studies, 1972), 205–12.

5. Seymour Martin Lipset and Earl Raab comment perceptively that the Birch Society ran into the same dilemma faced by earlier conspiracy theorists (such as Coughlin and McCarthy): "how to identify a corps of conspirators who are esoteric and mysterious enough to make their comprehensive power credible and yet concrete enough to make their existence visible to a mass audience. In a way, the very enthusiasm and vastness of Welch's conspiracy theory compound this problem." Lipset and Raab, *Politics of Unreason,* 251–52.
6. The speech is reprinted in Barry M. Goldwater, *Where I Stand* (New York: McGraw-Hill, 1964). It was largely drafted by Henry Jaffa, a scholarly disciple of Leo Strauss, a political theorist who taught adherence to constitutional principles informed by classical Greek philosophy.
7. The Sharon Statement is reprinted (with commentary) in William Rusher, *The Rise of the Right* (New York: Morrow, 1984), 90–91. On Buckley, see John B. Judis, *William F. Buckley, Jr.: Patron Saint of the Conservatives* (New York: Simon and Schuster, 1988), quote, 228.
8. Goldwater quoted in Philip A. Klinker, "Race and the Republican Party: The Rise of the Southern Strategy in the Republican National Committee, 1960–1964," Paper delivered at the 1992 convention of the American Political Science Association. I am grateful to Tom Sugrue for sending me a copy.
9. Smith quoted in Glenn Jeansonne, *Gerald L. K. Smith: Minister of Hate* (New Haven: Yale University Press, 1988), 166. On the pivotal nature of the 1964 results, see Thomas Byrne Edsall and Mary D. Edsall, *Chain Reaction: The Impact of Race, Rights, and Taxes on American Politics* (New York: Norton, 1991), 32–46. On Goldwater's record on race, see Michael W. Miles, *The Odyssey of the American Right* (New York: Oxford University Press, 1980), 289.
10. An excellent analysis of this shift is Gary Gerstle, "Working-Class Racism: Broaden the Focus," *International Labor and Working-Class History* 44 (Fall 1993): 33–40.
11. Thomas Sugrue, "Crabgrassroots Politics: Race, Home Ownership and the Fragmentation of the New Deal Coalition in the Urban North, 1940–1960," unpublished paper, in author's possession, p. 25; Arnold R. Hirsch, *Making the Second Ghetto: Race and Housing in Chicago, 1940–1960* (New York: Cambridge University Press, 1983). On protests against open housing in the 1960s see, for Philadelphia, Peter Binzen, *Whitetown, U.S.A.* (New York: Random House, 1970); and for Chicago, Ralph, *Northern Protest,* especially 124–30. In 1964, California voters repealed an open housing law by a wide margin.
12. Iver Bernstein, *The New York City Draft Riots: Their Significance for American Society and Politics in the Age of the Civil War* (New York: Oxford University Press, 1990), 17–42.
13. See Chapter 2, note 41.
14. T. Harry Williams, *Huey Long: A Biography* (New York: Knopf, 1969), 182; Chester M. Morgan, *Redneck Liberal: Theodore G. Bilbo and the New Deal* (Baton Rouge: Louisiana State University Press, 1985), 89; Carl Grafton and Anne Permaloff, *Big Mules and Branchheads: James E. Folsom and Political Power in*

Alabama (Athens: University of Georgia Press, 1985), 61. Bilbo had an acute sense of the class resentments of his audience. "Never speak to a Rotary club," he advised, "you speak to twenty on the inside and a hundred on the outside looking in are against you for being with the twenty." Morgan, *Redneck Liberal,* 17.

15. Quoted in David Alan Horowitz, "White Southerners' Alienation and Civil Rights: The Response to Corporate Liberalism, 1956–1965," *Journal of Southern History* 54 (May 1988): 178.
16. Grafton and Permaloff, *Big Mules,* 111, 201. Also see George E. Sims, *The Little Man's Big Friend: James E. Folsom in Alabama Politics, 1946–1958* (University: University of Alabama Press, 1985).
17. Bill Jones, *The Wallace Story* (Northport, Ala.: American Southern Publishing Co., 1966), 19. There are two serious, book-length biographies of Wallace, both by talented journalists: Marshall Frady, *Wallace* (New York: New American Library, 1968), and Stephan Lesher, *George Wallace: American Populist* (Reading, Mass.: Addison-Wesley, 1994). Professor Dan T. Carter of Emory University is completing the first scholarly biography. A sanitized, ghostwritten autobiography is George C. Wallace, *Stand Up for America* (Garden City, N.Y.: Doubleday, 1976).
18. Frady, *Wallace,* 53. Before her marriage, Wallace's mother, Betsy, gave lessons in classical piano.
19. Frady, *Wallace,* 82, 83.
20. Sims, *Little Man's Big Friend,* 63; Frady, *Wallace,* 104–5; interview with Dan T. Carter, *U.S. News and World Report,* 4 November 1991, 24; Dan T. Carter, personal correspondence, 13 June 1993.
21. Truman wasn't even listed on the Alabama ballot in 1948. Marshall Frady, "The American Independent Party," in *History of U.S. Political Parties,* vol. IV, 1945–1972, ed. Arthur M. Schlesinger, Jr. (New York: Chelsea House, 1973), 3433–34. At the 1948 convention, Wallace cast his vice-presidential ballot for Georgia Senator Richard Russell. Comparing Russell to William Jennings Bryan, Wallace said, "it gives me great pleasure to place in nomination . . . the man who will see that the South will not be crucified upon the cross of so-called civil rights." *Proceedings of Democratic Convention, 1948* (Washington, 1948), 280–81.
22. Sims, *Little Man's Big Friend,* 207–8; Philip Crass, *The Wallace Factor* (New York: Mason/Charter, 1976), 48–49. According to a biographer, Judge Wallace did deal fairly with individual black plaintiffs and defendants. Lesher, *George Wallace,* 92–96.
23. Patterson drew many sympathy votes due to his father's (and predecessor's) murder by a professional hit man.

    Quotes from *Birmingham News,* 22 April 1958, 7; 25 April 1958, 4; 2 May 1958, 1; 21 May 1958; Frady, *Wallace,* 124. In the runoff election, Wallace received the endorsement of most of the state's newspapers, including the establishment voices—the *News* and *Montgomery Advertiser.*
24. *Montgomery Advertiser,* 28 April 1962, 1; 27 April 1962, 1; 1 May 1962, 1; Grafton and Permaloff, *Big Mules,* 233. In order to head off Folsom, both the *Advertiser* and *Birmingham News* again endorsed Wallace.
25. Quoted in Lesher, *George Wallace,* 142.
26. Dan T. Carter has revealed that the inaugural address was secretly written by Asa Earl Carter, a prominent Klansman. More recently, Asa Carter (under the name Forrest Carter) published the best-selling novel *The Education of Little Tree.* I owe the

Saint George metaphor to Francis M. Wilhoit, *The Politics of Massive Resistance* (New York: G. Braziller, 1973), 87.

27. Wilhoit, *Politics of Massive Resistance,* 87–88; Taylor Branch, *Parting the Waters: America in the King Years, 1954–63* (New York: Simon and Schuster, 1988), 821–22. For a narrative history of the 1963 events and their background see E. Culpepper Clark, *The Schoolhouse Door: Segregation's Last Stand at the University of Alabama* (New York: Oxford University Press, 1993). For glimpses of Wallace at his first inauguration and in the confrontation with Katzenbach, see the widely available *Video Encyclopedia of the 20th Century* (CEL Educational Resources, 1986), disk 24, side B.
28. Quotes from Frady, *Wallace,* 173–75; Lesher, *George Wallace,* 271. The number of poll respondents answering in the affirmative ranged between 40 and 50 percent of the national total, but the figure was not broken down by race. If one assumes that nearly all blacks disagreed, then the percentage of whites who responded "too fast" was undoubtedly *over* 50 percent. The same polls registered even greater opposition to civil rights demonstrations, although a slim majority favored the civil rights *bill* then under consideration by Congress. For polls taken in the summer and fall of 1963, see *The Gallup Poll,* vol. 3, 1959–1971 (New York: Random House, 1972), 1828, 1832, 1836, 1838, 1844, 1852.
29. *Meet the Press,* 2 June 1963, videotape, Motion Picture and Broadcasting Division, Library of Congress; Jones, *Wallace Story,* 94. William Rusher recounts that on a television panel he shared with the Alabama governor (he gives no date), "I saw Wallace stare and point directly into a television camera—a highly professional (and thoroughly unnatural) thing to do—and tell viewers, 'This isn't Alabama's problem. It's *your* problem, and the federal government will be running your lives before long unless it's stopped.'" Rusher, *Rise of the Right,* 217.
30. Jones, *The Wallace Story,* 216–17. On the primary results, see Lipset and Raab, *Politics of Unreason,* 358–59; C. T. Husbands, "The Campaign Organizations and Patterns of Popular Support of George C. Wallace in Wisconsin and Indiana in 1964 and 1968," Ph.D. diss., University of Chicago, 1972, 48–60 and passim.
31. Quoted in Edsall and Edsall, *Chain Reaction,* 78.
32. A point suggested to me by Tom Sugrue, personal correspondence.
33. From *Meet the Press,* 30 June 1968, Recorded Sound Division, Library of Congress.
34. Introduction to Wallace address, National Press Club, 7 October 1968, Recorded Sound Division, Library of Congress; Edsall and Edsall, *Chain Reaction,* 77. Wallace had begun to recite a similar litany in the early 1950s when he was a state legislator. In 1951, he opposed a sales tax because "the lathe operators, the brick masons, the welders, the tool and die workers . . . the little man" would bear its burden. Quoted in Lesher, *George Wallace,* 85.
35. James Jackson Kilpatrick, "What Makes Wallace Run?" *National Review,* April 18, 1967, 400.
36. Wallace, *"Hear Me Out,"* 62; Lesher, *George Wallace,* 395; Paul DiMaggio, Richard A. Peterson, and Jack Esco, Jr., "Country Music: Ballad of the Silent Majority," in *The Sounds of Social Change,* ed. R. Serge Denisoff and Richard A. Peterson (Chicago: Rand McNally, 1972), 38–55; Bill C. Malone, *Country Music, U.S.A.,* rev. ed. (Austin: University of Texas Press, 1985), 318.
37. The David Levine drawing that illustrates the essay depicts Wallace as a mad dog

with a swastika carved into his chin. Elizabeth Hardwick, "Mr. America," *New York Review of Books,* November 7, 1968, 3.

38. Quoted by Jack Nelson of the *Los Angeles Times* in *George Wallace: A Rebel and His Cause,* ed. Patricia Sachs (New York: Universal, 1968), 35.

39. For praise of the police in this fashion, see Wallace's speech at Madison Square Garden, 24 October 1968, reprinted as an appendix to Frady, "American Independent Party," 3491–97. Such language reaped a direct benefit. In the 1968 election, large numbers of police officers and their unions supported Wallace. Lipset and Raab, *Politics of Unreason,* 365–67; quotes, ibid., 356–57.

For an analysis of the British style of "authoritarian populism" that targeted the welfare state and trade union power during the late 1970s, see Stuart Hall, "Moving Right," *Socialist Review* 11 (January–February 1981), 113–37.

40. Frank S. Meyer, "The Populism of George Wallace" (*National Review,* May 1967), reprinted in Meyer, *The Conservative Mainstream* (New Rochelle, N.Y.: Arlington House, 1969), 285–86; Judis, *Buckley,* 283–87. For a more positive view, see Kilpatrick, "What Makes Wallace Run?" In the fall of 1968, a poll taken by *Human Events* of over a hundred prominent conservatives recorded an overwhelming distaste for Wallace. Lipset and Raab, *Politics of Unreason,* 348.

41. In Pennsylvania, a Bircher named Frank Gaydosh ran an independent campaign for the United States Senate in 1968 under the slogan, "Wallace Cannot Do It Alone!" *South Philadelphia Review-Chronicle,* 31 October 1968. Thanks to Tom Sugrue for sending me this clipping.

On the Wallace movement, see Jody C. Carlson, *George C. Wallace and the Politics of Powerlessness: The Wallace Campaigns for the Presidency, 1964–1976* (New Brunswick, N.J.: Transaction, 1981), 72–77; Husbands, "Campaign Organizations," 143, 151, 153; Frank P. Mintz, *The Liberty Lobby and the American Right: Race, Conspiracy, and Culture* (Westport, Conn.: Greenwood Press, 1985), 94–98, 129; Crass, *The Wallace Factor,* 161–64; Lipset and Raab, *Politics of Unreason,* 351–58; Hixson, *Search for the American Right Wing,* 116–18.

42. Susan L. M. Huck, "Mr. Wallace: A Hard Look at the Candidate," *American Opinion,* September 1968, 25. For similar rhetoric from a remnant of the anti-Semitic Right, see "Wallace in '68?" *American Mercury,* 3. For the persistence of the original Birch Society rhetoric for recruitment purposes, see G. Edward Griffin, "This Is the John Birch Society: An Invitation to Membership" (Thousand Oaks, Calif.: American Media, 1970).

43. The AIP did issue a detailed platform, evidently written by several of Wallace's Alabama associates. It claimed to treat "those matters of deepest concern to the average American, his home, his family, his property, his employment, his right to freedom from interference and harassment from and by the government at all levels and, lastly, his pride in himself and his nation and all that it has stood for." But it was not widely circulated. Reproduced in Frady, "American Independent Party," 3447–76.

44. These and the following details of Wallace's 1968 campaign are drawn largely from the relevant sections of Carlson, *Politics of Powerlessness;* Theodore White, *The Making of the President 1968* (New York: Atheneum, 1969); Garry Wills, *Nixon Agonistes: The Crisis of the Self-Made Man* (Boston: Houghton Mifflin, 1970); Lesher, *George Wallace,* and especially Lewis Chester, Godfrey Hodgson, and Bruce Page, *An American Melodrama: The Presidential Campaign of 1968* (New York: Viking, 1969).

45. Wills, *Nixon Agonistes,* 49.
46. Wills, *Nixon Agonistes,* 50. To avoid caricaturing a particular speech pattern, I have altered Wills's rendering of the quotes in Southern idiom—"You jes' cum up t' the platform," for example.
47. Wills, *Nixon Agonistes,* 50–51; Carlson, *Politics of Powerlessness,* 131, 128.
48. Video Encyclopedia, disk 21, side A; Carlson, *Politics of Powerlessness,* 129–30.
49. Wallace was doing best among men, people in their twenties, residents of small towns, farmers and manual workers, Protestants, high school graduates, and, of course, white Southerners. *Gallup Poll,* vol. 3, 2162–64, 2166.
50. Hixson, *Search for the American Right Wing,* 150. Wallace would have preferred to select the affable A. B. (Happy) Chandler, a former governor and senator from Kentucky, who had once been the commissioner of major league baseball. But Chandler supported integration, and Wallace did not want to dilute electoral appeal. Chester et al., *American Melodrama,* 699; Michael Barone, *Our Country: The Shaping of America from Roosevelt to Reagan* (New York: Free Press, 1990), 450; Lesher, *George Wallace,* 424.
51. This discrepancy was obviously affected by the weakness of unions in the South. Lipset and Raab, *Politics of Unreason,* table, 380–81. For the official labor onslaught, see "Memo from COPE: George Wallace's Alabama"; "Homefront," September 1968; and other anti-Wallace materials in the folder "Politics—1968 Election," Civil Rights Papers, George Meany Memorial Archives. In one congressional district in suburban Detroit, a majority of AIP activists were blue-collar workers and union members. James Lewis Canfield, *A Case of Third Party Activism: The George Wallace Campaign Worker and the American Independent Party* (Lanham, Md.: University Press of America, 1984), 26–27.
52. Interpretations of Wallace's vote in 1968 are summarized well in Hixson, *Search for the American Right Wing,* 124–51. For statistical breakdowns by demographic group and issue preference, see Lipset and Raab, *Politics of Unreason,* 278–427.

CHAPTER 10. THE CONSERVATIVE CAPTURE: FROM NIXON TO REAGAN

1. Jonathan Rieder, *Canarsie: The Jews and Italians of Brooklyn Against Liberalism* (Cambridge: Harvard University Press, 1985), 6.
2. For an excellent case study of this shift in consciousness, see David Halle, *America's Working Man: Work, Home, and Politics Among Blue-Collar Property Owners* (Chicago: University of Chicago Press, 1984).
3. Aubrey Garrison of Shades Mountain Independence Church, quoted in Rebecca Klatch, *Women of the New Right* (Philadelphia: Temple University Press, 1987), 88–89.
4. Reverend Bailey Smith, past president of the Southern Baptist Convention, quoted in David Bennett, *The Party of Fear* (Chapel Hill: University of North Carolina Press, 1988), 388.
5. See the argument in Jerome L. Himmelstein, *To the Right: The Transformation of American Conservatism* (Berkeley: University of California Press, 1990), and the

evidence in John S. Saloma, *Ominous Politics: The New Conservative Labyrinth* (New York: Hill and Wang, 1984), and Sidney Blumenthal, *The Rise of the Counter-Establishment: From Conservative Ideology to Political Power* (New York: Times Books, 1987).

6. Lou Cannon, *Reagan* (New York: Putnam, 1982), 112–15; Garry Wills, *Reagan's America* (New York: Doubleday, 1987), 293–98.
7. Quoted in Alonzo Hamby, *Liberalism and Its Challengers: F.D.R. to Reagan* (New York: Oxford University Press, 1985), 290.
8. Nixon quoted in Herbert S. Parmet, "History, Historians, and Richard Nixon," *thesis* (journal published by Graduate School of City University of New York), Spring 1991, 11 (on Hiss); Hamby, *Liberalism,* 326. The best source on Nixon's beginnings is Roger Morris, *Richard Milhous Nixon: The Rise of an American Politician* (New York: Holt, 1990).
9. On Nixon's acceptance speech, see Lewis Chester et al., *An American Melodrama: The Presidential Campaign of 1968* (New York: Random House, 1969), 496–99. On the language of the campaign, see ibid., passim; Wills, *Nixon Agonistes,* 69, 71 (quotes) and passim; Buchanan, *Right from the Beginning,* 321. For a best-selling critique of the campaign's commercials (which seem quite mild in contrast with those of the 1980s and 1990s), see Joe McGinniss, *The Selling of the President, 1968* (New York: Trident, 1969).
10. Quote from Chester et al., *American Melodrama,* 496.
11. License plate in File 71913, Political History Collection, National Museum of American History. The short-lived Reagan presidential campaign that year used similar rhetoric about the need "to speak up for the aspirations of the taxpayers and home owners." M. Stanton Evans, *The Reason for Reagan* (La Jolla, Calif.: La Jolla Rancho Press, 1968), 10.
12. Nixon from 1968 television interview in Charlotte, North Carolina. Quoted in Edsall and Edsall, *Chain Reaction,* 76. For a similar statement in 1970, see Theodore White, *The Making of the President, 1972* (New York: Atheneum, 1973), 240. Jonathan Rieder, "The Rise of the 'Silent Majority,'" *The Rise and Fall of the New Deal Order, 1930–1980* (Princeton, N.J.: Princeton University Press, 1989), 261.
13. Phillips quoted in Wills, *Nixon Agonistes,* 265. The personal story is taken from my interview with him, 14 June 1989, Bethesda, Maryland. The fullest explanations of his argument can be found in his *The Emerging Republican Majority* (New Rochelle, N.Y.: Arlington House, 1969) and his neglected *Mediacracy: American Parties and Politics in the Communications Age* (Garden City, N.Y.: Doubleday, 1975). The parties that articulated their populism successfully, argued Phillips, were the Democrat-Republicans of Jefferson, the Democrats of Andrew Jackson, and the Democrats under FDR. Republicans from the Gilded Age through the 1920s were the only exception; the legacy of the Civil War and then the internally divisive candidacy of William Jennings Bryan explained that (rather large) discrepancy.
14. Phillips, *Emerging Republican Majority,* 37, 38; Wills, *Nixon Agonistes,* 266. Phillips's forecasts were prescient, if sometimes hyperbolic. He told Garry Wills during the 1968 campaign: "When Hubie loses, [Eugene] McCarthy and [Allard] Lowenstein backers are going to take the party so far to the Left they'll just become irrelevant. They'll do to it what our economic royalists did to us in 1936." But three

years later, he worried that Nixon was forsaking the fans of country and "white ethnic" music for the cultural avant-garde, a shift that might endanger his re-election. Wills, p. 269; Phillips, "Revolutionary Music," *Washington Post,* 6 May 1971, A19.

15. James Reichley, "Elm Street's New White House Power," *Fortune,* December 1969, 72.
16. One old conservative now talking like a populist was Frank Meyer. In early 1970, he wrote in *National Review* that the "vast 'producing majority' of Americans . . . were generating the developing revolutionary upsurge" against the liberal establishment. Quoted in George Nash, *Conservative Intellectuals,* 297. For the Nixon record, see A. James Reichley, *Conservatives in an Age of Change: The Nixon and Ford Administrations* (Washington, D.C.: The Brookings Institution, 1981), 1–261.
17. Spiro Agnew, speech of 13 November 1969, Des Moines, Iowa, at Midwest Regional Republican Committee Meeting, in John R. Coyne, Jr., *The Impudent Snobs: Agnew vs. the Intellectual Establishment* (New Rochelle, N.Y.: Arlington House, 1972), 268.
18. Patrick J. Buchanan, *The New Majority: President Nixon at Mid-Passage* (Philadelphia: Girard Bank, 1973), 22; Stephen E. Ambrose, *Nixon: Volume Two—The Triumph of a Politician, 1962–1972* (New York: Simon and Schuster, 1989), 310.
19. Nixon had just been defeated in a race for governor of California. Quoted in Ambrose, *Nixon,* vol. 2, 11.
20. Patrick J. Buchanan, *Right from the Beginning* (Boston: Little, Brown, 1988), 89–99. In 1972, Buchanan, who was born and raised in Washington, D.C., told Theodore White: "This hasn't been our town. They [the media, the bureaucrats, and the Supreme Court] live in Georgetown, with their parties; they never invited us, they ignored us. We were the vanguard of Middle America, and they were the liberal elite," quoted in White, *Making of the President, 1972,* 233.
21. Victor Gold, quoted in White, *Making of the President, 1972,* 233.
22. The term "new class" was borrowed from an earlier analysis of Stalinism made by independent socialists. For a discussion of its uses, see B. Bruce Briggs, ed., *The New Class?* (New Brunswick, N.J.: Transaction, 1979). On the craft of White House public relations, see Michael Kelly, "David Gergen, Master of the Game," *New York Times Magazine,* 31 October 1993, 62. On the long history of political merchandising techniques, see Robert B. Westbrook, "Politics as Consumption: Managing the Modern American Election," in *The Culture of Consumption: Critical Essays in American History, 1880–1980,* ed. Richard W. Fox and T. J. Jackson Lears (New York: Pantheon, 1983), 143–73.
23. Reichley, "Elm Street's New White House Power," 120, 122.
24. Adapting a trope from the world of mass entertainment, the presidential adviser John Erlichman used to ask of a particular Nixon speech or administration policy, "Will it play in Peoria?"
25. "Man and Woman of the Year," *Time,* 5 January 1970, 10–17.
26. Nixon quoted in Tom Wicker, *One of Us: Richard Nixon and the American Dream* (New York: Random House, 1991), 632. On the roots of the workers' actions, see Joshua B. Freeman, "Hardhats: Construction Workers, Manliness, and the 1970 Pro-War Demonstrations," *Journal of Social History* 26 (Summer 1993): 725–44. I saw the hard-hat buttons being sold at a pro-Nixon demonstration to "Honor America," held in Washington, D.C., on 4 July 1970.
27. Barone, *Our Country,* 483. Also see Himmelstein, *To the Right,* 71–72.

28. Lipset and Raab, *Politics of Unreason,* 522; *The Gallup Poll,* vol. 3, *1959–1971* (New York: Random House, 1972), 2209, 2238, 2296, 2335.
29. That fall, Schmitz, who was ignored by the media and ran only a minimal campaign, received about a million votes—one-tenth of Wallace's total in 1968 but still evidence of the hunger for an alternative right-wing politics.
30. Jack Bass and Walter DeVries, *The Transformation of Southern Politics: Social Change and Political Consequence Since 1945* (New York: Basic Books, 1976), 68; Video Encyclopedia, disk 38, side A; "800 Hear Wallace," *The Wallace Stand,* July 1971, 3. Except for the candidate's speeches, all copy in the campaign paper was written by the Montgomery journalist Joe Azbell. Carlson, *Politics of Powerlessness,* 139. On the 1972 campaign, see Lesher, *George Wallace,* 452–91.

    Running for governor in 1970, Wallace had vented his last public gasp of Jim Crow rhetoric. He published an ad that accused his main opponent (and former ally), Albert Brewer, of forming a "Spotted Alliance" of "Negroes and Their White Friends" and warned that it might be "Your Last Chance" to "save Alabama as we know Alabama." Quoted in Bass and DeVries, *Transformation,* 65.
31. Quoted by Garry Wills in an essay on Wallace published in March 1972. Wills, *Lead Time: A Journalist's Education* (Garden City, N.Y.: Doubleday, 1983), 146.
32. Michael Barone comments on the irony of this image as applied to the 1972 nominees: "McGovern, despite his flat midwestern accent, his corny manner, and his five children, clearly was seen as part of the adversary culture. Nixon, though he had lived at the sophisticated pinnacles of American public life for more than twenty years, seemed plainly Middle American in his sympathies." Barone, *Our Country,* 508. Nixon memo quoted in David Farber, "The Silent Majority and Talk About Revolution," in *The Sixties: From Memory to History,* ed. David Farber (Chapel Hill: University of North Carolina Press, 1994), 309.
33. Paddy Chayefsky wrote the screenplay for *Network.* Twenty years earlier, he wrote television dramas like *Marty,* which used naturalistic dialogue to illuminate, in his words, the "marvelous world of the ordinary." Quoted in Eric Barnouw, *Tube of Plenty: The Evolution of American Television,* 2nd rev. ed. (New York: Oxford University Press, 1990), 163.
34. To avoid confusion, I use *evangelical* as an umbrella term to encompass groups who sometimes disagreed with each other on theological grounds but spoke a similar language of politics in the 1970s and 1980s: fundamentalists, charismatics, pentecostals, and those who simply labeled themselves evangelicals. On the differences, see Robert Wuthnow, *The Restructuring of American Religion: Society and Faith Since World War II* (Princeton, N.J.: Princeton University Press, 1988), esp. 173–214; James Davison Hunter, *Culture Wars: The Struggle to Define America* (New York: Basic Books, 1991). On trends in church membership, see Dean M. Kelley, *Why Conservative Churches Are Growing: A Study in the Sociology of Religion* (San Francisco: Harper and Row, 1977).
35. Howard Phillips of the Conservative Caucus was a rare Jewish leader of the traditionalist Right.
36. Hunter, *Culture Wars,* 202. For a description and affirmation of the spiritual common ground, see Burton Yale Pines, *Back to Basics: The Traditionalist Movement That Is Sweeping Grass-Roots America* (New York: Morrow, 1982), 183–208.
37. Paul M. Weyrich, "Blue Collar or Blue Blood? The New Right Compared with

The Old Right," in *The New Right Papers,* ed. Robert Whitaker (New York: St. Martin's, 1982), 53.

38. Robert Wiebe, *The Search for Order, 1877–1920* (New York: Hill and Wang, 1967), 84. For a similar statement from Paul Weyrich, see Gillian Peale, *Revival and Reaction: The Right in Contemporary America* (Oxford: Clarendon Press, 1984), 66.
39. From a recording arranged by the Reverend Avis Hill. Used with permission. Quoted in James Moffett, *Storm in the Mountains: A Case Study of Censorship, Conflict, and Consciousness* (Carbondale: Southern Illinois University Press, 1988), 48. Notwithstanding such rhetoric, the protesters were part of a coalition that included the well-financed Businessman and Professional People's Alliance for Better Textbooks. Ann L. Page and Donald A. Clelland, "The Kanawha County Textbook Controversy: A Study of the Politics of Life Style Concern," *Social Forces* 57 (September 1978): 270–71. For a sensitive account of the textbook war, see Calvin Trillin, "U.S. Journal: Kanawha Country, West Virginia," *New Yorker,* 30 September 1974, 119–27.
40. Ronald Formisano, *Boston Against Busing: Race, Class, and Ethnicity in the 1960s and 1970s* (Chapel Hill: University of North Carolina Press, 1991); Anthony Lukas, *Common Ground: A Turbulent Decade in the Lives of Three American Families* (New York: Random House, 1985), 271–76.
41. Schlafly quoted in Klatch, *Women of the New Right,* 136–37.
42. See Klatch, *Women of the New Right,* and Kristin Luker, *Abortion and the Politics of Motherhood* (Berkeley: University of California Press, 1984).
43. On Schlafly's antifeminism, see Carol Felsenthal, *The Sweetheart of the Silent Majority* (Garden City, N.Y.: Doubleday, 1981), 232–97 (quote 281).
44. Quoted in Hunter, *Culture Wars,* 167. Hunter points out that opposing groups like Norman Lear's People for the American Way also employed "what the technicians in the industry call 'the devil factor.'" On the popularity of right-wing talk show hosts in the late 1970s, see Murray B. Levin, *Talk Radio and the American Dream* (Lexington, Mass.: D.C. Heath, 1987).
45. Richard Viguerie, "Ends and Means," in *New Right Papers,* ed. Whitaker, 31. Similarly, the liberal activist Morris Dees called direct mail a tool for "'raising the consciousness' of the people." Hunter, *Culture Wars,* 165.
46. Phillips, *Post-Conservative America,* 49.
47. For Jimmy Carter's self-presentation as an honest and compassionate problem-solver, see his campaign autobiography, *Why Not the Best?* (New York: Bantam, 1976). On his failure to capitalize on the religious and moral crisis, see Phillips, *Post-Conservative America,* 189–90; Leo P. Ribuffo, "God and Jimmy Carter," in *Right Center Left: Essays in American History* (New Brunswick, N.J.: Rutgers University Press, 1992), 214–48.
48. On the abortive third party, see William Rusher, *The Making of the New Majority Party* (Ottawa, Canada: Green Hill Publishers, 1975). There was also a short-lived Populist Forum that sought to link up activists from Kanawha County, South Boston, and other venues of grassroots resistance. The Forum helped the anti-textbook protesters record their songs and organized three small marches on Washington that brought together parents from West Virginia, Boston, Louisville, and several other areas. For a self-congratulatory account, see Robert J. Hoy, "Lid on a Boiling Pot," *New Right Papers,* 84–103.

49. Quoted in William E. Leuchtenburg, *In the Shadow of FDR: From Harry Truman to Ronald Reagan,* rev. ed. (Ithaca, N.Y.: Cornell University Press, 1985), 225. For Reagan's other borrowings from FDR, see ibid., pp. 209–35.
50. Peggy Noonan, *What I Saw at the Revolution: A Political Life in the Reagan Era* (New York: Random House, 1990), 143. For intelligent discussions of Reagan's style, see ibid. and Robert Dallek, *Ronald Reagan: The Politics of Symbolism* (Cambridge: Harvard University Press, 1984); Paul D. Erickson, *Reagan Speaks: The Making of an American Myth* (New York: New York University Press, 1985); Kathleen Hall Jamieson, *Eloquence in an Electronic Age: The Transformation of Political Speechmaking* (New York: Oxford University Press, 1988), 165–200; David Reid, "Public Eloquence," in *State of the Language,* ed. Christopher Ricks and Leonard Michaels (Berkeley: University of California Press, 1990), 265–75.
51. Eric McKitrick, "The Great White Hope," *New York Review of Books,* 11 June 1992, 36. The populist label was affixed by Richard Darman, Noonan, *What I Saw,* 263–64. About Reagan's career as a corporate PR spokesman, Noonan comments, remarkably, "In the fifties and early sixties, while the other people in power were joining government and learning its language, he was going from plant to plant for GE, shooting the breeze with the workers in the cafeteria, the guys on the line telling him what they thought. More than any other president since Jackson, he spent the years before power with the people, the normal people of his country." Noonan, *What I Saw,* 167.
52. From a speech given in Sedalia, Missouri, quoted in Erickson, *Reagan Speaks,* 109. In June 1984, the presidential adviser Richard Darman wrote a memorandum to guide the re-election campaign: "Paint RR as the personification of all that is right with or heroized by America," he wrote. "Leave Mondale in a position where an attack on Reagan is tantamount to an attack on America's idealized image of itself—where a vote against Reagan is in some subliminal sense, a vote against mythic 'America'." Ibid., 100.
53. Blumenthal, *Rise of the Counter-Establishment,* 330.
54. Reagan's popularity rating in the Gallup Poll was consistently below 50 percent from December 1981 through October 1983. Barone, *Our Country,* 760.
55. Reagan, 26 October 1984, quoted in Normon Solomon, *The Power of Babble* (New York: Laurel, 1992), 244.
56. Howard Jarvis quoted in Clarence Y. H. Lo, *Small Property Versus Big Government: Social Origins of the Property Tax Revolt* (Berkeley: University of California Press, 1990), 138; Terry Schwardron and Paul Richter, *California and the American Tax Revolt: Proposition 13 Five Years Later* (Berkeley: University of California Press, 1984), 3.
57. Quoted in Erickson, *Reagan Speaks,* 152.
58. The 1981 inaugural address is reprinted in Erickson, *Reagan Speaks,* 140; "Excerpts from Reagan's Labor Day Speech on Taxes in Independence," *New York Times,* 3 September 1985, D20. Also see the comments by Blumenthal, *Rise of the Counter-Establishment,* 321–22.
59. Kevin Phillips, *The Politics of Rich and Poor: Wealth and the American Electorate in the Reagan Aftermath* (New York: Random House, 1990), 80–86. On the debate surrounding the bill, see Timothy J. Conlan, Margaret T. Wrightson, and David R. Beam, *Taxing Choices: The Politics of Tax Reform* (Washington, D.C.: Congressional Quarterly Press, 1990).

60. Rabbit went on to disparage President George Bush: "With this new one you know he knows something, but it seems a small something." John Updike, *Rabbit at Rest* (New York: Knopf, 1990), 295.
61. Noonan, *What I Saw,* 211.
62. Noonan, *What I Saw,* 149, 152.
63. Richard A. Viguerie, *The Establishment vs. The People: Is a New Populist Revolt on the Way?* (Chicago: Regnery Gateway, 1983), 219; Viguerie, "The State of the Union: A Populist View," speech delivered to National Press Club, Washington, D.C., 26 February 1984, copy in my possession. For a sample Weyrich comment, see *The New Right at Harvard* (Vienna, Va.: The Conservative Caucus, 1983), 29.
64. Quote from a 1986 interview in Steve Bruce, *The Rise and Fall of the Christian Right: Conservative Protestant Politics in America, 1978–1988* (Oxford, Eng.: Clarendon Press, 1988), 54.
65. Lloyd Grove, "The Graying of Richard Viguerie," *Washington Post,* 29 June 1989, D1, 4; John B. Judis, "The Conservative Crackup," *The American Prospect* 3 (Fall 1990): 39–40.
66. Cited in John B. Judis, *Grand Illusion: Critics and Champions of the American Century* (New York: Farrar Straus Giroux, 1992), 243–44.

CHAPTER 11. CONCLUSION: POPULISMS OF DECLINE

1. John B. Judis, "The Conservative Crackup," *The American Prospect* (Fall 1990): 41. For an update during the 1992 campaign, see Judis, "The End of Conservatism," *New Republic,* 31 August 1992, 28–31.
2. The quotes from Jesse Jackson and Pat Robertson are drawn from Allen D. Hertzke, *Echoes of Discontent: Jesse Jackson, Pat Robertson, and the Resurgence of Populism* (Washington, D.C.: CQ Press, 1993), 69, 147. For more detail on this phenomenon and discussion of its meaning, see my article, "Populism: The Perilous Promise," *Socialist Review* 16 (September–October 1986): 99–106.
3. Advertisement for the HP DeskJet 1200C, published in *The New Yorker,* 1993; the Banana Republic ad appeared in the firm's Fall 1986 catalog. I keep a large file of such usages. The sources range from left-wing periodicals like the *Nation* and *In These Times* to conservative ones like the *Washington Times,* as well as the less contentious *Publishers Weekly* and *Spin* magazine, which titled one column, "The Fallacy of the New Populists: Middle America Just Wants to Get Laid." *Spin,* May 1986, 40.

   Critiques of an earlier wave of populist labeling that was mostly limited to political phenomena are George B. Tindall, "Populism: A Semantic Identity Crisis," *Virginia Quarterly Review* 48 (Fall 1972): 501–18; C. Vann Woodward, "The Ghost of Populism Walks Again," *New York Times Magazine,* 4 June 1972, 16.
4. Ian Shoales, *Morning Edition,* National Public Radio, 4 February 1992.
5. Ironically, the public does not seem to have embraced "populism" as a term. Few pollsters study the issue. But, in one survey, three times more people viewed "populist" unfavorably than favorably. *New York Times,* 24 November 1985, E5. The reason, suspects Kevin Phillips, is that the term still smacks of rebellion and upheaval. Author's interview with Phillips, May 1989.

6. See Bennett Harrison, *Lean and Mean: The Changing Landscape of Corporate Power in the Age of Flexibility* (New York: Basic Books, 1994).
7. Quoted by Sean Wilentz, "Pox Populi," *New Republic,* 9 August 1993, 29. Perot also ridiculed Clinton early in his administration for being so inexperienced that "you wouldn't consider giving him a job anywhere above middle management" in a private corporation. Dan Balz, "Perot Slams the President," *Washington Post,* 27 May 1993, A1.
8. Herbert Croly writing about the Progressive Party of 1924, quoted in David Kennedy, *Over Here: The First World War and American Society* (New York: Oxford University Press, 1980), 294.
9. "Putting People First," a short pamphlet distributed by Clinton/Gore National Campaign Headquarters, fall 1992, in my possession.
10. On Clinton's spiritual vocabulary, see Gustav Niebuhr, "President's Pulpit Has Ecumenical Echo," *Washington Post,* 10 March 1994, A1.
11. Kevin Phillips, *The Politics of Rich and Poor: Wealth and the American Electorate in the Reagan Aftermath* (New York: Random House, 1990).
12. Clinton, closing statement of the second presidential debate, *Washington Post,* 16 October 1992, A37.
13. On the baleful style of Walter Mondale and Michael Dukakis, see David Kusnet, *Speaking American: How the Democrats Can Win in the Nineties* (New York: Thunder's Mouth Press, 1992), 39 and passim. This little-known book, published in the spring of 1992, is a virtual primer of the type of populist campaign Clinton ran in the general election.
14. From Clinton's letter to Colonel Eugene Holmes, 3 December 1969, reprinted in *Washington Post,* 13 February 1992, A26.
15. Author's interview with Heather Booth, Washington, D.C., 19 July 1990.
16. A list of groups active in the late 1970s is appended to Harry C. Boyte, *The Backyard Revolution: Understanding the New Citizen Movement* (Philadelphia: Temple University Press, 1980), 210–21. On canvassing, see Harry C. Boyte, Heather Booth, and Steve Max, *Citizen Action and the New American Populism* (Philadelphia: Temple University Press, 1986), 69–83.
17. Booth, interview; author's telephone interview with Miles Rapoport, 15 March 1992. For a few years in the 1970s, Steve Max, who was still a democratic socialist at heart, concluded the two-week training session by quoting Sinclair Lewis: "When asked, are you a socialist? He said, I used to call it that but my wife tells me to call it Christianity." According to Heather Booth, the bad repute of "real world socialism" had negated the term's value: "You have to say, what your vision is, that word has now been taken to mean something else . . . you have to find a different way to talk about it." Booth, interview; Boyte, *Backyard Revolution,* 109–10.
18. See the insightful analysis by David Plotke, "Recent Populist Movements in the United States, Right and Left," presented at convention of the American Political Science Association, 2–5 September 1993.
19. Robert Kuttner, *The Life of the Party: Democratic Prospects in 1988 and Beyond* (New York: Viking, 1987), 5. For earlier arguments, see Jack Newfield and Jeff Greenfield, *A Populist Manifesto: The Making of a New Majority* (New York: Praeger, 1972); Fred Harris, *The New Populism* (New York: Saturday Review Press, 1973).

20. Quotes from Edsall and Edsall, *Chain Reaction,* 182; Stanley B. Greenberg, "Contesting Democratic Ideas," unpublished report for The Analysis Group, Inc., 2 April 1986, 5; Greenberg, "The Democratic State of Mind," unpublished report for The Analysis Group, Inc., 28 February 1986. Thanks to Jim Shoch for sending me copies of these documents.

    The perspective was later confirmed by Lee Atwater, campaign manager for George Bush in 1988. In a 1989 interview, Atwater said: "Simply put there is constantly a war going on between the two parties for the populist vote. The populist vote is always the swing vote. . . . The Democrats have always got to nail Republicans as the party of the fat cats, in effect, the party of the upper class and privilege. And the Democrats will maintain that they are the party of the little man, the common man. To the extent they're successful, Republicans are unsuccessful." Quoted in William Greider, *Who Will Tell the People: The Betrayal of American Democracy* (New York: Simon and Schuster, 1992), 274.

21. Greenberg, "Contesting Democratic Ideas," 2; Tom Daschle, Democratic Response to State of the Union Address, 4 February 1986 (courtesy of Democratic National Committee); Sidney Blumenthal, "Democrats Develop a Populist Strategy for Midterm Elections," *Washington Post,* 31 August 1986, A1, 6; Blumenthal, "Populist TV Ads Sold 3 Democrats to Voters," ibid., 6 November 1986.

    In the fall of 1985, Paul Kirk, Democratic National Committee chairman, had advocated a milder version of this strategy to articulate "the shared aspirations of average Americans." Quoted in Craig Reinarman, *American States of Mind: Political Beliefs and Behavior Among Private and Public Workers* (New Haven: Yale University Press, 1987), 227.

22. Quoted in "Jim Hightower on the Populist Moment," *The Texas Observer,* 8 November 1985, 9.

23. Reverend Jesse L. Jackson, *Straight from the Heart,* ed. Roger D. Hatch and Frank E. Watkins (Philadelphia: Fortress Press, 1987), 18.

24. For example, see his campaign announcement speech, 10 October 1987, *Keep Hope Alive: Jesse Jackson's 1988 Presidential Campaign,* ed. Frank Clemente and Frank Watkins (Boston: South End Press, 1989), 27–32, and his speech to the Cleveland City Club, 2 May 1988, ibid., 57–61.

25. In the 1988 Democratic primaries, Jackson received 92 percent of the black vote, 30 percent of the Latino vote, and 12 percent of the white vote. Clemente and Watkins, *Keep Hope Alive,* 236.

26. Quoted in Clemente and Watkins, *Keep Hope Alive,* 37.

27. On the reaction of Reagan Democrats to Jackson, see Edsall and Edsall, *Chain Reaction,* 226–27.

28. Text of inaugural address, *Washington Post,* 21 January 1993, A26. Just after the election, Paul Begala reflected, "The kind of people who hire us and like our philosophy are kind of populist in their outlook." ABC-TV "Nightline," 4 November 1992. On Macomb County, see Elizabeth Kolbert, "Michigan May Be Vital . . . ," *New York Times,* 24 September 1992, A23.

29. "Brown's Standard Campaign Speech: A New Vision of America," *New York Times,* 28 April 1992, A18. Buchanan quoted in Jack Germond and Jules Witcover, *Mad as Hell: Revolt at the Ballot Box, 1992* (New York: Warner Books, 1993), 236.

30. Quotes from Phillips, *Boiling Point,* 77; "Perot on Perot," *U.S. News and World*

Report, 29 June 1992, 27; Sean Wilentz, "Pox Populi," *New Republic,* 9 August 1993, 34. For a good brief analysis of Perot's links with the populist tradition, see Alan Brinkley, "Roots," *New Republic,* 27 July 1992, 44–45.

31. Michael Rogin, "Meet Mr. Perot," *Image* (magazine of the *San Francisco Examiner*), 26 July 1992, 12. Sean Wilentz likened Perot to the type of "village explainers" favored by Populists and other late-nineteenth-century critics of the emerging corporate order. Wilentz, "Pox Populi," 31–33.
32. Guy Molyneux and William Schneider, "Ross *Is* Boss," *Atlantic Monthly,* May 1993, 87.
33. In the spring of 1994, a woman angrily asked President Clinton at a North Carolina town meeting (a Perot innovation): "Are you one of us middle-class people, or are you in with the villainous, money-grubbing Republicans?" Quoted in Lloyd Grove, "Hail to the Cheese: Why the Big Guy Gets No Respect," *Washington Post,* 7 April 1994, C1.
34. For a glimpse of Perot's movement after the NAFTA debate, see Dan Balz, "United We Stand America Makes Plans, Struggles to Define Role," *Washington Post,* 7 February 1994, A7.
35. Ralph Nader, "Introduction: Free Trade & the Decline of Democracy," *The Case Against Free Trade: GATT, NAFTA, and the Globalization of Corporate Power* (San Francisco: Earth Island Press, 1993), 1. On the grassroots mobilization, see Peter T. Kilborn, "Opposites in California Join to Fight Trade Pact," *New York Times,* 13 October 1993, A16.
36. Reich quoted in William Raspberry, "Working-Class Vanishing Act," *Washington Post,* 17 November 1993, A23.
37. Debate between Gore and Perot, "Larry King Live," Cable News Network, 9 November 1993; Dan Balz, "Gore's Gamble in Debating NAFTA May Leave Perot a Weakened Foe," *Washington Post,* 11 November 1993, A8.
38. Elizabeth Kamarck Minnich, "Toward a Feminist Populism," *The New Populism: The Politics of Empowerment,* ed. Harry C. Boyte and Frank Riessman (Philadelphia: Temple University Press, 1986), 196; Cornel West, "Populism: A Black Socialist Critique," ibid., 208.
39. In the mid-1990s, radio talk-show hosts are a major source of such right-wing rhetoric. See Katherine Q. Seelye, "The Next Step for Talk Radio: Candidacies," *New York Times,* 16 April 1994, A1.
40. Murray Bookchin, "Were We Wrong?" *Telos* 65 (Fall 1985): 71; Mickey Kaus, *The End of Equality* (New York: Basic Books, 1992), 165.
41. Samuel Gompers, *Seventy Years of Life and Labour: An Autobiography,* vol. 2 (1925; reprint, New York: Augustus M. Kelley, 1967), 109.
42. See Todd Gitlin's probing analysis and critique, "The Rise of 'Identity Politics'," *Dissent* (Spring 1993): 172–77.

A NOTE ON METHOD

1. Lynn Hunt, *Politics, Culture, and Class in the French Revolution* (Berkeley: University of California Press, 1984), 54. Inevitably influenced by philosophers like Michel Foucault and Jacques Derrida, historians of France have been among the

more imaginative practitioners of this methodology. For examples, see the collection, *Rethinking Labor History: Essays on Discourse and Class Analysis,* ed. Lenard R. Berlanstein (Urbana: University of Illinois Press, 1993), and Joan Wallach Scott, *Gender and the Politics of History* (New York: Columbia University Press, 1988).

2. Quoted in Bryan Palmer, *Descent into Discourse* (Philadelphia: Temple University Press, 1990), 217. For the view of a political conservative, see Gertrude Himmelfarb, *On Looking into the Abyss: Untimely Thoughts on Culture and Society* (New York: Knopf, 1994).
3. Murray Edelman, "Political Language and Political Reality," *PS* 18 (Winter 1985): 12. For a good statement of this position, see James Farr, "Understanding Conceptual Change Politically," *Political Innovation and Conceptual Change,* ed. Terence Ball, James Farr, and Russell L. Hanson (Cambridge, Eng.: Cambridge University Press, 1989), 24–49.
4. Donald Reid, "Reflections on Labor History and Language," in Berlanstein, *Rethinking Labor History,* 46.
5. As J. G. A. Pocock has written, "It does not make the historian an idealist to say that he regularly, though not invariably, presents the language in the form of an ideal type: a model by means of which he carries on explorations and experiments." "Introduction: The State of the Art," in Pocock, *Virtue, Commerce, and History: Essays on Political Thought and History, Chiefly in the Eighteenth Century* (Cambridge, Eng.: Cambridge University Press, 1985), 11.

Good Reading

Hundreds of library shelves are filled with studies of the movements, people, events, and themes discussed in this book. But certain works were indispensable to my understanding of the nature and evolution of American populism. With gratitude, I list them here.

GENERAL WORKS

Anderson, Benedict. *Imagined Communities: Reflections on the Origin and Spread of Nationalism.* 1983.

Barone, Michael. *Our Country: The Shaping of America from Roosevelt to Reagan.* 1990.

Bennett, David H. *The Party of Fear: From Nativist Movements to the New Right in American History.* 1988.

Canovan, Margaret. *Populism.* 1981.

Foner, Eric. "Why Is There No Socialism in the United States?" *History Workshop* (Spring 1984).

Fraser, Steve, and Gary Gerstle, eds. *The Rise and Fall of the New Deal Order, 1930–1980.* 1989.

Green, David. *Shaping Political Consciousness: The Language of Politics in America from McKinley to Reagan.* 1987.

Ionescu, Ghita, and Ernest Gellner, eds. *Populism: Its Meanings and National Characteristics.* 1969.

Lipset, Seymour Martin, and Earl Raab. *The Politics of Unreason: Right-Wing Extremism in America, 1790–1977.* 1978.

McKenna, George, ed. *American Populism.* 1974.

Rodgers, Daniel. *Contested Truths: Keywords in American Politics Since Independence.* 1987.

Williams, Raymond. *Keywords: A Vocabulary of Culture and Society.* 1985.

Wills, Garry. *Under God: Religion and American Politics.* 1990.

CHAPTER 1. INHERITANCE

Boritt, Gabor S. *Lincoln and the Economics of the American Dream.* 1978.

Butler, Jon. *Awash in a Sea of Faith: Christianizing the American People.* 1990.

Cmiel, Kenneth. *Democratic Eloquence: The Fight over Popular Speech in Nineteenth-Century America.* 1990.

Dawley, Alan. *Class and Community: The Industrial Revolution in Lynn.* 1976.

Hatch, Nathan. *The Democratization of American Christianity.* 1989.

Meyers, Marvin. *The Jacksonian Persuasion: Politics and Belief.* 1957.

Peterson, Merrill D. *The Jefferson Image in the American Mind.* 1960.

———. *Lincoln in American Memory.* 1994.

Roediger, David. *The Wages of Whiteness: Race and the Making of the American Working Class.* 1991.

Stansell, Christine. *City of Women: Sex and Class in New York, 1789–1860.* 1986.

Tocqueville, Alexis de. *Democracy in America.* 1835, 1840.

Watson, Harry L. *Liberty and Power: The Politics of Jacksonian America.* 1990.

Wilentz, Sean. *Chants Democratic: New York City and the Rise of the American Working Class, 1788–1850.* 1984.

Wood, Gordon. *The Radicalism of the American Revolution.* 1992.

CHAPTER 2. THE RIGHTEOUS COMMONWEALTH OF THE LATE NINETEENTH CENTURY

Buhle, Mari Jo. *Women and American Socialism, 1870–1920.* 1981.

Destler, Chester McArthur. *American Radicalism, 1865–1901.* 1966.

Fink, Leon. *Workingmen's Democracy: The Knights of Labor and American Politics.* 1983.

Gaither, Gerald H. *Blacks and the Populist Revolt.* 1979.

Goodwyn, Lawrence. *Democratic Promise: The Populist Moment in America.* 1976.

Gutman, Herbert G. *Power and Culture: Essays on the American Working Class.* 1987.

Hicks, John D. *The Populist Revolt: A History of the Farmers' Alliance and the People's Party.* 1931.

Hofstadter, Richard. *The Age of Reform: From Bryan to FDR.* 1955.

Keller, Morton. *Affairs of State: Public Life in Late Nineteenth Century America.* 1977.

Laurie, Bruce. *Artisans into Workers: Labor in Nineteenth-Century America.* 1989.

McGerr, Michael. *The Decline of Popular Politics: The American North, 1865–1926.* 1986.

McMath, Robert C., Jr. *American Populism: A Social History, 1877–1898.* 1993.

Palmer, Bruce. *"Man over Money": The Southern Populist Critique of American Capitalism.* 1980.

Pollack, Norman. *The Just Polity: Populism, Law, and Human Welfare.* 1987.

Saxton, Alexander. *The Indispensable Enemy: Labor and the Anti-Chinese Movement in California.* 1971.

Thomas, John L. *Alternative America: Henry George, Edward Bellamy, Henry Demarest Lloyd and the Adversary Tradition.* 1983.

Woodward, C. Vann. *Tom Watson: Agrarian Rebel.* 1938.

CHAPTER 3. WORKERS AS CITIZENS: LABOR AND THE LEFT IN THE GOMPERS ERA

Brody, David. *Workers in Industrial America.* 1993.

Cronin, James, and Carmen Sirianni, eds. *Work, Community, and Power: The Experience of Labor in Europe and America, 1900–1925.* 1983.

Fones-Wolf, Ken. *Trade Union Gospel: Christianity and Labor in Industrial Philadelphia, 1865–1915.* 1989.

Forbath, William E. *Law and the Shaping of the American Labor Movement.* 1991.

Greene, Julia. "The Strike at the Ballot Box: Politics and Partisanship in the American Federation of Labor, 1881–1916." Ph.D. thesis, Yale University, 1990.

Karson, Marc. *American Labor Unions and Politics, 1900–1918.* 1957.

Kaufman, Stuart B. *Samuel Gompers and the Origins of the American Federation of Labor.* 1973.

Link, Arthur, and Richard L. McCormick. *Progressivism.* 1982.

Montgomery, David. *The Fall of the House of Labor: The Workplace, the State, and American Labor Activism, 1865–1925.* 1987.

Perlman, Selig. *A Theory of the Labor Movement.* 1928.

Salvatore, Nick. *Eugene V. Debs: Citizen and Socialist.* 1982.

———. Introduction to Samuel Gompers, *Seventy Years of Life and Labor: An Autobiography.* 1984.

Skocpol, Theda. *Protecting Soldiers and Mothers: The Political Origins of Social Policy in the United States.* 1992.

Weinstein, James. *The Decline of Socialism in America, 1912–1925.* 1967.

CHAPTER 4. ONWARD, CHRISTIAN MOTHERS AND SOLDIERS: THE PROHIBITIONIST CRUSADE

Blocker, Jack S., Jr. *American Temperance Movements: Cycles of Reform.* 1989.

———. *Retreat from Reform: The Prohibition Movement in the United States, 1890–1913.* 1976.

Bordin, Ruth. *Frances Willard: A Biography.* 1986.

———. *Women and Temperance: The Quest for Power and Liberty, 1873–1900.* 1981.

Clark, Norman H. *Deliver Us from Evil: An Interpretation of American Prohibition.* 1976.

Epstein, Barbara. *Politics of Domesticity: Women, Evangelism, and Temperance in Nineteenth-Century America.* 1981.

Handy, Robert T. *A Christian America: Protestant Hopes and Historical Realities.* 1971.

Kerr, K. Austin. *Organized for Prohibition: A New History of the Anti-Saloon League.* 1985.

Kyvig, David E. *Repealing National Prohibition.* 1979.

Levine, Lawrence W. *Defender of the Faith: William Jennings Bryan, the Last Decade, 1915–1925.* 1965.

Marsden, George. *Fundamentalism and American Culture: The Shaping of Twentieth-Century Evangelism, 1870–1925.* 1980.

McLoughlin, William G. *Billy Sunday Was His Real Name.* 1955.

Odegard, Peter. *Pressure Politics: The Story of the Anti-Saloon League.* 1928.
Timberlake, James. *Prohibition and the Progressive Movement, 1900–1920.* 1963.

CHAPTER 5. SOCIAL JUSTICE AND SOCIAL PARANOIA: THE CATHOLIC POPULISM OF FATHER COUGHLIN

Bayor, Ronald H. *Neighbors in Conflict: The Irish, Germans, Jews, and Italians of New York City, 1929–1941.* 1978.
Brinkley, Alan. *Voices of Protest: Huey Long, Father Coughlin, and the Great Depression.* 1982.
Dolan, Jay. *The American Catholic Experience.* 1985.
Fisher, James Terence. *The Catholic Counterculture in America, 1933–1962.* 1989.
Halsey, William M. *The Survival of American Innocence: Catholicism in an Era of Disillusionment, 1920–1940.* 1980.
Levine, Lawrence. *The Unpredictable Past: Explorations in American Cultural History.* 1993.
Marcus, Sheldon. *Father Coughlin: The Tumultuous Life of the Priest of the Little Flower.* 1973.
O'Brien, David J. *American Catholics and Social Reform: The New Deal Years.* 1968.
Ribuffo, Leo P. *The Old Christian Right: The Protestant Far Right from the Great Depression to the Cold War.* 1983.
Schlesinger, Arthur M., Jr. *The Age of Upheaval.* 1960.
Smith, Geoffrey S. *American Counter-Subversives, the New Deal, and the Coming of World War II.* 1973.
Susman, Warren. *Culture as History: The Transformation of American Society in the Twentieth Century.* 1984.
Tentler, Leslie Woodcock. *Seasons of Grace: A History of the Catholic Archdiocese of Detroit.* 1990.
Tull, Charles J. *Father Coughlin and the New Deal.* 1965.

CHAPTER 6. THE MANY AND THE FEW: THE CIO AND THE EMBRACE OF LIBERALISM

Bell, Thomas. *Out of This Furnace.* 1941 (repr. 1976).
Bernstein, Irving. *The Turbulent Years: A History of the American Worker, 1933–1941.* 1969.
Cochran, Bert. *Labor and Communism: The Conflict That Shaped American Unions.* 1977.
Cohen, Lizabeth. *Making a New Deal: Industrial Workers in Chicago, 1919–1939.* 1990.
Dubofsky, Melvyn, and Warren Van Tine. *John L. Lewis: A Biography.* 1977 (abr. ed. 1986).
Faue, Elizabeth. *Community of Suffering and Struggle: Women, Men, and the Labor Movement in Minneapolis, 1915–1945.* 1991.
Fraser, Steve. *Labor Will Rule: Sidney Hillman and the Rise of American Labor.* 1991.

Freeman, Joshua. *In Transit: The Transport Workers Union in New York City, 1933–1966.* 1989.

Gerstle, Gary. *Working-Class Americanism: The Politics of Labor in a Textile City, 1914–1960.* 1989.

Isserman, Maurice. *Which Side Were You On? The American Communist Party During the Second World War.* 1982.

Klehr, Harvey. *The Heyday of American Communism: The Depression Decade.* 1984.

Kraus, Henry. *The Many and the Few: A Chronicle of the Dynamic Auto Workers.* 1947 (repr. 1985).

Lichtenstein, Nelson. *Labor's War at Home: The CIO in World War II.* 1982.

Lichtenstein, Nelson, and Howell John Harris, eds. *Industrial Democracy in America: The Ambiguous Promise.* 1993.

Schatz, Ronald. *The Electrical Workers: A History of Labor at General Electric and Westinghouse.* 1983.

CHAPTER 7. A FREE PEOPLE FIGHT BACK: THE RISE AND FALL OF THE COLD WAR RIGHT

Allitt, Patrick. *Catholic Intellectuals and Conservative Politics in America, 1950–1985.* 1993.

Bell, Daniel, ed. *The Radical Right.* 1963.

Caute, David. *The Great Fear: The Anti-Communist Purge Under Truman and Eisenhower.* 1978.

Crosby, Donald F., S.J. *God, Church, and Flag: Senator Joseph R. McCarthy and the Catholic Church, 1950–1957.* 1978.

Griffith, Robert. *The Politics of Fear: Joseph R. McCarthy and the Senate.* 1987.

Heale, M. J. *American Anticommunism: Combatting the Enemy Within, 1830–1970.* 1990.

Hixson, William B., Jr. *Search for the American Right Wing: An Analysis of the Social Science Record, 1955–1987.* 1992.

Judis, John B. *William F. Buckley, Jr.: Patron Saint of the Conservatives.* 1988.

Nash, George H. *The Conservative Intellectual Movement in America Since 1945.* 1976.

Oshinsky, David. *A Conspiracy So Immense: The World of Joseph McCarthy.* 1983.

Pencak, William. *For God and Country: The American Legion, 1919–1941.* 1989.

Rogin, Michael. *The Intellectuals and McCarthy: The Radical Specter.* 1967.

Whitfield, Stephen J. *The Culture of the Cold War.* 1991.

Wuthnow, Robert. *The Restructuring of American Religion: Society and Faith Since World War II.* 1988.

CHAPTER 8. POWER TO WHICH PEOPLE? THE TRAGEDY OF THE WHITE NEW LEFT

Appy, Christian. *Working-Class War: American Combat Soldiers and Vietnam.* 1993.

Carson, Clayborne. *In Struggle: SNCC and the Black Awakening of the 1960s.* 1981.

DeBenedetti, Charles with Charles Chatfield. *An American Ordeal: The Antiwar Movement of the Vietnam Era.* 1990.
Echols, Alice. *Daring to Be Bad: Radical Feminism in America, 1967–1975.* 1989.
Evans, Sara. *Personal Politics: The Roots of Women's Liberation in the Civil Rights Movement and the New Left.* 1979.
Gitlin, Todd. *The Sixties: Years of Hope, Days of Rage.* 1987.
———. *The Whole World Is Watching: Mass Media in the Making and Unmaking of the New Left.* 1980.
Heineman, Kenneth J. *Campus Wars: The Peace Movement at American State Universities in the Vietnam Era.* 1993.
Hodgson, Godfrey. *America in Our Time.* 1976.
Horwitt, Sanford. *Let Them Call Me Rebel: Saul Alinsky—His Life and Legacy.* 1989.
Miller, James. *"Democracy Is in the Streets": From Port Huron to the Siege of Chicago.* 1987.
Mills, C. Wright. *The Power Elite.* 1956.
Rorabaugh, W. J. *Berkeley at War: The 1960s.* 1989.
Sale, Kirkpatrick. *SDS.* 1973.

CHAPTER 9. STAND UP FOR THE WORKING MAN: GEORGE WALLACE AND THE MAKING OF A NEW RIGHT

Carlson, Jody C. *George C. Wallace and the Politics of Powerlessness: The Wallace Campaigns for the Presidency, 1964–1976.* 1981.
Chester, Lewis, Godfrey Hodgson, and Bruce Page. *An American Melodrama: The Presidential Campaign of 1968.* 1969.
Coles, Robert, and Jon Erikson. *The Middle Americans: Proud and Uncertain.* 1971.
Edsall, Thomas Byrne, and Mary Edsall. *Chain Reaction: The Impact of Race, Rights, and Taxes on American Politics.* 1991.
Ehrenreich, Barbara. *Fear of Falling: The Inner Life of the Middle Class.* 1989.
Formisano, Ronald P. *Boston Against Busing: Race, Class, and Ethnicity in the 1960s and 1970s.* 1991.
Frady, Marshall. *Wallace.* 1968.
Halle, David. *America's Working Man: Work, Home, and Politics Among Blue-Collar Property Owners.* 1984.
Lesher, Stephan. *George Wallace: American Populist.* 1994.
Miles, Michael. *The Odyssey of the American Right.* 1980.
Sennett, Richard, and Jonathan Cobb. *The Hidden Injuries of Class.* 1972.

CHAPTER 10. THE CONSERVATIVE CAPTURE: FROM NIXON TO REAGAN

Bruce, Steve. *The Rise and Fall of the Christian Right: Conservative Protestant Politics in America, 1978–1988.* 1988.
Erickson, Paul D. *Reagan Speaks: The Making of an American Myth.* 1984.

Himmelstein, Jerome L. *To the Right: The Transformation of American Conservatism.* 1990.

Hunter, James Davison. *Culture Wars: The Struggle to Define America.* 1991.

Klatch, Rebecca. *Women of the New Right.* 1987.

Lo, Clarence Y. H. *Small Property Versus Big Government: Social Origins of the Property Tax Revolt.* 1990.

Luker, Kristin. *Abortion and the Politics of Motherhood.* 1984.

Noonan, Peggy. *What I Saw at the Revolution: A Political Life in the Reagan Era.* 1990.

Phillips, Kevin. *The Emerging Republican Majority.* 1969.

———. *Post-Conservative America.* 1982.

Rieder, Jonathan. *Canarsie: The Jews and Italians of Brooklyn Against Liberalism.* 1985.

Wills, Gary. *Nixon Agonistes: The Crisis of the Self-Made Man.* 1970.

CHAPTER 11. CONCLUSION: POPULISMS OF DECLINE

Boyte, Harry C. *CommonWealth: A Return to Citizen Politics.* 1989.

Boyte, Harry C., and Frank Riessman. *The New Populism: The Politics of Empowerment.* 1986.

Hertzke, Allen D. *Echoes of Discontent: Jesse Jackson, Pat Robertson, and the Resurgence of Populism.* 1993.

Kusnet, David. *Speaking American: How the Democrats Can Win in the Nineties.* 1992.

Kuttner, Robert. *The Life of the Party: Democratic Prospects in 1988 and Beyond.* 1987.

Phillips, Kevin. *The Politics of Rich and Poor: Wealth and the American Electorate in the Reagan Aftermath.* 1990.

Reinarman, Craig. *American States of Mind: Political Beliefs and Behavior Among Private and Public Workers.* 1987.

Index